A HISTORY OF PREACHING

A HISTORY
of PREACHING

O. C. Edwards Jr.

ABINGDON PRESS / Nashville

A HISTORY OF PREACHING

Copyright © 2004 by Abingdon Press

This book is printed on acid-free paper.

Library of Congress Cataloging-in-Publication Data

Edwards, O. C. (Otis Carl), 1928–
   A history of preaching / O.C. Edwards.
     p. cm.
   Includes index.
   ISBN 0-687-03864-2 (alk. paper)
   1.   Preaching—History. I. Title.

   BV4207.E39 2004
   251'.009—dc22

2004015607

06 07 08 09 10 11 12 13—10 9 8 7 6 5 4 3 2

MANUFACTURED IN THE UNITED STATES OF AMERICA

Dedicated
with much love and gratitude

---

to
Carl and his Jane,
Sam, Patricia, Adrian, and Phoebe,
and
Louise, Russell, Jane, and Charlie

CONTENTS

PREFACE

The determination to write this history of preaching came to me in the summer of 1983. I had just returned from a sabbatical in Nigeria that ended nine years of administrative duty and was preparing to assume my new duties as professor of preaching that fall. Although I had already written a couple of books on exegesis as a resource for preaching, it seemed appropriate (to say the least) to read more widely in the literature of the field before occupying the chair.

Among the stack of books on my desk was one recommended by a student with an evangelical bent, John Stott's *Between Two Worlds*.[1] Stott is of a generation that considers it improper to write a book about anything without including a chapter on the history of the subject matter. Stott warmly recommended the history of preaching as a discipline helpful to the practitioner, and mentioned his devotion to the two-volume work of Edwin C. Dargan, which by then was already more than seventy years old.[2]

Stott's chapter intrigued me so much that I stopped reading his book to open the only work on my bookshelves devoted to the subject: Yngve Brilioth's *Brief History of Preaching*.[3] Reading what the archbishop of Uppsala had to say about the preaching of the Fathers of the early church activated my instincts as someone trained in patristics, so I began pulling off the shelves the works to which Brilioth referred. And Brilioth and the Fathers together reminded me that all the great preachers of the early church had been trained as professional rhetoricians before their ordination. That drove me to Aristotle, Cicero, and Quintilian.

Apparently launched on an infinite regress of reading books to understand other books, I began to look around for a major work more recent than Dargan's and came rapidly to understand that there was none. The last thorough investigation of the subject had been made when the century that was about to close had just begun. Surely the intervening years had seen research in the area comparable to the progress made in other fields of study over the same period! An update of the history of preaching seemed a book just aching to be written.

Further, while in many ways I liked the work of Dargan very much, in other ways it frustrated me. He had written about preachers, trying to include everyone who had a reputation for excellence in Christian proclamation throughout history. Thus he gave as much biographical information about each as space and the state of knowledge would allow, and then made some observations about that person's preaching. He reflected a Romantic understanding of such oeuvre as a product of the genius of an individual.

But I was more interested in preaching than in preachers; compiling a homiletical prosopography had no appeal to me. My understanding of the historical enterprise is accounting for change over time. I wanted to know about movements, about what the sermons of an era had in common rather than how they differed. I wanted to know what preachers of a period thought they were accomplishing in the pulpit (or chair, or ambo[4]), and the strategy of persuasion they used to achieve that end. I wanted to know when there had been major shifts and why those had occurred.

This desire to understand what preachers were trying to do and how they went about doing it meant that I could not start out with my own theory of what constituted good preaching and use that as a criterion for distinguishing the "good guys" from the "bad guys" throughout history. To do so would be to display the provincialism of the cultural stay-at-home. Whether a sermon can be read with edification today does not really tell us much about how effective it was in the context in which it was originally delivered.

Allegorical biblical interpretation is a case in point. Brilioth refers to it as "one of the hereditary taints of scriptural preaching."[5] Yet, while some Reformers thought sermons should expound the literal grammatical sense[6] of the biblical passage on which they were based, allegorical interpretation remained a common ingredient in sermons well through the nineteenth century. It was not until 1888–89, for instance, that Adolf Jülicher succeeded in convincing most of the scholarly world that Jesus' parables were not to be understood that way.[7] Thus if one is to rule preaching based on allegorical biblical interpretation out of court, one will excommunicate the proclamation of well over three-quarters of the Christian era, including that of most of the Fathers of the early church. And this is but one example of the exclusions that will have to be made if a chronicler of preaching claims to know what distinguishes the good from the bad and goes through history sorting all sermons into these two categories.

However, once I had decided to have a go at bringing the history of preaching up to date, it soon became obvious that in several respects I would have to scale down my original hope. For example, even though the book would cover the Christian era, I could not consider all Christian preaching. I could try to treat preaching in both Latin and Greek through the Golden Age of the Greek Fathers, but would have to overlook sermons in Syriac. Through the Middle Ages, I could study only Western sermons in Latin and vernacular languages. I could discuss all the major traditions of the Reformation, but after that I would confine the history to preaching done in English. And for the twentieth century, I would pay more attention to American than British pulpit work. And so my intention became to produce a homiletical genealogy for those who preach the faith today in English—especially Americans, but British as well.

It was immediately obvious, however, that no one—and certainly not I—could do original research in every period. In fact, the most I could expect to accomplish was to summarize the available monographic literature. That meant the aspects of preaching considered would vary from period to period, because the specialists writing about them had not taken their cues from me about what to concentrate on! It also meant that my distinction between preachers and preaching could not always be scrupulously observed, since the characteristic preaching of a period or the transition to it is often epitomized in one individual or a few, so that talking about preaching in their time is to talk about what they did. In these ways, the book as originally conceived differs from the book that came to be written.

One thing that was clear to me all along, however, was that the historical survey had to be accompanied by a collection of documents—both sermons and theoretical treatments—that illustrated the development being traced. To do anything else would have been as senseless as a history of painting in which there were no pictures. And the selections would have to be complete. A collection of extended quotations would convey little sense of what it was like to be one of those who heard the sermon when it was originally delivered. Even then the experience would fall far short of the reality; a sermon is not black marks on paper but a transaction involving a preacher, a congregation, and, one hopes, the Holy Spirit. This collection of documents appears on the CD-ROM accompanying this volume.

An additional way of clarifying the purpose of this book is to distinguish it from others in the same field. I have already mentioned those of Dargan and Brilioth. When I began, a helpful short work was already available in German: Werner Schütz's *Geschichte der christlichen Predigt*,[8] but it is hardly more than an outline. Among multivolume treatments, the most obvious was *20 Centuries of Great Preaching*, edited by Clyde E. Fant Jr. and William M. Pinson Jr.[9] The great virtue of this set is the many sermons for which it provides an English text. Each of these is prefaced by a short biography of the preacher, but little effort was made to develop an interpretation of the overall development of preaching; only individuals are discussed.

And some of these individuals get more adequate treatment than others. The coverage of Rauschenbusch, for example, is an important contribution to the literature. But the editors admit to using seventeen "men" (who appear to have been seminarians) as aiding in preliminary research;[10] inadequate revision of their efforts could account for the way some of the biographies hardly rise above the level of hagiography.

An even more critical shortcoming in Fant and Pinson's treatment of the entire history of preaching is that the first seventeen and a half of the twenty centuries are dispatched in the first two volumes. Almost ten of the twelve volumes are confined to preaching in the nineteenth and twentieth centuries.[11]

During the eighteen years in which I wrote the present book, many works were published that provided important data and perspective to the history, but they are mostly monographs about a period or a person. There have been, however, two attempts to cover the entire history, and I have tried to distinguish between their purposes and that of this work.

One of the two projects was frustrated by the untimely death of the author, Ronald E. Osborn. A minister and pastor of the Disciples of Christ, Osborn had academic and editorial responsibilities for most of his ministry, teaching church history at the seminary level and serving as dean of Christian Theological Seminary in Indianapolis before his retirement. He was able to finish only one of the four volumes planned for his history, while another is to be completed by Joseph R. Jeter, who teaches preaching at the Brite Divinity School of Texas Christian University.

Thus the only volume to be published so far is Osborn's *Folly of God:*

The Rise of Christian Preaching,[12] which takes the history of preaching through the third century of the Common Era, the time of persecution. The book has many virtues, and it is sad that the author was not able to complete the task on which he had worked so long. The only caveat to be entered against it is that Osborn does not distinguish carefully between what is preaching and what is some other genre of writing. Thus this valuable work could have as easily been titled *Early Christian Literature and Its Greco-Roman and Jewish Antecedents*.

Hughes Oliphant Old, the author of the other survey, has been more fortunate than Osborn: so far four of the seven projected volumes of his *Reading and Preaching of the Scriptures in the Worship of the Christian Church*[13] have appeared. Old conducted his survey on the assumption that there are correct and incorrect ways of worship, and so he goes through history separating the sheep from the goats.

The correct ways are classified as those that treat preaching as an act of worship and see the reading and interpretation of scripture to be the major elements in the offering of the liturgical assembly of the faithful. While Old claims to find this pattern in the earliest traditions of Israel, what he really appears to treat as normative is the standard of American heirs of the Reform tradition. As fellow Presbyterian Thomas G. Long has said:

> Occasionally . . . Old is too eager to find biblical and patristic support for a Reformed understanding of the centrality of the preached Word in worship. The great march of preachers he presents (over 60 in [the first] two volumes) sometimes looks vaguely like a parade of precocious Presbyterians.[14]

In distinguishing my work from others, I have no illusion of its adequacy, much less perfection. Only one who has struggled with the vast expanse of the data can realize how difficult, if not impossible, it is to bring it into terse coherence. I make only three claims. The first is that trying to write this book has been the most enjoyable task I have ever undertaken. The second is that, since publication will occur in my seventy-seventh year, I have the sense of *ars longa, vita brevis* that must come to anyone who tries to survey two thousand years of the history of anything. And the third is that this is the best I can do.

Having stated how the idea for my history of preaching originally came to me, described what it intends to do and how that is gone about, and distinguished this from other works in the field, it is now necessary to acknowledge my indebtedness to a long list of persons and institutions whose help has made it possible for me to complete this undertaking. This should begin with an expression of gratitude for financial assistance. I was granted two sabbatical leaves from Seabury-Western Theological Seminary, where the Right Reverend Mark Sisk was dean at the time. Generous study grants were provided me by the Conant Fund of the Executive Council of the Episcopal Church in 1987 and 1989; the Pew Charitable Trust through the Association of Theological Schools in 1989–90; and the Lilly Fund of St. Paul's Episcopal Church, Indianapolis, in 1989.

The Newberry Library graciously made me a research associate in 1989–90, the College of Preachers welcomed me as Scholar in Residence and chaplain in 1994, and Seabury-Western accepted me back as Scholar in Residence in the fall of 2000. My thought on the history of preaching was developed through courses taught in that field at Seabury-Western, the University of Notre Dame, the Summer School of Vancouver School of Theology, the Association of Chicago Theological Schools' Doctor of Ministry in Preaching Program, the Divinity School of Duke University, the Doctor of Ministry Program at Emmanuel School of Religion, and the College for Seniors at the University of North Carolina-Asheville. I was also invited to give endowed lectures at Bexley Hall and the School of Theology of the University of the South.

In addition to the libraries of the institutions mentioned above, I am grateful for access to the libraries of the following: Northwestern University, the University of Chicago, Jesuit-Krause-McCormick, Cambridge University, Wesley Theological Seminary, the Virginia Theological Seminary, and Mars Hill College. There are three librarians who must be thanked personally: Newland Smith of the United Library of Seabury-Western and Garrett-Evangelical, Thomas Stokes of Emmanuel School of Religion, and James Dunkly of the University of the South. Without their constant help, this work could not have been completed in retirement in the mountains of North Carolina. Jim Dunkly, especially, was tireless in making bibliographical searches and doing other things to see that I had the books I needed. A different sort of bibliographical help came from Benjamin Cothran, who scanned and turned into editable text most of the documents reproduced on the CD-ROM, saving me many hours of work.

I have never ceased to be amazed at the helpfulness of other scholars, a number of whom—some perfect strangers—have sent me prepublication photocopies of their books. Others have provided me with copies of articles, read over parts of this work and made suggestions, supplied me with bibliographical leads, and otherwise assisted me in my research.

Their assistance is acknowledged in footnotes at the relevant places, an inadequate indication of my gratitude. They, of course, are not to be blamed for any misuse I have made of their erudition.

Colleagues in the Academy of Homiletics and Societas Homiletica have offered suggestions, criticisms, bibliographical leads, encouragement, friendship, and fellowship.

During most of the eighteen years I have worked on this book, I have benefited from the advice, skill, and warmth of my editor at Abingdon Press, Ulrike Guthrie. Only she knows the depth of my debt.

The support of Jane, my wife for forty-five years, has been the sine qua non of this, as well as of all my other undertakings.

Finally, this work is dedicated to our three children: Carl Lee Edwards, Samuel Adams Trufant Edwards, and Louise Reynes Edwards-Simpson. This is a long-delayed acknowledgment of what they mean to me. I had hoped to honor them before with my part in *The Bible for Today's Church,* but the official nature of that volume precluded my doing so. And then I had intended to dedicate a mystery novel I wrote to them, but that remains unpublished. The advantage of this deferred homage, however, is that they can now be joined by their spouses and children—for all of whom, I am profoundly grateful.

Notes

1. John Stott, *Between Two Worlds: The Art of Preaching in the Twentieth Century* (Grand Rapids, Mich.: Eerdmans, 1982).

2. Edwin C. Dargan, *A History of Preaching,* 2 vols. (1905–12; reprint, New York: Burt Franklin, 1968).

3. Yngve Brilioth, *A Brief History of Preaching,* trans. Karl E. Mattson, The Preacher's Paperback Library (Philadelphia: Fortress, 1965).

4. The architectural forerunner of a pulpit or lectern.

5. Ibid., 9.

6. This is a long way from what is meant today by the historical sense.

7. The fact that the Gospels themselves supply such interpretations gave the practice much authority. Nor is allegorical preaching yet dead. I once heard a fundamentalist radio preacher treat the ministrations of the good Samaritan allegorically because he could not believe that Jesus would have spoken approvingly of wine, even as a topically applied medicine.

8. Werner Schütz, *Geschichte der christlichen Predigt,* Sammlung Göschen, Band 7201 (Berlin: Walter de Gruyter, 1972).

9. Clyde E. Fant Jr. and William M. Pinson Jr., eds., *20 Centuries of Great Preaching,* 13 vols. (Waco, Tex.: Word, 1971).

10. Ibid., 1:viii-ix.

11. Volume 13 is devoted to an index.

12. Ronald E. Osborn, *Folly of God: The Rise of Christian Preaching* (St. Louis: Chalice, 1999). See my review in *STR* 44.1 (2000): 103-5.

13. Hughes Oliphant Old, *The Reading and Preaching of the Scriptures in the Worship of the Christian Church* (Grand Rapids, Mich.: Eerdmans, 1998–2002). See my reviews in *STR* 44.1 (2000): 105-8, and *PSB* 20 (1999): 351-52.

14. Thomas Long, review of *The Reading and Preaching of the Scriptures in the Worship of the Christian Church*, by Hughes Oliphant Old, *Christian Century* (December 2, 1998): 1154.

LIST OF ABBREVIATIONS

APR	Abingdon Preacher's Library
ASS	*Acta sanctae sedis*
AARDS	American Academy of Religion Dissertation Series
ARR	American Academy of Religion Studies in Religion
AJP	*American Journal of Philology*
AmUS	American University Studies
ABD	*The Anchor Bible Dictionary*
ACW	Ancient Christian Writers
ANQ	*Andover-Newton Quarterly*
ANF	*Ante-Nicene Fathers*
1 Apol.	*Apologia i (First Apology)*
ARG	*Archiv für Reformationsgeschichte*
AT	Author's Translation
ATR	*Anglican Theological Review*
BCP	Book of Common Prayer
CHR	*Catholic Historical Review*
CFS	Cistercian Fathers Series
CSS	Cistercian Studies Series
CWS	Classics of Western Spirituality
CO	*Calvini Opera*
CEP	*Concise Encyclopedia of Preaching*
Conf.	*Confessionum libri XIII* (Augustine: *Confessions*)
De Sacr.	*De sacramentis* (Ambrose: *The Sacraments*)
EncJud	*Encyclopaedia Judaica*
EEC	*Encyclopedia of Early Christianity*
ER	*The Encyclopedia of Religion*
ERE	*Encyclopedia of Religion and Ethics*
Ep.	*Epistulae* (Augustine: *Letters*)
FC	The Fathers of the Church
FZPhTh	*Freiburger Zeitschrift für Philosophie und Theologie*

GAO	Great American Orators
GOTR	*Greek Orthodox Theological Review*
Hist. eccl.	*Historia ecclesiastica* (Eusebius: *Ecclesiastical History*)
Hom. Act	*Homiliae in Acta apostolorum* (Chrysostom)
Hom. Col.	*Homilae in epistulam ad Colossenses*
Hom. 1 Cor.	*Homiliae in epistulam i ad Corinthios*
Hom. Matt.	*Homiliae in Matthaeum*
IDB	*The Interpreter's Dictionary of the Bible*
JHI	*Journal of the History of Ideas*
LCC	Library of Christian Classics
LPT	Library of Protestant Thought
LCL	Loeb Classical Library
LXX	Septuagint
MQR	*Mennonite Quarterly Review*
MGH	Monumenta Germaniae Historiae
NCB	New Century Bible
NIB	*The New Interpreter's Bible*
NovTSup	Supplements to Novum Testamentum
NPNF[1]	*Nicene and Post-Nicene Fathers*[1]
NPNF[2]	*Nicene and Post-Nicene Fathers*[2]
Or. Bas.	*Oration in laudem Basilii* (Gregory: *Orations*)
OBT	Overtures to Biblical Theology
ODCC	*The Oxford Dictionary of the Christian Church*
OECT	Oxford Early Christian Texts
PG	Patrologia graeca (= Patrologiae cursus completus: Series graeca) (J.-P. Migne)
PL	Patrologia latina (= Patrologiae cursus completus: Series latina) (J.-P. Migne)
PPL	The Preacher's Paperback Library
PSB	*Princeton Seminary Bulletin*
RB	*Revue biblique*
SBLSBS	Society of Biblical Literature Sources for Biblical Study
STRev	*Sewanee Theological Review*
SC	Sources chrétiennes
SWR	Studies in Women and Religion
NovTSup	Supplements to Novum Testamentum
TS	Texts and Studies in Religion
TDNT	*Theological Dictionary of the New Testament*
ThH	Théologie historique
TCP	*20 Centuries of Great Preaching: An Encyclopedia of Preaching*
VC	*Vigiliae christianae*

PART I

HOMILETICAL ORIGINS

THE EARLIEST CHRISTIAN PREACHING

There is no activity more characteristic of the church than preaching. Along with the sacraments, most Christian bodies consider the proclamation of the Word of God to be the constitutive act of the church.[1] No other major religion gives preaching quite the central role that it has in Christianity. Most major religions authorize persons to ritualize and storify their integrating myths; to preserve, interpret, and teach the current relevance of their sacred writings; to connect the past with the present and the future; and, in most cases, to win converts to the faith. But in the Christian religion, "the preacher, by and large, plays a more central role."[2] Judaism[3] and Islam[4] are the two other great monotheistic faiths in which homiletical activity approximating that of Christianity is most common.

The material included within or excluded from this account of the history of preaching was shaped and/or determined by the following basic definition of a "sermon":

> a speech delivered in a Christian assembly for worship by an authorized person that applies some point of doctrine, usually drawn from a

3

biblical passage, to the lives of the members of the congregation with the purpose of moving them by the use of narrative analogy and other rhetorical devices to accept that application and to act on the basis of it[5]

The overwhelming majority of Christian sermons have been delivered at regular worship services, especially those conducted on Sundays. Even most of the efforts to convert non-Christians through preaching have occurred at regular meetings of the Christian assembly. While there have been exceptions, such as open-air preaching, even that has often been accompanied by Scripture reading, prayer, and hymn singing, which turn the event into a service of worship. In addition to sermons in the ordered round of worship and those preached in missionary or evangelistic contexts, the other main category has aimed at instruction in the faith. Not all catechesis has been preaching within the definition given above, but at least the instructions in preparation for Christian initiation given by such early church fathers as Ambrose, Cyril of Jerusalem, and John Chrysostom fit within the genre of sermon. The subject of this investigation, then, is Christian preaching at the regular liturgy and in missionary/evangelistic and catechetical situations that falls within the definition of a sermon.[6]

Many will undoubtedly wonder why anyone would wish to bother writing or reading a history of preaching. Certainly the reputation of the activity in some quarters is such as to cause curiosity about it to appear perverse. Thus the third definition of *preach* in the first edition of the *Oxford American Dictionary* is "to give moral advice in an obtrusive way." Nor is it a compliment to call any discourse "preachy." The early-nineteenth-century wit Sydney Smith, himself a priest and even a canon of St. Paul's, said that

> preaching has become a by-word for long and dull conversation of any kind; and whoever wishes to imply, in any piece of writing, the absence of every thing agreeable and inviting, calls it a sermon.[7]

Even the most committed Christian has to acknowledge that there is more justice to such complaints than one wishes were the case. In spite of all that may be said against preaching, however, its history has proved to be of enormous interest to many scholars who have no personal bias in favor of the church. Indeed, most of the monographs in the field, those that make up so much of the bibliography of the present study, are the work of scholars whose field is not church history or homiletics. Many have been historians in other fields, whether political, social, or literary. Folklorists have studied African American preaching, scholars of Middle English have searched manuscripts for sermon illustrations that furnished the plot for early secular writings in the vernacular, and students of the American Revolution have read sermons to see how the decision to take up arms against the Crown was formed. Those interested in the evolution of public speaking have found secular rhetoric influencing homiletical theory, and styles in preaching shaping the work of those who engaged in other forms of public address. Nor has preaching been studied only for the light it could cast on something else; literary critics have found the styles of preachers in various periods to be worthy of attention in their own right. Thus many who have made no personal religious commitment have found *some* Christian preaching, at any rate, worthy of all the attention they could give it.

The attitudes toward preaching of "those who profess and call themselves Christians," however, are of a wholly different order. The most extreme claims have been made for the value of the activity. Paul, for instance, said:

> "Everyone who calls on the name of the Lord shall be saved." But how are they to call on one in whom they have not believed? And how are they to believe in one of whom they have never heard? And how are they to hear without someone to proclaim[8] him? And how are they to proclaim him unless they are sent? As it is written, "How beautiful are the feet of those who bring good news!" (Rom. 10:13-15)

Thus he can say: "God decided, through the foolishness of our proclamation, to save those who believe" (1 Cor. 1:21) and say of himself: "Woe to me if I do not proclaim the gospel!" (1 Cor. 9:16). The interpretation of the early church fathers that was collected into the most authoritative biblical commentary of the Middle Ages, the *Glossa Ordinaria*, found preaching represented allegorically on almost every page of the sacred text. The two greatest of the Reformers, Luther and Calvin, both assumed that the ordinary medium by which election to salvation is effected was preaching. Finally, the *Decree on the Ministry of Priests* of the Second Vatican Council says that "the primary duty of priests is the proclamation of the Gospel of God to all." Thus there are many, believers and nonbelievers alike, for whom investigating the development over time of Christian preaching is a worthy effort.

PREACHING IN THE NEW TESTAMENT

The obvious place to begin a history of Christian preaching would seem to be the New Testament, but when one investigates the matter closely, it becomes clear that there is little in the New Testament that fits the definition given above for Christian preaching. It is true, of course, that there is a larger sense in which everything in the New Testament is preaching. This has been recognized since at least 1918, when Martin Dibelius wrote:

> At the beginning of all early Christian creativity there stands the sermon: missionary and hortatory preaching, narrative and parenesis, prophecy and the interpretation of scripture.[9]

Norman Perrin has summarized the point of view by characterizing the New Testament literature as fundamentally proclamation *(kerygma)* and exhortation *(parenesis),* admitting at the same time that within these two major categories there are many subdivisions.[10] The proclamation involves both the preaching of the kingdom of God by Jesus and the early church's message that Jesus is the one through whom God acted decisively for the salvation of human beings, and the *parenesis* is exhortation that grows out of the proclamation. Hence the indicative declares the history of the Christ event, and the imperative spells out the implications of that event for living.

There is a sense, therefore, in which everything in the New Testament is preaching. And yet, paradoxically, there is another sense in which none of it is. In the strict terms of the definition above, there are probably no sermons as such in the New Testament, no texts that had been delivered orally to an assembly for evangelization, instruction, or worship.

Jesus' preaching could be thought to provide an exception, but it fails to do so on at least two counts. First, since its content was the breaking in of the reign of God and it refers only by implication to its proclaimer's role in that incursion, it is not, strictly speaking, Christian preaching. Second, while the Gospels contain long speeches that are placed on the lips of Jesus, scholars doubt that any of them reflect the content of a discourse he gave on any single public occasion. The Q material presented in Matthew and Luke as continuous speeches of Jesus is, on closer inspection, obviously made up of what seem a series of "one-liners" rather than a developed presentation of thought. Indeed, each verse could be a distillation of an entire sermon. By the same token, the discourses in the Fourth Gospel, which do sound like consecutive speeches, could have grown out of the evangelist's meditation over the years on a single statement of Jesus such as one of the synoptic verses.[11] Thus, while it is certain that preaching was the main form of communication employed by the founder of Christianity, none of his actual sermons are available to be studied for insight into the nature of Christian preaching.

Nor is it likely that any of Paul's sermons *as such* have survived. Paul makes it very clear that he had a strong sense of vocation to preach to the Gentiles the gospel of Christ crucified and risen, and he nowhere gives any indication of a similar sense of vocation to write letters to distant congregations. Yet the letters are what remain and not his missionary, catechetical, and presumably liturgical sermons. Many questions that have plagued New Testament scholars could be answered if we knew how Paul persuaded his Gentile converts to accept Christianity. Certainly there could be a more balanced understanding of his theology if we knew the content of the instruction he gave those converts in preparation for baptism. All that can be reconstructed, however, is what is implied in his letters. While a certain amount of overlap might be expected between the contents of the two kinds of communication, and it can be assumed that what was written later was consistent with what had been said earlier, it cannot be assumed that what he delivered orally was the same as what he wrote. To repeat, none of Paul's sermons have been preserved in a form in which they can be identified as such and analyzed as specimens of his preaching.

An exception to this conclusion is thought to be found in the Acts of the Apostles. A considerable portion of Acts, after all, is taken up with speeches of one sort or another,[12] many of them claiming to be the missionary sermons of Paul—or Peter or some other representative of the primitive church. All of these missionary sermons, however, have the same outline:[13] they begin with what is taken to be a prophecy from the Hebrew Bible, go on to claim that the prophecy was fulfilled in and by Jesus, document that claim by saying that the apostles were witnesses of its fulfillment, and call upon members of their audience to repent and believe the gospel. The unlikelihood that all of these preachers always followed the same outline means that the reports in Acts cannot be taken as transcripts of actual sermons. Indeed, since in a few short verses they present discourses that could have taken hours to deliver, their evidential value is further diminished. Their sounding so much like real speeches is evidence not of their historicity but of Luke's extraordinary literary skill in creating such convincing scenes. Thus, if the sermons in Acts convey any information at all about preaching in the early church, the most that can be assumed is that they tell what Luke thought the missionary preaching of his own day should be like.

7

Some scholars do believe that at least two New Testament books contain material that originated in oral proclamation: 1 Peter[14] and the Epistle to the Hebrews.[15] Even if those claims are justified, however, there seems to be little reason to think that the shape of Christian preaching in the New Testament period can be reconstructed—which is to say that, while true Christian preaching began much earlier, the *history* of Christian preaching cannot be traced back earlier than the middle of the second century.

While Christian preaching itself cannot be traced earlier, however, there are two pre-Christian movements, Jewish synagogue preaching and Greco-Roman rhetoric, that must be studied before we can understand the way Christian preaching developed.

SYNAGOGUE SERMONS

The New Testament suggests that the first Christian congregations did not understand themselves as part of a new religion, but rather as Jewish synagogues differing from their co-religionists only in claiming that Jesus was the Messiah. Thus it can be expected that their organization and worship would develop along the lines that were already established, making, at first, only the adaptations required by their devotion to Christ, such as initiation by baptism and celebration of the Eucharist. Since other synagogues were accustomed to sermons, it was only natural that churches should have them too. Passages from holy Scripture read at worship assemblies were interpreted and applied to the lives of the people. This knowledge, however, does not contribute as much to clearing away the mist that hovers over the origins of Christian homiletics as might be hoped, because little trace has been left of either the beginnings of the synagogue as an institution or the earliest kinds of preaching done in synagogues.

While most scholars still think the synagogue originated during the Exile in Babylon (sixth century B.C.E.) to provide the people of God with a way to "sing the Lord's song in a strange land" (Ps. 137:4 KJV), no evidence exists to prove that is so. Indeed, the earliest traces of the institution go back only as far as the Hellenistic period. The word *synagogue* itself is Greek *(synagōgē)*, which has a root sense of gathering or assembly. The other early term is *proseuchē*, a Greek word meaning either "prayer" or "a place of prayer." The first appearance in this connection of *proseuchē*, the older of these terms, is in the third century B.C.E.[16] The oldest synagogue building to have been identified was built on the island of Delos during the second century B.C.E. In Israel itself, the oldest synagogue remains are on the Golan Heights at Gamla; they date from just before or after the beginning of the Common Era. The next oldest are in two fortresses erected by Herod the Great, Masada and the Herodium (built on a hilltop near Bethlehem), but the religious use of these buildings may date only to their occupation during the revolt against Rome, 66–70 C.E. Yet by the first century of the Common Era, synagogues were very common both within Israel and throughout the Diaspora, as literary references in the New Testament, from Josephus, and elsewhere attest. It has been estimated, for instance, that there were 365 synagogues within Jerusalem itself by that time.

Our knowledge of the worship conducted in synagogues at the time of Christian beginnings is very slim, yet the little that is known of the patterns developed after the destruction of the Temple suggests that "a Jew of the first century would find himself at home in a synagogue of the twentieth century."[17] The Sabbath morning service was dominated by readings from the Torah and the Prophets (the latter called the *haftarah*), a homily, weekly hymns, and the fixed prayers that "constituted but a small, though significant part of the day's liturgy."[18]

While "nothing is known of [the] beginnings" of the synagogue sermon,[19] it may have begun with the *Targum*, the extempore translation of the reading from the Torah into Aramaic for the benefit of worshipers who did not understand Hebrew. The Targum was nearer a paraphrase than an exact translation, and it was often embellished with haggadic[20] expansion. By the time the Temple was destroyed, however, the Targum had become a much more straightforward translation, and the instruction and edification that had been incorporated into it had been transferred to the sermon. The sprightliness that had characterized the haggadic features of the Targum, however, was not completely lost in the sermon. Haggadic interpretation continued to make more obvious the relevance of Torah to daily life.

> By using at times daring methods of interpretation, the preachers succeeded in making the Bible an unceasing source of ever-new meaning and inspiration in which answers to the problems of every generation could be found.[21]

The preachers also knew that to get their messages across, they had to make them entertaining as well as edifying. They enlivened their sermons with all the techniques of popular speech that Christian preachers of later centuries also would employ.

While elements of thousands of synagogue sermons from the first four or five centuries of the Common Era have been preserved in later collections, seldom do any appear in exactly the form in which they were delivered. And most of those that do survive come from a period that was too late to influence the evolution of Christian preaching. While there was undoubtedly a period in the early days of the church when sermons heard in its assemblies would have closely resembled in form those heard in the synagogues, none from either tradition exist today to be compared.

The oldest synagogue sermons that have been passed down are very different from any Christian sermons. We can see this by taking a quick look at the two main forms of synagogue sermons in the ancient collections. One is called the *proem* type, taking its title from the term used by Greek rhetoricians to refer to the introduction of a speech. What is introduced in this homily form, however, is not the rest of the sermon, but the lection from the Torah. Such a sermon begins with another verse entirely, one from another section of the canon, that makes a point similar to that made in the first verse of that day's reading.[22] "From the 'remote' verse the preacher gives a series of explanations and clarifications that succeed in shedding new light on the Torah reading."[23] Such a sermon would end with the first verse of the Torah lection, and then that passage would be read by those assigned that responsibility.[24]

While the other sermon form to be examined is more like Christian sermons in that it involves exposition of the lection itself rather than serving as an introduction to its reading, it probably represents an even later development. Surviving examples are in collections known as *Tanchuma*, which have been so radically edited that what remains is a "literary" production that was never preached in the form in which it has come down. Nevertheless, it is possible to reconstruct the form of the sermon and even occasionally to extrapolate something close to what must have been delivered. The sermons in the *Tanchuma* seem to have been created as responses to questions about Jewish law, because they begin with the expression "Let our rabbi teach us" *(yelammedenu rabbenu)*.

In presenting an example of the genre, Stegner lists the elements that were generally included in sermons of this type:

1. The sermon begins with a statement of the first verse of the passage or several words from the first verse....
2. A key word or words are explained and emphasized throughout the sermon.

3. Other words and phrases from the whole passage (not just the initial verse) are explained and repeated in the sermon.

4. Other biblical verses are cited for purposes of illustration or for developing side points, etc.

5. Illustrations are drawn from Scripture or contemporary life.

6. If scriptural illustrations are used, the biblical story is frequently retold with imaginative additions to the text.

7. In the conclusion a word or words from the opening verse are repeated to indicate the sermon is ended.

8. Frequently, the main thrust of the sermon is summarized in the conclusion.[25]

Such an abstract description could leave the impression that *yelamme-denu* sermons were very similar to patristic Christian homilies, but actually they were quite different in form and, especially, in content. This can be seen clearly in the example of the type examined by Stegner. **(See Vol. 2, pp. 3-6,** for a translation of this sermon.) Its text is Genesis 9:20, "And Noah became a man of the soil."[26] For the preacher, the word *soil* carries a sense of defilement; it is as though the text read "And Noah became dirty," with all the connotations that expression might have. Thus the sermon is an exhortation to ritual purity and the study of Torah rather than to the lesser activities of human life. While the allegorical interpretation of Christian preaching from at least Origen on was as figurative as this, the difference in the way the case is argued and the ideal of the religious life held up have a very different atmosphere and bespeak quite different communities and cultures.

In short, while Christians learned from the synagogue to have sermons at their worship services and to base those sermons on biblical passages that were read at the services, the oldest synagogue sermons that have survived occurred too late to resemble the earliest Christian preaching very closely.

GRECO-ROMAN RHETORIC

The oratorical tradition of classical culture was another influence from the environment of the early church that, through the centuries, proved almost as powerful a force in shaping Christian preaching as the textual commentary of synagogue sermons. What is important for the history of preaching is not so much the *history* of Greco-Roman rhetoric as introducing *concepts* and *vocabulary* that will recur in the history of Christian preaching—especially in the golden age of the Fathers, when all of the great preachers had been trained as rhetoricians, and in the Renaissance, Reformation, and Romantic periods, when the recovery of classical rhetoric had considerable influence on preaching.[27]

Most cultures in the history of the world have produced great oratory. The difference between the ancient Greeks and the others is that Greece also developed a technical vocabulary about oratory that facilitated analysis of it. This conceptualization of public speaking was a result of there being no professional lawyers in Greece. Citizens had to argue their own cases in court, and some were better at it than others. Thus the conceptualization began in the fifth century B.C.E. when little handbooks about effective techniques to use started to appear. The great synthesis of Greek thought on the subject was the work of Aristotle,[28] who defined the aim of rhetoric as the discovery of the available means of persuasion. While many others also wrote on the topic, the Roman appropriation of rhetorical theory is best seen in the compilations of Cicero[29] and Quintilian.[30]

The three sorts of occasions on which Athenians might be called upon to speak in public were in the courts of law, in the legislative assembly, and at ceremonial events. Each required its own appropriate manner of speaking (what the Romans called *genus dicendi*). The law courts, for instance, had to decide what had happened in the past, the *boule* had to agree upon what needed to be done in the future, and ceremonial occasions called for praising or blaming someone or something in the present. These three types of oratory came to be called, respectively, the forensic, the deliberative, and the demonstrative or "epideictic."[31]

Classical thought divided the task of preparing to speak into five stages: invention (figuring out what to say to make one's case), disposition (the outline the speech should follow), elocution (style, especially in the sense of deciding what figures of sound and thought would best contribute to making one's case), memory (preparation for delivery), and delivery itself. Invention recognized the existence of three kinds of "proof": the trustworthiness of the speaker *(ethos)*, reason *(logos)*, and appeal to the emotions *(pathos)*. Each of these seemed generally more appropriate to one part of a speech than another: *ethos* should be established in the introduction, *logos* was necessary for the body,[32] and *pathos* was most effective in the conclusion. Instead of kinds of proof, Cicero spoke of the orator's duties. Since, however, these are to prove *(probare)*, to delight *(delectare)*, and to stir or move *(flectere)*, he obviously meant something very similar. Each of these duties could be connected with one of the levels of style: the plain for proof, the middle for pleasure, and the grand for moving. (The grand is not the most flowery; that is the middle, which is intended for the pleasure of the audience. The grand style aims at moving the audience to believe or do what the speaker is calling upon them to believe or do.)

"Disposition" identified the elements thought to be required for each type of speech. Since the forensic speech was taken as normative from the beginning, the textbooks usually did not discuss in such detail the outline of either of the other types. A forensic speech was expected to have six parts: introduction, narration, partition, confirmation, refutation, and conclusion. In the introduction the speaker had to make the audience well disposed, attentive, and receptive. The narration set the facts of the case before the jury. In the partition the audience was told what would follow in a list of either the points of disagreement or the points the speaker would try to prove. In the confirmation those points were made, and in the refutation the opponent's case was attacked. The conclusion involved a combination of summarizing what had been said and arousing feeling against the opponent and in favor of the speaker. The appropriateness of such a pattern for arguing a case in court at a time when each of the two speakers was given only one opportunity to speak is immediately apparent. What is not so apparent is the helpfulness of this pattern to a preacher trying to write a sermon, since this outline provides no place for the explication of the biblical text on which the sermon is based. However, that would not prevent many homiletical authorities in the future from insisting that preachers should follow it exactly.

The elements of a deliberative speech were essentially the same as those of a forensic speech, although stating the way the speech was divided into its points was not required, nor was a narration, although one could be included. The proof was divided into a series of "headings" *(kephalaia)*. Epideictic speeches had only three main parts—the introduction, body, and conclusion—but there were elaborate lists of topics that should be included in the body, dealing with the life of the person being celebrated or attacked or the quality being praised or blamed.

Good style was thought to have four virtues: (1) grammatical correctness; (2) clarity in expression and arrangement of ideas; (3) propriety in matching style to content; and (4) ornamentation with figures of sound and thought to amplify what was said, give it emphasis and distinction, and maintain contact with the audience. The three levels of style have already been mentioned. Over the centuries in which rhetorical theory was being refined, different writers disagreed over taxonomy, but one way to discuss the tasks of style was to divide the subject into the selection of individual words and of combinations of words. Issues in the choice of separate words included using the *mot juste,* how classical the word had to be, and figurative uses ("tropes") such as synecdoche, metonymy, hyperbole, metaphor, or deliberate misuse of a word.[33]

The combination of words was called *composition* and involved figures of sound, figures of thought, and groupings of phrases. Modern usage tends to combine the first two into "figures of speech," but the ancients recognized that some of these forceful uses of language work through their effect on the ear. Thus anaphora, alliteration, assonance, and *homoiteleuton* were called figures of sound. Other figures of speech, however, depended on the ideas they expressed. Such figures of thought included antithesis, rhetorical question, apostrophe, climax, chiasmus, and lingering on a subject while appearing to say something else *(expolitio).* Words usually were grouped in periodic sentences, that is, sentences consisting of a "number of elements, often balanced or antithetical, and existing in perfectly clear syntactical relationship to one another."[34] The opposite of such a way of organizing sentences is the "running" or "run-on" iterative style.

The two remaining stages in the preparation of a speech recognized by classical rhetoric were memory and delivery. It was assumed that speeches not given impromptu[35] were to be memorized, and the rhetoricians devised elaborate techniques for such feats of memorization; techniques that are taught today by authors of self-improvement books promising better memory. These, however, had little influence on the history of preaching. And advice on delivery then was not very different from what is familiar today. As such, little needs to be said about these topics to prepare the way for the appropriation of classical rhetoric by Christian homiletics.

THE OLDEST KNOWN CHRISTIAN SERMON

That there was preaching at Christian assemblies for worship from the earliest days is clear from a description of such assemblies written by Justin Martyr in the middle of the second century:

> On the day called Sunday all who live in cities or in the country gather together in one place, and the memoirs of the Apostles or the writings of the prophets are read, as long as time permits. Then when the reader has finished, the Ruler in a discourse instructs and exhorts to the imitation of these good things.[36]

14

After that the Eucharist continued. We know something of what that preaching was like from two works from the mid- to late-second century that meet the criterion of being texts written for oral delivery to a Christian congregation assembled for worship.

The first has been known since the fourth century as *The Second Epistle of Clement to the Corinthians,* under the belief that it was written by Clement of Rome.[37] Both 1 Clement and 2 Clement were associated with each other in the thought of the time and in the manuscripts.[38] Analysis of style, however, shows that they do not have the same author. And explicit references in the text identify 2 Clement as a sermon rather than a letter, e.g., such indications of the oral nature of the document as "now while we are being exhorted by the presbyters" (17.3).[39]

This sermon fills about ten pages of a modern book and can be read aloud in approximately half an hour. It begins with the strong christological claim that "we ought to think of Jesus Christ just as we do of God."[40] It appears that the sermon was a response to the reading of Isaiah 54:1, which says:

> Sing, O barren one who did not bear;
>> burst into song and shout,
>> you who have not been in labor!
> For the children of the desolate woman will be more
>> than the children of her that is married, says the LORD.

This verse is understood here, as it is in Galatians 4:27, to refer to the relative situations of the church and Israel. With that, however, the parallels of 2 Clement with Paul cease, since the sermon comes close to preaching salvation by works rather than grace.

The argument of the sermon is that since Jesus has shown such mercy on Christians by calling them to salvation, they must demonstrate their gratitude by living in a manner consistent with their calling so they will receive the reward that can be theirs. "If we do the will of the Father and keep the flesh pure and keep the commandments of the Lord, we shall receive eternal life" (8.4).[41] While the sermon rambles a bit, it has a relatively clear thread of thought, which is summarized by Grant and Graham:

1. God's gracious, creative action in Christ on our behalf (1:1–2:7)
2. The response of acknowledging him in deed (3:1–4:5)
3. The Christian warfare in this world (5:1–7:6)
4. Repentance in expectation of the world to come (8:1–12:6)

5. Repentance and faithful obedience in gratitude and in hope (13:1–15:5)

6. While we have time, then, let us repent, using present opportunities to prepare for the judgment to come (16:1–20:5)[42]

The sermon ends with a doxology:

> To the only invisible God, the father of truth, who sent forth to us the Saviour and prince of immortality, through whom he also made manifest to us truth and the life of heaven, to him be the glory for ever and ever. Amen.[43]

The argument is developed by frequent quotations from Scripture. These are remarkable not only for their quantity but also for the range of material regarded as canonical. In the twenty chapters, each of which is hardly more than a paragraph long, there are about sixty explicit quotations from or allusions to the Bible, not to mention other possible echoes. Most references to the Hebrew Bible are to the Prophets or Psalms. More surprisingly at so early a date, most of the books of the New Testament are also cited, the most obvious exception being all of the Johannine literature.[44] There are even a few quotations from apocryphal gospels, especially the Gospel of the Egyptians. Karl Paul Donfried has pointed out that many of the chapters in the midsection of the sermon (chaps. 3–14) follow the pattern of (1) statement of theme, (2) scripture quotation, (3) exhortation, and (4) scripture quotation. As to the way the quotations are used,

> they are illustrations of the point being made, yet, the very fact that these quotations are not simply taken from ancient worthies but carry the authority of the Jewish and early Christian traditions, allows them not only to illustrate but to support authoritatively that which is being said.[45]

Different scholars have assigned the provenance of 2 Clement to every major center of the early church, but, with the exception of Donfried, they agree that it was written in the middle of the second century. This makes it the oldest surviving Christian sermon. Wherever it was written, the author, to be literate, would necessarily have had some exposure to classical rhetoric, on which the educational system of the time was built. The effect on him of that exposure, however, was minimal. In this regard he was just the opposite of the writer of the next oldest sermon that has been preserved.

MELITO'S PASCHAL HOMILY

Known only by title and unidentified fragments before 1940, Melito of Sardis's *Homily on the Passover*[46] (see **Vol. 2, pp. 6-18**, for a translation) has become widely recognized for the light that it sheds on the early history of the Christian calendar and liturgy. Melito, bishop of a church in eastern Asia Minor during the last third of the second century, was the author of about twenty other works that are still lost except for fragments.[47] His contemporaries regarded him as one of the "great luminaries" of Asia, and Tertullian admired his prose style. Beyond his belonging to the Quartodeciman party, little else is known about him except what may be deduced from his homily.

Another source of insight into Melito's sermon, however, is knowledge of the situation in Sardis. Situated about sixty miles inland from Smyrna (modern Izmir) and Ephesus, Sardis was built as the capital city of the Lydian Empire, the last king of which had been the Croesus of legendary wealth. The city retained its importance under the Persians and Seleucids, and under Roman rule it was one of the leading cities of the province of Asia. Sardis was one of the seven churches of the Revelation: the seer was instructed to tell the angel of that church that it had a name for being alive, but was really dead (3:1). The most important thing about Sardis as background to Melito's homily, however, is the size and influence of the Jewish community there. The enormous synagogue that has been excavated there, which had a main hall that could accommodate as many as a thousand worshipers, was not acquired by the Jews until the early third century, but it nevertheless indicates how large the community must have been half a century earlier when Melito was bishop.

Awareness of the size of this community is necessary for understanding Melito, because "almost a third of the text of the Homily on the Passion is preoccupied with the condemnation of 'Israel.'"[48] While persecution of Christians in the Roman Empire was not nearly so intense as it would become in a little more than a century, theirs was not a religio licta, and they could be and were persecuted and martyred. Although such incidents were sporadic, local, and often mob actions rather than the result of judicial process,[49] they seem to have intensified in that area during this period. Another work of Melito, an apology[50] directed to Marcus Aurelius of which a fragment is preserved in Eusebius,[51] calls attention to this intensification in stating that "something that has never happened at all before, the race of the godly is persecuted, being harassed by new decrees throughout Asia."[52]

Near the time of Melito's sermon, eleven Christians from nearby

Philadelphia were martyred at Smyrna, as was also Smyrna's venerable bishop, Polycarp. And the *Martyrdom of Polycarp* links Jews with Greeks as those who agitated for his death (12.2). This was not unusual in Melito's time and area. "In the persecutions which were to wrack Asia in the reign of Marcus Aurelius [A.D. 161–80] the Jew was often in the background."[53] This should be remembered when one reads Melito's statement that "God is murdered. The king of Israel is destroyed by an Israelite hand" (96).[54] This fact does not excuse Melito's statement, but it does point to an extenuating circumstance.

Melito's sermon dates from the period when the paschal mystery was celebrated as a unified event including not only everything from trial to resurrection and ascension, but all Christ's work of redemption, including the incarnation. Thus the exact occasion on which it was preached cannot be tied down neatly according to the Christian calendar of today. The one night on which Melito preached celebrated everything from Christmas to Pentecost.

Melito's Quartodecimanism[55] is also important for understanding his sermon. The name of the group is derived from the Latin word for "fourteen" because of their distinctive belief that Easter—or, more properly, the Christian Passover—should be celebrated on the same day as the Jewish Passover. As long as the Temple existed, Passover lambs were slaughtered on the fourteenth day of the month of Nisan in preparation for the *Pesach*, which began at sundown that day. This is to say that the paschal observance did not ordinarily occur on a Sunday; the fast began on whatever day of the week Nisan 14 fell. It also means that the early part of Melito's liturgical celebration ran simultaneously with that of the synagogue in Sardis.

The paschal observance began with a fast during the day of Nisan 14 followed by a vigil that night.[56] At "cock crow" (the third watch of the night, which lasted from midnight until 3:00 A.M.) the fast was broken by an *agape* meal followed by the Eucharist.[57] During the vigil there was a reading of Exodus 12, and Melito's homily commented on that passage. For a fuller picture of the liturgical context, we should remember that in Melito's time, Christian assemblies were still held in private homes, there were no distinctive garments for clergy, and the bishop probably sat while he preached.

Essentially, the sermon is an interpretation of the account of the Passover in Exodus as a foreshadowing or "type" of the death and resurrection of Christ. It begins with a long account of salvation history, showing the necessity for a redeemer. That is followed by a statement of the principles of typological interpretation, which leads into an identification of the salvation wrought through Christ with all that was prefigured in the exodus, especially the Passover. Next comes an extended apostrophe to Israel, in which Israel is blamed for rejecting Christ and necessitating the crucifixion. The peak of emotional intensity occurs when Melito speaks in the voice of Christ, proclaiming and offering the salvation he brings. There follows an almost creedal summary of the work of Christ that leads into the doxological conclusion.

The homily is notable for the thoroughness with which it introduces classical rhetoric into Christian preaching, the indebtedness it may have had to Jewish Passover celebration, and the way it anticipates later Christian liturgical forms. Campbell Bonner, who published the text of Melito's homily in 1940, considered it to be the first example of Christian art prose, but he attributed its style to biblical and Oriental sources. Since then, patristic scholars have suggested instead that it represents the Asian school of classical rhetoric prominent in the Second Sophistic.[58]

The Asianic style of the Second Sophistic is notable for its use of what are called Gorgian figures. A representative of the First Sophistic and one of the first teachers of rhetoric in Athens, Gorgias went there originally as an ambassador from his native city, Leontius, in Sicily. The impression he made was striking enough to provoke Plato to write a dialogue against him.[59] What made Gorgias's public speaking so striking was his use of what have since been known as his "figures":

> These include phrases or clauses with contrasting thought (antithesis), often of equal length (parison); rhyme at the ends of clauses (homoeoteleuton); and a fondness for sound play of all sorts (paronomasia).[60]

In Melito's sermon we can find these figures and others as well, with anaphora, apostrophe, and personification being among the more conspicuous.

Most of these can be seen in the first three sentences of the homily:

> The scripture from the Hebrew Exodus has been read
>   and the words of the mystery have been plainly stated,
>   how the sheep is sacrificed
>   and how the people is saved
>   and how Pharaoh is scourged through the mystery.
> Understand, therefore, beloved,
>   how it is new and old,
>   eternal and temporary,

19

> perishable and imperishable
> mortal and immortal, this mystery of the Pascha:
> old as regards the law,
>> but new as regards the word;
> temporary as regards the model,
>> eternal because of the grace;
> perishable because of the slaughter of the sheep,
> imperishable because of the life of the Lord;
> mortal because of the burial in earth,
> immortal because of the rising from the dead.[61]

Antithesis gives the passage its basic structure, the contrasted clauses are of similar length, and the parallel phrases have the same ending in Greek. In the first sentence, for instance, the words for "stated," "sacrificed," "saved," and "scourged" all end in -*etai*.[62] Anaphora occurs in the way the last three phrases in that sentence begin with "how." Apostrophe occurs in Melito's address to Israel, and personification when he speaks in the voice of Christ. This small sample does not exhaust the rhetorical devices used in the homily but only indicates the density with which they occur.

Efforts to evaluate the homily say as much about the taste of the critic as they do the quality of the homily. Some consider the homily eloquent and beautiful while others find it showy. It can be said objectively, however, that the homily reflects both the influence of the Septuagint, especially the poetic books, and also that of the sort of rhetoric with which professional orators were dazzling Asia Minor at the time. From this point on, classical rhetoric will shape Christian preaching.

But, as noted above, this homily has liturgical as well as homiletical significance. It has been argued, for instance, that it reflects the influence of Jewish liturgy. Hall says that it "shows signs of direct debt to the Jewish Passover recitation called the Haggadah."[63] It has also been argued[64] that the homily is a direct ancestor of the *Exultet* sung at the Easter vigil in the Western rite, which begins:

> Rejoice now, all ye heavenly legions of Angels: and celebrate the divine mysteries with exultation: and for the King that cometh with victory, let the trumpet proclaim salvation.[65]

Assuming Talley's date for Melito's homily of "around 165,"[66] one can see that by Melito's time Christian preaching had been going on for more than a century and a quarter. Already it had begun to show two of the main characteristics that would characterize it throughout the patristic

20

period: (1) it would be based on the continuous exposition of a biblical text, and (2) it would utilize the techniques of Greco-Roman rhetoric. The remaining chapters of this section will explore how these characteristics were refined.

FOR FURTHER READING

Grant, Robert M. *First and Second Clement.* Vol. 2 of *The Apostolic Fathers: A New Translation and Commentary.* New York: Thomas Nelson, 1965.

———. *Greek Apologists of the Second Century.* Philadelphia: Westminster, 1988.

Kennedy, George A. *Classical Rhetoric and Its Christian and Secular Tradition from Ancient to Modern Times.* Chapel Hill: University of North Carolina Press, 1980.

Meyers, Erich L. "Synagogue." Pages 252-60 in vol. 1 of *ABD.* Edited by David Noel Freedman et al. New York: Doubleday, 1992.

Stegner, Richard. "The Ancient Jewish Synagogue Homily." In *Greco-Roman Literature and the New Testament.* Edited by David E. Aune. SBLSBS, no. 21. Atlanta: Scholars Press, 1988.

Sur la Pâque et fragments Méliton de Sardes. Introduction, critical text, translation, and notes by Othmar Perler. SC, no. 123. Paris: Cerf, 1966.

Notes

1. Some bodies speak of "ordinances" rather than sacraments, but most of them observe at least baptism and the Lord's Supper, the main exception being the Society of Friends, or Quakers.

2. Charles Rice, "Preaching," in *ER,* ed. Mircea Eliade (New York: Macmillan, 1987), 11:494. It is possible, however, that this position is overstated. Professor Frank Reynolds of the University of Chicago has informed me in a letter dated April 30, 1997, that preaching as defined in this chapter "has always and continues to be a central component in Buddhism." He is also of the opinion that preaching is important in Jainism, but says that little has been published on the subject. Mr. Alok Gupta told me that preaching is a regular part of the worship of his Hindu tradition and his congregation in Mysore, India.

3. I will say more about early Jewish preaching later in this chapter.

4. See D. S. Margoliouth, "Preaching (Muslim)," in *ERE,* ed. James Hastings et al. (Edinburgh: T&T Clark; New York: Scribner's, 1910), 10:221-24.

5. This is an adaptation of a definition I first gave in my *Elements of Homiletic: A*

Method for Preparing to Preach (New York: Pueblo, 1982), 7, and restated in my article "History of Preaching," in *Concise Encyclopedia of Preaching,* ed. William H. Willimon and Richard Lischer (Louisville: Westminster John Knox, 1995), 184. Each part of the definition is analyzed in *Elements of Homiletic,* 7-16. The version of the definition given above seeks to make it general enough to include the preaching that occurs in non-Christian religions, yet the present work will consider very little other than Christian preaching.

6. Standard Roman Catholic publications also list theological argument as a type of preaching and there have indeed been sermons in the history of the church that consisted largely of that. On the Roman Catholic classifications, see Fred A. Baumer, "Toward the Development of Homiletic as Rhetorical Genre: A Critical Study of Roman Catholic Preaching in the United States Since Vatican Council II" (Ph.D. diss., Northwestern University, 1985).

7. Saba Holland, *A Memoir of the Reverend Sydney Smith, by His daughter, Lady Holland* (London: Longman, Brown, Green, and Longmans, 1855), 1:43.

8. "To proclaim" and "to preach" are interchangeable translations of the verb Paul uses here, *kērussein.*

9. Dibelius's words are quoted by Norman Perrin in *The New Testament: An Introduction* (New York: Harcourt Brace Jovanovich, 1974), 19.

10. Ibid., 19-21.

11. See, for example, Barnabas Lindars, *The Gospel of John,* NCB (London: Oliphants, 1972).

12. "The speeches in Acts—Dibelius (*Studies in the Acts of the Apostles,* ed. Heinrich Greeven, trans. Mary Ling [New York: Scribner's, 1956], 150) has counted 24, of which 8 belong to Peter, 9 to Paul—occupy, in round figures, 300 of the book's 1000 verses." Ernst Haenchen, *The Acts of the Apostles: A Commentary,* trans., rev. and brought up to date by R. McL. Wilson (Philadelphia: Westminster, 1971), 104 n. 1.

13. For a summary of research on the speeches in Acts up until the time of writing, see Werner Georg Kümmel, *Introduction to the New Testament,* trans. Howard Clark Kee, rev. ed. (Nashville: Abingdon, 1975), 167-69.

14. Kümmel, however, does not believe any part of 1 Peter was ever a sermon. See ibid., 419-21.

15. Yet Kümmel does believe that Hebrews is a sermon to which there has been added an epistolary conclusion. See ibid., 398. Johann Berger proposed the homiletical origin of Hebrews as early as 1797.

16. This information on the history of the synagogue is based on Erich L. Meyers, "Synagogue," in *ABD,* ed. David Noel Freedman et al. (New York: Doubleday, 1992), 6:252-60. I also consulted Geoffrey Wigoder, *The Story of the Synagogue: A Diaspora Museum Book* (San Francisco: Harper & Row, 1986).

17. Wigoder, *The Story of the Synagogue,* 17.

18. Ben Zion Wacholder, "Prolegomenon" to Jacob Mann, in *The Bible as Read and Preached in the Old Synagogue* (1940; reprint, New York: KTAV, 1971), 1:xi.

19. Joseph Heinemann, "Preaching. In the Talmudic Period," in *Encyclopaedia Judaica* (Jerusalem: Keter, 1971), 13:994.

20. To oversimplify, rabbinic exegesis is usually classified as either *Halakah* or

Haggadah (also transliterated as *Aggadah*). Halakic interpretation is an analytical process aimed at deriving rules and principles, stating clearly what is involved in the observance of Torah. Haggadic interpretation is freer, more creative, analogical, and homiletic, and involves stories and examples. To make the matter more confusing, Haggadah is also the term used to refer to the liturgy for the Passover Seder.

21. Heinemann, "Preaching. In the Talmudic Period," 13:994.

22. The nearest Christian equivalent to the proem form comes in the thematic sermons of the late Middle Ages in which a "sermonette" (horrible word!) on a protheme (a biblical text differing from the text of the sermon proper) is preached while the congregation is assembling. The protheme had to make the same point that the theme of the sermon proper would make. In contemporary worship, children's sermons often seem to serve a similar purpose.

23. William Richard Stegner, "The Ancient Jewish Synagogue Homily" in *Greco-Roman Literature and the New Testament,* ed. David E. Aune, SBLSBS, no. 21 (Atlanta: Scholars Press, 1988), 53. Stegner provides a translation and an analysis of a proem homily, 55-58.

24. In time there would be lectionary cycles established, but it is not clear that those existed when the church was still under the influence of the synagogue. The cycles of Torah and Haftarah developed separately. The one-year cycle still in use began in Babylon, but a four-year (actually longer) cycle was followed in Palestine.

25. Stegner, "The Ancient Jewish Synagogue Homily," 58-62. The sermon translated is found on 60-62.

26. Modern English translations treat "man of the soil" as an appositive of Noah, but the homily depends on a more literal consideration of the Hebrew text.

27. The easiest access to the history of Greco-Roman rhetoric is through the numerous writings of George A. Kennedy, including *Classical Rhetoric and Its Christian and Secular Tradition from Ancient to Modern Times* (Chapel Hill: University of North Carolina Press, 1980); *New Testament Interpretation Through Rhetorical Criticism* (Chapel Hill: University of North Carolina Press, 1984); and *A New History of Classical Rhetoric* (Princeton: Princeton University Press, 1994). Also invaluable is Richard A. Lanham, *A Handlist of Rhetorical Terms,* 2nd ed. (Berkeley and Los Angeles: University of California Press, 1991); Brian Vickers, *In Defence of Rhetoric* (Oxford: Clarendon Press; New York: Oxford University Press, 1988); and James L. Golden, Goodwin F. Berquist, and William E. Coleman, *The Rhetoric of Western Thought,* 3rd ed. (Dubuque, Iowa: Kendall/Hunt, 1983).

28. The most common edition of the Greek text is that which appears in Aristotle, *The "Art" of Rhetoric,* trans. J. H. Freese, Loeb Classical Library (Cambridge: Harvard University Press, 1926; London: William Heinemann, 1926). George A. Kennedy has translated it more recently, with an introduction, notes, and appendices in *Aristotle on Rhetoric: A Theory of Civic Discourse* (New York: Oxford University Press, 1991).

29. In addition to being an orator, Cicero wrote extensively on the subject of rhetoric. His works on the subject, all of which are available in Loeb editions, include *On Invention,* written while he was still in his teens and destined to be the most popular rhetorical textbook of the Middle Ages; *On the Orator,* written as a dialogue; *Brutus,* a history of Greco-Roman rhetoric in the form of a dialogue; and *Orator,* in

which he states his own taste in rhetoric. A convenient English edition of *On the Orator* and *Brutus* is *Cicero on Oratory and Orators,* trans. or ed. by J. S. Watson, Landmarks in Rhetoric and Public Address (Carbondale: Southern Illinois University Press, 1970). Another handbook long thought to have been by Cicero and very influential in the Middle Ages is the anonymous *Rhetorica ad Herennium,* translated for the Loeb Classical Library by Harry Caplan (1954).

30. The Latin text of Quintilian's *Institutio Oratoria* and a translation by H. E. Butler appear in four volumes in the Loeb series (1921–36).

31. There are other English translations of these and indeed most of the technical terms of rhetoric.

32. Needless to say, a good bit of invention consisted of the discovery of arguments to be used in proof. Earlier, this was done by reviewing the appropriate *topoi* (Latin, *loci*), the "places" to look for arguments. Later, however, more attention was concentrated on *stasis* (Latin, *status*), which made the identification of the basic issue of the case the determining factor in the kinds of argument sought.

33. All of these differ from the "figures" proper in that they involve only one word. This is one of the more confusing distinctions to modern readers.

34. Lanham, *A Handlist of Rhetorical Terms,* 112-13. For an idea of how complex such a sentence could be, see the diagram of a sentence of Isocrates made by Kennedy in *Classical Rhetoric,* 36.

35. As declamations of the Second Sophistic were given.

36. *1 Apol.* 67. The translation used is that of *St. Justin Martyr: The First and Second Apologies,* trans. with intro. and notes by Leslie William Barnard, ACW, no. 56 (Mahwah, N.J.: Paulist Press, 1997).

37. Scholars often point out that *The Second Epistle of Clement to the Corinthians* is not by Clement, is not an epistle, and was not written to the Corinthians.

38. They were even considered by some in the early church to be part of the New Testament canon, as may be seen from their inclusion in Codex Alexandrinus, an important Greek manuscript of the entire Bible from the early fifth century.

39. Karl Paul Donfried claims we cannot call 2 Clement a sermon or homily because we cannot give a firm form-critical description for either classification. Then he calls it a deliberative speech, ignoring the classical form of that *Gattung* and at the same time discerning in the work a pattern altogether different from that of a deliberative speech. Finally, he says that the probable sociological setting for the pattern he discovers was "oral exhortation to an assembled Christian congregation" (48), which sounds remarkably close to the definition of preaching proposed above for this history of preaching. *The Setting of Second Clement in Early Christianity,* NovTSup, no. 38 (Leiden: E. J. Brill, 1974).

40. Quotations from 2 Clement are taken from either Kirsopp Lake's translation of *The Apostolic Fathers,* vol. 1, in the LCL (1912–13), or Robert M. Grant and Holt H. Graham's *First and Second Clement,* vol. 2 of *The Apostolic Fathers: A New Translation and Commentary* (New York: Thomas Nelson, 1965), depending on which makes clearest the sense to which attention is being called. The critical perspective taken is very close to that of Grant and Graham.

41. Grant and Graham, *First and Second Clement,* 120.

42. Ibid., 111.

43. Lake, *The Apostolic Fathers,* 1:163.

44. Some deviations of quotations from the text of the canonical Gospels raise the question of whether the author was quoting from oral tradition, written textual variants not otherwise known, or from inaccurate memory of the canonical text.

45. Donfried, *The Setting of Second Clement in Early Christianity,* 96-97.

46. The translation ordinarily quoted will be that in *The Christological Controversy,* trans. and ed. Richard A. Norris Jr., Sources of Early Christian Thought (Philadelphia: Fortress, 1980).

47. The fragments are collected, translated, and commented upon in *Melito of Sardis:* On Pascha *and Fragments,* texts and translations edited by Stuart George Hall, OECT (Oxford: Clarendon Press, 1979).

48. John Griffiths Pedley, "Sardis," in *ABD,* 5:984.

49. The process itself almost encouraged that since Roman law did not provide for governmental agencies to detect the commission of crimes and to prosecute the perpetrators. Rather, charges were brought into court by *delatores,* citizens who made the accusations.

50. The Apologists were the second group of Christian writers after the New Testament period. Whereas the Apostolic Fathers wrote practical treatises addressed to the church, the Apologists wrote defenses (which is what "apologies" means in this context) of Christianity. Many of the treatises were, like that of Melito, addressed to the current emperor and presented arguments against the persecution of Christians. On the Apologists in general see Robert M. Grant, *Greek Apologists of the Second Century* (Philadelphia: Westminster, 1988). His treatment of Melito is on pp. 92-99.

51. *Ecclesiastical History* 4.26.5-11. The Greek text of the fragment and an English translation appear in *Melito of Sardis:* On Pascha *and Fragments,* 62-65.

52. Ibid., 63.

53. W. H. C. Frend, *Martyrdom and Persecution in the Early Church: A Study of a Conflict from the Maccabees to Donatus* (Garden City, N.Y.: Anchor Books, 1967), 194.

54. Norris, *The Christological Controversy,* 46.

55. This term is slightly anachronistic since Quartodecimans were only labeled as such later in the century during the synods over the date of Easter. It is used here, however, because it calls attention to the nature of Melito's paschal celebration. I am grateful to Professor Thomas J. Talley for pointing this out.

56. By Jewish reckoning a day began at sundown rather than midnight, as in the modern usage, or at daybreak, as in the Gospels.

57. *Sur la Pâque et fragments Méliton de Sardes,* intro., critical text, trans., and notes by Othmar Perler, SC, no. 123 (Paris: Cerf, 1966), 25. For a thorough analysis of the observance of the paschal vigil up until the time of Nicaea, see Thomas J. Talley, *The Origins of the Liturgical Year* (New York: Pueblo, 1986), 1-37. What is known of the Quartodeciman vigil comes from a second-century apocryphal work, *Epistula Apostolorum,* which appears in *New Testament Apocrypha,* ed. Wilhelm Schneemelcher; English trans. R. McL. Wilson (Philadelphia: Westminster, 1963), 1:189-227. The relevant section is on pp. 199-200.

58. Hall provides the references to the literature in *Melito of Sardis* On Pascha *and*

Fragments, xxiii-xxiv. On the Second Sophistic see George Kennedy, *A New History of Classical Rhetoric,* 230-41; on Asianism, see pp. 95-96.

59. Brian Vickers concludes a devastating analysis of the dialogue by saying: "In a careful reading, then, Plato's case against rhetoric in the *Gorgias* is based on a calculated perversion of his own principles of dialectic. We can no longer be taken in by Socrates' claim that he is pursuing the truth." *In Defence of Rhetoric,* 84-120, with the quoted words appearing on the last page.

60. Kennedy, *A New History of Classical Rhetoric,* 20. In *Classical Rhetoric and Its Christian and Secular Tradition,* 29-30, Kennedy comes as close as one can in English to giving the effect of one of Gorgias's Greek sentences (taken from his description of Helen of Troy): "Born from such stock, she had godlike beauty, which taking and not mistaking, she kept. In many did she work much desire for her love, and her one body was the cause of bringing together many bodies of men thinking great thoughts for great goals, of whom some had greatness of wealth, some the glory of ancient nobility, some the vigor of personal agility, some command of acquired knowledge. And all came because of a passion which loved to conquer and a love of honor which was unconquered. . . ."

61. Hall, *Melito of Sardis:* On Pascha *and Fragments,* 3. Hall's translation is followed here, because he arranges it typographically to show the rhetorical structure.

62. The first has an *eta* instead of an *epsilon,* but the difference in sound would be small.

63. Hall, *Melito of Sardis:* On Pascha *and Fragments,* xxvi. He goes on to spell out what he means by that and to summarize other theories.

64. Perler, *Sur la Pâque et fragments Méliton de Sardis,* 24-29.

65. The translation used is that of *The People's Anglican Missal in the American Edition* (Mt. Sinai, N.Y.: Frank Gavin Liturgical Foundation, Inc., 1961), A 185.

66. Talley, *Origins of the Liturgical Year,* 32.

CHAPTER 2

THE HOMILY TAKES SHAPE

THE PATTERN OF CLASSICAL EDUCATION

While it is true that training in Greco-Roman rhetoric such as Melito of Sardis received was to have enormous influence on Christian preaching, another element of the classical education system was to play an even more decisive role in its development. Like the modern pattern of formally socializing children into a culture, classical *paidea* also had its elementary, secondary, and advanced stages. "In Rome as in Greece rhetoric belonged to the sphere of higher education and was its chief manifestation."[1] Elementary education in antiquity strikes modern people as very elementary indeed, consisting of little more than learning how to read, write, and count a little through a regimen of mechanical drill and corporal punishment.[2]

For the future of Christian preaching, it was secondary education that was decisive in its importance. For the Greeks and, in a derivative way, for the Romans, this schooling was initiation into the culture through study of its classic literature. Primarily this was a study of poetry, which was thought to be the best expression and summary of what the society was about. And among the poets the epic poets reigned supreme: Homer for the Greeks and Virgil for the Romans. But the lyric poets and the dramatists were read as well. Generally, the only prose writings studied were those of the historians, since the works of the orators were deferred to higher education in rhetoric.

The aspect of this education that was to be so determinative for preaching was the way the literature was taught by the schoolmaster, or grammarian *(γραμματικός)*. First, students were given a plot summary of the passage they were to study, an ancient Greek equivalent of Cliffs Notes. Next, since the copies the students had of the work being studied were handwritten, there was a certain amount of variation between them, and the instructor had to lead the students laboriously through the text to be sure they were all reading the same words. After that, other difficulties imposed by the manuscripts had to be dealt with. Since writing at the time did not separate words and did not make use of punctuation, students were required, after thorough preparation, to read the passage aloud expressively to show that they could make up for these deficits. Then, after the students had gone over the text so closely several times, they took the next step by memorizing it. With such preliminary work out of the way, students undertook the real task—the explanation of the text—which was called exegesis *(ἐξήγησις)*, the word Christians have taken over to mean "biblical interpretation." Explanation involved, first of all, defining words in the text; no small task since Homer's vocabulary was archaic by then. Next, the inflected forms of the words had to be noted and the grammatical structures indicated by those forms. Students studied etymologies as guides to meaning, and pointed out figures of speech. Then the persons (divine as well as human), places, times, and events mentioned in the text had to be identified, a process that was called "historical" study.

All of this analysis, however, was not considered to be an end in itself, nor was its purpose merely aesthetic. The program was designed to initiate the young into their culture and its values. Its end, therefore, was moral education. Teachers completed their presentation of a reading by pointing to the ethical example it held up. Over time, however, readers recognized that Homer, whose writings were valued as scripture to the Greeks, often depicted the immortal gods as engaged in unedifying activities. This meant that pointing out the moral was not always a straightforward task. It was often supposed that the poet was speaking symbolically and calling for an allegorical interpretation. This program of secondary education was, therefore, socialization into the life of a community. And the method by which the grammarian taught had great influence on the way the homily developed.[3] Before that can be

28

considered, however, it will be necessary to say something about what happened to preaching after Melito, especially in Egypt.

INTERPRETING THE WORD IN ALEXANDRIA

Several Latin homilies have come down from the early third century, most of pseudonymous attribution to Cyprian, and a few Greek homilies under the name of Hippolytus. The most influential homiletic development of the early church, however, came from Greek-speaking Egypt. As its name implies, Alexandria was founded by Alexander the Great when he conquered Egypt in 332 B.C.E. Located at the mouth of the Nile, Alexandria had access to all the Mediterranean area. Its strategic importance was recognized by Ptolemy I, one of Alexander's three *diadochoi* who inherited that part of his empire and who built it into one of the world's great cities. Ptolemy's descendants ruled his section of the empire until it passed into Roman hands after the well-known suicide of Cleopatra VII.

From the beginning Alexandria was intended to be a great cultural and intellectual hub. Ptolemy had erected there a large center dedicated to the Muses of all the arts and intellectual endeavors. In Greek the name of the center was the *Mouseion*, which, transliterated into its Latin form of *Museum*, passed on to so many later institutions. Ptolemy invited about a hundred scholars to make their homes in Alexandria, where they were supported by generous salaries. He also built and stocked the famous library there whose collection ran into hundreds of thousands of volumes. Thus from its beginning, Alexandria was the intellectual capital of the Mediterranean world, a title it continued to hold under the Romans most of the way through the third century of the Common Era.

The city had great commercial significance as well: its excellent harbor made it possible for Egypt to become the granary of the Roman Empire. The wheat trade, in addition to a variety of other products and forms of commerce, meant that the city was very prosperous, which, in turn, meant that it drew immigrants from other countries. Thus Alexandria had a Jewish population of nearly one million persons, more than twelve times the population of Jerusalem,[4] and certainly the largest community of the Diaspora. It was for this population that the Greek translation of the Hebrew Bible, the Septuagint, was made. Furthermore, several books written in Alexandria came to be included in copies of this translation. Among these apocryphal books are the Wisdom of Solomon and some of the books of Maccabees.

The most prolific author of the Alexandrian Jewish community was Philo, called "the Jew" *(Judaeus)*, who lived in the last two decades before and the first five of the Common Era. During his time there was considerable strife between the Jews and the other inhabitants of Alexandria, and Philo worked hard to overcome that. At the same time he was worried that many young Jews seemed dazzled by Greco-Roman philosophy and literature and were in danger of leaving their ancestral faith. Since he himself was deeply immersed in such studies, Philo wrote a number of books showing that Judaism and the Bible were consistent with the deepest insights of Stoic, Pythagorean, and Platonic thought.

In order to do this, he used the method by which the philosophers interpreted Homer to study the Hebrew Bible. The sort of allegorical interpretation made by the grammarians mentioned above began with Stoic philosophers who assumed that any anthropomorphic descriptions of the gods and their behavior in the Homeric poems were an indication that the passages were to be understood symbolically. For the Stoics, the names of gods were references to elements or forces of nature. While philosophers of other traditions did not adopt these Stoic interpretations, they did take readily to the hermeneutical method by which they were made, and allegorical interpretation became a standard technique for getting around stories whose literal meaning offended their sensitivities.[5]

No one is certain when or how Christianity first arrived in Alexandria. Eusebius cites an anonymous "they" as saying that "Mark was the first to be sent to preach in Egypt the gospel which he had also put in writing, and was the first to establish churches in Alexandria itself" (*Hist. eccl.* 2.6). While that legend is late, a recently discovered letter of Clement of Alexandria shows that it was believed in Egypt itself in the late second century.[6] What this probably means is that by the time of Clement, even the church in Alexandria did not remember how Christianity had been planted. The earliest Christian writers from the city who can be definitely identified were the early second-century gnostic heresiarchs Basilides and Valentinus.

The first orthodox teacher there whose name has come down to us was Pantaenus. Little is known about him other than that he had traveled in India and was involved in preparing catechumens for Christian initiation in Alexandria. An older generation of scholars liked to refer to "the catechetical school of Alexandria," but too little is known to claim the sort of succession in office they described. Clement appears to have arrived in Alexandria around 180 to study under Pantaenus and stayed on to teach, possibly holding school on the model of pagan philosophers and such Christian teachers as Justin Martyr. He appears to have left

Alexandria before 215 and possibly as early as 202. There is no direct evidence that Clement taught Origen, although the influence of his thought is unmistakable. All of this is to say that remarkable Christian teachers, heretical and orthodox, are known to have been in Alexandria in the second century. While a good bit is known about some of their thoughts through their writings, little is known about either the circumstances under which they taught or the church in the city at that time.

The earliest sermon-like document from Alexandria is a delightful piece produced by Clement of Alexandria near the beginning of the third century. Many scholars consider it a homily because it is a verse-by-verse analysis of Mark 10:17-31 that seeks to provide an answer to the question *Who Is the Rich Man Who Shall Be Saved?* It even ends with a wonderful legend about John. But, since it would take a couple of hours to deliver and it is not known whether Clement was ever ordained, the most that can be said is that, while it follows the literary pattern of a homily and does so remarkably well, one cannot know whether it was delivered orally to a congregation.

ORIGEN THE ORIGINAL

Credit for creating the classical form of the homily has to go to the one who is also known as "the first Christian systematic theologian," Origen. With him the study of Christian preaching moves from the vague to the definite. After the handful of sermons that remain from an earlier time— 2 Clement and Melito's homily, and the few others attributed to Cyprian and Hippolytus—there is suddenly a preacher from whose ministry more than two hundred sermons have survived. Admittedly, all but about twenty of them are preserved only in Latin translations that are by no means literal. Nevertheless, there is a large enough body of work to analyze. And from such analysis it is clear that he practiced a definite homiletical method. That method gave to Christian preaching the basic shape it was to keep until the High Middle Ages, the pattern of what is called the homily.[7] Since the preacher involved was one of the two or three greatest minds in the history of the church, there is no reason to assume that the pattern was created by anyone else. With Origen, Christian preaching not only emerges into the clear light of history, it can also be said to take shape.

Though I have already used superlatives to describe Origen, a sampling of what scholars have said about him might still be in order. One called Origen and Augustine the two greatest geniuses of the early church.[8] Another judged that "his only peers are Augustine and Thomas Aquinas and he remains the greatest theologian the Eastern Church has produced."[9] Another said:

> When changed conditions call the church's message into question, a theologian must develop an all-encompassing religious vision that enables other Christians to interpret their experience. Two theologians, more than any others, have accomplished this for the entire Christian church. Paul of Tarsus is one of them. . . . The other is Origen.[10]

The scholars quoted are the authors of the three general book-length studies of Origen that appeared in the last half of the twentieth century. A less specialized patristics authority, however, says that "compared with the achievement of Origen, the work of the earlier Fathers of the Church seems a mere prelude."[11] And a professional writer who has produced well-received books in diverse fields says, "No one ever wrestled with the inner meaning of Christianity with such formidable energy, such titanic power."[12]

While more is known about the life of Origen than the lives of most other ante-Nicene fathers, there are still major disagreements about many aspects of his life, most of which relate to how much credence should be given to later charges that he was a heretic. There is no doubt that he held opinions inconsistent with later orthodoxy. First of all, no Christian writer before the councils that established the norms in the doctrines of Christ and the Trinity had views completely consistent with the conciliar definitions. Beyond that, even those who admire Origen most have to admit that his speculations included the preexistence of human souls and the ultimate salvation of everyone. While there is general agreement that the teachings condemned as his by the emperor Justinian I and by the Second Council of Constantinople in 553 are more those of his later admirers than his own, the remaining question has to do with the extent to which his attachment to the teachings of Plato shaped the way he articulated Christian doctrine. These interpretations of Origen have divided along denominational lines. "Roman Catholic and Anglican scholars have tended to rely on the Origen of the Latin homilies and the *De Principiis* while Protestants have often used Greek fragments of the *De Principiis* and restricted themselves to works preserved in Greek."[13] Thus the latter have inclined to the more Platonic interpretation.

Present purposes, however, do not require coming down hard on one side or the other. One requires here only enough knowledge of Origen's life to understand how he developed into the preacher he came to be. It appears that he was born ca. 185 into a Christian family. His father, Leonidas, was probably a Roman citizen while his mother, whose name has not been preserved, may have been an Egyptian. His father may have been a grammarian. Certainly he educated his son thoroughly through the secondary level and also saw to it that he studied the Bible. When the boy was almost seventeen, his father perished in the persecution of Septimius Severus. His ardent adolescent son wrote urging him to be steadfast, and apparently was prevented from being martyred himself only by his mother's hiding all his clothes. In fact, martyrdom seems to have exercised a fascination for Origen all his life.

When Leonidas died, his property was forfeited to the state and the support of his mother and six younger brothers fell to Origen. He was enabled by the patronage of a wealthy woman to complete enough of his education to begin teaching grammar himself. Soon, however, the bishop of Alexandria, Demetrius, placed him in charge of preparing catechumens for baptism. In that role he thought he should put aside all secular study and sold his library of classical literature to provide himself with an annuity. His youthful zeal was such that he led a very ascetic life; indeed, he went so far as to take Christ's saying that "there are eunuchs who have made themselves eunuchs for the sake of the kingdom of heaven" (Matt. 19:12) in what Eusebius delicately describes as "too literal and extreme a sense" (*Hist. eccl.* 6.8.2).

Origen's teaching of the faith in Alexandria met with such an enthusiastic response that eventually he had to turn over basic catechesis to one of his pupils, Heraclas, while he himself concentrated on more advanced pupils and on his own scholarship. Somewhere along the way he also continued his own education by studying under the well-known Platonist philosopher Ammonius Saccas. His doing so calls attention to something important in his eventual homiletical development. It reminds us that the death of his father meant that Origen's education was interrupted at the end of the secondary level. He had mastered that well enough to teach its subjects and, out of necessity, he went to work, postponing his higher education. When his own teaching duties required more knowledge than he possessed, he went back to school. At that point, however, he did not begin rhetorical training, which was the standard form of advanced training, but instead devoted himself to philosophical study.

As H. I. Marrou points out, those who did so broke with the usual culture, which was literary, rhetorical, and aesthetic, and devoted themselves to an ascetic way of life as much as to an intellectual system.[14] This understanding meant that Christianity was considered a philosophy at the time, and the ascetically inclined Origen would have found Platonism with its rigorous intellectual and personal demands a far more promising road to improvement than was rhetoric. Indeed, the influence of Clement had already set him moving in that direction.

Thus he began to attend the lectures of Ammonius, who later taught the founder of Neo-Platonism, Plotinus.

> It is impossible to say just what Origen learned from Ammonius. It may be that, like other great teachers, Ammonius influenced his students more by instilling in them a sympathetic yet critical approach to a great tradition than by passing on his particular doctrines.[15]

What was probably most appealing to Origen about Platonism was the defense that it gave against the gnostic heresies that had been such a threat to Christianity for over half a century. Platonism insisted, as did Christianity, on the goodness of creation and the compatibility of divine providence with human freedom. It also offered something that Christianity lacked: "a rational understanding of God's purpose in which all of these seemingly disparate and contradictory doctrines formed a coherent whole."[16]

The theological equipment that Origen was acquiring was adequate for its purpose, as may be seen in the numbers who flocked to him for instruction in the faith. One of these, Ambrose,[17] a Valentinian gnostic he converted to orthodoxy, was to hold great significance in the rest of Origen's life and work. Ambrose, who was well-to-do, was so grateful for Origen's instruction that he provided him for the rest of his life with a team of stenographers to take down every word he said and copyists and calligraphers to publish what was recorded. This, among other things, accounts for the large number of Origen's surviving sermons.

Origen put all of his erudition to use in the service of the church not in theology proper, as one might expect from his philosophical training, although he did write what has been called the church's first systematic theology, as we shall see below. Rather, his overwhelming interest was biblical interpretation. He accomplished the amazing feat of writing on all the books of the Bible in one or more of three literary genres: commentaries, the sort of marginal notes called *scholia,* and homilies. To be sure, most of these works were never completed, and most of what was written down has perished, but the size of the undertaking and the relatively small numbers of his works in other fields indicate that he saw his basic vocation as that of an exegete—the first major exegete in the history of the church.

Some of his major works in other fields are closely related to his biblical study. What has been called his systematic theology, *On First Principles* (Peri Archōn; Περὶ Ἀρχῶν, *De principiis*), was apparently written to answer criticisms on his method of biblical interpretation that arose after some of his commentary on Genesis was first published. (For the section of *On First Principles* dealing with biblical interpretation, **see Vol. 2, pp. 19-40.**)

> *On First Principles* announces itself as simultaneously a philosophical treatise on the relation of God to the world (*archē* in the first range of meaning) and as a development of a coherent body of doctrine from the logical elaboration of the implications of the rudimentary doctrines of the Christian faith (*archē* in the second range of meaning), the implication being, as Origen intended, that the two procedures are identical.[18]

On First Principles begins with a statement of Origen's view of reality, which starts with the three divine persons of the Trinity and proceeds to consider rational creatures, including animate beings, angels, demons, and human beings. After that he looks at particular issues raised by the system stated in the first part. The last of these issues to be discussed, which is of a different order from the rest since it justifies the procedure by which the system had been arrived at, is how the Bible should be interpreted. Essentially this exegetical method was to dominate in the church until the Reformation. I will defer discussion of it, however, until it is seen in practice in the homilies.

While Origen worked for the church in Alexandria he was not ordained. His emasculation would have been an impediment to that. And, admittedly, over the years of his great productivity and popularity, he did not grow closer to Demetrius, the bishop who had appointed him. While it is commonly asserted that Demetrius was jealous of Origen's fame, there was probably an even more basic conflict, that between an intellectual and an organizer, as Joseph Trigg has pointed out.[19] Nor was the blame one-sided. While Demetrius was apparently unaware of what a treasure he had on his staff, Origen was equally blind to the necessity for other gifts in the church. The grace of baptism he attributed mainly to the discipline of the catechumenate, and he considered the Eucharist to be basically a symbol of the knowledge of God that comes through hearing the teaching of God's word. Nor was the church's penitential discipline the best way for a sinner to receive forgiveness; the pastoral attentions of a spiritual person were far more effective.[20] All this to say that the gifts most appreciated by either Demetrius or Origen were those each had.

By the time the break between the two had actually occurred, Origen had become known throughout the Mediterranean world and had even traveled through a good bit of it. In 215 he had been to Rome. For some reason, around 222 the governor of the Roman province of Arabia (modern Jordan) sent a military escort to accompany Origen on a visit to him.[21] Then in 230 Origen moved to Caesarea, possibly because it was in the Holy Land and also was a place where Origen could consult with Jewish scholars. At any rate, he was met with an official reception there very different from what he had at home. The bishop of Caesarea, Theoctistus, invited him to preach at a Eucharist over which the bishop presided and at which the bishop of Jerusalem was present. Demetrius heard of it and was furious. He fired off an angry letter to Theoctistus about the breach of ecclesiastical discipline involved in letting a layman preach in the presence of bishops. But he also sent two deacons to invite Origen to return home, which he did, if only temporarily.

The next year he left Alexandria again. Julia Mammaea, the mother of Alexander Severus, the emperor, was very interested in all religions and especially Christianity. Having heard of Origen's great brilliance, she arranged for him to visit her at Antioch. Not long after returning to Alexandria, Origen set out again, this time for Greece. While en route he passed again through Caesarea and while he was there, Theoctistus ordained him to the presbyterate. While Origen was spending a couple of years in Athens, Demetrius did everything in his power to have him deposed and declared a heretic. Eventually all of that got straightened out and Demetrius died before he could cause any more trouble, but Origen returned to Caesarea rather than Alexandria.

Once there he settled into an extremely productive period in which he taught, wrote, and functioned as a priest. Apparently he was able to teach on a fuller scale than had ever been possible in Alexandria. A testimonial to Origen survives in the form of a *Speech of Appreciation* given in 245 by one of his students at the end of five years of residential study.[22] It has been customary to attribute the speech to Gregory Thaumaturgus, but the more likely author was named Theodore. The oration outlines an elaborate curriculum designed to prepare the student for interpreting the Bible. The course of study began with all the branches of philosophy: logic, "physics" (the study of the natural world), and ethics, which were considered to be prerequisites for being able to understand theology. The theology Origen taught, which apparently Theodore did not stay for, was undoubtedly close to what he wrote in *On First Principles,* because there is little indication that he ever changed his basic beliefs.

By the time Theodore gave his valedictory address, Origen was probably sixty years old. For the rest of his life he continued in the activities that had occupied him up to that point: he continued to produce long and learned biblical commentaries; he traveled a little, going to Athens again; and he ran afoul of the hierarchy, with the bishop of Alexandria especially trying to prove that he was a heretic. He also wrote the work which, after *On First Principles*, was his most important book that was not a biblical study. His patron Ambrose brought to his attention an attack on Christianity called *The True Doctrine*, which had been written about seventy years earlier by a pagan philosopher named Celsus. Origen set out to refute it in the tradition of the apologies for Christian faith that had been written by such second-century worthies as Justin Martyr. Trigg is probably right in his conclusion that the *Contra Celsum* "did more than any other work of its time to make Christianity intellectually respectable," but not all specialists will agree with him that "it defended it as Platonism for the masses."[23]

Not long afterward, Origen almost got what he had longed for much of his life: martyrdom. Decius, the emperor who ascended the throne in 249, was determined to restore Rome's inner strength by a return to traditional values, especially those of Roman religion. He declared that everyone in the empire had to sacrifice to the gods and produce a certificate that proved they had done so. While many Christians did submit, leaving an enormous problem to the church of deciding what to do about them, Origen was made of different metal. Indeed, he was called *Adamantios*—the man of diamond or steel (*Hist. eccl.* VI.xiv.10). His judge thought the cause would be better served by Origen's recantation than by making a martyr of him, so he ordered the rack and threatened fire. While Origen survived the ordeal and outlived Decius, he was disabled the rest of his life, and his injuries were undoubtedly the cause of his eventual death. There is no definite information about him after he was released from prison. He probably died around 253, perhaps in Tyre.

THE PREACHER

As devoted as he was to biblical study, Origen did not preach until he was in his midfifties, and even then he appears to have preached for only a three-year period beginning in 239 or 240. The reason for the delay, of course, is that he was not ordained earlier. Why he stopped preaching is a matter of speculation. His sermons indicate that they were not always well received. Some objected to his allegorical interpretation, others to his altering the familiar text of the Septuagint. His belief in the pre-existence of souls and in the ultimate salvation of everyone may have offended some, while others may have taken issue with his criticisms of the clergy in Caesarea. Some scholars have assumed that Theoctistus, the bishop of Caesarea, may have relieved him of his pulpit duties, and even suggest that his doing so caused ill feelings between them for the rest of Origen's life. This is only inference; there is no explicit evidence that things happened this way. It is, however, consistent with the evidence that exists. If this explanation is accurate, it is replete with irony. It would mean that when the homily form was first introduced, it was not well received, and the preacher who gave to sermons the shape they would keep for almost a thousand years was not able to hold his audience.

All this brings up the question of what Origen's preaching was like. That subject has been treated so well and exhaustively by one scholar, Pierre Nautin, that what follows will simply summarize his findings.[24] He begins with a consideration of the circumstances under which Origen preached. The church in Caesarea in his time apparently celebrated the Eucharist every Sunday and Friday. On the other days of the week there was an assembly at which there was a sermon but no celebration of the sacrament. These weekday services took place before the workday began. The sermon was given by a priest, but not necessarily the same priest every day. There are passages not treated in the collections of Origen's homilies on a particular book, but it is not known whether those were handled by other priests or that there simply was not enough time to cover everything. On Sundays there were readings from the Hebrew Bible and from one of the Gospels, with a homily on each; there may have also been a lection from Acts or an epistle with an explanation of that as well. For the weekday services, however, only an Old Testament lesson was read and preached on. Such services concluded with a prayer.

All services took place in the church with the bishop and priests seated in a semicircle around the altar, the bishop's chair being distinct from the benches on which the priests sat. Deacons were at the door, among the congregation, or at the altar, depending on their duties for the day. The people sat for the sermon. Catechumens also were present for the sermon, this being a major part of their preparation for baptism. The daily services lasted about an hour, but the sermons varied in length. Of the twenty homilies on Jeremiah in Nautin's edition, six are longer than forty pages of the relatively small Sources chrétiennes volumes, in which half of the pages contain the Greek text while the other half carry the translation. One homily, however, is only four pages long, while the rest seem to average about twenty pages. And, as in all churches at all times, not everyone present paid attention to the sermon; some even left early. The deacons kept order much as others were to do during Puritan sermons in colonial New England.

When Origen preached he did so from a position raised above the congregation. His sermons were in effect a rereading of the text with a running commentary on it. This meant that he had a copy of the text open before him from which he read and to which he returned after commenting on each passage. Origen's preaching differed from that of anyone else because of the text that he had before him. As a good grammarian, he needed to begin by establishing the text of the passage on which he commented. Yet he knew that the Septuagint was a translation. For his text to be accurate, it had to match the original Hebrew. To this end, he had some time before prepared a copy of the Old Testament that set in parallel columns with the Septuagint a Greek transliteration of the Hebrew, the word-by-word translation of the Hebrew made by Aquila, a more idiomatic Greek translation by Symmachus, and another by someone named Theodotion.[25] After moving to Palestine he added two more Greek translations, producing what has been called the *Hexapla*. He had also developed a set of symbols that told him at a glance which words from one text were present in another. Thus while he was preaching he could correct the text of the Septuagint to match the Hebrew.[26] While he depended on the *Hexapla* for the text of the passage on which he was preaching, he quoted freely from other parts of the Bible in which the same words or a similar thought appeared, demonstrating a knowledge of Scripture that few have ever been able to match as he explained the Bible by the Bible.

The structure of Origen's homilies owed nothing to rhetorical theories of disposition; he confined himself to the grammarian's task of explicating a text. The nearest he came to providing any formal structure was often to have an introduction and to follow a set pattern for his conclusion. The introduction would begin with something other than the first verse of his passage in order to raise a question to be addressed in his interpretation. Usually these prologues were very short unless he was introducing a point of doctrine. Quite often, however, even such minor preliminaries were skipped. His conclusion, on the other hand, was usually a doxology based on 1 Peter 4:11, "To him [i.e., Jesus Christ] belong the glory and the power forever and ever." To get from biblical explication to these words there would often be a transition of several phrases that was usually an invitation to prayer and perhaps a reminder of death and judgment. Sometimes the shift was more abrupt.

The body of most of the sermons had no logical or rhetorical pattern, but consisted simply of verse-by-verse or phrase-by-phrase explications of the text. In dividing his comments, Origen paid particular attention to grammatical indications of transitions in the text's sentences. He had ways of signaling that he was returning to the text to take up the next bit. Thus he continued through the passage that had been read until either he had commented on its last verse or the time ran out.

In summarizing his description of the sermon form by Origen, Nautin said Origen wished only to explain Scripture as well as he could, and that he was inspired in that task by what he had done previously when he had been a grammarian and was explicating a text his students had in their hands, a passage from Homer or Hesiod rather than from the Bible.[27] Then Nautin goes on to remark how the content as well as the form of Origen's homilies reflect the practice of the grammarian. Origen establishes the correct text, he notes the order of words, he identifies who is speaking and who is spoken to in dialogue and how that relates to the character of each, he is aware when the narrator is not one of the characters, he attends to the significance of the order and choice of words, paying attention to the meaning of a word by noting its etymology or looking at parallel passages in which it appears, he points out figures of speech, and, while doing all of this, he uses the technical vocabulary of the grammarian.[28]

Thus, Nautin deserves credit for observing that the pattern of Origen's homilies is that of a grammarian's lecture. He does not, however, point out two reasons why that is significant. First, Origen's falling into that pattern is a function of the way that his education was interrupted by the death of his father and his teaching at the secondary level as soon as he had completed that level himself. There is a degree of good fortune to the church in his not having gone on to higher education in rhetoric because, as so many homiletical theoreticians failed to note later, none of the *genera dicendi* of classical rhetoric provided for the explication of a text. Origen's training as a grammarian provided him with precisely the genre of speech in the Greco-Roman world that was adaptable to preaching from the Bible. Second, most Christian preaching thereafter until the High Middle Ages and a good bit afterward would continue to follow the pattern of Origen's homily. Much preaching ever since has imitated Origen in giving grammarian's lectures on biblical texts.

Origen's purpose in preaching, however, was no more merely explaining a text than was the grammarian's. Both were concerned that the texts they explicated have the moral and spiritual effect they were intended to, that their intention (βούλημα) be realized. For Origen, therefore, two principles governed his interpretation. The first was the recognition that, since all Scripture is inspired by God, its meaning ought to be worthy of God and thus useful for edifying and nourishing the soul. The second principle was that nothing in the Bible—not a word, the choice of a word, even the repetition of a word—was there by accident. Everything had been placed in the text by God for a particular purpose.

Sometimes the edifying purpose of a passage could be achieved by interpreting it in its simple literal sense. That sense, however, was not always obviously and immediately edifying. For instance, at times the Bible reports scandalous events; at others it makes anthropomorphic references to God. In such cases it was assumed that the text should be interpreted allegorically because the allegorical meaning was the true meaning of the text, the meaning the Holy Spirit intended. As noted above, the grammarians did the same with Homer; Origen the Christian continued to practice his trade as a grammarian. He called his methods of application *moral* and *mystical*. The moral sense looked for the meaning of the passage for the soul, and the mystical sense sought what the passage meant in regard to Christ and the church. At other times Origen would refer to the *letter* and the *Spirit,* a distinction he borrowed from Paul (2 Cor. 3:6).

Allegorical interpretation had a long history when Origen began using it in preaching. We have already seen the way that it developed among Greek philosophers, and how Philo applied the method to the Hebrew Bible. He, however, was not the innovator. This method may already be seen in the book of Wisdom, the so-called *Letter of Aristeas,* and in Philo's predecessor Aristobulus. Now its firm place in the history of Christian biblical interpretation prior to Origen has to be acknowledged. Most of the New Testament bases its theology on interpreting passages in the Hebrew Bible as predictions of redemption in Christ. This kind of interpretation, which uses common principles operating between the historical situations in two periods to treat the first as a prediction of the second, was already in use by the community that produced the Dead Sea Scrolls, as seen in their *Habakkuk Commentary.* While this kind of *pesher* or typological interpretation is not identical with the allegorical method, the two at least share the assumption that the real meaning of some biblical texts is other than the literal, grammatical, historical sense; the New Testament has plenty of both. While the Gospel parables that are given allegorical interpretation (such as the parable of the sower in Mark 4 and parallels) were not scripture at the time the interpretation was given, they quickly came to be. Paul often resorted to allegorical interpretation of the Hebrew Bible, for example, in Galatians 4 when he interpreted the sons of Abraham by Sarah and Hagar as referring to the Jewish and Christian covenants. And the Epistle to the Hebrews could be described as an extended allegory. Thus, Origen may have pushed allegorical interpretation farther than any of his predecessors, but he did not invent anything new.

While Origen has been accused of arbitrary biblical interpretation down to the present century, several things need to be said to set such evaluations in perspective. First, "history," as the term is understood today—the verifiable reconstruction of past events—is an invention of the nineteenth century. When the Reformers, for instance, called for literal instead of allegorical biblical interpretation, they still assumed that the Christian creed was the hermeneutical key to the Hebrew Bible. Further, since the historical meaning of biblical passages is always in reference to their first readers, the only way that any preacher has ever been able to transfer those passages to the lives of latter-day parishioners has been to assume that there were analogies between the original situation and the situation in the congregation that made such a transfer of perspective valid. Analogical application is not very far from allegorical application.[29]

Next, to treat all allegorical application as invalid is to excommunicate most of the preaching in the history of the church. While it is true that allegorical interpretation cannot be used to prove Christian doctrine, it was seldom ever used for that purpose. More often it was used to illustrate Christian beliefs that had been arrived at on the basis of other evidence. Mostly it was a tool for extending the meaning of biblical passages to the lives of Christians of later periods. The impetus for allegorical interpretation both in the time of Origen and later was the basic assumption of biblical inspiration, the belief that God gave the Bible to the church as the main hermeneutical instrument for understanding its own life. Thus it was Origen's preaching that furnished the model for biblical interpretation that dominated for many centuries to come.

There are recurrent themes in Origen's preaching: the preacher's important role; defense of Christian faith against such opponents as those who deny Providence, the Jews, and gnostics; and Christian doctrine.[30] But we can gain a more immediate sense of what he was like as a preacher by examining one of his homilies. The question is how to choose among two hundred homilies. At first one might think one of the twenty on Jeremiah that have survived might be best since they are written in the Greek that Origen spoke, which was duly recorded by his stenographers. There are others, however, that better reveal him at his most typical: the two on the Song of Songs that have survived in Latin translation.[31] While we have noted above the shortcomings of Latin translations of Origen's homilies, those by Jerome are generally much closer to the original than those by Rufinus.[32] And in his prologue to these particular sermons, Jerome claims that he translated them "with greater faithfulness than elegance."[33] This is probably near enough to the Greek to justify looking at a homily on a theme so close to Origen's heart.[34] We will therefore examine the first of these two homilies.

In this homily, at any rate, Origen did not check his Septuagint closely against the Hebrew, for there are major differences between them, and the text he interprets is the Greek. To make what he says comprehensible to anyone who may check his commentary against an English Bible, it appears wise to set a modern translation of the passage based on the Hebrew text in parallel with an English translation of the Latin Vulgate, which is very close to the Septuagint.

NRSV	Vulgate
1:1 The Song of Songs, which is Solomon's. 2 Let him kiss me with the kisses of his mouth! For your love is better than wine, 3 your anointing oils are fragrant, your name is perfume poured out; therefore the maidens love you. 4 Draw me after you, let us make haste. The king has brought me into his chambers. We will exult and rejoice in you; we will extol your love more than wine; rightly do they love you. 5 I am black and beautiful, O daughters of Jerusalem, like the tents of Kedar, like the curtains of Solomon. 6 Do not gaze at me because I am dark, because the sun has gazed on me. My mother's sons were angry with me; they made me keeper of the vineyards, but my own vineyard I have not kept! 7 Tell me, you whom my soul loves, where you	1:1 Let him kiss me with the kiss of his mouth, for thy breasts are better than wine, (2) smelling sweet of the best ointments. Thy name is as oil poured out. Therefore, young maidens have loved thee. (3) Draw me; we will run after thee to the odor of thine ointments. The king has brought me into his storerooms. We will be glad and rejoice in thee, remembering thy breasts more than wine. The righteous love thee. (4) I am black but beautiful, O ye daughters of Jerusalem, as the tents of Cedar, as the curtains of Solomon. (5) Do not consider me that I am brown, because the sun hath altered my color. The sons of my mother have fought against me, they have made me the keeper in the vineyards; my vineyard I have not kept. (6) Show me, O thou whom my soul

pasture your flock, where you make it lie down at noon; for why should I be like one who is veiled beside the flocks of your companions? 8 If you do not know, O fairest among women, follow the tracks of the flock, and pasture your kids beside the shepherds' tents. 9 I compare you, my love, to a mare among Pharaoh's chariots. 10 Your cheeks are comely with ornaments, your neck with strings of jewels. 11 We will make you ornaments of gold, studded with silver.	loveth, where thou feedest, where thou liest in the midday, lest I begin to wander after the flocks of thy companions. (7) If thou know not thyself, O fairest among women, go forth and follow after the steps of the flocks, and feed thy kids beside the tents of the shepherds. (8) To my company of horsemen, in Pharao's [sic] chariots, have I likened thee, O my love. (9) Thy cheeks are beautiful as the turtledove's, thy neck as jewels. (10) We will make thee chains of gold, inlaid with silver.

Origen begins by pointing out the privilege of considering the song that is beyond all others, the Song of Songs, and then moves to determine the genre of the book, deciding with a critical acumen rare for his time that it is a drama and a marriage song, an epithalamium, in which there are four characters: the husband, the bride, her maidens, and the groom's companions. Immediately he identifies the allegorical significance of each: the groom is Christ, the bride the church, the maidens souls of believers, and the companions angels and "those who have come unto the perfect man" (268). In the commentary Origen wrote on the Song of Songs, he allows for two readings, this corporate reading and an individual reading in which the groom is the Logos and the bride a soul. In this homily, however, he gives only the corporate interpretation. That, however, is consistent with an individual application in that Origen calls upon his listeners to "make haste and understand it and to join with the bride in saying what she says, so that you may hear also what she heard" (ibid.).

He understands the bride's words "Let him kiss me with the kisses of his mouth" to be a prayer to God the Father to send the Son. "Thy breasts are better than wine . . . ," etc., is addressed to the Son himself, however. The odor of his perfumes refers to his being the Anointed, the Messiah, the Christ.[35] Such spiritual understanding of Scripture is needed to become worthy of spiritual mysteries, "of spiritual desire and love" (270). The superiority of Christ's breasts to wine indicates that such thoughts "do inebriate and make the spirit glad" (271).[36] The name of Jesus is "as a perfume poured forth" (272), as may be seen in the way that Jesus was anointed by two women, one a sinner and the other not. "As perfume when it is applied scatters its fragrance far and wide, so is the name of Jesus poured forth" (273).

At this point the bridesmaids show up, but they demonstrate their inferiority to the bride by only following the groom instead of walking beside him. They are "standing without because their love is only just beginning" (274), while the bride is able to say to them, "The king brought me into his chamber" (275). They, however, are happy in their subordination, being glad and rejoicing in her, loving her breasts more than wine. They tell the groom that Equity has loved him, thus indicating the sum of her virtues. But the bride's response to being praised is to say that she is "black but beautiful . . . as the tents of Cedar, as the curtains of Solomon," and she tells them not to look at her because she has been blackened by the sun's looking down on her. Her blackness, of course, means that she is not yet fully cleansed from sin, and members of the congregation should be careful not to be black with sin. *Cedar*[37] is a Hebrew word meaning "darkness," as Origen has been told by his Jewish teachers.

When the bride says that the sons of her mother have fought against her, she is referring to Jewish persecution of the church. This may be seen in the apostle Paul, of whom it could also be said that he was a keeper of the vineyard of others rather than of his own, because "he made himself the servant of all that he might gain all" (279). In one of the touching references to his own spiritual life that he makes from time to time in the homilies, Origen sees a parallel to the bride's experience in his own when the groom leaves her, as he often does in the Song.

> God is my witness that I have often perceived the Bridegroom drawing near me and being most intensely present with me; then suddenly He has withdrawn and I could not find Him, though I sought to do so (280).

Continuing in the first person, she asks the groom where he eats lunch and takes his noonday nap. "I ask about the full day-time, when the light is brightest and Thou dwellest in the splendour of Thy majesty" (280). Noting that Joseph's brothers ate at noon, the same hour Abraham entertained the angels, Origen makes his characteristic claim that "Holy Scripture never uses any word haphazard and without a purpose" (ibid.). We, like the bride, must see Christ at his most glorious so that we will not be tempted to leave him for others. Thus the groom warns the bride of the danger that leaving him would place her in, a danger of being among the goats rather than the sheep.

45

The groom then tells the bride that she is as superior to all other women as his own cavalry is superior to Pharao's[38] chariots. Her cheeks, the place where a woman's beauty supremely resides, are like those of a turtledove. The cheeks reveal the beauty of the soul while her lips and tongue are references to her intelligence. So great is her beauty that the bride's naked neck is adorned as if she wore a necklace. Having said all that, the groom takes his rest, but then his companions promise to make her "likenesses of gold with studs of silver" (LXX), but when the groom awakens, he will make for her not likenesses but the real thing.

From this homily it is easy to see that the goal of all of Origen's preaching was the spiritual formation of the congregation.[39] In sermons like this, Origen, the Christian grammarian, set the shape of preaching for centuries to come.

FOR FURTHER READING

Crouzel, Henri. *Origen.* Trans. by A. S. Worrall. San Francisco: Harper & Row, 1989.

Grant, Robert M. *The Letter and the Spirit.* New York: Macmillan, 1957.

Marrou, H. I. *A History of Education in Antiquity.* Trans. by George Lamb. New York: New American Library, 1964.

Origen. *The Song of Songs: Commentary and Homilies.* Trans. and annotated by R. P. Lawson. ACW. Westminster, Md.: Newman Press, 1957.

Trigg, Joseph Wilson. *Origen: The Bible and Philosophy in the Third-century Church.* Atlanta: John Knox, 1983.

Notes

1. H. I. Marrou, *A History of Education in Antiquity,* trans. George Lamb ("Mentor Books"; New York: New American Library, 1964; Madison, Wisc.: University of Wisconsin Press, 1982), 380. This study has become classic. A description of this form of advanced education is given on pp. 267-81, 381-90.

2. Ibid., 210-22, 358-68.

3. Ibid.

4. Jerusalem had a population of around eighty thousand in Jesus' time. "Jerusalem," *ABD,* 3:753.

5. On allegorical interpretation in Greek philosophy and education see Robert M. Grant, *The Letter and the Spirit* (New York: Macmillan, 1957), 1-30, and *The Earliest Lives of Jesus* (London: SPCK, 1961), 38-49.

6. The letter was published by Morton Smith in *Clement of Alexandria and a Secret Gospel of Mark* (Cambridge: Harvard University Press, 1973). Most scholars have accepted the document as a genuine letter of Clement, but are very dubious about the inferences Smith drew from it.

7. To the extent that "homily" is a technical term, it refers neither to the length of the sermon nor to the conversational nature implied by the word's etymology as some have claimed, but to verse-by-verse interpretation and application of a biblical passage. Thus, a homily is what would be called expository preaching today.

8. Jean Daniélou, *Origen,* trans. Walter Mitchell (New York: Sheed & Ward, 1955), vii.

9. Henri Crouzel, *Origen,* trans. A. S. Worrall (San Francisco: Harper, 1989), xi.

10. Joseph Wilson Trigg, *Origen: The Bible and Philosophy in the Third-century Church* (Atlanta: John Knox, 1983), 8.

11. Hans Freiherr von Campenhausen, *The Fathers of the Greek Church,* trans. Stanley Godman (New York: Pantheon, 1955), 40.

12. Robert Payne, *The Holy Fire: The Story of the Fathers of the Eastern Church* (New York: Harper, 1957), 43. Anyone without special training who would like to begin a study of the early church fathers could not ask for a more readable and painless introduction than this book.

13. Robert M. Grant in his foreword to Trigg, *Origen,* 1.

14. Marrou, *A History of Education in Antiquity,* 282.

15. Trigg, *Origen,* 67.

16. Ibid., 73.

17. Not, of course, to be confused with the great fourth-century bishop of Milan.

18. Trigg, *Origen,* 93.

19. Ibid., 130.

20. Ibid., 140-46, 191-200.

21. Scholars disagree over the dates of events in the life of Origen. The opinions of Joseph W. Trigg, which are those of Nautin, are accepted here.

22. A translation of the speech may be read in *ANF,* 6:21-39.

23. Trigg, *Origen,* 239.

24. Origen, *Homélies sur Jérémie,* ed. Pierre Nautin, trans. Pierre Husson and Pierre Nautin, Sources chrétienne (Paris: Cerf, 1976), 1:100-191. For other good treatments of the subject, see Trigg, *Origen,* 176-88; Joseph T. Lienhard, S.J., "Origen as a Homilist," in *Preaching in the Patristic Age: Studies in Honor of Walter J. Burghardt, S.J.,* ed. David G. Hunter (New York: Paulist Press, 1989), 36-52; and Origen, *Homilies on Luke, Fragments on Luke,* trans. Joseph T. Lienhard, S.J., FC (Washington: Catholic University of America Press, 1996), xxiv-xxxvi. For Origen's other homilies in English, see Ronald E. Heine's translation of *Homilies on Genesis and Exodus* (2002), and that of Gary Wayne Barkley for *Homilies on Leviticus 1–16* (1990). Both volumes appear in FC from Catholic University of America Press.

25. Apparently Origen got the idea from synagogues in Alexandria, which used the transliteration and the translations of Aquila and Symmachus in parallel columns.

26. Scholars argue over how much Hebrew Origen knew. Most will admit that he knew some, but doubt that he was very fluent in it.

27. Origen, *Homélies sur Jérémie,* 1:131.

28. Later on, Nautin points out that Origen's style is not oratorical, but pedagogical. Ibid., 183-91.

29. I am delighted to discover my position unintentionally supported by Richard B. Hays in his commentary on *Galatians* in *The New Interpreter's Bible:* In writing of the allegory in Gal. 4:21–5:1, he says: "Paul's figurative reading strategy depends from start to finish on delineating correspondences between the scriptural story and the events of his own time.... This sort of imaginative discernment of parallels between past narrative and present situation . . . is invariably employed whenever preachers see the circumstances of their own day illumined or prefigured by the stories of scripture. Thus all Christian preaching is inescapably allegorical in the Pauline sense. The function of preaching is not to give factual historical reports; rather, it is to make metaphors, linking the ancient text with the present life of the congregation in fresh imaginative ways so that the text reshapes the congregation's vision of its life before God" (Nashville: Abingdon, 2000), 11:309.

30. Origen, *Homélies Sur Jérémie*, 1:151-83.

31. Origen, *The Song of Songs: Commentary and Homilies,* trans. and annotated by R.P. Lawson, ACW (Westminster, Md.: Newman Press, 1957).

32. Lienhard's introduction to the *Homilies on Luke*, xxxii-xxxvi.

33. "*Fideliter magis quam ornate.*" Origen, *The Song of Songs*, 265.

34. Of Origen's commentary on this book, Jerome says: "While Origen surpassed all writers in his other books, in his *Song of Songs* he surpassed himself." (Ibid.)

35. Messiah and Christ are transliterations of the Hebrew and Greek words that mean "anointed."

36. Philo referred to mystical experience as a "sober inebriation."

37. This refers not to the tree but to the Latinized spelling of *Kedar*.

38. "Pharao" is another Vulgate spelling.

39. For an excellent summary of Origen's spirituality, see Crouzel, *Origen*, 87-149.

ELOQUENCE IN CAPPADOCIA

CHRISTIANITY BECOMES RESPECTABLE

The development of the homily form by Origen was the first major step in giving preaching the shape it would have for the first half of the Christian era. The next step was not taken for another century and a half and occurred in a church with a greatly altered position in the Roman world. From being a persecuted minority, Christianity had become the religion of the emperor, with all the favor and privilege that entailed. Under these new circumstances, bishops came to be chosen from the best-educated people of the time, the graduates of schools of rhetoric. Thus it happened that those who preached to the Christian community were thoroughly grounded in the techniques of effective public speaking. Verse-by-verse interpretation of a Scripture passage took on an eloquence it seldom had before. To understand how that came about, it is necessary to trace seismic social upheavals.

The Challenge of Size to the Empire

When Hadrian succeeded Trajan as Roman emperor in 117, he decided to draw back a little from boundaries established by his predecessor in order to keep the empire a manageable size.[1] In the west and north he

49

built a wall near what is England's Scottish border, and in the east he withdrew across the Euphrates from Parthian territory in Mesopotamia. The Rhine and Danube became the empire's northern borders. Roman settlement of Africa had never penetrated deeply beyond its Mediterranean coast and he left it that way. Palestine and Syria were as far east as he needed to go.

Even at that, the territory proved too unwieldy for easy government. This was reflected in changes in the way the empire was ruled. For some time emperors had been drawn from and imposed by the army. Their ethnic stock ceased to be Roman in the urban sense or even the Italian. Their effective capital was no longer the eternal city but wherever their headquarters were located. By 286 it was necessary to have two Caesars, one in the West and one in the East. The empire threatened to come apart under its own weight. The only person who succeeded in unifying it was Constantine, who reigned alone from 324 to 337.

Roman Unity, Christianity, and Arianism

Before Constantine became sole emperor, at the battle of the Milvian Bridge in 312, he converted to Christianity, and from then on, with the exception of the brief reign of Julian the Apostate (360–63), Christianity enjoyed governmental support.[2] Constantine had hoped that he could reunite the empire around his new religion, but found to his chagrin that Christianity itself was badly divided over its understanding of the person and work of Christ. The belief that was eventually to win out and become the orthodox Christian view was that our Lord was at once completely divine and completely human—that he, the Father, and the Holy Spirit were the one God in three hypostases.

The powerful countervailing view was the position of the Arians that Christ was inferior to the Father, occupying a position between full divinity and full humanity. Constantine tried to heal the breach by calling a council of bishops at Nicaea in 325 to settle the matter. The council accepted the orthodox position, but that did not cause Arianism to disappear. It was not ejected from the empire until 381, and even after that it held on to life among some Germanic tribes until the end of the fifth century. Meanwhile several emperors, including Constantine's son, Constantius II, took the Arian side and bestowed governmental favor upon it. Therefore, the empire remained divided religiously, but the contending forces were no longer pagan and Christian but variant Christian expressions instead.[3]

New Patterns of Leadership

During this time, the East became progressively more important in the control of the empire and thus Constantine built its new capital city, Constantinople, on the Golden Horn where Europe almost touches Asia. As a result of all these factors, the next important chapter in the history of preaching was written in the Roman province of Cappadocia, located in what today is east-central Turkey.[4] The province was largely rural and agricultural, and its social organization was feudal. Its population was largely peasant except for the few landowning families.

Sons of these families were the only Cappadocians who could afford rhetorical education, which had recently taken on a new significance. Under Constantine a new career pattern had been created for administrators in Roman governmental service: standard preparation for such a career came to be education in Greek rhetoric.[5] This meant that those who worked in the central bureaucracy, those sent out as provincial governors, and the local notables in the provinces to which the governors were sent shared a common background and common standards of behavior. No matter what part of the empire one came from, people like oneself would be found wherever one went. Most of the members of this new "aristocracy of service" were Christians. Not surprisingly, it was from the same talent pool that bishops came to be selected.[6]

THE CAPPADOCIAN FATHERS

Christian preaching finally became completely integrated with classical rhetoric in Asia Minor in the second half of the fourth century. Three of the greatest preachers of all time not only appeared in the same remote province of the empire, but were very close: two brothers and their best friend. All became bishops, and they are known to history by the names of their sees. The brothers were Basil of Caesarea (330–79) and Gregory of Nyssa (ca. 331–ca. 395), and their friend was Gregory of Nazianzus (ca. 329–390). The three exemplified many of the motifs that have occupied this chapter so far: they were all born into wealthy landowning Christian families, they were thoroughly trained in rhetoric and practiced as Sophists, they all felt a strong call to the contemplative life, they all became bishops, they were deeply involved in the christological controversies of their time, and they all were brought into close contact with emperors (negatively so for Basil, but positively so for the Gregorys).

51

Basil the Great

Life and Work

As closely related as these Cappadocian Fathers were, it is simpler to look at their lives and their contributions to preaching individually. Basil was the center of the group. His father, also named Basil, was a professional rhetor, originally from Pontus, who married into a Cappadocian family even wealthier than his own. Basil had nine siblings, two of whom also became bishops, and a sister, Macrina, who became a nun.[7] Under his father Basil began the rhetorical training that was the standard form of higher education at the time. The elder Basil died, however, when the younger was a teenager, and so the son went into Caesarea to continue his education. There he met Gregory Nazianzus, who was to become his closest friend. From Caesarea he went to Constantinople where he probably studied under the great Libanius and then finished up with six years of study in Athens where Gregory, also known as Nazianzen, was his classmate.

After returning home and teaching for a year, he toured the monasteries that had recently come into being in Mesopotamia, Syria, Palestine, and Egypt, and developed a strong attraction to the contemplative life. In his day, most believers in Christ feared the danger of postbaptismal sin and so delayed initiation until late in life, but after his tour, Basil was baptized and went to his father's estate in Pontus to found an ascetic community that included Macrina, their mother, and eventually Nazianzen. His love of the ascetic life and his understanding of it caused him to write a monastic rule that gives Greek and Slavonic monasticism its basic shape to this day. He and his friend Gregory also published a collection of passages from Origen, the *Philocalia,* that is still regarded as a spiritual classic.

Though he continued to feel drawn to the ascetic life, Basil was ordained a priest in Caesarea in ca. 362 and an auxiliary bishop in 364. He was devoted to the poor, and he helped avert a disaster in Cappadocia during the famine of 368. With an Arian emperor, Valens, on the throne, he felt a call to do battle with heresy both intellectually and politically. Inheriting the diocese in 370,[8] he soon had to cope with its division by the emperor and the assignment of the other half to an Arian. He and his opposite number each began a mad scramble to strengthen his cause by creating new bishoprics in his territory. Basil assigned his brother Gregory to the town of Nyssa and his friend Gregory to the village of Sasima, an injury his friend never forgot.

On the intellectual front, Basil wrote a treatise on the Holy Spirit and one against Eunomius. He and his two cohorts are credited with developing what was to be the ultimate Eastern statement of the doctrine of the Trinity as Augustine's was to be the ultimate Western statement. Theirs used the principle of coinherence *(perichorēsis)* to do justice to both the unity and the individuality of the three divine persons. Basil's death in 379 meant that he did not see the triumph of the Cappadocian position at the Council of Constantinople in 381. His contributions to theology, monasticism, social service, and the practical life of the church combine to make him truly deserving of the title "the Great" by which he is called.

Preaching

In considering the preaching of the three Cappadocians, Basil's best represents the types of priestly and episcopal preaching that were ordinary at the time—and even these are extraordinary in their quality. The exegetical homily, the most common sermon form from the patristic period, was the form in which the preponderance of Basil's sermons were cast, and slightly more than half of the few that have been preserved are in this form. There are two major collections of sermons on single books of the Bible: those on the *Hexameron,* the six days of creation in the book of Genesis, and those on Psalms.

His homilies, *On the Psalms,*[9] were not a continuous series, but appear to have been preached between 368 and 375, during the last years before and the first years after his consecration as bishop. Fewer than 10 percent of the psalms are interpreted in the collection that has come down, but these few appear to be real sermons that were delivered to a congregation. There are indications of orality in many of them and even of improvisation in some, so they must have been recorded in shorthand. His method of preaching was to explain every word of every sentence of the particular psalm, so he obviously could not have preached on a long psalm in the time available.

Although Christian congregations of the time were very familiar with the psalms, Basil appears to have preached with a text before him, possibly some form of Origen's *Hexapla.* The sermons are addressed to the general Christian public, many of whom would have been unbaptized, and they reflect the social conditions of the time. The theme of some of the homilies is that the righteous person should give thanks to God for the power that enabled that person to triumph over temptation. The overall thesis of the collection is that all other activity should be abandoned for the contemplation of God.[10]

The sermons on the *Hexameron*[11] are longer than those on the psalms: on average, fifty as opposed to fifteen minutes long. They were delivered as a series, probably during Lent, after Basil had become bishop; indeed, Jean Bernardi believes they were preached March 12-16, 378, the year before Basil's death, with two sermons each on Monday, Tuesday, Thursday, and Friday, and only one on Wednesday.[12] The series was not finished because his final illness was already troubling him.[13]

The series was preached to the congregation at Caesarea. In fact, Basil made reference to members of the congregation who were artisans, for whom the sermons had to be short so they could get to work on time. While Basil was still enough under the influence of Origen to use allegorical interpretation when he preached on the psalms, he had abandoned that method by the time he preached on the creation narrative. Charming comments on each work of the Creator reveal Basil as deeply informed of the science of his time and probably also a close observer of nature himself.[14]

Twenty-two of the sermons in the collection called *Diverse Homilies* are regarded as genuine works of Basil, some preached while he was still a priest but most from his episcopate.[15] Those delivered while he was still a presbyter aroused the envy of his bishop, a feeling the bishop eventually transcended when he recognized the value of Basil's gifts to the church. The sermons Basil preached after he became bishop show his awareness of pastoral problems. An Epiphany sermon urged those who were delaying baptism to receive their catechetical instruction that Lent. The fast was apparently observed by many of the unbaptized; there are two sermons on preparation for it, one for the rich and one for slaves. And there is a complimentary homily on avoiding excess in celebrating Easter. All of these sermons take the form of a liturgical homily.

Some of the *Diverse Homilies* take a different shape. Four of them are for feasts of martyrs; they are notable in several respects. They call attention to the development of the cult of the martyrs and also to the exchange of relics taking place between churches at the time and expressing networks being formed by bishops.[16] They also serve as a reminder that the danger of persecution still existed for the orthodox during the reign of the Arian emperor Valens. They also are clear examples of the way that Basil's rhetorical training prepared him for preaching, exemplifying as they do the genus of epideictic (praise or blame) in a scrupulous observance of its rules. Only a few of the *Diverse Homilies* deal with questions related to the doctrines of Christ and the Trinity, since most of Basil's hearers were as yet unbaptized and had not been initiated into the mysteries of these doctrines.

Basil's sermons clearly reflect his pastoral responsibilities. The spirituality they inculcate is deeply biblical. Forty-six of the eighty-nine sermons in the three series are exegetical homilies in form. Many of the others have Scripture as their point of departure, and biblical language permeates all of them. "In almost every line there appears a citation, a reminiscence, or an allusion to a passage of scripture" (AT).[17] The Bible was the reservoir of Basil's ideas and images; he used it the same way his pagan contemporaries used the literature of classical Greece. In his sermons he used the Bible to provide his congregation with a program of reflection and of life. While the eighty-nine sermons that remain are only a small sample of the total amount of preaching Basil did, they are representative of the ways in which he tried to build up his flock morally and spiritually through his preaching.

Gregory of Nazianzus

For several reasons the corpus of Gregory's sermons selected for preservation is very different from that of his friend Basil. First, his basic sense of vocation was to the contemplative life, so he did not have the years of continued pastoral activity in one place that his friend had. Second, the sermons he allowed to be published are intended more for special occasions than for the regular Sunday eucharistic assembly and thus have a more elevated rhetorical style.[18] And, as we shall see, he had different criteria for deciding which of his sermons would be published, a different purpose for the collection that dictated the inclusion of some types and the exclusion of others.

Activities and Contributions

Gregory's criteria for sermon selection, however, can best be understood in the context of his life story. Gregory's father, with whom he shared his name, was not only a Christian but a bishop. The family was affluent; the elder Gregory constructed the church building in Nazianzus largely at his own expense. The father had not been born into the faith, however; he had begun life in a hellenized Jewish sect called the Hypsistarians.[19] Shortly after his baptism, sometime around his son's birth, he was chosen as bishop of Nazianzus.[20]

In being chosen while still a layman, the elder Gregory represented the system that was usual before his distinguished son and his friends changed the rules. In the older generation a leader for a congregation was raised up from its midst with no prior training, his only qualification being the character of Christian leadership recognized by the congregation.[21] It was not even necessary that he serve as a deacon or priest before being chosen as bishop. And many of those chosen were married and had families. Basil and the two Gregorys, however, were to break that tradition. Ordained ministry became a vocation for which one prepared by receiving rhetorical education and ascetic formation in the contemplative life. The contemplative aspect of the life made it also a vocation to celibacy.[22] Thus an important shift in the nature of the episcopate took place between the Gregorys elder and younger.

Gregory's education was very similar to Basil's, though he began school in Nazianzus rather than at his father's knee, and between his stays at the Cappadocian Caesarea and Athens he studied at Caesarea in Palestine and Alexandria rather than at Constantinople. His famous teachers include Thespesius, Himerius, Proaeresius, and possibly Didymus the Blind. In his panegyric on Basil (*Or. 43*) he painted an idyllic picture of their friendship and achievements during their student days.[23] He was in Athens before Basil arrived and stayed after he left; he even taught there for a while before departing.

After Gregory returned home, he was baptized and joined Basil in Pontus in his ascetic retreat. All his life Gregory vacillated between his desire for the contemplative life and the conflicting desire to use his great natural talent for oratory and his excellent education in the service of his faith. He remained in Pontus less than a year and even wrote Basil a satirical letter about the experience, but he continued to go back for extended retreats and took refuge there on several of the flights that were his characteristic response to a crisis in his life.[24]

The first of these flights occurred at Christmastime 361,[25] a couple of years after he returned home from Pontus, when his aging father, in need of assistance in the church, imposed priestly ordination on him. Gregory returned home in time to help his father with Easter services the following spring, and preached his first sermons. He then remained in Nazianzus most of the time until 370, dividing his time between taking as much of the burden off his father as he could and trying to keep up "some of the monastic routine of prayer, vigils, and fasting within the semi-seclusion of his home."[26]

His friendship with Basil was severely tested in 370 when Eusebius died and Basil wanted to succeed him as bishop of Caesarea. Basil considered becoming bishop of Caesarea a necessary defense of the church against Arianism, but Gregory regarded it as "the business of power-mongers."[27] To make matters worse, the following year when Valens divided his jurisdiction, Basil began creating new sees within his remaining territory and consecrated Gregory as bishop of Sasima. Although he accepted the consecration, Gregory despised his assignment, considering it a "stopping-place . . . without water or vegetation, not quite civilized, a thoroughly deplorable and cramped little village."[28] Another flight ensued. After several months, however, he did consent to return to Nazianzus and help his father. Then, when his father died in 374 and there was an effort to make him successor to the see, he fled again, this time to Seleucia, where he lived for four years in the convent of St. Thecla.

From there he was called in 379 to the most productive period of his life as a preacher: half of his surviving forty-four[29] orations were sermons preached during the following two years. After the Arian emperor Valens died and was succeeded by the orthodox Theodosius I, the church in Constantinople was still in the hands of its Arian bishop, Demophilus. Gregory was called to the small orthodox Church of the Anastasis (Resurrection). When Theodosius finally came to Constantinople, however, he placed Gregory on the city's episcopal throne. Gregory's preaching did much to prepare for the triumph of Nicene orthodoxy at the Council of Constantinople in 381. Indeed, his five *Theological Orations* (*Or.* 27–31) have earned him the title in the Eastern Church of "the Theologian," an honor he shares with only the Fourth Evangelist.[30]

When the council actually convened, however, Gregory was caught in the ecclesiastical politics he so disdained. The bishop of Alexandria and his cohorts claimed that it was uncanonical for Gregory to leave Sasima and go to Constantinople. Rather than fight, he resigned as bishop—and president of the council—and went back home to Nazianzus. Finally, he agreed to be bishop there and served until he could train a cousin to succeed him. He then retired to the family estate at Arianzus and the contemplative life for which he had always yearned. During this period he also edited his writings, selecting and revising those to be published. He died in 390.

Orations

The effect of Gregory's editing is obvious in the corpus of his *Orations* as it has been handed down. Some of the speeches, like many others in the history of preaching, have been revised for publication, although not all of them have. But the most impressive aspect of the editing is its high degree of selectivity. While it is true that Gregory was often not involved in regular Sunday preaching, there were whole years when he was, and the number of sermons he preached must have been several times more than the amount that have come down. There is the further issue of the kinds of sermons Gregory edited for publication. While Basil's sermons are representative of pastoral preaching to a congregation, Nazianzen's are not. Indeed, there is only one exegetical homily among them (*Or.* 37). More were written for great public occasions than for ordinary Sunday assemblies.

In his study of the preaching of the Cappadocian Fathers, Bernardi has undertaken to account for Gregory's having chosen to publish just these sermons and no more. First, Bernardi points to the extraordinarily auto-biographical character of the sermons in the collection. He says that the preacher seems to have intended to familiarize us with the main periods of his life[31] and the essential aspects of his personality.[32] Beyond that, however, he appears to have selected orations that would be a sampler[33] of rhetorical preaching to show bishops how to go about their work of Christian proclamation. The sermons, then, were chosen to serve as models for other bishops in parallel situations; therefore they include most of the genres of Christian public address.

Gregory's entire oeuvre seems to have a similar purpose: his letters to his great-nephew Nicobolus furnish a guide to letter writing,[34] and his poetry shows how Christian verse should be composed. He had, after all, lived through the reign of Julian the Apostate, who had said that Christians should not teach or study classical literature because it told of pagan gods.[35] More important, the publication of Gregory's sermons and other writings served his desire to see the episcopate transformed in the way I discussed above, in which the vocation to ordained ministry would be prepared for through rhetorical education and contemplative formation.

Ruether identifies the genres of Nazianzen's speeches as "occasional orations, *apologiae* for his own actions, festal orations, and doctrinal sermons" in addition to eight orations of praise and two of invective.[36] These categories are useful. The occasional orations occur at such events as his becoming his father's auxiliary bishop (*Or.* 16), the consecration of Eulalius of Doara (*Or.* 13), or Gregory's enthronement in the Church of the Holy Apostles in Constantinople (*Or.* 36). The defenses of his own actions are generally given after flight from a crisis: *Or.* 1–3 after his ordination to the priesthood, 9–12 after his consecration to the episcopate, and 42 to the bishops assembled for the council just before he left Constantinople.

The festal orations are for feasts of the church year: *Or.* 1 and 45 for Easter; 38–40 for Christmas, Epiphany, and the Sunday after Epiphany (all on baptism); and 41 on Pentecost. Doctrinal sermons include the great *Theological Orations* (27–31) and the synopsis of the first three of these for the bishops of the council (20). The eight orations of praise should be divided into those for saints' days[37] and those for family members and friends.[38] The two invectives are against Julian the Apostate (4, 5), who was a student in Athens at the same time as Gregory.[39]

These categories, however, do not exhaust the genres of the *Orations*. Almost half of Gregory's sermons are models of preaching for the Sunday assembly, although most of these put more emphasis on doctrine than morals or exegesis. Yet both morals and exegesis are included, as, for example, in *Or.* 14, on love of the poor, and the famous *Or.* 37, his surviving exegetical homily, which is on Matthew 19:1-12, Jesus' teaching on divorce.[40] This homily, however, illustrates the difficulty of assigning many of his sermons to a single genre.[41] Although the basic subject is divorce, Gregory uses allegorical interpretation to apply the passage to heretical preaching, asking the Emperor, who was present, to put an end to it (which the Emperor did).[42]

The form of the sermon is a homily, in that it proceeds in verse-by-verse exegesis, but there is literal as well as allegorical interpretation, and that of an extraordinary sensitivity for his time. Gregory called upon Theodosius to make adultery as much a crime for men as for women and to give women authority over their children—revolutionary proposals in Roman society. Yet his ascetic convictions also come to the fore and he still regarded marriage as inferior to virginity.

In other orations he undertook even more tasks. His *Or.* 19, for instance, was intended both for a feast of martyrs when visiting clergy were present as well as for the local faithful. He addressed each of the groups separately and spoke to them of what obedience involved in their state of life. But the provincial tax assessor, an old friend of Gregory's, was also present, and the bishop publicly exhorted him to continue the tax benefits the clergy had enjoyed.

Apologies

While it is impossible in the space available to look at all genres of Nazianzen's preaching, much less each oration, we should pay attention to at least three of his sermon categories: his apologias, his doctrinal preaching, and his encomia. The apologias are defenses of his conduct, normally his fleeing in a time of crisis. Such crises usually occurred when someone was trying to force him to take a more public role than he felt comfortable with, one that would call him from the contemplative life he craved. While modern readers may get the impression that these speeches involved a good bit of rationalization, he was far too talented and too Christian to make them merely that.

A case in point is *Or. 2*,[43] one of his three efforts to account for his departure for Pontus when his father ordained him to the priesthood. Among his other orations, only his panegyric on Basil is as long as this one, but this one was probably not delivered orally. After beginning with several lesser reasons for his flight, he states the main reason: "I did not, nor do I now, think myself qualified to rule a flock or herd, or to have authority over the souls of men" (2.9). While admitting that unworthy persons have undertaken this ministry,[44] he dared not do so himself; one needed to be much farther advanced in the spiritual life than he to undertake so awesome a responsibility. In demonstrating the appropriateness of his attitude, he wrote the first great treatise on the priesthood in the history of the church.

> S. Chrysostom in his well-known treatise, S. Gregory the Great in his *Pastoral Care*, and Bossuet in his panegyric on S. Paul, have done little more than summarise the material or develop the considerations contained in this eloquent and elaborate dissertation.[45]

Doctrinal Preaching

The most obvious examples of Gregory's doctrinal preaching are his *Theological Orations* (*Or. 27–31*) delivered in Constantinople. As they have come down, these sermons betray the fact that they were turned into a treatise by an editing process that Bernardi refers to as "dissolving" or "melting."[46] The second of the orations does not appear to have been a part of the original series, but to have been fitted in during the editing process. The original oral character of the orations remains obvious enough, however, for their inclusion in a history of preaching.

These sermons reflect the theological ferment of the capital in the years just before the council when an Arian still sat on the episcopal throne in the Church of the Holy Apostles. Nazianzen acknowledged that theological chitchat had almost replaced gossip as the small talk of the social elite of Constantinople when he said:

> Every marketplace must buzz with their talking; and every dinner party must be worried to death with silly talk and boredom; and every festival be made unfestive and full of dejection, and every occasion of mourning be consoled by a greater calamity.[47]

The opponents Gregory attacked in these orations are sometimes identified as Eunomians or Anomoeans and Pneumatomachians.[48] It is more accurate to refer to them generally as Neo-Arians because Gregory seems more concerned to address the "pop" Arianism in Constantinople at the time than to refute the technical treatises of heresiarchs.[49] He makes it clear that he thinks many of his opponents are present for his sermon. Yet not all of those he spoke against were of one opinion or even one heresy.

The five orations differ from one another considerably. The first lays down the ground rules for who should dare to argue a position on such exalted subjects. "Not to everyone, my friends, does it belong to philosophize about God; not to everyone—the subject is not so cheap and low—and, I will add, not before every audience, not at all times, nor on all points" (27.3). The second, which was not originally a part of the series, is on God and begins by discussing the impossibility that an unaided human mind should understand the nature of God and moves on to the strange things that human beings, in their ignorance, have considered gods. Next he gives a list of worthies mentioned in the Bible who have received revelation, but insists that even they did not know God as God is in the divine being. The sermon ends with a demonstration of how God's unknowable richness can be seen in the diversity of creation. This passage (28.22-30) is reminiscent of Basil's sermons on the *Hexameron* in its knowledge of and fascination with nature; Kennedy rightly regards it as the high point of this oration and possibly that of the series as a whole.[50]

The third oration is the first of two on the Son. Gregory begins by stating the orthodox position of consubstantiality and then refutes the doctrines of his opponents. Its high point (29.19-20) is another list, like the *ekphrasis* (vivid description) of nature in the second sermon. This is a collection of antitheses and paradoxes involved in our Lord's two natures, and recalls the Gorgian figures of Melito's *Paschal Homily.*

The fourth oration is also on the Son, but Kennedy is wrong in calling it a homily.[51] While it is true that Gregory shows that ten biblical proof texts cited by his opponents do not have the Arian implications they claim, that is very different from a verse-by-verse exegesis and application of a continuous passage of Scripture, which is the form of a homily. Rather, the oration is a simple refutation of individual points in the first half and a consideration of the titles given Christ in the Bible in the second half. It has little rhetorical form, simply being an effort to cover a lot of ground and to get a number of issues out of the way.

In the fifth oration Gregory faced a major challenge. The Cappadocians were among the first Christian theologians to recognize the consubstantiality of the Holy Spirit, and they were faced with the difficulty that there is not nearly as much about that in the Bible as there is about the status of the Son. Most of the sermon, then, is an effort to show that the scarcity of explicit reference should not lead to negative conclusions. At the end Gregory quickly summarizes the positive evidence from Scripture in support of the position and ends by referring briefly to the lack of adequate symbols of the Trinity in the natural world—rejecting some that continue to be used to this day.

Thus he ends one of the important treatises on the Trinity in the history of the church. The *Theological Orations* are a rare demonstration of the extent to which the church's understanding of its faith can be advanced, not by technical treatises written for experts, but in a pastor's regular proclamation of the Word to his or her congregation. But, of course, clarifying the faith continuously through proclamation demands an extraordinary pastor.

Encomia

Among the many genres in which Gregory spoke, his funeral orations for family members and friends are probably the most cherished. They have a narrative quality that permits readers to feel that they are being given an inside view of the life of the early church. This effect is only increased by the way that Gregory reveals more of his own emotional involvement than almost any other writer from the period. (For an example of an enconium on a family member, the funeral oration for his brother Caesarius, **see Vol. 2, pp. 41-56**.) Of the encomia in praise of saints, family members, and friends, the greatest is undoubtedly the panegyric[52] on Basil. Indeed, George Kennedy, the great historian of classical rhetoric, says that this speech is "probably the greatest piece of Greek rhetoric since the death of Demosthenes."[53]

There are many reasons for its greatness. A uniquely gifted orator who reveals himself in his speeches takes as his subject by far the best friend he ever had, one who himself had made so many and such varied contributions to the life of the church that all succeeding generations have labeled him "the Great." Expressing grief and paying tribute, however, were not his only motives for the speech. One short section is another of Gregory's apologies. Much more important, however, is the purpose of using the fall of the great leader as an occasion to rally others behind the orthodox Trinitarian doctrine that Basil taught.

Beyond even that, Bernardi sees this speech as integral to the purpose for which Gregory edited his orations for publication: to turn them into a call for a new breed of bishops, far better qualified than their predecessors. He notes that the panegyric (*Or.* 43) is Gregory's first speech after the one he gave to the bishops at the Council of Constantinople upon his resignation and departure (*Or.* 42). That was a scathing attack on their lack of qualification. By painting Basil as the ideal bishop, Gregory is able to show what the council fathers should have been like and were not. Thus Basil is treated as exemplifying the ideal shape of the episcopate for the future. By concentrating on Basil's preparation for his vocation through his wide rhetorical education, his mastery of theology, and his ascetic formation as a contemplative, Gregory demonstrated what it would take to enable bishops to measure up to the demands of their office.[54]

It is interesting to go section by section through this great testimony to a friendship to see how the master rhetorician adapted the requirements of the classical rhetorical genre to serve his Christian purpose, as both Kennedy[55] and Ruether[56] have done. It is enough here to refer the reader to their treatments and even more to the panegyric itself. There, more than anywhere else, one can learn what Christian preaching's marriage to classical rhetoric did to enrich Christian preaching.

Gregory of Nyssa

Johannes Quasten, the great compiler of patristic handbooks, has succinctly summarized the distinctive contributions of each of the Cappadocian Fathers:

> Gregory of Nyssa was neither an out-standing administrator and monastic legislator like Basil, nor an attractive preacher and poet like Gregory of Nazianzus. But as a speculative theologian and mystic he is certainly the most gifted of the three great Cappadocians.[57]

He goes on to say that Nyssa is "by far the most versatile and successful author" of the three and that "his writings reveal a depth and breadth of thought," which surpass that of the other two.[58]

Yet the fact remains that Nyssa does not have the importance for the history of preaching that Basil and Nazianzen have. Only twenty-six of his sermons survive, and they date from a relatively short period of his episcopate, 379 to 388. Nothing remains from the first or the last seven years he was a bishop. The reasons why the early and late periods are not represented in the existing corpus are probably clear enough. During the latter years he was working on his great spiritual commentaries such as *The Life of Moses.*[59] For the early years, he was in exile part of the time, his attention may have been on other things, and he probably did not yet have the fame to merit a scribe to take down what he said. The main reason, though, is likely to be that most of his sermons during that time were exegetical homilies that were recycled into the spiritual commentaries.

Nyssa mastered rhetoric through private study rather than schooling, but went on to practice it professionally for about seven years. During this period he married and had a son. Strangely, he had great devotion to the ascetic ideals of his brother and their friend, and, at Basil's request, even wrote a treatise on the glories of virginity. Then, in 372, when Basil was trying to populate his territory with bishoprics, he asked his brother to go to the little town of Nyssa. At first Gregory was not an outstanding success. He was not an effective administrator, and he found that his flock took offense at his efforts to correct them.[60] The Arians were even able to have him deposed over alleged financial irregularities, but he was restored two years later.

His real prominence began after Basil's death when he was assumed to be his brother's successor in the campaign against heresy. He had a visible role in the Council of Constantinople and was often sent by the Emperor on diplomatic missions for the church. After his wife died in 385 he devoted himself to practicing and writing about the ascetic life. The only event known from his last years is his participation in the synod of Constantinople in 394, which was probably the year before his death.

Much of the interest in the small body of his extant sermons lies in their furnishing early evidence of preaching for liturgical occasions: Lent and the great feasts of the church year. His Lenten preaching during the first weeks seems to have been devoted to issues of morality. After that it was probably given over to teaching doctrine on the basis of a systematic exegesis of Scripture. In any case, what remains is but a small sample, since, for a number of years, he preached twice daily during the Lenten season, and only five Lenten sermons remain. Three are against the sins of usury, fornication, and not accepting reprimands, while the other two encourage love of the poor. These last two show Gregory at his best. Bernardi says that in them Gregory reveals himself to be a great master of preaching, which he defines as one who knows how—by the close blending of ideas, images, and feelings—to create an emotion and direct it toward efficacious action because he knows how those who hear him live and feel, and he observes carefully the people he passes in the streets of his town.[61]

The sermons for feasts include three for Easter[62] and one for the ascension that is probably the first record of the observance of that feast.[63] There is also one for Pentecost, but none for any other calendrical date until Christmas, which was also a new feast in the East. Already, however, the days immediately after Christmas were being observed. December 26 was the Feast of Stephen, and the next day commemorated

Peter and James as well as John (to whom alone the feast is assigned today in the Western calendar). And there are two Epiphany sermons, although some scholars think one is for the day after. Other feast days include those of martyrs. Three sermons have come down from Nyssa on the Feast of the Forty Martyrs of Sebaste, a commemoration that he says his mother introduced into Cappadocia. The other is for a soldier named Theodore, who, like the Forty, refused to participate in pagan worship. Only one of the sermons was delivered in a church, the others being given in the appropriate martyria. We can learn much from them about the development of the cult of martyrs.

Also in the epideictic genre are Nyssa's funeral sermons. Three of these are for bishops. That for Gregory Thaumaturgus (miracle worker) was a commemoration in his hometown of Neocaesarea in Pontus more than a hundred years after his death. Gregory Thaumaturgus had personal significance for Gregory because the elder Gregory had instructed his grandmother Macrina in the faith. Needless to say, Gregory's *paramythē-tikos* for his brother Basil is much closer to home, but, unlike the *epitaphios* by Nazianzus, his speech does not allude to a personal relation. Rather, it presents the case for Basil's canonization and suggests that his day should be December 28, immediately following the Feasts of Stephen and Peter, James, and John.

The funeral sermon was for Meletius of Antioch, which shows the prominence to which Nyssa had risen as his brother's heir, because he delivered it at the Council of Constantinople, at which Meletius had been presiding when he died. This status is further documented in Nyssa's having preached *paramythētikoi* for the emperor Theodosius's wife Flacilla and their seven-year-old daughter, Pulcheria. Two speeches by Nyssa at the council have also survived; from one of them comes one of Gregory's best-known utterances, a description of the atmosphere of Constantinople at the time as one in which one could not buy bread or order a bath without receiving Arian slogans in response.[64]

As Bernardi says, the twenty-six sermons that have been preserved show little of the personality or originality of the bishop of Nyssa.[65] As much as anything else, they show how much he traveled and how responsive he was to the life of the church at large. They may also show how little he was appreciated at home. At any rate, there is little indication in them of continuing pastoral activity. Rather, many of the sermons that have come down were preached somewhere other than Nyssa, generally for some big public occasion. Thus, as Bernardi also says, they show much of the accomplished orator, but little of Gregory himself.[66]

CONCLUSION

The sermons of the Cappadocian Fathers show the sort of marriage between Christian preaching and classical rhetoric that could occur after the church was not only no longer persecuted, but actually favored by the state. Sons of landowning families who had received rhetorical educations that would qualify them for the highest offices of government service could prepare themselves spiritually for ministry by ascetic retreat at a time when monasticism was already being regarded as "the moral equivalent of martyrdom." As a result, there was an extraordinary rush of talent and training into the episcopate. None represented that trend better than the Cappadocians.

Yet, as close as they were to one another, their surviving sermons give very different impressions. Basil's sermons reflect ongoing pastoral activity in a way those of the others do not. And he understood his pastoral task in preaching to be dispensing moral lessons on the basis of Scripture. Conversely, Basil chose few sermons that were used for grand public occasions for preservation; none, for instance, for funerals.

While Nyssa's sermons are also those of a bishop in charge of a flock, the exegetical homilies that were a majority among Basil's sermons are seldom found. Instead there are sermons for great public events. Part of the differences between these sermon collections has to do with the time of their writers' episcopates. Basil died before the triumph of orthodoxy in the accession of Theodosius and the victory at the Council of Constantinople. He always represented a tolerated minority while Nyssa was the voice of the dominant party.

In other respects, however, the two brothers' preaching topics show similar concerns that differ from those of Nazianzus's preaching. Nazianzus chose which of his sermons were to be published on the basis of their being examples for other bishops, used in instructing them how to preach in a variety of genres. In this way he contributed to changing the sort of person chosen to be bishop, a cause to which he was so devoted. In relating to their audiences, Nyssa was probably least successful. Basil shows himself closely in touch with his flock, and Nazianzen's sermons are so deeply personal that they inevitably made contact with his audience.

In summary, Bernardi says that *kerygma* does not exist in a pure state,[67] it is always the preaching of particular persons at certain places at given times, and always reflects that conditioning. The preaching of the Cappadocians—especially the minority of their sermons that were chosen for preservation—is by no means typical of preaching through the ages. Their corpus, for instance, includes few of the exegetical homilies that must have been their standard homiletical form, as it was almost the only sermonic genre in the church before the High Middle Ages. Rather, their sermons have a preoccupation with teaching morals, a concern appropriate for an age in which primary evangelization was no longer necessary, but deep teaching had not yet become possible. Nevertheless, their sermons are invaluable for showing the communicative skill by which rhetorical education can increase the effectiveness of preaching. And the very eccentricity of the selections published reminds later generations that the early church had a richer variety of homiletical genres than is usually apparent. The deepest legacy of the Cappadocians, however, is the way their preaching bears the fruit of the spirituality to which they were committed. Their contemplative asceticism still has power to call readers to a life of deeper holiness.

FOR FURTHER READING

Basil. *Exegetic Homilies*. Translated by Agnes Clare Way. FC. Washington, D.C.: Catholic University of America Press, 1963.

Bernardi, Jean. *La prédication des pères cappadociens: Le prédicateur et son auditoire*. Publications de la Faculté des Lettres et Sciences Humaine de l'Université de Montpellier, no. 30. Paris: Presses Universitaires de France, 1968.

The Easter Sermons of Gregory of Nyssa: Translation and Commentary: Proceedings of the Fourth International Colloquium on Gregory of Nyssa, Cambridge England, 11–15 September, 1978. Edited by Andreas Spira and Christoph Klock, with introduction by G. Christopher Stead. Patristic Monograph Series, no. 9. Cambridge, Mass.: Philadelphia Patristic Foundation, 1981.

Funeral Orations by Saint Gregory Nazianzen and Saint Ambrose. Introduction by Martin R. P. McGuire and translated (Gregory's orations only) by Leo P. McCauley et al. FC. New York: Fathers of the Church, Inc. 1953.

Gregory of Nyssa. *The Life of Moses*. Translated with introduction and notes by Abraham J. Malherbe and Everett Ferguson; preface by John Meyendorff. CWS. New York: Paulist Press, 1978.

Ruether, Rosemary Radford. *Gregory of Nazianzus, Rhetor and Philosopher*. Oxford: Clarendon Press, 1969.

Notes

1. Hugh Elton, *Frontiers of the Roman Empire* (Bloomington: Indiana University Press, 1996).

2. Averil Cameron studies how Christians attained power in the society through their use of traditional forms of oratory during this period, thus identifying themselves with deep roots in the culture. See *Christianity and the Rhetoric of Empire: The Development of Christian Discourse,* Sather Classical Lectures (Berkeley and Los Angeles: University of California Press, 1991), 55:120-54.

3. Paganism also continued as a force until 416 when non-Christians were not allowed to serve in the army. Within a generation, most of the holdouts in aristocratic families had converted.

4. While Christian Cappadocia is best known to travelers for the churches carved out of tall cones eroded from volcanic rock in the area of Göreme, those churches with their marvelous frescoes came along several centuries after the Cappadocian Fathers and are not located in the same region.

5. Much as Englishmen of the eighteenth and nineteenth centuries were prepared for administering their colonial empire by attending public schools where they studied Greek and Latin literature.

6. Peter Brown, *The World of Late Antiquity: From Marcus Aurelius to Muhammed* (London: Thames & Hudson, 1971), 22-33; *Power and Persuasion in Late Antiquity: Towards a Christian Empire* (Madison: University of Wisconsin Press, 1992); and *The Cult of the Saints: Its Rise and Function in Latin Christianity* (Chicago: University of Chicago Press, 1981).

7. Theirs must have been one of the few families in history to produce three siblings with feast days in the church calendar.

8. His predecessor was named Eusebius, but he should be distinguished from the church historian of the same name whose Caesarea was the Palestinian port city and who died when Basil was only ten years old.

9. For an English translation, see Basil, *Exegetic Homilies,* trans. Agnes Clare Way, FC (Washington: Catholic University of America Press, 1963).

10. I owe much of what I say on the sermons of Basil and the two Gregorys to Jean Bernardi, *La prédication des pères cappadociens: Le prédicateur et son auditoire,* Publications de la Faculté des Lettres et Sciences Humaine de l'Université de Montpellier, no. 30 (Paris: Presses Universitaires de France, 1968).

11. Also translated in Basil, *Exegetic Homilies.* An older translation is available in vol. 8 of *NPNF[2]*.

12. Bernardi, *La prédication des pères cappadociens,* 47.

13. Some scholars believe that the homilies found in the works of Gregory of Nyssa under the Latin title of *In verba faciamus* are based on notes given by Basil on what he would have said in the final sermons on the days of creation.

14. Way provides some delightful examples of this in her introduction to Basil, *Exegetic Homilies,* x-xiii.

15. PG 31:164-617. See Bernardi, *La prédication des pères cappadociens,* 55.

16. See Brown, The *Cult of the Saints,* especially chapter 5.

17. "*Presque à chaque ligne apparaît une citation, une réminiscence ou une allusion à un passage de l'Ecriture.*" Bernardi, *La prédication des pères cappadociens,* 89.

18. Indeed, they are referred to as "orations" rather than as "sermons" or "homilies," and they are collected with speeches of other sorts.

19. From the Greek *hypsistos,* the "Most High."

20. *Or.* 18.5-16.

21. While the choice of the congregation designated who would become bishop, it was, of course, ordination by other bishops that made the person a bishop.

22. Gregory of Nyssa was the only one of the three who married, but even he wrote treatises about the superiority of virginity over the married state.

23. *Funeral Orations by Saint Gregory Nazianzen and Saint Ambrose,* intro. Martin R. P. McGuire and trans. (of Gregory's orations only) Leo P. McCauley, S.J., FC (New York: Fathers of the Church, Inc., 1953), 27-99; the section dealing with Athens is on pp. 39-49. An earlier translation is in *NPNF*[2] 7:395-422.

24. Rosemary Radford Ruether, *Gregory of Nazianzus, Rhetor and Philosopher* (Oxford: Clarendon Press, 1969), 28-33.

25. Although this particular date is not disputed, the authorities disagree by a year or so over a number of other dates in Gregory's life.

26. Ruether, *Gregory of Nazianzus,* 33.

27. *Epistle* 40, quoted ibid., 34.

28. *Carm. de vita sua,* quoted ibid., 36.

29. There are forty-five orations assigned to Gregory in Jacques Paul Migne, *Patrilogia Graeca,* vol. 35, 36 (Paris: n.p., 1857–66), the standard printed edition of the Greek text, but *Or.* 35 is generally recognized to be spurious.

30. Another translation of *ho theologos* is "the Divine." The translators of the *Orations* in *NPNF*[2] say that the term is used "in the narrower sense of 'Defender of the Godhead of the Word.'" 7:200 n. 1.

31. The *Orations* come from every stage of Gregory's ordained ministry and include his first and last sermons.

32. Bernardi, *La prédication des pères cappadociens,* 256. See also Gerhard H. Ettlinger, S.J., "The Orations of Gregory of Nazianzus: A Study in Rhetoric and Personality," in *Preaching in the Patristic Age: Studies in Honor of Walter J. Burghardt, S.J.,* ed. David G. Hunter (New York: Paulist Press, 1989), 101-18.

33. Bernardi, *La prédication des pères cappadociens,* 256.

34. Gregory appears to have been the first Christian to preserve his letters for posterity. On Gregory's letters see Ruether, *Gregory of Nazianzus,* 123-28. A large number of his letters are translated in vol. 7 of *NPNF*[2].

35. In response to the same challenge, Apollinarius of Laodicea rewrote much of the Bible in the genres of classical literature.

36. Ruether, *Gregory of Nazianzus,* 107. George Kennedy cuts the number of genres down to three—moral, dogmatic, and panegyric—on the basis of what Gregory said about the sermons of Cyprian (*Or.* 24), and goes on to suggest that these correspond to the classical *genera dicendi*: deliberative, forensic, and epideictic (*Greek Rhetoric Under Christian Emperors* [Princeton: Princeton University Press, 1983], 217).

37. The Maccabees (*Or.* 15), Athanasius (21), Cyprian (24), and Hero (25).

38. His brother Caesarius (*Or.* 7), his sister Gorgonia (8), his father (18), and Basil (43).

39. Translations of twenty-four of the forty-four *Orations* can be found in vol. 7 of *NPNF²*. A slightly edited form of the *NPNF* translation of the *Theological Orations* appears in *Christology of the Later Fathers*, ed. E. R. Hardy with Cyril C. Richardson, Library of Christian Classics, vol. 3 (Philadelphia: Westminster, 1954), 128-214. Another translation appears in Frederick W. Norris, *Faith Gives Fullness to Reasoning: The Five Theological Orations of Gregory Nazianzen*, trans. Lionel Wickham and Frederick Williams, Supplements to *Vigiliae Christianae*, vol. 13 (Leiden: E. J. Brill, 1990), 217-99. The orations on Caesarius, Gorgonia, Gregory the elder, and Basil appear in McGuire and McCauley, *Funeral Orations of Saint Gregory and Saint Ambrose.*

40. This is not to say that no exegesis occurs in any of the other orations. *Or.* 17, for example, begins as a homily on Jeremiah 4:19, moves into a moral exhortation to the congregation, and ends with an address to the provincial governor who was present. And, of course, there are frequent quotations from or allusions to the Bible, although the incidence of these varies with the subject and genre.

41. Although those that are in a distinct classical form, such as the *epitaphios,* observe its rules as scrupulously as possible when the subject is a Christian.

42. Nazianzen was the first bishop ever to have an opportunity to preach before a baptized emperor, and he took advantage of it to urge legislation supportive of Christian standards.

43. For classical influences on this oration (referred to as the *Apologeticus*), see Kennedy, *Greek Rhetoric Under Christian Emperors*, 218-21.

44. His dissatisfaction with many of the clergy who were contemporaries of his is part of the reason he edited his *Orations* to be both a collection of model addresses for bishops and a dissertation on the model of ministry he shared with Basil and Nyssa.

45. Browne and Swallow, "Introduction to Oration II," *NPNF²* 7:204. The practical guidelines and criteria that Gregory used in his preaching are summed up in a section of his autobiographical poem, *Carm. de vita sua* (ll. 1190-1262), a translation of which appears in Ruether, *Gregory of Nazianzus*, 43-44.

46. Jean Bernardi, *"Sermons fondus en un traité," La prédication des pères cappadociens*, 181.

47. *Or.* 27.2. Bernardi interprets references made at the beginning and end of this oration to refer to the women's quarters of high imperial officials as being hotbeds of such theological discussion, agitated by the eunuchs who were attendants there. *La prédication des pères cappadociens*, 186.

48. Eunomius was a late Arian whose position has been caricatured as "anomoean." The Nicene position to which Gregory was loyal insisted that the Son and the Holy Spirit were of the same substance *(homoousion)* as the Father, while earlier Arians had said that the Son, at any rate, was of *like* substance *(homoiousion)* with him. A truly Anomoean position, then, would be that the Son was of *unlike* substance with him.

Pneumatomachians, sometimes mistakenly referred to as Macedonians, were said to have "warred against the Spirit" because they denied the consubstantiality of the Holy Spirit with the Father.

49. Norris, *Faith Gives Fullness to Reasoning*, 53-71.

50. Kennedy, *Greek Rhetoric Under Christian Emperors,* 225.

51. Ibid., 226.

52. Kennedy and Ruether disagree on the genre of this speech. Ruether says that "since it was preached some time after Basil's death and lacks any *threnos* or *paramuthetikos,* we must class it as an encomium rather than an *epitaphios*" (*Gregory of Nazianzus,* 120). Kennedy, on the other hand, follows Menander Rhetor in saying that an *epitaphios* was usually given some time after the death, "in contrast to a *paramythetikos* or monody, which reflects more immediate feelings of grief" (*Greek Rhetoric Under Christian Emperors,* 228). The explanation for this disagreement is probably that the rhetorical handbooks that set forth these definitions and rules were not always consistent with one another in the distinctions they drew.

53. Kennedy, *Greek Rhetoric Under Christian Emperors,* 237.

54. Bernardi, *La prédication des pères cappadociens,* 238-39.

55. Kennedy, *Greek Rhetoric Under Christian Emperors,* 228-37.

56. Ruether, *Gregory of Nazianzus,* 120-23.

57. Johannes Quasten, ed., *The Golden Age of Greek Patristic Literature from the Council of Nicaea to the Council of Chalcedon,* vol. 3 of *Patrology* (Utrecht: Spectrum, 1960; Westminster, Md.: Newman Press, 1960), 254.

58. Ibid., 255.

59. Gregory of Nyssa, *The Life of Moses,* trans. with intro. and notes by Abraham J. Malherbe and Everett Ferguson, and pref. by John Meyendorff, Classics of Western Spirituality (New York: Paulist Press, 1978). Extensive excerpts appear in Jean Daniélou and Herbert Musurillo, *From Glory to Glory: Texts from Gregory of Nyssa's Mystical Writings* (New York: Scribner's, 1961).

60. The problem continued. He preached a sermon "against those who do not bear reprimands" when he had been a bishop almost ten years.

61. Bernardi, *La prédication des pères cappadociens,* 279.

62. Five sermons for Easter are attributed to Nyssa in PG, but only the first, third, and fourth are regarded as authentic. These are among the few of his sermons that have been translated into English. The translation and a collection of essays about them appear in *The Easter Sermons of Gregory of Nyssa: Translation and Commentary: Proceedings of the Fourth International Colloquium on Gregory of Nyssa, Cambridge, England, 11–15 September, 1978,* ed. Andreas Spira and Christoph Klock, with intro. by G. Christopher Stead, Patristic Monograph Series, no. 9 (Cambridge, Mass.: Philadelphia Patristic Foundation, 1981). One of his Epiphany sermons and his funeral sermon for Meletius are translated in *NPNF*[2] 5:513-24.

63. Thomas J. Talley, *The Origins of the Liturgical Year* (New York: Pueblo, 1968), 67-68.

64. Quoted in Hardy, *Christology of the Later Fathers,* 117, and Bernardi, *La prédication des pères cappadociens,* 328, translating PG, vol. 46, col. 557.

65. Bernardi, *La prédication des pères cappadociens,* 331.

66. Ibid., 332.

67. Ibid., 407.

CHAPTER 4

HOMILETICS AND CATECHETICS: CHRYSOSTOM AND OTHERS

T his chapter will deal with two different kinds of preaching that were practiced with a rare degree of virtuosity by one man: John of Antioch and Constantinople, known to later generations as Chrysostom *(Chrysostomos)*, the Golden Mouth. His work alone will be considered in the discussion of the homily form in this chapter, but his contribution to catechetical preaching will be examined alongside that of others.

Although the homily was the standard form of preaching before the High Middle Ages, we have not studied it in its characteristic form so far in this volume. While the genre seems virtually to have been created by Origen, he had none of the rhetorical training and flourish that most of the great Fathers showed. The Cappadocians undoubtedly used this genre of preaching more than any other genre, but, as we saw in the last chapter, the homily is not prominently featured in the sermons they chose to have published.[1] The most common sort of homily will not even be seen in the works of John, though most of his surviving sermons are in the genre.[2] Ironically, John's reason for writing his homilies in a form other than the most common of the day—his lack of enthusiasm for the allegorical interpretation employed by most of the other homileticians—makes them more accessible to people today than most other patristic preaching.

The most typical form of homily with allegorical hermeneutics will be the subject of the next chapter, in which we will consider the work of Augustine. These two preachers, Chrysostom and Augustine, have an otherwise unequaled significance for the history of patristic homiletics, which we can see in the way that their writings alone take up the entire fourteen volumes of the first series of the *Nicene and Post-Nicene Fathers*—as much space as is devoted in the second series to the works of all the other writers of their period.[3]

THE GOLDEN MOUTH

Early Life

The one destined to be designated by a future pope as the patron saint of Christian preachers[4] was born in 349, give or take five years,[5] in Antioch on the Orontes River, into an affluent and socially prominent Christian family. His father, a highly placed civil servant in the secretariat of the commander in chief[6] of the Roman army in the Oriens diocese,[7] died while John was an infant, so he was brought up by his mother. His education was the common one of the time, the only exception being that he did not have to leave home to complete it. After elementary and grammar school he was able to remain in Antioch and study under one of the most distinguished rhetoricians of his day, Libanius.[8] He also studied philosophy with Andragatius. He must have been gifted because he learned to speak and write with an eloquence few have attained, causing one modern critic to say that he was "the only prose author of his epoch who could stand comparison with Demosthenes."[9] Indeed, an ancient account quotes the dying Libanius as saying that his successor "ought to have been John had not the Christians stolen him from us."[10]

The career for which John was preparing was probably not the law, as is generally believed, but, as J. N. D. Kelly says, service in the *sacra scrinia*, the Roman civil service responsible for phrasing imperial documents in "clear and dignified prose," a career that could be crowned with the award of senatorial rank.[11] That was not to be, however, for by the time he finished his studies at the age of eighteen, John already felt the attraction of another calling far more deeply, that of ascetic service to

73

his Lord. He was baptized the following Easter (probably 368) and soon began to serve as an aide to Meletius, bishop of the main body of orthodox Christians in Antioch, a capacity in which he served for three years.

During this same period he undertook an ascetic life not unlike that which had been the ideal of Basil and Nazianzus. He was considered a monk *(monachos)*, although he was not at that time either a hermit or a member of a community. Rather, he was what was called in Syria a "son of the covenant," one who had taken vows to wear a habit, remain celibate, abstain from meat and wine, and devote his life to prayer. While doing this he lived at home, but he and some friends had agreed to meet together and place themselves under the guidance of Diodore, an ascetic and biblical scholar who was later to become bishop of Tarsus.[12]

Attraction to Asceticism

After three years, when John was about twenty-three, the bishop made him a reader, a member of the order just below the diaconate in the East. The specific duty of the order was to read the lections other than the Gospel at the Eucharist, but it made John a member of the clergy and probably involved other liturgical, pastoral, and administrative duties. About this time, however, John was frightened by an effort of the church authorities to impose the priesthood upon him and his close friend Basil.[13] By a ruse John saw that their efforts were successful with his friend, but he eluded ordination himself, considering himself unworthy of so high an office at that stage of his spiritual development.

The outrage that greeted his refusal was undoubtedly one of the factors in his decision to pursue the ascetic life even more fully by joining the monks on nearby Mount Silpios.[14] There he placed himself under a spiritual director for four years while he struggled for mastery over his youthful sexuality and other desires of the flesh, striving as his fellow monks did to achieve uninterrupted communion with God. After that he felt sufficiently grounded to go off to a cave by himself, where he fasted as much as possible and tried to go entirely without sleep. During this period he learned the Old and New Testaments by heart, a feat that accounts for the extraordinary facility with which he could cite parallel passages in his extempore preaching.

Not surprisingly, his frail body could not take such punishment for more than two years. When his health finally forced him to return to Antioch, he did not feel that he had ceased to be a monk, but only that he was practicing his vows under the different set of circumstances that God had imposed upon him. Indeed, he regarded asceticism as the norm for all Christians. For the rest of his life he lived as abstemiously as possible, even when he became bishop in the capital city of the empire, though his asceticism horrified many he met there.

Ordained Life in Antioch

When John got back to Antioch, he discovered that Meletius had returned from exile under an Arian emperor to be sole bishop of the city. John resumed his old duties as reader for two years, after which he was elevated to the diaconate. This gave him a much more visible liturgical role and very demanding pastoral duties. Essentially, deacons were in charge of all the church's eleemosynary responsibilities, which were quite extensive at the time. The church in Antioch

> had to maintain upward of three thousand widows and virgins, not to mention a host of prisoners in gaol, people who were sick or hospitalized, others who were impoverished or maimed, others still who crouched by the altar in desperate need of food and clothing.[15]

It was while he was busy with those overwhelming responsibilities that John, not yet allowed to preach,[16] began his work as a Christian writer, producing some eight treatises on various subjects.

After serving as a deacon for five years, John was ordained priest in 386, when he was thirty-seven years old. This was the beginning of what must have been the happiest and most fulfilling period of his life. Now he concelebrated the Eucharist with the bishop and sometimes presided for him when he was absent. With the other priests he also continued to assist the bishop in his administrative responsibilities. But chiefly his duties were to preach and to instruct the people. It was the work for which he was born. "So for almost twelve years . . . John stood out as the leading pulpit orator of Antioch, building up an unrivalled reputation."[17] I will defer the discussion of his preaching, however, until I complete this biographical sketch. While Kelly refers to the years of his priesthood as John's "decade of development,"[18] we know little about his activities during that period other than what we can infer from his preaching. Therefore, it is time to move on to the next phase of his life, on which all too much information is available.

Episcopate

Near the end of 397, John was urgently summoned by the local governor, quietly gotten out of town, and then driven to Constantinople

where he was told that he was to be the new bishop.[19] He had been chosen by the eunuch Eutropius, superintendent of the sacred bedchamber,
who was the power behind the imperial throne. Arcadius, the Eastern
emperor at the time, had none of the commanding stature of Theodosius
I, and was likely to be dominated by someone, whether his eunuch or his
beautiful, capable, and determined wife Aelia Eudoxia. The royal couple
were at first very welcoming to their new bishop, a man just under fifty
years of age with an unprepossessing appearance,[20] a puritanical out-
look, and an almost unparalleled ability to move Christian congregations
by his preaching. John quickly won the hearts of the people by the obvious love he felt for them, a love he freely communicated in his preaching. Indeed, his standard way of addressing the congregation was to call
them "love."

Yet his austerity and imperiousness evoked a resistance that eventually brought him down. He expected that all the clergy would live as simply as he did and assumed that they had not been doing so and had to be
brought into line. He wanted monks to be subordinate to him rather
than their founder, to be more like the ascetics in the mountains around
Antioch than the monks who had adapted their life to the capital city of
the empire. The large number of bishops who were either living in
Constantinople or were there temporarily on business, those who came
to be called "the resident synod," had trouble relating to a bishop who
preferred to dine alone and who provided only abstemious entertainment
for guests. He offended Theophilus, the bishop of Alexandria, who had
pushed his own candidate for the chair of Constantinople and who was
eager to maintain his own as the most influential see in the East.

While he endeared himself to the masses by decrying the luxuries of
the wealthy and saying that they should give their resources to the poor
rather than lavish them upon themselves, the rich were less enthusiastic
about his message. Aracadius and Eudoxia vacillated in their devotion to
him, giving him passionate support one moment and turning against him
the next. It was hard for the queen, for instance, to be too pleased when
he preached against ornate and expensive feminine attire and called
attention to hers as an example of what he meant, or, when she expro-
priated the property of an ordinary citizen and he spoke in a sermon of
the sin of Jezebel, who had done the same thing.

Neither tact nor compromise seemed to be a part of his vocabulary or
character. While one has to admire both his own self-denial and his fear-
lessness in opposing what he considered to be evil, it is hard to resist the
feeling that he did a great deal to render inevitable his own undoing. It

took only about five years for all the powerful persons he had offended to form a coalition against him. In trying to help out other churches in the area, he overstepped canonical authority and gave an entrée to his enemies. He was sent into exile once, brought back, and sent again, this time permanently. After four years of great hardship and deprivation, he finally died in 407 when he was only fifty-eight years old. The entire story of the downfall of this holy but forbidding genius who gave his enemies too much ammunition to use against him is one of the saddest in the annals of the church, but the details are not relevant enough to the history of preaching as such to warrant recounting here.

HIS HOMILIES[21]

Chrysostom's congregations frequently broke out in applause when he preached. His sermons are peppered with remonstrations with them for doing so, saying that if they approved of what he said, they should show it by doing what he told them rather than by anything so easy as clapping. He was there for their salvation rather than their entertainment. Although he turned against Greek culture as a pagan and worldly distraction from the way to heaven, his talent had been honed by Libanius to reflexive virtuosity, and he probably could not state the time of day without some mark of rhetorical grace.

By and large, however, he did eschew the classical *genera dicendi,* speaking only in the rather amorphous homiletic genre that offers less room for oratorical display than most other types of speeches. As Robert C. Hill, the translator of his *Homilies on Genesis* said, there was "little of the original and spectacular in the structure of the homilies."[22]

> Normally, there was the opening reading of the day's verse(s). Chrysostom would then link the day's sermon with the previous day's, often through some such figure as the laying of a table; this [linking] could occasionally develop into a lengthy moral/dogmatic/polemical excursus unrelated to the *Gn* text and supported from other Scriptural loci. Then—sometimes with abruptness and difficulty after such a lengthy digression (disproportionate enough to discourage again an impression of perfect planning beforehand)—he would take up the day's text for exegesis/commentary. Finally, after a substantial time on the text, he would move to a parenetic conclusion, quite perfunctorily done by way of "supplying you with the customary *paraklēsis*," and not always arising naturally from the exegetical material.[23]

Other things being equal, this description will serve for any of his series of homilies. Sometimes there was no introduction and John began immediately to exegete the text verse by verse. The effect is strange to modern taste, because it often seems like a commentary being read aloud, and often there was no obvious connection between the interpretation of the biblical passage and the concluding exhortation. Even less fathomable to contemporary consciousness was John's habit of building the application not on the passage as a whole, nor on the most profound issues raised in the pericope, but on the last verse to be exegeted, whichever it happened to be.

Biblical Interpretation

As I noted above, however, John's biblical exposition is much more attractive to contemporary taste than the allegorical interpretation so common elsewhere at the time. In part, allegorical interpretation was so popular because anomalies in the text were as obvious to interpreters then as they are now. Yet those who used this method assumed that the discrepancy was inserted by the Holy Spirit to indicate that spiritual interpretation was called for. For someone like John, however, who did not take that way out, the anomaly was apparent and had to be dealt with in ways very similar to those used today.

Therefore, John raises questions about authorship and why only two of the apostles and two of their followers wrote Gospels, and shows familiarity with the tradition that Matthew was originally written in Hebrew and that Mark went to Egypt.[24] Inconsistencies between the Gospel accounts are regarded as an asset rather than a liability: "that discordance which seems to exist in little matters delivers [the Gospels] from all suspicion and speaks clearly in behalf of the character of the writers."[25] John also undertakes to explain why the only three women mentioned before Mary in Matthew's genealogy have something questionable about them.[26] In the second of the *Homilies on St. John,* Chrysostom says, in effect, that a sermon on the author should have the form of an encomium and deal with his family, country, and education, but the lack of anything remarkable about any of these is itself remarkable and indicative of the miracle of inspiration.

In the only extended patristic treatment of Acts, he notes that the Holy Spirit is the special topic of the book, that the greater part of it deals with Paul, and that it was written by Paul's companion Luke, referring to evidence that has been rehashed by most commentators since.[27] He notices that most of Paul's letters begin with thanking God for the congregation to which he writes.[28] And he deduces that Colossians must have been written after Romans and before 2 Timothy.[29] Modern scholars may question the Pauline authorship of some of these epistles, yet they continue to argue over the order in which the genuine ones were written. By being concerned with such matters, John seems more like a colleague to New Testament scholars today than most of his contemporaries.

Chrysostom's literal rather than allegorical interpretation was not just a personal proclivity but was characteristic of the church in Antioch in which he had been formed. Eustathius, the bishop who represented Antioch at the Council of Nicaea in 325, wrote *On the Witch of Endor Against Origen*, a book in which he claimed that Origen's allegorical exegesis deprived the Bible of its historical character. Diodore of Tarsus, under whom John and his friends had placed themselves for spiritual and theological formation in their youth, was the author of a book, now lost, called *What Is the Difference Between Theory and Allegory?* The key term of the debate was "theory," which the two schools understood very differently.

> Where the Alexandrines use the word *theory*[30] as equivalent to allegorical interpretation, the Antiochene exegetes use it for a sense of scripture higher or deeper than the literal or historical meaning, but firmly based on the letter.[31]

Thus, both schools thought that there was more meaning to the Bible than the simple literal sense, but the Antiochenes felt that any such meaning was rooted in and consistent with that sense.

John's friend Theodore, who had studied with him under Diodore and became bishop of Mopsuestia, was the greatest exegete and theologian of this school, but his reputation was clouded later when he was held responsible for the teaching of his pupil Nestorius.[32] It is now generally agreed that Nestorius did not teach the heresy associated with his name and that the school of Antioch was as orthodox as that of Alexandria, but two very different ways of doing theology made it virtually impossible for representatives of one school to understand those of the other.

There are many parallels between the careers of John and Nestorius, including their both serving as bishop of Constantinople and their being ousted from that position by a cabal in which the bishop of Alexandria at the time played a leading part. Church politics as much as anything else made it hard for historical biblical interpretation to receive its due in the fourth century.[33] Even then, however, Jerome, the greatest and most influential exegete among the Western fathers, was persuaded by

Chrysostom's biblical interpretation to abandon the allegorism that he had originally practiced.

Content and Style

One of the reasons John was not as profound a biblical interpreter as his friend Theodore was that he did not have as deep an interest in the meaning of the biblical text in its own right. What he sought in his scriptural study, and certainly what he wished to leave with his congregation, was moral and spiritual guidance to help them live the Christian life. Sometimes, as noted above, that guidance would be based on the day's last exegeted verse. At other times it grew out of something going on in the city and congregation. Or he might have a single virtue he wished to recommend or vice to oppose during the entire liturgical season and homily series. On occasion he would make one moral appeal in the introduction and another in the conclusion. His one overriding interest was in persuading the people of God to live consistently with their calling. As he said in his treatise *On the Priesthood,* "this is the ultimate aim of teaching: to lead their disciples, both by what they do and what they say, into the way of that blessed life which Christ commanded" (4.8).[34]

John's various homilies display a considerable difference in their degree of stylistic polish. Indeed, the lack of such finish is one of the main criteria by which critics have distinguished the series preached in Constantinople from those delivered at Antioch, the assumption being that the busy and often beleaguered bishop had less time to devote to his sermons. This rule of thumb is not completely reliable, however, there being some unpolished works with internal indications that they were produced in Antioch and some more refined works that clearly date from his episcopate. John did not write his sermons out in advance. Instead, his, like those of the Cappadocians, were taken down by a scribe during delivery. Hence, much of the difference in literary elegance depended on whether the author found time to revise a series before publication.

A lack of such editing is not entirely a disadvantage to those who are interested in how John actually preached. As John A. Broadus says:

> You see the sermon in about as imperfect, and sometimes distorted, a condition as it is seen in the actual delivery by many of the congregation. You see the frequent questions, the abrupt turns of phrase, the multiplied repetitions, by which a skilled and sympathetic preacher, keenly watching his audience, strives to retain attention and to insure a more general comprehension. You are drawn near to him, and almost stand by his side.[35]

In all that has been said about the Golden Mouth's preaching, there has been little to account for his great reputation in his own day and since. Partly that is because much of what made him so impressive can no longer be experienced. His sermons were transactions with a live congregation, not words on paper, much less translations of those words into other languages. We can know nothing of his electrifying presence as he sat in his chair in the ambo, much nearer to his audience than if he had preached from the customary position of the bishop's chair behind the altar in the apse. The interaction with the congregation, mentioned by Broadus, cannot be recaptured. What John's delivery was like, the way he used either his body or his voice, is unavailable to history. What the voice that came from the Mouth of Gold sounded like cannot be known. And those who experience his words only in translation cannot guess at the magic of sound or the precision of expression in his choice of words. All that is left is the judgment of his contemporaries that he was the best there was at a time when oratory was one of the most highly developed and critically appreciated art forms there was.

Even from printed translations it is possible, however, to see some of the ways in which John achieved his oral effectiveness. He made great use of metaphor and simile to help his hearers understand the points he was making, drawing especially on athletic, military, maritime, and agricultural images. He also made "abundant, even excessive, use of the stylistic devices of the sophists, especially tropes and figures involving pleonasm, such as anaphora, or sound, such as paronomasia, or vivacity, such as rhetorical question or question and answer."[36]

He created vivid scenes *(ekphrasis)* that brought things to life for his audience. He made comparisons *(synkrisis)* and employed the techniques of the Cynic-Stoic diatribe. Paradox was a common form of expression for him as for all Christian speakers. As much as he claimed to despise Greek culture, he was nevertheless aware that "the art of speaking comes, not by nature, but by instruction, and therefore even if a man reaches the acme of perfection in it, still it may forsake him unless he cultivates its force by constant application and exercise."[37] He constantly honed the skills in which Libanius had trained him.

The Sermons on the Statues

We can see an example of his preaching power in one of his most famous series of sermons, the one called *Concerning the Statues*. Considered by Kennedy to be John's most striking homilies,[38] these were preached when John had been a priest for only a year. (For a sermon in

81

this series, see **Vol. 2, pp. 57-70.**) Just after he began his Lenten sermon series in 387,[39] an event occurred that placed the entire city of Antioch in great danger. When notice of a new and exorbitant tax was read out at the courthouse, a mob led by a claque erupted in widespread vandalism against public buildings, culminating in portraits and statues of the emperor and his family being pulled down and defaced. As Kelly says, "To insult or show disrespect to the images of the reigning emperor was equivalent to insulting him personally, and therefore counted as high treason."[40] The emperor would have been within his rights to obliterate the city and its inhabitants, and he certainly seemed likely to exact some sort of terrible vengeance.[41] The aged bishop Flavian set off to Constantinople at once to beg Theodosius in the name of the God he worshiped to spare the city, leaving his priest to minister to his terrified flock.

In the weeks that followed, John preached twenty[42] sermons, most of which began with an effort to help the anxious congregation see the latest turn of events in a theological perspective. There is an almost breathless quality to these reports, a feel of bulletins from the front lines. John's basic attitude toward the series of events is to consider it a visitation for the city's sins. It does not seem to have occurred to him to suggest that the emperor was being too demanding in levying taxes. Those to blame for the immediate dangers were, in effect, outside agitators. For all his tendency to blame the problems of his congregation on themselves, there is still something very pastoral in John's message, something that must have given many Antiochene Christians the courage to endure a very frightening period.[43]

The modern reader may be astonished, however, to realize that the sermons are not all about the crisis. They are called homilies and correctly so, since most of them are expositions of lections for the Lenten liturgy, largely from Genesis. After the daily update on the crisis, John discussed the reading with very little transition or effort to interconnect these two parts of the sermon. Finally, the concluding exhortation for almost all of the homilies concerned one subject: swearing. It seemed as though, come hell or high water, Chrysostom wanted to stamp out cursing in Antioch that Lent.[44]

One can see John's eloquence in all of the sermons, but perhaps it is in its purest form in the first, the one preached before the riot occurred. It begins, as Kennedy says, with "a splendor worthy of Pindar."[45]

> Ye have heard the Apostolic voice, that trumpet from heaven, that spiritual lyre! For even as a trumpet sounding a fearful and warlike note, it

both dismays the enemy, and arouses the dejected spirits on its own side, and filling them with great boldness, renders those who attend to it invincible against the devil! And again, as a lyre, that gently soothes with soul-captivating melody, it puts to slumber the disquietudes of perverse thoughts; and thus, with pleasure, instills into us much profit. Ye have heard then today the Apostle discoursing to Timothy of divers necessary matters![46]

He continues to introduce the lection from 1 Timothy 5 that had just been read. After summarizing it he says that, because it would be impossible for him to interpret all of it, he will allow the congregation to pick the text on which he will preach.

The verse they chose was 5:23, "Drink a little wine for thy stomach's sake, and thine often infirmities" (KJV). He then tells them they have chosen a text so simple that it seems to have little promise, but they will be amazed at the riches it contains. He begins by asking how God could permit someone who trusted him as much as Timothy did to fall into chronic illness. That question is further complicated by the way the illness interfered with the work Timothy had to do for the Lord. Why did God allow the work to be interfered with? And, since both Timothy and Paul performed many healing miracles, why did they not heal Timothy?

John begins his response by calling attention to Timothy's great virtue and Paul's loving care. Yet Timothy did not presume on his virtue. Rather, knowing the dangers of youth, he preferred suffering of the body to that of the soul. In that perspective it becomes clear that Paul's admonition to Timothy was a counsel of abstinence rather than indulgence: not "use wine," but "a little wine." For "it is not the use of wine, but the want of moderation which produces drunkenness."[47] With that background John goes on to give eight reasons why God allowed Timothy to suffer. He follows that by citing a long paragraph of scripture supporting each of these reasons. (How could he keep the list in his memory at the time that he was searching it for so many parallel verses of scripture?)

John then begins the shift to his concluding moral exhortation by saying that we should not call God into account for what he does. Even Job did not do that, nor did many others who lost their fortunes while they were using them to help the poor. For a Christian to question God in that way would be blasphemy. With that transition negotiated, John is able to announce what will be his recurring theme throughout the twenty-one sermons: "But since our discourse has now turned to the subject of blasphemy, I desire to ask one favor of you all, in return for this my address, and speaking with you; which is, that you will correct on my behalf the blasphemers of this city."[48] He even gives them permission to use physical force in carrying out that mission. He promises them a spiritual reward for discharging the task and arranges to segue into the doxology with which he closed most of his sermons.

What a tour de force! One of the exercises by which future Sophists were trained in schools of rhetoric was extempore speaking on an assigned subject. Chrysostom took the practice into the pulpit and asked his congregation to tell him from which verse in the passage that had been read he should preach. The complex structure he gave the treatment of the verse by listing the reasons why God allowed Timothy to suffer are *topoi* and the long citing of scriptural parallels showed that he already knew which biblical passages treated each of the topics, that he had furnished his mind to speak on all these subjects—and many more besides. And, in the end, he brought the subject around to the exhortation he wanted to be thematic for that Lent. However much he may have liked to discredit Greek culture, in sermons like this he demonstrated how thoroughly he had mastered everything Libanius had to teach.

PREPARATION FOR INITIATION

While a few of John's sermons in various genres other than homiletic have come down, the catechetical are the only ones that can be mentioned here. Basic instruction in the faith is a task that has been performed in all the Christian centuries, but not all such teaching is preaching. To begin with, preaching requires a more or less formal occasion in which one person is making a continuous presentation, rather than one in which there is discussion back and forth. Beyond that, however, the difference between catechetical sermons and lectures informing or explaining is the purpose of forming the congregation through the medium of the speech, enabling them to experience change, to undergo at least a "mini-conversion." It is not enough for them to know and understand what Christians believe on a particular subject; they must come to accept that as their own belief, and allow that belief to become the motivating factor for their behavior.

Not all catechetical preaching has been immediate preparation for baptism. That done by Aelfric in Anglo-Saxon England, for instance, occurred at a time when infant baptism was the rule.[49] The period of Chrysostom, however, is unique because it was a time when Christians were no longer persecuted and former pagans were flocking to the church for initiation. It was also a time when many if not most Christians were deferring baptism until the storms of youth were over from fear of postbaptismal sin.

Shortly before the late-fourth century there would not have been the numbers desiring baptism that would make catechetical preaching the obvious preparation. Shortly afterward, infant baptism became the norm and candidates could not be catechized. For a while, though, preaching was the favored method of preparation in a number of locations. While it is impossible to know how widespread the method was, it is nevertheless true that four sets of catechetical sermons from that period have been preserved.[50] One was preached by John when he was still at Antioch, one by his friend Theodore of Mopsuestia, one by Cyril and possibly another preacher at Jerusalem, and one by Ambrose in Milan. These series differ enough from one another to make it impossible to treat them synthetically,[51] so we must consider each individually.

John Chrysostom

Most of the catechetical sermons by Chrysostom were unknown until 1955, when they were found in the Stavronikita monastery on Mount Athos in Greece by Antoine Wenger.[52] The discovery called attention to three others that had been published in an obscure Russian series in 1909.[53] Prior to that, only two of John's catechetical homilies were known, one of which is in the Russian publication.[54] It is now believed that the four sermons in the Russian work and in PG are part of the instruction John gave candidates in Antioch in 388, while the newly discovered series was delivered in 390.[55] John was still a priest then, and the task of catechizing seems to have been shared with other priests; his sermons were only part of the total preparation of the Antioch catechumens.

The preacher of the *Baptismal Instructions* is clearly the preacher of the homilies. In demonstrating that the Stavronikita instructions are the work of John, Wenger pointed to characteristics he considered "trademarks" of Chrysostom's preaching:

> the richness and concrete character of his language, the abundance of examples taken from the political and social life of his times, the predominance of moral considerations over speculative theology, the primacy of pastoral preoccupations, and, finally, an unflagging eloquence.[56]

Harkins also points to what he calls John's "almost invariable method of development."[57] It consists of: "(a) an affirmation often linked with an image or supported by a comparison; (b) proof of the affirmation drawn from Scripture, most often from St. Paul; and (c) a conclusion and further developments by which the thought progresses." These two characterizations are consistent with the description of Chrysostom's Sunday preaching in the previous section.

How, then, does his catechetical preaching differ enough from what we've already discussed to warrant separate treatment? To begin with, these sermons do not involve verse-by-verse exegesis of a biblical lection. These are occasional sermons, the occasion for which is preparing catechumens for baptism and the beginning of life as a Christian. But here John's instructions also differ from those of the other three catechetical preachers. Most have as their topics sections of the Lord's Prayer, the local baptismal creed, or the sacraments of baptism and Eucharist. John discusses only some elements of the baptismal rite in a few of his sermons, but even there the emphasis is on exhortation to lead the Christian life rather than on the rite itself.[58]

We can see the special quality of John's catechetical preaching in the topics treated in the longer series of sermons he is thought to have delivered in 390. The first is a welcome to the candidates and almost a pep talk to get them enthusiastic for the challenge that lies ahead—although it does show some of the preacher's characteristic concerns in warnings about women's dress and omens, oaths, and spectacles. The second is more similar to others' mystagogical sermons in that it analyzes the initiatory rites. The third is addressed to neophytes and is much like the first in spirit, although its metaphor is a wrestling match with Satan rather than a spiritual marriage with Christ. Baptism is also compared to the exodus. The fourth is more of the same, saying that the neophyte should shine especially by his conduct, and using an image that will recur often, that of baptism as a brightly clean garment. The title the manuscript gives to the fifth is: "Exhortation to the Neophytes to Abstain from Softness, Extravagance, and Drunkenness, and to Esteem Moderation in All Things."

The sixth is truly occasional, a diatribe against those who skipped church to go to the chariot races and gladiatorial games held that day. The seventh is also occasional, since it was preached on a feast of martyrs in the *Martyrion* where all the instructions were given. And the final instruction serves several purposes: it pays respect to monks who had come down from the mountain to be present, it holds before those about to be baptized the infinite superiority of invisible to visible goods, and makes the practical suggestion that the initiates stop by the church to pray at the beginning and end of their working day. This is all vintage

Chrysostom, but very unlike the mystagogy given by the other three catechetical preachers.

Theodore of Mopsuestia

John's catechetical sermons are as different as possible from those of Theodore, his old friend, fellow student of Diodore, and brother priest. Since the two of them must have been catechizing the neophytes at Antioch at about the same time, it is fascinating to imagine receiving one's instruction from the two in alternation. It would be like riding in a wagon drawn by a spirited racehorse yoked with a powerful ox. Both had great gifts, but not at all the same gifts.

John did not share Theodore's interest in biblical interpretation as a goal in itself. Both, however, were very much in the Antiochene tradition of literal interpretation, as opposed to the allegorism of Alexandria. The two sees also had their characteristic emphases in their understanding of the person and work of Christ. Alexandrine Christology stressed the unity of our Lord's human and divine natures, but in doing so often seemed to do less than justice to his full humanity. That of Antioch, on the other hand, affirmed Jesus' complete humanity so staunchly that at times it was hard to see how that was joined to his divinity.

Theodore's instructions were as doctrinal as John's were moral and ascetic. There were sixteen of them in all: ten on the creed, one on the Lord's Prayer, and five on the sacraments. With almost two-thirds of them being on the creed, a theological emphasis was inevitable. The future controversialist wished none who heard him to be mistaken in their beliefs. His care appears overdone. "His style is exceedingly diffuse and repetitive, and his homilies are more often quarried for information about the rites than read as sermons."[59] So much was this the case that Edward Yarnold removed some of the repetitions from his translation, carefully indicating, however, where he did so.[60] Even at that, his edition of the homilies of Theodore about the sacraments[61] takes eighty-eight pages, while those of the other three on the same subjects total only ninety-seven. Yet, translated into Syriac, Theodore's homilies became a catechetical textbook for the Nestorian church after it broke away.

Cyril of Jerusalem

If any of the series of catechetical homilies was prototypical, it was the one by the least famous preacher. Very little is known about Cyril other than that he wished to have an orthodox Christology without using the word *homoousios*.[62] Cyril was born near 313, the year in which Constantine began to side with Christianity, so Cyril's life and ministry were under the shadow of that emperor. Not only was the theological agenda for his lifetime set by the Council of Nicaea that Constantine called, the material conditions of Cyril's church were also greatly affected by him. One of the marks of Constantine's favor to his new faith was a number of churches he built in the Holy Land, especially in Jerusalem, the scene of Cyril's ministry.

Growing up in the Holy City, Cyril was ordained deacon around 335, served in that order for about ten years, and then for about five more years in the priesthood before he was made bishop. Cyril was exiled a few times, the last and longest being 367 to 378, because of a controversy over whether the church in Jerusalem was subordinate to that in Caesarea or instead had special honor because of its historical importance. Before the Council of Constantinople in 381, Cyril had become reconciled to the unbiblical term designating Christ's shared divinity with the Father and was one of the honored participants in those deliberations. He died five years later as a venerated leader, but left few writings other than his catechetical sermons.

These sermons take on a special interest because of where they were preached. While interest in the holy places stretches back at least to the time of Melito of Sardis,[63] it had been given a new vitality by imperial support for Christianity after 313, especially Constantine's building program in Jerusalem. The centerpiece of the building program was the complex made possible by the proximity to one another of the traditional sites of Jesus' crucifixion and resurrection and the place where Constantine's mother, Helena, discovered what was thought to be the true cross.[64] There was a rotunda called the *Anastasis* (the Greek word for "resurrection") built over the tomb of Joseph of Arimathea from which Jesus rose.[65] Next to it was the walled-in atrium or courtyard of the Holy Cross. In a corner of that stood the rock of Calvary, Golgotha, which was about twelve feet high and enclosed in a grille; this was known as *Ad Crucem* ("at the cross"). A cross was erected nearby to indicate where the crucifixion was thought to have occurred (*Ante Crucem*, "before the cross"). Behind that was a chapel called *Post Crucem*. The courtyard shared its west[66] wall with the *Anastasis*, while its east wall was the wall behind the apse of the main church, the *Martyrion*, built over the cave in which Helena was said to have found the cross. Other churches in Jerusalem erected by Constantine were Sion, on the traditional site of the Last Supper; the *Imbomon*, on the Mount of Olives where the ascension was believed to have occurred; and the nearby *Eleona* (from the Greek word for "olives"), the church built over a cave where Jesus was thought to have taught the apostles.

Less than twenty years after Cyril's death, a Spanish nun named Egeria spent about three years in the Holy Land in an effort to see the places where all the things narrated in the Bible happened.[67] About half of the account of her experiences, which she wrote for her sisters back in Spain, is devoted to describing "the ritual observed day by day in the holy places"[68] of Jerusalem. Included in this is a report on the way candidates for initiation were prepared. While her visit occurred after Cyril's death, it is believed that conditions had not altered. Thus she furnishes a rare eyewitness account of patristic preaching.

During the forty days of Lent,[69] those preparing for baptism would attend the early morning office at the *Anastasis* and be exorcised by the bishop when it was over. Then they would move into the *Martyrion* and cluster around the bishop's throne while he lectured, introducing them to the Bible during Lent. After five weeks[70] they were given the creed, which the bishop then began to explain phrase by phrase. These daily sessions lasted three hours and ended with hymns on the way back to the *Anastasis* for the office for Terce. On the Saturday before Holy Week, the catechumens would show they had learned the creed by reciting it to the bishop. The elaborate liturgies of Holy Week did not leave time for further instruction, but during Easter week the bishop explained to the newly initiated the sacraments of baptism and the Eucharist, which they had now experienced.[71]

Cyril's sermons have an interest of their own beyond that of their setting. They begin with a Procatechesis on the occasion of the solemn enrollment of the catechumens. The first two instructions are hortatory preparations of the candidates for what lies ahead, and the third is a discussion of baptism, although not the sort of detailed explanation of the rite that will follow their initiation on Easter. Then Christian belief is summarized in the fourth lecture as "Ten Doctrines." The fifth speaks of faith both as a system of belief and as an inward disposition; it ends with the impartation of the system of belief as summarized in the local form of the baptismal creed.

Lectures six through eighteen are devoted to phrase-by-phrase explication of the creed. The catechumens recite the creed back to the bishop the day before Palm Sunday, and there is no more instruction until Easter Monday when the five mystagogical lectures (i.e., those on the sacraments) begin. Some scholars think that the mystagogical lectures were not written by Cyril but by his successor in the see, John. For our understanding of how catechetical preaching was done in Jerusalem, the issue is not important, especially since Cyril's catechetical lectures seem to have set the pattern in Jerusalem for at least a century. Nor would it make any difference if, as seems likely, Cyril was still a priest when he first delivered his lectures.

The sermons are true homilies in the sense that each of them is based on a lesson read before it was preached. The texts cited at the beginning of each of the lectures are those assigned to those days in two Armenian lectionaries that reflect the usage of Jerusalem in the fifth century. Yet, while the readings do summarize the theme of the sermons, the true texts on which the sermons are based are the articles of the creed or the elements of the baptismal or eucharistic rites that are being explicated. The preacher shows a good bit of skill in weaving all these together for a unified impact. There is also a certain amount of rhetorical artistry that turns each of the homilies into an appeal for a commitment. And each of the instructions has a hortatory conclusion and ends with a doxology. It is easy to get as excited as Egeria about initiation in Jerusalem and to think about what a nice way that was to be formed as a Christian.

Ambrose of Milan

There are few figures in the early church about whom so much is known and so little understood as Ambrose. Biographers who try to move from the known events to the man behind come up with diametrically opposed interpretations.[72] The basic outline of his life, however, is clear enough. Ambrose's father was praetorian prefect in Trier when his son was born ca. 339, but he seems to have died the next year. His mother took the family to Rome so that Ambrose and his older brother Satyrus could receive the typical education in rhetoric that sons of landowning families received. During their stay in Rome, Ambrose's sister Marcellina, about ten years his senior, was accepted by Pope Liberius as a consecrated virgin. Ambrose was, in fact, the first of the Latin Fathers to have been born into a Christian family, as he was also the first to have come from the aristocracy.[73] After completing their education ca. 365, the two brothers became lawyers at the court of the praetorian prefect of Sirmium, the capital of the province of Illyria and thus the meeting place of East and West. Five years later Ambrose was appointed *consularis* (governor) of Aemilia and Liguaria, with his headquarters at Milan, which was often the seat of imperial government in the West.

The church in Milan had been under the control of Arians until the death of their bishop Auxentius in 374. Yet somehow the orthodox were meeting with them to elect his successor and a riot almost broke out. To prevent it the governor appeared and was suddenly elected by acclamation. He had to not only pass through the other orders but also be baptized before he could be consecrated. As a bishop he took a strong stand against Arians and traditional Roman religion. He had a good deal to do with the removal of the pagan Altar of Victory from the Roman senate house, and he refused to let the emperor's mother have a church in Milan for her Arian congregation. When Theodosius ordered the massacre of seven thousand citizens of Thessalonica for rioting, Ambrose required public penance of him before he was allowed to receive communion. Ambrose has many other claims on the church's memory: he is known, for example, as "The Father of Liturgical Hymnody" because of his innovations in that area, and he is one of the four Doctors of the Western Church.

Most of his many writings are series of homilies that he edited as treatises. While he was not an original thinker, he was an influential one. Part of the explanation is that he was one of the few Western bishops of the time who knew Greek and read the works of the Eastern Fathers. Although his own interests were primarily practical—a characteristic attitude of the Western church at the time—his study of the Greek Fathers made him aware, as few of his Western colleagues were, of the importance of the theological controversies in the East. Thus he became an ardent promoter of orthodox Trinitarian doctrine. Ambrose was greatly influenced by Alexandrine biblical interpretation and became an inveterate allegorizer. He also drew on Greek and Roman philosophy in his writings although, like many preachers, he seldom identified his sources.

Estimates of the quality of his preaching vary. It is common to see such comments as: "His rhetorical style, characterized by long periodic sentences interspersed with direct and pithy statements, was rich in imagery derived from nature, scripture, and classical sources."[74] Yet it is also recognized that the editing done before publication makes it difficult to know exactly what his sermons were like when delivered. Even so sympathetic a critic as Angelo Paredi misses the "lively particulars and spontaneous observations" that must have been eliminated in the editing process. The result, he says, "is like having a glass of champagne which has been standing too long, and which has lost its seething, sparkling bubbles."[75]

The present purpose, however, is not to discuss his preaching in general, but only his catechetical instruction. That is an extensive enough topic by itself, however, since the corpus of his works includes two treatments of the sacraments and a sermon in which the creed was delivered to the catechumens.[76] Although he left no detailed instruction on the creed and Lord's Prayer like those of Cyril or Theodore, Ambrose did direct his Lenten preaching to the preparation of the catechumens. Several of his series of exegetical homilies were also catechetical preaching, a function they must have shared with many exegetical homilies by other Fathers.[77]

His two works on the sacraments give insight into the difference between his homilies as they were delivered and the treatises into which some were edited, since *De Sacramentis* appears to be a stenographic transcript of six homilies as they were delivered and *De Mysteriis* a treatise edited from another series of the same sort. The thought of the two is very similar, and both show Ambrose's great facility in citing Scripture and the remarkable allegorical interpretations that he gives to the verses cited. The shorthand record of *De Sacramentis* is characterized as having such a "lack of cohesion . . . frequent repetitions, and . . . careless style"[78] that many scholars thought it the work of someone else until Otto Faller, Bernard Botte, and Henry Chadwick demonstrated its true nature. Yarnold says that "in these half-extempore sermons A[mbrose] often rambles away from the logical order,"[79] and Yarnold finds the argument so intuitive at times that he feels called upon to explicate it. The extreme example of this is the way that both the fifth and sixth homilies begin discussing aspects of the Eucharist and end explaining the Lord's Prayer rather than finishing one topic before the other is taken up.

We can see something of the effect of this in the second homily. It begins with a discussion of prefigurations of baptism and notes that while both pagans and Jews had ritual washings, they did not have real baptism.[80] This leads to a digression in which the story of the healing at the pool of Bethesda, which had been read the day before but had not been commented on, is recalled. Ambrose makes a christological interpretation of John 5:4, which is not in the best manuscripts of the Fourth Gospel. Next follows an allegorical interpretation of the way that only the first person to go down into the water was healed. He then explains the sick man's lack of someone to carry him to the pool as meaning that he had no mediator with God.

Next the story of the cleansing of Naaman, which had been discussed the day before, is seen as a type of baptism. "There you have one kind of baptism; the flood is another. You have a third kind when our fathers were baptized in the Red Sea. You have a fourth in the pool when the waters moved" (*De Sacramentis* 2.9). This discussion of prefigurations of baptism is followed by other discussions of the presence of the Trinity in the rite, the effects of the rite, and the elements of the rite itself, including the second anointing, to complete this homily. Yet so discriminating a critic of public speaking as Augustine said that when he first went to Milan as imperial professor of rhetoric, he "hung on" Ambrose's words intently, and "was delighted with the pleasantness of his speech, more erudite, yet less cheerful and soothing in manner, than that of Faustus."[81] Something must have been lost in the transcription.

CONCLUSION

These four examples show the variety of catechetical preaching being done in the short period in which it was the means used to socialize adults at last ready to make a full Christian commitment. These series of sermons suggest there must have been many more that were not preserved, including many exegetical homilies designed for the purpose of catechesis. While the time was unique and exactly that sort of catechetical preaching has rarely recurred, these early examples do serve as a reminder that the need to teach Christian faith by sermons that call for conversion and commitment would appear often in the centuries ahead. Along with regular Sunday preaching, which can be called homiletic, and evangelistic preaching, catechetical preaching makes up the third major genre of Christian proclamation.

In considering the four catechetical preachers, a major transition in the history of preaching has passed without comment. Ambrose was the first preacher who preached in Latin to have been considered. Yet from here on until the Reformation, we will study only Western preaching. One reason for that is that with the passing of the great men treated so far, Eastern preaching became derivative.

> The two generations from the middle of the Fourth Century to the beginning of the Fifth constitute the Golden Age of Greek Christian Eloquence. . . . A great deal of subsequent Greek preaching not only imitates Gregory and John, but quarries phrases, sentences, and whole passages from their works. Their achievements were never surpassed and rarely equaled. Already in the Fifth and Sixth Centuries there is a falling off.[82]

Yet, as we shall see, similar things could be said about Western preaching as well. The main reason for the shift is that since the whole history of Christian preaching cannot be studied in so short a work, I made the decision to make this a homiletical genealogy for contemporary preachers in English. Thus, the rest of this work will be confined to Western Christendom, with further tapering in store down the line.

FOR FURTHER READING

Kelly, J. N. D. *Golden Mouth: The Story of John Chrysostom: Ascetic, Preacher, Bishop.* Ithaca, N.Y.: Cornell University Press, 1995.

Paredi, Angelo. *Saint Ambrose: His Life and Times.* Translated by M. Joseph Costelloe. Notre Dame: University of Notre Dame Press, 1964.

St. John Chrysostom: Baptismal Instructions. Translated and annotated by Paul W. Harkins. ACW, no. 31. Westminster, Md.: Newman Press, 1963.

St. John Chrysostom: The Homilies on Genesis 1-17. Translated and edited by Robert C. Hill. FC, vol. 74. Washington, D.C.: Catholic University of America Press, 1986.

Westerhoff, John H., III, and O. C. Edwards Jr., eds. *A Faithful Church: Issues in the History of Catechesis.* Wilton, Conn.: Morehouse-Barlow, 1981.

Wiles, Maurice. "Theodore of Mopsuestia as a Representative of the Antiochene School." In *From the Beginnings to Jerome.* Vol. 1 of *The Cambridge History of the Bible.* Edited by P. R. Ackroyd and C. F. Evans, 489-510. Cambridge: Cambridge University Press, 1970.

Yarnold, Edward. *The Awe-Inspiring Rites of Initiation: Baptismal Homilies of the Fourth Century.* Slough: St. Paul Publications, 1972.

Notes

1. With the exception of Basil's sermons on the *Hexaemeron* and the Psalms.

2. Around seven hundred homilies survive, in contrast to just over one hundred in other genres. These numbers were tabulated from Johannes Quasten, ed., *The Golden Age of Greek Patristic Literature from the Council of Nicaea to the Council of Chalcedon*, vol. 3 of *Patrology* (Utrecht: Spectrum, 1960; Westminster, Md.: Newman Press, 1960), 433-59.

3. Six of the volumes are devoted to John. It takes eighteen volumes of the PG to contain all his writings, more than are required for any other Greek Father.

4. Pope Pius X, *Acta sanctae sedis* (1908), 594-95.

5. J. N. D. Kelly, *Golden Mouth: The Story of John Chrysostom: Ascetic, Preacher, Bishop* (Ithaca, N.Y.: Cornell University Press, 1995), 4. For the rationale for the

dates Kelly accepts for John's early life, see Appendix B, 296-98. The sources for John's life are Palladius's *Dialogue on the Life of St. John Chrysostom*, and the church histories of Socrates (6.21-23, 7.25-45), Sozomen (8.8-28), and Theodoret (5.27-36).

6. Not, as often thought, the commander in chief himself, according to Kelly, *Golden Mouth*, 4-5.

7. The emperor Diocletian divided the empire into twelve administrative districts called dioceses. That of the Oriens stretched from the Red Sea to the southeastern part of modern Turkey.

8. For the significance of Libanius, see George Kennedy, *Greek Rhetoric Under Christian Emperors* (Princeton: Princeton University Press, 1983), 150-63.

9. O. Bardenhewer, *Geschichte der altkirchlichen Literatur*, as cited by Kelly, *Golden Mouth*, 7 n. 4.

10. Sozomen, *Hist. Eccl.*, 8.2. Quoted in Kelly, *Golden Mouth*, 8.

11. Kelly, *Golden Mouth*, 15-16.

12. Ibid., 18-20. It was through the training of Diodore that John became committed to the Antiochene school of biblical interpretation, which did not embrace allegorical explanation.

13. About twenty years later, John wrote of this experience in his dialogue *On the Priesthood*. While most modern scholars have taken this account to be the sort of fictional setting that was common in the dialogue genre, the reasons Kelly sets forth (*Golden Mouth*, 27-28) for considering it historical are persuasive. He is also right in regarding the order to which the two were to be ordained as the priesthood rather than the episcopate.

14. For the location of Mount Silpios, see the map in Kelly, *Golden Mouth*, 303.

15. Ibid., 39.

16. In the introduction to his translation of *The Homilies on Genesis of St. John Chrysostom*, FC, vol. 74 (Washington, D.C.: Catholic University of America Press, 1986), 6, Robert C. Hill raises the possibility that these were preached during John's diaconate, but most scholars doubt a bishop at that time would delegate his authority to preach to a deacon.

17. Kelly, *Golden Mouth*, 57.

18. This is the title of chapter 7 of Kelly, *Golden Mouth*.

19. The titles "archbishop" and "patriarch" were not yet used in Constantinople.

20. The mosaic portrait in Hagia Sophia, though from a later period, is consistent with the unflattering description in the office books for the feasts of saints in the Eastern Orthodox Church. Ibid., 106.

21. Kelly, *Golden Mouth*, 55-71, 83-103, 128-44; Kennedy, *Greek Rhetoric Under Christian Emperors*, 241-54; R. A. Krupp, *Shepherding the Flock of God: The Pastoral Theology of John Chrysostom*, American University Studies, series 7, Theology and Religion, vol. 101 (New York: Peter Lang, 1991), 51-69; Geoffrey Wainwright, "Preaching as Worship" and "The Sermon and the Liturgy," *GOTR* 28 (1983): 325-49.

22. Hill, *St. John Chrysostom*, 10.

23. Ibid. So sympathetic and insightful a critic as John A. Broadus said that it was misleading to compare Chrysostom's sermons with the more tightly integrated

expository sermons favored at the end of the nineteenth century, claiming that prayer-meeting talks furnished a better analogy. "St. Chrysostom as a Homilist," *NPNF*[1] 13:6.

24. *Hom. Matt.* 1.5-7.

25. Ibid., 1.6.

26. Ibid., 3.5.

27. *Hom. Acts* 1.

28. *Hom. 1 Cor.* 2.1.

29. *Hom. Col.* 1.

30. The root meaning of *theôria* is "sight," and the cognate verb has extended meanings of watching, looking on, observing, perceiving, noticing, and experiencing.

31. Robert M. Grant and David Tracy, *A Short History of the Interpretation of the Bible*, 2nd ed., rev. and enl. (Philadelphia: Fortress, 1984), 66.

32. Maurice Wiles, "Theodore of Mopsuestia as a Representative of the Antiochene School," in *From the Beginnings to Jerome*, vol. 1 of *The Cambridge History of the Bible*, ed. P. R. Ackroyd and C. F. Evans (Cambridge: Cambridge University Press, 1970), 489-510.

33. G. L. Prestige, *Fathers and Heretics: Six Studies in Dogmatic Faith with Prologue and Epilogue* (London: SPCK; New York: Macmillan, 1940), 120-49.

34. Graham Neville, trans. *Saint John Chrysostom: Six Books on the Priesthood* (London: SPCK, 1964).

35. Broadus, "St. Chrysostom as a Homilist," *NPNF*[1] 13:v. As Kennedy said, "It must be remembered that he was primarily an orator and not a writer and that he was speaking to a congregation of varied intellectual abilities: he must dwell on his points if they are to be grasped." See *Greek Rhetoric Under Christian Emperors*, 252.

36. Kennedy, *Greek Rhetoric Under Christian Emperors*, 248. Cf. Sister Mary Albania Burns, *Saint John Chrysostom's Homilies on the Statues: A Study of Their Rhetorical Qualities and Form*, The Catholic University of America Patristic Studies, vol. 22 (Washington, D.C.: Catholic University of America Press, 1930).

37. *On the Priesthood*, 5.5.

38. George A. Kennedy, *Classical Rhetoric and Its Christian and Secular Tradition from Ancient to Modern Times* (Chapel Hill: University of North Carolina Press), 145.

39. At that time the Antiochene Lent lasted eight weeks.

40. Kelly, *Golden Mouth*, 74.

41. His initial decision was to strip the city of its status as a metropolis (provincial capital); close its theaters, racetracks, and public baths; and suspend the distribution of bread to the poor.

42. The first of the twenty-one was preached before the riot.

43. Kelly, *Golden Mouth*, 72-82.

44. The *Homilies on the Statues* have been interpreted in a number of different ways by scholars. See, e.g., David Hunter, "Preaching and Propaganda in Fourth-Century Antioch: John Chrysostom's *Homilies on the Statues*" in *Preaching in the Patristic Age: Studies in Honor of Walter J. Burghardt, S.J.*, ed. David G. Hunter (New York: Paulist Press, 1989), 119-38; Peter Brown, *Power and Persuasion in Late Antiquity* (Madison: University of Wisconsin Press, 1992), 106; and Averil Cameron,

Christianity and the Rhetoric of Empire: The Development of Christian Discourse (Berkeley and Los Angeles: University of California Press, 1991), 136-37.

45. Kennedy, *Greek Rhetoric Under Christian Emperors*, 247.

46. *NPNF*[1] 9:331.

47. Ibid., 9:335.

48. Ibid., 9:343.

49. See part 2, chapter 7, below. On trends in the methods by which Christians were formed in their faith see *A Faithful Church: Issues in the History of Catechesis*, ed. John H. Westerhoff III and O. C. Edwards Jr. (Wilton, Conn.: Morehouse-Barlow, 1981).

50. To these may be added four sermons on the Lord's Prayer preached by Augustine to *competentes* (*Sermons on Selected Lessons of the Gospels*, 6-9, *NPNF*[1] 7:274-89).

51. For an introduction to these series and for examples of homilies preached in this genre, see Edward Yarnold, *The Awe-Inspiring Rites of Initiation: Baptismal Homilies of the Fourth Century* (Slough: St. Paul Publications, 1972); see also Leonel L. Mitchell, "The Development of Catechesis in the Third and Fourth Centuries: From Hippolytus to Augustine" in Westerhoff and Edwards, *A Faithful Church*, 49-78. Yarnold's volume is the most convenient way to sample catechetical sermons from each of the four preachers, but he does not provide a full text from any. For that, see *St. John Chrysostom: Baptismal Instructions*, translated and annotated by Paul W. Harkins. ACW, no. 31 (Westminster, Md.: Newman Press, 1963); *The Works of Saint Cyril of Jerusalem*, 2 vols., trans. and intro. Leo P. McCauley and Anthony A. Stephenson. FC (Washington, D.C.: Catholic University of America Press, 1969); or *St. Cyril of Jerusalem's Lectures on the Christian Sacraments: The Procatechesis and the Five Mystagogical Catecheses*, ed. F. L. Cross (1951; reprint, Crestwood, N.Y.: St. Vladimir's Seminary Press, 1986); *St. Ambrose: Theological and Dogmatic Works*, trans. Roy J. Deferrari. FC (Washington, D.C.: Catholic University of America Press, 1963); Theodore of Mopsuestia, *Commentary on the Nicene Creed*, ed. and trans. A. Mingana (Cambridge: Woodbrooke Studies 5, 1932); Theodore of Mopsuestia, *Commentary on the Lord's Prayer and on the Sacraments of Baptism and the Eucharist*, ed. and trans. A. Mingana (Cambridge: Woodbrooke Studies 6, 1933). On the theology of these four series of catechetical homilies, see Enrico Mazza, *Mystagogy: A Theology of Liturgy in the Patristic Age*, trans. Matthew J. O'Connell (New York: Pueblo, 1989).

52. John Chrysostom, *Huit Catéchèses Baptismales*. SC, no. 5 (Paris: Cerf, 1957).

53. A. Papadopoulos-Kerameus, *Varia graeca sacra* (St. Petersburg, 1909). This volume contains a fourth homily that is the same as one of those in the Stavronikita manuscript. Cf. Paul W. Harkins, *St. John Chrysostom: Baptismal Instructions*, 10, 201 n. 14.

54. PG 49:221-40.

55. These appear in reverse order in Harkins's translation, the 390 series includes homilies 1-8, and the 388 series includes homilies 9-12. The dates, of course, are not certain.

56. Cited in Harkins, *St. John Chrysostom: Baptismal Instructions*, 14.

57. Ibid., 205 n. 1. Harkins goes on to say that the vocabulary is also typical of John.

58. Mitchell, "The Development of Catechesis in the Third and Fourth Centuries," 66.

59. Ibid., 70. The form of an individual homily began with a "Synthesis" that was a narrative of what was to be discussed—the succession of actions in a sacramental celebration, for instance. The body of the homily was a series of annotations on the text of the Synthesis with the tone of so many footnotes on the subject.

60. Yarnold, *The Awe-Inspiring Rites of Initiation,* 74.

61. As we shall see below, there is some variation between the series in which topics were lectured on before and which after Easter. John and Theodore instructed their catechumens on baptism before they received it, while Cyril and Ambrose thought it better for them to have the experience first and explanation afterward. All, however, postponed discussing the Eucharist until after their hearers had participated in it.

62. For Cyril's theological position, see Anthony A. Stephenson and Leo P. McCauley, introduction to *The Works of St. Cyril of Jerusalem,* especially 34-60.

63. Ibid., 17-21.

64. All of these are now enclosed in the Church of the Holy Sepulchre built by the Crusaders.

65. The surrounding rock was cut away so that what remained was little more than walls of the tomb formed by what was left of the living rock.

66. I am speaking geographically not ecclesiastically.

67. Most of the assertions in this sentence have been contested, but it represents the majority opinion of contemporary scholarship.

68. *Peregrinatio,* 24, trans. and annotated by George E. Gingras in *Egeria: Diary of a Pilgrimage,* ACW (New York: Newman Press, 1970), 89.

69. Since the Jerusalem church did not fast on Saturdays as well as Sundays, the forty days of Lent were spread over eight weeks. While Egeria says that instruction occurred every day, Cyril's series consists of only twenty sermons. The best explanation seems to be that the catechumens would include Syriac- as well as Greek-speaking persons, so each lecture had to be given twice.

70. There is some inconsistency here between Egeria's report and Cyril's instructions in which the creed was imparted immediately following the fifth lecture rather than after the fifth week.

71. *Peregrinatio,* 45-47. In Jerusalem and Milan, unlike Antioch, baptism was not explained until the *photizomenoi* (those being enlightened) had experienced it, both because of the tradition of withholding information from the uninitiated *(disciplina arcani)* and because of an assumption that it could not really be understood before one had undergone it.

72. Thus Angelo Paredi *(Saint Ambrose: His Life and Times,* trans. M. Joseph Costelloe [Notre Dame: University of Notre Dame Press, 1964]) interprets everything about Ambrose in the best light possible, while Neil B. McLynn *(Ambrose of Milan: Church and Court in a Christian Capital* [Berkeley and Los Angeles: University of California Press, 1994]) sees it all in the worst light. For a good short study by someone who has also written a longer one, see Hans von Campenhausen, *Men Who Shaped the Western Church,* trans. Manfred Hoffman (New York: Harper & Row, 1964), 87-128.

73. Specialists debate how aristocratic they were, but even the most skeptical concede to them a place on the margins of the Roman elite.

74. Lewis J. Swift, "Ambrose," in *EEC*, ed. Everett Ferguson et al. (New York and London: Garland, 1990), 30.

75. Paredi, *Saint Ambrose*, 258. McLynn goes so far as to accuse him of cultivating a biblical sound to his sermons so that in preaching he assumed the mantle of biblical authority and also says he acquired learning in order to parade it in his sermons. See *Ambrose of Milan*, 238-40.

76. The sermon on the creed is called *Explanatio symboli*, "symbol" being a term for a creed. The delivery of the creed was known as *traditio symboli,* and its recitation back to the bishop was called *reditio symboli.*

77. Mitchell, "The Development of Catechesis in the Third and Fourth Centuries," 72.

78. Maria Grazia Mara, "Ambrose of Milan, Ambrosiaster, and Nicetas," in *The Golden Age of Latin Patristic Literature from the Council of Nicea to the Council of Chalcedon*, vol. 4 of *Patrology*, ed. Angelo di Berardino, intro. Johannes Quasten, trans. Placid Solari (Westminster, Md.: Christian Classics, 1986), 172.

79. Yarnold, *The Awe-Inspiring Rites of Initiation,* 103 n. 17.

80. Ambrose thought Christian sacraments were older than the rites of the Jews. See, e.g., *de Sac.* 4.9.

81. Augustine, *Confessions* 5.13.23, *NPNF*[1], 88.

82. Kennedy, *Greek Rhetoric Under Christian Emperors*, 255-56.

CHAPTER 5

AUGUSTINE: THE SIGN READER

THE CHURCH LEARNS LATIN

With the exception of Ambrose's catechetical sermons, all of the preaching studied so far was done in Greek. This would have been true for a long time even if preaching at Rome had been notable enough to be included in this history, because Greek was the language of the Christian community there for some time after the church in Rome was founded. When the eternal city was first evangelized, it had more foreign than native inhabitants. This proportion shifted as time went on, but it was not until the middle of the third century that papal correspondence was in the local language, and it took another century for the liturgy to be translated into what had become the vernacular again.

The first theological treatise in Latin that may have been written in Rome was the *Octavius* of Minucius Felix, from the late-second or early-third century. Yet this work defends monotheism, immortality, and morality on a philosophical rather than a biblical or theological basis, and its author seems to have come from Africa rather than the Italian peninsula, so its claim to be either Roman or theological is somewhat qualified. The first major theologian in Rome to write in Latin[1] was Novatian, who went into schism in the middle of the third century over the easy restoration to communion of persons who had apostatized under persecution.

All of this is to say that a distinctly Latin Christian culture did not originate in Rome itself but in the empire's colonies in North Africa, especially around Carthage. It was there that a Latin version of the Bible first appeared, the liturgy was first celebrated in Latin, practical discussions of church affairs were held in Latin, and a Latin vocabulary for theology was coined.[2] Thus we may see that Latin was the standard language of the church and culture in North Africa, while it was exceptional in Rome. It was in Africa, therefore, that preaching in Latin first became the norm.

Roman Africa (to be distinguished from Egypt and Cyrenaica) was a strip along the Mediterranean coast of the continent that stretched from modern Libya through Tunisia and Algeria to Morocco. The area had been populated by the Berbers for several millennia by the time the Romans arrived. After the Berbers, the seafaring Phoenicians (descended from the ancient Canaanites) invaded and colonized North Africa in the ninth century of the previous era, building Carthage and other port cities. Their descendants were the Punic people with whom the Romans clashed. Carthage was destroyed by the Romans in 146 B.C.E., but was later refounded by Augustus to become the center of Roman administration and the only large city in the territory. Agriculture was the reason for the area's importance to Rome. As hard as it is to believe today, the area was very fertile then, producing grain and olive oil, foodstuffs badly needed by Rome.

To provide the services needed for this agriculture and commerce, there developed a network of country towns.

> For all their pride, these little Romes would have had populations of only a few thousand, living off the land in exactly the same way as the present inhabitants of a Spanish *pueblo* or a South Italian township.[3]

Great estates worked by tenant farmers and slaves occupied part of the area between the towns; as one moved inland, they became the norm. The first several centuries of Roman occupation were a time of great prosperity for the region, but during the fourth century, when Rome was constantly at war, taxes siphoned off much of what discretionary money there was. The Latin culture of North Africa was largely that of the townspeople and the owners of the estates. The language of tenants, slaves, and villagers was the local Berber dialect that the Romans anachronistically called Punic.

It was in this world that Latin Christianity developed as a culture. It was not confined to this world, however; as Latin became the language of the Western Empire, so it became the language of the Western church as a whole. By the end of the fourth century there had been a great deal of preaching in that tongue throughout the West. Yet very few examples of it survive. We have sermons of neither Tertullian, Cyprian, nor Hilary of Poitiers. There are sermon fragments of some sort from Zeno of Verona and two sermons by Pacianus of Barcelona. Nor is the quality of what remains uniformly high, as is shown by, for example, a number of sermons by Gaudentius of Brescia.[4] And, as I noted in the previous chapter, it is hard for modern students to accord Ambrose's preaching the respect that it received from Augustine. It is to Augustine himself, therefore, that one must go to see what preaching in Latin could be like at its best. As I also noted above, it was Augustine who completed the marriage of Christian preaching with Greco-Roman rhetoric by using allegorical biblical interpretation. It was in his proclamation of the Word of God that the homiletic sermon form took its classical shape.

MONICA'S SON

Aurelius Augustinus (354–430), known to history as Augustine of Hippo, was born into a family of the petty gentry in the Numidian town of Thagaste. His father was a pagan at the time, although he later became a Christian under the influence of his ardently devout wife, Monica. While few would quarrel with the judgment of Agostino Trapè that "Augustine is undoubtedly the greatest of the Fathers and one of the great geniuses of humanity, whose influence on posterity has been continuous and profound,"[5] this does not mean that his behavior was impeccable when he was young.[6] It is not too surprising that the young Augustine got into mischief, since most boys do in most places. It is less expected that the possessor of one of the great intellects of all time should have hated school. Nevertheless, his promise was obvious and his father made considerable financial sacrifice to send him to Carthage to acquire the rhetorical education that could open the way to a brilliant career and great financial reward.[7]

He was seventeen when he went to Carthage. His first couple of years there were spent in delayed adolescent rebellion, but then he settled down in relative respectability with a concubine with whom he was to live for fifteen years and by whom he had a son, Adeodatus. With that accommodation, he was able to concentrate on his studies. Among the books he read was the *Hortensius*, in which Cicero argues that happiness is not to be gained by indulging in physical pleasures but by devoting oneself to the pursuit of truth—or, in other words, to philosophy as it was understood at the time. In writing of the experience later Augustine said: "Suddenly every vain hope became empty to me, and I longed for the immortality of wisdom with an incredible ardour in my heart. I began to rise up to return to you."[8]

His return to God was sidetracked, however, when he associated himself with the Manichaeans, a radically dualistic sect resembling the gnostics of the second century. Doing so gave him a perspective through which he could reconcile having a mistress with his devotion to philosophy. A good bit of his later conversion, therefore, had to be disassembling the structure of his Manichaean belief.

After completing his training, Augustine set himself up as a teacher of rhetoric, first in Thagaste and later back in Carthage. In time, though, dissatisfaction with the students in Carthage led him to try his luck in Rome. His greatest success there was to attract the patronage of Symmachus, one of the most influential men in the empire, one who was able to appoint Augustine to the chair of rhetoric in the city of Milan.

> As the Imperial court resided in Milan, this was an important appointment. A professor of rhetoric would deliver the official panegyrics on the Emperor and on the consuls of the year. . . . The successful rhetorician would have found himself, in many ways, a "Minister of Propaganda."[9]

Thus, at the age of thirty, Augustine had arrived at the top of his profession.

He was to stay there for only a couple of years. As he later came to see it, God had other plans for him. And one of the main earthly instruments God used to effect those plans was his mother, Monica. She had determined notions of what her talented son should be and do, notions that combined sacred and secular ambitions for him, notions that were reinforced by dreams she interpreted as revelations from God. When as a boy he had a life-threatening disease, she tried unsuccessfully to get him baptized, and she did not let that intention go until it was eventually accomplished, although she had to wait most of the rest of her life. When he became an adolescent, she urged him to remain chaste; the most she was ever willing to settle for was that he be legally and advantageously married.

When he returned from Carthage to teach at Thagaste, it took a vision to persuade her to let him live in her house while he was a Manichaean.[10] When he went to Rome, he had to lie to her about his departure time to keep her from going with him. She did join him in Milan, however, when he became a professor there. Deciding that he was to become a provincial governor, she knew that he needed a rich wife and set out to find him one, insisting that he send home his Carthaginian concubine to clear the way for the marriage. She was happy to abandon that project when he became a Christian and committed himself to a celibate life. Her mission in life complete, she died in Ostia on their way home to Africa less than a year after his baptism. One of the last things the mother and son were to do together was to share in a mystical experience.[11] She was easily the most influential person in his life.

AUGUSTINE THE CHRISTIAN

Soon after he moved to Milan, Augustine was disillusioned about the Manichaean position and decided that being a Catholic catechumen was as good a thing as any to do while he was seeking the truth. In his quest he received help from a number of directions. He went to hear Ambrose, the bishop of Milan, preach, not so much for religious instruction as to study a capable orator, but he got more than he bargained for. Ambrose introduced him to allegorical interpretation in a way that overcame all his prejudices against the Bible.[12] At the same time, Augustine developed a group of friends who shared the ideal of philosophical retirement. With them he began to read the works of the Neoplatonists, from whom he learned the philosophical framework in which he was to state his theology the rest of his life. He also began to study Paul.

Then he was informed about the life of Anthony and the monks of Egypt who practiced a Christian form of retirement. In his reaction to that discovery, he had the experience regarded as his conversion, the impression of hearing a child's voice chanting, "*Tolle, lege; tolle, lege.*" Pick up and read, pick up and read. He took up the copy of Paul's letters next to him and it fell open to the thirteenth chapter of Romans: "not in reveling and drunkenness, not in debauchery and licentiousness. . . ." Immediately he was released from bondage to his sexual appetite and ready not only to be baptized but also to retire from his profession and devote himself to cultivating the Christian life. Soon his friends and he were on their way back to Africa.

At first they lived in community on some property Augustine owned in Thagaste. There they practiced a Christian form of retirement that was shaped by the African understanding of being a "Servant of God": "a baptized, dedicated layman, determined to live, in the company of bishops, priests and noble patrons, the full life of a Christian."[13] As time went on, their ideal approximated more and more closely that of monks.

This idyll lasted only three years. Then the thing happened of which Augustine had been afraid. Bishops in Africa were chosen then much as Ambrose had been in Milan, by acclamation of the congregation. It was not unusual for the episcopate to be forcibly imposed on a person thus chosen, so Augustine had become careful not to enter a town that had no bishop. But he went to Hippo Regius, a town of thirty or forty thousand inhabitants—second only to Carthage in Roman Africa—to bring spiritual counsel to someone who had asked for it. It ought to have been safe enough, because there was a bishop there, Valerius. But he was an old man and a Greek who did not speak Latin well. As he told the community, they needed someone who could speak their language and speak it eloquently. This was especially so because, like most Catholic churches in Africa, the local congregation was greatly outnumbered by that of the Donatists, the schismatic perfectionist movement that had swept through the region. Augustine, therefore, was made a priest so that he could stand in for Valerius, which made Augustine the first priest allowed to preach in Africa.

After four years, however, Valerius died and Augustine succeeded him as bishop of Hippo Regius, the position in which he was to remain the last thirty-five years of his life. It is hard to imagine someone who had known the glamour of the imperial court in Milan settling down in a small seacoast city in Africa, but most of the talented Africans who went to Rome and Milan in those days did return home to stay. Among these were Augustine's friends who had been his companions in retreat in Thagaste and followed him to Hippo as the monastic community in which he would live.[14]

Augustine settled in and devoted the rest of his life to being pastor to the Catholic community of Hippo. Aurelius, the bishop of Carthage, recognized the talent of his junior colleague and used him in every way possible to advance the Catholic cause in Numidia, often inviting him to preach in the capital city. Augustine became the Catholic champion in theological controversy, acting as chief spokesman against the Manichaean, Donatist, and Pelagian heresies. By his writings, Augustine achieved a worldwide prominence and authority. He was linked in correspondence to church leaders throughout the Mediterranean area. Yet his main and ordinary activity was to serve as head of the Catholic community in Hippo, counseling the anxious, settling disputes between members, and, most of all, thrilling his small-town flock week after week with some of the greatest preaching in the history of the church.

HOW TO TEACH THE FAITH

The way Augustine preached must be studied in detail. For that study a tool exists of a sort that has not been available for the analysis of the homiletical practice of any of his predecessors. Augustine provided a guide to his preaching method in the form of the first homiletics textbook ever written. Its title, *De doctrina christiana,* is often translated as "Concerning Christian Doctrine," which is misleading. It suggests that the book is concerned with the content of Christian teaching, its "doctrines." A brief glance, however, is enough to see that the book is about something else. The real subject is made clear by the author in the *Retractiones,* in which he reviewed and corrected all his writings near the end of his life. There he says of this work:

> I also added the last book, and thus completed this work in four books, of which the first three help in the understanding of the scriptures, while the fourth suggests how what we have understood is to be passed on to others.[15]

Edmund Hill, the most recent translator, says:

> *Teaching Christianity* is how I think the title of the work should be translated. Christianity is, or ought to be, pre-eminently taught by preaching; so the work leads up to the fourth book as to its goal. But Christian preaching is, or ought to be, in terms of scripture; so the would-be preacher must first be taught how to interpret the Bible.[16]

Augustine begins his hermeneutical methodology by saying that all teaching is about either things or signs. Things are not mentioned to signify something else but mean only themselves, while signs mean things other than themselves.[17] Thus, ultimately, all teaching is about things. The most important distinction to be made about things is between those that are to be used and those that are to be enjoyed. The only thing to be enjoyed—the only thing that is an end in itself—is the three-personed God. All other things are a means to the end of enjoying God. Sin keeps people from doing that; so many things have to be used in order to reopen the possibility of enjoying God. The whole Bible, therefore, is about using everything else as a means to enjoy God, to love God. God is to be loved for the sake of God, and neighbors are also to be loved for the sake of God. The Summary of the Law—love God and love your neighbor—is therefore the key to interpreting the whole Bible. Any interpretation that is not consistent with that message is a misinterpretation.

The subject of the first book of *Teaching Christianity* is things and that of the second book is signs.[18] A sign is defined as "a thing, which besides the impression it conveys to the senses, also has the effect of making something else come to mind" (2.1). There are two kinds of signs, natural and conventional. Natural signs are those that signify without intending to, the way that smoke signifies fire. The most common kind of conventional sign is words, with which the interpreter of Scripture is most involved. Difficulties in interpreting Scripture come from signs that are either unknown or ambiguous. This book deals with those unknown; much of the difficulty unknown words cause can be dealt with by learning Greek and Hebrew, the original languages of the Bible.[19] Readers very often have difficulty understanding signs that are metaphorical because they are not familiar with what the biblical thing is compared with. To solve that difficulty they must acquire knowledge of these things,[20] often from books by pagan authors.[21] One must take care in using such books, however, not to be contaminated with pagan errors.

Book 3 deals with signs that are ambiguous, a condition that may result either from the way that words are pronounced or a figurative use of them. The ambiguities of sound are either those dealt with by grammarians as they cope with the lack of punctuation and spacing between words in the manuscripts in use at the time of Augustine, or those that result from the mere fact that the words can be understood in more than one way. The dangers connected with figurative signs are that an expression intended to be understood literally is taken figuratively, or the opposite, that a figurative expression is understood literally. Augustine's rule of thumb for resolving these ambiguities is to say that whenever the literal meaning is inconsistent with Christian faith or morals, the words are to be interpreted figuratively—that is, what others call "allegorically." As noted in Book 1, everything in the Bible means that people should love God and their neighbors.[22]

Since the sermon form presupposed by Augustine is the exegetical homily, the first three books of *Teaching Christianity* are about preaching rather than a separate discipline of biblical interpretation. They deal with the classical rhetorical task of Invention when the task of deciding what to say in a speech is not the discovery of arguments but the explication of a text. Since Book 4 is about discovering "a way to put across to others what has been understood" (1.1), it approximates a little more closely than the first three books, however, what is usually understood as the subject matter of homiletics. (For the text of Book 4, **see Vol. 2,**

107

pp. 77-102.) Yet even there Augustine makes it clear that he has no intention of merely writing a treatise on rhetoric. Whatever value such treatises have, rhetoric is the sort of thing that is best learned in the schools. Those who did not learn it there can probably do better reading and listening to those who speak well.[23] Among the models of eloquence that one could study, the best are the writers of holy Scripture.

The only aspect of classical rhetoric to which Augustine gives extended attention in Book 4 is the three duties of the orator identified by Cicero: to prove, to delight, and to move. These Augustine relates to the three levels of style, with the plain for proving or teaching, the middle (the most ornate) for pleasing, and the grand for moving. While all have their purpose in preaching, the ultimate goal is conversion, and thus the grand style for moving is the most crucial. Finally, he says that the Christian teacher must practice what he preaches, and also emphasizes the importance of prayer for preaching effectively.

The most obvious thing about *Teaching Christianity* is that Augustine considered the Bible to be basically a book of signs that need to be interpreted. His choice of vocabulary demands attention. He did not use the traditional term "allegory," nor did he refer to the multiple senses of Scripture that were to be so much studied from Gregory the Great on.[24] Rather, he chose to think through in a new and disciplined way the whole matter of how meaning is conveyed in the Bible and how that meaning is to be discovered. In doing so he took as his key term the important biblical term "sign."[25]

While it is common to deplore the nonliteral interpretation of Augustine and most other preachers and exegetes before the rise of the modern historical-critical method, it is important to recognize that they had little choice. To begin with, they really believed the interpretations they came up with were what the passages meant, what God intended for them to learn from the words of the prophet or apostle. The New Testament itself used allegorical interpretation to arrive at the meaning of the Hebrew Bible and, even more consistently, interpreted it typologically and christologically. Further, that was one of the main ways the ancients knew to interpret any book, since grammarians used it to explain the meaning of the classical texts they taught schoolboys. And Augustine had an additional difficulty in the version of Scripture that was available to him. He believed as a matter of faith that every word in the Bible had been put there by God to convey some meaning, but a good bit of the text before him did not make any obvious literal sense. Writing before Jerome made the Latin Vulgate translation, he was dependent on the Old Latin version. Therefore, the text of Scripture he used was a rather slavish Latin translation of a rather slavish Greek translation of a Hebrew original that was often corrupt, especially in the Psalms. It was therefore full of both Greek and Hebrew modes of speech which had been quite distorted through translation into more or less meaningless expressions.[26]

No wonder he thought his task was decoding signs!

Peter Brown sees a further explanation of Augustine's interest in signs in the literary culture of the Late Roman period:

> Such a man [as Augustine] lived among fellow-connoisseurs, who had been steeped too long in too few books. He no longer needed to be explicit: only hidden meanings, rare and difficult words and elaborate circumlocutions, could save his readers from boredom, from *fastidium*, from that loss of interest in the obvious, that afflicts the overcultured man.[27]

Such an interpretation finds support in Augustine's statement to the effect that God placed obscurities in the text "in order to break in pride with hard labor, and to save the intelligence from boredom."[28]

Yet Brown saw the main reason for Augustine's regarding the Bible as a book of signs to be the nature of a subject that could not be approached too directly. "The mind must move from hint to hint, each discovery opening up yet further depths."[29] He also took a giant step in making Augustine's biblical interpretation comprehensible to contemporary consciousness by comparing his deciphering of biblical signs to Freud's interpretation of dreams.

We can achieve further insight into Augustine's figurative interpretation by noting when he thinks it is called for. In earlier works it appeared that his criterion for believing figurative interpretation was needed was that the passage otherwise would have a meaning that was absurd. This criterion was common not only to earlier Christian writers, but to pagan ones as well. Yet the criterion invoked in *Teaching Christianity* is much broader: "Anything in the divine writings that cannot be referred either to good, honest morals or to the truth of the faith, you must know is said figuratively" (3.10, 14). There are several reasons for Augustine's adopting this more inclusive criterion. One is that he took very seriously 2 Timothy 3:16, which says: "*All* scripture is inspired by God and is useful for teaching, for reproof, for correction, and for training in righteousness" (emphasis added). Furthermore, the method of examining a text taught in schools was sentence by sentence, word by word, rather than as part of a coherent document. This led to an atomistic exegesis in which a passage did not have to have a consistent meaning all the way through.

Perhaps the most important reason, though, is Augustine's assumption that the whole Bible has a consistent meaning, which is the Christian creed and the ethic of love.

> Given Augustine's view that the essence of Scripture is contained in the Creed and the commandments to love God and neighbor, the vast majority of the Bible would be *superfluum* and *stultum* unless it contained hidden meanings, enigmata, and figures to be understood by those who would seek to understand the word of God at a more profound level.[30]

While contemporary historical consciousness can doubt that the only things the sacred writers ever intended to teach were Christian faith and love, it is important to notice the spiritual maturity of Augustine's hermeneutical key to Scripture.

> The exhortation to look beyond the letter to the deeper spiritual meaning that had been issued by the more moderate representatives of the Alexandrian school reappears therefore in Augustine, but it is made here in the name of charity rather than of wisdom.[31]

While that which Augustine derived from the Bible through his hermeneutical method may not be the meaning historically minded contemporary readers believe the sacred writers intended, it is nevertheless so essentially Christian that they can still agree with the teaching he derived and even be deeply moved by it.

As valuable a document as *Teaching Christianity* is, it is not the best way to learn how Augustine interprets Scripture. "A complete treatise on Augustinian exegesis would have to start from his exegetical practice rather than from his rules for interpretation."[32] Since this principle applies to his preaching as well, it is time to turn from theory to practice.

SERMON TIME IN HIPPO REGIUS

While there is little in the way of eyewitness accounts of Augustine's preaching, a combination of archaeological study of North Africa and the countless topical references that occur in his sermons makes possible the reconstruction of a rather detailed picture of the bishop in action.[33] His basilica was situated in a complex of buildings that included residences for the bishop and his monastic community, for nuns, and for visitors. The church would not have been elaborately decorated. On great occasions as many as two thousand people could be in the congregation, all of whom stood, the men separated from the women. In the apse the presbyters sat on a semicircular dais, in the middle of which the bishop's chair was elevated. In front of the apse in the center aisle was the altar, surrounded by the chancel screens.[34] A fresco in the Lateran Library dating from around 600 depicts Augustine sitting on his *cathedra* in the center of the bench for the presbyters with an open Bible before him, looking little different from a grammarian teaching in a secondary school. There is no reason to doubt the essential accuracy of this portrayal.

The eucharistic liturgy would have begun with the peace and then the psalm. On set days the three lections were prescribed, but on others Augustine could indicate to the lector or, for the Gospel, the deacon the passage to be read. After standing for the Gospel, the bishop would preach from his chair, rising occasionally for emphasis.[35] Often the congregation would break into applause, but, like Chrysostom, Augustine was more interested in changed lives. Depending on the elaborateness of the liturgy to follow and other factors, including the preacher's voice, the sermon could last anywhere from a few minutes to an hour and a half. After the sermon Augustine and his clergy would move down to the chancel for the Great Thanksgiving.

Certain generalizations can be made about Augustine's preaching. Most of his sermons were extempore, growing out of no more immediate preparation than prayer or a short meditation on the biblical passages that had just been read.[36] That was possible because his remote preparation included not only a mastery of rhetoric, but memorization of much of the Bible, theological reflection that is almost unparalleled in the history of the church, and a deep life of prayer as well. Because he used the form of the homily, his outlines were developed by his explication of the biblical text rather than according to a rhetorical *dispositio*. Ideas would come to him as he went along, so digressions were not rare. But neither were they boring, and he usually got back to the subject. His sermons "were not speeches but talks like those which became common in the medieval pulpit, though they were woven according to the stylistic pattern of Antiquity and used Antiquity's vocabulary."[37]

As Augustine spoke he got progressively more into his subject, and his words came alive with an eloquence that grew out of his ardor for his subject rather than from any intentional display of virtuosity. He did not regard his speech as "a harmonious assemblage of prefabricated parts, which the connoisseur might take to pieces, but rather as the inseparable welding of form and content in the heat of the message."[38] One of the many qualities that separated his preaching style from the canons of the rhetoric he had taught and could practice with ease was that his speech was always popular. His vocabulary was that of everyday life, and he used figures of speech such as puns, assonance, rhymes, alliteration, and antithesis to give zest to his thought. He could always find an apt analogy that would make the most abstruse point seem clear and even obvious. His instinct for the right word was infallible, and well-turned phrases were the rule rather than the exception.

> This is the secret of Augustine's enormous power as a preacher. He will make it his first concern to place himself in the midst of his congregation, to appeal to their feelings for him, to react with immense sensitivity to their emotions, and so, as the sermon progressed, to sweep them up into his own way of feeling.[39]

Yet he never used his power of speech to wound his hearers; instead, he was reflexively pastoral. And, surprisingly, although it was an affliction he shared with many of the world's great orators, his voice was not strong.

What can one say of his subject matter? First, that it was always centered on the meaning of the Bible as he understood it, the elucidation of individual words and phrases in the manner of the grammar teacher expounding classical literature. The difference between what he did and what the grammarian did, however, was not just in the text explicated but in the quality of the thought as well.

> There is always wealth in that thought; there are almost always surprises, and the average reader will almost always be overwhelmed by it. Nobody can fail to be astonished at what Augustine can get out of a single text. . . . *His real secret, which he shares with all orators who really succeed in fascinating us, is that he has such an enormous amount to say.*[40]

That "enormous amount" is the system of spirituality he found in the Bible, which he stated in a vocabulary derived from Neoplatonism. "And what Plotinus had struggled to convey to a select classroom in Rome, the Christians of Hippo and Carthage could hear any Sunday in the sermons of Augustine."[41] The remarkable thing about his presentation is that what he communicated was his own best thought on the subject; there is no watering down here. While he did administer his teaching in bite-size units, the whole system was communicated. Ordinary citizens in a small North African town were deemed as capable of holiness as the most rarified spirits.

THE THEORY APPLIED

The method by which Augustine derived his system of spirituality from biblical texts is, of course, interpretation of the passages as figurative signs. We can see an example of how he went about that in the second of his sermons on Psalm 31.[42] (**See Vol. 2, pp. 102-23,** for the text of the second sermon after this one.) To understand the interpretation, however, it will help to set a translation of the relevant verses of Old Latin text on which he commented in parallel with a modern translation (NRSV) from the Hebrew original.

Psalm 31:9-15*a*

Augustine	NRSV
Have mercy upon me, O Lord, for I am being harried,	[9] Be gracious to me, O LORD, for I am in distress;
Vexed with wrath is my eye, my soul, and my belly.	my eye wastes away from grief, my soul and body also.
For my life has pined away in pain, And my years in sighs.	[10] For my life is spent with sorrow, and my years with sighing;
My strength is weakened in want,	my strength fails because of my misery,
And my bones are vexed.	and my bones waste away.
I have become a disgrace over all my enemies,	[11] I am the scorn of all my adversaries,
An excessive one to my neighbors, and a fear to my acquaintances.	a horror to my neighbors, an object of dread to my acquaintances;
Those who used to see me, ran away from me out of doors,	those who see me in the street flee from me.
I am forgotten like one dead, from the mind, I have become like a pot that is scrapped.	[12] I have passed out of mind like one who is dead; I have become like a broken vessel.
For I have heard the blame of many who are settled round about,	[13] For I hear the whispering of many—terror all around!—
While they gathered together against me, they plotted to catch my soul.	as they scheme together against me, as they plot to take my life.
But I have hoped in you O Lord, I have said: "You are my God,	[14] But I trust in you, O LORD; I say, "You are my God."
In your hands are my lots."	[15a] My times are in your hand.

Augustine begins his exposition by stating that in the psalms the speaker is Christ and reminding his congregation of one of Tyconius's principles, that what is said of Christ applies to his body the church as well.[43] Since the last verse commented on in the previous sermon said that the speaker's feet had been set in an open space, and the first verse here complains of being harried, the meaning is that churches have different experiences: some are in peace and others in trouble. The cause of trouble for those that experience it is that their love has grown cold (Matt. 24:12). The number of holy people in the church has always been small; there are many others who come on Easter but go to the amphitheaters or playhouses on Low Sunday.

The psalmist's reaction to the trouble is anger ("My eye is vexed with wrath") at the sins of others who brought the trouble on them. "Yet from that seemingly worthless pile of chaff a great heap of grain can be winnowed."[44] Nor should we let our anger become a sin of our own. With psychological insight that sounds modern, Augustine says, "When we are angry and can't let fly, but have to keep it in, we fume inwardly, our insides are vexed."[45] Those who have become holy remain on earth only to help others, so when they see others not profiting from their preaching and example, they feel their "life is weakened in want."[46] Bad Christians are worse than pagans, because there is hope for the pagans. "Something can still be made of them, just as something can be made from the logs in a carpenter's yard, in spite of all the knots and the twists and the bark.... But from the twigs and trimmings he cleans off the carpenter can make nothing, they are only fit for firewood."[47] "Bad Christians" are "an excessive disgrace to my neighbours, namely to those who were drawing nearer to me, and were on the verge of believing."[48] But the anger of the righteous is a serious temptation. "It is difficult to say which is worse, this self-satisfied pride, or that wicked life. So never go and say that you are the only one."[49]

Another concern of the righteous is Christians who have deserted to heretical and schismatic bodies. These are the ones referred to in the verse: "Those who used to see me, ran away from me out of doors." They (especially the Donatists) do not realize that the Scriptures foretold that the church would be a worldwide society. They should imitate the obedience of Abraham in the sacrifice of Isaac.

> What does it all mean? It means Christ, but all wrapped up and hidden, tied up in riddles. To get at this meaning the story has to be shaken apart, the riddles untied, the wrapping unwrapped. Then we see that Isaac, his father's beloved only son, stands for the Only Son of God, and

he carries the wood for his own sacrifice, just as Christ carried the cross.[50]

While what this story teaches about Christ is hidden, what it says about the church is clear—a contrast that is characteristic of Scripture. Because of his obedience, God promised Abraham that "in your seed shall all the nations of the earth be blessed" (Gen. 22:18),[51] an obvious prophecy of the church.

Because of the sins of bad Christians, a good one feels like "a pot that is scrapped," because all Christians are blamed indiscriminately for such inconsistent behavior by outsiders, those who are "settled round about."[52] Those who stay outside the church, by their taunts, hope to lure the Christians out from it.

Some of the bad Christians had been taken as models before their lapse, but we should not depend on human examples. Rather, the psalmist says, "I have hoped in you, O Lord." To depend on human examples "is to be a milk-sop, as they call big boys who are still being breast-fed."[53] But the bad conduct of fallen role models can be like the bad-tasting stuff wet nurses put on their breasts to wean milksops: it can break an unhealthy pattern of dependency. The one thus liberated can say, "In your hands are my lots."[54] Casting lots to decide on a course of action is seeking divine guidance and thus is not sinful in the way that consulting an astrologer would be. This verse reminds us of God's election: "[The psalmist] is calling the grace of God a sort of lottery, because in a lottery things happen not by choice but by the will of God.... Not finding in us any merits he could decide on, he saves us by the lottery of his own will."[55] Scripture confirmed this interpretation when Peter told Simon Magus, "You have no lot nor part in this [faith]" (Acts 8:21).[56] He thought he could buy grace with money, but grace is free. A lot means a portion, a share. "What is my share? The inheritance of the Church. And what are its limits? The ends of the earth."[57] And that is as much as there is time for. The rest of the psalm will be interpreted tomorrow.

So goes a fairly typical sermon by Augustine. One could have read over the six and a half verses of the psalm and never thought they contained so much. Nor would they if Augustine had not been an interpreter of signs. What he found was very different from the intention of the psalmist, but it is certainly consistent with the faith of the New Testament. What he came up with is the sort of thing one immersed in Christian faith and spirituality is likely to think when reading a psalm. The psalmist did not know all that was true, but the Christian does. So Augustine brings it all out and makes it available to his congregation. And he does so in a homily that is much more unified than many expository sermons—certainly more so than a homily of Chrysostom, who would go through interpreting verse by verse and only apply the last verse commented upon to the life of the people. It is easier to understand why the Catholic congregation in Hippo Regius considered their bishop to be an extraordinarily good preacher than it is to know why one who had enjoyed international fame as a speaker should seem so contented to remain in his sleepy North African seacoast town for thirty-nine years ministering to his small flock. Unless, of course, he was practicing what he preached.

FOR FURTHER READING

Brown, Peter Robert Lamont. *Augustine of Hippo: A Biography.* Berkeley and Los Angeles: University of California Press, 1967.

Nine Sermons of Saint Augustine on the Psalms. Translated and introduction by Edmund Hill. London: Longmans, Green, and Co., 1958.

St. Augustine: Confessions. Translated with introduction and notes by Henry Chadwick. Oxford World's Classics. Oxford and New York: Oxford University Press, 1991.

The Works of St. Augustine: A New Translation for the 21st Century. Sermons III/11: Newly Discovered Sermons. Translation and notes by Edmund Hill, edited by John E. Rotelle. Brooklyn, N.Y.: New City Press, 1997.

The Works of St. Augustine: A Translation for the 21st Century. Part I, Vol. 11: Teaching Christianity: De doctrina christiana. Introduction, translation, and notes by Edmund Hill, edited by John E. Rotelle. Brooklyn, N.Y.: New City Press, 1996.

Wills, Garry. *St. Augustine.* New York: Viking, 1999.

Notes

1. Hippolytus was earlier, but he wrote in Greek.

2. The two most influential ante-Nicene theologians to write in Latin were the Carthaginians Tertullian (ca. 150–ca. 220) and Cyprian (ca. 205–258). African Christian Latinity may be synchronized with Roman by noting that scholars debate over whether Tertullian influenced Minucius Felix or if it was the other way around and whether or not Novatian corresponded with Cyprian. Tertullian, it should be noted, was a transitional figure who also wrote a few treatises in Greek.

3. Peter Robert Lamont Brown, *Augustine of Hippo: A Biography* (Berkeley and Los Angeles: The University of California Press, 1967), 20. In 2000 Brown issued a

new edition of this standard biography to which he added an epilogue in which he reviewed the advances in scholarship since the first edition. These advances include two discoveries of unknown or partially known works of Augustine, a collection of twenty-nine letters discovered by Johannes Divjak (*St. Augustine: Letters, Vol. 6*, trans. Robert B. Eno. FC, vol. 81 [Washington, D.C.: Catholic University of America Press, 1989]), and a collection of thirty sermons identified by François Dolbeau (*The Works of St. Augustine: A New Translation for the 21st Century. Sermons III/11: Newly Discovered Sermons*, trans. and notes Edmund Hill, ed. John E. Rotelle [Brooklyn, N.Y.: New City Press, 1997]). Both the sermons and the letters permit a more intimate view of Augustine than had been available before. Other advances in scholarship occur in new information about Augustine's contemporaries, the time and place of his ministry, and particular aspects of his works. Another important recent work on Augustine is Garry Wills's short but perceptive *St. Augustine* (New York: Viking, 1999). These works appeared too late to affect more than the footnotes of this chapter.

4. Their "style, thought, and oratory" did not impress Edwin Dargan, *A History of Preaching* (1905–12; reprint, New York: Burt Franklin, 1968), 1:98.

5. Agostino Trapè, "St. Augustine," in *The Golden Age of Latin Patristic Literature from the Council of Nicea to the Council of Chalcedon*, vol. 4 of *Patrology*, ed. Angelo di Berardino, intro. Johannes Quasten, trans. Placid Solari (Westminster, Md.: Christian Classics, 1986), 342.

6. Such a statement can be made with some certainty because more is known of Augustine's life from birth through his first professional activity than of any other person in antiquity, especially from an interior perspective. His autobiographical *Confessions* gives an account of the developing consciousness of an individual that is unparalleled before the modern era. (Wills is correct, however, in saying that *The Testimony* is a more accurate translation of the title than *Confessions* [*St. Augustine*, xiii-xiv].) Although his *Confessions* was written as a prayer praising God for preveniently directing him toward conversion throughout his early life, it is also very informative about what he was like as a boy. For the Latin text, see *Augustine: Confessions*, trans. William Watts. LCL, vols. 26-27 (Cambridge: Harvard University Press, 1912). An excellent translation into contemporary English is *St. Augustine: Confessions*, trans. with intro. and notes Henry Chadwick, Oxford World's Classics (Oxford and New York: Oxford University Press, 1991).

7. Part of the cost of his education was borne by his friend Romanianus, one of the wealthiest citizens of Thagaste.

8. *Conf.* 3.4.7, Chadwick trans.

9. Brown, *Augustine of Hippo*, 69.

10. Her husband had died three years earlier.

11. *Conf.* 9.10.24-26. Most of Book 9 from 8.17 on is about Monica's life and death.

12. Like everyone trained in classical literature, he had regarded the Bible as crudely written.

13. Brown, *Augustine of Hippo*, 132.

14. Most of them, however, were called to be bishops of other towns in the region, and therefore had to be replaced in the monastery.

15. *The Works of St. Augustine: A Translation for the 21st Century. Part I, Vol.*

11: Teaching Christianity: De doctrina christiana, intro., trans., and notes Edmund Hill, ed. John E. Rotelle (Brooklyn, N.Y.: New City Press, 1996), 98. This edition also contains three introductory essays by different scholars, although the rationale for including just these three is not stated. The translator's study of this work and of Augustine's preaching extends over forty years.

16. Ibid., 97. Hill also theorizes why Augustine wrote the book and accounts for the thirty-year lapse between the writing of the first three books and the completion of the fourth. Briefly, Hill says that Augustine was asked to write it by Aurelius, his primate, to train clergy who were to have the responsibility of preaching. After completing the third book, he wrote to Aurelius to get his approval for using the rules of Tyconius (see note 22 below). Either Aurelius never answered or he disapproved, so Augustine set the book aside and forgot about it until he wrote the *Retractiones* thirty years later. That reminded him of the value of the project, and he completed it at that time. Ibid., 96-97.

17. "Thing" is used here in a sense much broader than "an inanimate object." So broad, in fact, that it stands for "whatever is or may be an object of perception or knowledge or thought." First meaning, *Oxford American Dictionary,* 1st ed. In this sense, even God is a thing—without, of course, being reified.

18. A convenient precis of *De doctrina* appears in J. F. Shaw's translation in *NPNF*[1] 2:517.

19. Augustine, although he didn't have an enormous knowledge of Greek, knew enough of the language to translate the Septuagint Psalter into Latin. His knowledge of Hebrew was limited to the explanation of a few words that he had picked up from someone else.

20. What German exegetes refer to as *Sachkritik.*

21. Augustine does not mention it, but he refers to works like Pliny's *Natural History,* which contains most of the information (and misinformation) the ancient world had about nature.

22. Augustine ends the third book of *Teaching Christianity* with a list of seven rules for resolving ambiguities in the Bible that he borrowed from a Donatist theologian named Tyconius. The first of these is "About the Lord and his body," and states that "since Christ and his church form a single person, it is perfectly legitimate to pass from the head to the body." The second is "About the twofold body of the Lord," which takes cognizance of the way that saints and sinners will coexist in the church until the end of time and says that passages that seem to praise or curse Israel or the church are to be understood as referring only to the appropriate group within it and not to all its members. Rule Three, "About the promises and the law," is what Augustine called "about the spirit and the letter" or "about grace and commandments." Augustine considered this "as more a very large question than a rule to be applied to the settling of questions." "About species and genus," Rule Four, Augustine understands as "about the part and the whole." Whatever Scripture says about a part of a whole may be applied to the whole. Although neither he nor Tyconius says so, this is simply the rhetorical figure known as *synecdoche.* The next rule, Five, "About times," seems to be synecdoche used in statements of time. Rule Six, "Recapitulation," means that "when the scriptures do not carefully observe the temporal order of events or confuse the before and after, it is up to the reader to

restore the missing order." The final rule, "About the devil and his body" is the same principle as the first, but applied to the wicked rather than the church.

23. The two methods of learning are roughly equivalent to Kennedy's distinction between "technical rhetoric" (the sort learned from the handbooks) and "sophistic rhetoric" (the sort acquired by apprenticing oneself to a master). George A. Kennedy, *Classical Rhetoric and Its Christian and Secular Tradition from Ancient to Modern Times*, rev. and enl. (Chapel Hill: University of North Carolina Press, 1999), 16-17.

24. Multiple, that is, in the sense of Literal, Allegorical, Tropological, and Anagogical. Augustine believed that a given passage could mean more than one thing and delighted in that realization.

25. For the significance of the term see, for example, the article on *semeion* in *TDNT*, ed. Gerhard Kittel and Gerhard Friedrich, trans. Geoffrey W. Bromiley, abridged in one volume by Geoffrey W. Bromiley (Grand Rapids, Mich.: Eerdmans, 1985), 1015-22.

26. Edmund Hill, trans. and intro., *Nine Sermons of Saint Augustine on the Psalms* (London: Longmans, Green & Co., 1958), 27. Of course, only the Old Testament had a Hebrew original.

27. Brown, *Augustine of Hippo*, 259.

28. Hill, *Teaching Christianity*, 2.6, 7.

29. Brown, *Augustine of Hippo*, 260.

30. Roland J. Teske, "Criteria for Figurative Interpretation in St. Augustine," in De doctrina Christiana: *A Classic of Western Culture*, ed. Duane W. H. Arnold and Pamela Bright (Notre Dame: University of Notre Dame Press, 1995), 118. Teske's article is the basis for this paragraph and the one before.

31. Luigi Alici, "Sign and Language," in *Teaching Christianity*, 45.

32. Prosper Grech, "Hermeneutical Principles," ibid., 92.

33. Brown, *Augustine of Hippo*, 244-58; George Lawless, O.S.A., "Augustine of Hippo as Preacher," *Saint Augustine the Bishop: A Book of Essays*, ed. Fannie LeMoine and Christopher Kleinhenz (New York and London: Garland, 1994), 13-37; and, most important, Frederik van der Meer, *Augustine the Bishop: The Life and Work of a Father of the Church*, trans. Brian Battershaw and G. R. Lamb (London and New York: Sheed & Ward, 1961). While Part 3 of this work (405-67) is devoted to Augustine's preaching practice and his two books on teaching the faith, *De doctrina christiana* and *De catechizandis rudibus* (Instructions for Beginners), almost the entire book is helpful to anyone wishing to imagine what it must have been like to hear Augustine preach. There is a description of the region, its population, and its history; a report of other religious bodies in the area; an account of pastoral activity; an examination of the laity, clergy, and ascetics who made up the community; a description of liturgical practice in Hippo; and a study of popular piety in North Africa.

34. In *Augustine the Bishop*, facing p. 25, there is a drawing of a reconstruction of an African town church that must be very much like that of Hippo.

35. Brown says that from his *cathedra*, Augustine was only about five yards from the first row of the congregation and roughly at their eye level. *Augustine of Hippo*, 251.

36. Since Augustine wrote out few of his sermons, the fact that almost a thousand

of them survive is due to the scribes who took them down. For a breakdown of this figure into the various categories of Augustine's sermons, see Lawless, "Augustine of Hippo as Preacher," 13-15.

37. Van der Meer, *Augustine the Bishop,* 419. This paragraph is largely based on his chapter on the subject.

38. Brown, *Augustine of Hippo,* 256.

39. Ibid., 251.

40. Van der Meer, *Augustine the Bishop,* 432. Emphasis added.

41. Brown, *Augustine of Hippo,* 245. Augustine's basic understanding of what he was doing when he preached was "breaking bread" and "feeding the multitude." Ibid., 252.

42. Psalm 30 in the Vulgate and Septuagint. The translation of the sermon that follows is from Edmund Hill, *Nine Sermons of Saint Augustine on the Psalms,* 122-35. Another translation appears in *St. Augustine on the Psalms,* vol. 2, trans. and notes Dame Scholastica Hebgin and Dame Felicitas Corrigan. ACW, no. 30 (Westminster, Md.: Newman Press; London: Longmans, Green & Co., 1960), 2:28-44, where it is called the third sermon on the psalm, the first being "brief, dry notes of exegesis" probably dictated to a stenographer early in Augustine's ministry. The translation of *Enarrationes in Psalmos* in NPNF[1] vol. 8, is painfully abridged. *NPNF* does better by the *Tractates on the Gospel of John* and the *Homilies on the First Epistle of John* (vol. 7) and *Sermons on Selected Lessons of the New Testament* (vol. 6; these are Sermons 51-147 on the Gospel(s) in the Benedictine edition). John Burnaby included ten homilies on 1 John in his *Augustine: Later Works.* LCC, vol. 8 (Philadelphia: Westminster, 1955). Festal sermons are translated in *St. Augustine, Sermons for Christmas and Epiphany,* trans. and notes Thomas Comerford Lawler. ACW, no. 15 (Westminster, Md.: Newman Press; London: Longmans, Green & Co., 1952), and *Selected Easter Sermons of Saint Augustine,* intro., text of thirty sermons, notes, and commentary Philip T. Weller (St. Louis: Herder, 1959). These are the only sermon translations I have consulted, although others exist, some of which are listed in Lawless, "Augustine of Hippo as Preacher," 36. See also *Patrology,* vol. 4, 398-99.

43. As offensive as the notion is to contemporary historical consciousness, that is the way the psalms are always understood liturgically and homiletically. Otherwise, the monastic offices could not have had the Psalter as their core for all these centuries, nor could clergy be so nourished by the recitation of the daily offices or sermons be preached on texts from the psalms. This christological interpretation of the Psalter is already well developed in the New Testament.

44. Hill, *Nine Sermons of Saint Augustine,* 124.

45. Ibid., 125.

46. Ibid.

47. Ibid., 126-27.

48. Ibid., 127.

49. Ibid., 128.

50. Ibid., 130. This quotation from the sermon is an excellent summary of Augustine's understanding of the interpretation of signs. His interpretation of the sacrifice of Isaac is the standard patristic one. New Testament allusions to the passage see Abraham as exemplifying obedience (Jas. 2:21) and faith (Heb. 11:17).

51. Ibid., 130-31.

52. Ibid., 131.

53. Ibid., 132.

54. Ibid., 133. This is an example of the corrupt and at times meaningless Latin text Augustine had to comment on. As we can see in the parallel column above, the Hebrew says, "My *times* are in your hands."

55. Ibid., 132.

56. Ibid., 134.

57. Ibid.

PART II

THE MIDDLE AGES

CHAPTER 6

THE TREK TO THE MIDDLE AGES

In Augustine the Latin homily reached its peak. By the time of his death on August 28 in A.D. 430, the Vandals, who were Arian Christians, had already begun their conquest of North Africa. A year later they captured Hippo and burned part of it. The town was evacuated. Catholic Christians were persecuted by these Arians for a century before Africa was reconquered by Justinian's general, Belisarius. Then, a little over a century and a half later, the Muslims took Carthage, and Latin-speaking Christianity became almost extinct in North Africa, where it had begun.

By that time, the circumstances under which Latin Christianity existed elsewhere were vastly changed. The year 476 saw the abdication of the last Roman emperor in the West. For a while, exarchs in Ravenna provided the church and people in the West with some sort of contact with the imperial government in Constantinople, but even that became less as years passed. The time in which these changes took place was the beginning of what used to be called the Dark Ages, under the illusion that it was a period of intellectual stagnation.[1] Much more is known about the era now and it is recognized as a time of vigorous life.[2]

The titles of two historical surveys, *The End of Ancient Christianity*,[3] which deals with the period from 400 to 600; and *The Rise of Western Christendom*,[4] which traces events to 1000, show this shift. The end of ancient Christianity was the beginning of Western Christendom. These titles serve to divide the time between the era of the empire in the West after Diocletian and the era of the Germanic kingdoms that emerged in what had been the Western provinces of the empire. We will study the transition period, during which the inhabitants of the territory moved from understanding themselves to be part of the Western Roman Empire to thinking of themselves as Europeans.[5]

We may perceive other dynamics as well. Mediterranean civilization had been a civilization of cities, but this new world had few with as many as twenty thousand people; towns of five thousand were much more the rule. By the late-sixth century, Rome itself had fewer than fifty thousand inhabitants. Or, again, it is customary to refer to the movements of peoples that so disrupted the empire as "barbarian" invasions, but the designation is value charged.[6] The important distinction to be made is between *nomads* such as the Huns, who made occasional forays into civilized areas, and the *settled farmers*, who moved nearer to Roman territory for protection when they were disrupted by the nomads. As effective administration from the central government declined, the Romans on the frontier mixed with these Germanic peoples until the two populations became indistinguishable.[7]

The conversion of the population to Christianity adds a further dynamic of crucial importance to this study. Estimates as to the portion of Roman citizens who were Christians at the time of Constantine's conversion are as low as 10 percent.[8] But by A.D. 800,

> a peculiarly determined form of Catholic Christianity became the mandatory faith of all the regions, Mediterranean and non-Mediterranean alike, that had come together to form a post-Roman western Europe. . . . Large regions of northwestern and central Europe came to be joined, slowly but irrevocably, to the former territories of the Roman Empire in a shared Catholicism, that would soon stretch as far as Scandinavia and into parts of eastern Europe.[9]

The time, then, when the patristic period of church history shifted into the medieval, was an era of great vitality. One of the changes that occurred during this era, however, is the basis for the assumption that the age was dark: the decline of classical Roman culture, particularly of the Latin language, literacy, an educational system, and Greco-Roman

126

rhetoric.[10] What remained was being blended with Germanic cultures into the rich mix that would become the medieval synthesis, but for the time being, much that had been regarded by the Romans as the core of their heritage was in abeyance.

This decline of Latin culture was of great significance for the history of preaching. This is not to say that preaching stopped. Far from it! Such mass evangelization could not have occurred without it. But the sermons were in many languages, they were preached by persons who had not been trained in rhetoric—or much else that was academic, and they were not written down. Thus evidence is lacking for reconstructing most of what was occurring in homiletics during this period. What remains is limited to preaching in Latin and is thus highly atypical.

It is possible, on the other hand, to see how the minor amount of preaching that was done in Latin survived. We can gain that knowledge by looking at four preachers who mark its trajectory. Two of them were popes: the only two ever called "the Great" and the only two from the patristic period from whom we have a body of sermons, Leo I and Gregory I. Leo's reign began ten years after Augustine's death. He was the last pope of the patristic era to use the full range of rhetorical effects taught in classical education. While Gregory came from the most exalted circles of Roman society and had a good education, an audience capable of appreciating such art was not available just 150 years after Leo. The third preacher, Caesarius of Arles, was born halfway between the two pontiffs, and he reflects what was happening to preaching in non-Italian territory that had been a part of the empire for centuries. Finally, the Venerable Bede indicates the degree of classical culture that came to be preserved in and by the monasteries of Britain at the edge of what had been the Roman world.

LEO THE GREAT (CA. 390–461)

Virtually nothing is known of Leo's early life and very little of anything he did before his pontificate. While there is a suggestion that he was a Tuscan, it seems more likely that he was born in Rome during the last decade of the fourth century. The only evidence of his having received a first-rate education is the elegant prose that he came to write.[11] He became archdeacon of Rome and was alert, as few Westerners were, to the seriousness of the christological controversies going on in the East. It was he who warned Pope Celestine against Nestorius and also helped Sixtus III deal with the Pelagian Julian of Eclanum. Leo was on a peacemaking mission in Gaul when Sixtus died and he was elected to succeed him.

Even for the period of his pontificate there is little personal information about Leo. Neither his sermons nor his letters, the two genres of his writing, reveal Leo the man. What is known instead are the official acts, which were noteworthy indeed, justifying his designation as "the Great." One of his accomplishments was to cause the papacy to become "self-conscious."[12] Previously the church at Rome had emphasized its foundation by two apostles, Peter and Paul, and bishops elsewhere had assumed that Jesus' naming Peter as the rock on which he would build his church was their corporate charter rather than that of Rome alone. Now Leo insisted that only Rome spoke with the voice of Peter and that doing so gave her authority *(principatus)* over the whole church.[13] While no one ever subordinated himself to his role more than Leo, it is also true that few have ever so maximized their role.

That maximization is clear in his participation in the Council of Chalcedon (451), which gave the definitive formula for Catholic teaching about the person and work of Christ. This council had been called to undo the work of the "Robber Council"[14] of Ephesus in 449, which had been controlled by Monophysites who upheld the heresy of Eutyches.[15] Leo had prepared a statement for Ephesus that set out in Western terms the position that Chalcedon was to affirm, but it was ignored. At neither Ephesus nor Chalcedon did Leo sit down as a peer or even *primus inter pares,*[16] but was represented by legates instead. He expected them to preside over the council as his representatives and that the council would not debate the issue, but merely subscribe to the letter ("Tome") he had prepared for Ephesus on the subject. It was to be a case of *Roma locuta, causa finita* (Rome has spoken, the case is closed). But the Eastern bishops did not see it that way. The patriarch of Constantinople presided and, while Leo's Tome was eventually accepted as an adequate statement of orthodox Christology, that occurred only after long discussion. "The *Tome* of Leo to Flavian was accepted *on merits,* and not because it was issued by the pope."[17]

Leo was a very eloquent man. He persuaded Attila the Hun not to invade Italy and even did something to ameliorate the effects of the Vandal capture of Rome. We can see the same persuasiveness in his sermons. Ninety-six of his sermons have been preserved.[18] The odd assortment is the result of Leo's arranging for two collections to be made to preserve their dogmatic content.[19] This accounts for the fact that a great majority of them were preached in the first five years of his pontificate and most of the rest were preached in the next nine.

It probably accounts also for most of them having been delivered on the fasts and great feasts of the church year. Five were preached for the anniversary of his consecration (September 29), six for the collection for the poor taken in November at the time of a pagan celebration, nine for the December Ember Days,[20] ten for Christmas, eight for Epiphany, twelve for the Lenten Ember Days, one for the transfiguration, twenty-one for Holy Week,[21] two for the ascension, three for the Feast of Pentecost, and four for the Ember Days after it, two for the Feast of Peter and Paul, one in commemoration of Alaric's sack of Rome, one in honor of the Maccabees, one for St. Lawrence, nine for the September Ember Days, one on the Beatitudes, and one against Eutyches.

The first thing that strikes the modern reader about Leo's sermons is how short they are. They average slightly less than four pages each in the Fathers of the Church translation.[22] This brevity could be related to the pope's liturgical duties at that time. The surviving documents do not permit detailed reconstruction of the papal liturgy during this period, but when Leo was pope there were already at least twenty churches in the city of Rome. Although the full system of station days[23] does not appear to have developed before Gregory the Great, it seems likely that the pontiff was already presiding regularly at different churches in the time of Leo. Thus, he and his retinue would proceed to the designated church as a group. Entering it, they would make their way toward the apse, with Leo perhaps greeting those he knew as he passed among them. All this means that the bishop of Rome did not have a regular congregation of his own to preach to each Sunday. He was the distinguished visitor who had come in such pomp. Even more, the voice in which he spoke and the words that he said were more Peter's than his own.

These words take on a kind of objectivity and sound like liturgical prayers. "The rhythm of his phrases is accommodated to the sound of the liturgy, its forms are similar to many preserved by the Roman missal, which, through the sacramentaries, is often inspired by him."[24] As Lietzmann observed, Leo's expression is concise and apposite, and often has a brilliant terseness and a painstakingly formal development that would well repay careful study.[25] He also cited studies that point out Leo's punctiliousness in observing the rules for the cadence of final clauses in periodic sentences—an attention to the rhythms of speech important in classical rhetoric that has not received the attention it deserves in modern public speaking.[26] According to Yngve Brilioth, Leo furnished the model for the "majestic and polished style" of later popes and the *cursus leoninus*: "His balanced prose rhythm became normative for the style of the Roman curia and also set its stamp on the construction of the Roman collects."[27]

A surprising feature of Leo's preserved sermons to those familiar with patristic preaching is that they are not exegetical homilies. They are very biblical in the sense that they are saturated with allusions to the sacred text.[28] Yet there is more to it than that; Jean Leclercq is undoubtedly correct in saying that while Leo does not give a commentary on the text of the Gospel passage read at the liturgy, his teaching in the sermon is nevertheless in respect to it. And while Leo does not follow its text strictly, he explains its content as a whole and pays attention to the details in it that are needed to understand the "mystery" of the day. Therefore, regarding the form of the sermons, it can be said that

> Leo constructed his sermons very carefully—with an introduction, a theme with examples, and a definite conclusion. Content and structure form an admirable, logical whole.[29]

If one wishes to study what Leo's sermons are like, a good place to begin is with his thirtieth, preached on Christmas Day in 454. He begins by saying that although he has often preached to his flock on that occasion, no human eloquence is adequate to the event commemorated. Yet something must be said because so many have gone astray in their understanding of what happened. He will summarize the heresies into which people have fallen concerning the relation between our Lord's divine and human natures. Since Christ's birth proved that "he was the real son of a human being," some have decided that he was "nothing more than a mere man." Others have been so impressed with his teaching and miracles that they feel there could be nothing human in so divine a being, and that his flesh, therefore, must be an illusion. And still others adopted an intermediate position by which "the humanity in Christ would have been false by virtue of the fact that it did not have its own substance, and the divinity would have been untrue by virtue of the fact that it was defective through mutability."

The church, however, has crushed such heresies, and, since the church is his body, "we are his flesh, the flesh that had been taken up from the Virgin's womb." Thus, as Paul said, "In him dwells all the fullness of the divinity according to the flesh, and you have been filled in him" (Col. 2:9-10).[30] "As nothing of his majesty remains that does not dwell in the dwelling filled by it, so nothing of the body remains unfulfilled by his indwelling."[31] This means that the miracle of Christ's birth infinitely exceeds all the miraculous births of the old dispensation, including those of Adam, Eve, Isaac, Jacob, Jeremiah, Samuel, and John the Baptist.

Heretical Christologies should "go far away and recede into their own shadows" and Christians should not be "weakened . . . in the plan of God's mercy." As John 5:25-27 shows, "the Son of God is also the son of a human being." That truth is in no danger of contradiction. And it was to justify human beings that God's Only Begotten became one of them himself. Thus, "although one [of our Lord's natures] remains from eternity and the other began in time, both have nevertheless come together in a unity." Those who believe that are true Christians, as the Gospels show. No one can doubt, therefore, that "there is no other name under heaven given to human beings by which they can be saved" (Acts 4:12).[32]

CAESARIUS OF ARLES (CA. 470–542)

The difference between the world in which Leo lived and that of Caesarius is greater than one would anticipate, even allowing for the time that had elapsed or the distance between them. The territory of classical Gaul was roughly that occupied by modern France. Caesar's *Gallic Wars* is the last chapter of the story begun centuries earlier of the incorporation of this land and its Celtic population into the Roman Empire. By the middle of the second century there were Christian communities in Lyons and Vienne, as Irenaeus, their bishop at the end of the century, indicates. Sixteen Gallic bishops attended the Council of Arles in 314, while a similar number could not be present. The Gallic church even produced a widely known saint, Martin, the soldier who became bishop of Tours late in the fourth century.

Germanic peoples, the Franks, Visigoths, and Burgundians began to move into the territory in the early-fifth century, being accepted as allies of Rome at first, and establishing kingdoms of their own when Roman authority in the West flickered out. The newcomers accommodated themselves to the culture they found in Gaul and in time became hardly distinguishable from the Romanized Celtic natives. Not only did they accept Latin as their language, they even shared the Christian religion, although they were Arians.

Caesarius of Arles, who was born a few years before Romulus Augustus stepped down as emperor in the West in 476, had to contend with these Germanic settlements; his see passed from under Visigothic rule to that of the Ostrogoths and then to that of the Franks. He was not originally from Arles, but came instead from a prosperous family in Châlon (Latin: Cabillonum), a busy port on the Saône river about seventy-five miles north of Lyons. When he was seventeen he took minor orders and transferred from his father's authority to that of his bishop. Two years later, however, he went to test his vocation at the monastery of Lérins,[33] which had become the cradle of the Gallic episcopate.

Caesarius spent only a few years at the monastery before his austerities necessitated his being nursed back to health. He was sent to Arles to recuperate rather than home to Châlon: it was much closer and Aeonius, the bishop there, was a relative. But Lérins had made its mark on him: "a set of habits, ideas, and values that would have a profound impact on his career as a bishop, preacher, pastor, and reformer."[34] These included an ascetic way of life, knowledge not only of the spiritual tradition of his monastery but of all Latin patristic literature, and an Augustinian understanding of the nature of Christian community as an imperfect but nonetheless real manifestation of the true *civitas dei*.

The city where he went to recover his health was very different from his home in Châlon on the edge of the Roman world or the peaceful island monastery to which he had gone. Arles was in Provence, the "province" that had been Roman for six centuries and was as much a part of the Roman world as Italy. Located at the first crossable spot on the Rhône as it left the Mediterranean and moved into the heartland of Gaul, Arles was almost as important a port as nearby Marseilles. And, as to be expected of a city so strategically located, Arles was always a political and administrative center. It had been the capital of Gaul under Rome and had great if lesser importance under the Visigothic rule that began in 476. It is not surprising that the bishop of Arles had metropolitan rights over surrounding dioceses, although these were constantly being contested.

As Caesarius was recovering his health, his kinsman Aeonius had opportunity to observe him and discover his promise. He asked the abbot of Lérins to release him so that he could become one of the diocesan clergy of Arles. Caesarius served for about eight years, first as a deacon and then as a priest, before Aeonius appointed him to succeed the recently deceased abbot of the local monastery in 499. He was about thirty at the time, and Aeonius began to make it clear that he wanted this young relative to become his successor, which did happen in 502.

By the time he was consecrated, Caesarius already had a clear idea of what he or any other bishop ought to be like. One of the people he had come to know in Arles was the distinguished rhetor Julianus Pomerius. Caesarius became his student. Although it is not mentioned in his *Life*,[35] he must have already received a good secondary Latin education or he could never have written so correctly in both simple and sophisticated prose forms.[36] The *Life* also records, however, that Caesarius had a dream not unlike that in which Jerome came to fear that he was not a Christian but a Ciceronian (1.9). In response, he is reported to have discontinued his training under Pomerius.

Rhetoric, however, was not the main thing that he learned from his teacher. Pomerius was a Christian ascetic as well as a teacher of oratory and had written a treatise called *The Contemplative Life,* in which he set forth the Augustinian ideal of a bishop as a monk who lived in community with his clergy. This was in contrast to what had been the practice in Gaul: electing a local aristocrat who would continue to live in much the way he had before. By this time churches were wealthy and had estates that needed to be administered. It was easy for bishops to give more attention to such responsibilities than to teaching the faithful and caring for the poor. Indeed, they could say that the prestige of the church required that they dress richly and entertain at sumptuous banquets. But Pomerius taught Caesarius that all that should change.

At this point the reader could have a sense of having sat through this before, since the Cappadocians, Chrysostom, and Augustine all represented a stage in the development of their churches when the monk was replacing the aristocrat as the favored type of candidate in episcopal elections.[37] But the earlier Fathers represent a time when the empire was still functioning and changes were being made from a more local to a more central form of administration. The Gallic shift in favor of monks, on the other hand, reflects developments that occurred between the late-fourth and the early-sixth centuries. By the later date there was no longer a Roman government in the West, and the rulers of Germanic kingdoms in Gaul needed to rely heavily on bishops for effective local administration. Luckily, a "graduate" of Lérins who had been further schooled under Pomerius was well prepared for such responsibilities.

During his forty-year episcopate, Caesarius upheld the Augustinian and Pomerian ideal both by having its principles turned into law by a number of councils in Gaul and also even more radically by practicing it himself. He was known, for instance, for buying people out of captivity, whether they had been on his side of the conflict in which they had been captured or the other. He also fed the poor and is famous for having founded a monastery (as it was called) for women that was to be free of the control of the local bishop. But, as is appropriate for one espoused to the Augustinian ideal of the episcopate, there is no cause to which Caesarius gave himself so wholeheartedly as that of preaching.

Some 250 of his sermons have been preserved,[38] but only a few were identified as his before the painstaking and groundbreaking work of the Maurists in the seventeenth century—who found about half of them among works attributed to Augustine—and Dom Germain Morin, who identified most of the rest. Much of that obscurity is due to Caesarius's own actions. He not only believed that he himself should preach, but that all bishops and priests should, and that even deacons could read sermons of the Fathers.[39] Therefore, the form of his sermons that has been preserved is not that in which he delivered them, but that into which he edited them to be used by any cleric who could not or would not compose sermons of his own.

This accounts for two peculiarities of the series. One is that he often borrowed wholesale from the Fathers in composing his own sermons, simplifying their words for Gallic audiences. The other is that he often identified one of his own sermons as being the work of an eminent patristic authority, in the hope of making it more likely to be read in church (See **Vol. 2, pp. 127-32**, for an example). The purpose of what Morin called this "pious ruse" was not pride of authorship but a desire for the edification of the people of God.[40]

Not all of the sermons were preached by Caesarius himself; some were only compiled to be distributed for use by others. At his cathedral he had a training center for future clergy, and he used the students there to produce collections of fifteen to fifty sermons to be passed on in this way. The better students would pick out passages from the Fathers they thought would be helpful to Gallic congregations and the bishop would edit them, adding an introduction or conclusion, simplifying the vocabulary and eliminating unnecessary words. These collections proved quite popular and were used over and over again, for instance, by the great missionary bishops in the seventh to ninth centuries.[41]

Caesarius's sermons were sorted by Morin into five groups: 1-80, admonitions on various topics (which do not have the form of homilies); 81-186, exegetical sermons (which do); 187-213, sermons for seasons of the church year; 214-32, those for saints' days and other feasts; and 233-38, addresses to monastic communities.[42] The admonitions cover a wide range of concerns for the behavior of Gallic Christians. The first eight have to do with the value of the written and the proclaimed Word of God. These are followed by a few on creedal or doctrinal subjects, which in turn lead into a group on the Christian life. A series on charity then prefaces a group on almsgiving, which is followed by several on loving one's enemies. Next come warnings against sexual sins and drunkenness and against superstitious pagan practices. Then come admonitions that Christians be prepared for judgment day, followed by some on the value of confessing one's sins and discussions of penitence. The volume ends with instructions on how to behave in church, whether it be how to chant the psalms or the value of such devotional gestures as genuflecting or bowing the head.

While all of these sermons teem with frequent scripture citations, the next 106 are exegetical homilies as such, commenting on the readings at the liturgy and applying them to the lives of the people. In those based on lections from the New Testament as well as the Old, the method of interpretation is uniformly allegorical. Following Origen and Augustine, for instance, the ten plagues of the exodus are related to the Ten Commandments in Sermons 99 and 100. The range of his preaching is well summarized in his *Life:*

> He delivered sermons suited to particular feasts and scriptural passages, and also against the evils of drunkenness and lust, against discord and hatred, against anger and pride, against the sacrilegious and fortune-tellers, against the utterly pagan rite of the Kalends of January, and against augurs, worshipers of trees and springs, and vices of different kinds. (*Life* 1.55)

Unlike other bishops of the time who came from prosperous families and had been educated in rhetoric, Caesarius did not preach in the high style that could be understood only by those with similar backgrounds, but preached instead in the Latin of ordinary people: "What is said to simple souls can, indeed, be understood by the educated, but what is preached to the learned cannot be grasped at all by the simple."[43]

Another way in which Caesarius strove to make his preaching effective was by doing it extemporaneously. The term used in his *Life* (1.54, 2.20), *memoriter,* could suggest that he memorized his sermons, but the more likely meaning is that he remembered an outline and preached from that. This would have been true even of sermons in which he incorporated large sections from the sermons of the Fathers, since he had a "wonderfully retentive memory" (*Life* 1.16) and could recite at will long passages from these works he had studied so attentively.[44]

Other ways in which he tried to make his preaching more effective were to speak loudly enough to be heard, to reinforce his words with gestures and facial expressions, and to keep his sermons short. As Klingshirn said, "Caesarius worked hard to deliver sermons that were clear, convincing, and above all memorable."[45] In doing so he used all the rhetorical techniques advocated by Augustine in *De doctrina christiana.* Even in the way he preached, Caesarius practiced what he preached. It is no wonder that his sermon collections were copied often and used extensively in the centuries to come.

Yet in some ways his preaching forebodes the decline of proclamation at the beginning of the Middle Ages. To a degree, his Latin is already on the way to becoming French[46]—not a bad thing in itself, but evidence that the culture is changing. Caesarius's borrowing from the sermons of his predecessors also prepares the way for the homiliaries at a time when clergy will not trust their own exegesis, but will only repeat what has been said by one of the giants of the past. Additionally there is an emphasis on the miraculous in his sermons as well as in his *Life* that is more akin to the spirit of the age that lies ahead than to that of the age gone before. Caesarius was at once a voice crying in the wilderness of his own generation and a harbinger of the future, a prophet in both the senses of forthtelling and foretelling.

GREGORY THE GREAT (CA. 540–604)

The year in which Caesarius died was close to that in which Gregory was born, but Gregory lived in a world different from that of Caesarius and even more different from that of Leo, his predecessor on the throne of Peter of a century and a half before. Leo had been pope before the Roman Empire in the West had ended. Caesarius flourished in the time when Germanic tribes were in control of the West. Shortly before Gregory was born, however, much of Italy had been reclaimed from the Ostrogoths by the Eastern emperor Justinian. That did not mean, however, that life in Rome had become more secure. The hold of the Eastern emperors on the Italic peninsula never became sure. It was constantly being challenged by the Germanic tribes, and control of Rome itself was not nearly so important to Constantinople as dealing with threats in the East. Even the emperor's exarchs in Ravenna did not give the welfare of Roman citizens in Italy significant priority.[47]

Constant wars and imperial indifference were not the only problems, however. In 542, possibly the year of Gregory's birth, there began a series of outbreaks of the plague that would trouble Europe for the rest of the century, the first killing about a third of the population of the affected areas. During his lifetime there were also famine, disease, floods of the Tiber, inflation, panic, and at times even riots.

After Gregory was consecrated in 590, he had to cope with all these distresses to a degree unprecedented in previous papacies. Before I turn to address the way he did that, however, it is appropriate to consider his life before his elevation to the Holy See. He came from an old and wealthy Roman family, although not one of the highest aristocracy.[48]

They were also deeply involved in the life of the church; indeed, his great-great-grandfather was Felix III, who served as pope a little over a century before Gregory did.

Gregory, however, was the first member of the family to hold an important civil office in Rome. When he was in his midthirties, he became one of the last prefects of the city. While it is hard to know exactly what Gregory's duties as prefect were, it seems likely that a good bit of the responsibility for government rested on his shoulders during the short term of his office.

His reaction to that responsibility is the first statement of a theme that would become dominant in his life, the struggle between his own desire to devote himself to the life of prayer and the many calls he received to look after the needs of others. This time he responded by doing what he must have wanted to do for a long time; he became a monk after his term of office was over.

He sold all of the family property he had inherited and used the proceeds to establish six monasteries in Sicily and a seventh at his family home on the Caelian Hill in the center of Rome, which he himself entered. Founding it, however, did not mean that he wished to govern it. Such duties must have seemed too much like what he was trying to get away from. He wished to begin the contemplative life of a monk; that is what he was fleeing *to*.

The needs of the church in those tumultuous times were too great, however, for so talented a person to be allowed to devote himself uninterruptedly to the life of prayer. He could have been a monk for only five years or so when the pope at the time made him a deacon. This is probably to say that he was put in charge of ecclesiastical administration for one of the seven districts into which Rome was divided. In 579 Pope Pelagius sent him to be his representative *(apocrisiarius)* to the imperial court in Constantinople, a duty with which he was charged for seven years. Gregory took to Constantinople with him a large group of his fellow monks, and his first major book, his *Morals on the Book of Job,* was begun there as conferences he led for his brothers.[49] Yet he was faithful as well in the duties for which he was sent to the capital.[50]

In 590, when he had been back in Rome about four years, one of the victims of that year's outbreak of the plague was Pope Pelagius. Gregory succeeded him as soon as imperial approval was received. The difficulties with which he would have to cope were enormous. Not only had the plague returned, but so had war. The Lombards, who occupied much of the peninsula, were attacking again. Floods of the Tiber devastated the countryside. And, with no effective civil government in the West, all the responsibility for the safety and welfare of the people would fall on Gregory's shoulders.

The Roman church at that time had the most extensive landholdings in Italy, not to mention others in Corsica, Sardinia, Dalmatia, Gaul, and North Africa. These resources made it possible for the church to assume responsibility for most of the services provided at other times by civil government—everything from feeding thousands to bankrolling imperial military operations. This, of course, was in addition to providing for all the expenses of the church, its clergy and religious, buildings, cemeteries, and charities. As one scholar put it, "The capital had become, especially economically, a papal Rome."[51]

It was possible for Gregory to oversee all of that because by talent and, undoubtedly, experience—especially that of being urban prefect, but also the management of the family estates—he was a marvelous administrator. He created an effective bureaucracy for the administration of the papal estates, seeing that everything was under a unified central control. The overall impression is that one of the reasons Gregory found administration so onerous was that he did it so thoroughly and efficiently.

This should not leave the impression, however, that he capitulated completely to his organizational duties and put aside his spiritual life. Rather, he remained a monk and continued to live in community, being the first to take the episcopal ideal of Augustine and Pomerius to the Holy See, the first monastic pope. Thus he still understood the church's main business as the salvation of souls. Indeed, his consciousness of that priority was intensified by his conviction that the world would end very soon.

Granted, then, that he continued to feel acutely the tension between his own desire for the contemplative life and the care for all the churches, which fell upon him daily, it is not surprising that he devoted much thought to how not only he but others as well should resolve that conflict and exercise authority in the church. An outgrowth of his thought on the subject is his conviction of the importance of preaching[52] and his understanding of what makes it important.[53] That understanding and acceptance were not arrived at immediately, however, or without a struggle. It is significant that when he was returned to the active life by being sent as *apocrisiarius* to Constantinople, the biblical figure with whom he most identified was long-suffering Job.[54] And it is also significant that in the first few months of his pontificate, he devoted himself to writing his treatise on pastoral care, his *Regula pastoralis*.

Gregory's eventual resolution of the conflict was more experiential than theoretical. He came to recognize that precisely what is needed by those under one's pastoral care is the fruit of one's contemplation of holy scripture. Thus, instead of seeing the active and contemplative lives as two different stages in spiritual development, he came to regard them as serving one another reciprocally. "The two lives are dynamically related, they foster and nourish each other in the individual person, as well as in the community."[55]

Gregory achieved this ideal on two levels. On the first, he conveyed the fruits of his own contemplation directly to the laity (the *coniugati*, the "married," as he called them)[56] in sermons he preached at the public liturgy. On the second, he preached about his understanding of how they all should carry out their joint responsibility to others with the duty of preaching.[57] Two very different kinds of sermons are involved.

Of his popular preaching there remain only the *Forty Gospel Homilies*.[58] These appear to have been preached early in his pontificate. Some are for Sundays spread through the Christian year, others for the feasts of martyrs and other saints, and still others are for ordinary weekdays. Some were probably preached in stational churches or martyria while others were delivered in the "Golden Basilica" of the Lateran, which served as Rome's cathedral at the time.[59] It would be hard to characterize these homilies better than Jeffrey Richards has: "simple, straightforward and accessible to ordinary people, a pastoral, allegorical, inspirational form of culture which laid great stress on the character, spirituality and endurance of the holy man."[60]

While no one was a more important theological influence on Gregory than Augustine, there are many differences between what they have to say. Most of them are functions of the differences between the worlds in which they lived.[61] In Augustine's North Africa, there were still many non-Christians and also many heterodox Christians. Accordingly, Augustine preached theological sermons not only because of his own disposition but also because of the needs of his hearers.

By the time of Gregory, however, Christian faith could be assumed to be what sociologists of knowledge refer to as "reality taken for granted." Thus the subject matter of Gregory's preaching was very different from that of Augustine's.

> Compared with Augustine, Gregory could take for granted the settled contours of his spiritual landscape. Christianity had come to give definitive shape to a "totalizing discourse." The boundaries of Gregory's intellectual and imaginative worlds were thus the horizons of the scriptures. How to be a Christian, how to live the fullest Christian life: this was Gregory's central preoccupation in all his preaching; and this was the question into which the anxieties of his

age had shaped themselves. Naturally, it helped to give his exegesis a predominantly moral direction.[62]

Gregory's exegesis, however, was more complex in his "metapreaching" than it was in his popular preaching, and consideration of that needs to be deferred. Before moving on to his preaching to preachers, it is necessary to note one way in which his popular preaching was extraordinarily influential on all later preaching. As Dudden said, "Gregory was the first great preacher who attempted, in anything like a systematic fashion, to introduce non-scriptural illustrations into his instructions, to drive home a religious truth with the help of an apposite story."[63] (**See Vol. 2, pp. 133-40,** for a sermon with two of these illustrations.) These illustrations reflect Gregory's expectation that the world would soon end and thus have much in common with many stories told through the ages by preachers urging sinners to repent while there was still time.

There is a story of a man who did not begin his deathbed repentance in time and another of one who did. A beggar has a holy death, and a sinner who becomes a monk in repentance is forgiven. Angels surround a devout abbot at his death, and the funeral of a saintly nun is celebrated by the angels while she is dying. In a number of the stories, the death of a virtuous person is accompanied by the odor of sanctity. The flavor of these *exempla* may be sampled in the shortest of the lot:

> In the time of the Goths there was a married woman of good family, very religious, who used to come frequently to the church of these martyrs. On a certain day, when she had come to pray as her custom was...she saw two monks clothed as pilgrims. She believed them to be pilgrims, and ordered that they be given alms. Before the one who performed this service for her had approached to bestow the alms, they stood close to her and said: "You are helping us now. On the day of judgment we will seek you out, and do whatever we can for you." When they had said this, they were taken out of her sight. Frightened, she returned to her prayers, shedding more copious tears. After this she became more zealous in her prayers, as she was convinced of the promise.[64]

This, then, was the beginning of what has become an important ingredient of sermons.

Gregory became so fond of these anecdotes that he wrote a collection of them, setting it in a genre of philosophical writing that had been popular since Plato. These *Dialogues*[65] contain stories about miracles of the saints of Italy. Most of the stories told in the homilies are repeated in Book 4 of the *Dialogues*. Book 2 is the earliest available account of the life of the great monastic pioneer Benedict of Nursia. The *Dialogues* went on to become, in effect, a "cyclopedia of sermon illustrations" for the great revival of preaching by friars in the thirteenth and fourteenth centuries, offering as they did some of the first *exempla* to be widely incorporated into thematic sermons.[66]

Gregory's metapreaching, his "preaching to preachers about preaching," occurs in such works as his *Morals on the Book of Job* and his *Homilies on Ezekiel*, but is also presented in nonsermonic form in his *Regula pastoralis*.[67] It is well known that the third book of the *Regula*, which is almost twice as long as the other three books put together, consists of suggestions for constructing what later came to be called *ad status* sermons, sermons for persons in various stations in life.[68] In addition, the short fourth book deals with the temptations that come to a preacher after a sermon is delivered.

Preaching is also greatly emphasized in the first two books. The first has to do with "the difficulties of the pastoral office and the requirements it places on him who is called to it."[69] While it refers more generally to the *pastor* and speaks of "the pastoral office" *(magisterium pastoralis)* and "the government of souls" *(regimen animarum)*, it nevertheless contrasts those who wish only to withdraw to contemplation with those who are "of service to the neighbor by preaching" (*Regula pastoralis* 1.5).

While the moral qualifications of *rectores* discussed in Book 2 can be seen to fit one with any sort of responsibility in the community, some of them, such as being discreet in silence and speech (chap. 4), exercising sternness toward the vices of those who do evil (chap. 6), not being too eager to please (chap. 8), and meditating on the Scriptures (chap. 11), seem particularly relevant to preachers. Hence it could be said that preaching is the main subject of the *Regula*. This is not surprising, since, as noted above, the importance of preaching is one of the most consistent themes in Gregory's writings.[70] It was one of the most consistent themes in his preaching to preachers.

In his metapreaching as well as his popular preaching, Gregory anticipates trends of medieval homiletics. For his metapreaching, that anticipation is in interpreting Scripture in several senses. While at least three senses had been mentioned as early as Origen, in practice most preachers had confined themselves to two, the historical and the allegorical. Gregory did not yet have the fourfold system that was to be so popular throughout the Middle Ages, but he was moving in that direction. This may be seen in the letter he wrote to Leander as the dedication of the *Moralia*:

Be it known that there are some parts, which we go through in a historical exposition, some we trace out in allegory upon an investigation
of the typical meaning, some we open in the lessons of moral teaching
alone, allegorically conveyed, while there are some few which, with
more particular care, we search out in all these ways together, exploring them in a threefold method. (Ep. iii)

This program is not carried out in a consistent manner. Indeed,
Markus calls the *Moralia* a "scarcely penetrable jungle,"[71] and says that

Little is to be gained by attempting to disentangle the oddly haphazard
vocabulary; the moral sense sometimes appears as part of the historical,
sometimes as part of the allegorical; his language is fluid. Gregory cared
little for neatness of terminology, and was in any case apt to conflate
his three senses of the scriptures with a dichotomy he thought more
fundamental.[72]

This is merely to say that in his understanding of the multiple meanings of Scripture, Gregory is a transitional figure. Even so, the understanding of ministry and especially of preaching that he finds in his
interpretation of Job is essentially the same as he states in his *Pastoral
Care,* an understanding that has a great deal to be said for it.

Scholars enjoy debating whether Gregory is the last of the Fathers or
the first great medieval theologian. In his preaching he was very important for what was to come. Few of the Fathers were quoted more often
in, for example, the *Glossa ordinaria,* the great patristically annotated
volume that was for all practical purposes the Bible of the Middle Ages.
For him the work of the pastor in communicating the Bible's hope of salvation through preaching was the one necessary thing. In the allegorical
interpretation of the *Morals,* the sons of Job stand for the apostles, the
definitive work of whom is preaching (1.14.18), an interpretation that is
developed consistently throughout the whole work. The reason preaching is so important is that it is the means by which pagans are converted,
the faithful are instructed in the Christian life, heretics are reconciled,
and the church reformed.

As Gregory says:

The church is called "adult" when being wedded to the Word of God,
filled with the Holy Spirit, by the office of preaching she is with young
in the conception of children, with whom by exhorting she travails,
whom by converting she brings forth.[73]

THE VENERABLE BEDE (CA. 673–735)

Britain had been part of the Roman Empire for about four centuries before it was abandoned in 410, and Roman Christians had taken their faith to Britain with them. While the tradition that Joseph of Arimathea brought the Holy Grail to Glastonbury shortly after the death of Christ is unreliable, it does appear that the gospel arrived in the island quite early. The first British martyr, Alban, seems to have died around 208. Writing in the third century, both Hippolytus and Origen refer to Christians in Britain, and British bishops were present at the Council of Arles in 314.

When the Romans withdrew, the British felt a need for protection of the sort the legions had provided and contracted with warriors from Germanic tribes—designated by Bede as the Angles, Saxons, and Jutes—to serve as mercenaries. The newcomers liked what they saw and decided not only to stay themselves but to bring their relatives as well. The process was long and drawn out, but by the end of the seventh century the English, as they could be called by then, had succeeded in confining the British to what is now Wales (where they became the Welsh) and occupied all of what is England today.[74]

While some of the British remained Christian, they apparently made no effort to share their faith with their conquerors. They did, however, share it with a number of other groups, other Celtic peoples in Wales, Brittany, Scotland, and Ireland. The missionary zeal of these Celtic Christians was shown in the fruit of their efforts in the lands they evangelized. This zeal was communicated to their mission territory, and produced there other missionaries who even spread the faith to the Anglo-Saxon (or English) conquerors of Britain.

All of this was taking place near the beginning of the seventh century, the very time that Roman missionaries sent by Gregory the Great were arriving in Kent. Thus while the English conquest of Britain was still going on, the invaders were being converted to Christianity by two groups of missionaries representing different traditions of their religion. The differences between the two groups were settled at the Synod of Whitby in 664, however, and after that there was one English church, embracing most of the country's people, in communion with the Catholic Church in the West under the bishop of Rome.

Evangelization often began with the conversion of a king and his nobles. The church then prospered intellectually and materially, especially in its monasteries. A case in point is the sister monasteries in which Bede spent his life, Wearmouth and Jarrow. They were founded by

Benedict Biscop, who had been a thane before becoming a monk. In his lifetime he made five trips to Rome, each time returning with things and people to enrich his monasteries: paintings, vestments, glaziers, and the archchanter of St. Peter's in Rome, who would teach his monks to conduct their worship in the Roman manner. Most important of all, however, were the books he brought back, the foundation of a library that was at the time one of the best in the world.[75]

And so it came about that in a monastery in the back of beyond, Christian learning was preserved. Indeed, a monk there became one of the last polymaths in history, one of the last people to know almost everything that was known at his time. He is the last of the preachers to be studied in this tracing of the survival of learned Latin rhetorical patristic preaching in the West after its acme in Augustine, and he by no means represents its nadir. The monk Bede has been known as "the Venerable" at least since the Council of Aachen in 836. This honorific did not mean that he was an archdeacon as it would in the English church today. Indeed, he held no office, not even in his monastery. Rather, in reference to him the term "venerable" has a root meaning of one worthy of respect, a sense in which he applied the designation to many others. Yet for him the term seemed so apt that history has treated it as part of his name.[76]

It is extraordinary that one whose name is so well known and for whom so many have a sense of affection should have left so little information about his life. Most of the biographical information that exists, however, comes from a short section at the end of his history:

> I was born on the lands of this monastery, and on reaching seven years of age, I was entrusted by my family first to the most reverend Abbot Benedict and later to Abbot Ceolfrid for my education. I have spent all the remainder of my life in this monastery and devoted myself entirely to the study of the Scriptures. And while I have observed the regular discipline and sung the choir offices daily in church, my chief delight has always been in study, teaching, and writing.
>
> I was ordained deacon at the age of nineteen, and priest at the age of thirty, receiving both of these orders at the hands of the most reverend Bishop John at the direction of abbot Ceolfrid. From the time of my receiving the priesthood until my fifty-ninth year, I have worked, both for my own benefit and that of my brethren, to compile short extracts from the works of the venerable Fathers on Holy Scripture and to comment on their meaning and interpretation.[77]

After that follows a list of his writings. Beyond this very little is known. A story recorded by someone else that must be about Bede is that of a "little lad" who was the only member of the community besides the abbot left at Jarrow after the outbreak of the plague in 686. The two of them, however, continued to sing the offices alone until new monks were recruited.[78] From his writings it is possible to discover that Bede did go to Lindisfarne once and to York and that he visited another monastery, but there the information ends. Otherwise, he appears to have settled into the monastic life to which his parents gave him as an oblate and happily spent all his years within the walls of his monastery.

Despite so little biographical data, it is possible, as Benedicta Ward has said, "to know Bede more intimately than any man of his time, whether in his relationship to Christ and his view of salvation or in his opinions on sex and his admiration for the fashion in beards." The reason this is so, as she pointed out, is that "it is through his writings that Bede is known in this face to face encounter."[79] Through all of them shines the personality of the author and, with his as with other favorite books, the reader would very much like to know the author personally and yet, at the same time, in a deeper sense knows her or him already.

The list of writings that follows the short autobiographical entry in the history is a long one indeed. While it is for his *History of the English Church and People* that he is best known, Bede did not consider it the most important of his writings. He understood his primary role to be that of an interpreter of Scripture. His list of works includes sixteen titles[80] on the Old Testament and eight on the New. These works usually take the form of commentaries and combine a summary of patristic interpretation with his own insights. They seem to be designed, on the one hand, to help monks in their meditation on the lections read at their offices throughout the day and, on the other, to furnish biblical insight to English clergy who were involved in the evangelization of their people.

Moreover, equipping clergy for their work seems the primary motivation of all his writing. "His pupils were monks who had a definite purpose in mind in studying at all and their learning is best understood as part of their work in the conversion of England rather than as essential to their monastic life."[81] His efforts fit into a program of education for ministry inaugurated by the great Greek archbishop of Canterbury, Theodore of Tarsus (668–90), and his African companion, Hadrian, who founded a school at their see city.[82]

Bede seems to have been charged with the responsibility of training novices at Jarrow, where their education extended from the basic three R's to Latin, which opened to them the wider world of Christian knowledge. He taught them about poetry both in Latin and in their own language, how to calculate the dates of feasts in the church year (involving some astronomy as well as mathematics), and about the world they lived in as understood by science at the time. He even encouraged translations into Anglo-Saxon for people who did not have the leisure to learn Latin. And, in order to be able to teach these subjects, he wrote textbooks on many of them.

All of this other study, however, was, as noted above, mere preparation for the study that would be useful in the evangelistic task. Such study, as indicated, was basically study of the Bible, but it included other things as well. Especially it included getting a vision of what the Christian life was to accomplish. This is to say that it involved learning about the holiness of the saints.

Included in the list of Bede's writings on the Bible are two books of *Homilies on the Gospels*. The first question prompted by the appearance of that title is: why would Bede have preached, since most monastic preaching was done by abbots and he was not an abbot?[83] As one of the priests of the community, Bede would have presided at Eucharist on occasion. He could thus have preached his homilies during one of his abbot's frequent absences from the monastery or when he was prevented from celebrating and preaching by some other reason. Since all the homilies are on the Gospel pericopae appointed for the eucharistic lectionary, that would have been a natural occasion for their being preached, but they could also have been preached at chapter or at the night office.[84]

There are fifty homilies, so the collection does not cover the entire church year. Rather, it clusters around the two great seasons of the nativity and resurrection, with a few homilies provided for some saints' days and other holy days. For the Christmas season there are: four for Advent, one for Christmas Eve, three for the different masses of Christmas Day, one each for the Feasts of St. John and the Holy Innocents, one for the octave day[85] of Christmas, one for the Feast of the Epiphany and five for the following Sundays, and one for the Purification (or Presentation, or Candlemass).

The cycle for the paschal mystery includes: seven homilies for Lent, four for Holy Week, one for the Vigil, one for Easter, five for Sundays after Easter, one for the Rogation Days, one for ascension and another for the following Sunday, one for Pentecost and one for its octave. Bede provided three homilies for the feasts of John the Baptist, one for the Roman martyrs James and John, one for Peter alone and another shared with Paul, and one for the founder of Bede's monastery, Benedict Biscop. There were also two homilies for the dedication of a church.

Precisely this selection raises the question of why these and not others. Part of the explanation may lie in the fact that Bede admired Gregory the

Great above all people, and only one of Bede's fifty homilies is on the same pericope as any of Gregory's forty. Thus he may have had a sense of supplementing the legacy of Gregory. It is certainly true that in general development the homilies of Bede are very similar to those of Gregory—although Bede does not imitate his model in the use of narrative illustrations. It is also obvious that Bede had read Augustine's *De doctrina christiana* and followed its precepts both in the interpretation of Scripture and in the use of rhetoric. While there is a simplicity to these homilies, they often achieve real eloquence. But Bede's homilies follow the story line of the pericope more closely than Augustine's and are perhaps even more integrated than Gregory's.

The outline of Bede's homilies is very simple. There is a short introduction, stating why his congregation should ponder the words of the Gospel passage that has just been read to them. Then the passage is examined, but Bede does not feel compelled to comment on every word or even every verse, because it is the pericope as a whole that he wishes to be understood. He explicitly teaches a fourfold interpretation, but seldom deals with more than the literal and perhaps one spiritual meaning. He uses allegorical interpretation regularly but with restraint, and he has the capacity to cite parallel passages from the entire canon without leaving a modern reader feeling that the meaning is forced.

The chief difference between his homilies and his commentaries is that the sermons do not cite nonbiblical authors, while the commentaries scrupulously note from which church father a particular insight comes. This does not mean, however, that the homilies are not indebted to previous interpreters; the lack of citation is rather a function of the difference of genre. In an oral communication for edification, bibliographical references are simply distracting.

Bede has been unfairly accused of having no original thoughts and of merely repeating what was said by his elders and presumably betters. Lawrence Martin, however, has shown how unjust that assessment is. In a detailed analysis of Bede's homily for the Feast of the Purification (2.18),[86] he shows that, while Bede's use of sources differs between the commentaries and homilies, in neither case is it simply a matter of parroting what others thought and said. In the commentaries, he uses the Fathers to strengthen the position he arrived at in his own study, while in the homilies, "Bede often draws on the fathers for motifs to enrich and ornament his own words, quite freely adapting his predecessors' work to suit his own homiletic themes and purposes."[87]

The third part of a homily by Bede is a short application of the teaching of the Gospel lection to the lives of his congregation. It is here that his preaching differs most markedly from that of his predecessors, because he had a different audience. He did not preach to a lay congregation as the bishops did, nor was he doing the sort of metapreaching—preaching to preachers—that Gregory did. Although most of the patristic preachers studied thus far were monks, no great series of monastic conferences has come down from them.[88] Bede thus is a precursor of the Middle Ages when a great deal of such preaching was done, much of which survives.

> Bede's main concern is with the spiritual meaning of the gospel stories, their meaning for the spiritual life of the monk. There is little exhortation about specific moral problems, as we find, for example, in the sermons of Caesarius of Arles. Bede does, however, refer to the specific details of the prayer life of the monastery, and he includes passages of direct address which speak to the concerns of his monastic audience.[89]

Bede's influence on the spiritual life of monks was not of the uninterrupted sort for which he would have hoped. Within a century of his death, England came to be harassed by Viking raids that were especially devastating to the coastal retreats and islands where many monasteries were located. Since *Norman* means "Northman," it could be argued that these disruptions did not end before the victory of William the Conqueror in 1066. By then, however, Bede was well known on the Continent, and most of his works have survived. He was honored in many ways, such as having much of his commentary incorporated into the *Glossa Ordinaria* and in such works of the friars as Thomas Aquinas's *Catena Aurea*. His writings are abundantly quoted in the Roman breviary. The judgment of the ages upon him is summed up in his having been declared a Doctor of the Church by Leo XIII in 1899.

This completes the path followed by the learned Latin rhetorical homily after Augustine. It represents only a fraction of the preaching done during the period that saw the conversion of Europe to Christianity, but its very literary character ensured its preservation, while the more abundant vernacular preaching can only be inferred from its results. While a minority tradition, this is by no means an ignoble one. Its practitioners saved from extinction a Christian cultural inheritance that would reemerge during the Middle Ages and at the Renaissance.

Those who preached at this time share much with their distinguished predecessors regarding Latin rhetorical culture. They also are signs of things to come in medieval preaching. Of the four men studied, the first, Leo the Great, has least in common with the others. He still preached in an elegant Latin that would set the style for the curia in later centuries. Caesarius, Gregory, and Bede were all well trained in rhetoric, but they knew their congregations were not, and they preached to them in words they could understand. The three in their various ways all showed great concern for encouraging others to preach. They also anticipated later preaching in several ways, especially in their elaboration of the multiple senses in which Scripture was to be understood and their emphasis on miracles. And all three were monks on the eve of a era in which Latin Christian culture, both classical and patristic, would remain alive only in the monasteries. The four, then, are key figures in the transition from the end of ancient Christianity to the rise of Western Christendom.

FOR FURTHER READING

Bede the Venerable: Homilies on the Gospels, 2 vols., trans. Lawrence T. Martin and David Hurst, pref. Benedicta Ward, intro. Lawrence T. Martin, Cistercian Studies Series 111. Kalamazoo, Mich.: Cistercian Publications, 1991.

Blair, Peter Hunter. *An Introduction to Anglo-Saxon England*. 2nd ed. Cambridge and New York: Cambridge University Press, 1977.

Brown, Peter Robert Lamont. *The Rise of Western Christendom: Triumph and Diversity A.D. 200–1000* (The Making of Europe). 2nd ed. Oxford and Cambridge, Mass.: Blackwell Publishers, 1996.

Gregory the Great: Forty Gospel Homilies. Translated by David Hurst. Cistercian Studies Series, no. 123. Kalamazoo, Mich.: Cistercian Publications, 1990.

Klingshirn, William E. *Caesarius of Arles: The Making of a Christian Community in Late Antique Gaul*. Cambridge and New York: Cambridge University Press, 1994.

St. Leo the Great: Sermons. Translated by Jane Patricia Freeland and Agnes Josephine Conway. FC. Washington, D.C.: Catholic University of America Press, 1995.

Straw, Carole. *Gregory the Great: Perfection in Imperfection*. Berkeley and Los Angeles: University of California Press, 1988.

Notes

1. See, for example, the definition of "Middle Ages" in *Merriam Webster's Collegiate Dictionary*, 10th edition.

2. Peter Robert Lamont Brown, *The Rise of Western Christendom: Triumph and*

Diversity A.D. 200–1000 (The Making of Europe), 2nd ed. (Oxford and Cambridge, Mass.: Blackwell Publishers, 1996), xi.

3. R. A. Markus, *The End of Ancient Christianity* (Cambridge and New York: Cambridge University Press, 1990).

4. Brown, *The Rise of Western Christendom.*

5. The term "Europe" came to be applied to the territory in the tenth century, although references to "Europeans" go back as early as the eighth century. J. M. Roberts, *History of the World* (New York: Oxford University Press, 1993), 312.

6. The term "barbarian" comes from a Greek word involving the nonsense syllables that foreigners' speech seemed to consist of.

7. Brown, *The Rise of Western Christendom*, 3-17.

8. This figure seems much too low to other scholars.

9. Brown, *The Rise of Western Christendom*, 17.

10. The very things that make up "civilization," as the term is understood in Thomas Cahill's popular book, *How the Irish Saved Civilization: The Untold Story of Ireland's Heroic Role from the Fall of Rome to the Rise of Medieval Europe* (New York: Nan A. Talese [Doubleday], 1995).

11. Even at that, Leo never alludes to pagan classical literature in any of his writings.

12. John Meyendorff, *Imperial Unity and Christian Divisions: The Church 450–680 AD*, The Church in History, vol. 2 (Crestwood, N.Y.: St. Vladimir's Seminary Press, 1989), 148.

13. Ibid., 148-58. As Meyendorff points out, however, it would be anachronistic to see in Leo's position an anticipation of the papal infallibility and universal ordinary jurisdiction promulgated by the First Vatican Council (1870).

14. *Latrocinium*, so designated by Leo.

15. While Eutychianism is a heresy, most of the Monophysites who did not accept the Council of Chalcedon and went into schism were not heretical and could have remained in communion but for some tragic mistakes on both sides of the controversy.

16. "First among equals."

17. Meyendorff, *Imperial Unity and Christian Divisions*, 156.

18. The excellent article by Francis X. Murphy, C.SS.R., "The Sermons of Pope Leo the Great: Content and Style," in *Preaching in the Patristic Age: Studies in Honor of Walter J. Burghardt, S.J.*, ed. David G. Hunter (New York: Paulist Press, 1989), 183-97, has more to say about content than style. Dom Jean Leclercq's introduction to the Sources chrétiennes edition of Leo's sermons is also more concerned with theology than homiletical method. See the introduction to *Léon le Grand: Sermons*, trans. and notes Dom René Dolle, 2nd ed., SC, no. 22 (Paris: Cerf, 1964). The introduction to *St. Leo the Great: Sermons*, trans. Jane Patricia Freeland, and Agnes Josephine Conway, FC (Washington, D.C.: Catholic University of America Press, 1995) is so restricted in its page allotment that it furnishes little guide to what follows.

19. Basil Studer, "Italian Writers Until Pope Leo the Great," in *The Golden Age of Latin Patristic Literature from the Council of Nicea to the Council of Chalcedon*, vol. 4 of *Patrology*, ed. Angelo di Berardino, intro. Johannes Quasten, trans. Placid Solari, 597.

20. The Ember Days were fast days observed in the church four times a year: the

Wednesday, Friday, and Saturday of the first week of Lent; the week following Whitsunday (Pentecost); and the first weeks after the middle of September and the middle of December. Their emphasis has varied over the centuries, and they have been optional observances since Vatican II. "Ember" is the English corruption of *Quattuor Tempora* (four seasons), as is the German *Quatember* and even the Japanese *tempura*.

21. Most of the Holy Week sermons were preached in two parts, one on Sunday and the other on Wednesday, the exception being three for Good Friday and two for Holy Saturday. One of the Good Friday sermons is paired with one of those for Holy Saturday. All the Holy Week sermons have the same theme, the passion, while the other sermon for the vigil on Holy Saturday is on the resurrection; there are no Easter sermons as such.

22. Hans Lietzmann says that Sermons 6 and 7 could not have lasted more than three minutes each. "Leo I, der Grosse," A. F. von Pauly and Georg Wissowa, *Real-Encyclopädie der classischen Altertumswissenschaft* (Stuttgart: J. B. Metzler, 1894–1963), Halband XXIV, cols. 1971-72. In translation these two sermons take less than a page each.

23. Station days were the eighty-seven or so days in the year for which the pope celebrated the liturgy at a designated church.

24. "*Le rhythme de ses phrases est accordé au ton de la liturgie, ses formules sont semblables à beaucoup de celles qu'a conservée le Missel romain qui, à travers les sacramentaires, s'est souvent inspiré de lui.*" Leclercq, intro. to *Léon le Grand*, 1:22-23.

25. *Dafür ist der Ausdruck knapp und treffend, von oft glänzender Prägnanz und sorgfältiger formaler Durchbildung, die eindringendes Studium wohl lohnen würde.* "Leo I, der Grosse," XXIV, 1972.

26. Leo's precise expression led John Henry Newman to conclude that he preached from a manuscript. *The Idea of a University*, ed., intro., and notes Martin J. Svaglic (Notre Dame: University of Notre Dame Press, 1982), 315.

27. Yngve Brilioth, *A Brief History of Preaching*, trans. Karl E. Mattson (Philadelphia: Fortress, 1965), 62. On the issue of Leo's influence on the collects, Josef Jungmann says, "Many Sunday orations [prayers, that is, the Sunday collects] and several prefaces [the seasonal introductions to the *Sanctus*] which we still recite today contain terms and phrases strikingly in accord with Leo the Great's phraseology. Even the rhythm of the language is the same. Thus the assumption that he is the author of many of the prayers in the Leonine Sacramentary is well founded." Josef A. Jungmann, *The Early Liturgy to the Time of Gregory the Great*, trans. Francis A. Brunner, Liturgical Studies, vol. 6 (Notre Dame: University of Notre Dame Press, 1959), 236.

28. A random check of ten pages revealed forty-four quotations or allusions.

29. Freeland and Conway, *St. Leo the Great: Sermons*, 13.

30. Ibid., 127.

31. The original of this sentence is an excellent example of the way Leo used the Latin language: "*Totum igitur corpus implet tota divinitatis; et sicut nihil deest illius majestatis, cujus habitatione repletur habitaculum, sic nihil deest corporis, quod non suo habitatore sit plenum.*"

32. Freeland and Conway, *St. Leo the Great: Sermons*, 131.

33. Located on an island off what today is the coast of Cannes.

34. William E. Klingshirn, *Caesarius of Arles: The Making of a Christian Community in Late Antique Gaul* (Cambridge; New York: Cambridge University Press, 1994), 31.

35. This *Vita* was written by friends and appeared just a few years after his death (*Caesarius of Arles: Life, Testament, Letters*, trans. with notes and intro. William E. Klingshirn, Translated Texts for Historians, vol. 19 [Liverpool: Liverpool University Press, 1994]). See also "Introduction," in *St. Caesarius of Arles: Sermons*, trans. Mary Magdeleine Mueller, , FC, vols. 31, 47, 66 (Vol. 1, New York: Fathers of the Church, Inc.; Vols. 2 and 3, Washington, D.C.: Catholic University of America Press, 1956–73), 1:v-xxvii; and Klingshirn, *Caesarius of Arles*. Another important volume synthesizing over twenty-five years of intensive study of medieval preaching by a number of scholars is *The Sermon*, directed by Beverly Mayne Kienzle, *Typologie des sources du moyen âge occidental*, fasc. 81-83 (Turnhout, Belgium: Brepols, 2000). The chapter covering the period of this and the next chapter is Thomas N. Hall, "The Early Medieval Sermon," 203-69. Hall's point of view is similar to the one I've taken here.

36. Klingshirn, *Caesarius of Arles*, 19.

37. Although admittedly many of the monks came from aristocratic families.

38. The 238 sermons in G. Morin's standard edition, *Sancti Caesarii episcopi arelatensis Opera omnia nunc primum in unum collecta*, 2 vols. (Maretoli, 1937–42), plus an additional sermon published by Anna Maria Giorgetti Vichi in *Academie e biblioteche d'Italia* XXI (1953), 335-42, are included in Mueller's translation of *St. Caesarius of Arles: Sermons*. Klingshirn, however, says that more than 250 of his sermons have survived. Introduction to *Caesarius: Life, Testament, Letters*, xiv. The others may be found in the bibliography to his *Caesarius of Arles*, with their editors listed on p. 288 and the sermons listed in the Secondary Sources section under the names of their editors.

39. Sermon 1.12-15, in *Sermons*, 1:6-16. This sermon, which is four or five times as long as any of Caesarius's others, concerns the duties of bishops and focuses especially on seeing that preaching occurs. It may not have ever been delivered orally; it could have been passed around as a circular letter instead. At the Council of Vaison in 529, his suffragan bishops gave permission for priests to preach and deacons to read patristic sermons. Klingshirn, *Caesarius of Arles*, 230.

40. In his edition, Morin used typography to indicate the degree of Caesarian authorship, using full-size type for sermons that were almost entirely the work of the bishop of Arles, smaller type for those to which he had contributed only an introduction or conclusion, and regular type set off by a dagger (†) for those in which there were extensive borrowings, but not such as to obscure their author/editor's style and thought. Mueller's translation, however, uses an asterisk (*) to indicate both the second and third categories. By the time she got to her third volume she realized that something more was needed, so for each of the sermons in that volume she supplied a footnote indicating Morin's conclusions about it and gave similar notes for the sermons in the first two volumes in an appendix. This makes it possible to know what non-Caesarian material is used in sermons attributed to the bishop, but the only indication that a sermon attributed to someone else is really by Caesarius is that it has a

title like "St. Augustine's Sermon on Charity" while nevertheless appearing among the collected sermons of Caesarius with none of Morin's typographical indications of another provenance.

41. This paragraph is based on a long passage from Morin, "The Homilies of St. Caesarius of Arles," in *Orate Fratres* XIV (1939–40), 481-86, quoted in Mueller, *St. Caesarius of Arles: Sermons*, 1:21-23. On "The Legacy of Caesarius," see Klingshirn, *Caesarius of Arles*, 273-86.

42. The first volume of Mueller's translation comprises the first category, the second volume comprises the second, and the third volume the last three.

43. Mueller, *St. Caesarius of Arles*, Sermon 86.1. Cf. Klingshirn, *Caesarius of Arles*, 81-82.

44. Klingshirn, *Caesarius of Arles*, 12-14.

45. Klingshirn, *Caesarius of Arles: The Making of a Christian Community in Late Antique Gaul*, 150. This sentence begins a paragraph in which Klingshirn gives an excellent summary of the rhetorical techniques Caesarius used to make his preaching effective. This paragraph comes at the end of a very fine discussion of his preaching overall, 146-53.

46. Mueller, *St. Caesarius of Arles: Sermons*, 1:xx, citing a study by Morin.

47. For the general historical background, see John Julius Norwich, *A Short History of Byzantium* (New York: Knopf, 1997), 57-97. For the implications of the political history for the church, see Meyendorff, *Imperial Unity and Christian Divisions*, 207-332, especially 293-332.

48. The most helpful secondary source for this section has been R. A. Markus, *Gregory the Great and His World* (Cambridge; New York: Cambridge University Press, 1997). The classic biography is still F. Homes Dudden, *Gregory the Great: His Place in History and Thought*, 2 vols. (London and New York: Longmans, Green & Co., 1905). Other works will be cited in reference to particular points.

49. Translated as *Morals on the Book of Job by S. Gregory the Great, the First Pope of that Name, Translated with Notes and Indices*, 3 vols. (Oxford: John Henry Parker; London: J. G. F. and J. Rivington, 1844–50).

50. While there he even refuted the heresy of the ecumenical patriarch Eutychius, who had denied the resurrection of the body.

51. Erich Caspar, *Geschichte des Papsttums von den Antängen bis zu Höhe der weltherrschaft* (Tübingen: JCB Mohr, 1930–33), 2 vols. 1:338. Quoted in Markus, *Gregory the Great and His World*, 122 n51.

52. On this issue, see O. C. Edwards Jr., "Preaching in the Thought of Gregory the Great," *Homiletic* XVIII (1993), 5-8.

53. Gregory's spirituality is excellently presented in Carole Straw, *Gregory the Great: Perfection in Imperfection* (Berkeley and Los Angeles: University of California Press, 1988).

54. This should not be pressed too far, because in the letter to Leander of Seville by which he begins the *Morals*, Gregory sees physical suffering to be the main thing he has in common with Job.

55. Markus, *Gregory the Great and His World*, 24. Cf. Gregory's statement in *Morals on the Book of Job*, 2:ii.11.

56. Gregory recognizes three categories of members within the Christian community, the married laity *(coniugati)*, those under religious vows *(continentes)*, and the *ordo praedicatorum*. This order of preachers includes all those who have the *officium praedicationis*. These groups, however, are not mutually exclusive.

57. Jean Batany has distinguished between Gregory's works of *exégèse parénétique* (Homilies on the Gospels) and <<*métaparénétiques*>> *qui prêchent aux prêcheurs* (Morals, Regula pastoralis, and Homilies on Ezekiel). *"Le vocabulaire des fonctions sociales et ecclésiastiques chez Grégoire le Grand,"* in *Grégoire le Grand: Chantilly, Centre culturel Les Fontaines, 15-19 septembre 1982*: Actes / publiés par Jacques Fontaine, Robert Gillet, and Stan Pellistrandi, Colloques Internationaux du Centre nationale de la recherche scientifique (Paris: Éditions du Centre national de la recherche scientifique, 1986), 171.

58. *Forty Gospel Homilies*, trans. David Hurst, Cistercian Studies Series, no. 123 (Kalamazoo, Mich.: Cistercian Publications, 1990). The Latin text is in PL, LXXVI.

59. Gregory's is one of the few episcopal thrones or *cathedrae* surviving from the early church. Its present location is a chapel on the south side of the sanctuary of San Gregorio Magno church in Rome (built on the grounds of his family estate). It is the earliest piece of church furniture from which any of the sermons discussed in this book were delivered. A picture of it may be seen in Jeffrey Richards, *Consul of God: The Life and Times of Gregory the Great* (London and Boston: Routledge & Kegan Paul, 1980), plate 4; or F. van der Meer and Christine Mohrmann, *Atlas of the Early Christian World*, trans. and ed. Mary F. Hedlund and H. H. Rowley (London: Nelson, 1958), 136.

60. *Consul of God*, 261. Richards was talking about not only the homilies but Gregory's *Dialogues* as well, which, he said, "epitomize the new folk-preaching that was so influential in the Middle Ages and represent the new form of learning that Gregory and the Gregorians stood for" (ibid.). While there is truth to his statement, it is now being recognized that Gregory's own education was surprisingly good for the time. Compare, for example, Markus, *Gregory the Great and His World*, 34.

61. Markus, *Gregory the Great and His World*, 40-41. Markus was so impressed by those differences when he originally set out to write his study of Gregory, he realized that before doing so he would first have to account for them. This resulted in his writing *The End of Ancient Christianity* (see p. xi of this work).

62. Markus, *Gregory the Great and His World*, 41.

63. Dudden, *Gregory the Great*, 1:255. This statement concludes a discussion of how Gregory's preaching practice differed from that of those who preceded him and of the influence of Gregory's example on later homiletics.

64. Homily 32 in both Migne's edition and Hurst's translation. The order of the first twenty homilies in the manuscripts varies, so Hurst arranged these twenty in the sequence of the liturgical year rather than following the order in which they appear in Migne, but kept Migne's order for the last twenty. *Exempla* may be found in the following homilies (Migne's number first followed by Hurst's in parenthesis where it differs): 12 (10), 15 (12), 19 (11), 32, 34, 35, 36, 37, 38 (in which there are two, one of which is the same as that in 19 [11]), 39, and 40.

65. *Life and Miracles of St. Benedict: Book Two of the Dialogues*, trans. Odo J. Zimmermann, FC, no. 39 (Washington, D.C.: Fathers of the Church, Inc., 1959).

66. See below, 217-32.

67. *Pastoral Care,* trans. and annotated Henry Davis, ACW, no. 11 (Westminster, Md.: Newman Press, 1950).

68. This list of opposed pairs of types of person puts flesh on a skeletal outline in *Morals* XXX:iii, which in turn is developed from a list by Gregory Nazianzen, *Orat.* 2, 16-34. See Batany, "Le vocabulaire des fonctions sociales et ecclésiastiques chez Grégoire le Grand," 173.

69. Davis, *Pastoral Care,* 4.

70. Inflected forms of *praedicare, praedicator,* and *praedicatio,* for instance, appear over thirty-three hundred times, according to the index of *Thesaurus Sancti Gregorii Magni,* curante CETEDOC, Universitatis Catholica Lovaniensis Lovani Novi, Corpus Christianorum Thesaurus Patrum Latinorum (Turnhout, Belgium: Brepols, 1986). Or, to resort to an older guide, the entries related to preaching in the index of subjects and opinions in PL run to almost twelve columns, which is to say, four folio pages of references.

71. Markus, *Gregory the Great,* 16.

72. Ibid., 46-47. This quotation is from an excellent chapter on the importance of the Bible to Gregory and his method of interpreting it, 34-50.

73. *Morals on the Book of Job,* 2:409. Citations in Gregory's works supporting the statements made in this paragraph can be found conveniently in Claude Dagens, *Saint Grégoire le Grand: Culture et expérience chrétiennes* (Paris: Études augustiniennes, 1977), 312-44, by following paragraph titles.

74. For a description of this process see Peter Hunter Blair, *An Introduction to Anglo-Saxon England,* 2nd ed. (Cambridge; New York: Cambridge University Press, 1977), 1-54.

75. Bede wrote of Benedict Biscop not only in his history, but more extensively in his *Lives of the Abbots of Wearmouth and Jarrow,* 1-7 (translated in *The Age of Bede,* ed. with intro. D. H. Farmer, trans. J. F. Webb [Harmondsworth, Middlesex, England; New York: Penguin Books, 1965; reprint, with a new introduction, 1983; reprint, 1988], 185-91), and in a sermon for his feast day (Homily 1:13 in *Homilies on the Gospels,* 2 vols., trans. Lawrence T. Martin and David Hurst, with preface by Benedicta Ward, and introduction by Lawrence T. Martin [Kalamazoo, Mich.: Cistercian Publications, 1991], 1:125-33).

76. John Marsden, *The Illustrated Bede,* rev. ed., with translation by John Gregory, photography by Geoff Green (Edinburgh: Floris Books, 1996), 202. Marsden also reports the more charming if less likely explanation of the term's application to Bede, that it was supplied by the monastic mason carving his epitaph when his bones were moved to Durham cathedral. The stone carver wished to use the rhyme "*Hic sunt in fossa/ Baedae . . . ossa*" and the blank was miraculously filled during his absence with *venerabalis,* which fit his meter perfectly.

77. Bede, *A History of the English Church and People,* trans. with intro. Leo Sherley-Price (Baltimore: Penguin, 1955), 5:24.

78. The story appears in an anonymous life of Ceolfrid translated by D. S. Boutflower and is quoted in Benedicta Ward, *The Venerable Bede,* Outstanding Christian Thinkers Series (London: Geoffrey Chapman, 1990), 4.

79. Ibid., 2.

80. "Titles" is used to refer to these works because, on the one hand, some cover only a section of one biblical book while others treat a number of canonical writings, and, on the other, the length of these works varies, and Bede's list often gives the number of books into which each title is divided.

81. Ward, *The Venerable Bede,* 2.

82. It is due to their influence that Bede knew Greek better than the other preachers studied in this chapter and, indeed, better than Augustine.

83. Monastic preaching as such is treated in part 2, chapter 8, below.

84. Martin seems to favor the idea that the homilies were not composed for delivery but for being read, for example, as *lectio divina.* While that is possible, the reasons advanced for questioning delivery are a good bit short of persuasive.

85. One week later than the feast.

86. The fifty homilies are divided equally between the two volumes and thus are cited by volume number (1 or 2) followed by homily number (1-25 for each volume, although the break between the volumes is arbitrarily in the middle of sermons for Lent).

87. Martin and Hurst, *Bede the Venerable,* 1:xxii. In his analysis Martin showed the difference between what Bede said and what each of the fathers on whom he had drawn had written. In his translation of the homilies, footnotes indicate all the resonances between Bede's work and that of earlier preachers and commentators so that the reader can look up the citations and perform the sort of comparison Martin made in his analysis of 2°:18.

Ward distinguishes between the format of the homilies and that of the commentaries in regard to their purpose: "The special mark of the homilies is the direct application of biblical passages to a specific audience; whereas the commentaries gave other preachers the material for sermons, here Bede himself made the application" (Ward, *The Venerable Bede,* 65).

88. With the exceptions mentioned above of Gregory's *Moralia* and *Homilies on Ezekiel,* which are treated here as metapreaching rather than monastic conferences.

89. Martin and Hurst, *Bede the Venerable,* 1:xi.

THE EARLY MEDIEVAL PERIOD

MISSIONARY PRELUDE

Periodization in historiography is always somewhat arbitrary. Life is a continuum and it is only in retrospect that points in the flow are labeled as "starts" and "stops," and even these apply only to severely restricted sets of phenomena within the total activity of that moment. Observers correlate beginnings and ends that are relatively synchronistic and seem to them to be interdependent and call these by titles such as "era" and "period," but the patterns discerned are at least as much a function of the organizing intelligence of the observer as they are intrinsic to the events observed. As a result, individual interpreters can and do consider different patterns of synchronicity to be significant. For example, while historians generally concur that there was an "age" that can appropriately be called "middle," they disagree by numbers of centuries about when that age began.

For the purposes of this history of preaching, the shift to the Middle Ages seems to have occurred when the language of preaching in the West shifted from Latin to vernacular tongues. The previous chapter traced the survival of learned Latin preaching through the period in which it had become the exception. This one will recount a time that overlaps that one to some extent, the time when vernacular preaching became the norm.

The easiest point from which to trace this is the evangelization of northern Europe by missionaries from Britain. A contemporary of Bede, Willibrord (658–739) carried the gospel to the Frisians in what is now Holland and Belgium, and Boniface (680–754) became the apostle of Germany. The next stage of missionary expansion would owe more to armies than to monks as Charlemagne began to make conversion one of the terms of peace with the peoples he conquered. The so-called Dark Ages were a time when many new peoples were being led to the Light, were being included in the Christian faith.

Yet, while one cannot doubt that all this missionary activity involved a good deal of preaching, unfortunately no written trace of it survives. Migne contains fifteen sermons attributed to Boniface (PL 89, 843-72). The first fourteen of these seem to be catechetical instruction of the sort called for by Carolingian reforms to be considered below. The last, which seems to have been written earlier, deals catechetically with what is renounced and what is promised in baptism. There is also a pastoral manual written to serve as a model for preachers that has been attributed to St. Pirmin, the founder of the monastery at Reichenau ca. 724, but this attribution seems to derive from the desire of a copyist to have transcribed some work of this worthy rather than from any direct connection with him. Thus missionary sermons prior to the time of Charlemagne do not appear to have survived.[1]

HOMILIARIES

The lack of surviving missionary sermons from the period before Charlemagne means that the study of medieval preaching in the vernacular must begin somewhere else. Before that can be considered, however, it is necessary to look at the way Latin sermons were given an afterglow in collections called homiliaries.[2] These collections come from a time when preachers were experiencing a loss of nerve. With the demise of Latin culture, clergy no longer considered themselves or their contemporaries to be competent to interpret the Scriptures. Instead, they ransacked the sermons of the Fathers for words through which their own generation could be guided safely into the harbor of truth. It is these gleanings that scholars have labeled "homiliaries." More precisely, homiliaries are collections of homilies arranged to follow the liturgical lectionary. The category does not include all collections of patristic sermons made during the Middle Ages; anthologies of sermons by the same author, for instance, or those of homilies on the same topic would not be homiliaries. The collection of sermons by different church fathers must be arranged according to the liturgical calendar.

This is not to say, however, that the only or major purpose of such collections was to provide clergy with sermons to deliver at the liturgy in place of those of their own composition. As we shall see, they were used for a variety of purposes that ranged from being read aloud at the Night Office or during meals in monasteries, to being read privately for personal edification, to being studied by clergy who were composing their own sermons.

One may question the inclusion of such material in a history of preaching on the grounds that activities other than proclamation at the liturgical assembly are being contemplated. Yet these homiliaries constitute the most abundant homiletical remains from the early Middle Ages, when almost no new sermons were being written. Since, then, they are what we have, since their contents originated in proclamation, and since these texts were very influential on later preaching, they must be discussed.

The compilation of homiliaries seems to have begun in Africa with such works as the mid-fifth-century homilies that Victor of Cartenna composed for the edification of his brothers and the eighty sermons from the fifth or sixth century incorrectly ascribed to Fulgentius. From Africa such collections were taken by exiles into Europe where they had their principle diffusion from Naples and Arles. Indeed, as I noted in the previous chapter, the sermons of Caesarius of Arles had much in common with those in a homiliary, often being largely reworkings of sermons by the Fathers. By this time, although the bishop was still regarded as the normative preacher and teacher of the flock, there were places where bishops were not numerous enough to be the head of the congregation in every town and village, and in such places presbyters[3] could preach and deacons could at least read sermons of the Fathers.[4] And Caesarius's own collection of sermons demonstrates the value of having a supply of patristic sermons on hand for anyone responsible for composing sermons.

The usefulness of such collections as homiliaries for monasteries is made apparent in the *Rule of St. Benedict* where it discusses how many psalms and lessons are to be read at the Night Office (chap. ix).[5] There it is stated that

> the books to be read at the Night Office shall be those of divine authorship, of both the Old and New Testament, and also the explanations of

them which have been made by well known and orthodox Catholic Fathers.[6]

Monasteries also drew upon homiliaries for reading during the silence at meals.[7]

From Benedict's reference to the texts to be read as *expositiones* it is clear they were not to function so much homiletically as exegetically; they were to serve in an auxiliary role to *lectio divina,* the meditative study of scripture that was such a basic part of the monastic discipline. Here the use of homiliaries moves in the direction of private devotion, and prefaces to some of the collections make it clear that those responsible for compiling them expected them to be used devotionally as well as exegetically.

Many homiliaries have been preserved. The more important ones are identified briefly by Barré and are discussed at length by Grégoire, being designated either by the name of their collector or by the provenance or locality of the manuscripts in which they have been preserved. These include St. Peter of Rome, Verona, Fleury-sur-Loire, Wolfenbuettel 4096, Vatican lat. 3828, Vienna 1616, Toledo, Agimond, Alan of Farfa, Paul the Deacon, Alcuin, and Ottobeuren. One of the most significant of these, that of Paul the Deacon, will furnish an example of what such collections were like.[8] His was drawn up at the request of Charlemagne because the text of other homiliaries used by monks for the Night Office was so corrupt as to be unintelligible.

Paul's efforts were so successful that his collection continued to be used for a thousand years. It consists of 244 sermons and homilies for every Sunday and feast day in the entire liturgical year, with several provided for occasions when more preaching was expected. He includes fifty-seven sermons or homilies attributed to Bede, fifty to Maximus, thirty-five to Leo the Great, thirty-two to Gregory the Great, nineteen to Chrysostom, eighteen to Augustine, eight to Jerome, six to Origen, five to Ambrose, four to Fulgentius, two to Isidore of Seville, and one each to Severianus and Eusebius of Caesarea. Cyril Smetana considers Paul to have been very discriminating for his time in being able to recognize which sermons are correctly attributed and which are not.[9] One can see that this collection of one or more homilies for each of the Gospel pericopes for the liturgical year, taken from respected Fathers and presented with accurate texts, would have proved very popular not only for readings at the Night Office but for a number of other uses as well. It is no wonder that it was copied as often as it was over so long a period.

Scholars make a distinction between patristic homiliaries, which were basically intended for liturgical use, and Carolingian ones assembled for private reading. These latter were not comprised of complete sermons but consisted instead of quotations from patristic commentaries. This personal usage meant that these homiliaries could be expanded very naturally to include lectionary epistles along with Gospels. Among the more important Carolingian types are the Mondsee homiliary, two composed by Hrabanus Maurus, the homiliary of Chartres, and those of Haymo and Heric of Auxerre.[10] By referring, however, to Paul the Deacon, Carolingian homiliaries, and Hrabanus Maurus, this discussion has already reached a point where it is necessary to take stock of the reforms in the church in general and in preaching in particular that are associated with the reign of Charlemagne.

THE CAROLINGIAN REFORM

There is no more romantic figure in history than Charlemagne, yet surviving documents do not make it possible to learn what he was really like as a person.[11] It is possible to see, however, that during his reign the territory of the Franks was doubled, that he was crowned by the pope as the Roman emperor, and that he built his capital at Aachen and tried to administer his empire from there. He associated his program closely with that of the church and made great use of clergy in his administration, from Alcuin, Theodulf, and Paul the Deacon, who were among his closest advisors, to the bishops he had appointed as ecclesiastical heads of the territories (whereas counts served as civil ones), down to the clerics who were also paired with laymen as his *missi dominici*, "the lord's emissaries." His armies evangelized the lands through which they moved, making conversion one of the conditions of peace. His *Admonitio generalis* tried to set standards for Christian education and behavior for all his territory and many of his captularies deal with programs to implement those standards. (**See Vol. 2, pp. 141-43,** for an example.) At the center of his reforms was a program for educating the clergy, providing them with the skills and tools they needed to do their job of conducting the church's worship and educating their people in Christian faith and morals.

Although it is possible to speak of a Carolingian renaissance, one must be very careful about what the expression means.

> This was no New Athens finer than the Old: it was intellectual reform and textual criticism as the indispensable preliminary to the reform of the clergy and to the performance of the *Opus Dei*.[12]

And, it should be noted, at the same time that Charlemagne was making it possible for the church to be the church, he was also supplying himself with enough literate people to make the administration of his empire possible.

An emphasis on preaching was a necessary part of the Carolingian reform.[13] Preaching was expected to furnish basic catechesis in the Christian faith for Saxons and even Franks who had but recently been converted from paganism and who had only the most rudimentary knowledge of what it means to be a Christian. Preaching could be included with the learning and good letters that J. M. Wallace-Hadrill says were no mere hobbies of the Carolingians and their friends. "They were conditions of survival."[14] Indeed, one of the things that makes learning and good letters necessary is that they are preconditions of the preaching.

"Charlemagne and his clergy legislated for the propagation of the Christian faith, and promoted the sermon to be one of the principal vehicles for the instruction of the people."[15] In his *Admonitio generalis* of 789 Charlemagne instructed his bishops that they should see that the presbyters whom they sent to parishes should preach rightly and virtuously.[16] The content of this preaching is also prescribed. As Rosamond McKitterick summarizes it, it should be:

> the "Triune God, omnipotent and sempiternal," of his Son Jesus Christ, who "was made man and came to judge men according to their respective merits," and of the resurrection of the dead and the eternal rewards to be received.[17]

The *Admonitio* also specified the sins against which the people were to be warned: fornication, uncleanness, lust, witchcraft *(veneficia)*, enmities, controversies, jealousies, animosities, wraths, quarrels, dissensions, heresies, sects, envies, grudges, murder, drunkenness, revelries, and similar things. The opposing virtues to be encouraged were also listed. What it all boils down to is that the people were to be thoroughly instructed in Christian faith and morals.

Sermons were expected at Mass on all Sundays and holy days.[18] The Council of Arles in 813 made it clear that this was not to be done only in cathedrals *(civitatibus)* but in parish churches *(paroechiis)* as well.[19] This expectation is expressed in the communications of such bishops as Gerbald of Liège, his successor Waltcaud, Riculf, Hincmar of Reims, and the author of "All glory, laud, and honor," Theodulph of Orléans. Council attendees also expected their clergy to have such homiletical aids as Gregory the Great's *Forty Homilies on the Gospels* and a homiliary containing sermons for all Sundays and holy days.

The Reform Councils of 813 are also quite insistent that this preaching occur in the language of the people.[20] By the Carolingian period Latin seems to have disappeared as a spoken language in Frankish territory and it was only the renaissance of learning Charlemagne encouraged that made it possible for his clerics to use it; any understanding of it by the laity would have been unlikely.[21] The sort of accommodation made in the sermons' language was also necessary in their content. One of the purposes of the preaching the Carolingian reform urged was to make it possible for laypeople to understand the creeds, but that had to be done a step at a time. McKitterick has compared surviving vernacular sermons with both the complex exposition in Heiric of Auxerre's homily for Trinity Sunday and the use of homiliaries made by Aelfric. She concludes that

> the subject matter of each sermon was simplified and reduced to the most directly relevant essentials, not because the language could not cope, but because the priests felt that they would be more readily comprehensible to an illiterate audience unused to, and possibly not vitally interested in, the deeper profundities of Christian doctrine.[22]

Even though there have been intermittent centuries in which preachers could expect their congregations to follow the most intricate theological arguments, the situation in the time of Charlemagne does not seem greatly different from that of today; in both ages the basics in Christian doctrine could not be assumed to be a part of the common culture of the people.

HRABANUS MAURUS

For insight into what the preaching of the Carolingian reform was actually like it is helpful to turn to one of those most deeply involved in encouraging it, Hrabanus Maurus (ca. 776–856). Hrabanus, a pupil of Alcuin at Tours, was a member of the second generation of reformers. He went on to become abbot of Fulda and then archbishop of Mainz where his activities as an encourager of the reform won for him the title of *praeceptor Germaniae*.[23] A very prolific author for the time, Hrabanus wrote books on most of the theological disciplines; this work is not original, but is instead mostly a retelling of patristic lore. He is an excellent figure in whom to study the reform as it related to preaching because he not only compiled two homiliaries but also provided in his *De clericorum institutione* what is in effect the first in a long line of medieval textbooks on preaching.

De clericorum institutione is virtually a curriculum in pastoral theology by itself. The first book deals with major and minor orders of ministry, their vestments, and the two "dominical" sacraments, with a section on the catechumenate incorporated into the discussion of Christian initiation. The second is largely liturgical, and deals with the full round of daily offices; confession, litanies, fasts, penance, and reconciliation; the feasts and seasons of the church year; and church music and the lectionary. The final book concerns what those in holy orders ought to know, but concentrates on the two closely related topics of biblical interpretation and preaching.[24] This first medieval preaching manual would be more exciting if there were anything new in it, but as Joseph M. Miller has pointed out,

> none of the material is original; he merely takes large chunks of Augustine's *De doctrina christiana,* IV, and reproduces them almost verbatim, sometimes rearranging sections, but never altering the text. . . . One who wishes to read [Hrabanus], then, will do well to return to Augustine.[25]

Hrabanus's two homiliaries were compiled forty years apart, the first begun in 814 when he was master of the monastery school of Fulda and the second in 854 when he was archbishop of Mainz.[26] The collections also are very different: the first was dedicated to Haistulf, a predecessor in Mainz, and was intended to be preached by parish clergy to their congregations[27] while the second was dedicated to the Emperor Lothar and was verse-by-verse catenae of patristic exegesis of the epistles and Gospels for every day of the church year assembled for the devotional reading of the Emperor—although Lothar said that clergy could profitably preach these sermons to their people. This is to say that, according to the distinction made above, the first is a "patristic" and the second a "Carolingian" homiliary.

Hrabanus is very explicit about the purposes of the seventy sermons in the first collection:

> I have composed a book of sermons to be preached to the people, on all subjects which I considered necessary for them. That is, firstly, in what manner they ought to observe the principal festivals which occur in the course of the year. . . . After that, we have written discourses for them concerning the various kinds of virtue. . . . And after this we

have added another series of discourses on the various seductions of errors and vices....[28]

(**See Vol. 2, pp. 143-44** for a specimen of his preaching.) Hrabanus did not assemble these sermons into a book but sent them to the archbishop as they were written. For that reason, they have not often been copied as a unit and there is only one manuscript that has most of the collection, which is printed in Migne.[29] These sermons borrow heavily from those of Caesarius of Arles, Augustine, Gregory the Great, Bede, Maximus of Turin, and the *Vitae Sanctorum*.

McKitterick has summarized the technique of the sermons for feasts by saying that

> Hrabanus' method...was to divide his instruction into two parts. First there was a statement and exposition of the Gospel for the day, followed by an exhortation on whatever subject the pericope or event had suggested.[30]

This description is accurate if one recognizes that the exposition of the Gospel did not look anything like verse-by-verse exegesis; that was much more characteristic of the homilies in the collection made for the Emperor.

Since the first half of the sermons in the first collection ended in exhortations and since the others were about virtues and vices, one may deduce what is indeed true, that these sermons were aimed at encouraging Christian living among masses recently converted from paganism. The main inducement for doing so is eschatological: that they may escape hell and enjoy heaven.[31] Thus the homilies of Hrabanus meet the stipulations set forth by the Synod of Tours in 813:

> It is our unanimous opinion that each bishop should have homilies containing needful admonitions by which his subjects may be taught, that is, concerning the catholic faith, in order that they may be able to embrace it, concerning the perpetual retribution of the good and the eternal damnation of the evil, concerning the coming general resurrection and last judgment and by what works one may merit eternal life and by what works be excluded from it. And that each should be diligent to translate clearly the same homilies into the rustic Romance language or German, in which all may the more easily be able to understand the things that are said.[32]

Hrabanus sent his homiliary for Lothar in three sections: from Christmas through Lent, from the Easter vigil to the fifth Sunday after

Pentecost, and the rest of the year. A single manuscript of the first part survives, the second is printed in PL[33], and the third section may be hidden in the manuscript in which the first section appears.[34] Its technique of verse-by-verse exegesis has already been mentioned. Since, however, it was intended for private devotional reading rather than delivery to congregations, it need not be considered here.

ANGLO-SAXON CATECHETICAL PREACHING

A major goal of promoting preaching in the Carolingian reform was socializing new peoples into the Christian faith. The success of that effort depended on teaching the basic elements of the Christian faith to people in their own languages. One may see from Hrabanus's first homiliary that such efforts were successful to a degree, but surviving texts document an even fuller realization of those accomplishments in England 150 years after Hrabanus's death.

On the eve of the end of the first Christian millennium a political and religious situation had developed in which such preaching could take place. During the last century or so of their occupation of Britain, the Romans had invited in Germanic tribesmen to assist them as mercenaries in maintaining Roman control. These mercenaries and their families stayed and they were followed by great numbers of their kinsmen—Angles, Saxons, Jutes, and Frisians—in the fifth century. Together they drove the Celtic-speaking British people back into what is now Wales, Ireland, and Scotland, and made their own language the language of the land. Scholars call this language "Old English" and they call "Anglo-Saxon" the culture that lasted until the Norman invasion.

So much for political conditions. The religious situation was the English manifestation of the monastic expansion that is associated in Europe with the Cluniac reform. The English version, however, was not closely connected with Cluny, which was fiercely independent of external connections. Instead, it derived from Ghent and was encouraged by and gave great support to the Crown. This monasticism did not seclude itself in cloisters but replaced secular priests in cathedral chapters[35] with monks. It was not long before England's bishops came to be recruited from these communities.[36] This attachment of religious to congregations of laypeople meant that the learning of the monks could be harnessed for the instruction of the laity. The monks had already begun to translate some of their own documents into Old English and there had been effort to furnish Anglo-Saxon people with vernacular religious instruction since the days of Bede and King Alfred. Thus monastic expansion in England created a climate in which learned monks could turn their attention to the religious instruction of the laity in their own language.

Another factor in the religious situation that called for increased teaching of the laity was the replacement of adult baptism with that of infants, a change that involved the separation of catechesis from initiation. With the loss of instruction such as that in the catechetical preaching of Cyril of Jerusalem and Ambrose, it became necessary to devise new ways in which laypeople could be socialized into the Christian faith.[37] The result was replacing the preaching done to catechumens during the Lent and Easter of their baptism with basic instruction on the Christian faith in sermons to the entire congregation who had already been baptized.

Aelfric, "the greatest scholar and literary leader of the English Benedictine Revival" responded to this need for basic Christian catechesis in Old English.[38] While he was still a monk of Cerne Abbas in Dorset and before he became abbot of Eynsham, Aelfric translated into Old English a series of forty sermons that was followed later by a second series. (**See Vol. 2, pp. 144-51** for one of his catechetical sermons.) He stated his reason for doing this in his preface:

> I have seen and heard of much error in many English books, which unlearned men, through their simplicity, have esteemed as great wisdom: and I regretted that they knew not nor had not the evangelical doctrines among their writings, those men only excepted who knew Latin, and those books excepted which king Alfred wisely turned from Latin into English, which are to be had.[39]

Aelfric's preaching has been studied extensively and given a suggestive interpretation by Milton McC. Gatch.[40] He sees it as contributing to the call of the Reform Councils for replacing liturgical preaching with catechetical instruction. This catechetical preaching was to be done at a vernacular office developing at the time that came to be called "Prone." This office, although it could occur separately, usually took place after the Gospel at the Eucharist. It "consisted of a translation and brief explanation of the pericope, announcements of forthcoming liturgical events, catechetical instruction based on the Creed and Lord's Prayer, and biddings of prayers and other devotions."[41]

Gatch sees this tendency to replace the liturgical homily with catechetical preaching in the office of Prone manifested in several features of Aelfric's *Sermones catholici*. A number of these are "sermons" in the strict sense of not being exegetical liturgical homilies. Series 1, for instance, begins with a sermon on the beginning of creation that is reminiscent of the great patristic catechetical expositions of the six days of creation. Moreover, the title matter of this sermon has the rubric that it is to be preached *quando volueris*, "whenever you wish."[42] Therefore it was not an exposition of a lectionary reading. Further, the sermons for the Rogation Days[43] in the first series are the most basic catechesis possible, expositions of the Lord's Prayer, Apostles' Creed, and Nicene Creed.

Gatch argues that Rogationtide "became in the late-Saxon church a conventional collecting-place for general catechetical and parenetic or hortatory sermons."[44] And he finds in the *Sermones* what are in effect the sort of liturgical announcements that are only to be expected at Prone. Finally, he points to the material tacked on to the end of the manuscript on which Thorpe's edition was based, which includes translations into Old English of the creeds, the Lord's Prayer, a collection of prayers, an instruction on Lenten penitence, and other things, all of which are appropriate to a collection of essentially catechetical materials.[45] Thus he is able to argue that the *Sermones,* rather than being liturgical homilies, are catechetical preaching of a purer form than had been developed earlier on the continent. And he can say this in spite of the fact that many of Aelfric's sermons include the verse-by-verse exegesis of a pericope characteristic of a homily.

Aelfric apparently expected such preaching at Prone to occur every other week and he provided two series of sermons to be preached so that the faithful would not become bored by frequent repetition. The second series provided for even greater variety since it gave the preacher some choice about which of the materials provided were to be used in the sermon, while the sermons in the first series were expected to be read to the congregation largely as Aelfric had written them.[46]

Yet what Aelfric does in his catechetical sermons is not a totally new departure in the history of preaching. He used patristic comments on his biblical texts to guide his interpretation, and his source for those comments seems to have been a form of the homiliary of Paul the Deacon.[47] Gatch's argument, which seems cogent, is that while Aelfric used traditional materials from homiliaries, he did not use them to create exegetical liturgical homilies but to write catechetical sermons to be delivered at Prone instead.

The preaching of Aelfric's contemporary Wulfstan shares a similar concern for basic Christian instruction just as there is also a shared eschatological emphasis. There is, however, a great deal of difference between the preaching of the two—in spite of the fact that Wulfstan often used Aelfric's sermons as a source for his own. Much of the difference can be attributed to a difference of responsibility since Aelfric became an abbot but Wulfstan left the cloister to become first bishop of London and then bishop of Worcester and eventually archbishop of York. Wulfstan was always the practical man of affairs, one who became an invaluable counselor of kings, and there was an attendant moral emphasis to all of his preaching.

He did not, as Aelfric did, write sermons to be delivered by others throughout the Christian year, and there are indeed few of his sermons that can be assigned to particular liturgical occasions, nor did he have even the exegetical interest that Aelfric did. Instead, he left us with the sort of general sermons that would do for many occasions that busy prelates often produce to this very day. His editor Dorothy Bethurum has grouped his sermons into categories that she labels as (1) eschatological, (2) the Christian faith (including catechetical), (3) episcopal functions, and (4) evil days (including especially the *Sermo ad Anglos*[48] in response to the Danish invasions of the time).[49] Among the catechetical sermons, 8 a, b, and c deal directly with baptism; 7 and 7 a concern the Lord's Prayer and the Creed; 9 with the gifts of the Holy Spirit; and 10 a, b, and c spell out the implications of the baptismal vows for Christian living. Bethurum concludes that these catechetical sermons must have been some of Wulfstan's first compositions after becoming an archbishop, and notes that, while he probably wrote them for his own use, he would not have been blind to the possibility that his diocesan clergy might take them for models as well.[50]

This survey has not said all that could be said about Old English preaching in Anglo-Saxon England. It has not dealt with all of the sermons of Aelfric and Wulfstan, being limited to their catechetical preaching. And the other sermons that have survived from that period, such as the anonymous ones in the Blickling and Vercelli collections, have not even been mentioned.[51] Since, however, the purpose of this section has not been to give a definitive review of Anglo-Saxon preaching but rather to take a look at a particular movement in the history of preaching, a particular kind of catechetical preaching, such omissions are inevitable.

CONCLUSION

In trying to survey the various kinds of preaching in the vernacular that are the homiletical legacy of the early Middle Ages, one senses a very mixed batch. We have considered a number of different kinds of sermons. Yet there is an underlying theme that gives unity to the period: the incorporation of newly converted pagans into the Christian faith. Missionary preaching (of which we have no surviving samples) attempted to precipitate such acceptances of the gospel. A good bit of the Carolingian reform was precisely about socializing the newly conquered and christianized masses into their new religion, as the preaching of Hrabanus Maurus shows. Anglo-Saxon catechetical preaching, then, was a response to much the same situation as earlier preaching on the Continent. Even the Latin homiliaries were not irrelevant to catechetical preaching in the vernacular, serving as they did as some of the sources most frequently mined by its practitioners for their teaching material. The homiletical goal of the early Middle Ages was, to use Peter Brown's title, "the rise of Western Christendom."

FOR FURTHER READING

Barré, Henri. "Homéliaires," Columns 597-606 in *Dictionnaire de Spiritualité. Ascétique et mystique, doctrine et histoire. Publié sous la direction de Marcel Viller, S.J., assisté de F. Cavallera et J. de Guibert, S.J., avec la concours d'un grand nombre de collaborateurs.* Paris: G. Beauchesne et ses fils, 1932–95, 7.

Gatch, Milton McC. *Preaching and Theology in Anglo-Saxon England: Aelfric and Wulfstan.* Toronto and Buffalo: University of Toronto Press, 1977.

Grégoire, R. *Homéliaires liturgiques médiévaux: Analyse de manuscrits,* Biblioteca degli 'Studi Medievali,' no. 12. Spoleto: Centro italiano di studi sull'alto Medioevo, 1980.

The Homilies of the Anglo-Saxon Church: The First Part, Containing the Sermones Catholici, or Homilies of Aelfric in the Original Anglo-Saxon, with an English Version. 2 vols. Edited and translated by Benjamin Thorpe. London: Aelfric Society, 1844; reprinted New York: Johnson Reprint, 1971.

McCracken, George E. Pages 302-13 in *Early Medieval Theology.* LCC, vol. 9. Philadelphia: Westminster, 1957.

McKitterick, Rosamond. *The Frankish Church and the Carolingian Reforms, 789–895.* London: Royal Historical Society, 1977.

Neale, J. M. *Mediæval Preachers and Mediæval Preaching.* London: J. C. Mozley, 1856.

Notes

1. Jean Longère, *La prédication médiévale* (Paris: Études augustiniennes, 1983), 48-51.

2. The best short introduction to homiliaries is the article on that subject by Henri Barré in *Dictionnaire de Spiritualité* 7, 597-606. See also R. Grégoire, *Homéliaires liturgiques médiévaux: Analyse de manuscrits,* Biblioteca degli 'Studi Medievali,' no. 12 (Spoleto: Centro italiano di studi sull'alto Medioevo, 1980), 3-39.

3. It is less confusing for this period to refer to the three major orders as bishop, presbyter, and deacon since, for example, Caesarius can refer to bishops as priests.

4. Longère, *La prédication médiévale,* 30-31.

5. For a fuller discussion of monastic preaching, see chapter 8.

6. "*. . . Expositones earum quae a nominatis et orthodoxis catholicis Patribus factae sunt.*" St. Benedict, *Rule for Monasteries,* trans. Leonard J. Doyle (Collegeville, Minn.: The Liturgical Press, 1948), 30.

7. Barré, "*Homéliaires,*" *Dictionnaire de Spiritualité* 7, col. 603.

8. Cyril L. Smetana, "Paul the Deacon's Patristic Anthology" in *The Old English Homily and Its Backgrounds,* ed. with intro. Paul E. Szarmach and Bernard F. Huppé (Albany: State University of New York Press, 1978), 75-97.

9. Paul's collection grew as it was recopied through the centuries and the version of it in PL 95 (1159-1566) is taken from a printed edition of the sixteenth century to which fifty-four sermons have been added and other changes made. Ibid., 87-88.

10. Longère, *La prédication médiévale,* 41-46.

11. J. M. Wallace-Hadrill, *The Barbarian West, 400–1000,* 3rd. ed. (Oxford and New York: Basil Blackwell, 1967), 87-114.

12. Ibid., 102.

13. Rosamond McKitterick, *The Frankish Church and the Carolingian Reforms, 789–895* (London: Royal Historical Society, 1977), 80-114.

14. Wallace-Hadrill, *The Barbarian West,* 99.

15. McKitterick, *The Frankish Church and the Carolingian Reforms,* 81.

16. *Recte et honeste. Admonitio generalis,* c. 82, MGH Cap. I, p. 61.

17. McKitterick, *The Frankish Church and the Carolingian Reforms,* 82.

18. *Ut omnibus festis et diebus dominicis unusquisque sacerdos evangelium Christi populo praedicet. Capitula a sacerdotis poposita,* c. 4. MGH Cap. I, p. 106. Any citations of the capitularies in MGH not explicitly referred to may be found in the notes to the McKitterick chapter noted above.

19. This distinction could also be translated as being between cities and rural areas, but for all practical purposes there is no difference between the two translations. Indeed, it could be argued that one could just as well see this as a distinction between the preaching of bishops and that of presbyters.

20. Tours, "in *rusticam romanam linguam, aut thiotiscam* (Germanic) *quod facilius cuncti possint intellegere*"; Rheims, "*secundum proprietatem linguae*"; the summary of the councils, "*iuxta quod intellegere vulgus possit.*"

21. McKitterick, *The Frankish Church and the Carolingian Reforms,* 85. See also Longère, *La prédication médiévale,* 161-64.

22. McKitterick, *The Frankish Church and the Carolingian Reforms,* 86-87.

23. This title was later given to Luther's disciple Melanchthon as well.

24. The chapter on rhetoric is translated and annotated by Joseph M. Miller in *Readings in Medieval Rhetoric*, ed. Joseph M. Miller, Michael H. Prosser, and Thomas W. Benson (Bloomington: Indiana University Press, 1973), 125-27.

25. Ibid., 127.

26. Hrabanus's homiliaries are discussed in Henri Barré, *Les homéliaires carolingiens de l'école d'Auxerre: authenticité, inventaire, tableaux comparatifs, initia*, Studi e testi, 225 (Vatican City: Biblioteca apostolica vaticana, 1962), 13-17; Longère, *La prédication médiévale*, 41-42, and McKitterick, *The Frankish Church and the Carolingian Reforms*, 97-102.

27. Hrabanus's prefatory letter to Haistulf is translated by John Mason Neale in *Mediæval Preachers and Mediæval Preaching* (London: J. C. Mozley, 1856), 30-31.

28. Ibid.

29. PL 110. That manuscript is Clm 14629 from St. Emmeram.

30. McKitterick, *The Frankish Church and the Carolingian Reform*, 98.

31. Several sermons from this collection are translated respectively by Neale, *Mediæval Preachers and Mediæval Preaching*, 32-43, and George E. McCracken in *Early Medieval Theology*, LCC (Philadelphia: Westminster, 1957), 9:302-13.

32. Canon vii, trans. Milton McC. Gatch, "Basic Christian Education from the Decline of Catechesis to the Rise of Catechisms," in *A Faithful Church: Issues in the History of Catechesis*, ed. John H. Westerhoff III and O. C. Edwards Jr. (Wilton, Conn.: Morehouse-Barlow Co., 1981), 92.

33. PL 110, 135-468.

34. The remark of Longère, *La prédication médiévale*, 42, is not clear.

35. A cathedral chapter was its staff of clergy.

36. P. A. Stafford, "Church and Society in the Age of Aelfric," in Szarmach and Huppé, *The Old English Homily and Its Backgrounds*, 11-42.

37. Gatch, "Basic Christian Education from the Decline of Catechesis to the Rise of Catechisms," 79-91.

38. "Aelfric," ODCC, 2nd ed. (New York: Oxford University Press, 1974).

39. *The Homilies of the Anglo-Saxon Church: The First Part, Containing the Sermones Catholici, or Homilies of Aelfric in the Original Anglo-Saxon, with an English Version*, ed. and trans. Benjamin Thorpe (London: Aelfric Society, 1844), 1:3.

40. Milton McC. Gatch, *Preaching and Theology in Anglo-Saxon England: Aelfric and Wulfstan* (Toronto; Buffalo: University of Toronto Press, 1977).

41. Ibid., 37.

42. Thorpe, *The Homilies of the Anglo-Saxon Church*, 1:8-9.

43. The Monday, Tuesday, and Wednesday before the feast of the Ascension, days of solemn supplication, at the time of planting, for a good harvest.

44. Gatch, *Preaching and Theology in Anglo-Saxon England*, 53.

45. Thorpe, *The Homilies of the Anglo-Saxon Church*, 2:594-609.

46. Gatch, "Basic Christian Education from the Decline of Catechesis to the Rise of Catechisms," 98.

47. Cyril L. Smetana, "Aelfric and the Early Medieval Homiliary," in *Traditio* 15 (1959): 163-204.

48. For a detailed discussion of this sermon see Rachel Jurovics, "*Sermo lupi* and the Moral Purpose of Rhetoric" in Szarmach and Huppé, *The Old English Homily and Its Backgrounds*, 203-20.

49. Dorothy Bethurum, *The Homilies of Wulfstan* (Oxford: Clarendon Press, 1957).

50. Ibid., 299. Bethurum discusses Wulfstan's preaching on pp. 85-98. Gatch also gives an excellent short introduction to the preaching of Wulfstan in *Preaching and Theology in Anglo-Saxon England*, 18-22.

51. For a perspective on these sermons see Gatch, ibid., 119-28. They are discussed in their own right in two articles in Szarmach and Huppé, *The Old English Homily and Its Backgrounds:* Marcia A. Dalbey, "Themes and Techniques in the Blickling Lenten Homilies," 221-40, and Paul E. Szarmach, "The Vercelli Homilies: Style and Structure," 241-67. The Early English Text Society published R. Morris's edition of *The Blickling Homilies of the Tenth Century* (London: published for Early English Text Society by N. Trübner & Co., 1880) and reprinted it as one volume in 1967. For printed editions of the Vercelli manuscript, see the notes at the end of Szarmach's article.

CHAPTER 8

THE RENAISSANCE OF THE ELEVENTH AND TWELFTH CENTURIES

THE PERIOD

The title of this chapter is borrowed from a great historian of monasticism and medieval thought, David Knowles.[1] As applied to the history of preaching, it refers to a shift in consciousness away from the traditionalism that hardly dared to create sermons that were more than a pastiche of patristic quotations. Loyalty to patristic authority remained, but with a difference. There was coming to be the kind of confidence that is reflected in a well-known statement of Bernard of Chartres to the effect that he and his contemporaries were like dwarfs sitting on the shoulders of giants. Though their stature was obviously much, much less than that of their predecessors, the mere fact that they looked out from the vantage point of the accomplishments of the Fathers enabled them to see farther than the Fathers had. While Bernard's words did not refer to preaching in their original context, they nevertheless exemplify the new willingness to risk originality that distinguishes the preaching of this period from what preceded it.

THE REEMERGENCE OF TEXTBOOKS

Guibert of Nogent

We may see the new spirit characteristic of this period in a thirty-year-old monk of St. Geremar Abbey who began to write a commentary on Genesis shortly before 1084. Guibert, who was later to become abbot of Nogent himself, shocked his abbot by daring at such an early age to begin comment on such an exalted topic as the Hexaemeron, the six days of creation, a task undertaken previously by only the most learned and holy Fathers.[2] He continued with the project in secret and was able to complete it shortly after his abbot's death. To this commentary he added what he called "A Book About the Way a Sermon Ought to Be Given."[3] (For the text of this work, see **Vol. 2, pp. 152-63.**)

With the stipulation that Hrabanus's work[4] was a catena of quotations rather than an original work, one can agree with the judgment of Joseph M. Miller that

> none of the writers from the period between the death of Augustine (430) and the First Crusade (1095) had attempted any organized manual for preachers; rather they had confined themselves to exhortations concerning the need for the preacher to live a virtuous life and to know the Bible.[5]

Thus Guibert's homiletical addition to his commentary on Genesis is the first new homiletics textbook since Augustine's *De doctrina christiana*.

Guibert begins his treatise with the sound statement that "it is extremely dangerous for (one) who has the obligation of preaching ever to stop studying." Then he immediately goes off on a digression about the reasons why people try to avoid preaching, apparently under the impression that the duty of preaching should not be confined to bishops or abbots or even to priests, but should be extended to all who "live virtuously and continently" and who "have acquired any knowledge of the sacred page."[6] He even introduces a numerological argument that would lay the duty of preaching on all who are baptized and confirmed.

Such an assumption raises the question of what Guibert meant. Does it include personal witness and private moral instruction? Since Guibert himself was a Benedictine monk, he would not ordinarily have been expected to preach publicly, but he does dedicate his work to a bishop and it may therefore reflect the bishop's needs more than his own. The point is small and the question unanswerable, but it is also nagging because Guibert devotes so much of his discussion to arguing that some persons who were not doing so should be preaching. Who were they? Whatever the answer may be, Guibert reinforces his position by arguing that even preaching undertaken for such an unworthy motive as a desire for fame can be efficacious.

With his exhortation to reluctant preachers out of the way, Guibert then settles down to a lot of sound practical advice on preaching that would be worth following in any age. Preachers are advised to begin their sermons with prayer so that their own devotion will kindle the hearts of their hearers, "for a tepid sermon, delivered half-heartedly, cannot please even the preacher."[7] Sermons that are not going well should not be allowed to go on too long; indeed, even the best should be brief since repetitions and irrelevancies anger the audience and cause them to forget the good they have heard. Only after spiritual and intellectual preparation should the preacher give thought to issues of style. The preacher, however, should always keep in mind those who will hear the sermon. "Though he preaches simple and uncomplicated matter to the unlettered, at the same time he should try to reach a higher plane with the educated."[8]

For Guibert as for Augustine, a preaching manual needs to say something about biblical interpretation because for both preaching is essentially teaching, *doctrina,* and that teaching consists of helping the congregation to know and understand what the Bible teaches. Yet what the Bible teaches is not immediately apparent to all who read it; this teaching must be ascertained through interpretation. Medieval biblical interpretation was based completely on patristic interpretation, and there is very little difference between the hermeneutics of Guibert and Augustine.

Since, however, the Middle Ages did organize the theory of the Fathers more systematically than they themselves had done, the concise statement of the abbot of Nogent is interesting as one of the first clear enumerations of the four senses of Scripture universally accepted in the medieval period.

> There are four ways of interpreting Scripture; on them, as though on so many scrolls, each sacred page is rolled. The first is *history,* which speaks of actual events as they occurred; the second is *allegory,* in which one thing stands for something else; the third is *tropology,* or moral instruction, which treats of the ordering and arranging of one's life; and the last is *ascetics,* or spiritual enlightenment, through which we who are about to treat of lofty and heavenly topics are led to a higher way of life (italics added).[9]

This accords very well with a little verse in circulation as late as the sixteenth century that has been translated as follows:

The letter shows us what God and our fathers did;
The allegory shows us where our faith is hid;
The moral meaning gives us rules of daily life;
The anagogy shows us where we end our strife.[10]

In actual practice, however, sermons seldom dealt with more than one sense. On the whole, the literal, historical sense held little interest, nor were the doctrines that grew out of allegorical interpretation in the strict sense thought appropriate subject matter for preaching. The real concern was the daily lives of Christians and so the tropological sense was emphasized, although occasional glances were given to the anagogical (eschatological) as a way of reinforcing the moral application. Guibert voiced a strong preference in favor of these. And he thought it well to preach negatively about vices as well as positively about virtues:

It seems to me that no preaching is more efficacious than that which would help man to know himself, that which brings out into the open all that is deep within him, in his innermost heart, that which will shame him, finally, by forcing him to stand clearly revealed before his own gaze.[11]

Such preaching can grow out of what the preacher learns of the interior life from reading Gregory and Cassian, but this reading has to be measured against the preacher's own experience. Just as stories of battle are told very differently by those who have been in battle and those who have not, so preaching about moral struggle also profits from obvious existential involvement. The purpose of Guibert's commentary is to supply material for such tropological preaching.

Alan of Lille

After Guibert's, the next textbook on preaching we have is from roughly a century later, *The Art of Preaching* by Alan of Lille.[12] Alan's learning was so conspicuous in his time that he was given the title *Doctor universalis*. He taught at Paris and possibly at Montpellier prior to becoming a Cistercian before his death in 1202, and he wrote a vast number of works ranging not only from philosophical to practical theology but even to poetry as well.[13] While he was basically a theologian, he apparently had, as Gillian Evans has said, "an eye for a gap in the literature of any subject which he himself was competent to fill"[14] and thus he produced works in a number of fields of practical theology, including his preaching manual.

Although there are senses in which the works of Guibert and Alan are
very similar, and while Alan's is very different from the technical *artes
praedicandi* that would begin to appear in such proliferation less than a
generation after his death, so much had transpired in the century after
Guibert wrote that the two books seem to represent different thought
worlds. This was the period in which higher education was passing from
monastic and cathedral schools through the era of individual teachers to
the beginning of the universities. It was also the time in which dialectic
began to dominate theological discussion.[15] This becomes very clear in
Alan's discussion of the outline *(dispositio)* of the sermon. While Alan's
directions for sermon construction and his own homiletical productions
do not yet achieve anything like the formality and complexity recommended for thematic sermons so soon after his death, it is nevertheless
true to say that "several features of Alan's method, especially in the
Sermons themselves, suggest that the manuals of the thirteenth century
formalized a method of preaching which had already been well-tried in
practice."[16]

One of the distinctions of Alan's *Ars* is that in it he gives what James
J. Murphy has described as "the first formal definition (of preaching) in
the 1200-year history of the church":[17]

> Preaching is an open and public instruction in faith and behavior,
> whose purpose is the forming of [persons]; it derives from the path of
> reason and from the fountainhead of the "authorities."[18]

What Alan meant by this definition, especially the roles of reason and
authorities, will emerge as we analyze his method.

The preface to the work is an allegorical interpretation of Jacob's
ladder.

> The ladder represents the progress of the catholic man *(viri catholici)* in
> his ascent from the beginning of faith to the full development of the per-
> fect man. The first rung of this ladder is confession; the second, prayer;
> the third, thanksgiving; the fourth, careful study of the scriptures; the
> fifth, to inquire of someone more experienced if one comes upon any
> point in scripture which is not clear; the sixth, the expounding of scrip-
> ture; the seventh, preaching.[19]

This high evaluation of preaching is something that had not been
heard in the church for quite some time, but shows that it was coming to
be in vogue. The saying has a contemporary parallel in Peter the
Chanter's enumeration of the three stages of biblical study as reading,

disputation, and preaching, "which, like a roof, completes the building of which *lectio* is the foundation and *disputatio* the walls."[20]

Alan begins his manual with a list of what he hopes to accomplish that sounds promising:

> First, then, we must see what preaching is, what form it should take—in the surface aspects of its words, and in the weight of its thoughts—and how many kinds of preaching there are. Secondly, we must consider who the preachers should be; thirdly, to whom the sermon should be delivered; fourthly, for what reasons, and fifthly, in what place.[21]

The question of what preaching is seems to be settled in the definition quoted above, which immediately follows this outline. The form that preaching should take appears also to be dealt with in the treatment of *dispositio* in the first chapter. In the same chapter the three kinds of preaching are said to be that by the spoken word, by the written word, and by deed. At the end of that chapter, though, the treatise seems to get off track with a couple of chapters giving material for sermons about spiritual attitudes. These are followed by seven chapters (4 to 10) supplying homiletical ammunition against vices, after which there are two more on spiritual attitudes, and thirteen on virtues (13-25). Next there are preaching notes on three evil practices followed by nine on devout practices (29-37).

Only in chapter 38, then, does Alan get to his second question of who should preach (prelates, by which he apparently means bishops and abbots, since he refers to the symbolism of their pastoral staffs pointing back toward themselves).[22] In the next chapter he lists the classes to whom preaching should be delivered, following that with chapters on how to preach to eight of the classes mentioned (40-47). All that he says about the reasons for and the site of preaching seems to be in the first chapter: it is for the edification of people and should be done in public.

Why does so much of the treatise seem to be devoted to something other than the topics in the outline? Murphy refers to these chapters as "sample sermonettes" like those provided by Gregory in the *Regula pastoralis* and says elsewhere that Alan's "method in respect to his own definition is the same one he uses elsewhere to amplify ideas in the forty-seven sample sermonettes."[23] Gillian Evans, however, must be correct when she argues that these chapters are not model sermons or sermons in miniature, but are instead rhetorical *topoi*, "stock examples, illustrations, and other commonplaces."[24] Alan's own sermons are always based on only one text, but often in these chapters he suggests a number of possible additional texts. Together with the other material in these chapters, the various texts are,

> as Cicero defines them (in Aristotelian terms), "seats of argument," not arguments fully developed into sequences of argumentation. They are simply collections of source material, and the preacher is intended to draw upon them selectively, taking what he needs for a particular sermon, rather than expanding them as they stand into full-length sermons.[25]

In other words, they are very similar in function to many homiletical aids published today.

Alan begins describing the form of preaching by saying that it should develop from a theological authority, that is, from a quotation from an authoritative document such as the Bible or a work by one of the church fathers. To use the vocabulary of a more modern era, the patristic homily was expository preaching while sermons of the High Middle Ages tended to be textual.

The authority—the biblical verse—that furnished what today would be called the text of the sermon was in those days called the theme. A difference between Alan's preaching textbook and the *artes praedicandi* to come is that sermons constructed according to his method did not develop by dividing the text into three or more parts, and then commenting on several aspects of each. He was more interested in developing the content of the authority/theme/text than in verbal analysis of its component parts. In his opinion, the best texts for preaching come from the Gospels, the psalms, Paul's Epistles, or the books of Solomon. Although Alan does not say so in so many words, the Gospel verses he recommends as texts are Jesus' sayings rather than stories about him, since authorities had to be abstract rather than narrative statements.[26]

Next Alan says that "the preacher must win the good will of his audience through the humility he shows in his own person (what Aristotle called the proof of *ethos*), and through the profitableness of his subject matter."[27] The initial development of the text should not be done in too great a hurry. Other authorities should be used to confirm the first, and even the words of pagan writers can be introduced to good advantage. The preacher "may introduce moving words which soften hearts and encourage tears"[28]—which is to say that the proof of *pathos* may be employed. And the use of examples is encouraged (although by the end of the Middle Ages the church will have had enough of them for a while). Yet, however good the contents of the sermon, it should not be too long. This is the counsel that Alan has to give about developing a sermon.

How well did he follow his own advice? A large number of sermons attributed to him have survived.[29] Unfortunately, relatively few of them have been published. A number of manuscripts contain a *Liber sermonum* of twenty-eight sermons, which accompany *The Art of Preaching* and are intended to exemplify its principles. Evans has translated these, but they have not yet been published.[30] (For one of the sermons from Evans's translation, see **Vol. 2, pp. 163-67.**) Until they are, the best place to sample Alan's preaching is in d'Alverny's book.[31] There she edits:

> three sermons from the *Liber sermonum* (for Epiphany, Palm Sunday, and Michaelmas);
> Six from the *Sermones varii* (for Trinity Sunday, the Birth of St. Augustine, and Ash Wednesday, and occasional sermons for: scholars, a crusade *[de cruce Domini],* and priests at a synod); and
> A cosmological sermon on a pagan text to the effect that God is an intellective sphere of which the center is everywhere and the circumference nowhere.[32]

With the exception of the last mentioned sermon, Alan shows himself to be a good and at times eloquent practitioner of his own principles. In the sermon on the Epiphany, he interprets the gifts of the magi allegorically as representing three of the four senses of Scripture (historical, tropological, and anagogical), showing how basic to biblical interpretation the four senses had become. The sermon on St. Michael and All Angels is also theological, being a homiletical treatise on angelology.

The "authority" or text for his Palm Sunday sermon is Matthew 21:2, "Go into the citadel over against you."[33] The sermon is based on an analogy Alan sees between the governance of a city and the rule of the universe. In a city, those who have wisdom govern, the knights defend the city, and the people obey. In the universe, the Trinity reigns, the angels execute God's orders, and the people are subject to God. With that background Alan proceeds to recite salvation history as though it were a medieval romance in a manner that must have been quite comprehensible and fascinating to a popular audience. This is an example of the way that Alan's sermons are based on a single verse of scripture rather than on an extended passage as a patristic homily would have been. And yet, unlike the later thematic sermon, his is not developed by a division of the authority, but by an exploration of its content. This is to say that he is a transitional figure in the history of preaching.

He preached his sermon promoting the third crusade on the Feast of the Exaltation of the Cross, which celebrated the recovery of the cross from the Persians by the emperor Heraclius in 629. This, of course, was the cross discovered by Helena, the mother of Constantine, which occasioned the erection of the Church of the Holy Sepulchre in Jerusalem in 335. Alan was urging his auditors to do again what Heraclius had done, but he also took time to attribute the loss of the cross to the characteristic sins of different groups of Christians, the sort of *ad status* preaching suggested by his *Ars*.

Alan's synod sermon, based on the Song of Solomon 3:8, identifies Solomon with Christ and the guards of Solomon's litter with the high church officers attending the synod, and is a fearless attack on the sins of the clergy. For all of his mastery of the contemporary hermeneutical and rhetorical arts, Alan shows himself to be committed to the moral improvement of Christian people of all ranks, and both his sermons and his textbook on preaching are means to that end.

MONASTIC PREACHING[34]

While the manuals of Guibert of Nogent and Alan of Lille are principally concerned with preaching to the laity, much of the preaching done during the eleventh and twelfth centuries was addressed to monks. This, of course, had been the case for some time, as we can deduce from the development of homiliaries used in connection with the Night Office.[35] While it is hard to know exactly how much preaching was done on a regular basis in either parishes or monasteries, clearly there was a great renewal of monastic life in the eleventh and twelfth centuries, and preaching was an important aspect of that renewal.

During this period the revival occurred not so much in the great classical order from the patristic period, the Benedictines, as in new forms the religious life was taking.[36] The Benedictines had begun to devote so much of their energy to the elaboration of their liturgy that the amount of time left for the activities that formed the basis of their Rule was diminished. Further, their endowments came to support progressively smaller numbers of monks.

Two kinds of movements arose to fill the gap left by the departure of the Order of St. Benedict from its original vision, the one more practical and the other more contemplative. The more practical reflected the desire of groups of clergy and laity alike who felt called by God to follow a life devoted to good works in the world while living together under a rule. The rule required them to share their possessions completely, wear identical habits, observe set times of prayer together, and obey a superior. Such groups are called Augustinian[37] canons because their very general rules are based on a letter of advice that Augustine wrote to a group of women who wished to live together in community.[38] A good example of this sort of order is that formed by St. Norbert at Prémontré called Norbertines or Premonstratensians.

The more contemplative tendency of these orders is reflected in their desire to return to what was considered a stricter interpretation of the Rule of St. Benedict than contemporary Benedictines seemed capable of making. The principal manifestation of this tendency was formed in 1098 by Robert of Molesme and his companions at Citeaux, who were thus called Cistercians.[39]

What the monastic movement at its best was about was precisely an attempt to "press on toward the goal for the prize of the heavenly call of God in Christ Jesus" (Phil. 3:14). Or, as it was expressed very simply by a modern writer who has sought to discover what the Rule of St. Benedict has to offer laypersons trying to live out their Christian vocation in the world: "the Rule is simply an aid for us to live by the Scriptures."[40] In the prologue of his Rule, Benedict says: "This message of mine is for you, then, if you are ready to give up your own will, once and for all, and armed with the strong and noble weapons of obedience to do battle for the true King, Christ the Lord" (*RB* 1980, 157).

That he was not advocating works rather than grace is seen a little later when he addresses the question raised in Psalm 15:1, "Who will dwell in your tent, Lord, who will find rest upon your holy mountain?" (*RB* 1980, 161). Part of his answer is as follows:

> These people *fear the Lord,* and do not become elated over their good deeds; they judge it is the Lord's power, not their own, that brings about the good in them. *They praise* (Ps 14[15]:4) the Lord working in them, and say with the Prophet: *Not to us, Lord, not to us give the glory, but to your name alone* (Ps 113[115:1]:9). In just this way Paul the Apostle refused to take the credit for the power of his preaching. He declared: *By God's grace I am what I am* (1 Cor 15:10). And again he said: *He who boasts should make his boast in the Lord* (2 Cor 10:17). [*RB* 1980, 163]

The monastic movement at its best was always a way presented to souls so in love with Christ that they would leave all to follow him. Not surprisingly, then, its preaching was always counsel on how that might be done most efficaciously. Indeed, Benedict calls his monastery "a school for the service of the Lord" and a "workshop."[41]

The Sanctification of Time

In order to understand monastic preaching, it is necessary to know something about the context in which it occurred. The daily schedule of the monastery was built around carrying out in the most literal way possible the words of the psalmist: "Seven times a day have I praised you" (118[119]:164 RSV) and "At midnight I rose to give you praise" (118[119]:62 RSV). Thus there is the Morning Office[42] (called Lauds because the psalms of praise are recited). That is followed by Prime at the first hour of the day, Terce at the third, Sext at the sixth, None at the ninth, Vespers in the evening, and Compline before retiring. The monks rise at the eighth hour of the night (2:00 A.M.) for the Night Office (Vigil or Matins).[43]

The monastic day is built around the schedule of the oratory.[44] During these offices the entire Psalter is recited every week, and almost the entire Bible is read during the course of a year. To these biblical elements are joined hymns, responses, and prayers, but the psalms are the core of the office. It is, therefore, no wonder that all monastic preaching is thoroughly sprinkled not only with allusions, especially to the psalms, but also to the rest of the Bible as well. In contemporary American homiletics, probably only African American preachers in the classical tradition are so immersed in biblical language. This life of constant corporate prayer was called *opus Dei,* the "work of God."

Just as prayer is considered to be work, so physical labor is understood as a form of prayer. *Opere est orare,* "to work is to pray," is one of the monks' sayings. The Rule of St. Benedict calls for a number of hours a day to be spent in manual labor on the grounds that "idleness is the enemy of the soul" (chap. 48).[45] As time went on monasteries began to produce, in addition to agricultural products, such things as manuscripts for their own use and that of others, and nonmanual labor came to replace manual labor for some monks, though some sort of work was always expected from all.

The third sort of activity by which monks were expected to fill all their waking hours except those set aside for eating or rest was called *lectio divina,* "sacred reading" in the sense that what was read was sacred. However, this reading involved much more than is normally encompassed today in the concept of spiritual reading. To begin with, people generally read aloud in those days, and there was a good deal of bodily engagement in the process. The reading was a very reflective kind of reading, an activity close to meditation, an activity that involved thinking about what was being read, fixing it in memory, and learning it. This reading was basically biblical but it also included works of some by the Fathers, especially such spiritual writers as Basil and Cassian.[46]

To complete this total preoccupation with the things of the Spirit, silence was observed most of the time and there was reading aloud during meals. It is hard to imagine a life more calculated to remove everything that distracts one from wholehearted concentration upon the things of God.

An enormous amount of monastic homiletical literature has survived from the eleventh and twelfth centuries. In his treatment of it, Jean Longère has parceled it out among the various orders as a means of allowing himself to list the members of each whose sermons have been preserved, enabling him to make concise observations about the preaching of each.[47] Jean Leclercq, however, has argued in *The Love of Learning and the Desire for God* that there is essentially one monastic theology for this period, a theology that stands in marked contrast with the scholastic theology that developed shortly afterward. Since the purpose of this book is to understand movements in the history of preaching rather than to list the names of all famous preachers, it will be convenient to study all of monastic preaching in the work of its greatest practitioner, Bernard of Clairvaux.[48]

Bernard's Life and Significance

Jean Mabillon, the seventeenth-century patristics scholar responsible for the edition of Bernard's works taken over by Migne, made an estimate of Bernard's significance that still has cogency. He called Bernard "the last of the Fathers, but certainly not unequal to the earlier ones."[49] His meaning is similar to Leclercq's thesis that monastic theology is very different from the scholastic theology that succeeded it because monastic theology is simply a continuation of the spirituality of the patristic *expositores* of the Latin Bible.[50] Any just estimate of Bernard's significance must begin with his stature as a spiritual master since all his other accomplishments that made him one of the most respected persons of his age derive from the authenticity and authority of that spirituality.

His life through his early maturity, however, gave no one reason to believe that he would become one of the most influential people in Europe. Born near Dijon in 1090 into a noble family, he seems not to have been intended for the knightly military career followed by his father and commenced by his brothers. He was sent instead to a nearby school of the Canons Regular where he received the sort of good basic education in Latin that was more characteristic of those going into the church than of those who were to bear arms. When he was twenty-one he not only became a monk himself but also took along thirty others to be professed with him. Four of these were his brothers; another brother and his father would follow them later. Some of the thirty left wives, and Bernard also persuaded his sister to trade her husband's house for a convent. His great powers of persuasion were obvious from an early age.

Reflecting the changes in the monastic life that were taking place at the time, he did not go nearby to the historic and powerful Benedictine abbey of Cluny, but instead went a little farther to Citeaux, where Robert of Molesme had founded the Cistercians only fourteen years before. When Bernard arrived, the infant order seemed likely to succumb to an early death, but his recruits gave it a renewed vigor. In only three years he was sent off with a group of companions to found another monastery at Clairvaux. By the time of Bernard's death the order had grown to 350 houses, slightly fewer than half of which were under his authority; he had founded sixty-eight of these himself.

The Rule of St. Benedict depicts the abbot's primary responsibility as forming the monks under him spiritually by his teaching and example (chap. 2), primarily through preaching. At Cluny, for instance, and in other monasteries, this preaching took place twice a day. In the morning before manual labor was begun, the abbot preached to the monks in the cloister, probably on the book being read at meals in the refectory. Then, in the evening when the day's work was over, he delivered, in the fields or wherever the work had been done, a "conference" or "collation" on a text from Scripture, the Rule, or some patristic writing.[51]

For the first nine years after Clairvaux's founding, this preaching was Bernard's main channel of influence. By 1124, however, his reputation for spiritual wisdom had become so widespread that his own monks wanted him to write down some of the things he said to them, and other religious communities began asking him to undertake writing assignments for them, sharing his deep insight into the religious life. By letters and treatises his influence began to radiate even at a time when his austerities were taking their toll on his frail body.

From teaching on the monastic life he expanded first to talk about the differences between the visions of the Cistercians and those of Cluny. Then he was asked to say what the life and work of bishops should be like. He became involved in the organization of the Knights Templar, trying to show how an order of military men could live a communal life of devotion even when engaged in warfare. Next he rallied the French church and then the Italian church behind Innocent II against the antipope Anacletus, a struggle that took eight years.

During all this time he still taught his monks when he was able to stay in Clairvaux, wrote books that have become spiritual classics, and even persuaded a number of students at the University of Paris to become monks. He became involved in trying to point out errors in faith; his role in the condemnations of Abelard and Gilbert de la Porrée is almost the only aspect of his life that is ever criticized—and even then the importance of the theological issues he raised is recognized. He was sent to the south of France to preach against the heretical teachings of Peter of Bruy and his disciple Henry of Lausanne, who were in some respects predecessors of the Waldensians. When one of his former disciples became pope as Eugenius III, Bernard acceded to his request and preached the second crusade. After his unsuccessful efforts to give the crusade the spiritual dimension that had become obscured, he was blamed for the crusade's failure.

In response to another request from Eugenius, he wrote a treatise on papal spirituality entitled *Consideration*—which, among other things, contained a violent attack on the Curia. Time and time again he was called from the monastery he loved to serve the church in some reconciling faction. He lived a life so devoted to the love of God that, less than a century after his death, Dante would see him replacing even the beloved Beatrice as guide when the poet arrived at the Empyrean. Bernard was the one who introduced Dante to the Blessed Virgin Mary, preparing the way for his beatific vision of God. Few preachers in the history of the church have been so admired as he both by his contemporaries and by Christians of all varieties who came after him.

Bernard the Preacher

As Gillian Evans has said: "Bernard was above all a talker; almost everything he wrote arose out of his sermons or discourses."[52] The standard edition of his works runs to thirty-five hundred pages, of which roughly twenty-one hundred purport to be sermonic literature, and even more grew out of what had originally been sermons.[53] How close any of this is to the words this great talker actually spoke, however, is a question of enormous complexity.[54] The question has less to do with whether Bernard is the author of these works than it does with their literary genre.

While there are at least three major manuscript traditions for most of his works, these usually represent different stages in his writing process rather than efforts of others to create bernardine pseudepigrapha. There is often an earlier, shorter recension; a later, longer one; and then a final version that he edited near the end of his life. So most of the works are genuine enough; the real question is whether they are sermons in the sense of being words that he spoke to a congregation. Certainly they follow the literary genre of sermons and include many conventions of oral presentation, such as an aside to his audience that he had to break off his talk because visitors to the monastery were waiting for him. Nevertheless, the systematic treatment given to topics, often extended over a number of sermons, indicates that in the developed form in which we have them, these writings are to be understood as treatises cast in the literary genre of sermons.[55]

That being the case, one might ask whether such writings should be considered in a history of preaching. There are cogent reasons why they should. First, it seems likely that these works usually had their origin in Bernard's preaching, giving us some indication not only of what he said but also of how he talked about it. Second, they are still the best indication we have of what the sermons of one of the great preachers of all time must have been like. Furthermore, there is one section of the literature that gives good promise of going back to the actual oral delivery of Bernard himself.

The materials categorized as *Sentences* and *Parables* seem to represent either sketches of the arguments of Bernard's sermons or stories that he told in their course taken down by members of his audience either while he was delivering them or shortly afterward. They give us an authentic flavor of Bernard's actual preaching and furnish criteria to distinguish between the elements of his treatises in the genre of sermons that reflect his preaching practice and those that do not.

Finally, treatises written in the genre of sermons were often intended either to be read aloud to monks in the place of live preaching or to be used by them in their *lectio divina;* in either case they served much the same function as actual sermons in the spiritual formation of monks. For instance, Bernard's *Homilies in Praise of the Virgin Mary,* which are among his earliest works, were written when illness caused him to be separated from the monks of his monastery and were used as a substitute for what he would have said to them if he had been with them.[56]

From the remaining materials a picture emerges showing the way that Bernard preached to his monks. As noted above, the purpose of this preaching was to enable them to forsake all bondage in self-will so that they could give themselves completely to God. The content of this preaching was profoundly biblical and patristic, and it dealt much more with practical issues of the spiritual life than it did with speculative thought. Most of his sermons were in the form of commentary—usually on a passage from the Bible, although a text could be taken from the Rule of St. Benedict or the writings of the Fathers.

Although Bernard's sermons at times involved the detailed study of short passages (he wrote a commentary on the Song of Songs consisting of eighty-six sermons without getting past the first verse of the third chapter), his exegesis was spiritual rather than academic. He certainly did not engage in multiple divisions of texts of the sort that thematic preachers would carry to excess a few years after his death. Rather, his preaching shared the fruits of his own *lectio divina*, his own meditation on the Scriptures to which he, like other monks, devoted time not required for corporate prayer and work. The purpose of modeling his own *lectio* was to show the monks how to deepen their own. As Gillian Evans has said,

> No one who had heard Bernard expound the text of the Bible could read it afterwards without perceiving new depths in it. This is what Bernard intended—to form habits of perceptive and reflective reading in his monks which they could use in their own private *lectio divina*.[57]

Bernard's Homiletical Writings

With this background it is now possible to look at Bernard's various preaching materials either grouped together by him as continuous works or collected by others. This survey will illustrate not only the range of Bernard's proclamation but the variety of monastic preaching in general as well. It will show especially what portions of Scripture were most influential in the spiritual formation of religious, both male and female.

Sentences and Parables

The word *sententia* has a number of possible meanings in classical and medieval Latin, but when used to describe Bernard's work it has the sense of résumé or outline. Since many of the sermons summarized are organized around a number of different categories of something (two advents, three degrees of obedience, four animals, etc.), one may assume that the outline is accurate enough. There are many sermon collections in monastic literature, some taken entirely from one preacher and others from a variety. The content of the sermons thus epitomized is typical monastic preaching, summing up the accepted wisdom of what it means to be faithful to one's vocation in a manner reminiscent of *Words of the Elders* in the earliest monastic tradition.

These sermons tend to be quite short, especially in the first two series of Bernard's *sententiae* that were already collected as early as Mabillon and therefore appeared in Migne. Sometimes they are no longer than a "sentence" in its modern English sense of one complete statement; the 231 *sententiae* of the first two series occupy only fifty-one pages of the Leclercq and Rochais edition. Those collected and established as authentic since the time of Mabillon, which make up the third series of Leclercq-Rochais, tend to be much fuller (127 *sententiae* in 196 pages). However

189

detailed the outline, the content still consists of practical advice on how to advance in the spiritual life by fidelity to one's monastic vows.

As the name suggests, the *Parabolae* are not sermon outlines but sermon illustrations taken from Bernard's preaching.[58] While the Leclercq-Rochais edition of Bernard's works has only eight of these grouped together under this rubric, others appear in the *sententiae* and elsewhere in Bernard's sermons. The titles of these eight suggest the kinds of stories they are: the king's son, the conflict of two kings, the king's son sitting on a horse, the church that was captive in Egypt, a king's three sons, the Ethiopian woman married by the king's son, the eight beatitudes, and the king and the beloved servant. To anyone acquainted with New Testament scholarship, these illustrations will seem more like allegories than true parables in that they are decoded term by term. Unlike Anselm, who told his story first and then applied it, Bernard made his identifications as he went along, which gave him greater narrative spontaneity.

Sermones per Annum

Bernard's sermons for use throughout the church year[59] include some for both Sundays and saints' days. The *temporale* covers the time from the first Sunday in Advent to Pentecost, including the fixed feasts between Christmas and Epiphany, but makes little provision for the Sundays after Pentecost. Lent is provided for by the series on "Qui habitat," the Ninety-first Psalm,[60] which also appears as a separate work in the manuscript tradition. The *sanctorale* is largely limited to New Testament saints and events, with provision for only a few postbiblical commemorations: those of Benedict, Malachy (an Irish archbishop who had recently died), Martin, Clement, and the superior general of the Dominicans, Humbert of Romans.

Leclercq has discovered two kinds of evidence that point overwhelmingly to the literary character of the collections of liturgical sermons. First, all the sermons for a particular season, such as, for instance, Epiphany, fit together as a "logical and organized treatise" on the significance of that season.[61] Further, the sequence of thought within individual sermons and the collection as a whole indicates that the entire collection was envisaged by Bernard as a vast commentary on the liturgical year, given its shape by the succession of seasons and feasts.

The other sort of evidence is the degree of literary polish in the sermons. Bernard was one of the greatest preachers of all time, but even he could not have attained such literary perfection speaking from a brief outline. And, even if he could, no one at the time could have taken it all down, since there was no system of shorthand in use then. Besides, we have examples of Bernard's familiar style, and it is not similar to the style of these sermons. Thus the great liturgical sermons are to be viewed as examples of Bernard's written rather than oral art.

Sermones de Diversis

The *Sermons on Various Subjects* are exactly what the name suggests, a collection lacking homogeneity.[62] Sometimes this has also been called "Short Sermons," but that description does not fit everything included in the collection. The variegated nature of the material and its history of having been garnered by a succession of editors from many sources render it inevitable that every stage between oral and literary sermons be represented here.[63] This variety also means that it is much harder in this collection to distinguish what is genuinely bernardine than it is in other series. About all that can be said about these sermons is that most are based on biblical texts, they often receive their outline from a list of categories, and they are applied to the spiritual lives of monks.

Sermones super Cantica Canticorum

Bernard's *Sermons on the Song of Songs*[64] are at once his acknowledged masterpiece and the portion of his work that is most alien to contemporary consciousness. It is hard for people who have been brought up on historical-critical biblical interpretation to take seriously the idea that the Bible's great paean to human sexual love is about the soul's growing attachment to God. Many find it embarrassing to take an expression so graphically carnal as "Let him kiss me with the kiss of his mouth" as an expression of their feelings about God. Yet this tradition goes back far beyond Bernard. The doubt in Origen's mind was whether the bride referred to the individual soul or to the church. In the latter interpretation he had the precedent of Jewish exegesis that understood the bride as Israel. As Brevard Childs has said,

> The theological reasoning behind the allegorical interpretations was not obscure. The Song of Songs formed part of the canon of sacred scripture, indeed, in the Jewish tradition it was read as part of the passover liturgy. Did it not then follow that the book must have a sacred meaning if it had been incorporated into this sacred context?[65]

Add to that the fact that the best analogy human beings have ever been able to find to the love of God has always been their own erotic/romantic love, and the perennial appeal of such spiritual interpretation of the Canticles is not hard to understand.[66]

Certainly the theme was popular enough in Bernard's day. Bernard himself testifies to that in what is probably his best-known work, his treatise *On Loving God (De diligendo Deo)*.[67] Longère is able to list five other commentators on the Canticles from Bernard's Cistercian order alone.[68] Bernard lived, after all, in the age of the troubadours and minstrels, the age of courtly love. It was not only in Christian Europe, however, that a spirituality of love emerged in the twelfth century. During this same period Jewish kabbalistic mystics were also writing commentaries on the Song of Songs; Muslim Sufi masters were celebrating the lovableness of God in the divine beauty; Hindus were composing their own equivalent to the Canticles, their *Gita Govinda;* and Buddhists were experiencing their Tantric and Pure Land movements.[69] How fascinating it would be if historians using the methodology of the sociology of knowledge could come up with an explanation for why this same powerful motif sprang up in so many different and widely separated cultures simultaneously.

Refuting the conclusion of previous research that "St Bernard's *Sermons on the Song of Songs* appeared in book form and were also delivered as talks," Leclercq has argued cogently from a variety of evidence that the sermons as we have them constitute a treatise on the monastic life in the literary genre of a series of homilies.[70] In this series, however, it is possible to see how a treatise of Bernard disguised as sermons related to sermons he had really preached. In his account of the life of Bernard, William of St. Thierry tells of how the two of them lay sick together shortly after Bernard became abbot and Bernard expounded to him the moral sense of the Canticles.[71] Further, various disciples of Bernard have recollected hearing him preach on the Canticles, and there are several sermons in the *Sentences* on texts from this biblical book, some of which employ illustrations that are used in the *Sermons* for the same texts. Finally, Mabillon and Migne after him published William's work entitled *Brevis Commentatio ex Sancti Bernardi Sermonibus Contexta* that appears to be "the frame on which Bernard wove his work on the *Sermons*."[72]

Thus Leclercq concludes:

> We do not have the actual spoken sermons which Bernard delivered on the Song of Songs. But we can well believe that they were more developed than the text of the *Brevis Commentatio,* and on the other hand less polished than the text of the published *Sermons*.[73]

192

In both his literary *Sermons* and the homilies that he actually delivered in chapter, Bernard wooed monks to progress in their spiritual lives through the love of God, "devotion to the sacred humanity" of Christ.[74]

Sermones in laudibus Virginis Matris

"To this fervent love for Jesus Christ was joined a most sweet and tender devotion toward his glorious mother."[75] This estimate of Pope Pius XII is confirmed by Henri Barré, who called Bernard the "Marian Doctor *par excellence*."[76] This is not to say, however, that Bernard contributed anything to the elaboration of Marian doctrine, especially not in the three developments occurring during his lifetime, the belief that Mary was conceived without inheriting original sin, that her body was assumed into heaven when she died, and that she is the spiritual mother of all Christians. Instead, Bernard drew all of his understanding of the Blessed Mother from the Bible and the Fathers. "But what our author lacks in theological adventuresomeness (a lack which some of us will be inclined to applaud), he more than makes up for in intensity and beauty of expression."[77] This intensity and beauty of expression are probably seen at their best in the second of his homilies when he picks up on Jerome's etymological interpretation of the name Mary as meaning "Star of the Sea."

Bernard's *Four Homilies in Praise of the Virgin Mother* are his earliest writing on the subject and his most complete treatment of it.[78] They were written shortly after he became abbot at a time when he had become ill over his exertions and also over some estrangement from his monks that was already being healed. The bishop of Châlons, William of Champeaux, asked that the young abbot be placed under his spiritual direction for a year, an extremely unusual measure justified by the need to save Bernard's life. This time was spent in retreat and recuperation in a shack similar to those built for lepers.

There, in order to maintain some contact with his monks, he composed these sermons.[79] Because they are on texts from the story of the annunciation, they are also known as the sermons on *Missus est*, the first words of the story in the Vulgate ("The angel Gabriel *was sent*"). Obviously, because he wrote them for his monks when he was away from the monastery, these sermons were not delivered, but they were written to be read to the community in his absence. They nevertheless serve the same essential purpose as all his monastic preaching: "The purpose of all Bernard's preaching on the Virgin and her Son is to make the reader alive to the detailed implications of the Nativity story for his own spiritual and active life."[80]

Ad Clericos de Conversione

Bernard not only preached to those who were already monks but to secular clerics as well to persuade them to become monks. The clergy in question were not all in major orders; most students of the time were at least in minor orders, and it was to students that the original oral form of this "sermon" was addressed. The "conversion" in question was not that of becoming Christians but of becoming monks. As Marie-Bernard Saïd has pointed out, the situation Bernard was addressing was essentially that described in Helen Waddell's *The Wandering Scholars:* "Among the vagrant student population there were genuine scholars, but there were also those of the 'baser type, the unfrocked or runaway monk or clerk.'"[81]

Bernard was debatably the most influential person in Europe when his duties took him through Paris sometime between Lent 1139 and early 1140. The bishop asked him to preach, but at first he refused. The next day, however, he felt moved by God to do so, and a number of clerics gathered to hear him. At least three of them were persuaded to become monks, including Geoffrey of Auxerre, who later became his secretary and then biographer.[82]

On Conversion: A Sermon to Clerics exists in two manuscript editions, one shorter and the other longer. The shorter ends with section 31 at the conclusion of a commentary on the Beatitudes where Bernard says, "But I am tiring you with this rambling sermon."[83] It is assumed that this shorter version is what Bernard actually preached and that the longer version represents his later polishing of the text for publication, together with the addition of some remarks about the morals of clergy at the time and a depiction of the faithful pastor's life. Saïd observes that Bernard makes this treatise do for the priesthood what *De moribus et officio episcoporum* does for bishops and *De consideratione* does for the pope.[84]

This, however, is an afterthought, because the basic thrust of the preached shorter edition, which is approximately four-fifths the length of the longer, is the affirmation that the surest way to heaven is afforded by the opportunity the monastic life gives to rid oneself of every distraction and devote oneself completely to the love of God.

Bernard's Other Sermons

Not all of Bernard's preaching was monastic, but all that has been preserved is. It is especially regrettable that all examples of his preaching in support of the crusades against heresy and for the recovery of the tomb of Christ are lost. There are, however, some indications of the sorts of things he might have said. Sermons 65 and 66 on the Canticles seem to have been written in response to a request from Eberwin (or Evervin) of Steinfeld, prior of a Premonstratensian community near Cologne, for Bernard to speak out against heretics of a Catharist variety in his vicinity.[85] There are also several indications of what Bernard's preaching of the second crusade may have been like. It was Bernard who wrote the Rule for the great crusading order, the Knights Templar, and he also wrote a treatise, *In Praise of the New Knighthood*.[86] There also exists an exciting account of his preaching the crusade at Vézelay on Palm Sunday 1146, when so many came forward to receive the cloth cross that signified their enlistment that Bernard had to tear up his own clothing to make more crosses.[87] At first he opposed the crusade, but when his former pupil Pope Eugenius III asked him to preach it, he complied without question. Yet Bernard's feeling for the Templars was a result of their being a religious order so that even in preaching the crusade there is some sense that Bernard's preaching was monastic preaching.

De Psalmo "Qui habitat"

So far this section has looked at the various collections of Bernard's sermonic material rather than at any particular sermon. It has also emphasized types of monastic preaching rather than the specific content of such sermons. Justice is done to this tradition and its greatest exemplar only by looking at an individual sermon. A good example of the body of work in general, and one that comes closer to oral preaching than many, is the sixth of the Lenten sermons on Psalm 91. (For this sermon, see **Vol. 2, pp. 167-71**.)

Manuscripts of this sermon series fall into three categories: (1) a short form in which commentary is made on only the first six verses of Psalm 91, (2) a longer form that extends the commentary through verse 10, and (3) the final form that makes this series a commentary on the sixteen verses of the psalm, the only commentary from Bernard other than the sermons on the Song of Songs.[88] Since the short manuscripts divide their six sermons into thirty fragments, these may closely resemble notes from which Bernard actually preached to his monks over one Lenten season. The complete form of the work, however, shows too many signs of overall design and finished prose style to be anything but a treatise written in the literary genre of the sermon. Or, more properly, it is written in the literary genre of the homily, since the sermons are verse-by-verse expositions of the passage.

The commentary, of course, is not so much concerned with the literal, historical meaning of the psalm as it is with applying the psalm's meaning to the lives of monks.[89] We may see the way that is done in Sermon 6 on the second part of verse 5 and all of verse 6,[90] which read as follows:

> You will not fear the terror of the night;
>   nor the arrow that flies by day,
> nor the bogy that prowls in the darkness,
>   nor assault, nor the noonday devil.[91]

The sermon identifies the four dangers listed with temptations faced by monks. The terror of the night is fear of the vexations of the body that appear as temptations during the night. The arrow that flies by day is the vainglory of those who have overcome carnal temptations and thus appear fervent. The bogy that prowls in the darkness is not considered to be an external enemy like the first two, but the treason from within of ambition. These three are equated with the three temptations that came to Jesus (in the Matthean order), but the Tempter did not try on him the fourth: the noonday devil. This is the temptation to regard what is evil as though it were not only good but perfect. After showing how these temptations have beset the church throughout its history, Bernard ends by reminding the brothers that he had dealt with these temptations in one of his sermons on the Song of Songs (Sermon 33), where he connected the noonday devil with the noonday rest of the bridegroom.

Scripture is used here not to inquire into how this psalm reflects the experience of those who journeyed to Jerusalem for one of the pilgrim feasts, the literal, historical meaning of the text. Rather, it borrows familiar language that is recited at least once a week to put into words the monks' experiences in evading temptation. Bernard belonged to a community so saturated with the vocabulary of the Bible that it was the most natural thing in the world to borrow its phrases to describe whatever was going on.[92] In this sermon he makes use of the words not only of Psalm 91 but of much of the rest of the canon as well; Sermon 6 fills only seven pages printed with very wide margins, but there are fifty-seven biblical allusions. This incidence of allusion is by no means exceptional.

Jean Leclercq is able to say that Bernard uses Scripture in both senses of the word:

> First, it is a text that predates his own experience and thinking. . . . He was able to interpret his experience only because it had its continual source in the Church. He could thus similarly understand the solution that the Spirit of God brought to his problems, or more exactly, to the problem that he had with himself.[93]

It is also a pretext in that it becomes an occasion to talk about God's love for souls. "God continues to speak in the words he has left us and through his Spirit, who continues in us the work he began with the biblical writers."[94] Thus

> We are asked to remove the cover and find the hidden contents within; in this way, sacred history, which is universal, objective, impersonal, and external, becomes *our* history.

This is to say that Bernard did what all good preachers have done down through the ages: he applied the Scriptures to the lives of his hearers. This shows the fundamental kinship of monastic preaching with all effective preaching. It also shows that monastic preaching was an important expression of the homiletic aspect of the eleventh- and twelfth-century renaissance.

"YOUR DAUGHTERS SHALL PROPHESY"[95]

Another aspect of this renaissance was the appearance of women who preached with the approval of the Catholic Church in the West. While it seems very likely that women preached in the subapostolic church and perhaps into the second century,[96] records of who they were, what they said, and how they said it have been lost or expunged.[97] Through the ages, schismatic and heretical bodies—from the early Montanists to the Waldensians and Catharists to be studied in the next chapter—have been much more open to women's voices than the Great Church. The twelfth century, however, proves an exception to the rule: a number of women are known to have preached with church approval. Some of these were abbesses addressing their own nuns in the absence of a priest, but the best-documented examples are of women who invoked a different justification for their activity in the face of culturally engrained misogyny, tradition, and explicit biblical statements such as the Pauline prohibition: "Women should be silent in the churches" (1 Cor. 14:34). As Carolyn Muessig has said, "When a teaching or preaching woman is encountered in twelfth- or thirteenth-century medieval sources, her ability to speak about divine matters is generally attributed to a charism of prophecy rather than intelligence."[98]

These women include Rose of Viterbo[99] and Umiltà of Faenza.[100] There is no doubt, however, that their most impressive representative was Hildegard of Bingen. This is true not only because of her preaching, but also because of the range of her activities. No other medieval woman and few men of the time wrote as extensively as she did, or in as many genres. She produced three massive theological tomes in a visionary format. She wrote works of science, including a medical guide. She provided the words and music for liturgical texts and created the first morality play—the only one in which all parts are sung except that of the devil. She was consulted personally and through correspondence by a variety of persons, including bishops and heads of religious houses, members of the nobility, and ordinary people. Her correspondents included a pope, an emperor, and even Bernard of Clairvaux. And, besides preaching to her sisters, she went on several long preaching tours, stopping at monasteries, convents, and cathedral cities as a welcome guest of the hierarchy. She overcame obstacles of opposition by male officials and held on to what she thought she should do. And all of this was accomplished despite her being sick a great deal of the time.

Born in 1098 as the tenth child of wealthy and well-connected parents, Hildegard was precociously religious, having her first visionary experience before she was five. When she was eight, her parents offered her as a tithe of their children to the religious life. She was enclosed—literally, walled up—as an anchoress in a cell attached to the Benedictine monastery of Disibodenberg, where she served as a sort of apprentice hermit under Jutta, the young, beautiful, talented, devout, and determined daughter of a local count. The deep spirituality of the pair quickly attracted disciples, and their cell was transformed into a Benedictine community for women. Hildegard made her profession when she was fifteen.

Almost nothing is known of her next twenty-three years. But in 1136 Jutta died, and Hildegard succeeded her as abbess. Although she had continued to have visions, she had revealed them only to Jutta, who in turn spoke of them to Volmar, one of the monks there who was destined to become one of Hildegard's closest collaborators. In 1141, however, she had a vision that surpassed anything she had experienced before. It left her with the feeling that she "knew the meaning of the exposition of the scriptures, namely the Psalter, the Gospel, and the other catholic volumes of both the Old and the New Testaments."[101] With the understanding came a command from God to write the visions she had received. For a long time she resisted the command, but when she fell into sickness, she interpreted that as a sign of divine disfavor, so she began the ten-year-long process of writing what she had seen and heard and the understanding of it she had received. While she was writing, her project came to the attention of Pope Eugenius, who read what she had done and commanded her to finish the work.

While she was still at work on this book, which she called *Scivias* (a contraction of the Latin for "Know the ways of the Lord"), the project attracted a great deal of attention. Suddenly Hildegard announced that God had commanded her to move the convent thirty kilometers away to Rupertsberg, a hill overlooking the Rhine near the town of Bingen. When the abbot of Disibodenberg refused to let them go for various reasons, she fell ill again, until he was convinced that her illness was a sign and allowed them to make the move. *Scivias* is an enormous book, running to just under five hundred pages in the Hart and Bishop translation. It recounts twenty-six visions and their much longer interpretations, but the subject, as the name implies, is the virtues needed by persons in various walks of life to attain paradise.

Her second great work, *Liber vitae meritorum (The Book of Life's Merits)* on which she worked from 1158 to 1163, is devoted to the vices that oppose the virtues considered in the *Scivias*. Then, from 1163 to 1174 she composed her most ambitious work, *Liber divinorum operum (Book of Divine Works)*. This book

> can be seen as a triumph of synthesis in which Hildegard brings together her theological beliefs, her physiological understanding, her speculations on the working of the human mind and of the structure of the universe, into a unified whole.[102]

During the time she was at work on these three volumes of her visionary *summa*, she was also busy as the head of a religious community, occupied with an international correspondence and preaching tours, composing music for the liturgy, and aging—turning seventy-six the year she finished the *Liber divinorum operum*. This makes it all the more astonishing that during the same period, she also summed up and may even have contributed to her age's knowledge of nature in two large scientific works, her *Physica (Natural History)* and a medical treatise, *Causae et curae (Causes and Cures)*. The *Physica* has sections on plants, the elements, trees, jewels and precious stones, fish, birds, animals, reptiles, and metals, and is primarily concerned with their medical use. This work and *Causae et curae* have led to speculation over whether Hildegard filled her spare time by serving as the convent's infirmarian.

While it would be interesting to discuss the haunting beauty of Hildegard's liturgical music, now accessible through a number of recordings, or the vivid illustrations that illuminate her visionary trilogy, it is her preaching that is the proper concern of these pages. Although she took four preaching tours, preaching before both religious houses and the clergy and laity at large, what is best preserved is the preaching she did as the one responsible for the formation and ultimately for the salvation of her own community. While she included copies of some of her sermons in her correspondence, the main source for her sermons is *Expositiones evangeliorum (Expositions of the Gospels)*.[103] These are homilies on the Gospels for twenty-four days in the liturgical calendar.

In addition to her mandate as an abbess, Hildegard based her authority to preach on the prophetic calling responsible for her great visionary trilogy, which also was the justification for her advising a pope, an emperor, bishops and abbots, members of the nobility, and laypersons through correspondence. It is not surprising, therefore, that some of the main themes of the *summa* recur in both the letters and in the homilies.[104] These themes are also reflected in the fact that, while there is only one homily in the *Expositiones* for many of the feasts, for others there are two, three, and even four, each with its distinctive interpretation.

While Hildegard's interpretation is invariably allegorical, it does not correspond to the traditional four levels of meaning in medieval exegesis: literal/historical, allegorical, moral, and anagogical. Rather, she is closer to Origen's distinction between literal and spiritual meaning. But there are four themes or patterns to her interpretation, themes that are tantalizingly and confusingly close to the four traditional meanings, but are never coextensive with them. These themes are: (1) the collective struggle of humankind in salvation history, (2) the journey of the faithful soul, (3) the individual and collective battles against sin that the nun and her community wage in monastic life, and (4) the cosmological theme of the harmony of cosmic elements reestablished with the soul's restoration.[105]

We may see how this plays out in Hildegard's reading of the Gospel for the First Sunday of Advent, Luke 21:25-33, the only Gospel on which four homilies have been preserved. (For the text of these sermons, see **Vol. 2, pp. 172-77.**) There are two elements in this pericope from Luke's version of "the Little Apocalypse," the signs of the end of the age and the *Parousia,* and the parable of the fig tree's leaves as a sign of the times. Hildegard is rare among medieval exegetes in interpreting the parable and connecting it with the signs of the end.

While the first of her homilies for the day is designated in a manuscript as dealing with the literal meaning, it also has a cosmological dimension. The signs of the end are seen as indications of the reaction of the cosmos and angels to human sin. In the fourth homily, the interpretative pattern is that of the drama of the individual soul. A typical theme of the war between virtues and vices can be observed in this psychodrama of both the individual nun and the community as a whole. We can see in these two homilies a familiar Hildegardian theme of playing off microcosm versus macrocosm. The second homily, designated in the manuscript as allegorical, demonstrates Hildegard's concern in resisting the spread of Catharism from France to the Rhineland. And the third homily, which employs the motif of the battle between vices and virtues, seems to have been an expression of Hildegard's concern over the schism in Germany from 1159 to 1177 when her patron, the emperor Frederick Barbarossa, supported anti-popes against the one to whom she was loyal.

As Kienzle says,

> The set of four homilies highlights the spiritual meaning of the text. One is primarily historical-literal, concerned with salvation history, Christ's coming and redemption; another, a psychodrama, is highly allegorical with elements of anagogy. Two moral interpretations relate to contemporary society. . . .[106] Nonetheless, all are primarily spiritual and three of four include a cosmological dimension. These four homilies... demonstrate the richness of Hildegard's exegetical range in the entire corpus of *Expositiones*.[107]

There have been many attempts to account for Hildegard's visions psychologically or medically. Sabina Flanagan, for example, offers a plausible case for regarding them as a function of migraines.[108] Since allowing women to preach not only then but down through the twentieth century has been justified by stating they were prophets rather than clergy, such interpretations need assessment. There is no need to reject such analyses: much of what God does in human history is mediated through the ordinary processes of nature (themselves the creations of God). But the analysis alone can be reductionistic, implying that the visions were nothing but migraine, or hallucination, or delusion. The difficulty with this analysis is that from biblical times onward, some of the human beings most honored for their contributions to human spirituality and morality have claimed that their insights were communicated to them in manners that today could result in their being certified as insane. If these people were crazy, we all should be so crazy. Yet there have been those who insisted that they were prophets who were either victims of pathology or charlatans. The question becomes how to distinguish between true and false prophets. The only criterion still seems today to be the pragmatic one offered by Jesus: "You will know them by their fruits" (Matt. 7:16, 20).

The stage in the history of preaching represented by Guibert, Alan, Bernard, and Hildegard was truly a renaissance. As such, it was the homiletical manifestation of the vigorous intellectual awakening of the eleventh and twelfth centuries, and its quality was consistent with all the best of the movement's other aspects. Thus it has significance in its own right and also constitutes necessary preparation for the great outburst of preaching that was about to occur.

FOR FURTHER READING

Alan of Lille: The Art of Preaching. Translated with an introduction by Gillian R. Evans. Cistercian Studies Series, no. 23. Kalamazoo, Mich.: Cistercian Publications, 1981.

Bernard of Clairvaux. *Bernard of Clairvaux, Sermons on Conversion: On Conversion, A Sermon to Clerics, and Lenten Sermons on the Psalm, "He Who Dwells."* Translated with an introduction by Marie-Bernard Saïd. Cistercian Fathers Series, no. 25. Kalamazoo, Mich.: Cistercian Publications, 1981.

Evans, G. R. *Alan of Lille: The Frontiers of Theology in the Later Twelfth Century.* Cambridge and New York: Cambridge University Press, 1983.

Flanagan, Sabina. *Hildegard of Bingen, 1098–1179: A Visionary Life.* London and New York: Routledge, 1989.

Guibert of Nogent. "The Way a Sermon Ought to Be Given." In *Readings in Medieval Rhetoric.* Translated by Joseph M. Miller, edited by Joseph M. Miller, Michael H. Prosser, and Thomas W. Benson, 162-81. Bloomington and London: Indiana University Press, 1973.

Hildegard of Bingen. *Hildegard of Bingen: Expositions of the Gospels.* Translated by Beverly Mayne Kienzle and Fay Martineau. Kalamazoo, Mich.: Cistercian Publications, forthcoming.

Leclercq, Jean. *The Love of Learning and the Desire for God: A Study of Monastic Culture.* Translated by Catharine Misrahi. New York: Fordham University Press, 1961, 1974.

Notes

1. David Knowles, *The Evolution of Medieval Thought* (New York: Vintage Books, 1962), 71-149.

2. Guibert's account of this event is recorded in a portion of his *Memoirs* in *Rhetoric in the Middle Ages: A History of Rhetorical Theory from St. Augustine to the Renaissance*, trans. James J. Murphy (Berkeley and Los Angeles: The University of California Press, 1974), 301. For the complete work, see *A Monk's Confession:*

The Memoirs of Guibert of Nogent, trans. with intro. Paul J. Archambault (University Park, Pa.: Pennsylvania State University Press, 1996).

3. *Liber quo ordine sermo fieri debeat*, PL 156, cols. 21-32. A translation of this by Joseph M. Miller appeared in *Today's Speech* 17 (1969), 46ff.; reprinted in *Readings in Medieval Rhetoric*, ed. Joseph M. Miller, Michael H. Prosser, and Thomas W. Benson (Bloomington: Indiana University Press, 1973), 162-81.

4. Discussed in chapter 7.

5. Miller, Prosser, and Benson, *Readings in Medieval Rhetoric*, 162.

6. Ibid., 164-65. *Sacra pagina* was a technical term for the study of the Bible made by medieval students who had completed their studies of the liberal arts. It was undertaken both for instruction in their private religious duties and as preparation for a pastoral charge. See Beryl Smalley, *The Study of the Bible in the Middle Ages* (Notre Dame: University of Notre Dame Press, 1964), xv.

7. Miller, Prosser, and Benson, *Readings in Medieval Rhetoric*, 168-69.

8. Ibid., 170.

9. Ibid.

10. *Littera gesta docet, quid credas allegoria, Moralis quid agis, quo tendas anagogia.* Quoted in Robert Grant and David Tracy, *A Short History of the Interpretation of the Bible*, 2nd ed., rev. and enl. (Philadelphia: Fortress, 1984), 85.

11. Miller, Prosser, and Benson, *Readings in Medieval Rhetoric*, 173.

12. *Alan of Lille: The Art of Preaching*, trans. with intro. Gillian R. Evans, Cistercian Studies Series, no. 23 (Kalamazoo, Mich.: Cistercian Publications, 1981) from *Ars praedicandi*, PL 210, cols. 109-35. In Latin, Alan's name is Alanus de Insulis and is sometimes translated into English as Alan of the Isles as, for example, in the translation of chaps. 1, 38, 39, and 41 (the theoretical chapters) by Joseph M. Miller, which appears in Miller, Prosser, and Benson, *Readings in Medieval Rhetoric*, 228-39. The term, however, refers to the French city of Lille.

13. While all of PL 210 is devoted to Alan, it does not include all of his works. A list of the known works and editions of them is given in G. R. Evans, *Alan of Lille: The Frontiers of Theology in the Later Twelfth Century* (Cambridge and New York: Cambridge University Press, 1983), 14-19.

14. Evans, *Alan of Lille: The Frontiers of Theology*, 87.

15. Knowles, *The Evolution of Medieval Thought*, 71-149. See also Mark Zier, "Sermons of the Twelfth Century Schoolmasters and Canons," in *The Sermon*, directed by Beverly Mayne Kienzle (Turnhout, Belgium: Brepols, 2000), 325-62.

16. Evans, *Alan of Lille: The Art of Preaching*, 6.

17. Murphy, *Rhetoric in the Middle Ages*, 307.

18. *Praedicatio est, manifesta et publica instructio morum et fidei, informationi hominum deserviens, ex rationum semita, et auctoritatum fonte proveniens.* Alanus de Insulis, *Ars praedicandi*, PL 210 (cols. 109-35).

19. Evans, *Alan of Lille: The Art of Preaching*, 15.

20. Evans, *Alan of Lille: Frontiers of Theology*, 89-90. The work of Peter referred to is his *Verbum abbreviatum*, which, in the opinion of Evans, "has, on the face of it, a strong claim to be set beside Alan's *Art of Preaching* as the first manual of preaching in the university tradition" (89).

21. Evans, *Alan of Lille: The Art of Preaching*, 16.

22. This limitation seems strange since Alan himself, who was neither a bishop nor an abbot, has left a number of sermons.

23. Murphy, *Rhetoric in the Middle Ages,* 304, 307.

24. Evans, *Alan of Lille,* 95.

25. Ibid.

26. Alanus de Insulis, *Ars praedicandi* 210 (PL col. 113). This discussion of form *(dispositio)* begins in col. 113 of PL 210 and on p. 20 of Evans's translation.

27. *Alan of Lille: The Art of Preaching,* 20-21.

28. Ibid., 22.

29. Johannes Baptist Schneyer listed 227 in *Repertorium der lateinischen Sermones des Mittelalters für die Zeit von 1150–1350 (Autoren: A-D),* Beiträge zur Geschichte der Philosophie und Theologie des Mittelalters, Band 43, Heft 1; Münster Westfalen: Aschendorffsche Verlagsbuchhandlung,1969), 699-83. A shorter list is given in M. T. d'Alverny, *Alain de Lille: Textes inédits avec une introduction sur sa vie et ses oeuvres,* Études de philosophie médiévale, no. 70 (Paris: Librairie philosophique J. Vrin, 1965), 125-40.

30. I am grateful to her for sending me a copy.

31. D'Alverny, *Alain de Lille: Textes inédit,* 241-87, 297-306. Printed editions of Alan's other sermons are listed in Evans, *Alan of Lille: The Art of Preaching,* 19.

32. *Deus est sphaera intelligibilis cuius centrum ubique, circumferentia nusquam.* This is a pseudo-hermetic text that Alan, depending on a florilegium, thought was from Cicero.

33. As rendered in Gillian Evans's unpublished translation.

34. Important works on this topic that appeared too late to influence this chapter are *Medieval Monastic Preaching,* ed. Carolyn Muessig, Brill's Studies in Intellectual History, vol. 90 (Leiden and Boston: Brill, 1998), and Beverly Mayne Kienzle, "The Twelfth-Century Monastic Sermon," in *The Sermon,* directed by Kienzle.

35. See p. 159 above.

36. "Religious" is used here in its technical sense of persons bound by life vows, usually of poverty, chastity, and obedience, to be members of a community. This use of the word is based on the derivation of the Latin noun *religio* from the verb *religo,* "to bind fast." Thus it has the same sense as "regular," which means living under a rule. It is contrasted with "secular" in the sense of living "in the world." That is, a religious or regular priest is one who is a member of an order, while a secular priest is under a diocesan bishop and usually serves in a parish. Many of the religious were (and are) members of the laity, of course.

37. Or, using an earlier English form of the word, "Austin."

38. Augustinus, *Ep.* 211:33 (PL col. 958-68). An English version is *The Rule of Saint Augustine, Masculine and Feminine Versions,* introduction and commentary Tarsicius J. Van Bavel, trans. Raymond Canning (Garden City, N.Y.: Image Books, 1986).

39. A clear introduction to this revival, especially in its social and economic aspects, is given in R. W. Southern, *Western Society and the Church in the Middle Ages,* Penguin History of the Church, vol. 2 (Harmondsworth: Penguin, 1970), 214-

72. In succeeding sections Southern also discusses other developments in the religious life, the rise of the mendicant orders and what he calls "fringe orders and anti-orders," which will be important later in the history of preaching. See also George Zarnecki, *The Monastic Achievement*, Library of Medieval Civilization (New York: McGraw-Hill, 1972).

40. Esther de Waal, *Seeking God: The Way of St. Benedict* (Collegeville, Minn.: Liturgical Press, 1984), 32.

41. *Rule*, prologue, chap. 5. The authoritative edition is *RB 1980: The Rule of St. Benedict*, trans. Timothy Fry, O.S.B. (Collegeville, Minn.: Liturgical Press, 1981).

42. These services are called "offices" because the Latin *officium* has a range of meanings that includes a kindness or favor, a ceremonial occasion, and an obligation or duty, all of which are nuances of the way that these liturgical acts are understood.

43. This scheme varied both seasonally, depending on how close dawn was to six o'clock, and locally, when some services were combined. E. C. Ratcliff, "The Choir Offices," in *Liturgy and Worship: A Companion to the Prayer Books of the Anglican Communion*, ed. W. K. Lowther Clarke and Charles Harris (London: SPCK, 1932), 257-66. Modern readers may be surprised by the lack of obvious reference to the Eucharist in the Rule of St. Benedict, but apparently in the sixth century Benedict himself expected it to be celebrated only on Sundays and feast days, if that often. See *RB 1980*, 410-12.

44. Since the Latin verb *orare* means both to give a speech and to pray, the English transliteration is identical for *oratoria*, the art of public speaking, and *oratorium*, a place of prayer.

45. *RB 1980*, 249-53.

46. Jean Longère, *La prédication médiéval*, Séries Moyen Âge et Temps Modernes, 9 (Paris: Études Augustinienne, 1983), 54-68.

47. Jean Leclercq, *The Love of Learning and the Desire for God: A Study of Monastic Culture*, trans. Catharine Misrahi (New York: Fordham University Press, 1961, 1974), 16-22.

48. The names of the others can be garnered either from the section of Longère cited in the previous note or from Leclercq's notes.

49. Jean Mabillon, *Bernardi Opera, Praef. generalis*, n. 23 (PL 182:26 n23). Pope Pius XII picked up this phrase in *Doctor Mellifluus*, the encyclical he wrote in 1953 to commemorate the eight-hundredth anniversary of Bernard's death. One of the best short studies of Bernard's life and importance is Thomas Merton, *The Last of the Fathers: Saint Bernard of Clairvaux and the Encyclical Letter, Doctor Mellifluus* (1954; reprint, New York: Harcourt Brace Jovanovich, 1981).

50. Leclercq, *The Love of Learning and the Desire for God*, 111.

51. Ibid., 207.

52. Gillian Evans, *The Mind of St. Bernard of Clairvaux* (Oxford: Clarendon Press; New York: Oxford University Press, 1983), 49.

53. *Sancti Bernardi Opera*, ed. J. Leclercq, C. H. Talbot, and H. Rochais, 8 vols. (Rome: Editiones Cistercienses, 1957–78). See also Jean Leclercq, *Recueil d'études sur St. Bernard et ses écrits*, 3 vols. (Rome: Edizioni di Storia e litteratura, 1966–92).

54. This is a major problem with all medieval preaching and, indeed, with written sermons from all ages.

55. The exact situation of Bernard's sermons varies from series to series, but the general process is very similar in all and is well presented in Marie-Bernard Saïd's introduction to the volume she translated, *Bernard of Clairvaux, Sermons on Conversion: On Conversion, A Sermon to Clerics, and Lenten Sermons on the Psalm, "He Who Dwells,"* Cistercian Fathers Series, no. 25 (Kalamazoo, Mich.: Cistercian Publications, 1981), 90-94.

56. *Magnificat: Homilies in Praise of the Blessed Virgin Mary by Bernard of Clairvaux and Amadeus of Lausanne,* trans. Marie-Bernard Saïd and Grace Perigo with intro. Chrysogonus Waddell, Cistercian Fathers Series, no. 18 (Kalamazoo, Mich.: Cistercian Publications, 1979), xiv, 3.

57. Evans, *The Mind of St. Bernard of Clairvaux,* 106. Cf. p. 99.

58. Evans gives a detailed analysis of Bernard's use of *parabolae* in ibid., 52-69.

59. Leclercq, Talbot, and Rochais, *Sancti Bernardi Opera,* vols. 4-6. Some or all of them appear in *St. Bernard's Sermons for the Seasons and Principle Festivals of the Year,* trans. Priest of Mount Melleray (Westminster, Md.: Carroll Press, 1950), vols. 1-3, a work I know only from citation in Clyde E. Fant Jr. and William M. Pinson Jr., eds., *20 Centuries of Great Preaching: An Encyclopedia of Preaching* (Waco, Tex.: Word, 1971), 1:149.

60. Psalm 90 in the Vulgate.

61. *Recueil d'études sur St. Bernard et ses écrits,* III, 139.

62. Leclercq, Talbot, and Rochais, *Sancti Bernardi Opera,* 6:1.

63. Ibid., 6:59.

64. Leclercq, Talbot, and Rochais, *Sancti Bernardi Opera,* vols. 1-2. While there are many English translations of excerpts, the most scholarly translation of the complete work is *Bernard of Clairvaux: On the Song of Songs,* trans. Kilian Walsh and Irene Edmonds, with intro. M. Corneille Halfants, 4 vols., Cistercian Fathers Series, nos. 4, 7, 31, and 40 (Kalamazoo, Mich.: Spencer, Mass., 1971–80).

65. Brevard S. Childs, *Introduction to the Old Testament as Scripture* (Philadelphia: Fortress, 1979), 571.

66. On the novelty that Bernard introduced into Christian spirituality and the possible dangers of excess in this innovation, see the chapter entitled "Eros: Or, Devotion to the Sacred Humanity," in G. L. Prestige, *Fathers and Heretics: Six Studies in Dogmatic Faith with Prologue and Epilogue* (London: SPCK, 1958), 180-207.

67. *Bernard of Clairvaux: Selected Works,* trans. with foreword G. R. Evans, intro. Jean Leclercq, and preface Ewert H. Cousins, Classics of Western Spirituality (New York: Paulist Press, 1987), 173-205.

68. Gilbert of Hoyland, Geoffrey of Auxerre, John of Ford, William of St. Thierry, and Alan of Lille, found in Longère, *La prédication médiévale,* 58-60.

69. Ewert H. Cousins in his preface to *Bernard of Clairvaux: Selected Writings,* 5-7. For his information he draws on an apparently unpublished paper by Richard Payne entitled "A Mystical Body of Love."

70. "Were the Sermons on the Song of Songs Delivered in Chapter?," introduction to vol. 2, *Bernard of Clairvaux: On the Song of Songs,* vii-xxx. The quotation is from p. xxx. In "The Making of a Masterpiece," his introduction to vol. 4, Leclercq makes a fascinating reconstruction of the way that the writing and editing of the *Sermons* can be correlated with what is known of Bernard's life (ix-xxiv).

71. William of St. Thierry, *Vita Sancti Bernardi* (PL 185:258-59).

72. Ibid. (PL 184:407-36). This work is also referred to as *Brevis Commentatio in Cantica.* The quotation from Leclercq is from Bernard of Clairvaux: *On the Song of Songs,* 2:xxx.

73. William of St. Thierry, *Brevis Commentatio ex Sancti Bernardi Sermonibus Contexta,* 2:xxx.

74. This phrase comes from the title of one of G. L. Prestige's 1940 Bampton Lectures, *Fathers and Heretics: Six Studies in Dogmatic Faith with Prologue and Epilogue* (London: SPCK, 1958), 180.

75. From the encyclical *Doctor Mellifluus,* trans. Thomas Merton in *The Last of the Fathers,* 112.

76. Quoted by Chrysogonus Waddell in his introduction to *Magnificat,* xviii.

77. Ibid., xvii.

78. Leclercq, Talbot, and Rochais, *Sancti Bernardi Opera,* 4:1-58; trans. Saïd, *Magnificat,* 1-58.

79. Preface, translated in *Magnificat,* 3.

80. Evans, *The Mind of St. Bernard of Clairvaux,* 136.

81. Bernard of Clairvaux, *Sermons on Conversion,* 18.

82. Geoffrey of Auxerre, *Vita Prima* IV.ii.10 (PL 183, 327).

83. Bernard of Clairvaux, *Sermons on Conversion,* 69.

84. Ibid., 19.

85. Eberwin of Steinfeld, *Epistolae* (PL 182:676-80). See the note in Bernard of Clairvaux, *On the Song of Songs,* 3:189. See also Leclercq's statement in 2:xi-xiii.

86. *De Laude Novae Militiae,* trans. Conrad Greenia in *The Works of Bernard of Clairvaux: Volume 7, Treatises III,* Cistercian Fathers Series, no. 19 (Kalamazoo, Mich.: Cistercian Publications, 1977), 125-67. The Rule of the Templars is found in PL 166:853-76.

87. Author, *Vita prima* 3.iv.9 (PL 185:308-9). On the whole issue of Bernard's involvement with the crusade, see Evans, *The Mind of St. Bernard of Clairvaux,* 24-36.

88. Leclercq, Talbot, and Rochais, *Sancti Bernardi Opera,* 4:119-22; Saïd, *Bernard of Clairvaux, Sermons on Conversion,* 97-99. There are seventeen sermons on the sixteen verses; sermon six continues the discussion of verse five begun in sermon five and also discusses verse six.

89. "This is to be more than an exegetical exercise. It is to change men's hearts. Bernard says that he has chosen the Psalm expressly because it is concerned with the battle with temptation which is fought especially hard in Lent." Evans, *The Mind of St. Bernard of Clairvaux,* 101.

90. *"De ultima parte eiusdem et de sexto versu."* The form of the Psalter Bernard used did not have the same verse divisions as modern editions of the Hebrew and translations made from them. As a result, what Bernard considers to be only the last part of verse 5 of Psalm 91 is the entire verse in modern editions. His edition puts the words "his truth will cover you with a shield" in verse 5, while they are the ending of verse 4 in modern editions. (They are more correctly translated in the RSV as meaning, "his faithfulness is a shield and buckler" [Ps. 91:4*b*].) Sermon 5 was devoted to these words and Sermon 6 comments on what are verses 5 and 6 in

modern editions. Verse divisions were not introduced until Robert Estienne ("Stephanus") placed them in his 1551 edition of the Greek New Testament. Chapter divisions were created by Stephen Langton, the archbishop of Canterbury who brought about the signing of the Magna Carta in 1215.

91. Saïd, *Bernard of Clairvaux, On Conversion,* 143.

92. Rather in the way that those who engage in amateur theatricals find that lines from the current play make appropriate observations on a wide variety of occasions.

93. Leclercq, *Bernard of Clairvaux: Selected Works,* 32.

94. Ibid.

95. "Then afterward I will pour out my spirit on all flesh; your sons and your daughters shall prophesy, your old men shall dream dreams, and your young men shall see visions" (Joel 2:28).

96. Elisabeth Schüssler Fiorenza, *In Memory of Her: A Feminist Theological Reconstruction of Christian Origins* (New York: Crossroad, 1983); Karen Jo Torjesen, *When Women Were Priests: Women's Leadership in the Early Church and the Scandal of Their Subordination in the Rise of Christianity* (San Francisco: HarperSanFrancisco, 1993).

97. There is no complete history of preaching by women. The best treatment of the subject available is a collection of essays by different scholars, *Women Preachers and Prophets Through Two Millennia of Christianity,* ed. Beverly Mayne Kienzle and Pamela J. Walker (Berkeley and Los Angeles: The University of California Press, 1998).

98. Carolyn Muessig, "Prophecy and Song: Teaching and Preaching by Medieval Women," in ibid., 147.

99. Darlene Pryds, "Proclaiming Sanctity Through Prescribed Acts: The Case of Rose of Viterbo," in ibid., 173-95.

100. Catherine M. Mooney, "Authority and Inspiration in the *Vitae* and Sermons of Humility of Faenza," in *Medieval Monastic Preaching,* ed. Carolyn Muessig, Brill's Studies in Intellectual History, vol. 90 (Leiden and Boston: E. J. Brill, 1998).

101. *Hildegard of Bingen: Scivias,* trans. Mother Columba Hart and Jane Bishop, intro. Barbara J. Newman, pref. Caroline Walker Bynum (New York: Paulist Press, 1990), 59.

102. Sabina Flanagan, *Hildegard of Bingen, 1098–1179: A Visionary Life* (London and New York: Routledge, 1989), 142.

103. The standard edition of the Latin text is in *Analecta Sanctae Hildegardis,* ed. Jean-Baptiste Pitra, *Analecta Sacra,* vol. 8 (Monte Cassino, 1882), 245-347. Beverly Mayne Kienzle and Carolyn Muessig are preparing a new edition from the best manuscripts for Corpus Christianorum Continuation Mediaevalis. Kienzle is also translating the *Expositions* for Cistercian Publications with Fay Martineau. I am indebted to Professor Kienzle for copies of her articles on Hildegard's preaching and for her Latin text and translation of the twenty-fourth set of homilies.

104. In what follows I depend on Beverly Mayne Kienzle's article "Hildegard of Bingen's Teaching in her *Expositiones evangeliorum* and *Ordo virtutum*" in *Medieval Monastic Education,* ed. George Ferzoco and Carolyn Muessig (London and New York: Leicester University Press, 2000), 72-86.

105. While Hildegard's visions were communicated in vivid symbolic experience, their result was not mystical experience as in Meister Eckhart or apocalyptic scenar-

ios as in Savonarola (for the two, see chapter 10), but solid intellectual understanding of issues of faith and morals.

106. Such external reference is a very rare thing in monastic preaching.

107. Kienzle, "Hildegard of Bingen's Teaching in her *Expositiones evangeliorum* and *Ordo virtutum*," 81.

108. Flanagan, *Hildegard of Bingen*, 193-213.

CHAPTER 9

THE EXPLOSION OF PREACHING IN THE THIRTEENTH AND FOURTEENTH CENTURIES

THE CONTEXT

Seldom in the history of the church has there been such a rapid and widespread increase in the amount of preaching along with a corresponding proliferation of interest in that preaching as that which began early in the thirteenth century and continued through the fourteenth. One way of documenting this increase is to point to the sheer volume of sermons that have survived from the time. A compiled list of sermons from the years 1150 to 1350 consists of nothing other than the beginnings and endings of sermons along with an identification of the manuscripts in which those sermons are to be found. Nonetheless, the list runs to nine volumes that have a cumulative seventy-three hundred pages. If the average number of sermons per page is consistent with a sample of more than forty pages, more than eighty thousand sermons have been preserved in manuscripts.

In those days when writing materials were so precious and the time needed to inscribe a manuscript was so great, it is doubtful that any of those were written down to be preached just once or even by only one preacher. (Originality was valued less highly then than it is now!) And, of course, it is likely that far more manuscripts have been lost than have been preserved. When all of these factors are taken into consideration, it becomes obvious that the total amount of preaching during this period must have been enormous.[1]

Many of the reasons for such an outburst of preaching are well known. A period of economic expansion had been going on in Europe since before the first crusade (1096–99). An expanding population and more efficient farming methods had produced both prosperity and the need for developing trade. That in turn caused cities to spring up.

Since the parochial system had been tied to the land under feudalism, the church was ill prepared to minister to the new urban masses until a new kind of religious order had developed that could take the gospel to these people where they were. The most notable of these orders, the Franciscans (founded 1209) and the Dominicans (founded 1215), were not, at first, tied to monasteries in remote places as the Cistercians were, but rather lived as wandering beggars who were free to go where the people were.

In order to prepare themselves for this ministry of preaching, these mendicants took advantage of the universities being founded at the time, institutions stimulated by the recovery in the West of the thought of Aristotle. Thus the friars, as members of these orders were called, developed a system that had never existed before for training preachers. In this intellectual and evangelical ferment, a complete support system or infrastructure, one that included the provision of numerous homiletical aids, was established to enable these preachers to do their work. I will address this in more detail later. First, it is necessary to notice that the friars were not the first to respond to the evangelical impulse that seemed to be in the air at the time.

Irregular Preachers

The social ferment described above caused the dislocation of great numbers of people and psychological displacement among others. Old institutions and ways of thinking were brought into question. Not surprisingly, the church and its teaching were among those up for reassessment. The church had grown so large, rich, and powerful that it had been able to challenge even the authority of kings. It began to occur to many, especially among the homeless poor, that such pomp and luxury was a strange development of the religion of the Son of Man who had no place to lay his head (Matt. 8:20; Luke 9:58).

As early as the mid-eleventh century, the Augustinian canons had announced their standard to be the apostolic life *(vita apostolica);* for them, the primary sense of this phrase was the community of goods.[2] In the last quarter of the century, though, the ideal came to be expressed first in the lives of hermits and then in the lives of wandering preachers. Even before their message became heretical, there was great indignation against it among the clergy because these itinerants were often laypersons who were not licensed to preach. The preachers responded by questioning the worthiness of the priests, accusing them of simony, luxury, and unchastity. Inevitably, charges of disobeying spiritual authorities when they refused to give up their preaching drove many of these *Wanderprediger* out of the church so that heresy followed almost inevitably. Originally, though, the charges against them were disciplinary rather than doctrinal.[3]

The period under discussion is that in which the Augustinian canons and the Cistercians were founded and the lay preaching movements reflect some of the same impulses in the piety of the time. Indeed, other religious orders grew out of these beginnings. Robert of Arbissel was a priest who became a hermit before becoming a wandering preacher. The large number of followers who responded to his preaching—"Christ's Poor," as they called themselves—forced him to settle down and form a double monastery[4] at Fontevrault around 1100. Not all wandering preachers, however, were able to stay within the church as Robert did. An Augustinian canon and pupil of Abelard, Arnold of Brescia, taught that the church should give up its wealth and power. He led in the founding of communes in Brescia and Rome to oppose clerical abuses until he was burned at the stake under Hadrian IV. Peter of Bruys and his disciple Henry the Monk preached in France that individuals are responsible for their own salvation and that the entire sacramental and ecclesiastical systems are therefore of no use. Peter was burned by a crowd for what it regarded as sacrilege, and Henry's followers were the targets of a preaching mission by Bernard of Clairvaux (**see chap. 8, pp. 187-97**).

These movements in the first half of the twelfth century were paving the way for much larger ones that dominated the last half of the century, the Waldenses and the Cathars or Albigensians. The Waldenses are the only medieval sect that still exists—although it has changed much through the centuries. In the mid-1170s, its founder, a wealthy merchant of Lyons named Valdès,[5] responded to Christ's "counsel of perfection" to sell all that he had (Matt. 19:21) by making provision for his family and giving the rest of his goods to the poor. Taking Jesus' instructions to the apostles (Matt. 10:5-23) as his standard, he began to travel around preaching repentance, receiving his support entirely from alms.

Soon he attracted followers who assisted in this ministry; they were known as "the Poor in Spirit" or "the Poor of Lyon" and quickly spread through France and over into what are modern Germany and Italy. In Italy they attracted into their company similar local groups, both those known as the *Humiliati* and former followers of Arnold of Brescia.

At first the church's only objection to their work was that they preached without license, and they were excommunicated around 1182 for this disobedience. Even afterward their main doctrinal variations were directed toward a biblical literalism that objected to anything in the church that lacked explicit scriptural warrant. Their leaders were a group called the Seventy who obeyed all the Gospel instructions for the apostolic mission. Since these passages in the New Testament say nothing of gender, women as well as men were permitted to preach and to officiate at the Eucharist.[6]

Very different are the Cathars, who were heretics from the beginning.[7] And that beginning could have been very early; one may trace an unbroken succession between them and the Gnostics of the second century.[8] In the classical way, they were dualists who saw two opposing principles or even two gods fighting against one another in the universe. One was spiritual and therefore good, and the other responsible for the existence of the material universe and therefore evil. Salvation came through receiving the *consolamentum,* a sort of "waterless baptism," and committing themselves to celibacy and to eating no foods regarded as products of sexual intercourse (eggs, meat, milk, and cheese, but not, according to their thought, fish).

Only a few, the "Perfects," received this consolation before death appeared imminent; those who did became, in effect, the clergy of the Cathars and had the duties of preaching, teaching, and administering the *consolamentum.* Ordinary believers *(credentes)* were not expected to practice such asceticism; their hope lay in receiving the *consolamentum* before they died and supporting the Perfects in the meanwhile. Considering human sexuality as a creation of the Evil One, the Cathars regarded distinctions of gender as even less important than the Waldenses did. Women could receive the *consolamentum* as well as men. Having received it, they had the duties of administering it to others and preaching. They were not itinerant, however, and thus did not become deacons or bishops, though the rationale for that restriction seems to have been a practical one of the hardship of the life rather than a theoretical one of their not being qualified.

In Montaillou, at any rate, the main inclination to heresy arose from resentment of the tithes imposed by the church.[9] The combined impact of the Cathars and Waldenses was so great that between them they "threatened to carry the entire region from the Alps to the Pyrenees out of communion with the Roman Catholic Church."[10] To oppose their preaching, the church had to have even more effective preachers of its own.[11] The need for these preachers is one of the immediate causes for the mendicant orders' formation.

The Coming of the Friars

It is hard to imagine two men more different than the founders of the two orders most responsible for the explosion of preaching, the Franciscans and Dominicans,[12] orders that inevitably get lumped together. Francis was still in his late twenties when his personal example began to attract others to imitate his way of life. The son of a wealthy merchant, he had given up earlier ambition to become a knight and, thus, to enter the nobility, in order to practice a simple, direct, and apparently naive spirituality. He had an ardent desire to lead the apostolic life that caused him to embrace poverty, pray constantly, and show love to outcasts to the extent of kissing the sores of lepers. He obeyed Gospel injunctions literally to the extent that he rebuilt decayed churches with his own hands. He had a mystic ardor and charism that make it easy for modern Christians, on the one hand, to regard him as the most obvious saint who ever lived and, on the other, to be uncomfortable with what today seem like symptoms of pathology. He was not an organizer and administrator; he was much more an envisioner, and even before he died it had become obvious that it would be as easy to institutionalize his vision as to domesticate a rainbow.[13]

Dominic, on the other hand, was in his midforties when he established his order. He was a well-trained scholar and a member of the Augustinian canons, from whom he had learned the ideal of the apostolic life. As a canon associated with the cathedral of Osma, he entered a period of close association with the bishop of the diocese, Diego of Acevedo. In 1206 when the two were traveling through France, an incident occurred that was determinative for the rest of Dominic's life.

> In the land of the Albigensians [Bishop Diego] met the legate of Pope Innocent, with a great council of archbishops and bishops and twelve Cistercian abbots; they received him with honor and asked his advice about what ought to be done for the defense of the faith. On his advice, they abandoned all their splendid horses and clothes and accoutrements, and adopted evangelical poverty, so that their deeds would demonstrate the faith of Christ as well as their words.[14]

Diego knew that it would be impossible to compete with the heretics' preaching without matching their example of apostolic living.

He and Dominic joined in this ministry for two years before Diego started for home to raise funds to support it. Along the way, however, Diego died and Dominic was left to carry on without him. He continued with the support of Fulk, the bishop of Toulouse, and Simon de Montfort, the Englishman in charge of the military crusade against the heretics. As time went on he was joined by others who wished to assist. When he was given three houses for his followers in 1215, it appeared to be time to begin regularizing their efforts. In the same year the Fourth Lateran Council forbade the creation of new religious orders, but the next year when Dominic proposed a modification of the Rule of St. Augustine under which he already lived, Pope Honorius III recognized his order.

It was the pope himself who recommended that they be called the order of preaching brothers, a recognition that from the beginning the Dominicans understood themselves as a group committed to a homiletical mission. This was less true of the Franciscans, who saw themselves following Francis in his imitation of Christ. For Francis, "the initial motivation of his preaching is basically the recognition that it is part of the whole program of Luke 10. . . . Diego and Dominic, by contrast, start preaching because preaching is needed."[15]

Dominic lived only a few years after his order was recognized, but he had already discovered before he died that the need for preaching was not confined to the Languedoc with its Albigensian crisis. In 1217 he sent seven of the brothers to Paris and two to Spain while he himself went to Rome, leaving only four to carry on the work in Toulouse. He had also recognized that preaching requires thought and thought requires study. At first he had asked for theological scholars to come from Paris so that his friars could be trained, but he recognized later that it was better for the friars to go to the universities than for the universities to come to them. By the third quarter of the century Dominic's spiritual sons, Albert the Great and Thomas Aquinas, would dominate the intellectual life of Paris.

Preaching by the Friars

This multiplication of preachers raises the question of who was permitted to preach in the church at that time. The answer is simple: bishops were still regarded as the only ones who could preach in their own right. Others were only auxiliary preachers, preachers *per accidens*. Almost a century after the event, Jordan of Pisa could say that when Dominic proposed an order of preachers, the pope wondered to himself,

"Who is this man, who wants to found an Order consisting entirely of bishops?"[16] Yet as Innocent III had said, bishops at the time were like "dumb dogs" (Isa. 56:10 Vg.), not daring to bark because they were ignorant, and leaving the church in a condition of "evil silence" *(pessima taciturnitas).*[17]

Obviously, many people other than bishops had preached for some time. But that raises the question of what qualifies as preaching. "Public preaching exercised for the enlightenment of a whole assembly of the faithful, generally gathered for liturgy" qualifies.[18] One could see that the mission of parochial priests constituted an extension of the bishops' ministry, and the authority to preach could be assumed to be delegated. But did priests have the authority by virtue of order, or by virtue of having a pastoral responsibility? Could priests without "a cure of souls," such as monks, preach? And what about self-appointed preachers like Valdès, or priests who left their parishes to become wandering preachers? Admittedly, bishops and even popes leaned over backward at times to encourage what seemed beneficial.

The preaching orders emerged in the context of this chaotic lack of universally accepted criteria, though the situation was very different for the two. Dominic was a learned priest and attracted similar sons. Thus in 1221 Honorius III gave members of his order authority to preach everywhere; it was their own constitutions that set limits as to who among them could preach, what education they needed to do so, and where they could preach. The decision as to who could preach was based on evidence of the candidate's having the "grace of preaching" *(gratia praedicationis),* understood as a charism, "the super-natural vocation of one who is certain that the Spirit may speak in him and through him."[19]

Francis had preached since he had heard the Gospel containing Christ's instructions to the apostles for their mission and had responded by saying, "This is what I want; this is what I long for with all my heart."[20] In 1210 Innocent III gave permission for the Franciscans to preach, under the conditions that their preaching be concerned with penitence and not doctrine, and that each friar who was to preach be given personal permission by Francis. The earlier form of the Rule said that only those who had been given permission should preach. "All the brothers, however, should preach by their deeds" (chap. xvii). Yet Francis provided an "exhortation and praise" that could be used as a model sermon by those who were not licensed to preach (chap. xxi); penitence is a major theme in it.[21] By 1219, though, Honorius III wrote to bishops, saying that he wanted the friars to "sow the seed of the divine word after the manner of the apostles,"[22] and from then on there were Franciscan preachers of doctrine as well as exhortation. By then there were also educated friars, and it became harder and harder to distinguish their preaching from that of anyone else.

PREACHING AS AN ART

Franciscans and Dominicans were prominent among those who developed a new way to preach. Previously, most preaching had been done in the form of homilies that expounded one of the biblical readings appointed for the liturgy and applied it to the lives of the people. Now a new style of sermon was developed. Its form can be conveyed from an analogy of the way that a tree branches. For example, there is a drawing of a tree in a fifteenth-century manuscript illumination; its trunk and limbs are labeled to show which parts of the tree correspond to which parts of a sermon. About halfway up, the trunk separates into three large boughs, each of which later divides into three limbs. This tree represents the way that a sermon should be based on a text, which, like the tree, is divided into three points, with each point then broken down into three subpoints.[23]

One can understand more easily when one sees how a particular text could be developed; the illumination shows that in relation to the Summary of the Law (Matt. 22:37, 39, 40). The text (or *thema,* as it was called) is divided into three questions, to each of which three answers are given:

I.   (Why should you love God?) ...
  A. Because of His creation of the world.
  B. Because of His goodness.
  C. Because of His fatherhood.
II. (How does one love his neighbor?)
  A. Favor and good-will.
  B. Compassion.
  C. Acts of love.
III. Why do the whole Law and Prophets hang on these two commandments?
  A. Because love is the avoidance of all evil.
  B. Because love is the doing of all good.
  C. Because love is also the happy and eternal consummation.

The pattern can be completed with three additions. First, there are a couple of sawn-off limbs under the main division; these indicate the possibility of a protheme (a "mini-sermon" on an entirely different text that makes the same point as the theme), which leads into a prayer. Second, there may be a "prelocution," a sort of introduction consisting of an analogy, a moralization, or a proverb. Finally, each of the nine subdivisions may use a different means of "dilating" or developing the point.[24] Although not indicated by the illumination, there is an expectation that each affirmation made in the sermon will be confirmed by at least one "authority" *(auctoritas),* a quotation of a biblical proof text. This, in turn, may be backed up by a quotation from one of the Fathers, and then possibly even a quotation from a pagan writer. (For an example of such a sermon, **see Vol. 2, pp. 202-6.**)

This kind of sermon has been variously designated. The most common term has been "university sermon," but that seems less than appropriate because (1) this is a technical term referring to sermons preached before a university, and (2) it appears uncertain that the style originated in university circles. "Scholastic sermon" connects this style of preaching with the contemporary philosophical and theological method of that name, but, as we shall see below, that connection's validity is unclear. For want of a better term, Richard Rouse and Mary Rouse have called it the "school sermon," but the identity of the schools in question is not obvious.[25] The textbooks that taught the method for preaching such sermons refer to them as "modern," but that relative term is even more confusing here than elsewhere.

The two least misleading terms seem to be those used by James J. Murphy: "artistic sermons" and "thematic sermons."[26] While "artistic" calls to mind the designation of the manuals in which this preaching style is taught as *artes praedicandi* ("arts of preaching"), artistic preaching is suggestive of a wider aestheticism. Since "thematic sermon" indicates that this type of sermon is based on interpretation of a *thema*—a text, a verse from the Bible—it appears to be the term that is least likely to lead to confusion and is thus the one that I will follow here.

The form of thematic sermon depicted in the tree illumination represents its fully evolved state. The sermons of Alan of Lille (**see above chap. 8, pp. 177-82**) represent a starting point. There the outline is a sequence of lists rather than formal divisions and subdivisions. These early sermons also lack both the *auctoritates* and the frequent use of *exempla* characteristic of the fully developed thematic sermon.[27] This development from the end of the twelfth century to the full complexity of the form in the middle of the fourteenth century is gradual but steady.[28]

Before concluding this discussion of the thematic sermon genre, it is necessary to deal with three other questions: (1) Were such sermons addressed exclusively to learned audiences? (2) What language was used for popular preaching? and (3) Was thematic preaching the only genre practiced during the period? The answer given by recent research to the first of these questions is surprising: Far from appealing only to learned audiences, thematic sermons have a number of features that made them especially appealing to popular lay audiences.[29] In order to help the most popular audience to follow, understand, and remember a sermon, speakers would divide the sermon into numbered parts; divide the sermon into a few broad parts; number them; use the protheme to introduce the visiting preacher to his new audience, giving time for latecomers to arrive, and leading the congregation into prayer; and use scriptural authorities to give instruction in the Scriptures, vary the preacher's language, and lend authority to the points made; in addition to using exempla.

The question of popular preaching's language would seem to be a non-issue were it not for one particular sort of evidence. One must agree with David d'Avray: "That the friars achieved their undoubted successes by preaching in a language which their audience could not understand is so wildly implausible that the onus of proof is on those who propose it."[30] Yet the embarrassing fact is that very few surviving thirteenth-century manuscripts contain sermons in vernacular languages. The explanation seems to be that sermon manuscripts were created for the clergy and not for the laity.[31] These manuscripts were used as model sermons from which outlines, authorities, and other matter could be taken for creating new sermons. Having the original in the friars' basic language made it easier for them to draw on it when they put together sermons in a variety of vernacular languages. A possible exception to this rule is "macaronic" sermons, that is, sermons in a mixture of Latin and a vernacular. While it is clear that such sermons were written (manuscripts of them exist), it is not so evident that these sermons were preached in this confusion of tongues.[32]

Knowing whether thematic sermons were the only preaching genre of the period is more important than it sounds. This leads one to question who was preaching. Thematic preaching was overwhelmingly the style of the mendicants, who were itinerants. What sort of preaching, if any, were the secular clergy doing? D'Avray has argued that the lack of elementary instruction in the Christian faith, basic catechesis, in the sermonic literature of the friars implies that such instruction was done by parish priests in catechetical sermons much like the *prônes* of seventeenth-century France. Such catechetical preaching, reminiscent of Aelfric's sermons, had ordinarily replaced homilies (in the technical sense) as the standard pulpit fare from parochial clergy.[33] The very existence of thematic preaching, then, implies that local pastors were laying down a solid foundation in the Christian faith, the foundation upon which the friars built.

Artes praedicandi

Amazingly early in the development of the thematic sermon a profusion of textbooks began to appear telling preachers how to construct this type of sermon.[34]

> By the year 1200 . . . the Christian Church had produced only four writers who could by any stretch of the imagination be called theorists of preaching: Saint Augustine, Pope Gregory, Guibert of Nogent, and Alain de Lille. . . . But within twenty years of 1200 a whole new rhetoric of preaching leaped into prominence, unleashing hundreds of theoretical manuals written all over Europe during the next three centuries. . . . Several hundred such preceptive manuals still survive in various European libraries.[35]

As often as not, the title of one of these textbooks was *Ars praedicandi.* Thus the plural form, *artes praedicandi,* refers to the entire group.

Throughout the history of instruction in public speaking, there have been two main ways in which people learned, the "technical" and the "sophistic."[36] "Technical" is derived from the Greek *technē,* which is close to being a synonym for the Latin *ars.* Technical rhetoric instructs through "how-to-do-it" manuals; by studying such books and applying their principles, almost anyone can become a competent speaker. Yet one cannot acquire virtuosity in this way; that comes only from following the example of acknowledged artists. In ancient Greece these were the Sophists, from whom the sophistic tradition takes its name. The sophistic method consisted of being apprenticed to one of these acknowledged virtuosos. In terms of this distinction, the *artes praedicandi* obviously inculcated a technical rhetoric.

The first *artes* seem to have appeared almost out of thin air. Not only do they predate the earliest manuscripts of sermons constructed according to the method, "there is reason to believe that the basic elements of this new approach were available outside the universities before they were taken up and popularized by academics."[37] Alexander of Ashby, an Englishman, produced such a treatise around the year 1200, stating the whole theory of thematic preaching when he said: "The mode of preaching consists in the parts of a sermon, and in its delivery. There are four parts of a sermon, to wit: prologue, division, proof, and conclusion. The entire material of the sermon is proposition and authority."[38]

An important and easily overlooked aspect of this new form is that it represents the beginning of the assumption that sermons ought to have a pattern instead of taking their shape from the biblical passage expounded. Within a few years of Ashby's work, there appeared an even greater work that both discusses the new nomenclature of preaching (theme, antetheme, division, etc.) and also sets such preaching within the intellectual framework of the period, the *Summa de arte praedicandi* of Thomas (Chabham or Chobham) of Salisbury.[39] The *artes* of Thomas Waleys and Robert of Basevorn, coming a century to a century and a half after those of Alexander and Thomas, represent the full flowering of the form. (For an abstract of the *Ars* of Basevorn, **see Vol. 2, pp. 179-93.**)

With this background, it is possible to look at the preaching method it inculcates.[40] The first step in preparing such a sermon is to choose an appropriate theme (i.e., text). To be a good theme the text has to be from the Bible—using its exact wording—and it must be a passage that has significant meaning and uses words that recur often in Scripture. It should also have three main words so that it may easily be divided into points with the preacher citing the biblical book from which it comes by chapter alone, since verses have not yet been numbered. To give late-comers time to gather, the sermon should begin with a protheme (also called an antetheme), which will culminate smoothly in a prayer for grace, such as the *Veni sancte Spiritus,* the Lord's Prayer, or the Hail Mary.

The prayer said, the preacher will repeat his text, introduce the sermon, divide the text, and then proceed to develop the parts into which the theme has been divided. The introduction should be short, and it should really introduce (*ducere intro,* "lead into") what follows. Introductions may be in either the "narrative" or the "argumentative" mode, although neither of these terms means in this regard exactly what it signifies to modern readers. Narrative introductions make use of an analogy or a quotation that employs one of the words of the theme. The argumentative mode may be built around an induction, an illustration,[41] a syllogism, or an enthymeme.[42] Illustrations may be drawn from nature (e.g., the busyness of bees), history (classical or hagiographic), or art. (It may seem picayune to list these, but apparently these sermons were judged on the basis of the rigidity with which they adhered to the form, and faults and merits were as obvious to cognoscenti of the medium as they are to judges at a dog show.)

After the theme is introduced, it is divided. The three or more "branches" into which the sermon is going to split must be announced in advance, often by some phrase such as "in which words (i.e., the text) three things are touched upon" *(in quibus verbis tria tanguntur).*[43] The preacher may be assisted in such divisions by making use of distinctions between the various possible meanings of a word in the text (e.g., genuine and feigned penitence) or accepting a plurality (as in noting that there are three requisites for genuine penitence: contrition, confession, and satisfaction).

There are also other conditions that an "artistic" division must satisfy. First, "the words which correspond to the three parts of the division must terminate in syllables which give the same sound."[44] Then the division also should be made in the right cadence, that is, each punctuation mark should be preceded by the right number of the right kind of metric feet (but this works only for someone preaching to clergy in Latin). The key words of the theme or text are the basis of the division, but these words are not used to name the parts into which the text is divided. Even words built on the same roots are not used. Rather, synonyms of the key words that are built on different roots must be used. The parts of the division must be presented in the order in which the words come in the text. Finally, the division will take into proper account the meaning of the theme and of the individual words in it.

The division is followed by the declaration and confirmation of the parts in which the division is paraphrased, justified, and proved by the citation of biblical "authorities" or proof texts. After all of that, each of the points is developed (the *dilatatio*); for this phase, "everything that has gone before is merely a preamble, a skeleton."[45] There are three means by which this dilation is done:

1. The citation of biblical authorities.
2. The advancement of rational arguments.
3. The use of *exempla.*

This seems almost anticlimactic in its simplicity—and, indeed, Basevorn does go on to discuss such "ornaments" of the sermon as digression, correspondence, congruence of correspondence, circulation, convolution, and unification—but the method of constructing a thematic sermon has been communicated.

Presented like this, the method seems artificial in the extreme. Thomas-Marie Charland, a scholar close to the medium, could conclude his analysis of it by saying, in effect, that "one would have to know 'a hell of a lot' to preach so badly."[46] Yet contemporaries did not understand the style that way. One has only to read the introductory chapter to Waleys's *ars praedicandi* to recognize what a deeply spiritual man he was and how seriously he took the vocation of preaching.[47] Interpreting Jesus' preaching on the mountain allegorically, he says that the preacher must live on a higher plane than the congregation, that anyone in a state of mortal sin should not preach. He then says that the preacher should not preach to show off but for the glory of God and the edification of the faithful. Thus the most important preparation for preaching is the spiritual preparation of prayer.

Thereafter, Waleys begins to discuss practical issues of homiletics: The preacher's dress should be neither showy nor contemptible. This is followed by some sound advice on delivery. Gestures should be used in moderation so that the preacher is neither "an immobile statue" nor does his bodily movement suggest that he is "in a duel with someone."[48] The preacher should speak neither too loudly nor too softly, nor should his voice go up and down in a singsong way. And the preacher should avoid speaking so fast that no one understands what he says. Waleys is opposed to memorizing sermons; rather, their substance should be so familiar that the preacher can easily find language in which to express the gospel naturally and forcefully.

> When he is in the fervor of his spirit, his heart is so immediately joined to the hearts of his hearers that he will not perceive his tongue nor his hearers' ears, but it will appear to him almost as if his words flowed and proceeded into the hearts of his hearers without any mediation.[49]

The preacher should not even pay too much attention to *artes praedicandi* out of a desire to preach impressive sermons. Nor should sermons be allowed to go on too long; preachers in danger of going overtime should have a friend signal them when the time is up. Finally, new preachers should practice off in the woods by themselves until they have enough skill for preaching to people.

Thematic Preaching and Scholasticism

For over a century it has been popular to associate thematic preaching with the scholastic movement in theology. The reasons for the association are obvious enough: at about the time scholasticism had its beginning, there appeared a new form of preaching that, instead of being formless as previous preaching had been, had its parts carefully coordinated according to a central plan.[50] Thus what thematic preaching and scholasticism have in common would be systematic division of one form or another.

Yet scholasticism as such did not use just any form for division. Scholasticism was a method of arguing theological questions based on the dialectic of Aristotle and the rhetoric of Cicero. It proceeded by posing *quaestiones* formally, presenting the conflicting points of view held by different authorities and the arguments by which these were supported, and arguing to a solution that did justice to all the issues raised.[51] But thematic preaching did not proceed by formal argument to establish propositions. Rather, it proceeded by dividing a theme into progressively smaller portions and confirming each stage of division or subdivision by quoting authorities. Therefore, scholastic method as such is not used in thematic preaching.

What this preaching and scholasticism do have in common is "a passion for dividing and subdividing."[52] This common element is seen more readily in scholastic commentaries than in the *quaestiones*, since the latter do not lend themselves to numbered sections and subsections. Both the sermons and the commentaries show the working of minds that like to begin with a single point and fan out artistically. D'Avray speaks of such an attitude as exhibiting "the subdividing mentality."[53]

While he argues correctly that any theory about how this subdividing mentality came to penetrate preaching in the thirteenth century would have to be based on a still-unmade study of the sermons themselves, it is not surprising that the same minds could be capable of arguing *quaestiones* and preaching thematic sermons. After all, Aristotle himself insisted that dialectic and rhetoric have their distinctive methods of persuasion. One thing at stake is the difference between written and oral discourse. What one detects in both scholasticism and thematic preaching is an exuberant joy in the God-given powers of the human intellect.[54]

Preaching Aids

One index of the importance assigned to preaching by the mendicant orders is the variety and great abundance of tools provided to assist preachers in their sermon preparation. The *artes praedicandi* already mentioned are a case in point. Although they have received a great deal of scholarly attention, d'Avray argues that in comparing the relatively small number of *artes* manuscripts with the quantity of other preaching aids, these may not have been so important as has been thought.[55]

Reference books are so taken for granted today that the achievement of the human intellect in creating the genre may be overlooked. Many of the techniques helpful in producing searchable reference tools to make it possible for preachers to produce thematic sermons were developed during the thirteenth century and have been in common use ever since. Richard Rouse and Mary Rouse distinguish between the attitudes toward reference works held in the twelfth century and those held in the thirteenth century. They say that the first "represent efforts to assimilate and organize inherited written authority in a systematic form" while "the tools of the thirteenth century represent efforts to search written authority afresh."[56] This new interest in searching written authority was closely connected with the emerging understanding of the preaching task.

To make such searches possible, techniques had to be devised, including alphabetical arrangement, layout, and reference symbols, including Arabic numerals.[57] There even developed among the stationers of the University of Paris, the most important center for the diffusion of these preaching tools, a system by which these reference works could be mass-produced. When a work was in demand, the stationers would provide themselves with exemplars that were written in *peciae*, quires of four or eight folios. Scholars who wished to copy the work would rent the *peciae* a few at a time until they had as much of the work reproduced as they wished.[58]

The first sort of preaching tool to be devised, the *collection of distinctions*, is not surprising in an age with a "subdividing mentality." For example, the number of different senses in which a word is used in the Bible could provide an outline for a sermon. We can see an example of the way lists of such distinctions worked in a compilation of the meanings of the word "horse" in various passages: preacher, temporal dignity, the easy life, and the present age.[59] It was not until this period that verbal concordances to the Scriptures came into existence; they hardly could have existed earlier since the Bible was not divided into chapters until Stephen Langton did so in the early-thirteenth century. Since verses were not numbered until much later, the relative location in a chapter citation was signified by a letter between A and G in the original concordance produced by the Paris Dominicans in 1239. The practice of providing alphabetical subject indexes to books can also be dated to this time. Even such obvious tools as library catalogs owe their origin to the needs of preachers during the thirteenth century.

Another genre of preaching aids was the *florilegium* ("gathering of flowers"), an anthology of earlier writers, a collection of quotations that could serve as *auctoritates* to confirm the points made by preachers. One of the greatest of these was Thomas of Ireland's *Manipulus florum*, a collection of six thousand extracts from the works of the church fathers, a few classical writers, and Maimonides. These are arranged under an alphabetical list of 266 topics, most of which were moral or ethical. The extracts vary from several lines to half a column in length. Within the topic the quotations are arranged alphabetically by author, and cross-references are made to related topics.[60]

Another collection of quotations was made by John of Wales, who did a great deal more besides. A British Franciscan, who studied and taught at Oxford and Paris in the last half of the thirteenth century, John served as Regent Master of Theology at Paris and went on an embassy to Wales for Archbishop Pecham. In his lifetime he was as well known as his contemporaries at Paris: Roger Bacon, John Pecham, Bonaventure, and Thomas Aquinas. What he was principally known for was his production of preaching aids. Scholars now recognize some eighteen works as being his; they include biblical commentaries and sermon collections, themselves useful to preachers, but reference books as well. Among these are a book of advice to princes consisting largely of *exempla* about the virtuous behavior of rulers in classical antiquity, a collection of material useful for creating sermons for different types of people,[61] a summary of the lives and sayings of pagan philosophers, and a similar volume on Christian saints. These handbooks

> aimed to cover all sorts of topics, giving an authoritative view, a number of named authorities in support of this view, a series of *exempla* and appropriate extracts for use in preaching, and suggestions for further reading.[62]

His *Communiloquium*, for instance, contains 2,389 quotations from biblical, classical, and patristic writings, fruits of his own study used to make cogent points. The erudition that went into the production of these reference books for preachers is remarkable.

Treatises on virtues and vices were another common type of homiletical tool. Rouse and Rouse say that eleventh-century preaching not intended for monks had a largely missionary function; it was aimed at converting nonbelievers. A thematic sermon of the style that developed in the thirteenth century, however, "never strays far from the function of teaching."[63] A great deal of that teaching was moral. Siegfried Wenzel has made available to English readers one of these treatises, *Fasciculus morum*, an early-fourteenth-century tool for preaching on the seven deadly sins and their opposing virtues.[64] It takes the form of a series of sermons on each of the sins and its opposing virtue.

The subdividing mentality is seen in the way that each of the sins and virtues is broken down into its components. Lechery, for example, has its nature delineated, its occasions listed (sight, conversation, touching, kissing, and the sex act itself), its branches enumerated (fornication, violating a virgin, adultery, incest, and sodomy), and the reasons it is to be hated (it is offensive to God, hateful to the angels, harmful to the person who commits it, harmful to one's neighbor, and renders service to the devil). Then chastity is discussed, examples of it are given, the method of acquiring it described, and its end effect noted.

The treatment of each of these topics is a sermon, beginning generally with a distinction between the various forms of the phenomenon under consideration,[65] the offering of theses on that subject, and the support of each thesis by biblical, patristic, and classical authorities, and by appropriate *exempla*.

One may see from several features that this collection is intended as a tool for preachers rather than merely a collection of edifying sermons to be read. Frequently a biblical passage or an *exemplum* is introduced without expansion; instead there is interjected the instruction *"expone"* (explain or expound). Then the prologue says that the collection was made "to comfort you and to help the unlettered." Finally, the book ends with the words *"Finis sermonum fit hec collectio morum,"* which Wenzel says can mean, "This collection of moral matters is for the end (purpose) of sermons."[66] Thus the translator has given the person who does not know Latin a rare opportunity to study a medieval preaching tool in its entirety.

What may be regarded as "the most important single genre of preaching aid," however, is *collections of model sermons*.[67] Such collections generally include sermons for the Sundays or the saints' days of the church calendar, that is, ordinary liturgical sermons. Others, however, are collections of *ad status* sermons, sermons addressed to different categories of persons on their state of life. Sermons on the dead appear as well. The pattern of all these sermons, however, is that of the thematic sermon rather than that of the homily. These collections are usually published in a very small format, the sort of "vade-mecum books" that friars could take—along with other preaching material, confessional handbooks, Bibles, and breviaries—as they went from place to place in their preaching travels. Produced in the *peciae* system at the University of Paris, these sermon collections were used by Franciscans especially to enable them to preach on very short notice, whatever the occasion.

Often the model sermons are simply outlines, sometimes in rhyming form, with a scriptural text to confirm each heading.

> The contents of preachers' vade-mecum books brings it home
> to us that the preaching offensive of the friars, which was

undoubtedly successful, depended to a significant extent on
ready-made sermons and other kinds of stereotyped material.[68]

The sort of preaching aid that has been even more studied than the
artes praedicandi, however, is *collections of* exempla. Folklorists have
combed through these collections looking for popular tales, social historians have sought details of medieval life in them, and literary scholars
have studied them to find sources for early creative writing in various
vernacular languages. While these efforts called attention to this type of
preaching aid and made it accessible to scholars by their producing editions and analyses, they tended at the same time to draw attention away
from the primary function of these collections, their usefulness to the
writers of sermons.

Before looking at that usefulness, however, it is necessary to specify
more precisely the kinds of illustrations and support material that are
included in the category of *exempla*. There have been many efforts to
enumerate the appropriate categories for such a taxonomy, but more
recent study has suggested that the elements that go into the classification of *exempla* are: (1) their source or origin, (2) the nature of the information, (3) the nature of the characters in the story, and (4) the formal
or logical structure of the exemplum.[69]

While this bare list may seem dull enough, the variety of data
embraced by these categories is consistent with the liveliness of the genre
itself. Sources, for instance, can be as diverse as the Bible, the patristic
writings most influential in shaping medieval thought (Boethius,
Cassiodorus, Gregory the Great, Isidore of Seville, Bede, and *Vitae
Patrum*), stories from classical antiquity, *illustrations* from the
Carolingian renaissance, and stories collected by the compilers of *exempla* collections from their own contemporaries.

Even this does not adequately suggest the variety. An older listing has
presented the variety of sources in the following way, one that does
greater justice to the wealth represented here:

> (1) such incidental material as was afforded by
> historical works, secular and ecclesiastical;
> poems and prose fiction, ancient and medieval;
> contemporary events;
> incidents and stories brought personally to the attention of the
> writer;
> (2) collections of tales, fables, anecdotes, and saints' lives, not originally
> designed to serve as exempla but offering plentiful and convenient mat-
> ter for such; these are represented respectively by

the numerous early collections of Latin stories,

Aesopic fable collections,

the historical anecdotes of Valerius Maximus, and

the *Legenda Aurea* of Jacobus de Voraigne;

(3) elaborate moral and didactic treatises which make use of a large number of exempla in illustration of the points discussed; to this class belong

the *Dialogues* of Gregory,

the *Disciplina Clericalis* of Petrus Alphonsus,

and *Jacob's Well*;

(4) collections especially designed for the use of preachers and moralists and properly designated as "example-books"; of this class there are four varieties:

(a) collections containing exempla unclassified and without accompanying moralizations, such as the early compilations from the sermons of Jacques de Vitryo;

(b) collections containing exempla classified under topics alphabetically but without moralizations, such as the *Alphabetum Narrationum* formerly ascribed to Étienne de Besançon;

(c) collections containing exempla moralized but not classified, such as the *Gesta Romanorum*;

(d) collections containing exempla both alphabetically classified and moralized, such as the *Scala Celi* of Johannes Junior.[70]

The other issues in classification (nature of the information, sort of characters involved, and formal and logical structure) are directly related to the usefulness of *exempla*. While some illustrative materials had been used in sermons before, they became an important element in the strategy of persuasion of the thematic sermon. To understand this it is necessary to look at the elements that go into defining the *exemplum*. These begin with its narrative character, which makes it more consistent with the proclamation of a faith that looks back historically to its founding and forward eschatologically to its consummation rather than to abstract reasoning from eternally valid principles.

A second element is the brevity necessary for oral presentation. Then there is the element of authenticity given by relating what is either historical or history-like. The example is not the whole argument; it is a component of a total presentation of an argument. Yet it does occupy the culminating position in the argument; it climaxes and completes it. The sort of argument involved is essentially sermonic; thus the use of *exempla* in other forms of medieval literature is derivative from homiletical use.

This homiletical use presupposes a rapport between the preacher and the audience, a community of the faithful. In this situation, the purpose of the *exemplum* is always to teach, its function is pedagogical. Yet this teaching is never for any merely temporal benefit, whether entertainment or moral suasion, but is always directed toward the eternal welfare, the salvation, of the souls of the congregation. From these elements one may construct a definition of the *exemplum*. It is a short narration given as truthful and intended to be inserted into a speech (usually a sermon) to convince an audience by means of a salutary lesson.[71]

With this background, it is possible to see how the other criteria for classifying *exempla* assist in understanding how these stories do their work in thematic sermons. The "nature of the information" refers to the means through which the preacher or collector acquired the *exemplum*, through either reading or conversation. This information is contained in the way the illustration is introduced, whether by the words, "I have heard," or by "it is written."[72] In either case this introduction makes the argument more persuasive by giving it one of the two great forms of cultural authority known in the Middle Ages, that of the written word and that of the word of persons with credibility (clergy, elders, neighbors, and distinguished people). Further, the types of characters who spoke in *exempla*, whether supernatural beings, humans, or animals, were all vested with authority in this kind of story.

The formal or structural logic of these stories could be of one or two sorts. In the first case the argument is analogical and is thus authoritative for whoever falls into a position parallel to that of a character in the story. That is, what is said in a fable about an animal carries a message to all who behave like that animal. In the second category of stories the argument is metonymic: what is said in the tale about one member of the class has implications for all members of the class; for example, what is said about a member of a religious order in a personal narrative is a warning to all religious.[73] All of which is to say that the rhetorical function of *exempla* in thematic sermons contributes greatly to their effectiveness.

While the variety of *exempla* collections is too great to permit cataloging, it is worthwhile to look at one of the most highly developed to get some idea of what the genre was like at its pinnacle. It is the work of John (de) Bromyard, an English Dominican who was chancellor of Cambridge University in the late fourteenth century, vicar of the Dominicans at Oxford, and staunch opponent of Wyclif. A widely traveled man, Bromyard brings to his vast collection a cosmopolitan perspective. This work is entitled "a treatise on preaching that is by far the most useful and indispensable for all shepherds of the Lord's flock, proclaimers of the divine Word, ministers of faithful souls, and planters of the sacred writings,"[74] a title that seems to incorporate a publisher's blurb.

Yet the work itself almost lives up to this billing. In a printed edition it occupies almost one thousand folio pages and has illustrations arranged alphabetically under 189 headings. The seven under the letter "L," for example, are: *labor, laus, lex, liber, loqutio, ludus,* and *luxuria* (work, praise, law, book, speaking, play, and lust). Each of these topics has a series of *exempla* provided under titles that are theses proved by the illustration. Under the heading of *praedicator* there are thirty-eight such theses that could provide a theology of preaching by themselves, all in narrative form. Happy indeed was the preacher who had such an aid in sermon preparation!

Popular Preaching

With such an armory of tools, the itinerant preacher of thematic sermons was well prepared to preach the Word "in season, out of season" (2 Tim. 4:2 KJV) to people in the new cities. Many who did were enormously successful. If this were a work devoted to preachers rather than preaching, it would be a pleasant indulgence to recount the accomplishments of Jacques de Vitry, William of Auvergne, Bernardino of Siena, Juan of Capistrano, Anthony of Padua, and many others. None, however, seems to have been more effective than the one reported by the inveterate chronicler of the friars, Salimbene:

> Take note that Brother Bertold had the special grace of preaching from God. And everybody who has heard him says that from the days of the Apostles till the present day he has not been matched in the German tongue. A great multitude of men and women followed him, sometimes from as much as sixty or a hundred miles around, sometimes from a large number of cities, in order to hear the eloquent and saving words which came forth from the mouth of him who gives "his voice the voice of power" [Ps. 67:34] and who gives "the word to them that preach good tidings with great power" [Ps. 67:12]. He would go up in a *bettefredum* or a wood tower built like a bell tower which he used in the fields as his pulpit. And in the top of this tower had been constructed a wind-indicator, so that the people could tell by the direction of the wind where to sit in order to hear best. Thus, marvelously, he could be heard and understood as well by those sitting at a distance as those near at hand. And nobody got up and left until his sermons were ended. And when he preached on the Last Judgment, they all trembled like a reed in the water. And they begged him for the love of God not to preach on such subjects, because it terrified them so much to hear him.[75]

Salimbene goes on to confirm the power of Berthold's preaching by telling of two miracles accomplished by it. One occurred to a peasant who wished to hear Berthold, but was prevented from doing so by his lord, who insisted that he spend the day plowing. But when Berthold preached, the peasant heard him as clearly from thirty miles away as if he had been right under the tower. Not only that, but he memorized the entire sermon and, when he resumed plowing, got as much done during the day as he would have if he had not been interrupted. The other involved a noble lady who had followed Berthold for six years, not missing a sermon. In doing so she used up her fortune. When, at the end of that time, she had her first audience with him, he instructed her to go to a certain dishonest banker whom she was instrumental in converting. Supporting her then became one of the ways he repaid his ill-gotten gains.

These stories seem to be hyperbolic ways of testifying to the real power of preaching to the masses done by the sons of Francis and Dominic, who utilized the thematic form of the sermon and their abundant array of preaching aids to assist them in their proclamation. This truly was an explosion of preaching. This was the medium through which the church responded to the crisis of the time and the new urban masses of the High Middle Ages had their commitment to the Christian faith reinforced. Although the medium was effective for its age, no single strategy of persuasion is effective at all times and in all places. The time was coming when the friars, with their thematic sermons, their subdividing mentality, the exempla, and their whole infrastructure for preaching, would come under attack.

FOR FURTHER READING

D'Avray, D. L. *The Preaching of the Friars: Sermons Diffused from Paris before 1300.* Oxford: Clarendon Press; New York: Oxford University Press, 1985.

Early Dominicans: Selected Writings. Edited with introduction by Simon Tugwell, and preface by Vincent de Couesnongle. CWS. New York: Paulist Press, 1982.

Murphy, James J. *Rhetoric in the Middle Ages: A History of Rhetorical Theory from Saint Augustine to the Renaissance.* Berkeley and Los Angeles: The University of California Press, 1974.

Rouse, Richard H., and Mary A. Rouse. *Preachers, Florilegia, and Sermons: Studies on the Manipulus florum of Thomas of Ireland.* Studies and Texts, no. 47. Toronto: Pontifical Institute of Mediæval Studies, 1979.

Smyth, Charles. *The Art of Preaching: A Practical Survey of Preaching in the Church of England 747-1939*. London: SPCK; New York: Macmillan 1940.

Wenzel, Siegfried, ed. and trans. *Fasciculus Morum: A Fourteenth-Century Preacher's Handbook*. University Park: Pennsylvania State University Press, 1989.

Notes

1. The list in question is found in J. B. Schneyer, *Repertorium der lateinischen Sermones des Mittelalters für die Zeit von 1150-1350*, Beiträge zur Geschichte der Philosophie und Theologie des Mittelalters, Band 43, Heften 1-9 (Münster Westfalen: Aschendorffsche Verlagsbuchhandlung, 1969-80). Two more volumes of the *Repertorium* have appeared since 1980, but, since they are index volumes for the first nine, they do not change the total number of sermons. See also D. L. d'Avray, *The Preaching of the Friars: Sermons Diffused from Paris Before 1300* (Oxford: Clarendon Press; New York: Oxford University Press, 1985), 1.

2. They appealed to the authority of Isidore of Seville, who says that monks should be "keeping the apostolic life, having all things in common after the apostolic example." *Regula monachorum* 83 (PL col. 870).

3. Stanislaw Trawkowski, "Entre l'orthodoxie et l'hérésie; Vita apostolica et le problèm de la désobéissance," in *The Concept of Heresy in the Middle Ages (11th-13th c.): Proceedings of the International Conference, Louvain, May 13-16, 1973*, ed. W. Lourdaux and D. Verhelst, Mediaevalia Lovaniensia, series 1, studia 4 (Leuven: University Press, 1976), 157-66.

4. That is, one for both men and women.

5. The designation of him as Peter comes more than a century after his death and is the result of an effort to link him with the apostle.

6. No early Waldensian sermons have survived; indeed, by the nature of the case, it is doubtful that any were ever written down. For contemporary records of the movement see Walter L. Wakefield and Austin P. Evans, *Heresies of the High Middle Ages: Selected Sources Translated and Annotated* (New York: Columbia University Press, 1969), 189-241.

7. Also known as Albigensians in southern France from the town of Albi that was one of their important centers. The term *Cathar* is often related etymologically to the Greek word *katharos* ("clean" or "pure"), although some scholars account for it differently.

8. Steven Runciman in *The Medieval Manichee: A Study of the Christian Dualist Heresy* (Cambridge: Cambridge University Press, 1947; reprinted 1960). For a different interpretation of Catharism, see Anne Brenon, "The Voice of the Good Women: An Essay on the Pastoral and Sacerdotal Role of Women in the Cathar Church," in *Women Preachers and Prophets Through Two Millennia of Christianity*, ed. Beverly Mayne Kienzle and Pamela J. Walker (Berkeley and Los Angeles: The University of California Press, 1998). A detailed reconstruction of the life of a Cathar

233

community is given in Emmanuel LeRoy Ladurie, *Montaillou: The Promised Land of Error,* trans. Barbara Bray (New York: Vintage Books, 1979). See also John Arnold, "The Preaching of the Cathars," in *Medieval Monastic Preaching,* ed. Carolyn Muessig (Leiden; Boston: Brill, 1998), 183-205. Although representing a later period, a remarkable novel by the medievalist and semioticist, Umberto Eco, recreates the religious confusion of tongues of this age: *The Name of the Rose,* trans. William Weaver (San Diego: Harcourt Brace Jovanovich, 1983).

9. Ladurie, *Montaillou,* 327-41 and *passim.*

10. Williston Walker, Richard A Norris, David W. Lotz, and Robert T. Handy, *A History of the Christian Church,* 4th ed. (New York: Scribner's, 1985), 300.

11. Two preachers already studied, Bernard of Clairvaux and Hildegard of Bingen, preached against the Cathars and Waldenses. See Beverly Mayne Kienzle, "Defending the Lord's Vineyard: Hildegard of Bingen's Preaching Against the Cathars" in Muessig, *Medieval Monastic Preaching,* 163-81.

12. The official name of the Dominicans is *Ordo Praedicatorum,* the Order of Preachers, and that of the Franciscans is *Ordo Fratrum Minorum,* literally, the Order of Smaller Brothers, but generally rendered as the Order of Friars Minor. The Dominicans are also known as Black Friars from the color of their cloaks. Franciscans are called Gray Friars from the original color of their habits (which are now brown).

13. The sources for the life of Francis are the two *vitae* written by Thomas of Celano, a document produced by some of Francis's first associates *(Scripta Leonis et Sociorum Eius),* and the *Legenda maior* of St. Bonaventure. This last is translated in *Bonaventure: The Soul's Journey into God, The Tree of Life, The Life of St. Francis,* trans. and intro. Ewert Cousins, pref. Ignatius Brady, CWS (New York: Paulist Press, 1978). Much of the charm associated with Francis comes across in a historically less reliable source from the fourteenth century, *The Little Flowers of St. Francis,* available in numerous translations and editions. See John R. H. Moorman, *The Sources for the Life of S. Francis of Assisi* (Manchester: Manchester University Press, 1940).

14. Jean de Mailly, "Life of St. Dominic," in *Early Dominicans: Selected Writings,* ed. with intro. Simon Tugwell, pref. Vincent de Couesnongle, CWS (New York: Paulist Press, 1982), 54. Biographical materials for the less charismatic Dominic are rarer than they are for Francis; most of the contemporary accounts are included in the Tugwell volume. A sound modern treatment is M.-H. Vicaire, *Saint Dominic and His Times,* trans. Kathleen Pond (New York: McGraw-Hill, 1964).

15. Tugwell, *Early Dominicans,* 18.

16. Quoted in ibid., 14.

17. Quoted in Guy Bedouelle, *Saint Dominic: The Grace of the Word,* trans. Mary Thomas Noble (San Francisco: Ignatius Press, 1987), 121. On the importance of Innocent and the Fourth Lateran Council for preaching, see Richard H. Rouse and Mary A. Rouse, *Preachers, Florilegia, and Sermons: Studies on the Manipulus florum of Thomas of Ireland,* Studies and Texts, no. 47 (Toronto: Pontifical Institute of Mediæval Studies, 1979), 55-59.

18. Much of what follows is based on Bedouelle, *St. Dominic,* 121-29.

19. Ibid., 125.

20. Bonaventure, *Legenda maior,* 3.

21. *Francis and Clare: The Complete Works,* trans. and intro. Regis J. Armstrong and Ignatius C. Brady, pref. John Vaughn, CWS (New York: Paulist Press, 1982). Quote of xvii on 122, quote of xxi on 126.

22. Quoted in John R. H. Moorman, *A History of the Franciscan Order from Its Origins to the Year 1517* (Oxford: Clarendon Press, 1968), 273.

23. Otto A. Dieter, "*Arbor picta*: The Medieval Tree of Preaching," in *The Quarterly Journal of Speech* 51 (1965), 123-44.

24. Those indicated on the tree branches in the illumination are: concordance of authorities, discussion of the words, properties of things, exposition of more than one sense of interpretation, parables and facts of nature, alleging the opposite (making a correction), comparing adjectives, interpreting a name, and multiplying synonyms. There is nothing sacrosanct about this order nor are these the only "ornaments" recognized.

25. Rouse and Rouse, *Preachers, Florilegia, and Sermons,* 66 n. 1.

26. James J. Murphy, *Rhetoric in the Middle Ages: A History of Rhetorical Theory from Saint Augustine to the Renaissance* (Berkeley and Los Angeles: The University of California Press, 1974), 311-44.

27. I will explain *exempla* in greater detail below, but for the moment they may be thought of simply as sermon "illustrations."

28. Rouse and Rouse trace this development stage by stage in *Preachers, Florilegia, and Sermons,* 68-90.

29. Ibid., 76-77, 84-87. Cf. D'Avray, *The Preaching of the Friars,* 193-95. Since this chapter was written, thematic sermons have been treated in N. Bériou, "Les sermons latins après 1200" in *The Sermon,* directed by Beverly Mayne Kienzle (Turnhout, Belgium: Brepols, 2000), 363-447, and in most of the chapters on vernacular sermons in that volume.

30. David d'Avray, *The Preaching of the Friars,* 94. On the language in which popular preaching was done, see 91-95. Giles Constable notes that the question is very complicated in "The Language of Preaching in the Twelfth Century," in *Viator, Medieval and Renaissance Studies,* 25 (1994), 131-52. I am grateful to A. Gary Shilling for bringing this article to my attention. Kienzle discusses the matter in the conclusion of *The Sermon,* 971-74, summarizing the views of the other contributors to the volume expressed *passim.*

31. An exception is German sermons copied in the vernacular as spiritual reading for nuns. D'Avray, *The Preaching of the Friars,* 91-93. For reason to believe that exceptions were more extensive, see Kienzle, *The Sermon,* 968-70.

32. This conclusion is brought into doubt by Siegfried Wenzel, *Macaronic Sermons: Bilingualism and Preaching in Late-Medieval England,* Recentiores: Later Latin Texts and Contexts (Ann Arbor: The University of Michigan Press, 1994).

33. D'Avray, *The Preaching of the Friars,* 82-90. The catechetical sermons of Thomas Aquinas referred to below would have served as an excellent model for this kind of preaching.

34. The earliest surviving collection of such sermons was published in Marie Magdeleine Davy, *Les sermons universitaires parisiens de 1230–1231: Contribution à l'histoire de la prédication médiévale.* Études de Philosophie Médiévale, no. 15 (Paris: Librairies philosophique J. Vrin, 1931). But, as we shall see, the oldest surviving *artes* go back before that.

35. Murphy, *Rhetoric in the Middle Ages*, 309-10. The study of these textbooks has gone through a number of different stages. The first major work on thematic preaching in England was G. R. Owst, *Preaching in Medieval England: An Introduction to Sermon Manuscripts of the Period c. 1350–1450*, Cambridge Studies in Medieval Life and Thought (Cambridge: The University Press, 1926); the *artes* are dealt with on 309-54. A list of the manuscripts containing these textbooks is found in Harry Caplan, *Mediæval Artes Praedicandi: A Supplementary Handlist*, Cornell Studies in Classical Philology (Ithaca, N.Y.: Cornell University Press; London: H. Milford, Oxford University Press, 1934) and its *Supplement*, which appeared in 1936. Thomas-Marie Charland edited the Latin texts of two of the most important of the *artes*, those of Thomas Waleys and Robert of Basevorn, in *Artes Praedicandi: Contribution à l'histoire de la rhétorique au moyen âge*, Publications de l'Institute d'Études Médiévales d'Ottawa, no. 7 (Paris: Librairie Philosophique J. Vrin; Ottawa: Institute d'Études Médiévales, 1936). The Murphy volume is the major study of developments within this literature. Murphy has provided translations of *artes* in *Three Medieval Rhetorical Arts* (Berkeley and Los Angeles: The University of California Press, 1971).

36. George A. Kennedy, *Classical Rhetoric and Its Christian and Secular Tradition from Ancient to Modern Times*, rev. and enl. (Chapel Hill: The University of North Carolina Press, 1999), 16-17. What Kennedy calls "technical" rhetoric is designated as "preceptive" in Murphy, *Rhetoric in the Middle Ages*, 296.

37. Murphy, *Rhetoric in the Middle Ages*, 311.

38. Quoted in ibid., 313.

39. Ibid., 317-26.

40. This summary is based on Charles Smyth, *The Art of Preaching: A Practical Survey of Preaching in the Church of England 747–1939* (London: SPCK; New York: The Macmillan Company, 1940), 20-35.

41. An *exemplum*. See below.

42. According to Aristotle, dialectic uses syllogisms while rhetoric uses enthymemes, which are incomplete or implied syllogisms; that is, only one of the premises is explicit in an enthymeme, the other being presupposed as something the audience believes. For him, rhetoric is oratory, and audiences cannot be expected to follow rigorous argument when it is presented orally. Thus the enthymeme is the syllogism accommodated to oral presentation.

43. There is still a proverbial homiletical wisdom to the effect that you should "tell them what you are going to tell them, tell them, and tell them what you've told them." Many homileticians today (including the author) question the desirability of doing this, but some highly regarded preachers still practice it, for example, the distinguished Jesuit patristics scholar, Walter Burghardt. One of his *divisiones* is as follows: "Three stages to my journey into Jonahland: (1) the man, (2) the meaning, (3) the message. Who was he? What was his importance for Israel? What might he say to you and me now?" See Burghardt, *Grace on Crutches: Homilies for Fellow Travelers* (New York: Paulist Press, 1986), 100.

44. Smyth, *The Art of Preaching*, 27. He illustrates this principle by dividing a sermon to be preached to bishops on Psalm 141:5 (Vulgate 140:5): "Let the righteous strike me in mercy" *(Corripiet me justus in misericordia)*, which I translate as follows:

> A prelate is described
> > with respect to state *(statUM)*:
> > "righteous" *(justus)*,
> > with respect to deed *(actUM)*:
> > > "let him strike" *(corripiet)*,
> > with respect to manner *(modUM)*:
> > > "in mercy" *(in misericordia).*

45. Ibid., 34.

46. *"Il fallait savoir prodigieusement pour prêcher si mal."* See *Artes Praedicandi,* 224.

47. O. C. Edwards Jr., "Thomas Waleys: A Fourteenth-Century Colleague," in *Homiletic* 14 (1989), 1-4.

48. Ibid., 2.

49. Ibid., 3.

50. This section is based on d'Avray, *The Preaching of the Friars,* 163-80. Although d'Avray denies that thematic preaching is scholastic, Daniel R. Lesnick unsuccessfully refutes that claim in *Preaching in Medieval Florence: The Social World of Franciscan and Dominican Spirituality* (Athens: University of Georgia Press, 1989), 96-97.

51. One has only to open one of Thomas Aquinas's *Summae* to any page to see the method in full form.

52. D'Avray, *The Preaching of the Friars,* 176.

53. Ibid., 177.

54. For a long time it was believed that there was an *ars praedicandi* written by Thomas Aquinas, but that appears to be the work of a later Thomist, according to Harry Caplan, *Of Eloquence: Studies in Ancient and Mediæval Rhetoric,* ed. with intro. Anne King and Helen North (Ithaca, N.Y.: Cornell University Press, 1970), 48-76. There are, however, sermons preached by Thomas that have survived: Lenten sermon conferences on the Apostles' Creed, the Ten Commandments, the Lord's Prayer, and the Hail Mary. See *The Sermon-Conferences of St. Thomas Aquinas on the Apostles' Creed* trans., ed., and intro. Nicholas Ayo (Notre Dame, Ind.: University of Notre Dame Press, 1988).

55. D'Avray, *The Preaching of the Friars,* 78.

56. Rouse and Rouse, *Preachers, Florilegia, and Sermons,* 4.

57. Ibid., 26-36.

58. Ibid., 169-80.

59. Ibid., 8. Allegorical interpretation is needed to account for some of these. For example, the understanding of the horse as a preacher comes from Gregory the Great's exegesis of Job 39:19: "Wilt thou give strength to the horse, or clothe his neck with neighing?" (Rheims-Douay).

60. The work of Rouse and Rouse is an important pioneering study of such a preaching tool. It could be said to have focused attention of medieval sermon studies on tools other than *artes praedicandi* and collections of *exempla.*

61. *Ad status* sermons.

62. Jenny Swanson, *John of Wales: A Study of the Works and Ideas of a Thirteenth-Century Friar,* Cambridge Studies in Medieval Life and Thought, 4th series (Cambridge; New York: Cambridge University Press, 1989), 16.

63. Rouse and Rouse, *Preachers, Florilegia, and Sermons,* 43, 67.

64. *Fasciculus Morum: A Fourteenth-Century Preacher's Handbook,* ed. and trans. Siegfried Wenzel (University Park: Pennsylvania State University Press, 1989). The popularity of the genre is reflected in a quotation from a manuscript of the time: "There be so many books and treatises of vices and virtues and diverse doctrines, that this short life shall rather have an end of any man, than he may either study them or read them" (spelling modernized). See Owst, *Preaching in Medieval England,* 278.

65. For example, incest includes intercourse not only between those who are related by blood but also between those related by spiritual kinship. Thus it is the sin of religious who break their vow of chastity. See Wenzel, *Fasciculus Morum,* 682-83.

66. Ibid., 731.

67. D'Avray, *The Preaching of the Friars,* 78.

68. Ibid., 61.

69. Jean-Claude Schmitt, *L'"Exemplum,"* Typologies des sources du moyen âge occidental, fasc. 40 (Turnhout, Belgium: Brepols, 1982), 27-38. For a summary of their general perspective see *Prêcher d'exemples: Récits de prédicateurs du Moyen Age,* intro. Jean-Claude Schmitt (Paris: Stock, 1985), 9-24.

70. Joseph Albert Mosher, *The Exemplum in the Early Religious and Didactic Literature of England,* Columbia University Studies in English (New York: Columbia University Press, 1911), 6-7. Tabular presentation added.

71. Schmitt, *L'"Exemplum,"* 37-38.

72. A cartoon in *The New Yorker* some years ago showed several clergy sitting together on a train like a group of traveling salesmen. One of them was saying, "Let me tell you a parable I heard in Scranton." This conveys the mood of the personal *exempla,* which, as Smyth says, "are mostly at second or third hand, the godly gossip of the cloister or of the preaching tour." See *The Art of Preaching,* 60.

73. Schmitt, *L'"Exemplum,"* 41-42.

74. *Summa Praedicantium omnibus dominici gregis pastoribus, divini verbi praeconibus, animarum fidelium ministris, et sacrum literarum cultoribus longe utilissima ac pernecessaria.* From the title page of the printed edition of 1614 published by Hieronymus Verdussi in Antwerp.

75. *The Chronicle of Salimbene de Adam,* trans. Joseph L. Baird, Giuseppe Baglivi, and John Robert Kane (Binghamton, N.Y.: Medieval & Renaissance Texts & Studies, 1986), 566. So great was Berthold's reputation that most mendicant sermons from Germany, whether in Latin or German, are attributed to him, although only a few can be assigned to him with certainty. Hans-Jochen Schiewer, "German Sermons in the Middle Ages," in *The Sermon,* directed by Kienzle, 868-69.

CHAPTER 10

A HOMILETIC
MISCELLANY

W hile the designation of periods is always arbitrary, there is
often an ebb and flow of events that makes it easy to feel as
though history does occur in eras. After the preaching explosion of the thirteenth and fourteenth centuries, there seems to have been
a settling down, the calm before the next storm, that of the Protestant
Reformation. This chapter, therefore, will deal with odds and ends, the
wisps of mist that appeared on the horizon, wisps that could either be
burned out by the sun on a clearing day or instead burgeon into massive
thunderheads that would darken and then drench the landscape. This
meteorological mixed bag is filled with spirituality, on the one hand, and
negative responses to either thematic preaching or the institutional life of
the church or both, on the other.

A SPIRITUALITY OF PREACHING

The first of the phenomena to be surveyed is wispy indeed, a single
volume, and one that was so little valued at its appearing that only four

manuscripts of it remain, none of which contain the entire work.[1] Yet it had every reason to be received enthusiastically, having been written by the fifth master of the Order of Preachers after his resignation from that post. The skill with which he had discharged that responsibility is perhaps suggested by his having been offered the patriarchate of Jerusalem when he stepped down; he had also received a few votes in a papal election. His duties even involved him with royalty. When he was elected master, one of his first duties was to receive a daughter of the king of Hungary as a Dominican nun. He became godfather to a son of the king of France and advised the king on how to settle disputes between some of the most powerful families of his realm. There is no doubt about the respect in which his contemporaries and successors held the author, Humbert, from the town of Romans-sur-Isère[2] (ca. 1200–1277).

Why, then, was his book not more popular? The opinion of the editor and translator of the work, Simon Tugwell, is that "its failure as a book is one symptom of the originality (eccentricity, some would say) and difficulty of the whole notion of a religious order defined as an Order of Preachers."[3] Dominican spirituality never had the emotional fervor of Bernard's exhortations to Cistercians who had gone into the wilderness to give their souls completely to God. The Dominicans' "spiritual exercises were designed to make them better preachers, and their own spiritual progress was not sought as a goal in its own right, but rather as a kind of spin-off from their service of others."[4] They sought not the desert, but the marketplace where the people were. The concept, however, was so novel that even the Dominicans themselves were not ready for a book spelling out the principle: "For those called to be preachers, it is precisely the *gratia praedicationis*, the 'grace to be a preacher,' that must be the nucleus of their whole spiritual life."[5]

Such a book, however, is *The Formation of Preachers*.[6] Appearing two-thirds of the way through the thirteenth century, it was written very much in the manner of the sermons of the time. A point is stated but hardly developed. It may be paraphrased or a reason for it may be stated and then an authority for it quoted, but there is no "dilation" beyond that. What d'Avray calls "the subdividing mentality"[7] is the obvious principle of organization. Each topic is broken down into a number of subheadings—which often sound like a list of all the permutations the author could think of.

Modern logic is offended by a considerable overlap of categories; it seems as though everything that could be said is said, even if its substance has been included in what was said before. This is especially true when biblical metaphors for a thing are being cataloged (e.g., the scriptural symbols of the preacher in 2.6). Biblical interpretation may reflect any of the four senses and quite often depends on the exegesis of the passage in question given in the *Glossa Ordinaria*, that great collection of patristic commentary that was, for all practical purposes, what the Bible meant to the Middle Ages.

This, too, can be disconcerting for modern readers, as when the point that without preaching the church would never have been established is being made on the basis of Job 38:4: "Where were you when I laid the foundation of the earth?" Gregory says: "When scripture refers to foundations, we understand the preachers, who were the first to be established in the church by the Lord, so that the whole structure which follows rests upon them."[8] When, however, one becomes accustomed to the form of reasoning employed, one can see that it is not so superficial as it first appears. Indeed, the spiritual principles involved are very deep and still valid.

Humbert was not reflecting on the vocation to preach in general, but on what it meant to be a member of the Dominican order that had been founded precisely as a preaching order. The treatise is about the implications of that identification. Thus he begins with the nobility of the preacher's job and goes on to the necessity of preaching, its acceptability in the sight of God, and the benefits that accrue to the preacher both in this life and the life to come. Then he speaks of the usefulness of preaching, which is coextensive with that of the Word of God. This means that it is needed by many categories of people. Then the difficulties of the job are discussed, with a recognition at the end that they can be relieved by study, learning from others, and prayer. The requirements to be a preacher (**see Vol. 2, pp. 207-19,** for this section) are compiled under the headings of quality of life, knowledge, speaking ability, and merit, which can be lost in a number of ways. The preacher's person is exhausted in a short list of physical requirements (including maleness). Next, the scriptural symbols of the preacher are set down, and then right and wrong ways of becoming a preacher are detailed.

The section devoted to the actual performance of preaching is not concerned with the how-to-do-it issues covered in such profusion by the *artes praedicandi*, but looks instead at cases in which one should preach, inadequate reasons for failing to do so, undiscriminating ways of preaching and the conditions under which it is done well, ending with the reasons that those with the vocation should preach gladly. An analysis is made of the ways in which people come to be deprived of preaching and the harm occasioned by that lack. Then all the possible results of preaching, good and bad, are examined together with the conditions that make for each.

Since Dominicans were an itinerate preaching order, all the dangers and opportunities of travel must be noted. Further, the conduct of the traveling preachers while out of the pulpit comes in for a lot of discussion, focusing especially on their conversation. Finally, a bit of advice is given over such purely practical issues as the hearing of confessions, whether prothemes are used, and the kinds of homiletical aids to be taken in the friar's knapsack.

When spirituality is understood not just as a set of devotional exercises, but as the total way of life by which a Christian's vocation is lived out, it becomes clear that a spirituality can be built that derives entirely from the obligation to preach. By clearly delineating the purposes of preaching and then discussing the way life must be organized and lived out by persons who are called to accomplish those purposes, Humbert did indeed set forth a spirituality growing out of what it means to be a member of an order of preachers.

SPIRITUALITY THROUGH PREACHING

Meister Eckhart

In addition to the possibility of a spirituality growing out of the obligation to preach, there can also be a spirituality communicated largely through preaching. A spirituality of this sort also developed within the Dominican order, but it was preached as much to nuns as to friars. The setting for this development was the Rhineland in the early fourteenth century. The form of preaching that was the medium for this spirituality is an exception to the rule that says thematic preaching replaced classical patristic homilies as the genre of preaching during this period. Indeed, a technical description of the sermons of these mystics would be reminiscent in many ways of the monastic preaching of Bernard and his contemporaries. Most of the distinctions to be drawn between these two periods of preaching to religious have first to be made on the basis of content before they can be spelled out in terms of form. That, however, will come out as the homiletical careers of two of the leading Rhineland mystics, Meister Eckhart (ca. 1260–1327) and John Tauler (ca. 1300–1361), are presented.

Eckhart's first name may have been Johannes, but he has been called so exclusively by the title of Master given him by the University of Paris that certainty about what his parents called him is impossible. He was born around 1260 in the Thuringian town of Hochheim and entered the Dominican order in nearby Erfurt. After preliminary formation and education, he was sent to Cologne, where he may have studied under Albert the Great. From there he went to Paris and began his career as a writer and teacher.

Under the Dominican practice of rotating its university lecturers, Eckhart was next returned to Erfurt for the first in a series of administrative positions. He began as prior of Erfurt and then became the Thuringian representative of the Dominicans' provincial prior of Germany. Next he directed the newly created subdivision of Saxony, becoming after that the general vicar of the province in Bohemia. In 1310 he was elected prior provincial of Teutonia, but the general chapter of the order decided that he should return to Paris instead. After a three-year stint he was sent back to Germany, first to Strasbourg and then Cologne. In both places he attracted great attention for the essential Dominican work of preaching, being especially popular in convents of Dominican nuns.

He also caught the unfavorable attention of the archbishop of Cologne, a Franciscan, who began raising questions about his orthodoxy, questions that resulted in a papal condemnation for heresy not published until after his death in 1327.[9] The extent of any lapses from orthodoxy was a matter of debate at the time and has remained so. The questions arose out of the perennial difficulty mystics have of putting their experiences into words. One of Eckhart's favorite expressions referred to the birth of the Son in the soul of the Christian. Some of his paradoxical ways of talking about that sounded like a unitive mysticism in which the worshiper becomes so at one with the worshiped that the union is ontological and the two are no longer distinguishable. A pantheistic interpretation of the same doctrine was given by some.

Whatever the case, Eckhart expressed regret before his death for any heretical interpretations to which his statements could have given rise; his own intention was always devoutly orthodox. His condemnation did not terminate his influence; Tauler and Henry Suso (Heinrich Seuse) carried on with more judicious expressions of his thought. In this century his ideas have again become an occasion of controversy; "at different times Eckhart has been viewed as a pantheist, a forerunner of the Reformation, a prophet of German national religion, a Zen master in disguise, and a proto-Marxist."[10]

The present relevance of Eckhart, however, is not in his possible heresy, but in his homiletics. Perhaps the best approach to that is to look at the way he develops a particular sermon.[11] The second in the collection of his German sermons is preached from the text of Luke 10:38 (**See Vol. 2, pp. 219-24,** for this sermon). The text was read to its audience of religious in the Latin of the Vulgate: "He entered into a certain village *(castellum)*; and a woman named Martha welcomed him to her house." Despite the use of a word for the village that has as its primary meaning "a fort, camp, or castle," there is little surprising in that. The surprise begins, however, when Eckhart translates the text into German: "Our Lord Jesus Christ went up into a little castle and was received by a virgin who was a wife." That begins to sound like a text from which a mystic might wish to preach!

The sermon is a commentary on this verse and gives no evidence of the subdividing mentality of thematic sermons. Instead, it is a straightforward treatment of the words of the text. These words are understood allegorically,[12] of course, but so were the texts from which Bernard preached. The difference almost seems to be in the spiritualities of the two preachers, the classical patristic and monastic approach of Bernard and the more mystical and philosophical approach of Eckhart.

From this it should not be assumed, however, that Eckhart is to be thought of as a mystic or philosopher who followed his personal interests while wearing the habit of the Order of Preachers. His understanding of his vocation, and indeed that of biblical interpretation, was homiletical and Dominican to the core.

> True philosophy—what we would call theology—is based on the study of the scriptures and has as its goal the work of the preacher, however much it may strive to make use of natural reasons and examples. This is the perspective from which Eckhart wrote and preached. . . . The majority of his surviving Latin works are exegetical in character, and his numerous Latin and German sermons are also based on biblical texts.[13]

"Martha" is understood to mean "wife" through a traditional method of interpreting biblical names. Since she received Jesus into *her* house, she was the mistress of the house, so she is assumed to be a wife. The means by which the "woman" is identified as a virgin depends on Eckhart's principle of finding the hidden meaning under the letter. Neither "wife" nor "virgin," however, is to be applied in its literal sense. *Virgin* here is to mean "a human being who is devoid of all foreign images and who is as void as he was when he was not yet."[14]

Behind this lies Eckhart's belief, derived from Albert the Great, in the preexistence of human beings in their ideal state before birth. In that state they did not know by images, but knew things in their own nature as God knows them. A return to that virginal state of pure knowing is the goal of human beings, and that is to be achieved by detaching oneself completely from these images and thus from any sense of things as one's own property.

Jesus, by his knowing as God knows, was virginal in this sense. To be united with him, a soul must be pure, as he is pure. In order to be united, though, the virgin must become a wife, must become creative and conceive, so that the Son of God is born in the soul. This is the fruit of complete detachment: "to reintegrate the primitive freedom before the self disperses itself among images."[15] Freedom from images is much more fruitful than attachment to them; it can give birth "a hundred, a thousand times a day"[16] rather than just once a year. The difference is between the fruit the *attached* person conceives and the fruit the *detached* person conceives in union with God.

Eckhart goes on to show that the power in which this conception occurs is neither in the intellect nor the will. It occurs in the one and simple ground of the mind that he calls the "little castle" *(castellum)*. This is to say that it consists of regaining "the original identity with the self, in the ground of the mind to which God gives himself in his being."[17] While this doctrine is appropriately called mystical, it is not otherworldly; it is not flight from this world but a call to find God by being in the world but not of it. The Meister's interpretation is not the first thing that pops into one's mind today when reading Luke 10:38, but it was the "hidden meaning under the letter"[18] that he saw in this passage.

John Tauler

Although greatly influenced by Eckhart, John Tauler did mystical preaching in a very different way. A fellow Dominican, he nevertheless was always much more the spiritual director than the professor and philosopher, more the *Lebmeister* than the *Lesmeister* (director of studies). Born around 1300, twenty-seven years before the death of Eckhart, Tauler grew up in a prosperous family in Strasbourg and spent most of the rest of his life as a friar in his native city and in Basle. His work was largely with the seven convents of Dominican sisters in Strasbourg and with the communities there of Beguines (women living together in a religious community without taking life vows). These religious houses had a combined population of almost a thousand women, about 5 percent of the total population of Strasbourg.[19] His sermons to them were also open to the laity. Tauler and Henry Suso, his friend and fellow disciple of Eckhart, were leaders of the Friends of God, a movement in the

Rhineland and Switzerland of mystics who stressed transformation through the union of their souls with God.

Little is known about the life of Tauler, but several pieces of evidence come together to suggest a spiritual crisis around the time of his move to Basle in 1339.[20] The first is that a visit to Cologne that year seems to have been the occasion of a revived interest in the work of Eckhart. Also, he says in one of his sermons that "until a man has reached his fortieth year, he will never attain lasting peace, nor be truly formed into God, try as he may."[21]

These two reports are consistent with a beautiful legend about Tauler. It tells of a devout layman who had been instructed in a dream to go hear him preach. Following this instruction, making his confession to Tauler and receiving his Communion from him, the man then asked him to preach on "how a man may attain to the highest and utmost point it is given to us to reach in this present time." When Tauler had done so, the layman returned to him and told him that the sermon was excellent, but that the preacher himself did not live by its precepts. Shocked, Tauler asked for instruction. After a discipline of two years' silence in the pulpit, he began to preach again with the power that he is known to have had.[22]

Not much in addition to that is known about his life, although he lived in the exciting years of the Avignon papacy and the Black Plague, dying during its second outbreak in 1361. During his lifetime his orthodoxy, unlike that of Eckhart, was never in doubt. When, after the Reformation, his works were translated into Latin along with a number of others attributed to him (only about sixty of his genuine sermons remain), he was interpreted in a quietistic way and Pope Sixtus V temporarily placed his works on the Index.[23]

While Tauler drew much of his understanding of the spiritual life from Eckhart, his sermons are very different from those of the Meister. In form, they are fairly straightforward biblical homilies much in the pattern of the monastic preaching of Bernard, the difference being in the spirituality inculcated rather than in the rhetorical form. Taking a text from one of the liturgical lections for the occasion, Tauler would draw out the lessons he found in it for the development of the spiritual lives of the nuns and laypersons in his congregation. These are far more accessible than the teaching of Eckhart.

Indeed, Tauler's are some of the few sermons that have come down from previous centuries that can still be read today with a sense of immediate applicability, so great is their simplicity, directness, and complete commitment to doing "the one thing necessary." They are less abstract, philosophical, and theoretical than those of Eckhart. Then, too, they seem to depend less on Neoplatonism and more on the example of Jesus.

Gabriele von Siegroth-Nellessen has conducted a study of the styles of Eckhart, Tauler, and Suso that involved a statistical analysis of syntactic patterns and idiosyncrasies. She came to the conclusion that Tauler is "the most spontaneous and audience-oriented preacher of the three." She says that while Eckhart uses the written style of the treatise even when he is preaching, Tauler "relates to the everyday context of the audience."[24]

There is no doubt, however, that the basic mystical thought of Tauler comes from Eckhart. That thought is expressed in Eckhart's own words:

> Whenever I preach, I usually exhort detachment and that man should free himself of himself and of everything. Secondly, that one should become embedded ... into the one-fold good that is God. And thirdly, that one should contemplate the great nobility that God has implanted into the soul so that man comes in mysterious ways into God. And fourthly, of the purity of divine nature—of the light that is in divine nature, which is truly ineffable.[25]

There are important differences between the mystical thought of Tauler and that of his teacher, and these undoubtedly had implications for the differences in their preaching styles, but they need not concern us here. For the moment it is enough to recognize that the two of them in their mystical fervor created a distinctive genre of preaching in fourteenth-century Germany. Through his influence on the *Theologia Germanica*, Tauler was an inspiration even to Martin Luther as he was an influence on spiritual renewals and mystical-theological controversies as late as the eighteenth century.[26] Any history of preaching would be incomplete without some reference to the homiletical activity of the Rhineland mystics.[27]

A PULPIT OF PROTEST

Wyclif

A late contemporary of Tauler was engaged in a very different sort of production of sermons in England. Not a Dominican like the other major figures studied in this chapter, John Wyclif[28] (ca. 1330–84) was a secular priest. Having grown up in a comfortable Yorkshire family, he arrived at Oxford in the mid-1350s, where he was first a fellow of Merton and then master of Balliol. Being master of Balliol at the time amounted to little more than heading a lodging house for students, and the position provided him with scant support; he gave it up as soon as he could. In 1365, however, he was given a more prestigious appointment; he was made head of Canterbury Hall, an experimental college in which both monastic and secular clergy would live together (there being few members of the laity in the university then). When, however, he tried to eject all of the religious from the college, he was relieved of his position.

During Wyclif's era (and for centuries after the Reformation), it was possible for a cleric to receive the income from a church appointment without living in the place or performing the ministry. Someone else could be hired to do the actual work while the incumbent did something else, such as studying in a university. Indeed, one might be appointed to several such benefices and live in none of them. Such absentee pluralism was the major source of Wyclif's income while he was at Oxford.

Since the Oxford degree nomenclature at the time was the same as it is in modern universities, Wyclif's career can sound a bit confusing. Advancement from the bachelor to the master of arts involved several years of lecturing, and the master's, given after a total of six or eight years of study, was the standard teaching degree. Wyclif did not receive his doctorate until he had been at Oxford almost eighteen years.

His first lectures were in logic; he quickly identified himself as a realist, in opposition to the nominalists who had ruled the turf at Oxford since William of Ockham had taught there in the previous generation. While his argument is too subtle to be explored here, it is enough to note that he claimed an ethical motivation for it:

> All envy or actual sin is caused by the lack of an ordered love of universals . . . because every such sin consists in a will preferring a lesser good to a greater good, whereas in general the more universal goods are better.[29]

Stated in terms of simple ethical choices, the acknowledgment of categories of persons could lead one to promote the welfare of the entire class of human persons rather than of just those closely related to oneself. However foreign such a philosophical vocabulary sounds today, it was very much that of the time—and it is hard to argue with the conclusion. This and other ventures in the field of logic led in time to Wyclif's becoming one of the most influential minds in the university. For most of his career, any fame he had rested on his skill as a logician. With the completion of his first work in theology as such, a study of the incarnation, he received his doctor of divinity degree in 1372.[30] After that he began work on a theological *summa*, an undertaking that occupied eight years. Before it was completed, however, his life underwent a number of changes.

Like many scholars of today, Wyclif's reputation for learning caused him to be called into government service. Popes had long claimed the right to tax clergy anywhere in the Western world. When, however, the papacy moved to France and came under the protection of the French Crown, the English began to feel that such taxes were taking their money to arm their enemies against them. In 1371, Parliament had just levied a large tax on the English clergy to help pay for the war against France when the pope levied another to finance a war to recover papal territories in Italy. Wyclif was invited to be a member of the second of two unsuccessful English delegations to Bruges to negotiate the matter with papal officials.

This involvement led Wyclif to begin to think about government. In the treatise on civil dominion in his *Summa*, he argued the thesis that no one in a state of sin has a right to exercise authority. God may allow someone to occupy such a position in a state of sin, but that person does so without any divine claim to the position. He drew a number of inferences from this, including the principle that Christians ought to have all things in common. Yet he applied his thesis very differently to civil and church governments. Even a bad king should be obeyed, as Christ obeyed Pilate, but

> whenever an ecclesiastical community or person habitually abuses its wealth, kings, princes and temporal lords can take it away, however much it may be established by human tradition.[31]

By the time of publication in 1376, when Wyclif was in his mid-forties, he took the first step toward his later recognition as a heretic, that of siding with the Crown against church government at any level when the latter could be accused of using its wealth for itself rather than to help the poor. Why he chose to work out the implications of his thesis for church government alone and not for civil as well, no one knows.[32]

Needless to say, his opinions were more welcome to political than to religious leaders. As a result, Wyclif enjoyed the protection of John of Gaunt, son of the king and one of the most influential men at court. John invited him to London to preach a series of sermons against the worldliness of the bishops of London and Winchester. When the bishop of London summoned him to trial for these sermons, Wyclif was accompanied not only by four advocates but also by John and the marshal of England, and the trial ended in a riot.

By this time the pope had condemned eighteen propositions from Wyclif's *On Civil Dominion* and had asked the king, the senior bishops, and Oxford to condemn him. The king died, but the royal council hired Wyclif as a consultant; the bishops forbade only his teaching those doctrines in a way that might scandalize the laity; and Oxford found the condemned theses to be true. Then the pope died and was succeeded by one from whom reform was expected. When that pope inspired the election of an anti-pope, Wyclif was safe from prosecution by Rome until after his death.

After this London episode Wyclif turned his attention to the doctrine of holy Scripture. His lectures on the Bible had already allowed him to complete a commentary on every book in it that was rich in knowledge of patristic interpretation, the only such commentary that survives from the second half of the fourteenth century. His treatise *On the Truth of Sacred Scripture* (1377–78) argues that the Bible is free from error and thus authoritative, that all truth is in it, and that it is thus the yardstick by which all other claims to truth are to be evaluated. Because it is the inerrant statement of truth, it should be available to all Christians.

Yet Wyclif was no fundamentalist; all his life he used allegorical interpretation, and he considered patristic interpretation to be the guide to true biblical understanding. He certainly did not believe in what was later to be called "plenary verbal inspiration."

> What is on the paper is not scripture without its relation to the mental understanding; and what is in the mind is not holy unless it is a grasping of the objective scripture. Hence the need to compare manuscripts together, and check them against the common faith of the whole Church.[33]

His belief that Scripture should be open to all Christians does not mean, as was long thought to be the case, that he himself translated any of it or even supervised the translating activity of others. There is no doubt, however, that the two English translations from his time were made by his followers. After he left Oxford in 1381, the leader of his party at the university, Nicholas of Hereford, did a pedestrian rendering that employed Latin cognates and constructions; and his companion at Lutterworth, John Purvey, was probably the one who revised that into a more idiomatic version.[34]

In 1378–79 Wyclif continued to develop his thoughts about civil and religious government. In doing so he worked out his doctrine of the church, which he defined as consisting of the predestined, those elected to salvation. He distinguished between being in a state of grace and being predestined. At a given moment someone not predestined may be in a state of grace, while someone who is predestined may be in a state of sin. No matter; only those who will persevere are considered actually to be part of the church. Thus he approaches the distinction between the visible and the invisible church.

Yet, in connecting these thoughts with what he has to say about civil dominion, he makes it clear that it is being in a state of grace rather than being predestined that entitles a leader to obedience. Thus if the pope is in grace, even if he is not predestined, he should be obeyed by as much of the Western church as is in communion with him (although this is a "poor particular church cramped in a corner" rather than the holy catholic church).[35] Not being head of the universal church, the pope has no claim to the obedience of all secular lords.

Grace can be communicated to Christians without its having to go through the pope. Nonpredestinate clergy can administer valid sacraments so long as they are in a state of grace (a variation on the Donatist view). Thus, while it is necessary that there be a pope, an actual pope not in a state of grace may even be an Antichrist and thus forfeit any right to be obeyed. A true pope would leave secular matters entirely alone and be a model of charity and holiness. Because of this it had been hard for a bishop of Rome to be a true pope ever since the Donation of Constantine endowed the Roman church and made it wealthy.

Up through this attack on the papacy, Wyclif had the support of many leaders in the church as well as the government, especially the friars who agreed with his standard of apostolic poverty. When, however, he turned his critical eye to eucharistic doctrine, he lost this following. His quarrel was not with the real presence of Christ in the Eucharist; indeed, he died hearing Mass. But he could not make logical sense of the claim that while all the accidents of bread and wine remained, the substance had been totally transformed into the body and blood of Christ. He did not believe that accidents can subsist without a substance, nor did he believe that any substance can be annihilated. Further, as he pointed out, the early fathers had not believed or known the unscriptural doctrine of transubstantiation. All of these arguments depend, of course, on an analysis of reality that grows out of Aristotle's distinction between substance and accident.

Friars at Oxford caused a university commission of twelve doctors to be set up in 1380 to examine this doctrine, which they found to be heretical and dangerous to Catholic faith and the reputation of the university.

Anyone teaching it should be imprisoned, suspended from university functions, and excommunicated. This doctrine also cost Wyclif the support of John of Gaunt. Meanwhile, one of the leaders of the Peasants' Revolt, John Ball, claimed to have learned from Wyclif the doctrines that justified the rebellion. While Wyclif would not have condoned this application of his theory, the association of his name with the revolt did him no good.

Soon afterward he withdrew from Oxford and settled in the nearby parish of Lutterworth, a benefice he had held for a number of years. From there he continued to pour out polemical writings for the three years that remained of his life, although many of his closest followers were either recanting or fleeing. Meanwhile, in 1382 his old enemy the bishop of London, who had become archbishop of Canterbury, called a conference of bishops and theologians to meet at Blackfriars' and examine twenty-four of Wyclif's teachings. Ten were declared heretical and the other fourteen erroneous.

One of Wyclif's activities during the waning days of his life was to edit his Latin sermons for publication. It is ironic that the reason for his consideration in this volume is hardly mentioned before he was near to death. As an absentee pluralist, however, he would have done little preaching in the parishes to which he had been presented. Some of his Latin sermons were preached to the university and numbers of them have no distinctive Wycliffite doctrines, yet most represent his short stay at Lutterworth and the majority of these were never preached by him. They "were a literary production, composed in the sequence in which they now stand, and were probably intended for the use of other preachers."[36] "Of sermons actually preached by Wyclif only a relatively small number survive as the *Sermones Quadriginta*,"[37] which appear in the last volume of the Loserth edition.

There also exists in English a cycle of 294 sermons that are homilies in form and constitute a series (for an example of these sermons, **see Vol. 2, pp. 224-27**). The series comprises sermons on both the Epistles and Gospels for every Sunday in the Sarum calendar,[38] including Gospels shared by the feast days of a number of saints ("commons"), those for a particular saint's day ("propers"),[39] and Gospels for certain weekdays in the church year ("ferias").

Until recently, it was assumed that Wyclif wrote these sermons or that they were translations made by others of the similar series of Latin sermons he had composed but not preached at Lutterworth. Now, however, "it seems clear that, whatever their debt to Wyclif's Latin works, and whatever the link with his *Sermones* in their extant or previous forms, the English sermons as they stand are very unlikely to have been written by Wyclif himself."[40] Indeed, they seem to have been written after his death, with 1389–90 the most likely date.[41] The series appears to have had either an unknown single author or at least an overseer of the entire project. That person was someone closely related to a university who was familiar (a) with most of the corpus of Wyclif's writings, (b) with many works of patristic and earlier medieval biblical scholarship, and (c) with issues before the church at the time of writing. Yet that person was also capable of lapses in Latin usage and showed other gaps in learning.[42]

The manuscripts of these series are very fine and appear to have been produced under tight control. This fact has a number of implications. First, it appears that there were wealthy Wycliffites (or Lollards, as they were called) who could bear the expense and provide the facilities where such manuscripts could be produced in safety.[43] Next, the preaching to be done was neither the extempore nor the written efforts of the preachers, nor even their variations on appointed themes; the sermons were to be read as official teaching.[44] They were bound into handsome volumes appropriate for use at liturgical assemblies and so were not prepared for street preaching, but for the regular worship of congregations who followed the official calendar. From this fact it would appear that there was an organized circuit of Lollard congregations, congregations, moreover, that were prepared to listen to four or more sermons a week.[45]

While it used to be thought that Wyclif himself organized groups of "poor priests" to wander over England giving extempore sermons based on his English translation of the Bible, little of that belief is now credible. The translation was made by others, only a few of Wyclif's supporters have left records of preaching tours in his lifetime, and no evidence exists to prove that he organized them. Yet, obviously, congregations did come into existence, and they were founded by people influenced by the teaching of Wyclif. It does not push the evidence too far to suggest that he was in favor of such developments, but there is no ground for saying that he was responsible for their initiation.

Little is known about how the movement spread. One scholar has suggested that it did so through the efforts of sympathetic Oxford colleges to appoint Wycliffites to parishes to which they had the power of appointment.[46] At any rate, the doctrines did spread until the failure of Sir John Oldcastle's[47] Lollard rebellion against Henry V in 1413–14.[48]

The English cycle, however derivatively, reflects Wyclif's thought about preaching. He never tired of saying how important he thought it was.[49] That, of course, does not make him very different from the friars. Indeed, on the whole, his thoughts about preaching remind one of nothing so much as the early days of the friars. Their emphasis on having learned priests go about preaching from the Bible is very similar, as is also their emphasis on poverty and their objections to avarice and worldliness among the clergy. Even the picture that has survived of the "poor priests" Wyclif was supposed to have sent out (which could be an accurate representation of Lollards who went out later) sounds very Franciscan:

> Bare-foot, clad in a long coarse cloak of dark-red colour which was the symbol of hard labour and poverty, a long staff in hand signifying their pastoral office, they wandered in the dioceses of Leicester (and of London) from town to town, from village to village. In churches, chapels and alms-houses, wherever they could get a few hearers together, they preached of the glory of God's law. Although mocked at by some for their coarse garb and for their manner of teaching, they were beloved by the people.[50]

This raises the question of why Wyclif opposed the friars so much. It can be pointed out that he did not do so until his eucharistic doctrine met their disfavor. After that he began to teach against begging; he also criticized thematic preaching and, especially, the use of *exempla*. While it does appear likely that, as time went on, some *exempla* were a bit coarse and others appear to have been told more for their entertainment than their illustrative value, it is hard to know what Wyclif had against *exempla* in general, unless it was merely that his philosopher's mind preferred the abstract to the concrete.

The form of Wycliffite sermons, both those of the master in Latin and those of his followers in English, was essentially that of old-style homilies that fell into two divisions, exegesis and application. The former was the shorter of the two and was by no means confined to the literal, historical meaning of the passage. Yet, as Kinney says: "All too often Wyclif uses an episode in Christ's life, or a scriptural text, merely as a peg on which to hang an attack on his *bêtes noire*."[51]

Since Wyclif's preaching has often been claimed to be "sermons of the Reformation age rather than of medieval times,"[52] it is interesting to read the evaluation of a distinguished mid-twentieth-century Lutheran historian of preaching:

> We expect great things of Wycliffe and his school; the study of his extant sermons has, however, disappointed those who wish to see in him a "precursor" of the Reformation. Though his Latin sermons are wholly Scholastic in character, the English sermons are a practical, popular proclamation based upon the Bible. The allegorical method does,

however, hold him in its sway and when he interprets scripture literally it becomes primarily a law of God which demands application to the contemporary situation in church and state. Because of this Wycliffe did not find the true living water of the gospel. It was in rapture over the law of God that the Lollards left on their travels.[53]

The significance of Wyclif and his preaching is seen not only in his inspiration of the Lollards, but also in his having been the primary theological and homiletical influence on John Hus and his Bohemian followers. Whole passages of the sermons of Hus can be set down in parallel with those of Wyclif and be seen to have extensive verbal dependence.[54] Thus Anne Hudson has summarized Wyclif's importance in the history of preaching by saying:

> Directly, Lollardy prepared the ground for the reformation in England, by establishing groups of men who were accustomed to radical ideas on the church and authority within it, and who regarded the text of the Bible in the vernacular with special reverence. Indirectly, Wyclif's theories, through the medium of Hus's writings and of Hussite copying, reinforced those of the later reformers.[55]

Pulpit Apocalypse

It could be thought that any history of preaching, even one devoted to movements rather than practitioners, would be incomplete without reference to so famous a preacher as Girolamo Savonarola (1452–98). One of the most authoritative interpreters of the Florentine friar, however, has insisted that the attention he deserves generally and not just homiletically does not spring so much from his uniqueness as from his being at home in his environment. As Donald Weinstein says:

> The central methodological problem has been the tendency to treat Savonarola monolithically, either as a man without a history or as one whose history serves to illustrate a solid, unchanging core of personality, rather than, as with ordinary men, to provide the experience that shaped his personality.[56]

That experience, as Weinstein noted a few pages earlier in *Savonarola and Florence,* is very much a part of the Florentine world of his time. "He is just such a combination of popular zealot, conservative theologian, and radical millenarian as could have existed only in the milieu of Italy before the Reformation and the conquest of Hapsburg Spain."[57] He could have also said that Savonarola exemplifies the apocalyptic preaching so common in the Middle Ages.

Few persons in the history of preaching, including Meister Eckhart and Wyclif, have been the subject of more varied interpretations offered by more fervent partisans. In an excellent summary of scholarship over the last century, Weinstein refers to those who love Savonarola as "the New *Piagnoni*," the term by which his contemporary followers were designated.[58] They are those who think that the church should regard him as a saint rather than as the heretic he was burned for being. These devotees could be divided into those who consider him a precursor of the Reformation and those who think he should be canonized by the Roman Catholic Church. Others consider him proud and deluded, not to mention doctrinally devious and dangerous. More secular modern interpreters are apt to regard anyone who claimed to be the recipient of divine revelation as emotionally disturbed. Others are content to think of Fra Girolamo as a political thinker: the restorer of the Florentine republic, a herald of Italian unification in the nineteenth century, or a dictator. Variations have been played on all these themes.

Whatever the interpretation, there is general agreement on the data. Born in 1452 into a middle-class professional family in Ferrara, Savonarola was always a serious and severe person, even when he was studying philosophy as part of his premedical education. His love of Thomas Aquinas undoubtedly had something to do with his running away from home to join the Dominicans when he was twenty-two. In 1482 he was sent to Florence for the first time.

He did not show great promise as a preacher, however, until he was preaching in the church at San Gimignano near Siena two years later. There, for the first time, he began to incorporate into his preaching what he considered to be the revelations he was receiving, revelations to the effect that the church was to be scourged,[59] then it would be renewed, and all of that was going to happen very soon. After several years on a preaching tour in northern Italy, he was ready to return to the Dominican community of San Marco as prior in 1491 and see the beginning of his remarkable success in the city of Florence.

From the beginning, his prophecies seem to have been closely related to the political scene. His predictions of the death of Lorenzo de Medici and the conquest of Florence by the king of France, Charles VIII, were seen by the people as signs that his message came from God. He was a member of the embassy that Florence sent to arrange terms with Charles, and, when those terms were lenient, he was regarded as the savior of the city. So high was his stock that he not only played an important role in the establishment of a sort of theocratic democracy, but also began a period of ascetical moral reform there.

His attacks on the church continued, however, and brought him to the unfavorable attention of Pope Alexander VI.[60] By this time, too, political, economic, and financial difficulties in Florence, as well as restiveness under his puritanical standards, had begun to foster disaffection among powerful elements within the citizenry. In 1495 the pope suspended the friar from preaching, a ban he observed for about six months. On the whole, Alexander was very patient and did not excommunicate Savonarola until 1497. The friar's response was to start requesting the secular powers to call an ecumenical council to depose an unworthy pope. After that there seemed no alternative but to arrest him, wring a confession out of him by torture, and turn him over to the secular authorities for execution.

In order to understand the sermons of Savonarola, it is necessary to know something about the apocalyptic framework in which they were set. Learning that is not as simple as it could have been because, as Weinstein pointed out, the framework changed in midcourse. His original revelation had been little more than that the church was to be purged by God from its wickedness and then restored to purity in the near future. But

> at a certain moment his Christian universalism narrowed to a partisan civic focus, with Florence taking shape in his mind as the New Jerusalem and the future of her government and worldly fortunes becoming part of the divine plan.[61]

As Weinstein has shown, the new elements in Savonarola's vision were derived from "the myth of Florence" widely believed at the time. "Strongly optimistic millenarian hopes centered on Florence as the harbinger of the renovated church" had been a motif in Florentine self-understanding for some time,[62] and the seer came to this more positive view of his adopted city as the very success of his earlier prophecies generated a wider acceptance of him and his message within the city.

Savonarola's confidence in his own revelation, however, demanded that he see his point of view as having been consistent all along. The way he explained it to himself and others was as follows:

> As Almighty God saw the sins of Italy multiply, especially in her ecclesiastical and secular princes, he was unable to bear it any longer and decided to cleanse his Church with a great scourge. . . . Since Florence is located in the middle of Italy, like the heart in a man, God himself

deigned to choose her to receive this proclamation so that from her it might be widely spread through the other parts of Italy, as we have seen fulfilled in the present. Among his other servants he chose me, unworthy and unprofitable as I am, for this task, and saw to it that I came to Florence in 1489 at the command of my superiors. That year, on Sunday, August first, I began to interpret the book of the Apocalypse in public in our Church of San Marco. Through the whole of the same year I preached to the people of Florence and continually stressed three things: first, the renovation of the Church would come in these times; second, God would send a great scourge over all Italy before that renovation; and third, these two things would happen soon. I worked at proving and establishing these three conclusions by firm arguments, by figures from the Holy Scriptures, and by other likenesses or parables formed from the things that are now happening in the Church.

I urged the case at that time only with these arguments and kept secret the fact that I had also received knowledge of them from God in another way, because it seemed that the state of souls was not then ready to receive that mystery. In the following years, finding minds more ready to believe, I sometimes introduced a vision, not disclosing that it was a prophetic vision but setting it forth to the people only in the manner of a parable.[63]

Savonarola says that he received his revelations in all of the ways that such things come. He always received a supernatural light that was a form of participation in God's eternity; from this he learned that the revelation was true and came from God. The medium of the revelation varied, however: sometimes it came directly into the intellect without any images, sometimes the imagination was imprinted with different figures and images, and sometimes God set forth things to the exterior senses.

Beginning with a sermon at Santa Reparata's in Florence during 1490, however, he came to realize that God sent him the visions so that he could make them known. From that time on he did so, and the response was overwhelming. "My faithful listeners know how fittingly my expositions of the scriptures always agreed with the present times."[64] A climax in this process came when everyone knew that Charles VIII was about to invade Italy. In his continuing exposition of Genesis he came to the text "Behold, I will bring waters upon the face of the earth." When he announced that text, "many were immediately astonished and acknowledged that this passage of Genesis had been gradually prepared by God's hidden inspiration to fit the times."[65]

With most of Savonarola's recorded sermons, there is some difficulty in knowing exactly how closely they approximate what he actually said in delivery, because his faithful amanuensis, Lorenzo Violi, did not always seek to write down what he said word for word.[66] In part Violi's interest grew and in part his skill improved, especially after the friar began to assist him by looking over what he had taken down in a shorthand that appears illegible to others.[67] For some of Savonarola's sermons before Violi began to record them there remain the author's Latin notes, but these are very sketchy and incomplete. Later scholars have published some of these earlier series of sermons in a form that seems imaginative expansions from such notes into full sermons. It can be assumed, however, that for the last sermons on which Violi had the cooperation of the preacher, the text is close to what was actually delivered.

When one looks at the sermons of Savonarola,[68] it is obvious that the friar returned to a patristic practice of *lectio continua*, doing series of sermons on individual books of the Bible rather than preaching on one of the lections for the liturgical occasion. Yet the sermons are preached from a short text rather than from an extended passage, and the preacher shows virtually no interest in the historical meaning of the text. Rather, he is concerned with its applicability to the situation in Florence as that is understood within the framework of his basic revelation.

Thus, after pointing out that Savonarola adhered to the traditional medieval fourfold interpretation, Weinstein goes on to say:

> But not even skill in the fourfold exegetical method was enough to reveal all the mysteries contained in Scripture. Only the prophet illuminated by God could uncover the history of the future recorded therein; Savonarola's Biblicism was inseparably linked with his prophetism and inevitably subordinated to it: "And this I have not by Scripture nor by the revelations of any man who is under heaven."[69]

The only way in which the flavor of that can be communicated is through extended quotation. This sample comes from his sermon for All Saints' in 1494 when Charles VIII was threatening to attack:

> *Vox dicentis clama.* A voice cries out saying: O Italy, *propter peccata tua venient tibi adversa.* All you cities of Italy, now is the time for all your sins to be punished. O Italy, for your lust, your avarice, your pride, your ambition, your thieving and extortion, there will come upon you many adversities and many scourges. *Vox dicentis clama.* A voice cries out saying: O *Florentia, propter peccata tua venient tibi adversa.* O Florence, O Florence, O Florence, for your sins, for your brutality, your avarice, your lust, your ambition, there will befall you many trials and many tribulations. *Vox dicentis clama.* On whom do you call? O Clergy, Clergy, Clergy, *propter te orta est haec tempestas*—O clergy,

who are the principal cause of so many evils, through your evildoing comes this story; by your sins have been prepared so many tribulations; woe, woe, I say unto those that bear the tonsure! *Vox dicentis clama,* a voice still calls. On whom further should I call? *Clama, ne cesses, annuntia populo huic scelera eorum,* cry out without ceasing, declare unto the people their wickedness. It calls and says, keep on: *Annuntia populo huic scelera eorum. . . .* I have said it so many times, I have cried out so often, I have wept for you so many times, Florence, that it should suffice. *Orate,* pray for me to the Lord, *ut Deus consoletur me.* O Florence, I have wished to speak this morning to you and each and every one openly and sincerely, for I could do no other. And still the voice cries out: *vox dicentis clama,* the voice of One speaks forth and calls. And whom else should I call? I have called each one to repentance. *Clama ad Dominum Deum tuum,* call and cry out to the Lord, thy God. I turn to thee, O Lord, Who died for love of us, and for our sins. *Parce, Domine, populo tuo.* Forgive, forgive, Lord, this Thy people; forgive, Lord, the people of Florence, who desire to be Thy people![70]

All preaching is predicated on the assumption that a common principle is operating between the situation in the text and the situation in the congregation. That is what justifies the transference of the perspective in the text to the congregational situation. But even if one assumes that the Holy Spirit inspires the preacher into awareness of these parallels, only an apocalyptic preacher, one who assumed that he or she had a direct message from God, would ever suggest that the only reason the Holy Spirit had inspired the biblical writer to say something was because of its future applicability to the situation of the apocalyptist. That is what Savonarola did when he said that the Genesis text "Behold, I will bring waters upon the face of the earth" had been "gradually prepared by God's hidden inspiration to fit the times."[71] In doing this he points to what makes apocalyptic preaching a distinct homiletical genre. While his own apocalyptic preaching received extraordinary attention both while it was occurring and ever since, it is representative of the genre not only in the Middle Ages but whenever it has appeared, from New Testament times on.

Revolutionary Conservatism

With the exception of the homiletical spirituality of Humbert of Romans, this chapter has dealt with movements in preaching that have not followed the supremely medieval pattern of the thematic sermon. The Rhineland mystics used a form of preaching little different from that of Bernard of Clairvaux; the difference that did exist was in the content. The reform preaching of the Wycliffites and the apocalyptic sermons of

Savonarola also employed variations on the traditional pattern of the homily. At least the latter two represented movements critical of the mainstream life of the church at the time, and thus the change of homiletical pattern was probably not entirely an accident.

There were other oscillations of the weathercock on the steeple of the medieval church, suggesting that winds of change were in the air. The "subdividing mentality" seen alike in scholasticism and thematic preaching was probably an effect of the confidence in the powers of the human mind given to the medieval world by the recovery of Aristotle, especially his logic. The distinctions it allowed theologians to make opened to them the possibility of breaking down issues into their component parts. By the middle of the fifteenth century, however, the minds of Europe were being excited by the recovery of other writings from classical antiquity, especially the rhetorical works associated with the names of Cicero and Quintilian. This recovery was, of course, a part of a passionate interest in every aspect of classical antiquity, that movement of the human spirit known as the Renaissance. The coincidence of that with the movement known as the Reformation marks the next turning point in the history of preaching.

FOR FURTHER READING

Early Dominicans: Selected Writings. Edited, translated, and introduction by Simon Tugwell, and preface by Vincent de Couesnongle. CWS. New York: Paulist Press, 1982.

Johannes Tauler: Sermons. Translated by Maria Shrady, with introduction by Josef Schmidt and preface by Alois Haas. CWS. New York: Paulist Press, 1985.

Kenny, Anthony. *Wyclif.* Past Masters. Oxford: Oxford University Press, 1985.

Meister Eckhart: The Essential Sermons, Commentaries, Treatises, and Defense. Translated and introduction by Edmund Colledge and Bernard McGinn, with preface by Huston Smith. CWS. New York: Paulist Press, 1981.

Selections from English Wycliffite Writings. Edited and introduction, notes, and glossary by Anne Hudson. Medieval Academy Reprints for Teaching, no. 38. Cambridge: Cambridge University Press, 1978; repr., Toronto: University of Toronto Press for the Medieval Academy of America, 1997.

Weinstein, Donald. *Savonarola and Florence: Prophecy and Patriotism in the Renaissance.* Princeton, N.J.: Princeton University Press, 1970.

Notes

1. *Early Dominicans: Selected Writings,* ed. with intro. Simon Tugwell, and pref. Vincent de Couesnongle, CWS (New York: Paulist Press, 1982), 181.

2. Near Valence.

3. Tugwell, *Early Dominicans,* 2.

4. Ibid., 2.

5. Ibid., 6.

6. The Latin title is *De eruditione praedicatorum* and the standard edition is Humbertus de Romanus, *Opera de vita regulari,* ed. J. J. Berthier, 2 vols. (1889; reprint, Turin: Marietti, 1956). Another element in the mystery of the lack of notice that *The Formation of Preachers* received is the fact that Humbert joined to it a collection of model sermons, mostly of the *ad status* variety. Since it represented a more familiar genre, the model sermon collection was copied more often than the work on spirituality.

7. D. L. d'Avray, *The Preaching of the Friars: Sermons Diffused from Paris Before 1300* (Oxford: Clarendon, 1985), 177.

8. *The Formation of Preachers* 1.3.12. in Tugwell, *Early Dominicans,* 188. Gregory's exegesis here obviously reflects Ephesians 2:20 and a hermeneutical principle acknowledged since at least the time of Hillel that a word means the same thing whenever it appears in the canon, the word in this case being *foundation.* Also involved is Gregory's identification of the essential task of the apostles as being preaching.

9. The year 1327 is not known with certainty.

10. *Meister Eckhart: The Essential Sermons, Commentaries, Treatises, and Defense,* trans. and intro. Edmund Colledge, and Bernard McGinn, pref. Huston Smith, CWS (New York: Paulist Press, 1981), xvii. The entry in *ODCC* adds that he has also been regarded as a forerunner of Kantian critical idealism.

11. Cf. *Meister Eckhart: Mystic and Philosopher,* trans. and commentary Reiner Schürmann, Studies in Phenomenology and Existential Philosophy (Bloomington: Indiana University Press, 1978), 3-47.

12. "Allegorical" here is used in the general sense of any figurative meaning. Eckhart did not refer to the four senses of Scripture (literal, allegorical, topological, and anagogical) in the commonly accepted way, but instead spoke of two senses, the "more evident" and that hidden "under the shell of the letter" (McGinn in Colledge and McGinn, *Meister Eckhart,* 28). A convenient presentation of this perspective in Eckhart's own words occurs in the prologue to *The Book of the Parables in Genesis,* ibid., 92-95.

13. Ibid., 28.

14. Schürmann, *Meister Eckhart,* 3.

15. Ibid., 47.

16. Ibid., 5.

17. Ibid., 47.

18. Ibid., 10.

19. In the collection of *ad status* sermons included as the second half of *The Formation of Preachers,* Humbert of Romans provided a number for women in various states of life.

20. Strasbourg had sided with Louis of Bavaria against Pope John XXII, and so was one of the cities placed under Interdict. Thus Dominicans there had to be transferred to cities not under the ban.

21. "Sermon for Ascension II," trans. Maria Shrady, in *Johannes Tauler: Sermons*, intro. Josef Schmidt and pref. Alois Haas, CWS (New York: Paulist Press, 1985), 72.

22. *The History and Life of the Reverend Doctor John Tauler of Strasbourg; with Twenty-five of His Sermons,* trans. Susanna Winkworth (London: Smith, Elder & Co., 1857), 1-71.

23. Haas, *Johannes Tauler: Sermons,* xiv.

24. *Versuch einer exacten Stiluntersuchung für Meister Eckhart, Johannes Tauler, und Heinrich Seuse,* Medium Aevum Philosophische Studien (Munich: Wilhelm Fink Verlag, 1979). Schmidt reviews her analysis in *Johannes Tauler: Sermons,* 18-19.

25. Translated by Schmidt from Eckhart's Middle High German in a passage cited by Alois Haas, "Meister Eckharts geistliches Predigtprogramm," *FZPhTh* 29 (1982), 192-93. (*Johannes Tauler: Sermons,* 13). The final line of the quotation has been altered in the interest of intelligibility in English.

26. Haas, *Johannes Tauler: Sermons,* xiii.

27. To set this in the context of German homiletics, see Hans-Jochen Schiewer, "German Sermons in the Middle Ages" in *The Sermon,* dir. Kienzle, 861-961.

28. There are variations on the spelling of the name, but Wyclif is that preferred by specialists.

29. *De Universalibus,* ed. I. Mueller, P. Spade, and A. Kenny (Oxford: University Press, 1978), 77. Quoted in Anthony Kenny, *Wyclif,* Past Masters (Oxford: University Press, 1985), 10.

30. To this day, the D.D. is not an honorary degree in England as it is in the United States, but is rather a very high earned degree.

31. *De civili dominio,* ed. R. L. Poole (London: Wyclif Society, 1885), 286. Quoted in Kenny, *Wyclif,* 49-50.

32. Scholars disagree drastically about the reasons, depending on their overall attitude toward Wyclif. Herbert B. Workman sees Wyclif as more interested in metaphysical groundwork than in working out in life the doctrine of lordship. *John Wyclif: A Study of the Medieval Church* (Oxford: Clarendon Press, 1926), 1:259. K. B. McFarlane considers his motivation to have been pique at being passed over for a canonry in *John Wycliffe and the Beginnings of English Nonconformity,* Teach Yourself History (London: English Universities Press Ltd., 1952), 30, 66-69, 84-85. Gordon Leff insists that it is important to remember that "Wyclif was also a theorist who gave to his hostility to the church a far-reaching theoretical framework." *Heresy in the Later Middle Ages: The Relation of Heterodoxy to Dissent c. 1250–c. 1450* (Manchester: University Press; and New York: Barnes and Noble, 1967), 2:497.

33. Kenny, *Wyclif,* 61.

34. Margaret Deansley, *The Lollard Bible and Other Medieval Biblical Versions,* Cambridge Studies in Medieval Life and Thought (Cambridge: At the University Press, 1920), 252-67; *Selections from English Wycliffite Writings,* ed., with intro., notes, and glossary Anne Hudson, Medieval Academy Reprints for Teaching, no. 38 (Cambridge: Cambridge University Press, 1978; reprint, Toronto: University of Toronto Press for the Medieval Academy of America, 1997), 163.

35. Kenny, *Wyclif,* 71.

36. Hudson, *Selections from English Wycliffite Writings*, 3. For the Latin sermons, see *Iohannis Wyclif Sermones Now First Edited from the Manuscripts with Critical and Historical Notes*, ed. Johann Loserth, 4 vols. (London: Trübner & Co. for the Wyclif Society, 1887–90).

37. Ibid.

38. The calendar used in the Diocese of Salisbury, which, with most other liturgical usage there, became standard for Britain in the late Middle Ages.

39. In the Wycliffite tradition, only New Testament saints are provided for (with rare exceptions).

40. *English Wycliffite Sermons*, ed. Pamela Gradon and Anne Hudson, vol. 4 (Oxford: Clarendon Press, 1996), 28.

41. Ibid., 21.

42. Ibid., 28-37.

43. Sir Thomas Latimer is a case in point.

44. Although, as with other model sermons, there are times when a particular point is left to be developed by the preacher.

45. Anne Hudson, "A Lollard Sermon-Cycle and Its Implications," *Medium Aevum* 40 (1971): 142-56.

46. A. K. McHardy, "The Dissemination of Wyclif's Ideas," *From Ockham to Wyclif*, ed. Anne Hudson and Michael Wilks (Oxford: Basil Blackwell for the Ecclesiastical History Society, 1987), 361-68.

47. It is ironic that this Lollard leader should have been in his youth the companion of the future Henry V, on whom the character of Falstaff is based.

48. McFarlane, *John Wycliffe and the Beginnings of English Nonconformity*, 146; Anne Hudson, *Selections from English Wycliffite Writings*, 1:7.

49. Loserth, *Iohannis Wyclif Sermones*, 1:iii-vi.

50. Quoted by Loserth, *Iohannis Wyclif Sermones*, 1:xviii, from R. Buddensieg, *Johann Wiclif und seine Zeit* (Gotha: n.p., 1885), 169-70. Workman says that Wyclif "copied the methods of St. Francis" (*John Wyclif*, 1:201).

51. *Wyclif*, 97.

52. Workman, *John Wyclif*, 2:213-14.

53. Brilioth, *Brief History of Preaching*, 91-92. Brilioth obviously thought that Wyclif wrote the English as well as the Latin sermons. Much of this evaluation is conceded by Workman, who says: 'The student who turns from these glowing precepts (i.e., Wyclif's theory of preaching) to Wyclif's actual sermons will be disappointed, even if he bears in mind that there is nothing which so changes from age to age as the standard of effective pulpit oratory." *John Wyclif*, 2:212. Workman's understanding of Wyclif's preaching and his responsibility for the work of the "poor preachers" is presented in ibid., 2:201-20.

54. Loserth, *Iohannis Wyclif Sermones*, 1:xxii-xxvii.

55. Hudson, *Selections from English Wycliffite Writings*, 4. In a survey of preaching in English between ca. 1370 and ca. 1500, H. Leith Spencer says compilers of English sermon collections generally appear to have been persons of Wycliffite sympathies before the clamp-down on Lollardy by Archbishop Arundel in his *Constitutions* of 1407, but after that the more traditional influence of John Mirk's *Festial* was more prevalent. *English Preaching in the Late Middle Ages* (Oxford: Clarendon Press, 1993). Spencer expresses this view more concisely in "Middle English Sermons" in *The Sermon*, dir. Kienzle, 597-660.

56. Donald Weinstein, *Savonarola and Florence: Prophecy and Patriotism in the Renaissance* (Princeton: Princeton University Press, 1970), 18.

57. Ibid., 15.

58. Ibid., 3. The term means "the tearful ones" or "the mourners" and was originally used pejoratively, but it soon lost negative connotations. The summary of recent scholarship is found on pp. 3-26.

59. It is often thought that Wyclif and Savonarola were lone voices condemning the sins of the clergy of their day, but G. R. Owst has made it clear that the corrupt morals of some of them was one of the standard topoi of late medieval preaching. *Literature and Pulpit in Medieval England: A Neglected Chapter in the History of English Letters and of the English People* (Cambridge: University Press, 1933), 236-86.

60. An entertaining journalistic (but generally reliable) account of the clashes of Savonarola with the pontiff whose name has become a symbol for everything wrong with the Renaissance papacy is Michael de la Bedoyere, *The Meddlesome Friar: The Story of the Conflict between Savonarola and Alexander VI* (London: Collins, 1958). Alexander's reputation is not entirely deserved.

61. Weinstein, *Savonarola and Florence*, 77. This is the essential thesis of Weinstein's study.

62. Ibid., 27-66. The phrase quoted is from Bernard McGinn's preface to his translation of Savonarola's Compendium of Revelation in his book *Apocalyptic Spirituality: Treatises and Letters of Lactantius, Adso of Notier-en-Der, Joachim of Fiore, Franciscan Spirituals, Savonarola*, pref. Marjorie Reeves, CWS (New York: Paulist Press, 1979), 188.

63. McGinn, *Apocalyptic Spirituality*, 195-96.

64. Ibid., 196-97.

65. Ibid., 197.

66. *Savonarola: Prediche Italiani ai Fiorentini*, ed. Francesco Cognasso, Documenti di Storia Italiana (Perugia, Venice: Nuova Italia, 1930), 1:xiii. See also Roberto Ridolfi, *The Life of Girolamo Savonarola*, trans. Cecil Grayson (London: Routledge and Kegan Paul, 1959), 111-12.

67. E.g., Pierre Van Paassen, *A Crown of Fire: The Life and Times of Girolamo Savonarola* (New York: Scribner's, 1960), 174.

68. By no means an easy thing for the English reader to do. I know of only three translated sermons that are generally available. Petry has sections of the "Sermon for All Saints," 1494, in *No Uncertain Sound*, 296-99. An Ascension Day sermon appears in *20 Centuries of Great Preaching: An Encyclopedia of Preaching*, ed. Clyde E. Fant Jr. and William M. Pinson Jr. (Waco, Tex.: Word, 1971), 1:273-81. Then a "Sermon for the Octave of the Annunciation" is incorporated into Savonarola's *Compendium of Revelation*, in McGinn, *Apocalyptic Spirituality*, 208-70. Whole paragraphs of sermons are translated, however, in the English version of Ridolfi's *Life*, which also discusses the various series of sermons. The best critical edition of the sermons in Italian is that of "Edizione nazionale delle opere di Girolamo Savonarola" published in Rome by A. Berladetti (1955–74); the individual volumes in this series have different editors. Since Petry gives only an excerpt from a sermon, the sermon in McGinn occupies sixty-two printed pages, and the sermon in Fant and

Pinson has been reprinted often since it first appeared in 1908, no sermon from Savonarola is included in Volume 2. The flavor of Savonarola's preaching, however, is communicated in the excerpt from his sermon for All Saints' Day in 1494 that is included in this chapter.

69. Weinstein, *Savonarola and Florence,* 184. The internal quotation is from the *Sermons on the Psalms,* 1:45, in the edition that Weinstein was using.

70. Ridolfi, *Life,* 80-81.

71. McGinn, *Apocalyptic Spirituality,* 197.

PART III

FROM THE RENAISSANCE AND REFORMATION TO THE ENLIGHTENMENT

CHAPTER 11

ERASMUS AND THE
HUMANISTS

CHANGING TIMES

At the height of the Middle Ages there was a universal culture in Europe that found its unity expressed in the papacy. By their end, however, that culture was in disarray. Factors that contributed to the dissolution of the medieval synthesis include the growth of national sentiment among the European nations, skepticism about the hierarchy of the church, a resort to mysticism as an alternative to the sacramental spirituality of the church, the success of nominalism in undercutting scholastic theology, and the rise of humanism.[1] Most of these factors' impact on preaching were discussed in the previous chapter; the impact of humanism will begin this one.

The significance of the dissolution, however, is not so much that something old had ended as that something new was about to begin. A spiritual vacuum had been created that many exciting new movements would rush in to fill. Since this process resulted in divisions in Western Christianity that still exist, some effort is necessary at this point to evade the partisanship that has characterized many discussions of these monumental changes in the past. One way of going about that is to note that

269

systems do not have to be treated as wholes; they may be separated into aspects that can be studied individually. For example, no one denies that there was much wrong with the church in the West at the beginning of the sixteenth century, but we do not have to see efforts to improve that situation as so confined to one group that a horrible past can be contrasted to an ideal present or that faith communities are seen as either heroes or villains.

Major aspects of changes in church life in the sixteenth century include at least morality, theology, and scholarly method. To begin with the first, the inconsistency that can exist between the ethical ideals of the church and its own behavior was most conspicuous at the highest level. From a time when popes could appear to make good their claim to have power over kings and emperors, they had moved to one in which they could be pawns of rulers and there could be two or even three popes at the same time, each chosen by and for different political interests. In this milieu they often functioned like other monarchs, even to the extent of leading troops into battles over territory. Thus secularized, their interests and means assimilated to those of their opponents. The church's lands and treasures were treated as personal possessions, and efforts were made to create dynasties by the appointment of relatives and even offspring to key posts in civil and religious governments. Vast funds were needed to support both these efforts to acquire or maintain power and extensive building operations that expressed the glory and the taste of the papacy. The power to forgive sins came to be treated as a marketable skill, and the hawking of indulgences was the distribution system devised to maximize its profitability.

No one at any time, however, considered such conditions to be ideal. This can be seen in Alexander VI, Savonarola's nemesis, who appeared to incarnate all that was wrong with the Renaissance papacy but yet was capable of designing an excellent program for purifying the church when he was devastated by the murder of his son Juan. Both before and after the separation of others, there were always persons of the highest standards who remained loyal to the papacy at the very moment that they called for its reform. In the Counter or Catholic Reformation their standards of ecclesial rectitude were put into practice and have remained in force to an extraordinary degree to this day. Furthermore, church bodies that originated in the sixteenth century and continued in existence have discovered that all religious institutions have their ups and downs, times when they exemplify their ideals more and less adequately. Therefore, while moral reform of the church was very much an issue at this time, it cannot be identified as the agenda of any one group to the exclusion of all others.

In addition to the impetus for moral improvement, there was in the air a call for theological change. This is the area in which the greatest differences can be discerned between the various faith communities that existed at the end of the period. And, while these theological positions had serious implications for the way that preaching was understood and practiced and will have to be considered at the appropriate juncture, this is not the forum in which to adjudicate among them and to opt for the superiority of one over the others. Rather, it will be assumed that faithful representatives of all traditions held their convictions in integrity and with intelligence.

The third noteworthy aspect of the changes of the sixteenth century is in scholarly method. This is closely connected with the effort to recover classical antiquity that was so prominent a characteristic of the Renaissance.[2] The scholars involved in this quest are known as "humanists," not because of any implied contrast with interest in the Divine, but because of their preoccupation with the "humanities": the liberal arts of grammar, rhetoric, poetry, history, and moral philosophy.[3] For present purposes the most relevant aspect of their recovery of antiquity is Greco-Roman rhetoric. Manuscripts of the major works by or attributed to Cicero and Quintilian were discovered and published, and Aristotle's treatise came once again to be regarded as a textbook on eloquence instead of being read primarily as a work on politics and morals.[4] This interest in rhetoric was central to the humanists. As Hanna Gray says:

> It is essential to understand the humanists' reiterated claim, that theirs was the pursuit of eloquence. That claim, indeed, reveals the identifying characteristic of Renaissance humanism. The bond which united humanists, no matter how far separated in outlook or in time, was a conception of eloquence and its uses.[5]

EPIDEICTIC AT THE VATICAN

The implications of Renaissance humanism for other aspects of scholarly method will be considered as they come up. For the moment, however, the implications for preaching can easily be imagined. By changing notions of what was to be admired in public speaking in general, this newly recovered classical theory of rhetoric was bound to have its impact on the way people thought preaching ought to be done. Although the medieval *artes praedicandi* would continue to influence preaching in some quarters for centuries to come, a major shift in homiletical theory was already under way.

The question was not whether thematic preaching would be replaced by sermons shaped according to the standards of classical rhetoric, but which classical standards should apply. Renewed study of classical rhetorical theory caused homileticians to reflect on the three genres into which public speaking had been divided by the ancients: the forensic oratory of the law courts, the deliberative oratory of legislative bodies, and the epideictic oratory used for praise and blame. In Christian adaptations of this theory, many practitioners accepted the view that since preaching did not call upon its listeners to decide what happened in the past, its genre was not forensic. Nor were they to come to decisions about future policy, so it was not deliberative. Instead, sermons urged upon them sets of positive and negative value judgments about persons (divine as well as human) and patterns of behavior, and thus their genus was epideictic.

John W. O'Malley has demonstrated that this shift can be traced at the very heart of the medieval church, the papal court.[6] The shift from thematic to epideictic preaching can be seen in the manuscripts and printed copies of sermons preached at solemn masses in the papal chapel during the period under investigation.

In order to argue his case, O'Malley established six categories for analyzing the differences between thematic and epideictic preaching: Latin style, sources, structure, unity, *res* or materials preached about, and purpose. Differences in Latin style could easily be seen in the use of a scholastic or a classicizing vocabulary. Further, the epideictic genre (known in Latin as the *genus demonstrativum*) has a lyrical quality.

Epideictic did not quote statements from the Bible or ancient writers as proof texts or "authorities" as thematic sermons did. Instead, it incorporated allusions and paraphrases into a more literary use of these sources. Like thematic preaching, epideictic preaching cited the Bible and the church fathers, but, unlike it, the new style did not draw directly on medieval theologians. Classical writers were cited less frequently, though classical history was occasionally invoked. In neither case, though, was the pagan writing thought to be the source of the Christian point of view; rather, the argument was *quanto magis,* "how much the more!"

In epideictic, the thematic sermon's shape of the spreading tree has been replaced by the *dispositio* of the pagan orator's speech. Such sermons began with an *exordium* emphasizing the impossibility of the orator's task and ended with a peroration that summarized the speech and roused the congregation to an emotional climax. When the sermon was for a saint's day, it often followed all the *topoi* of a classical speech of praise.[7] Going through these *topoi* gave a unity to the speech that the thematic sermon had lacked with its "fanning out." Indeed, it was assumed in all the genera of classical oratory that every element of the speech would contribute to a single unified impact and conclusion—that a person had been guilty or not guilty, a proposed policy should be accepted or rejected, or that a person or thing was to be praised or blamed. The Christian *genus demonstrativum,* like its classical exemplar, was a unified call upon its audience to join the speaker in being grateful for or alarmed about the sermon's subject.

The subject matter of thematic preaching was points of doctrine or ethics. The form of argument was thus abstract. That of epideictic preaching, on the other hand, was very concrete. It was more historical in its orientation, dealing with the deeds, acts, mighty works, or benefits of God. The verbs used in reference to such things are "look," "view," "gaze upon," or "contemplate." In other words, argument has been replaced by narrative and word pictures. This is to say that while the principal source of both types of preaching was the Bible, the way that it was used had changed considerably. It was no longer treated as a data bank for doctrine; it had come instead to be regarded as a book of sacred history.[8] With the Bible viewed in this way, the purpose of preaching based upon it was to evoke a response from the congregation of "veneration," "admiration," and "praise." The audience was called upon to imitate. Since the liturgy of the papal solemn masses was supposed to approximate as nearly as possible the worship of the heavenly sanctuary, it is no wonder that the sermons preached at them also sought to draw the listeners into a sense of awe and wonder at beholding and praising the very glory of the divine presence.

While such preaching has value, there are ways in which it can be a disservice. The admiration that it elicits can make people complacent even if solemn warnings are intercalated into it, as they were in the papal court. Such complacency can cause people not to take seriously enough the signs in the outside world that conditions are changing rapidly and that others elsewhere do not find the status quo such an occasion for rejoicing. Yet, ironically, the change in the style of preaching itself should have shown that the world was no longer satisfied with the way things had been. Sermons at the solemn masses in the court of Renaissance popes could have alerted the court to the truth that the Middle Ages were over.[9]

THE ERASMIAN WATERSHED

With the recovery of Greco-Roman rhetoric, it became inevitable that *artes praedicandi* would be replaced with textbooks that advocated the construction of sermons in accordance with the standards of classical oratory. The earliest efforts to produce such works did not meet with much response. The *Margarita eloquentiae castigatae* of Lorenzo Guglielmo Traversagni seems to have been "singularly ignored by his contemporaries," the effort of the great Hebraist Johann Reuchlin "did not have much impact on contemporaries," and the works on preaching as such by Philipp Melanchthon and Veit Dietrich were "sketchy, partisan, and extremely brief works of pamphlet size that did not have immediate or broad influence."[10]

Therefore, since the text published by Erasmus in 1535, *Ecclesiasticus*, was a long and thorough work (a modern edition would run to about a thousand pages without notes)[11] and a successful one (going through ten editions in as many years and thus "one of the best sellers of the decade"),[12] O'Malley is able to call the text "the great watershed in the history of sacred rhetoric."[13] (For a résumé of this work, **see Vol. 2, pp. 231-47.**)

Such a judgment might be surprising to anyone who has not kept up with recent scholarship about Erasmus, since an earlier generation of scholars tended to regard him either as a Reformer who did not have the courage to go all the way with Luther or as a precursor of the Enlightenment. That his character had many sides cannot be denied. Roland Bainton has suggested that each of the three artists who depicted his features caught a different aspect of the man: Dürer showed the scholarly editor of the church fathers, Holbein the ironical author of satires, and Metsys the author of *Contempt of the World* and *Preparation for Death*.[14]

> No matter how one chooses to label Erasmus, however, one can no longer deny that he was deeply concerned about ministry, doctrine, theology, and theological method and that he saw all those as closely related to *pietas*, to *pie beatque vivendi ars*.[15]

Thus it is that his last and longest work was a treatise on preaching.

The title of the work is *Ecclesiastes, sive Concionator evangelicus*.[16] These alternative designations are important clues to Erasmus's understanding of how preaching should be done. The first is the same as the Greek title of the biblical book that he took as the equivalent of the Hebrew *Koheleth* and the Latin *Concionator*, all of which can be rendered in English as "Preacher." He had a particular sort of preaching in mind, however, the sort of sermon he calls *concio*. "The *concio* was a specific type of deliberative oratory in which a leader addressed, not sophisticated statesmen gathered in the Senate, but a popular and perhaps unruly audience of ordinary people."[17] Before his time, this term had seldom been used to designate Christian preaching, but afterward it became quite common. More will be said later of the significance of this choice of term when Erasmus's understanding of the relation of preaching to the genera of classical oratory is discussed.

The first of the four books of *Ecclesiastes* is devoted to the importance of preaching and the consequent virtues and training needed by the one who preaches.[18] Indeed, it would not be too much to call it a spirituality of preaching. Erasmus says preaching is the most important duty of clergy and more important than any task of rulers.

> The most important function of the priest is teaching by which he may instruct, admonish, chide, and console. A layman can baptize. All the people can pray. The priest does not always baptize, he does not always absolve, but he should always teach. What good is it to be baptized if one has not been catechized, what good to go to the Lord's Table if one does not know what it means?[19]

The skills of preaching can be taught: "If elephants can be trained to dance, lions to play, and leopards to hunt, surely preachers can be taught to preach."[20] Even more important than the skills, however, are the virtues the preacher ought to have.

> The preacher should exhibit purity of heart, chastity of body, sanctity of deportment, erudition, wisdom, and above all eloquence worthy of the divine mysteries. Let him remember that the cross will never be lacking to those who sincerely preach the gospel. There are always Herods, Ananiases, Caiaphases, Scribes and Pharisees. There are men of Ephesus who incite the mob and there are those like the Jews before Pilate who cried, "Crucify him! Crucify him!"[21]

Hence the life of the preacher must be a lived sermon.[22]

In Book 2, Erasmus follows Augustine in deeming the three duties of the preacher to be to teach, to please, and to move. For him the first is the most important, although after the turgidity of thematic sermons, a humanist like Erasmus has to find a place, however humble, for pleasing. These duties are to be met by following the techniques of classical rhetoric. Thus the parts of a speech, the genera of speeches, and the topics to be discussed are presented. Book 3, like Book 2, shows great debt to Cicero and Quintilian, dealing as it does with disposition and style. "In Book IV, Erasmus presented a *topicon* for the Christian orator, 'an index of materials in which the Christian orator must be versed.'"[23] These include most of the tracts of theology.

Weiss has analyzed *Ecclesiastes* brilliantly, showing that in it Erasmus not only advocates rhetorical training for the preacher but also models its benefits in a virtuoso manner and thus reveals that for him, rhetoric is an entire epistemology, greatly superior to dialectic, a way of knowing especially congenial to a man as irenic as he.

In the construction of his last and longest book, Erasmus was able to bring together the themes of most of the other works that he had given a lifetime to writing.

> *Ecclesiastes'* style and method reveal not only the richness of the rhetorical approach in itself but also the very texture of Erasmus' mind. We find this thread of method running through the fabric of all his thought. Or rather, this thread discloses the seamless quality of the fabric. In talking ostensibly about one thing, the rhetorician can talk about many things. And in a comprehensive handbook of Christian rhetoric, Erasmus talked about everything.[24]

And, although Erasmus never preached a sermon himself that we know about,[25] James Weiss is able to say that "the mirror of the Christian orator reflects the full-length image of Erasmus himself."[26]

Saying this, however, is not the same as saying that *Ecclesiastes* is a satisfactory homiletics textbook. Even O'Malley, who considers the book to represent a watershed in the history of sacred rhetoric, recognizes faults in it. He points out that however little entitled Alfonso Zorilla was to say so, some truth lies in his charge that *Ecclesiastes* was "diffuse, prolix, and confused."[27]

The other main contemporary question about the work had to do with the propriety of Christians drawing on pagan sources. While having no quarrel with that propriety as such, O'Malley raises four questions that grow from the difficulty of constructing an adequate Christian preaching method out of pagan rhetoric. The first is, granting Christian belief in "the divine, or supra-human, nature of the word of God," one must recognize that this belief "requires that any treatise on preaching must have a component lacking in the classical treatises on rhetoric: a theology of the divine word and the minister of that word."[28] This issue was recognized by Erasmus and addressed by him to a degree in Book 1, but such considerations do not appear to greatly influence the rest of the book.

The next difficulty has to do with the way that most Christian preaching has been a "text-related enterprise," involving as it does a desire to bring words of scripture to bear on the lives of the people of God.[29] Classical oratory has no genre related to *explication de texte*. Rather, as noted often above, the preacher needs to turn from the rhetorician to the *grammaticus* for classroom techniques of exegesis.

In the Renaissance, however, there was an additional resource to be drawn upon. In the ancient world, rhetoric had been the theory of oratory, speaking effectively in public, but by the sixteenth century the term came also to be applied to the analysis of works of literature. The earlier, more exclusive use of the term is "primary rhetoric" while the later, literary use is "secondary rhetoric." This secondary rhetoric of Erasmus's time also offered preachers help in their exegetical task. Before that time, however, from the age of Origen to the development of the thematic sermon, Christians had not used any of the classical genera for preaching, but had instead employed the homily form. This was done also by Erasmus's much admired friend, the Franciscan Jean Vitrier.[30]

The extent to which Erasmus dealt with this problem, however, was in his treatment of the three genera of classical rhetoric. He understood the basic task of preaching to be teaching, and he believed that teaching could be accomplished in all three genera: judicial, deliberative, and epideictic. He felt, however, that the adversarial relations demanded by judicial rhetoric were inappropriate to Christian preaching. To meet the needs of Christian proclamation, he developed the deliberative genus into four others: the persuasive, the exhortative, the admonitory, and the consolatory. Retaining epideictic as the laudatory genus, he thus had a system of five genera of preaching.[31] These subdivisions, however, concentrate on the purpose of the various types of sermon rather than on how text commentary is to be incorporated into them. Perhaps Erasmus's own lack of experience in preaching left him insufficiently aware of the practical problems posed by squeezing biblical interpretation into classical rhetorical forms.

Further, Erasmus also seems insensitive to the liturgical setting of the sermon in the Eucharist. He appears unaware that it should, in the words of William Skudlarek, tell the congregation why they should lift up their hearts.[32] Thus the sermon is reduced to mere instruction and exhortation, "just an address on a sacred subject to a popular audience, which would be a fair rendering of Erasmus' understanding of it."[33]

The last problem that John O'Malley found with Erasmus's preaching theory also has to do with genera, but is different from that of making allowance for the sermon's need to explain a biblical text. The Lutheran Melanchthon, as will be seen below, created a distinctive genus, the *genus didascalicum* or *didactium,* in order to treat doctrinal instruction as the characteristic purpose of preaching. Erasmus, however, "was more concerned with inculcating and persuading to good morals and ethically correct behavior,"[34] thus helping to promote a moralistic strain in Catholic preaching that was already strong.

Although he located preaching within the charism of prophecy, "not confrontation, but the teaching of prescriptive and ethics-related wisdom was the task of the Erasmian prophet." This understanding of the preaching task undoubtedly has something to do with his hitting upon the classical category of *concio* as that to which preaching should be assigned. The purpose of such speeches was "to explain to the promiscuous multitude the edicts, promises, and will of the supreme prince and to persuade that multitude to accept them."[35] With such a definition, it is not surprising that a moralistic model of preaching occurs. But Erasmus must have felt something of the inadequacy of such an understanding, for he seems to have shown some nostalgia for the homily even though it did not fit comfortably among the classical genera.[36]

If *Ecclesiastes* fell short of being a perfect homiletics textbook, what can be made of O'Malley's claim that it represents "the great watershed in the history of sacred rhetoric"?[37] A surprising amount, actually. First of all, it appears to have represented the death knell of thematic preaching. Although the form continued in use for a while, no new *artes praedicandi* seem to have been published after Erasmus's work appeared.[38]

Then, too, Erasmus's *Ecclesiastes* was innovative in the extent to which it drew explicitly on classical rhetoric. While Augustine presupposed the discipline, he used only elements of it in *De doctrina Christiana* because, on the one hand, the genre in which he preached, the patristic homily, did not fit any of the classical *genera dicendi,* and, on the other, he thought that rhetoric could be studied profitably only as a schoolboy. In his huge textbook, Erasmus was the first to attempt to teach the entire discipline of classical rhetoric as an element in preparing readers to preach.

But what of its influence on later homiletical literature? Since, as has been seen, all of Erasmus's works were placed on the index in 1549, and *Ecclesiastes* is not quoted in Catholic manuals after that, there would seem to be little chance of its shaping the future of that tradition. And, since Luther disagreed so strongly with Erasmus on theology, one would not expect his followers to quote Erasmus with approval. Frederick J. McGinness, however, has studied the reforms in preaching made by the Council of Trent, reforms that have shaped Catholic preaching down almost until the present, and he concludes that although the name of Erasmus is not invoked, the ideas are largely his:

> No one other than Erasmus had anticipated so clearly every single component in the Tridentine decree on preaching, and had spelled out thoroughly what each component entailed: that bishops and their preachers be feeders of their flocks—teachers—concerning themselves with the gospel of Jesus Christ, preaching the things one needs to know for salvation, [word omitted] upon them with briefness and plainness of speech the vices that they must avoid and the virtues they must cultivate, in order that they may escape eternal punishment and obtain the glory of heaven.[39]

The influence on Lutheran homiletics is also very probable. As will be seen in the next chapter, Luther's own preaching was not much imitated by his followers. Rather, the rhetorical manuals of his disciple Melanchthon, a humanist who was indebted to Erasmus, set the standard. Certainly Erasmus was very influential on the English Reformation, and he helped to create an atmosphere in which the public school curriculum was to be shaped by classical literature and rhetoric. The main Reformation tradition not directly shaped by Erasmus was the Calvinist. Although Calvin was certainly formed by humanism, and even wrote a commentary on a work of Seneca before he turned to theology, his approach to preaching was much more in the tradition of the *lectio continua* of the patristic homily (i.e., the tradition of the grammarian) rather than that of the rhetorician.

With such innovation in content, such replacement of the previous norms, and such influence on most succeeding homiletics, it is by no means too much to claim that *Ecclesiastes* represents a watershed in textbooks on preaching. That will become more evident in the chapters ahead.

FOR FURTHER READING

Bainton, Roland H. *Erasmus of Christendom.* New York: Crossroad, 1982.

Erasmus, Desiderius. *Ecclesiastes, or the Evangelical Preacher.* Translated by James Butrica, edited by Frederick J. McGinness. Collected Works of Erasmus. Toronto: University of Toronto Press, forthcoming.

O'Malley, John W. *Praise and Blame in Renaissance Rome: Rhetoric,*

Doctrine, and Reform in the Sacred Orators of the Papal Court, c. 1450–1521. Duke Monographs in Medieval and Renaissance Studies, no. 3. Durham, N.C.: Duke University Press, 1979.

―――. "Erasmus and the History of Sacred Rhetoric: The *Ecclesiastes* of 1535." In vol. 5 of *Erasmus of Rotterdam Society Yearbook*, 1-29. 1985.

Renaissance Eloquence: Studies in the Theory and Practice of Renaissance Rhetoric. Edited by James J. Murphy. Berkeley: University of California Press, 1983.

Notes

1. Justo L. González, *A History of Christian Thought* (Nashville: Abingdon, 1975), 3:11-24.

2. For a dated and misleading but still exciting treatment of this see Jacob Burckhardt, *The Civilization of the Renaissance in Italy*, trans. S. G. C. Middlemore, int. Benjamin Nelson and Charles Trinkaus, Harper Torchbooks (New York: Harper & Brothers, 1958 [German original, 1860; Eng. trans. of 15th ed., 1890]), 1:175-278. The introduction to the volume indicates what aspects of the treatment are upheld by modern scholarship. Much of the mood of the period is captured in *Romula*, George Eliot's novel set in the Florence of Savonarola. For a contemporary view, see Ronald Witt, "The Origins of Italian Humanism," *Centennial Review* vol. xxxiv (1990): 91-109.

3. Hanna H. Gray, "Renaissance Humanism: The Pursuit of Eloquence," *JHI* 24 (1963): 499.

4. George A. Kennedy, *Classical Rhetoric and Its Christian and Secular Tradition from Ancient to Modern Times* (Chapel Hill: University of North Carolina Press, 1980), 190. For the recovery of classical rhetoric in the Renaissance, see ibid., 195-219. See also Brian Vickers, *In Defence of Rhetoric* (Oxford: Clarendon Press; New York: Oxford University Press, 1988), 254-93. On the difficulties in writing a complete history of rhetoric in the Renaissance, see the essays in *Renaissance Eloquence: Studies in the Theory and Practice of Renaissance Rhetoric,* ed. James J. Murphy (Berkeley: University of California Press, 1983), especially Paul Oskar Kristeller, "Rhetoric in Medieval and Renaissance Culture," 1-19; James J. Murphy, "One Thousand Neglected Authors: The Scope and Importance of Renaissance Rhetoric," 20-36; and Dominic A. LaRusso, "Rhetoric in the Italian Renaissance," 37-55.

5. Gray, "Renaissance Humanism," 498. By "eloquence," of course, she means rhetoric and goes on to say: "By 'rhetoric' the humanists did not intend an empty pomposity, a willful mendacity, a love of display for its own sake, an extravagant artificiality, a singular lack of originality, or a necessary subordination of substance to form and ornament.... True eloquence, according to the humanists, could only arise out of a harmonious union between wisdom and style; its aim was to guide men toward virtue and worthwhile goals, not to mislead them for vicious or trivial purposes."

6. John W. O'Malley, *Praise and Blame in Renaissance Rome: Rhetoric, Doctrine, and Reform in the Sacred Orators of the Papal Court, c. 1450–1521,* Duke Monographs in Medieval and Renaissance Studies, no. 3 (Durham, N.C.: Duke University Press, 1979).

7. For a list of these, see the description of *epideictic* in the orations of Gregory of Nazianzus in Kennedy, *Classical Rhetoric and Its Christian and Secular Tradition from Ancient to Modern Times,* 228-37, or Rosemary Radford Ruether, *Gregory of Nazianzus, Rhetor and Philosopher* (Oxford: Clarendon Press, 1969), 120-23.

8. For this insight, I am indebted to a letter from Father O'Malley written December 7, 1990.

9. John A. McManamon has detected in funeral sermons a similar shift from thematic to epideictic preaching in "Innovation in Early Humanist Rhetoric: The Oratory of Pier Paolo Vergerio the Elder," *Rinascimento* 22 (1982): 1-32, arguing that the transition was pioneered by Vergerio (who also figures in O'Malley's treatment). For a fuller treatment of Renaissance funeral sermons, see McManamon's *Funeral Oratory and the Cultural Ideals of Italian Humanism* (Chapel Hill: University of North Carolina Press, 1989).

10. John W. O'Malley, "Erasmus and the History of Sacred Rhetoric: The *Ecclesiastes* of 1535," *Erasmus of Rotterdam Society Yearbook,* vol. 5 (1985), 6-8. On textbooks for this period, see also his "Content and Rhetorical Forms in Sixteenth-Century Treatises on Preaching" in *Renaissance Eloquence,* 238-52.

11. Ibid., 18.

12. Ibid., 2.

13. Ibid., 13. Compare his statement on p. 29: "The *Ecclesiastes* is not simply a major work by Erasmus. It is a major monument in the long history and continuing influence of classical tradition in western culture. Above all, it is a major monument—perhaps *the* major monument—in the history of sacred rhetoric." He sees its only rival to be Augustine's *De doctrina christiana.*

14. Roland H. Bainton, *Erasmus of Christendom* (New York: Crossroad, 1982), 237-38.

15. John W. O'Malley, "Introduction," *Spiritualia: (vol. I) Enchiridion, De Contemptu Mundi, De Vidua Christiana,* Collected Works of Erasmus, vol. 66 (Toronto: University of Toronto Press, 1988), xiv.

16. Originally published by Froben at Basel in 1535 and, as noted above, reprinted often in the next ten years in both authorized and pirated editions, *Ecclesiastes* fell on hard times afterward. Luther's opposition to Erasmus and the placing of all Erasmus's books on the first Index of Prohibited Books by a fanatical pope in 1559 caused the work to fall into obscurity. Thus the standard Latin edition was still *Opera omnia,* ed. J. Clericus, vol. 5 (Leiden: 1703–6), until a new one appeared, *Opera Omnia Desiderii Erasmani Roterodami recognita et adnotatione critica instructa notisque illustrata,* ordo 5, tome 4 (Amsterdam: North-Holland, 1991–). Thomas Bray, founder of both the SPCK and the Society for the Propagation of the Gospel, published a Latin edition of the first part of the work in London in 1730 (Robert Kleinhans, "Erasmus' Ecclesiastes and the Church of England," *Historical Magazine of the Protestant Episcopal Church* 39 [1970]: 307-14). No English translation of the entire work has been published before now, but that oversight will soon

be remedied with a translation by James Butrica and edited by Frederick J. McGinness that is forthcoming in the Collected Works of Erasmus being published by the University of Toronto Press. I am grateful to Professor McGinness for a copy of the page proofs. The Latin edition consulted for the first draft of this chapter was the Froben of 1554.

17. O'Malley, "Erasmus and the History of Sacred Rhetoric," 14-15.

18. The following summary is based on James Michael Weiss, "*Ecclesiastes* and Erasmus: The Mirror and the Image," *ARG* 65 (1965): 83-108; Marc Fumaroli, *L'Age de l'éloquence: Rhétorique et <<res literaria>> de la Renaissance au seuil de l'époque classique,* Hautes études médiévales et modernes 43 (Genève: Librairie Droz, 1980): 106-9; and Charles Béné, *Érasme et Saint Augustin ou influence de Saint Augustin sur l'humanisme d'Érasme,* Travaux d'humanisme et renaissance," no. 103 (Genève: Librairie Droz, 1969), 372-425.

19. Translated in Bainton, *Erasmus,* 268-69. He takes the statements *passim* from volume five of the Leiden edition, giving page numbers on p. 275.

20. Ibid., 268.

21. Ibid.

22. Weiss, "*Ecclesiastes* and Erasmus," 87, citing the Leiden edition, 783-90.

23. Ibid., 88. The interior quotation is from the Leiden edition, 5:1071C.

24. Ibid., 107.

25. O'Malley, "Erasmus and the History of Sacred Rhetoric," 21.

26. Weiss, "*Ecclesiastes* and Erasmus," 107.

27. O'Malley, "Erasmus and the History of Sacred Rhetoric," 18. Zorilla's *De sacris concionibus recte formandis,* published in 1542, plagiarized Erasmus's work—not to mention that of Melanchthon, Dietrich, and Johannes Hepinus (Hoeck)—on a wholesale basis.

28. Ibid., 19.

29. Ibid.

30. Ibid., 20. See also Bainton, *Erasmus of Christendom,* 64ff.

31. Weiss, "*Ecclesiastes* and Erasmus," 98-101. The relevant sections of *Ecclesiastes* are found in the Leiden edition, 858-92.

32. *The Word in Worship: Preaching in a Liturgical Context,* Abingdon Preacher's Library (Nashville: Abingdon, 1981), 70.

33. O'Malley, "Erasmus and the History of Sacred Rhetoric," 22.

34. Ibid., 24.

35. Ibid., 26, quoting from the Leiden edition, 770.

36. Ibid.

37. Ibid., 13.

38. Ibid. See also a paper delivered by Frederick McGinness at the Sixteenth Century Studies Conference, Cleveland, Ohio, on November 3, 2000, "Erasmus and the Reform of Preaching Between Luther and the Council of Trent," 10. I am indebted to Professor McGinness for a copy of this paper, which is a draft of part of the Introduction he was preparing for the University of Toronto translation of *Ecclesiastes.*

39. McGinness, "Erasmus and the Reform of Preaching Between Luther and the Council of Trent," 16. Professor McGinness said in his cover letter that he would probably make last-minute changes in the text of the paper before he delivered it.

CHAPTER 12

THE REFORMATION PREACHING OF LUTHER AND MELANCHTHON

GENESIS

Few people in history have been more influential or effective in shaping the future development of preaching than Martin Luther. So it comes as a surprise both that his followers did not imitate his style more and that his own preaching has not been much studied.[1] Yet every student of preaching, of whatever ecclesial allegiance, must admit that there is much in his style worthy of study and imitation. Part of the explanation for this neglect must be that his talent was so individual that the challenge of measuring up to his example was daunting.

Luther's preaching and theology were shaped to a large extent by his personal experience. The basic story is well known. Being frightened by a thunderstorm in 1505 when he was twenty-one years old, the moody young man made and kept a vow to Saint Anne that he would become a monk in order to prepare for a holy death. Even though he became a very ascetic member of the Augustinian Hermits, he was never able to quiet his conscience, and so he lived with the conviction that he merited damnation. To assist him in dealing with his scrupulosity, his superior assigned him the task of earning his doctorate and becoming a professor of Scripture. At some point between receiving his degree and beginning his teaching career in 1511, and his being made vicar over eleven monasteries in 1515, he had what is called his "tower experience" *(Turmerlebnis),* which resolved all his doubts and at the same time gave him the theological basis for his eventual break with Rome.

His own words best describe that event and its significance for him:

> I greatly longed to understand Paul's Epistle to the Romans and nothing stood in the way but that one expression, "the justice of God," because I took it to mean that justice whereby God is just and deals justly in punishing the unjust. My situation was that, although an impeccable monk, I stood before God as a sinner troubled in conscience, and I had no confidence that my merit would assuage him. Therefore I did not love a just and angry God, but rather hated and murmured against him. Yet I clung to the dear Paul and had a great yearning to know what he meant.
>
> Night and day I pondered until I saw the connection between the justice of God and the statement that "the just shall live by his faith." Then I grasped that the justice of God is that righteousness by which through grace and sheer mercy God justifies us through faith. Thereupon I felt myself to be reborn and to have gone through open doors into paradise. The whole of Scripture took on a new meaning, and whereas before the "justice of God" had filled me with hate, now it became to me inexpressibly sweet in greater love. This passage of Paul became to me a gate to heaven.[2]

Luther felt that the basic hermeneutical key to understanding Christian theology had been communicated to him through this experience. Christians do not have to earn their salvation through ascetic and charitable works, but rather it is freely given by God. It took some time, however, for him to work out the implications of that view to the point where a breach with the pope seemed necessary. Salvation through works had involved a calculus in which the exact value of all acts, evil or virtuous, could be ascertained and expressed in terms of the number of days a soul would have to spend in purgatory as temporal punishment for sins. Such punishment had to be endured even if the sins had been forgiven. On the other hand, days of plenary remission of such punishment were given as reward for merit.

Much of this calculus was based on an understanding of Matthew 16:18-19 that saw the pope, by virtue of his succession from Peter, as having the "keys of the kingdom" that would allow him to bind or loose the sins of Christians and thus to increase or decrease the time they would have to spend in purgatory. This view was connected with another in which the saints were regarded as persons who had accumulated more merit than was required to expiate for their own sins. Their surplus, therefore, was translated to the "treasury of merit," which the pope could apply to sinners. His remissions of this temporal punishment for sins were called indulgences.

Indulgences at first were given for such major acts of penance as participation in a crusade, but during the Renaissance when papal need for money became acute, they came to be sold outright on a wholesale scale. As early as his trip to Rome in 1511, Luther had come to doubt the efficacy of various pious activities connected with pilgrimages to holy places as a means of reducing time to be spent in purgatory. When Johann Tetzel preached at nearby Jüterbog in 1517 and offered an indulgence granted by Leo X to raise money to renovate St. Peter's basilica at Rome, parishioners in Wittenberg were disturbed. Luther was driven to post his Ninety-five Theses on the church door, inviting the debate that ended in his break with Rome and the beginning of the Reformation.[3]

LUTHER'S UNDERSTANDING OF SALVATION

Martin Luther's theological thought developed in such an integrated way that it is impossible to understand his theory of preaching without knowing the overall dynamic of his thought. A convenient way of entering the dynamic that immediately reveals the enormous importance of preaching in Luther's thought is to begin with his doctrine of the Word of God.[4] God's Word is seen in three manifestations: the second person of the Trinity (the incarnate Word), the Holy Scriptures (the written Word), and the preaching of the church (the proclaimed Word). Thus he was completely traditional in his understanding of the Trinity and the person and work of Christ. The Word who became flesh and dwelled among us is also the Word by which the Father created the universe. The intimate connection between God the Son and the Bible is that the whole purpose of Scripture, Hebrew and Christian, is to reveal Christ. The authority of Scripture for Luther is therefore not that of the canon, the authoritative list of writings, but that of the writings that proclaim the gospel. While any biblical book is to be interpreted in light of the intention of its author, that intention was always basically to proclaim the gospel. Finding that proclamation, then, is the hermeneutical key to the book. Such discovery is not basically an exercise of the human intellect, however, because the guidance of the Holy Spirit is necessary for finding and receiving that gospel.

The written Word has two aspects, law and gospel. Law is God's will, God's moral requirement of human beings. It cannot be identified exclusively with the Hebrew Bible, nor is the gospel to be associated exclusively with the New Testament. Each may be found in either testament and indeed in the same passage, but law is found outside the Bible as well, while gospel is discerned only with the aid of the Spirit. Law, for instance, can be known by the unaided human intelligence as natural law. It is enacted as positive law, civil law, to restrain the wicked and provide the order necessary both for people to live together in society and for the gospel to be proclaimed.

At the same time, since no one can live up to its standards, law also serves the function of convincing all human beings that they deserve damnation and are in need of redemption. When they hear the gospel, though, they know that God has shown his love for them in the redemption made available through Christ and thus they are liberated from the law by God's attribution to them of the righteousness of Christ. This attribution is their justification—which does not mean that they cease to be sinners, but does mean that they are redeemed sinners, justified (accounted righteous) by the grace and faith given to them.

Such extreme measures are necessary because fallen humanity has entirely lost its capacity to respond to God or to do good. Human sin is so all-encompassing that persons cannot even learn of their sinful state without its being revealed to them. And, knowing about it, they have no power of their own to resist it. The only capacity left to them is to be turned in a new direction by God.[5] That capacity, however, has no inherent virtue. It is only the place where the power of God can be exerted. That power is God's absolution, God's reclassifying of human beings as saved rather than damned.

While this justification is appropriated by faith, faith is not to be understood as an intellectual or volitional good work, but rather as the work of the Holy Spirit in the soul. This justification is absolution, but it is not a restoration of the pre-fall capacity to live without sin. Yet by it God does lead the justified into righteousness, allowing them to have some experience of the status attributed to them. Luther described the state of such a person as *simul justus et peccator*—a righteous person and a sinner at the same time. Good works then become not a way to earn salvation, but a demonstration that it has been freely given. To the person who has been justified, the law ceases to be the hateful reminder of damnation and becomes the sweet will of the loving Father.

Luther's doctrine of justification is not individualistic. Rather, he believes that there is no salvation outside the church. The church, however, is not constituted by apostolic succession, but by the Word of God. Both preaching and sacraments are functions of the Word, through which the Spirit speaks to human beings and they are justified. Since this church is not invisible but an institution on earth, many of the Word's means of grace had been preserved in the papal church and there was even true Christianity and sanctity in that body.

LUTHER'S THEORY OF PREACHING

Luther considers preaching to be the most important office in the world, more important than even that of officiating at sacraments.[6] It is more important than prayer (21:228). It is a matter of life and death (3:347) because it is the medium through which salvation is bestowed. Unlike the Muslim religion, which is spread by the sword, Christian faith is spread by preaching (44:179). People who are deprived of preaching often lose their faith (44:175). Thus David, in saying, "I shall not want" (Ps. 23:1), means that he will have all the bodily and spiritual blessings bestowed through preaching (12:157). Preaching constitutes the church (32:73). For that reason, "the Word of God does not assail trifles, baubles, or bubbles, but kingdoms, great kings, and nations on earth, as Psalm 2:2 declares" (23:387). Preaching is the means by which Christ will slay the antichrist (35:387). So, clergy who do not preach do not deserve the name of clergy (36:91).

Because preaching is the one necessary thing, Luther took his own proclamation with the utmost seriousness. He said, "I, Dr. Luther, am convinced that the birds, the stones, and the sand of the sea will have to attest to my preaching" (23:239). And he made a number of references to the frequency with which he did preach. He walked to church to preach so often that it would not be surprising if, in addition to wearing out his shoes, he had worn out his feet as well (54:206). Often he preached four times a day; one whole Lent he preached at two services and gave a lecture every day (54:282). (The lecture involved was the sort of course preaching he did, giving expositions of entire books of the Bible [48:320].) This commitment to preaching did not begin with the Reformation, but already existed when he was a vicar of the Augustinians (48:27-28, 113).

For Luther, preaching is as fully the Word of God as the incarnate Lord and the written Scripture. Therefore, any preacher who has finished a sermon should not pray for the forgiveness of its deficiencies, but should rather say, "In this sermon I have been an apostle and a prophet of Jesus Christ." Anyone who cannot boast like that should give up preaching, "for it is God's Word and not (the preacher's) and God ought not and cannot forgive it, but only confirm, praise, and crown it" (41:216). The distinction between the incarnate and the proclaimed Word is that "the former Word is in substance God; the latter word is in its effect the power of God, but isn't God in substance, whether it's spoken by Christ or by a minister" (54:395). Thus it can be said that "the preaching of the gospel is nothing else than Christ coming to us, or we being brought to him" (35:121).

Luther placed great emphasis on the orality of preaching. In an allegorical interpretation, he identified the star of Bethlehem as "the new light, preaching, and the gospel, oral and public preaching." (For Luther, allegory always relates to the Word; he never entirely ceased doing allegorical interpretation.) Oral preaching took precedence over even the written Word. "In the New Testament, preaching must be done orally and publicly, with the living voice, to produce in speech and hearing what prior to this lay hidden in the letter and in secret vision" (52:205). Such oral preaching is "the way the Lord, our Ruler, establishes his kingdom" (12:114; cf. 170). The superiority of the oral to the written Word is developed at length in Luther's exegesis of Malachi 5:7: "For the lips of a priest guard knowledge" (18:401).[7]

With this perspective, then, he can say:

> For just as in legal disputes whatever judgment is passed on the basis of the reports of witnesses is arrived at by hearing alone and believed because of faith, since it cannot be known in any other way, neither by perception nor by reason, so the Gospel is received in no other way than by hearing. (29:145)

When one moves from Luther's view of the importance of preaching to his understanding of how it should be done, it becomes apparent how accurate Carl Braaten's statement is that "the law/gospel distinction is the classical Lutheran homiletical principle."[8] This distinction is phrased in other ways as well by Luther; it is the same as the letter/Spirit and the *Schrift/Predigt* dichotomies, and the basic difference between the Old and New Testaments.

This does not mean, however, that Christian preaching should include no element of law. Quite the contrary, such preaching is necessary before the gospel can be heard, and every valid sermon will contain both law

288

and gospel. Such preaching of the law leads people to an awareness of their need for the gospel and opens them to hearing its word of forgiveness and grace.

> Even though we are already in the New Testament and should have only the preaching of the Spirit, since we are still living in flesh and blood, it is necessary to preach the letter as well, so that people are first killed by the law and all their arrogance is destroyed. Thus they may know themselves and become hungry for the Spirit and thirsty for grace. So [the letter] prepares the people for the preaching of the Spirit. (39:188)[9]

Hence the proof for the seventeenth theological thesis in the *Heidelberg Disputation* reads: "It is apparent that not despair, but hope, is preached when we are told that we are sinners. Such preaching concerning sin is a preparation for grace" (31:51).

Since law is preached to enable people to recognize that they are sinners, the basic content of the gospel and, therefore, Christian preaching is the forgiveness of sins. "This is the gist of your preaching: *Behold your God!* Promote God alone, his mercy and grace. Preach Me alone" (17:14). Those New Testament books that reflect this emphasis are to be preferred: in Romans and 1 Peter "you do not find many works and miracles of Christ described, but you do find depicted in masterly fashion how faith in Christ overcomes sin, death, and hell, and gives life, righteousness, and salvation" (35:362). For the same reason, John is "the one, fine, true and chief gospel."

More is required for such preaching to be effective than merely hearing it physically, however eloquently it is proclaimed. Faith is also necessary. "For whoever does not accept the Word on its own account, is never inclined to accept it on account of any preacher, even if all the angels were preaching to him" (52:32). Yet it is through preaching that faith is communicated. Christendom, the people of the King, is constituted by "the Word of the gospel (that) brings them to the point where they willingly cling to him by faith" (13:291). This faith, however, is no achievement of their own, but is a gift of God administered through preaching: "God has so ordered it that the Holy Spirit ordinarily comes through the Word."[10]

Election occurs through preaching: "When the Word is revealed from heaven, we see that some are converted and freed from condemnation" (2:16-17). Their own unwillingness is the reason some are not converted, but faith is given only to those God chooses.

> The Holy Spirit, ordinarily, gives such faith or his gift to no one with-
> out preaching or the oral word or the gospel of Christ preceding, but
> ... through and by means of such oral word he effects and creates faith
> where and in whom it pleases him (Romans 10[:14ff.]). (38:87)
>
> Thus to the end of the world we preach to those who await the com-
> ing of Christ, but we preach not at all to the others, the ungodly. (17:344)

Election, however, does not mean that one ceases to sin (23:234). The
Christian is *simul justus et peccator.* As a result, "every preacher and
minister of the Word is a man of strife and judgment and because of his
office he is compelled to reprove whatever is wrong" (2:20). This is the
preaching of the law that must take place before the gospel can be heard.

Since preaching is the very vehicle of salvation, it is the most important duty of clergy and the main purpose for which people are ordained.
"Whoever does not preach the Word, though he was called by the church
to do this very thing, is no priest at all, and that sacrament of ordination
can be nothing else than a certain rite by which the church chooses its
preachers" (36:113; cf. 23:342; 38:186).

That clergy are ordained to preach, however, does not mean that only
the ordained preach. Luther understood the priesthood of all believers to
mean that all the faithful are capable of preaching. Thus if Adam had not
fallen, he would have preached publicly to his family (1:82, 105). The
sacrifices of Cain and Abel were not offered without preaching because
"God is not worshiped by a speechless work" (1:248). Noah and
Abraham are also seen as preachers (2:22, 26, 84, 98, 333). "The only
true, genuine office of preaching, like priesthood and sacrifice, is common to all Christians.... Not many of you are to preach at the same
time, although all have the power to do it" (36:149).

In order to show that laity could preach, Luther wished to persuade
Melanchthon to do so (48:308). Yet his understanding of preaching was
much broader than such formal proclamation in assemblies for worship;
he recognized that in the apostolic church, preaching was not confined
either to worship services or to the ordained clergy (48:311). The preaching office extended not only to pastors and preachers, but also to teachers, lectors, chaplains, sacristans, schoolmasters, and others (46:220).
Heads of households had a responsibility for seeing that members,
whether children or servants, attended the preaching service (51:145).
"Father, mother, master, or mistress" can also preach at home (41:264).

Although the Roman Catholics quote 1 Corinthians 14:34 as authority for denying that believers who are women can preach, Luther replies
that while all have the right to preach, only those who are most skilled
should exercise that right:

> Because it is much more fitting for a man to speak, a man is also more
> skilled at it. . . . Therefore order, discipline, and respect demand that
> women keep silent when men speak; but if no man were to preach, then
> it would be necessary for the women to preach. (36:152)

He even lists a number of women in the Bible who may be said to have
preached and elsewhere sums up his position by saying, "If the Lord
were to raise up a woman for us to listen to, we would allow her to rule
like Huldah" (28:280).

While all the faithful may preach, there is a procedure for deciding
which ones will.

> We are the Christian Church, or a segment of it. This church has the
> power to engage pastors. The church selects such as are able and com-
> petent, not for their own sakes but for the welfare of the church. And
> in an emergency everyone must take care of his own needs. Yet not all
> are authorized to preach, but only one is to preach to the entire con-
> gregation. (22:480)

If any Christian is the only one in a certain place, "here it is his duty to
preach and to teach the gospel to erring heathen or non-Christians." If
there are others, however, the preacher should wait until he is called and
chosen (39:310).

The call is based upon skill, and some talents are required: "The person who wishes to preach needs to have a good voice, good eloquence, a
good memory, and other natural gifts" (36:152). But education is needed
as well: "A preacher must be instructed in the Word of God in order that
he may be able to defend the church" (51:182). Luther thought that his
doctorate conferred authority to preach (54:100), and he was greatly
annoyed by "these fellows who know nothing and yet dispute our
preaching" (51:223). To see that there was always an ample supply of
clergy was one of the reasons children needed to have more than the minimum education required by business (46:251). One of the uses to which
old monasteries could be put was as school buildings in which young
people could prepare to be "bishops, pastors, and other servants of the
church" or other Christian vocations (37:364).

Education, however, is not the only essential qualification for preaching: "No matter how learned a man may be, if he has no sure call and
does not rightly teach the scriptures, he may talk as he will but there is
nothing behind it" (51:224).

The preacher should not be intimidated by the presence in the congregation of people better educated than he; rather, "think of yourself as the

most learned man when you are speaking from the pulpit" (54:158). Besides, when preaching, one should not aim the sermon at scholars.

> I spoke to Bucer in Gotha and suggested that he and Osiander should refrain from erudite preaching. Philip (Melanchthon) doesn't need to be instructed, and I don't teach or lecture for his sake, but we preach publicly for the sake of plain people.... Good God, there are sixteen-year-old girls, women, old men, and farmers in the church, and they don't understand lofty matters!... Someday I'll have to write a book against artful preachers. (54:383-84; cf. 235-36)

Furthermore, "practice must agree with preaching" (52:243).

> The preacher's first message is to teach penitence, remove offenses, proclaim the Law, humiliate and terrify the sinners. No one can do this but a godly preacher. Hypocrites cannot preach this way because they do not truly feel sins (17:277).

Even when preaching is completely sincere and skillful, however, the response to it is not always positive. Luther can say of his own experience,

> I would rather be stretched upon a wheel or carry stones than preach one sermon. For anyone who is in this office will always be plagued.... If I were to follow my own impulse I would say, "Let the damned devil be your preacher!" (51:222)

Indeed, he hardly preached at all for the first nine months of 1530.

In the last sermon of his life, he said that people get tired of preaching when it occurs often (51:390). At another time he observed that certain "bigwigs and towns" despise the office of ministry and "trample the ministers and preachers underfoot and treat them more cruelly than the peasants treat their hogs" (21:226). "The nearer the punishment, the worse the people become; and ... the more one preaches to them, the more they despise his preaching" (35:281). The devil wants preachers to become despondent over their work so that they will give it up (24:289; cf. 29:9).

On top of everything else, clergy are not even paid well: "We have let the peasants and noblemen starve us" (51:222; cf. 17:343; 23:7). That should not be too surprising since "God's Word must suffer persecution in the world"; "where God's Word, the dear gospel is preached and proclaimed, the devil does not rest or take a holiday" (12:183). Hence the lack of persecution is a sign that one is not preaching the gospel (51:112).

Much of the resistance to what Luther considered good preaching came from the two fronts on which he was constantly fighting, from Roman Catholics on the one hand and those he called *Schwärmer* on the other. Roman priests were objected to either because they said private Masses and did not preach at all or because of the sort of preaching they did. On the one hand it might be said: "A priest was a man who could say mass, even though he could not preach a word and was an unlearned ass" (46:221). Or, on the other,

> the reason why the world is so utterly perverted and in error is that for a long time there have been no genuine preachers. There are perhaps three thousand priests, among whom one cannot find four good ones— God have mercy on us in this crying shame! And when you do get a good preacher, he runs through the gospel superficially and then follows it up with a fable about the old ass or a story about Dietrich of Berne, or he mixes in something of the pagan teachers, Aristotle, Plato, Socrates, and others, who are all quite contrary to the gospel and also contrary to God. (51:63-64)[11]

The radical reformers whom Luther called *Schwärmer* were originally limited to Münzer, Karlstadt, and the others who pushed changes in Wittenberg after the Diet of Worms when he was seeking asylum in Wartburg, but later he came to include Zwingli in this category. Usually translated "enthusiasts" or "fanatics," the word is derived from the verb used to refer to the swarming activity of bees, which had taken on a secondary sense of "raving" (37:18 n). Luther was willing to include Oecolampadius in this category for saying that since the Word is available through preaching, the Eucharist is rendered redundant (140). These people "take the greatest offense if unworthy men baptize, celebrate Mass, preach, etc. They do not see that they themselves may be more offensive before God" (188). "Sectarians," "fanatics," and "visionaries" of a spiritualist tendency "despise the oral word" because they do not realize that "it takes toil and trouble to engender faith in people by the God-ordained means of the preaching ministry, absolution, and the sacrament" (22:48). Yet such divisions were inevitable: "If the preaching is God's Word, sects arise, and the same thing happens" as that reported in John 7:43 (23:290).

In short, Luther considers preaching the most important activity in the world because it is the instrument by which election occurs, and he gives a great deal of attention to how it should be done. In doing so, he raises the question of who can preach and what qualifications they should have. Preaching is not always effective, however, when all due precautions are taken. There will always be people who resist the Word of God, whether they be papists or enthusiasts, or merely ordinary sinners.

LUTHER'S HOMILETICAL PRACTICE

About twenty-three hundred of the more than four thousand sermons Luther preached are included in the twenty-two volumes devoted to them in the Weimar edition of his works. By this count, a very high percentage of his sermons have survived, although, as will be seen below, we have almost nothing in the exact form in which it was delivered from the pulpit. Such prodigious homiletical production, even stretched out over half a century, represents frequent preaching. Although Luther was neither the pastor nor the only preacher at the church in Wittenberg, its preaching schedule accounts for the quantity. The first service on Sunday began at 5:00 A.M. and included a sermon on the Epistle appointed for that day in the lectionary. The text for the ten o'clock morning sermon was the Gospel, while the afternoon sermon was either on a passage from the Hebrew Bible or on the catechism.[12] There were also catechetical sermons on Mondays and Tuesdays, with Matthew furnishing the text for Wednesdays, the Apostolic Letters for Thursday and Friday, and the Gospel of John for Saturday afternoon. It is known that Luther also did courses of homiletical lectures on books from both Testaments and that he preached to his household, including whoever might be staying with him, on Sunday afternoons.[13]

Involved in this preaching were a number of different genres of sermons. Sunday sermons were generally on lectionary passages; their form will be discussed below. In the traditional way, catechetical sermons expounded texts from the Creed, the Lord's Prayer, or the Ten Commandments. Course lectures on individual books of the Bible took the homiletical form of verse-by-verse exposition.[14] Occasional sermons varied with the demands of the occasion.

Since Luther preached from an outline (from which he departed frequently), there are no manuscripts containing the full text of what he said. What have survived are notes taken by members of his inner circle; sometimes several produced reports of the same sermon and the printed edition is a synthesis of these. Such notes were usually macaronic, combining the German words that Luther uttered with Latin terms that the scribes could fill in more quickly. About the only sermons published by Luther himself were literary revisions of what he had preached, which he issued when he did not like the notes published by someone else. On the whole, though, it is thought that the printed versions of sermons come very close to what Luther actually said in church, especially when the transcriber was Georg Rörer.

There is, however, a significant body of sermonic material, material that has exercised influence on Lutheran preaching through most of the succeeding centuries and can be traced in its existing form to the pen of Luther. Unfortunately, for the purpose of re-creating his homiletical practice, this material is entirely literary and was never delivered in precisely that form by Luther at divine service. Rather, it was written as an aid to clergy in their sermon production. The work in question is Luther's *Church-* or *Wartburg Postil.* The word *postil* comes from the Latin *postilla*, which has the sense of "exposition," being itself a corruption of *post illa verba sacrae scripturae* ("after these words of sacred scripture"), the words with which expository sermons usually began.

Luther completed only the portion of the postil that covers Advent through Lent. Stephan Roth provided for the remaining Sundays of the year and for feast days in a form that was only partially acceptable to Luther; eventually he commissioned Kaspar Cruciger Sr. to redo the summer postil. Confusingly, the term "postil" is also used to refer to an additional body of Lutheran homiletical material. Between 1531 and 1535, when Luther's health prevented public preaching, his household sermons for the church year were published as the "house postil."[15]

Like most other great preachers, Luther did not emerge with his style full-blown, but had to evolve one. Naturally, he began in the medieval tradition of the thematic sermon. One of the oldest two surviving sermons is outlined on the medieval scheme[16] of: Who, What He Gave, To Whom, With What Motive, What He Accomplished, For What. Another characteristic of thematic preaching that appears in the early sermons of Luther is numbering points. Then, too, he also reflected the medieval sense of the multiple meanings of scripture.[17] Indeed, he only gradually and incompletely restrained himself from allegorical interpretation.

In time, however, Luther developed a method of preaching that was virtually unique. It has often been compared to the patristic homily, but ordinarily he did not engage in verse-by-verse exegesis. Rather, it was the method of *schriftauslegende Predigt*, "expository preaching." Instead of looking at every word in the text sequentially in the sermon, he would discover in his own exegetical preparation what could be called the *Sinnmitte* (center of meaning), *Herzpunkt* (heart point), or *Kern* (kernel) of the passage.[18]

Then, rather than having a formal introduction, he would begin by stating that point, the message he felt the text had for his congregation that day. To illustrate, he begins a Lenten sermon based on the story of the raising of Lazarus with these words:

> Dear Friends of Christ. I have told you the story of this Gospel in order
> that you may picture in your hearts and remember well that Christ our

> God, in all the Gospels, from beginning to end, and also all writings of
> the prophets and apostles, desires of us nothing else but that we should
> have a sure and confident heart and trust in him. (51:44)

The sermon consists of his efforts to extract that meaning from the
story.[19]

Other than that, there is no set pattern by which his sermons are developed. Indeed, Johann Gerhard characterized their structure as "heroic
disorder."[20] Luther would take an outline *(Konzept)* into the pulpit, but
he was notorious for departing from it. Yet that is not to say he did not
prepare thoroughly for his preaching. That preparation, however, consisted of immersing himself in the text until he had penetrated to its
Sinnmitte and developed a *Konzept* that would allow him to get that
point across. His favorite structural device was to set up an antithesis,[21]
to set things in opposition to one another. As noted above, the law/gospel
contrast is the most characteristic form of this, but he also used sin/grace,
Satan/God, and bound will/free will.

There is more to this than rhetoric, however. Preaching was a life-and-
death matter for Luther because he believed that it was the medium
through which election occurred, and in every sermon judgment and
gospel were experienced anew. As John Doberstein says:

> Luther's sermons are therefore real battles in the eschatological struggle
> between Christ and the adversary; their aim is to make Christians of the
> hearers through the Word of God and thus hurl the power and victory
> of Christ against the power of evil.[22]

This accounts for the popular, conversational style, his "characteristic
use of direct address, dialogue, and the dramatic form."[23] This accounts,
too, for his addressing his sermons not to the forty or so doctors and
masters in the congregation, but to the hundreds and thousands of young
people and children in attendance (54:235). It is for their souls that the
eschatological struggle is being waged and its outcome is eternal. (For an
example of a sermon by Luther, see **Vol. 2, pp. 248-54**.)

One could deduce from this description that the study of rhetoric had
nothing to do with Luther's preaching, that he was unaffected by the
humanist movement. Recent investigation, however, has cast important
new light on this issue, light that also helps clarify both the relation of
Luther to his disciple Melanchthon and part of the reason that Luther's
followers did not more closely imitate his homiletical style. John
O'Malley has summarized and added to this literature in an important

article[24] in which he points to the humanistic studies of grammar and rhetoric going on in Luther's time and notes that each of the two categories can be subdivided. The distinction between primary and secondary rhetoric has long been taken to be that between rhetoric as the study of oratory and rhetoric as other uses of oratorical strategies, such as, for example, in letter writing and historical narration.

This sort of secondary rhetoric moves in the direction of grammar, which traditionally taught more than the elementary skills of reading and writing. "The 'grammarian' taught literature, especially poetry, for it was from poetry that the rules of grammar were originally derived."[25] This study of literature involved the interpretation of texts at two levels: a word-by-word or line-by-line philological reading and a search for philosophical or theological meaning that was determined allegorically or "poetically."

With O'Malley's distinctions, we can say immediately that Luther "fits, first and foremost, into the tradition of 'the Christian grammarian,' and that it is in this category that he was most palpably influenced by the patristic and Renaissance adaptation of the classical tradition."[26] From there it becomes clear that Luther understood the Bible primarily as a book of doctrine. As a scholastic he had been trained in dialectic, and he had defined preaching as *doctrina et exhortatio*. This is to say that preaching is a pedagogical art involving dialectics for persuasion.

Adding to that insight Luther's emphasis on popular preaching, one is reminded of the definition of *contio*[27] as deliberative speech addressed to popular assemblies, as Birgit Stolt has pointed out.[28] This association connects Luther to primary rhetorical theory, theory that, as will be shown, was easily available to him through Melanchthon. It also associates his preaching with the kind recommended by Erasmus 274-79. Thus Luther combined the grammarian's concern for explicating a text with the rhetorical techniques of the *contio* for persuading popular audiences to take a course of action.

On the basis of this analysis, O'Malley is able to point out three features of Luther's sermons that make them rhetorically effective, features that are not only good rhetorical practice, but also very appropriate to the Reformer's personality, theology, and existential situation:

1. "Clear and untiringly repeated doctrine" ("his message, in other words, had a clear center" and Lutheran preaching ever since has aimed at "precise doctrinal content").

2. Clear isolation of enemies (papists and *Schwärmer*), giving a sense of "present danger," and, therefore, urgency.

3. "An agenda for the hearers that was specific and immediate, yet fraught with implications for a better order to come."[29]

In the preaching of Luther, then, there was a perfect marriage of content and method. His grammarian's analysis of the text allowed him to discover its meaning for the congregation, and the form of the *contio* enabled him to direct that insight powerfully to their attention. And the doctrine of justification itself was not just something to be explained; it was a call for a response, a demand for a decision.

> Abstract though the doctrine of justification might be in its slogan-like formulation, it had, as expounded by Luther, an immediate impact on the way those who heard it viewed themselves and acted. It clashed dramatically with received opinions and with what other preachers had been saying. As such, it had to make an impression.[30]

MELANCHTHON'S INFLUENCE ON LUTHERAN PREACHING

In his effort to account for the relative neglect of Luther's preaching art—even within Lutheran circles—John O'Malley points out that "unlike so many of his contemporaries and near-contemporaries, he left no specific treatise on how to preach."[31] He could well have gone on to say that Luther's right-hand man, Philipp Melanchthon, did leave such a treatise; indeed, he left a number of them.

Insight into Melanchthon can be garnered by noting that the etymology of his family name is Greek rather than German. He had been baptized as Philipp Schwarzerd, but, while he was receiving attention as a prodigy during his university training, he indulged in the scholarly fad of adopting a Greek equivalent of his family name. Since *Schwarzerd* means "black earth," he combined the genitive forms *melanos* (of the black) and *chthonos* (soil). In those days of humanist excitement over all things Greco-Roman, it was natural that this grandnephew of Johann Reuchlin should follow the graecicizing fashion by which, for example, Neumanns were becoming Neanders.

Envy of his brilliance as a young classical scholar caused his superiors at first Heidelberg and then Tübingen to deny him the advancements he so obviously deserved. Recognition finally came, however, when he was called in 1518, at the age of twenty-three, to become professor of Greek at a center of humanism, Frederick the Wise's new university in Wittenberg.[32] That was ten years after Luther had begun to lecture there, seven after he had become a doctor and professor, and a year after he had begun to preach against Tetzel and indulgences. So quickly did Melanchthon become a friend of Luther and a party to his cause of reform that the following year he supported him in the Leipzig Disputation. His *Loci communes* of 1521 was "the first ordered presentation of Reformation doctrine."[33] In later years he was one of the chief Lutheran representatives in various important negotiations (e.g., he was the leading presence at the Diet of Augsburg in 1530 and the main author of the Confession produced by it).

The humanism of Melanchthon was not abandoned in his enthusiasm for the Reformation cause, nor was it unimportant for the history of Lutheran preaching. Indeed, the epithet by which Melanchthon is known is "the preceptor of Germany." The educational system he devised was essentially rhetorical, and it not only furnished the basic pattern of German education for centuries to come, but that of English and American education as well.[34]

Much of his continuing influence was through the textbooks he wrote on rhetoric. He did write a book solely on preaching, *De officiis concionatoris*, the third edition of which, appearing in 1535, was the first one dated. Up until that time, it could be said of this work and a similar textbook by Viet Dietrich that they were "sketchy, partisan, and extremely brief works of pamphlet size that did not have an immediate or broad influence."[35] The real influence of Melanchthon on preaching was thus exercised through his treatment of it in his work in rhetoric.

In 1519, Melanchthon published his first book on rhetoric, *De rhetorica libri tres*. Two years later his lectures on rhetoric at Wittenberg were published as the *Institutiones Rhetoricae*. In 1531, he produced his own textbook, the *Elementa rhetorices* and revised it slightly in 1542.[36]

Thus Luther himself accepted Melanchthon's secondary rhetoric as the major tool of biblical exegesis, but made use of his primary rhetoric only to the extent of adopting the *contio* form for his sermons. Yet it was Melanchthon's primary rhetoric, his theory of preaching, that was more determinative for the future shape of Lutheran homiletics than was the preaching of Luther himself. As a humanist, Melanchthon was committed to the revival of classical rhetoric. Instead of accepting the *contio* form favored by Luther and Erasmus for Christian preaching, he dealt with the essential difficulty of fitting *explication de texte* into the three classical genera by creating a fourth genus especially for preaching and classroom lecture, which he called *genus didascalicum*. (For

Melanchthon's treatment of this, see **Vol. 2, pp. 254-61.**) But this designation reflects Luther's understanding that preaching is essentially the teaching of sound doctrine and that the method for doing so is dialectic, a combination of *doctrina et exhortatio*.

In classical dialectic there are both simple and complex questions. The *loci* for a simple question are: What is the thing, what are its parts or species, what are its causes, what are its effects, what things are related to it, and what things are opposed to it?[37] Using these *loci*, the preacher can "invent" (i.e., discover) what is to be said about any simple question. The *loci* for complex questions are essentially the same. By asking themselves such questions, clergy can find what needs to be said about every biblical topic.

The three classical genera are the judicial or forensic *(genus iudicialis)*, the legislative or deliberative *(genus deliberativum)*, and the epideictic *(genus demonstrativum)*. Melanchthon did not think that the judicial had any part in Christian preaching and felt that epideictic did so only to the extent that it was an "ornamented" version of the *didascalicum*. The deliberative, however, was homiletically useful if it was broken up into two sub-genera: the *epitrepticum*, which exhorts to faith; and the *paraneticum*, which exhorts to good morals.[38]

In his textbooks, Melanchthon taught pastors to write sermons in the didascalic, the epitreptic, and the paranetic genera. These homiletical forms, rather than the *contio* of Luther, became the standard patterns of Lutheran preaching for centuries to come. The man who influenced Luther by his knowledge of secondary rhetoric influenced the followers of Luther with his primary rhetoric.[39] In doing so, he became the preceptor not only of Germany but of the majority of Lutheran preachers for centuries to come.

FOR FURTHER READING

Bainton, Roland H. *Here I Stand: A Life of Martin Luther.* New York: Abingdon-Cokesbury, 1950.

La Fontaine, Mary Joan. "A Critical Translation of Philipp Melanchthon's *Elementorum Rhetorices Libri Duo*," Latin text with English translation and notes. Louisville: Westminster John Knox, 1995.

Luther, Martin. *Luther's Works.* American ed. Edited by Jaroslav Pelikan and Helmut T. Lehmann. Vols. 51-52, *Sermons I-II*, edited by John A. Doberstein. St. Louis: Concordia Publishing House; Philadelphia: Fortress, 1959.

Meuser, Fred W. *Luther the Preacher.* Minneapolis: Augsburg, 1983.

O'Malley, John. "Luther the Preacher," *The Martin Luther Quincentennial,* ed. Gerhard Dünnhaupt. Detroit: Wayne State University Press for *Michigan Germanic Studies,* 1985.

Wengert, Timothy J. *Philipp Melanchthon's Annotationes in Johannem in Relation to Its Predecessors and Contemporaries.* Travaux d'Humanisme et Renaissance, no. 220. Geneva: Librairie Droz S.A., 1987.

Notes

1. The reason that Luther's style was not copied is that his disciples followed instead the pattern set forth in the textbooks of his assistant Melanchthon, as will be seen below (pp. 298-300). That his preaching has not been studied is a commonplace (see, e.g., Elmer Carl Kiessling's University of Chicago dissertation, *The Early Sermons of Luther and Their Relation to the Pre-Reformation Sermon* [Grand Rapids, Mich.: Zondervan, 1935], 5; and Fred W. Meuser, *Luther the Preacher* [Minneapolis: Augsburg, 1983], 9).

2. Roland H. Bainton, *Here I Stand: A Life of Martin Luther* (New York and Nashville: Abingdon-Cokesbury, 1950), 65, from the Weimar edition of Luther's works, 54:185. In his book, written in English, Bainton provided the English translation of the passage on 455 cited in this note, which was originally in German.

3. Historians are no longer sure the breach occurred in precisely this way, but there is no doubt that it did occur at that time over these issues.

4. The presentation of Luther's thought that follows is based on Justo L. González, *A History of Christian Thought: From the Reformation to the Twentieth Century,* vol. 3 (Nashville: Abingdon, 1975), 25-62.

5. Luther does not speak of "the capacity to be turned in a new direction," but the phrase seems to express his thought.

6. Documentation for this section will be drawn from *Luther's Works,* American ed., Jaroslav Pelikan and Helmut T. Lehmann, eds. (St. Louis: Concordia Publishing House; Philadelphia: Fortress, 1958–86). Citations appear parenthetically in the text with the volume number followed by a colon and the page number (e.g., the documentation for the statement for which this note is given is 39:314).

7. Luther even sees a powerful homiletical dimension to sacraments. See 35:105; 13:377.

8. Carl E. Braaten, *Justification: The Article by Which the Church Stands or Falls* (Minneapolis: Fortress, 1990), 148.

9. See also 12:17, 71; 13:316-17; 17:7-8, 210, 260, 277; 23:278; 31:241, 364; 35:166.

10. 23:174. The Word here is not just the proclaimed Word, but is the incarnate and written Word as well.

11. Passages of the sort quoted in this paragraph are too common to list.

12. The view stated is that of Meuser, cited below, 37-38. But Prof. Timothy

Wengert told me during conversations held over March 13-16, 1991, that catechetical sermons were preached only during the Ember seasons—a traditional time for such sermons from at least the time of Aelfric. Wengert said that when Luther preached such sermons, he was filling in for the pastor of the church. He referred to the 5:00 A.M. service as Matins, the 10:00 A.M. as Mass, and the afternoon as Vespers. His reference was Bruno Jordahn, "Katechismus-Gottesdienst im Reformationsjahrhundert," *Luther: Mitteilungen der Luthergesellschaft* 30 (1959): 64-77.

13. Meuser, *Luther the Preacher,* 37-38.

14. For example, it took Luther twenty-eight lectures to get through the first four chapters of Galatians (26:ix).

15. Hans J. Hillerbrand, "Introduction," in *Luther's Works,* 52:ix-xiii. This volume contains a translation of slightly more than half of the *Christmas Postil.* See also Yngve Brilioth, *A Brief History of Preaching,* trans. Karl E. Mattson, The Preacher's Paperback Library (Philadelphia: Fortress), 108-9; and Meuser, *Luther the Preacher,* 37. Other short treatments of Luther's preaching occur in Bainton, *Here I Stand,* 348-58; Werner Schütz, *Geschichte der christlichen Predigt* (Berlin: Walter de Gruyter, 1972), 90-96; Harold J. Grimm, "The Human Element in Luther's Sermons," in *ARG* 49 (1958): 50-60; James Mackinnon, *Luther and the Reformation* (London, New York, and Toronto: Longmans, Green & Co., 1930), 4:304-18; and John W. Doberstein, "Introduction," in *Luther's Works,* 51:xi-xxi. Volume 51 is a good collection of characteristic sermons preached at various periods of Luther's career.

16. Based on the dialectics of Aristotle, from which Melanchthon was to derive the *loci* of his Didactic genus of speaking.

17. Kiessling, *The Early Sermons of Luther and Their Relation to the Pre-Reformation Sermon,* 60-67.

18. Although scholars at times refer to this as "literal, historical, grammatical" interpretation, these terms can be misleading, since Luther was not involved in the task of modern historical-critical exegesis, that of discovering what the sacred writer intended his/her first readers to understand. Rather, the Scriptures were taken as addressed to the contemporary church. The "literal" meaning of a passage from Galatians, for instance, would not be what it had meant to Christians in the community founded by Paul in the region of Ancyra, but what it meant to Wittenbergers.

19. Meuser, *Luther the Preacher,* 46-48.

20. Quoted by Kiessling, *The Early Sermons of Luther and Their Relation to the Pre-Reformation Sermon,* 60.

21. Meuser, *Luther the Preacher,* 48.

22. Doberstein, "Introduction," in Luther's Works, 51:xix-xx.

23. Ibid., 51:xi-xxi.

24. "Luther the Preacher," *The Martin Luther Quincentennial,* ed. Gerhard Dünnhaupt (Detroit: Wayne State University Press for *Michigan Germanic Studies,* 1985), 3-16.

25. Ibid., 6. O'Malley's interpretation is consistent with what was said above about Origen, 31-46. Indeed, his "secondary rhetoric" is essentially the concerns of the classical *grammatikos.*

26. Ibid., 8.

27. A variant spelling of *concio.*

28. O'Malley, "Luther the Preacher," 9. The reference is to Stolt's *"Docere, delectare, und movere bei Luther,"* *Deutsche Viertejahresschrift für Literaturwissenschaft und Geistesgeschichte* 44 (1970): 433-74.

29. O'Malley, "Luther the Preacher," 12.

30. Ibid., 12.

31. Ibid., 3.

32. For the atmosphere of the university at the time, see Maria Grossmann, *Humanism in Wittenberg 1485–1517* (Nieuwkoop: B. DeGraaf, 1975). It must be admitted, however, that Grossmann stresses more than most recent scholars an anti-Christian spirit in humanism and an opposition to humanism on the part of Luther. For German humanism, see also Mary Joan La Fontaine, "A Critical Translation of Philipp Melanchthon's *Elementorum Rhetorices Libri Duo,"* Latin text with English translation and notes (unpublished Ph.D. dissertation, University of Michigan, 1968), 6-18; and Helmut Schanze, "Problems and Trends in the History of German Rhetoric" in *Renaissance Eloquence: Studies in the Theory and Practice of Renaissance Rhetoric,* ed. James J. Murphy (Berkeley: University of California Press), 105-25.

33. *ODCC,* 898.

34. La Fontaine, "A Critical Translation of Philipp Melanchthon's *Elementorum Rhetorices Libri Duo,"* 30-38.

35. John W. O'Malley, "Erasmus and the History of Sacred Rhetoric: The *Ecclesiastes* of 1535," in *Erasmus of Rotterdam Society Yearbook,* vol. 5 (1985), 8.

36. Timothy Wengert, "Melanchthon, Philipp," in *Concise Encyclopedia of Preaching,* ed. William Willimon and Richard Lischer, 328-29.

37. La Fontaine, "A Critical Translation of Philipp Melanchthon's *Elementorum Rhetorices Libri Duo"* (Louisville: Westminster John Knox, 1995), 99.

38. O'Malley, "Sixteenth-Century Treatises," in *Renaissance Eloquence: Studies in the Theory and Practice of Renaissance Rhetoric,* ed. James J. Murphy (Berkeley: The University of California Press, 1983), 242-43.

39. This is not to say that his secondary rhetoric was not also very influential on subsequent Lutheran exegesis. The *Loci communes* was even more of an exegetical tool of secondary rhetoric than it was a theological treatise as such. For the use of rhetorical categories in Melanchthon's exegesis, see Timothy J. Wengert, *Philipp Melanchthon's Annotationes in Johannem in Relation to Its Predecessors and Contemporaries,* Travaux d'Humanisme et Renaissance, no. 220 (Geneva: Librairie Droz S.A., 1987), 167-212. For a translation of *Loci communes,* see *Melanchthon and Bucer,* ed. Wilhelm Pauck, LCC, vol. 19 (Philadelphia: Westminster, 1969), 18-152.

CHAPTER 13

CALVIN AND THE REFORM TRADITION

THE SWISS REFORMATION

Luther's particular type of reforming activity, although the inspiration or occasion of the efforts that followed, succeeded only in spreading to other Germanic-language areas. The tradition that was to influence the rest of the world arose in Switzerland. The movement there began very soon after that in Germany, but apparently without Lutheran influence in the beginning. Indeed, Ulrich Zwingli, its first founder, was eager to escape association with Luther even after he became acquainted with his writings; he considered the Wittenberg Reformer to have been too conservative, too supportive of aspects of the old religion. Besides, they were operating out of different presuppositions and preoccupations. Zwingli had never been a monk involved in an effort to achieve a sense of acceptance by God, and he never acquired the deep immersion in scholasticism that Luther's doctorate betokened. Rather, his training had alerted him to the revival of classical and patristic learning among the humanists. Instead of Luther's emphasis on justification, he was more involved in the humanist's desire to return to the sources *(ad fontes)*, and thus he wanted to emphasize the Bible as the exclusive source of Christian doctrine. His battle cry was not *sola fide*, but *sola scriptura*.[1]

Although Zwingli's reform teaching was the earliest in Switzerland, it was not to be the form that predominated. Nor was his own example of preaching to be the most influential. In fact, very few of his sermons have survived. Only two aspects of what was to become the standard pattern of Swiss preaching can be traced to him. The first is that he did not preach from the lectionary for the church year but instead did course preaching through books of the Bible. The second is that he designed a liturgy for which the sermon, rather than the Eucharist, provided the shape.[2]

> The Sunday service was again given a new form with the sermon as the central point. The sermon itself, loosed from its liturgical context, became the basic motif in the creation of new liturgy.[3]

As important as these changes were, the initiative for innovation was to lie elsewhere. Zwingli's early death as a casualty of the second war between Switzerland's Catholic and Protestant cantons in 1531 meant that he was no longer on the scene when John Calvin, the Frenchman who was to give the Swiss Reformation and its preaching their distinctive patterns, made his appearance.

Radical Reform

Calvin's, however, was not the first attempt to alter the pattern Zwingli had begun to construct in Zurich. That impulse came from Zwingli's own city and from his circle of friends. The ostensible issue of the first disagreements was the legitimacy of infant baptism, although more was at stake than the nature of one sacrament; the whole nature of the church and its relation to the state was involved.[4] The first disagreement was in debates about the Mass, especially Zwingli's decision to let the town council decide the timing for discontinuing the Mass. Anabaptists felt the council had no right to legislate on an issue governed by the Word of Scripture—it was thus a disagreement about the relationship of church and state.

Yet the event has traditionally been discussed in terms of stands on infant baptism. Those who quarreled with Zwingli claimed that it had no legitimacy (a point on which he agreed with them at first), and thus argued that adults should be baptized even if they had been christened as babies. From this position they came to be known as "Anabaptists," advocates of rebaptism. They rejected the term, however, saying that no one could be rebaptized if the ceremony through which they had previously gone was not true baptism.

The argument still goes on about the proper way to refer to the groups that grew out of or otherwise resemble Zwingli's opponents at Zurich. For a while it was popular to refer to the movement as "the left wing of the Reformation," a tendency growing out of Ernst Troeltsch's analysis, which envisioned

> a spectrum of religious practice ranging from medieval and reactionary, on the far right, to liberal and modern, on the far left.... By this measure Catholics were the most medieval and reactionary; Lutherans, conservative to moderate; Calvinists and Zwinglians, moderate to liberal; and the radical reformers—Anabaptists, Spiritualists, and Evangelical Rationalists—liberal and modern.[5]

Part and parcel of this interpretation has been assigning to these groups the credit for three principles that are taken for granted in contemporary North American Christianity: "the voluntary church, the separation of church and state, and religious liberty."[6] For Troeltsch, this makes them forerunners of modern humanism and liberal Protestantism, but it disregards their differences from modern groups and ignores how much they had in common with medieval Christianity.[7]

The appropriateness of retrojecting contemporary political categories into the sixteenth century has been further questioned by George H. Williams, who has suggested instead that the groups be referred to collectively as "the radical Reformation."[8] As a way of avoiding the confusion of some of these groups with others that have very different views and dynamics, Williams also proposed a taxonomy that distinguishes between a number of different types of radical reform movements. It lists three kinds of Anabaptists (revolutionary, contemplative, and evangelical), three kinds of Spiritualists (revolutionary, evangelical, and rational), and Evangelical Rationalists.[9]

Before the recent scholarship reflected in the previous paragraphs, there was a tendency to lump all of these groups together and to study them in terms not of their own writings, but of what their enemies, especially Lutherans, Calvinists, and Zwinglians, had to say about them.[10] Luther tended to confuse later movements with the group who had disturbed the Wittenberg church while he was in Wartburg after the Diet of Worms and with radicals in the north German town of Münster. In 1534 these latter instituted a theocracy that put into practice many positive Old Testament social ideals, providing work for everyone, which at the same time revived charismatic prophecy and polygamy. Luther thus dismissed all radical reform movements as "enthusiasts" *(Schwärmer)*, and assumed that all were revolutionary and antinomian. Yet there seems to have been little if any influence of either group on the Zurich, southwest German, and Dutch radicals from whom later Anabaptists appear to have originated.

The basic doctrines of at least evangelical Anabaptistry begin with a primitivist assumption that the apostolic age was the golden age of the church, a normative period in which the church enjoyed a perfection from which it later fell. That fall was often associated with the time of Constantine, when indiscriminate baptism occurred and unbelievers were allowed into the church. This was seen as the beginning of the use of coercion by the state for religious conformity.

The Radical Reformers, however, saw themselves as called by God to inaugurate a new period in history, the time of the restitution of Christianity to its New Testament pattern. They were energized by an eschatological belief that the end was at hand.[11] In their system, religious behavior was to be voluntary and therefore sincere. This meant not only that there would be no use of police power to enforce conformity, but also that only adults who freely chose to make the commitment would be baptized. The Anabaptists thus called for an end to religious establishment enforced by the state and a beginning of tolerance for dissent. They themselves foreswore any use of force and committed themselves to a pattern of pacifism and passive resistance, even when they knew that it could very well lead to martyrdom.[12]

As in the time of Tertullian, the blood of martyrs proved to be seed from which the church sprang up in vigorous new growth. The "Fourth Reformation"[13] became an aggressive missionary movement. The Anabaptists' missionary activity, like the rest of their ministerial activity, involved a great deal of lay participation. Those who had taken on responsibility for their own religious commitment also took on responsibility to share it with others.

Since the historical recovery of the Radical Reformation is still under way, it is not surprising that there have not been many studies of its preaching so far.[14] Furthermore, the nature of the case is such that few written sermons have survived from the early days of the movement. While the founders had been ordained as Catholic priests and were often learned, almost all were included among the martyrs of the first generation. After that, those chosen for ministerial office (by lot at first, though later by election) came from the congregation and had no academic training in theology. Further, sermons that were not extempore were distrusted at first. There is little surprise, then, that few were taken down by stenographers and published.

The early Anabaptist sermons were without doubt conceived as simple forthright declarations of a hortatory and devotional character, except when used for evangelistic purposes. They were certainly not expected to be rhetorical orations prepared and finished according to the practice of learned men. It was assumed that any member of the church could admonish the congregation out of his general knowledge of the Scriptures, his experience in life, and the help of the Holy Spirit.[15]

The life pattern of such congregations probably means that what Roy Umble said about the American preachers of 1864–1944, whom he studied, could apply equally well to any generation after the first (except for the extent to which it suggests a central place for the sermon):

With the Bible as the background and focus of the preaching, these men illustrate a certain uniformity in method of organization and proof. Sermons usually followed a lengthy devotional period consisting of congregational singing, Scripture reading and prayer. The minister began with a Scripture text, announced a theme or related the Bible verse to the occasion, and proceeded to explain or expand and then apply the teaching.[16]

In time and in various places, this pattern changed. While the extempore pattern continued in Switzerland and south Germany, there developed in Prussia and Russia a practice of writing out sermons and reading them. This was followed by a time when it was thought prideful to preach a sermon of one's own composition, so only the written sermons of the past could be read. At least as late as the 1950s, in Hutterite congregations of Canada and the northwest United States, newly elected preachers copied by hand notebooks full of sermons from mid-seventeenth-century Slovakia to read at worship services.[17]

In the Anabaptist tradition, on the other hand, only one sermon in German survives from the sixteenth century and one in Dutch from the seventeenth. By the eighteenth century, though, sermons were printed frequently. These were not read from the pulpit, although they probably were thought of as models. Their main purpose was to be read in family devotions; by the beginning of the twentieth century, such collections were published with the explicit statement that they were *zum Gebrauch für Hausgottesdienst*.[18] This custom reflected the influence of Pietism.

Regrettably, this is about all that can be learned about a preaching tradition that was rich, and very meaningful to those who experienced it.

THE CAREER OF A REFORMER

When Luther did or did not post his Ninety-five Theses on the door of the Wittenberg church on All Hallows' Eve, 1517, John Calvin was an eight-year-old boy, the fourth son of a notary in service of the clergy in the cathedral town of Noyon in Picardy. Recognizing the opportunities for advancement that the church offered to a young man of talent, Gérard Cauvin[19] began early to plan on a priestly career for his precocious son. The father's connections made it possible for young John to receive the tonsure and to be appointed to several benefices when he was only twelve.

Two years later, the lad was enrolled in the Collège de la Marche at "the Sorbonne," the University of Paris. This meant that he found himself "in the greatest of universities and at the heart of the greatest of nations."[20] Five years after that, when he had completed his M.A., his father, now involved in quarrels with the cathedral clergy that would eventually result in his excommunication, caused John to take up the study of law. He was enrolled first at Orléans and then at Bourges, although he returned to Paris for regular intervals of study during the five years that he was a law student. After John became *licencié* in the law in 1533, he was free to pursue his own interests, his father having died the year before.

While Calvin was well exposed to scholasticism during his years of study, he was most impressed by the humanists among his teachers.[21] His ideals during those days were Erasmus and Jacques Lefèvre d'Étaples (latinized as Jacobus Faber Stapulensis), librarian of the monastery of St. Germain-des-Prés and humanistic biblical scholar.[22] The greatest monument of Calvin's own humanistic activity and his first book as well was a commentary on Seneca's treatise, *De clementia*,[23] which he published the year before he finished his legal studies.

The teachers who influenced him most during this period were humanists who were critical of abuses within the Roman Catholic Church while remaining loyal to it. That seems to have been the situation of his close friend Nicholas Cop, who took advantage of his position as rector of the University of Paris to preach a sermon on All Saints' Day, 1533, criticizing the scholasticism of the Sorbonne faculty from an Erasmian perspective that Bouwsma calls "evangelical humanism."[24] In the fallout from this sermon, not only Cop but also Calvin had to flee Paris. Authorities disagree over whether Calvin's danger was the result of his having shared in the composition of the sermon or was merely guilt by association. In any case, most scholars now believe that Cop's sermon, critical as it was of the religious establishment, stopped short of recommending a breach with Rome.

In point of fact—and remarkably so—one of the most disputed issues in the study of Calvin's life is that of exactly when his own criticism of the Catholic Church's conduct and thought led him to decide that conscience required him to leave it. It has long been recognized that virtually the only autobiographical evidence on the question is contained in the dedication at the beginning of his commentary on the Psalms:[25]

> I was called back from the study of philosophy to learn law. I followed my father's wish and attempted to do faithful work in this field; but God, by the secret leading of his providence, turned my course another way.
>
> First, when I was too firmly addicted to the papal superstitions to be drawn easily out of such a deep mire, by a sudden conversion He brought my mind (already more rigid than suited my age) to submission [to him]. I was so inspired by a taste of true religion and I burned with such a desire to carry my study further, that although I did not drop other subjects, I had no zeal for them. In less than a year, all who were looking for a purer doctrine began to come to learn from me, although I was a novice and a beginner.

But what exactly does that mean? It obviously involved the reorientation of his life, but if it also involved a cataclysmic emotional experience, he does not describe it. Clearly it was not his passing over from a dissolute life of irreligion or atheism to a life of Christian belief and commitment. Indeed, Bouswma seems to deny that he had a conversion at all, at least in the manner of Paul or Augustine. Pointing out that Calvin always seemed to minimize Paul's experience and to emphasize "the gradualness rather than the suddenness of conversion," he makes the startling claim that "Calvinism was the creation of a devout sixteenth-century French Catholic."[26] More measured and probably nearer the truth is his statement on the following page that Calvin's conversion "did not obliterate but built upon his evangelical humanism."[27] I would prefer to say that his conversion occurred when it became obvious to him that his loyalty to evangelical humanism forced him to leave the Roman church and become one of its critics and opponents.

The date for this reorientation of Calvin's life is also a matter of dispute. At present, however, most scholars consider the first act that decisively indicates a change of heart to have been Calvin's visit in May 1534 to his hometown of Noyon to surrender his benefices; apparently he felt that he could not receive income from a system in which he did not believe. This dating is supported negatively by the lack of any distinctively Protestant sentiments in his Seneca commentary of 1532. It is easy to speculate that Calvin's visit to Lefèvre d'Étaples near the time he went to Noyon must have been for the purpose of consulting his aging humanistic ideal about his decision to abandon the Roman communion.

Calvin spent the next two years traveling in France and Italy and putting his newfound convictions into expression. During this time he produced the first edition of *Institutes,* his "instruction" in the reformed faith that he used also as an apologia to the French king Francis I, urging him to grant amnesty to returning religious exiles. The book did not succeed in its apologetic purpose, and so its patriotic author had to spend the rest of his life as an exile. As a textbook in Protestant thought, however, it has no near rival. Continuing to revise and expand it (to five times its original length) until five years before his death in 1564, Calvin had already decided by the second edition that it was not to be merely a handbook for the faithful; it was also to be the authoritative guide for theological students in their interpretation of the Bible.[28]

Calvin had tried to remain anonymous out of a desire for scholarly retreat, but his name on the title page of the *Institutes* made that impossible. A temporary amnesty for religious exiles permitted him to return briefly to settle his affairs in France. From there he set out for Strasbourg in hopes of finding the peace and quiet that study requires. He was, however, forced to take a detour through Geneva, and word of his overnight presence there brought to his inn the local Reformer, Guilliaume Farel. The religious situation in the city was tense. Its traditional ruler had been its prince-bishop, who had exercised his oversight through a town council. Huguenot exiles, however, had negotiated an alliance with Fribourg and Bern that toppled the prelate and handed his power over to a concentric series of councils. Bern then sent Reform missionaries to the city under the leadership of Farel. After a series of disputations, the town council accepted the Reformation on May 25, 1536. Two months later, Calvin arrived in town. Farel, who is described by McNeill as "Lefèvre's most aggressive pupil, a second-rate scholar, and a hot gospeler,"[29] recognized both the tenuousness of the religious situation in Geneva and his own limitations. He tried to persuade Calvin, who was twenty years his junior, to stay and help.

How Farel overcame Calvin's reluctance is best stated in Calvin's own words in the preface to his Psalms commentary that also contains the story of his "conversion":

> Since the wars had closed the direct road to Strasbourg, I had meant to pass through Geneva quickly and had determined not to be delayed there more than one night.

A short time before, by the work of the same good man [Farel], and of Peter Viret, the papacy had been banished from the city; but things were still unsettled and the place was divided into evil and harmful factions. One man, who has since shamefully gone back to the papists, took immediate action to make me known. Then Farel, who was working with incredible zeal to promote the gospel, bent all his efforts to keep me in the city. And when he realized that I was determined to study in privacy in some obscure place, and saw that he gained nothing by entreaty, he descended to cursing, and said that God would surely curse my peace if I held back from giving help at a time of such great need. Terrified by his words, and conscious of my own timidity and cowardice, I gave up my journey and attempted to apply whatever gift I had in defense of my faith.[30]

After that, it would be appropriate to say, "And the rest is history," except for one thing, namely, that in less than two years the town council expelled Farel and Calvin from Geneva, unwilling to grant them the power of excommunication they felt their reform program called for. Thus Calvin finally got to Strasbourg, where he assisted Martin Bucer by serving as pastor to a congregation of French exiles. There he accomplished many things, including writing his first biblical commentary (on Romans),[31] revising and expanding the *Institutes,* and learning much from Bucer about how to be a Reform leader in a Swiss city.

After a little more than three years, however, he reluctantly accepted the recall of the Genevan town council and went back to the position of leadership that he was to keep until his death in 1564. During that time he met with opposition, but gradually those who opposed him emigrated. Meanwhile, Geneva became the city of refuge for many whose zeal for reform had necessitated their flight from other countries; in time these refugees totaled 30 percent of the population. For them Geneva was the epitome of all their hopes and dreams because Calvin had succeeded in getting accepted there his full program of religious reform.

Le Prédicateur Méconnu de Genève

After Calvin returned to Geneva in 1541, he asked the council to appoint a committee to draft *Les Ordonnances ecclésiastiques de l'Église de Genève* to govern the religious practices of the city and its citizens. These ordinances, as approved by the council, called for a rich diet of preaching. On Sundays at daybreak there was a sermon in the larger two of the three churches. There were sermons in all three churches at nine o'clock and again at mid-afternoon. Then there were sermons during the week on Mondays, Wednesdays, and Fridays.[32] In 1549 the sermons during the week became daily. Calvin's associate and successor, Theodore Beza, estimated that Calvin preached an average of 290 sermons a year.[33]

Preaching was very important to Calvin's understanding of what the church exists to do. In listing his criteria by which a genuine church was to be recognized, he said:

> Wherever we see the Word of God purely preached and heard, and the sacraments administered according to Christ's institution, there, it is not to be doubted, a church of God exists.[34]

He never did achieve his sacramental ideal of having the Eucharist every Sunday. It was not until 1557, when the power of excommunication was granted to the Consistory, that he realized his disciplinary ideal for the administration of the sacraments.[35] He could hardly complain, however, that the Word of God was not purely preached.

This singular success in the area of preaching makes it all the more amazing that Richard Stauffer could claim that Calvin the preacher is unappreciated and ignored. This inattention goes back to Calvin's lifetime. While it is true that arrangements were made for Denis Raguenier to take down Calvin's extemporaneously delivered sermons in shorthand, that was not done until 1549. Only eight hundred of the transcribed sermons were published before Calvin died. These amounted to only a fraction of the contents of the forty-four folio volumes of these transcripts made by Raguenier; his catalog of Calvin's sermons lists 2,042.

These manuscripts remained in the Public and University Library of Geneva until 1806 when the librarian sold them by the pound as wastepaper. In 1823 eight of the volumes were discovered in a used clothing shop by some theological students, who recognized them for what they were and began the effort to reassemble the collection. Although other volumes have been recovered, it is estimated that around a thousand sermons were lost. The Corpus Reformatorum edition of *Calvini Opera* contains 872 sermons. More than two hundred others began to see the light of day, however, in 1961 when the series of *Supplementa Calviniana* started to appear.[36] Such tardiness in the publication of these sermons supports Stauffer's claim that Calvin the preacher has been unappreciated and ignored.[37]

Calvin's Doctrine of Preaching

Calvin did not go as far as Luther did in identifying preaching as the Word of God.[38] The minister cannot assume that God is speaking through his[39] preaching:

A man whose holy life is given up to the service of God may preach irreproachably scriptural doctrine, applied with a profound psychological insight to the needs of the congregation, and yet nevertheless it cannot be taken for granted that God is speaking to His Church. Rather, Calvin would say, preaching *becomes* Revelation by God adding to it His Holy Spirit.[40]

Nevertheless, preaching is the ordinary channel through which the Holy Spirit speaks:

Outward preaching is vain and useless unless the Spirit himself acts as the teacher. God therefore teaches in two ways. He makes us hear his voice through the words of men, and inwardly he constrains us by his Spirit. These two occur together or separately, as God sees fit.[41]

When the Spirit speaks internally to someone, however, no insight is granted that is not already expressed in Scripture. "The Spirit will not be a maker of new revelations."[42] Yet through this preaching it may be expected that the older revelation will be extended to the congregation:

The task of the preacher of the Word is to expound the scripture in the midst of the worshipping Church, preaching in the expectancy that God will do, through his frail human word, what He did through the Word of His prophets of old, that God by His grace will cause the word that goes out of the mouth of man to become also a Word that proceeds from God Himself, with all the power and efficacy of the Word of the Creator and Redeemer.[43]

In this perspective it may be said that preaching is the Word of God in at least two senses. The first is that "it is an exposition and interpretation of the Bible, which is as much the Word of God as if men 'heard the very words pronounced by God himself.'"[44] The Bible and nothing but the Bible is the matter of preaching; Calvin was determined to speak where the Scriptures speak and to be silent where they are silent. Thus "the teaching of a minister should be approved on the sole ground of his being able to show that what he says comes from God."[45] When such preaching occurs, it can be taken as a sign of the presence of God and the instrument through which Christ's rule is established, a Word that is effective to accomplish its commands and promises. This is to say that it is "efficacious for the salvation of believers (and) abundantly efficacious for the condemning of the wicked."[46]

The second sense in which it may be said that preaching is the Word

314

of God is that the minister is called precisely for the proclamation of the Word of God. His vocation comes through the Holy Spirit and is ratified by his call to serve in a congregation. In the confidence of this double calling, he speaks as an ambassador of God and as though God personally were speaking.

> Now we must not find this strange, for when the servants of God speak thus, they attribute nothing to themselves, but show to what they are commissioned and what charge is given them; and thus they do not separate themselves from God.[47]

Calvin's conviction that it takes the Holy Spirit's ratifying of the sermon to make it the Word of God, his belief in double predestination, and his generally low estimate of the value of human activity did not mean that he considered the qualifications of pastors to be a matter of indifference.

> Clearly not everyone is fitted to be a pastor; knowledge of the Scriptures and soundness of doctrine must be joined to faithfulness, zeal, and holiness. As important as any of these, however, and without which no man can be a good preacher, is the gift of teaching.[48]

Such qualities are external evidences of an inward call and are thus prerequisites for ordination. And the most important duty of the minister is preaching the Word of God; that was believed to be "the constituting essential of the ministry."[49]

Purely Proclaiming the Word of God

Anyone moving from Calvin's theory of preaching to his practice of it will not be surprised at the consistency between them. His own knowledge of the Scriptures, theological erudition, high standards of personal behavior, and pedagogical skill are well known. Further, his humanistic training developed all of his natural rhetorical ability. He knew the misuses to which rhetoric could be put, but knew as well its value when rightly used:

> That eloquence, then, is neither to be condemned nor despised, which has no tendency to lead Christians to be taken up with an outward glitter of words, or intoxicate them with empty delight, or tickle their ears with its tinkling sound, or cover over the Cross of Christ with its empty show as with a veil; but, on the contrary, tends to call us back to the

native simplicity of the Gospel, tends to exalt the simple preaching of the Cross by voluntarily abasing itself, and, in fine, acts the part of a herald.[50]

His rhetorical skill may not be immediately apparent to modern readers of his sermons, however, for two reasons: (1) his preaching, though carefully prepared for, was always extempore, and (2) he used the homily form of verse-by-verse analysis, which undercuts the overall unity of a sermon. He used the homily form as he engaged in course preaching through entire books of the Bible, having theological qualms about chopping the Scriptures into liturgical lections. Doing that, he felt, suggested that parts of Scripture were unnecessary, less inspired, and not of a unity with the rest of the canon in their teaching.

Parker has drafted the outline of a typical Calvin sermon on a text of two phrases or clauses:

1. Prayer.
2. Recapitulation of previous sermon.
3. (a) Exegesis and exposition of first member.
   (b) Application of this, and exhortation to obedience or duty.
4. (a) Exegesis and exposition of second member.
   (b) Application of this, and exhortation to obedience or duty.
5. Bidding to prayer, which contains a summary of the sermon.[51]

This diagram, however, suggests a sharper division between exegesis and application than one often feels in reading one of Calvin's sermons. Rather, Parker captures that experience much more adequately when he analyzes the construction of a particular sermon, that on Job 21:13-15. (For another sermon in the same series, see **Vol. 2, pp. 263-76.**) His outline is as follows:

The text is chapter 21. 13-15: "They pass their days in good, and in a moment they descend to the sepulchre. Yet they say to God, 'Depart from us, for we do not wish to know thy ways. What is the Almighty that we should serve him? or what profit will there be to pray to him?'"

1. He reminds the congregation of what he said yesterday.
2. Verse 13. "God will permit the despisers of his majesty *to go to the sepulchre in a minute of time,* after they have had a good time all their life." Psalm 73:4ff. (of which a brief exposition) may be compared with this passage.
   There is a "contrast between frequently easy deaths of the ungodly and pains of believers."

But God defers his judgments to the next world; and therefore we must raise our minds above this fleeting world, when God will judge the ungodly.

Therefore, let us not be like those who despise God and have all their happiness in this world. But rather let us prefer to be wretched here and look to God to give us his bounty hereafter.

"See what believers are admonished of here."

3. Verse 14. "Now Job consequently declares how the wicked reject God entirely. *They say to him, 'Depart from us, for we do not wish to know thy ways.'*"

The wicked wish to be free from God. We see them trying to get away from him by claiming they can do as they like.

"*We do not wish for thy ways.*" To be near God or far from him does not refer to his essence and majesty. It is to be obedient or disobedient to his Word.

"Now *voici* a passage from which we can gather good and useful teaching."

(1) The root and foundation of a good life is to have God always before us.

> (a) How can a man leave the evil to which he is prone?
> (b) He must be reformed by God, since he cannot reform himself.
> (c) We are so blind that we do not know the right way. We think evil is good "until God enlightens us."

"So then, do we wish to walk as we should? Let us make a start at this point—that is, of drawing near to our God. How do we draw near? First of all, let us know that nothing is hidden from him; everyone must come to a reckoning before him, and he must be the Judge, even of our thoughts" (CO 34:232[7-13]).

"*Voilà*, so much for the first."

(2) "God will judge us by His Word," the two-edged sword.

> (a) Therefore we must draw near to Him.
> (b) And this means, to him in his Word, in which he comes to us.
> (c) Therefore "our greatest misery" is to be without God's Word; "our greatest blessing" is when he gives it to us.
> (d) "Those who will not submit to the Word" show that they are God's enemies.
> (e) Let us always be willing and obedient.

"*Voilà* what we have to note from this passage—that we may not only have God before our eyes, but also love him to care for us and lead us" (CO 34:234[8-11]).

4. Verse 15. "Now, after Job has shown here such blasphemy on the part of the wicked and the despisers of God, he adds that they say, '*What is*

the Almighty, that we should serve Him? and what profit" will it bring us to "pray unto him?"'

(1) "The pride of the wicked."

    (a) "Pride is the chief vice" of the wicked, as humility is the sovereign virtue in believers—"the mother of all virtues."

    (b) "Their pride is . . . trust in their own wisdom."

    (c) Swollen with presumption, they do just what they like.

(2) *"What is the Almighty, that we should serve Him?"*

    (a) They do not use these words, but this is in their mind; and sometimes God makes them betray themselves.

    (b) They "acknowledge God's existence, but not His authority."

    (c) "But believers must submit themselves to God" as those that are his children, "created in His image," "redeemed by the death" and passion of his only Son, and called to be his household, as "children and heirs."

"When, then, we have made all these comparisons—I pray you, if we have hearts of iron or steel, ought they not to be softened? If we are swollen with arrogance and bursting with it, must not all that poison be purged, that so we may come with true humility to obey God?" (CO 34.236[33-40]).

    (d) He refers to the preface to the Ten Commandments: "I am the Eternal, thy God."

        (i) "The Eternal—that is, the Creator."

        (ii) "Thy God"—the Father of his people.

        (iii) "that brought thee out of the land of Egypt, out of the house of bondage"—that is, redeemed us from the depths of hell by our Lord Jesus Christ.

        (iv) Therefore we must dedicate ourselves entirely to the service of God.

        (v) God adds promises to his service, that he will be our Father, the protector of our life, that he will pardon our sins, and will accept our feeble service without examining it rigorously and hypercritically.

(3) *"What is the profit of serving God?"*

    (a) If we flee from God, we become servants to our own desires or to the devil.

    (b) "Freedom from God's service is bondage."

    (c) The service of God is more honorable than possessing a kingdom.

(4) "Moreover, let us extend this even further, as Job has done."

    (a) The wicked think they can live well or ill as they like, because God's punishments are not apparent.

    (b) But we must hold to the truth of what Isaiah said: "There is good fruit for the righteous" (5:10). When we see confusion in the world and it seems a mockery to serve God, we must trust in him that he will not disappoint our hope.

(c) God himself is our reward, as it says in Ps. 16:5 and Gen. 15:1.

5. "Now, there is still one word to note. It is that after Job had spoken of the service of God, in the second place he put prayer."

(1) Although service to our fellows is service to God, more is required—"prayers and orisons."

(2) A life unstained by gross vices and yet without religion or faith is not acceptable to God.

(3) The principal service of God is to call upon him.

(4) The conclusion: A life approved and accepted by God is one that trusts in him and has recourse to him and is loving towards our neighbors. "When, then, our life is thus ruled, it is the true service of God."

Bidding to prayer, relevant to the substance of the sermon.

The style in which Calvin constructed such sermons is exceedingly plain, but also exceedingly clear:

> Thought follows thought in careful, orderly arrangement without muddle, and each idea is expressed clearly, and often in two or three different ways, so that every member of the congregation might be able to understand.[52]

He is, indeed, one of the pioneers of French prose and the original model of that *clarté* on which the language has always prided itself.

Yet, as Parker has said, "He walks, and rarely soars."[53] His style of preaching is conversational and, in the service of being clearly understood, he sacrifices most of the ornaments that decorate writing. For instance, he seldom quotes anyone, although he was arguably the most learned man of Europe in his time. Yet neither does his preaching descend to the coarseness of Luther's—although he does employ the invective conventional in the polemical writing of the period. Nor does he often illustrate his points with stories or even employ imagery.

> His sermons are characterized by a gravity and earnestness springing from a profound realization of the urgency of the situation. Those to whom he preached were, he believed, either in a fearful plight under the wrath of God for their sin, or they were believers who needed to be encouraged and urged to strain every effort to arrive at the salvation which was theirs in heaven.[54]

So great was Calvin's earnestness that people asked: "Can they not preach without being angry?"[55] All of which is to say that his style was matched perfectly to his understanding of what he was hoping would be accomplished through the pulpit.

Preaching as Exegesis

Since Calvin understood preaching to be the exposition of the Word of God to the people assembled for worship, it is important to know how he went about the task of exegesis. Otherwise there is a danger of evaluating his accomplishment anachronistically. His humanistic training had developed in him a deep sense of need to return *ad fontes*, to the original languages of the texts he was interpreting, in order to recover the original meaning of the sacred writers. And his mastery of biblical languages was impressive.

Yet his understanding of "original meaning" was not the same as that of historical-critical biblical scholars of today. He lived before the Enlightenment, and he certainly did not have a modern fear of historical relativism. Furthermore, he acted out of two hermeneutical assumptions that are contrary to contemporary biblical interpretation: he postulated without question the unity and perfection of the Scriptures.[56] For instance, he presupposed without question the christological interpretation of the Hebrew Scriptures made by New Testament writers. This was not only their interpretation but the true interpretation—inspired by the Holy Spirit, who can be accurately spoken of as having dictated the sacred writings.

Thus what Calvin understood as the original meaning of a passage could be very different from what a modern exegete might understand. Nor would he assume that his interpretation of any key passage was just one theory proposed among many. The Spirit guided the faithful interpreter (and thus Calvin *a fortiori*) to discover in a passage the meaning the Spirit intended that passage to have. And this passage would be completely consistent with any other in the Holy Book because all had been dictated by the same Spirit to communicate the same gospel, and it was impossible for such divine efforts to meet with ambiguous or inconsistent results. Therefore, any apparently natural interpretation of a passage at odds with this overall teaching of the Bible was illusory and had to be explained away.

The overall teaching of the Bible is related to what Calvin meant by one of his key concepts, that of knowledge. He began the *Institutes* with the statement: "Nearly all the wisdom we possess, that is to say, true and sound wisdom, consists of two parts: knowledge of God and of our-selves" (1.1.1). Since this knowledge is acquired from Scripture, it amounts to the faith system Calvin found in the Bible. For him this most important knowledge, which he called the knowledge of faith, had to do with the doctrine of salvation of the elect through grace.

> In understanding faith it is not merely a question of knowing that God exists, but also—and this especially—of knowing what is his will toward us. For it is not so much our concern to know who he is in him-self, as what he wills to be toward us. Now, therefore, we hold faith to be a knowledge of God's will toward us, perceived from his Word.[57]

This understanding of the meaning of the Bible is not only communi-cated through true preaching but is also given to the elect believer by the Holy Spirit. Indeed, it could almost be said that justification and the communication of this knowledge are the same act. For the elect believ-er, this knowledge, then, is knowledge of the gratuitous mercy of God.

> This knowledge of faith contains within itself the broad outlines of a more or less complete system of theology. It suggests a doctrine of man as incapable of saving himself. It points to Jesus Christ as the revelation of the divine will. Moreover, it proclaims that man's ineptness is over-come and Christ's work made effective through the work of the Holy Spirit. In short, one may say that Calvin's doctrine of faith summarizes in a general way the major themes discussed in Book II and Book III of the *Institutes*.[58]

In addition to this knowledge of faith, however, there is, as suggested above, a wider knowledge that includes knowledge of the Creator (the subject of Book 1) as well. Calvin also recognized a very propositional kind of knowledge, a kind of *fides quae creditur* in addition to the *fides qua creditur*, which was the knowledge of faith.[59] This knowledge is also important because the perfection of the Bible means there is nothing in it that it is not necessary for believers to know—otherwise the Spirit would not have dictated it.

Thus there is a full range of knowledge that is a matter of cognition, knowledge that may be arrived at deductively from reading the Bible. But the knowledge of faith, on the other hand, is a "firm and effectual confidence," a knowledge that has its seat in the heart rather than the head.[60] The knowledge of faith is saving knowledge, through which the believer is secure in being the object of the grace of Christ, and thus is enabled to participate in Christ.

This knowledge is communicated to the elect in two ways. One is directly into the heart by the Spirit. But the other is through preaching. These two reinforce one another. No wonder that Calvin, believing this, preached with such earnestness and solemnity.[61]

FOR FURTHER READING

Bouwsma, William J. *John Calvin: A Sixteenth-Century Portrait*. New York and Oxford: Oxford University Press, 1988.

Calvin, John. *Sermons from Job*. Translated by Leroy Nixon. Grand Rapids, Mich.: Eerdmans, 1952.

Calvin: Institutes of the Christian Religion. Edited by John T. McNeill, translated and indexed by Ford Lewis Battles. LCC. Philadelphia: Westminster, 1960.

Parker, T. H. L. *Calvin's Preaching*. Edinburgh: T&T Clark, 1992.

Spiritual and Anabaptist Writers. Edited by George H. Williams and Anjel M. Mergal. LCC. Philadelphia: Westminster, 1957.

Notes

1. Steven E. Ozment, *The Age of Reform (1250–1550): An Intellectual and Religious History of Late Medieval and Reformation Europe* (New Haven, Conn.: Yale University Press, 1980), 318-24.

2. Calvin, who gave the definitive form to Swiss Reform preaching, did not want this sort of liturgy, preferring instead for the Eucharist to be celebrated every Sunday. He could never persuade the town council of Geneva to support him in this ideal, however.

3. Yngve Brilioth, *A Brief History of Preaching*, trans. Karl E. Mattson, The Preacher's Paperback Library (Philadelphia: Fortress, 1965), 152.

4. This chapter has been revised in the light of a conversation with Prof. Thomas Finger of Eastern Mennonite Seminary, held over March 13-16, 1991, in Irving, Texas. Assertions growing out of that discussion will be documented as "Finger conversation."

5. Ozment, *The Age of Reform*, 340.

6. Ibid., 341, quoting from Roland H. Bainton, *Studies in the Reformation*, collected papers in church history, series 2 (Boston: Beacon Press, 1963), II, 199.

7. Bainton, *Studies in the Reformation*. See the Finger conversation.

8. *Spiritual and Anabaptist Writers*, ed. George H. Williams and Anjel M. Mergal, LCC (Philadelphia: Westminster, 1957), 21. Williams's interpretation of these movements is developed on an impressive scale in *The Radical Reformation* (Philadelphia: Westminster, 1959).

9. *Spiritual and Anabaptist Writers,* 19-38.

10. For an account of this recent process of rehabilitation see Franklin H. Littell, *The Origins of Sectarian Protestantism: A Study of the Anabaptist View of the Church* (New York: Macmillan, 1964, 1958, 1952). This work was originally published as *The Anabaptist View of the Church.*

11. Finger conversation.

12. This reconstruction is based on Littell, *The Origins of Sectarian Protestantism,* and is in accord with what is said by Williams and others. It should be noted, however, that not all accept this understanding. See Ozment, *The Age of Reform,* 340-51.

13. So called to distinguish it from the Lutheran, Calvinist, and Anglican movements.

14. In "An Annotated Bibliography on Published Mennonite Sermons," *Mennonite Quarterly Review* 27 (1953): 144, Harold S. Bender and N. P. Springer say, "The only known published discussion of the history of Mennonite preaching outside of Holland is that by H. G. Mannhardt in *Mennonitische Blätter,* 38:18f., 22f., 37f. (1891)." Reference is then made to Roy Umble's Northwestern University dissertation, "Mennonite Preaching," which is summarized in the same issue of *MQR,* pp. 137-42. Bender, however, was to expand his bibliographical annotations into the article on "Sermons" in *The Mennonite Encyclopedia* (1959), occasionally using the same phraseology. This article, in turn, is followed by one on "Sermons, Hutterite" by Robert Friedmann, thus extending the coverage to the other main body existing today that grew out of Anabaptistry per se. Evangelical Rationalism did influence modern English and American Unitarianism through Socinius's impact on England. Hans J. Hillerbrand includes a reference to C. J. Dyck, "The Role of Preaching in Anabaptist Tradition," *Mennonite Life* 27 (1962): 21-26, in *A Bibliography of Anabaptism, 1520–1630. A Sequel—1962–1974,* Sixteenth Century Bibliography 1 (St. Louis: Center for Reformation Research, 1975), 51, but I have not been able to see the Dyck article.

15. Bender, "Sermons," 4:503. Finger says that evangelism was probably the chief use of sermons. Anabaptist gatherings probably consisted of informal teaching, prayer, and mutual exhortation in which many participated. Holy Communion was also held frequently. The centrality of preaching in Reformation worship grows out of an assumption that many church members were unconverted, an assumption the Anabaptists did not make. Further, it presupposes one main leader in worship, which the Anabaptists did not have. Finger conversation.

16. Umble, "Mennonite Preaching," 141.

17. Friedmann, "Sermons, Hutterite," 4:505. Actually, two types of sermons were copied and read, *Lehren* and *Vorreden.* The *Lehren* were verse-by-verse exegeses of entire chapters of the Bible, while the *Vorreden* were expositions of single verses. Seldom are *Lehren* read in their entirety anymore, although sections from them make up the second half of the service, with a *Vorrede* serving as a part of the devotional first half. The sermons are read in High German, although the community speaks a Tyrolean-Bavarian dialect in ordinary conversation. Yet they are very fond of this preaching that they call "sharp" because of "the outspokenness of the instruction concerning the meaning of the scriptural texts and its application to everyday life, realizing that it is this biblical radicalism which distinguishes their piety and life from all their surroundings" (ibid.).

18. "For use in home worship."

19. John (Jean, Joannes) latinized the family name to Calvinus when he went to the University of Paris.

20. John T. McNeill, *The History and Character of Calvinism* (New York: Oxford University Press, 1954), 94. This biographical sketch is derived from McNeill, 93-234, and William J. Bouwsma, *John Calvin: A Sixteenth-Century Portrait* (New York and Oxford: Oxford University Press, 1988). Not long after arriving at Paris, Calvin transferred to the Collège de Montaigu, a college noted for its orthodoxy and discipline that numbered both Erasmus and Rabelais among its disgruntled alumni.

21. For a list of the teachers and their individual contributions, see McNeill, *The History and Character of Calvinism*, 95-106. For another good but slightly different analysis of the intellectual influences on Calvin during his student days, see Thomas F. Torrance, *The Hermeneutics of John Calvin* (Edinburgh: Scottish Academic Press, 1988). See also the chapter on "John Calvin and the Rhetorical Tradition" in Quirinius Breen, *Christianity and Humanism: Studies in the History of Ideas*, ed. Nelson Peter Ross (Grand Rapids, Mich.: Eerdmans, 1968), 107-29.

22. Calvin consulted him on the eve of his break with Rome, but nothing is known of Lefèvre's advice.

23. *Calvin's Commentary on Seneca's De Clementia*, ed. with intro., trans., and notes Ford Lewis Battles and André Malan Hugo (Leiden: E. J. Brill for the Renaissance Society of America, 1969). For a concise statement of the nature of the commentary and Calvin's purposes in writing it, see pp. 72-74.

24. Bouwsma, *John Calvin: A Sixteenth Century Portrait*, 9 and *passim*.

25. The Dedication to the commentary on the Psalms is quoted in the translation of Joseph Haroutunian in *Calvin: Commentaries*, LCC (Philadelphia: Westminster, 1958), 51-57, especially p. 52. The standard edition of the works of Calvin in the original Latin and/or French is *Joannis Calvini Opera quae supersunt omnia*, ed. G. Baum, E. Cunitz, and E. Reuss, Corpus Reformatorum (Brunswick and Berlin: C. A. Schwetschke et filium, 1863–1900; reprint, New York and London: Johnson Reprint Corp., 1964). Not included in this are a number of sermons to be discussed later. The standard English version of Calvin's Old Testament commentaries is the nineteenth-century Calvin Translation Society edition published in Edinburgh. There is a translation of the New Testament commentaries edited by David W. and Thomas F. Torrance, published in Grand Rapids between 1963 and 1974.

26. Bouwsma, *John Calvin: A Sixteenth Century Portrait*, 11.

27. Ibid., 12.

28. John T. McNeill, "Introduction," *Calvin: Institutes of the Christian Religion*, ed. John T. McNeill, trans. and indexed Ford Lewis Battles, LCC (Philadelphia: Westminster, 1960), 1:xxxv.

29. McNeill, *The History and Character of Calvinism*, 131.

30. Haroutunian, *Calvin: Commentaries*, 53.

31. I regret that I was not able to consult Benoit Girardin, *Rhétorique et Théologique: Calvin, Le Commentaire de l'Épitre aux Romans*, ThH, no. 54 (Paris: Éditions Beauchesne, 1979), before writing this chapter. It would have contributed a great deal to my understanding of Calvin's humanistic perspective and the way that theology and rhetoric were intertwined in his biblical interpretation and, therefore, preaching.

32. T. H. L. Parker, *The Oracles of God: An Introduction to the Preaching of John Calvin* (London and Redhill: Lutterworth, 1947), 33. Since this chapter was written, Parker has published a much longer study, *Calvin's Preaching* (Edinburgh: T&T Clark, 1992). It was impossible to recast the entire chapter in the light of this later work, but insights from it are incorporated where they seemed most to demand inclusion.

33. Richard Stauffer, *Un Calvin méconnu: le prédicateur de Genève, Bulletin de Société de l'histoire du Protestantisme français* 23 (1977): 188.

34. *Institutes,* 4.1.9.

35. McNeill, *The History and Character of Calvinism,* 188.

36. The series, under the general editorship of Erwin Mülhaupt, is published by Neukirchener Verlag des Erziehungsvereins in Neukirchen-Vluyn. Accounts of the misadventures of the manuscripts can be found in Stauffer, *Un Calvin méconnu;* Erwin Mülhaupt, "Calvin's 'Sermons inedits': *Vorgeschichte, Überlieferung und gegenwärtiger Stand der Edition,*" in *Der Prediger Johannes Calvin: Beiträge und Nachrichten zur Ausgabe der Supplementa Calviniana,* ed. Karl Halaski (Neukirchen-Vluyn: Neukirchener Verlag des Erziehungsvereins, 1966), 25-33; and T. H. L. Parker, *Supplementa Calviniana: An Account of the Manuscripts of Calvin's Sermons Now in the Course of Preparation* (London: Tyndale, 1962). See also John H. Leith, "Calvin's Doctrine of the Proclamation of the Word and Its Significance for Today," in *John Calvin and the Church: A Prism of Reform,* ed. Timothy George (Louisville: Westminster John Knox, 1990), 207.

37. When one turns to English translations of Calvin's sermons, the neglect is even more obvious. An advertisement of *A Selection of the Most Celebrated Sermons of John Calvin, Minister of the Gospel, and One of the Principal Leaders of the Protestant Reformation,* ed. John Forbes (New York: S. & D.A. Forbes, Printers, 1830), says that "Calvin's Sermons were translated and published in England, about the year 1580; since which date we have no account of an edition having been published." When William B. Eerdmans of Grand Rapids reprinted the Forbes edition in 1950, their advertisement said that it was "the only sizeable collection of John Calvin's sermons translated into the English language since the sixteenth century and the only volume ever published in America." The Forbes volume was copied in 1831 by T. Desilver Jr. of Philadelphia. In 1950 Eerdmans began to issue a series of volumes of sermon translations by Leroy Nixon. These include *The Deity of Christ, and Other Sermons* (1950), *Sermons from Job* (1952), and *The Gospel According to Isaiah* (1953). To this all too short list may be added *Sermons on Micah by Jean Calvin,* trans. Blair Reynolds, Texts and Studies in Religion, vol. 47 (Lewiston: Edwin Mellen, 1990), a translation of vol. 5 of *Supplementa Calviniana* and thus a volume that allows English readers to get a sense of what Calvin's course preaching must have been like.

38. This section is based on Parker, *The Oracles of God,* 45-64, and Haroutunian, *Calvin's Commentaries,* 392-406.

39. Calvin did not believe that women should speak in church. *Inst.* 4.15.20-22.

40. Parker, *The Oracles of God,* 55.

41. Commentary on John 14:26, *Calvini Opera* (hereafter referred to as CO) 47:334-35. Quoted in Haroutunian, *Calvin: Commentaries,* 397. This volume is

arranged to present topically the doctrine Calvin teaches in the commentaries, with the squibs quoted following citation of the biblical verse on which the comment is made. Thus the only indication of the particular commentary from which the quotation is extracted is the naming of the book from which the verse is taken.

42. Ibid.

43. Ronald S. Wallace, *Calvin's Doctrine of the Word and Sacrament* (Edinburgh and London: Oliver & Boyd, 1953), 83.

44. Parker, *The Oracles of God*, 50. His reference is to CO, 25:646.

45. Haroutunian, *Calvin's Commentaries*, 396.

46. Calvin's comment on Isaiah 55:11 as quoted in Wallace, *Calvin's Doctrine of the Word and Sacrament*, 93.

47. CO 26:66.

48. Parker, *The Oracles of God*, 57.

49. J. L. Ainslie, *The Doctrine of Ministerial Order in the Reformed Churches of the Sixteenth and Seventeenth Centuries*, 43, quoted by Parker, *The Oracles of God*, 61.

50. Quoted from the translation of the commentary on 1 Corinthians in the Calvin Society edition of the *Works*, 77 (CO 49:322) by Parker, *The Oracles of God*, 65. This section will draw heavily upon ibid., 65-80. Virtually useless for an understanding of the manner (as opposed to the content) of Calvin's preaching is Leroy Nixon, *John Calvin, Expository Preacher* (Grand Rapids, Mich.: Eerdmans, 1950), 27-45, which consists almost exclusively of extended quotations from hagiographic turn-of-the-century histories of preaching.

51. Parker, *The Oracles of God*, 71-72. The following outline is taken from Parker, *Calvin's Preaching*, 133-36.

52. Parker, *The Oracles of God*, 77.

53. Ibid., 75.

54. Ibid., 75-76.

55. Ibid., citing CO 35:12.

56. What follows is closely based on H. Jackson Forstman, *Word and Spirit: Calvin's Doctrine of Biblical Authority* (Stanford: Stanford University Press, 1962), 106-23. His treatment of Calvin's understanding of the unity and perfection of the Scriptures occupies pp. 109-12.

57. John T. McNeill, translation of *Inst.* 3.2.6 in *The History and Character of Calvinism*.

58. Forstman, *Word and Spirit*, 92.

59. Ibid., 89-105.

60. Ibid., 101. Quoted from Calvin's commentary on Romans 10:10.

61. For a very similar interpretation but one that grows out of an analysis of Calvin's thought in terms of influences upon it, see Torrance, *The Hermeneutics of John Calvin*, Part II: "The Shaping of Calvin's Mind," 61-165. See also Parker, *Calvin's Preaching*, 93-107.

CHAPTER 14

THE PREACHING OF CATHOLIC REFORM

In this more ecumenical age of church historiography, the sixteenth-century reforming activities of those who remained within the communion of Rome are no longer seen as merely a reaction to the threat to the church posed by Protestant separation.[1] Rather, they are seen to have antedated that and to have a validity of their own, representing the same impulses as those reflected in the work of the Reformers. Thus Steven Ozment can say:

> Modern historians interpret the Counter Reformation of the sixteenth century as less a reaction to the success of Protestantism than the continuation of late medieval efforts to reform the medieval church.[2]

He goes on to cite the conclusion of H. O. Evennett:

> The Reformation on its religious side and the Counter Reformation on its religious side can reasonably be regarded as two different outcomes of the [same] general aspiration toward religious regeneration which pervaded late fifteenth and early sixteenth century Europe.[3]

So much is this the case that the traditional term, "Counter Reformation," is now questioned as the definitive categorization to use when discussing this movement. Originated by polemical German Protestant scholars to suggest that any reforming activity within Rome was a purely defensive reaction to what Luther and Calvin had done, the term was picked up by other scholars to refer to what was considered to be the repressiveness of the movement's institutions. Then Italian intellectuals like Benedetto Croce adopted it to designate Italian baroque, a cultural decline they blamed on the church after the Council of Trent.[4]

So pervasive has this negative understanding of Counter Reformation been that it has affected the judgment of even Catholic scholars on the worth of its products. An example of this trend in the area of homiletics is the way that J. B. Schneyer "dismisses the whole phenomenon of Renaissance preaching in Italy and Spain with four pages in his *Geschichte der katholischen Predigt* (Freiburg, 1969)."[5]

It would, however, be possible to overcorrect, to act as though none of the motivation for reform within the Roman communion were occasioned by the successes of Protestants. Hubert Jedin has proposed using the term "Catholic Reform" to designate the movement in its aspect of continuity, and "Counter Reformation" when referring to it as a response to the Protestant Reformation.[6] This distinction makes it easier to be precise and to avoid value-laden vocabulary.

THE ROLE OF PREACHING

A very important place is assigned to preaching in both of these aspects of Catholic renewal. This may be seen in four of the most important channels of reform: religious orders in general, the Jesuits in particular, the Council of Trent, and missionary activity.

The Religious Orders

Besides humanism, the three reforming movements that A. G. Dickens traces back to the fifteenth century are all related to communities of monks and friars.[7] These include the *devotio moderna*, developed among the Augustinian canons of Windesheim and spread to the Brothers of the Common Life; the Observant movement, arising among the Franciscans; and the renewal of the Carthusians. In addition to these, the fire of Savonarola and the passion of Luther testify to spiritual vitality among the Dominicans and Augustinian friars. While it was among these groups that the real vitality remaining in the religious life at the end of the fifteenth century was to be found, all of these were more concerned with developing the spiritual lives of their members than with reforming the church at large. The mendicant orders still supplied most of the trained and skillful Catholic preachers, but it was time for new orders to be created to minister to the overwhelming needs of a new generation.

The first indication of the changes to come was not an order as such, but only a confraternity for laity and clergy interested in working to increase their personal holiness and practical charity, the Oratory of Divine Love.[8] The first Oratory was founded at Vicenza in 1494 and the second at Genoa. The movement spread to Rome and between 1517 and 1527 came to involve a group of outstanding persons who were to have significant roles in the reforming activity that changed the religious face of the Roman church. Among these were a number of bishops: Jacopo Sadoleto of Carpentras, Giovanni Matteo Giberti of Verona, and Giovanni Pietro Caraffa of Chieti.[9] Luigi Lippomano was one of Giberti's successors in Verona while Gaetano da Tiene, along with Caraffa, was founder of the Theatine order and was later to be canonized as Saint Caejetan. When driven from the city by the sack of Rome in 1527, this group fled to Venice, where they added a number of other distinguished colleagues to their ranks.

Pope Paul III recognized their abilities and made six of them cardinals. Later he largely committed to them the task of drawing up a plan for reform of the church. Presented to the pope in 1537, the plan bore the title of *Consilium delectorum cardinalium ... de emendanda ecclesia*. After stating that the main cause of everything wrong with the church was the belief that the pontiff could sell benefices as though they were personal property, they listed particular abuses, most of which had to do with practices that interfered with the effectiveness of clergy. The spiritual welfare of the people in their care should be the only consideration in their appointment. Other abuses such as absenteeism and pluralism were also attacked, and stricter discipline was advocated for religious orders. The ability to teach the faith and to deal with sin was crucial to the effectiveness they sought. Thus the *Consilium* said: "Care must be taken that their preachers and confessors are fit men, and not admitted to their office except after examination by their bishop."[10] The report was so devastating and so embarrassing to the papacy that it was not published officially, but it undoubtedly did a great deal to prepare the way for Trent.[11]

As important as the Oratory of Divine Love was, there existed a widespread recognition that the cause of reform needed stronger ties than the loose association of a sodality; the life vows of religious communities seemed called for. Gaetano da Tiene considered the poor quality of secular clergy to be the main thing wrong with the church. His idea for reform was not unlike that of the Augustinian canons of the early Middle Ages: an order of clerks regular who would live together in community under vows of poverty, chastity, and obedience while carrying on parochial ministry.[12] In founding the order, the practical skills of Caraffa were united with the vision of Gaetano. Though the Theatines, as they were called, lived the life of the poor, they came from the aristocracy and many became bishops.

Three other orders of regular clerics were formed. The Paulines, who came to be called Barnabites after they took charge of the St. Barnabas church in Milan, were more at home among the masses. They were concerned with the religious instruction of the young and general pastoral care. Open-air preaching missions were one of their most effective tools. The bishop of Milan, Charles Borromeo,[13] made great use of them. The Somaschi were founded to take care of children who were orphaned or rendered homeless in the wars that had ravished the Italian peninsula. Intellectually, one of the most vigorous of the new orders was the Oratorians,[14] founded by Philip Neri through what had started out as informal gatherings of students and young clergy for conferences and music.[15] This order also spread rapidly, although in France it took a form slightly different from its form in Italy.[16]

A different type of new order was the Capuchins, a reform movement within the Franciscans devoted to Saint Francis's ideals of care for the poor and suffering, and preaching to the people. Unfortunately for them, their leader and most popular preacher, Bernardino Ochino, was so attracted to the cause of Reformation that he went over to the Protestants, serving in several countries and churches before ending up as a Polish Unitarian. Yet the Capuchins survived the adverse publicity and were by far the largest and most important of the new orders.

What Owen Chadwick said of the entire movement describes especially well the spirit of these religious communities:

> If we seek a single theme running through the reforming endeavors of the Catholic Reformation, it would be the quest for a more adequate clergy—better-trained and better-instructed priests, priests resident in their parishes, bishops resident in their sees, pastors fervent and self-sacrificing and missionary-minded, trained as confessors, celibate, mortified, able to teach in school, wearing canonical dress; a priesthood uncorrupted and incorruptible, educated and other-worldly.[17]

While he does not explicitly list preaching among these desiderata, others did. The place it occupies in such a program is obvious.

The Society of Jesus

If all the new orders exemplified the ideals of the Catholic Reformation as listed by Chadwick, none did so more than the Jesuits. Indeed, the papal bull confirming the order[18] contains a similar summary, describing the Jesuits as

> a Society founded to concern itself above all for the advancement of souls in Christian life and doctrine, for the propagation of the faith by public preaching, spiritual exercises and works of charity, and in particular for the Christian education of the young and the unlearned, as well as for the hearing of confessions.[19]

When Don Inigo de Onez y Loyola entered adult life, he had no thought of founding a religious order. Fond of the sort of courtly romances that inspired Don Quixote, Inigo lived at a time when there were still wars to be fought. When he was thirty and fighting in Charles V's defense of Pamplona against Francis I, he was wounded in both legs by a cannonball and spent a long time recovering. During his recuperation, a shortage of his favorite literature forced him to read devotional books for lack of anything else.

Being converted in the process, he left his sword on an altar of the Blessed Virgin Mary at Montserrat, took the dress of a beggar, and began a year's retreat in a cave near Manresa. During this time his own meditations gave him the insight to make an initial draft of his *Spiritual Exercises*. After making a pilgrimage to the Holy Land, he returned to Spain where he began to educate himself for the work that he felt lay ahead. In order to make sure that his foundation was firm, he sat in Latin class with schoolchildren in Barcelona before going on to university training in Alcalá and Salamanca. He preached in the streets until he was imprisoned twice by the Inquisition. Transferring to the University of Paris, he began to gather the nucleus of his order.

They left Paris intending to go on a missionary crusade to the Holy Land if possible, but resolving to stay in Rome and put themselves under the pope if the Middle East was closed to them. War between Venice and the Turks rendered eastern travel impossible. Thus they sojourned in Rome, where their distinctive vocation began to emerge in practice and to be spelled out in their preliminary draft of a rule. They felt that most devotions should be performed more often than had become customary.

They advocated more frequent confessions and Communions and even more frequent preaching, it being the custom in Rome at the time to have sermons only in the penitential seasons of Advent and Lent. Once again their enthusiasm caused them to be suspected of heresy, but investigation brought exoneration. Ignatius (he had begun to use this Latin form of his name) was ordained at Venice and thus was able to say his first Mass on Christmas Day in 1538. In less than two years, their preliminary rule was accepted and summarized by the pope in the bull in which he confirmed it.[20]

The apostolic, missionary, catechetical, and homiletical character of the Jesuits' ministry was obvious from the very beginning. Salmeron's sermons at Brescia and Belluno, for instance, began to attract huge crowds. Lainez's congregations at Florence must have rivaled those of Savonarola half a century earlier. Peter Cannisius was able to reclaim southern Germany from the Reformation. Francis Xavier took the gospel to India and Japan.

The tasks of preaching and teaching were combined in one particular homiletical genre, that of the sacred lecture.[21] In addition to preaching both at the liturgy and in the open air, Jesuits who were in a city for a protracted time gave series of lectures on Sunday afternoons or at other convenient times. Most often these would be on consecutive sections of biblical books, although they could be on such other topics as catechetical issues or "cases of conscience."

There were pre-Reformation precedents for such preaching, especially among the mendicant orders; some of the preaching of Savonarola is a case in point. It also resembles the sort of course preaching that Luther and others did at Wittenberg. Not surprisingly, some of the Jesuit lectures were Counter Reformation preaching in the strict sense of being used to refute such Protestant positions as the Lutheran interpretation of the Epistle to the Romans.

These sacred lectures differed from university courses on biblical books in both the popular audience for which they were prepared and the application of the teaching to people's lives. They represent the sort of aggressive effort put forth by the Jesuits to instruct the faithful that characterized the early life of their society.

The Council of Trent

From as early as the thirteenth century, there had been a strain of thought that became quite pronounced in the fifteenth, in which the supreme authority in the church was a general council. During the time of the Avignon papacy, councils were thought of as the way to resolve the claims of rival popes, and the Councils of Pisa (1409) and Constance (1414–18) had been resorted to as the means of healing the Great Schism. After there ceased to be multiple claimants to the papal throne, there then arose the problems associated with the Renaissance holders of the chair of Peter, not the least of which were the political activities that saw the Holy See competing militarily and diplomatically with the world powers of the time. Some conciliar theorists appealed to the example of Constantine assembling the bishops at Nicaea as justification for saying that the initiative for assembling a council lay with the civil authority. Popes had resisted appeals over their head to councils; Pius II went so far in 1460 as to promulgate *Exercrabilis,* a bull forbidding such actions.

After the Reformation had begun to divide his territory into warring factions, the emperor Charles V began to urge a council as a way of reuniting his realm. The empire and the papacy, however, were not the only vested interests within the Catholic world. Francis I was so eager to pursue French interests against the Holy Roman Empire that he would even resort to alliance with Muslim Turks. And, devoted as he was to the defense of the Catholic faith, Philip II also had his own course to pursue in the interests of Spain.

Charles appeared to be on the way to an initial success in 1541 when, concurrently with an imperial diet there, a colloquy was held in Regensberg or Ratisbon, the hometown of the popular medieval preacher Berthold. The Protestants had such distinguished representatives as Melanchthon, Martin Bucer, and a very young John Calvin, while the Catholic delegation included a range of opinion from irenic Erasmians to the aggressive Johannes Eck.

The most influential Catholic, though, and the pope's representative, was Cardinal Contarini, one of the old members of the Oratory of Divine Love. He had enough sympathy with an Augustinian theology to approve a statement on justification, which seemed to open the possibility of compromise and negotiation. When the discussion moved on to sacraments, however, he was so firm in his commitment to transubstantiation that agreement would have been impossible, even if all parties on both sides had been willing to accept the statement on justification— which they were not. And so the most promising effort to reunite European Christendom foundered.

After a great deal of maneuvering back and forth, Paul III called a council that finally convened in 1545 at a town in the Italian Alps called Trent.[22] Contrary to everyone's expectations, it dealt with the issues at hand, spreading its deliberations over three periods and eighteen years.

By the time the council actually met, the emperor was the only one still interested in reunion. The results could be roughly summarized by saying that *theological* decisions in general had the effect of reaffirming medieval positions against Protestant efforts at revision, while *practical* decisions were usually in the direction of reforming abuses.[23] The council's efforts were remarkably successful. Its decisions stood the test of time and in retrospect appear far more nuanced than anyone would have guessed when they were being made. It is quite appropriate, therefore, that the character of church life achieved by the Counter Reformation is called post-Tridentine.

The practical reforms achieved by Trent bear out Chadwick's contention that the most consistent theme of the Catholic Reformation was the search for a more adequate clergy. In this program nothing was more important than preaching. At the Fifth Session (June 17, 1546) there was passed a Decree on Reformation, which began by providing lectureships on Scripture for schools at every level and quickly went on to discuss preachers of the Word of God:

> But seeing that the preaching of the Gospel is no less necessary to the Christian commonwealth than the reading thereof; and whereas this is the principal duty of bishops; the same holy Synod hath resolved and decreed, that all bishops, primates, and all other prelates of the churches be bound personally—if they be not lawfully hindered—to preach the holy Gospel of Jesus Christ.[24]

Those who are "lawfully hindered" must appoint competent substitutes. Anyone with a cure of souls

> shall, at least on the Lord's days, and solemn feasts ... feed the people committed to them with wholesome words, according to their own capacity, and that of their people; by teaching them the things which it is necessary for all to know unto salvation, and by announcing to them with briefness and plainness of discourse, the vices which they must avoid, and the virtues which they must follow after, that they may escape everlasting punishment, and obtain the glory of heaven.[25]

There follows a provision of disciplinary measures to be taken against those who neglect this duty. Next are regulations concerning the licenses needed by members of religious orders who preach, the steps to be taken when someone preaches heresy, what to do about religious who live outside their houses and try to preach, and prohibition of preaching by anyone in quest of alms.

Many of these provisions are repeated in chapter 4 of the Decree on Reformation promulgated at the twenty-fourth session, with the additional stipulations that daily or at least triweekly sermons be preached during Advent and Lent, that the people be admonished to attend sermons, and that

> the said bishops shall also take care, that, at least on the Lord's Days and other festivals, the children in every parish be carefully taught the rudiments of the faith, and obedience towards God, and their parents, by those whose duty it is.[26]

Closely connected with this concern for preaching is the desire of the council that clergy be trained so that they can exercise responsibly their duty of preaching, which is reflected in the directive that seminaries be established:

> The holy Synod ordains, that all cathedral, metropolitan, and other churches greater than these, shall be bound, each according to its means and the extent of the diocese, to maintain, to educate religiously, and to train in ecclesiastical discipline, a certain number of youths . . . in a college to be chosen by the bishop for that purpose.[27]

The relevance of the curriculum for homiletics is obvious:

> They shall learn grammar, singing, ecclesiastical computation, and the other liberal arts; they shall be instructed in sacred scripture; ecclesiastical works; the homilies of the saints; the manner of administering the sacraments, especially those things which shall seem adapted to enable them to hear confessions; and the forms and rites of the ceremonies.[28]

Provision is then made for the adequate financing of the seminaries and for the appointment of competent faculty.

One can see the extent of change these standards imply by looking at the system in France, where the decree on seminaries was late in being implemented. "The idea that an advanced secular education and a decent family were sufficient qualification for the cleric held good until the second half of the (seventeenth) century."[29] Trent was destined to make a great deal of difference in the emphasis placed on preaching and the training for it in the Roman Catholic Church.

Missionary Activity

For a number of reasons, missionary activity—whether directed at reviving the faithful at home, wooing back adherents who had been proselytized, or evangelizing non-Christian foreigners—was much more characteristic of Catholic Reform than it was of the Protestant Reformation. "It is perhaps in this sphere that true originality and enterprise found their most congenial spheres within the Counter Reformation church."[30] Sufficiently preoccupied with preserving their competitive edge against one another or resisting Counter Reformation efforts to recover lost flocks, the Reformed churches often found themselves left with little attention to devote to new fields. Then, too, efforts to convert the unsaved seemed blasphemous to thoroughgoing double-predestinarians. And most of the voyages of discovery were conducted by representatives of countries that remained in communion with Rome.[31] To give some degree of consistency to this worldwide missionary enterprise, the *Congregatio de Propaganda Fide* was formed in 1622. As always in the history of Christian missionary activity, preaching was an important medium for spreading the faith.

THE BEGINNINGS OF THE REVIVAL

In an essay published in 1988, Peter Bayley discussed the current state of the investigation of preaching from the early modern period in the history of Catholicism. After showing how disadvantaged the historian of preaching in this period is compared with patristic or medieval colleagues, he outlines the work that needs to be done: the search of libraries for sermons and preaching aids from the period, the coordination of knowledge of composition principles followed in sermon writing, and the pooling of information for a more comparative perspective. The completion of these scholarly tasks, he says, will permit the evaluation of the best hypothesis that the current state of knowledge will permit. He phrases his hypothesis in this way:

> that the ideals of Trent, coinciding as they did with the revival of antique rhetoric, evolved into theories in strong Counter Reformation centers like Borromeo's circle in Milan and, fertilized by contact with cultivated Renaissance minds like Luis de Granada in Spain and disseminated by innumerable handbooks, became by those very methods of dissemination the stuff and texture of the European Catholic sermon for two hundred years.[32]

Although Bayley warns that attempts at general surveys in the history of preaching "end up as compilations of out-dated second-hand material and opinions,"[33] the writers of such surveys have little choice but to accept the conventional wisdom in each discrete area of research and synthesize it with findings from other periods. A single scholar could never hope to do for all periods what the combined efforts of specialists in those periods have not been able to accomplish for them individually.

Thus, having observed the factors in Catholic Reform that dictated a renewed emphasis on preaching, it is now time to begin to state what is known about how that preaching developed. After a look at the work of Borromeo, there will be a summary of studies of sermons and the theories on which they were constructed in the two countries on which such investigations have been made, Spain and France.[34] In the look at French preaching, Bayley can at least have the consolation that the "out-dated second-hand materials and opinions" are his own.

Charles Borromeo

Although many of the abuses of the Renaissance papacy resulted from the tendency of its occupants to treat the Holy See as a family business, there is one occasion upon which all authorities will agree that nepotism was a good thing: the time in 1560 when Pius IV made his nephew Charles Borromeo cardinal and archbishop of Milan. This appointment made it possible for Borromeo to become the preeminent example of how a bishop went about translating Trent's decrees into policy and action. (For a sermon about Borromeo, see **Vol. 2, pp. 277-95.**) In no area was his leadership more important than in the implementation of the Tridentine decrees on preaching. Taking seriously the statement that preaching is the principal duty *(praecipuum munus)* of bishops, he was an indefatigable preacher himself, he issued an instruction to his clergy about their obligation, and he encouraged others to write treatises on preaching.[35]

In order to assess the role of Borromeo in the history of Catholic Reform preaching, John O'Malley began by looking at the homiletics textbooks produced under the influence of the archbishop of Milan. He points out that at the beginning of the sixteenth century, the only treatise on the subject in print other than the *Artes praedicandi* of medieval thematic preaching was Augustine's *De doctrina christiana*. The great turning point came in 1535 when Erasmus published his *Ecclesiastes,* which introduced classical rhetoric and patristic homiletics as furnishing alternatives to thematic preaching. While, for a variety of reasons given in chapter 11, Erasmus's work was more important as a milestone than as a ready tool, Catholics were ready for a new method of preaching by the time the Tridentine decrees were published—a method that would move beyond not only the thematic sermon but also the patristic homily, one that would reflect on how the principles of classical rhetoric could be combined with the Christian necessity of explicating biblical texts.

It was at this point Borromeo entered the scene. His contribution reflects his background. Having been only twenty-one when his uncle ascended to the Holy See and, in the Renaissance tradition, immediately appointed him as his secretary of state, Borromeo had a humanistic university education but no formal schooling in theology. In Rome he had helped organize the *Noctes Vaticanae*, a group that studied classical and patristic writers, including rhetoricians and Stoic philosophers.[36] When he took up residence in Milan, then, and began to put the Tridentine legislation into practice, much of his understanding of what preaching, the "principal duty of bishops," should be like was shaped by his study of rhetoric and pagan ethics. This, connected with the Franciscan language of the conciliar decree on preaching, meant that when he was in the pulpit, he continued the moralistic emphasis of the Middle Ages.

Although regard for preaching was characteristic of the provincial synods Borromeo held in Milan, it was not until 1576 that he issued his own developed statement on the subject, *Instructiones praedicationis verbi Dei*.[37] His understanding there of the subject matter of sermons is "sins, occasions of sin, virtues, and, finally, the sacraments and other holy usages of the church"[38]—in other words, the moralistic emphasis expected. Missing is "any developed 'theology of the Word' or 'theology of the minister of the Word.'"[39] He does deal with the *ethos* of the preacher, which turns out to be a very clerical style of life. His lack of theological training made it inevitable that the instruction would be somewhat lacking as a theoretical statement, but, coupled with his indefatigable example[40] in exercising the *praecipuum munus*, it meant that he was extraordinarily influential in recommending the implementation of the Tridentine legislation about preaching.

Like many other preachers, his practice was better than his theory, moving beyond Stoic morality to a deep grounding in the Christian understanding of creation and redemption. The sermons take cognizance of the liturgical occasion and are based on the appointed lections. Francis de Sales pointed out that while Borromeo's theological knowledge was meager, it was sufficient for effective preaching.[41]

More important than his own theoretical work in preaching is that which he inspired and commissioned in others. Since Erasmus's work had been placed on the Vatican's Index of Prohibited Books, several Catholic manuals were published that stressed classical rhetoric and showed various degrees of dependency upon such Protestant writers as Melanchthon and Hyperius. Borromeo, however, asked his friend Agostino Valier (Valerio), Bishop of Verona, to produce a volume of "ecclesiastical rhetoric." Valier's *De rhetorica ecclesiastica* was first published in 1574 and reprinted often. Soon it was followed by similar works by the Spanish authors Luis de Granada and Diego de Estella.

> These three books were characterized by their comprehensiveness, their easy intelligibility, their organizational clarity, and their grasp of both the classical and patristic traditions.... They mark a great watershed not only for the sixteenth century but for the entire history of preaching in the Roman Catholic Church.[42]

All of these works and others as well owe at least some of their inspiration to the archbishop of Milan, but they do not exhaust his contributions to preaching. He also imported effective preachers into his archdiocese to teach his clergy by precept and example. Quoting Fumaroli to the effect that Borromeo created an "atelier for preaching established at Milan," O'Malley corrects him by saying, "It would be more adequate to the reality to speak of a huge 'industry.'"[43] He goes on to conclude that Borromeo "is a major figure and a chief promoter of the extraordinary enthusiasm for the ministry of the Word in the sixteenth century, which . . . was just as characteristic of Catholicism as it was of Protestantism."

Catholic Reform Preaching in Spain

Anticipating O'Malley's comment, Hilary Dansey Smith says:

> Catholics and Protestants seem to have been possessed of an equally voracious appetite for sermons, to judge by the numbers of them to appear in print as the (seventeenth) century progresses, and by the persistent homiletic strain which runs through contemporary prose fiction, particularly in Spain.[44]

These sermons were preached not only in churches but in hospitals and out of doors as well. Even "processions of flagellants and *autos-de-fe* were accompanied by sermons."[45] The sermons were preached by some bishops, by priests with a cure of souls, and by religious who were licensed to do so. During Lent and Advent, there were extra sermons in the afternoon in addition to those preached at Mass. As time went on, the recognition made by Trent that education was required to do such preaching became more general, the increase in the quantity of sermons having created a demand for a similar increase in quality.

Many Spanish sermons from the period were published. Some appeared individually as occasional sermons *(sueltos)* for such events as funerals or saints' days; these were occasionally collected into books. Others were published in *sermonarios* that "represent a preacher's personal selection of his sermons, often spanning the whole of his preaching career."[46] The choice was made on the basis of the sermons' ability to serve as models for young clergy just learning the homiletical craft. While some of the *sermonario* sermons were *ad status,* most had been composed for either the temporal or the sanctoral lectionary cycle.

Since most of the sermons were originally delivered from notes, the published form does not represent a verbatim account of what was actually said. Instead, it could depend either on what the preacher wrote up for publication or on—sometimes quite accurate—notes taken by members of the congregation. Such collections were also used as devotional reading by the laity. From their published form it can be seen that the sermons were delivered in the vernacular; this genre was one of those through which written Spanish was being developed. The average published sermon must have taken about an hour to deliver. In terms of style,

> what distinguishes this genre is a particular form, or *dispositio,* which ... lends itself to parody by virtue of being quite easy to recognize. There is always a single main text *(thema),* and always a division of the text, traditionally a tripartite one in honour of the Trinity.[47]

Various types of outlines were followed in these sermons: the *sermón de un (solo) tema, homilia, paradoxon,*[48] or *panegyrico.*

Whichever sort of sermon was preached, all tried to fulfill Cicero's three duties of an orator: to prove, to please, and to move. These are usually met in the parts of the speech in which they were classically expected, so that pleasure was communicated in the exordium, reason in the proposition and confirmation, and emotional appeal in the peroration. The three most common figures of thought were exempla, comparisons (similes in which "the more concrete, visible term of comparison illuminates the abstract, invisible one"),[49] and conceits.

The textbooks of the time used various poetic ways of talking about all this. They also offered advice about gestures. Some preachers extended these latter to include "audiovisuals" and other dramatic effects, the least of which was holding a crucifix while they preached. Others, however, were willing to rely upon words alone to create what has been called "virtual experience," a sense of having participated in a described event.[50]

While the revival of classical rhetoric was very much an element of the golden age of Spanish speaking, there were inevitable questions about what constitutes the difference between Christian preaching and other forms of public speaking. At times this was phrased in terms of two kinds of "spirits," natural and supernatural. Any good speech depends upon a certain amount of *brío*, but the sanctification of souls is the work of God. Yet that divine work requires a degree of cooperation from the one who preaches, the human instrument through whom the purposes of God are accomplished. Thus holiness of life is more important to effective preaching than any amount of rhetorical talent and training. In the context of such a discussion, there were, of course, differences on what Christian eloquence sounded like:

> On the one hand, the apostolic ideal leads to the conclusion that sincerity and plain-speaking are the only acceptable forms of Christian preaching, and that all the rest is dangerous sophistry.... On the other hand, if one looks back to the Fathers one finds quite another kind of eloquence, and even elegance.[51]

Such considerations of style lead to questions of content: Should Christian preaching draw on pagan thought, especially philosophy? Could one "spoil the Egyptians" without being contaminated? Or, for that matter, could poets—pagan or modern—be quoted from the pulpit? As on most questions, the Spanish preachers were divided, some taking one side, some the other, and most in between. Similar discussions occurred over the use in sermons of that popular seventeenth-century form of imagery, the emblem.[52]

Spanish preaching participates in the pervasive moralism of Catholic Reform, and its homiletical literature deals not only with confronting congregations with their sins, but also with the preacher's need for a blameless life and with issues of professional ethics in the choice of methods by which others' sins are opposed. Yet the preachers also felt obliged to teach the faith, and the popularizations of doctrines they published in their sermons make them useful documents for the historian of doctrine.

In these, as all other aspects of preaching in Spain's golden age, it is possible to see how important preaching was in Catholic Reform and to see also how well it could be done.

The French Experience

Catholic Reform preaching in France has been studied by Peter Bayley.[53] He points out that the sermons that were published and thus have survived were not the relatively short homilies delivered at Sunday Mass:

> The full dress sermon was normally delivered at a separate time, often in the afternoon, on certain major feast days, on Sundays in fashionable town churches, and above all during Lent and Advent.[54]

Other published genres include sermons for preaching missions, for the professions of members of religious orders, and for the funerals of distinguished persons.

These occasions suggest what is indeed the case, that the preaching in question involved more self-conscious virtuoso performances than the regular weekly doses of the proclaimed Word of God. And from this it follows that there had to be a culture to support such an activity, which also proves to be true. One of that culture's bases was the dominance of school curricula by rhetoric in the late-sixteenth and early-seventeenth centuries. The principal difference between one school and another was likely to be whether the rhetoric taught was purely classical or, instead, had been influenced by the theories of Peter Ramus; there was a slight probability that more Roman Catholics were trained in the purely classical tradition and more Protestants in the Ramist tradition.[55]

When one moves beyond general education in the schools and universities to discover the sort of rhetorical training future clergy received, there is less to be learned than might be expected. "The Council of Trent's decree on the subject of the seminarian movement was one of the last to be accepted by the French Church, and the seminarian movement of the 1630s and 1640s aimed at only a very brief training in essentials prior to ordination."[56] All clergy except Jesuits were expected to learn to preach from published treatises on the subject after they had entered the practice of their priesthood. At first these treatises were translations of the Italian and Spanish works mentioned earlier, including those of Granada and Estella, propagated by Borromeo and by their own intrinsic merit. Jesuits, however, did receive preordination training in preaching, and those who demonstrated aptitude were given additional preparation, for which special textbooks were developed within the order.[57]

When post-Tridentine homiletical literature began to originate in

France itself, the works produced fell into two categories, elaborate theoretical works and practical manuals of instruction. While some of the former seem to represent an antirhetorical bias, closer inspection shows that they are really concerned with the spiritual life of the preacher. It is in the "how-to-do-it" manuals that there can be discerned the characteristic element of baroque preaching. Whether these are translations of works by Italian or Spanish writers such as Panigarola or Estella, or the original compositions of a Frenchman like Francis de Sales, what they have in common is an insistence upon the use of preaching aids that is reminiscent of the heyday of thematic preaching.

Perhaps the most important of these is the commonplace book compiled by the preacher himself. One gets the impression that the main reason for a preacher's reading is the discovery of quotations or illustrations that can be copied out against the day when they will be what is needed to "prove" the theme of a sermon. But, in order to assure an adequate *copia* of such material, the preacher will also need encyclopedias, concordances, and digests compiled by others.

With this emphasis on the accumulation of such material, it is not surprising that the major differences between the styles of sermons constructed during this period are in the ways the contents of such collections are employed in the construction of sermons. Most published sermons from the end of the sixteenth and beginning of the seventeenth centuries represent "a kind of preaching which sees the sermon in much the same terms as the long poem or the expository tract"—that is to say, preaching in either the "poetic" or the "plain" style. In the latter part of that period, however, there began to develop "a type of pulpit oratory in which the preacher's main function is the presentation and connection of a wide range of anecdotes, illustrations, and analogies." This is the sort of preaching for which commonplace books and digests are prerequisites. Bayley calls such sermons "thesaurus preaching."[58]

Since it is difficult to communicate the flavor of such preaching without quoting extended passages, Bayley calls upon the most similar works of literature with which the average reader may be familiar, the essays of Montaigne:

> Just as Montaigne's essays developed from a commentary on a selection of favourite anecdotes and passages from the classical writers, so the chief sources of this type of preaching are the thesauri, encyclopedias, and collections of *exempla* which ... were constantly recommended by the manuals.[59]

Since such preaching had the tendencies of becoming flabby and monotonous on the one hand, and of creating in its published volumes of sermons what are essentially new thesauri to be plundered by other preachers on the other, reactions against it were inevitable. One of these produced what Bayley considers to be "the most highly individual technique of sermon construction in our period," the "catenary preaching" of Jean-Pierre Camus.[60] The catenary style consists of

> the *"enchaînement des images"* … the nonchalant linking together of strings of analogies, allusions, anecdotes, Scriptural figures and quotations which combine, [Jean Descrains] says, to form a sort of *"prose poétique."*[61]

Camus accepts calmly the knowledge that a large part of the public buying volumes of sermons will consist of clergy quarrying inspiration for their own preaching. "He has deliberately shaped his work so that it can serve not only as a model for direct imitation, but as a conceptual framework for the sermons of others."[62]

Etienne Molinier objected to the catenary sermon. He considered writing sermons mainly to serve as resources for others who were writing sermons to be a perversion of the preacher's calling. The purpose of preaching was to inspire souls to flee from sin to the love of God, and the accomplishment of that purpose required an affective development of the sort seen so well in the New Testament preaching of Paul. In catenary preaching Molinier could find no intention to instruct or persuade, duties of a Christian orator recognized since Augustine wrote *De doctrina christiana*. This is not to say that Molinier and his allies objected to the use of material garnered from commonplace books and encyclopedias; instead, they insisted that it be embedded in passages of consecutive writing stating the argument the quotations were to ornament.

It was by such a combination of argument and ornament that the desired emotional appeal could be created. Indeed, the existence of a strong line of argument set the commonplace material free to do its work fully. "Since the *conception* no longer has to play the double role of both proof and ornament, the element of the decorative wittiness can be exaggerated; word-play and ingenious analogies unite to form conceits of extreme brevity."[63] Which is to say that extreme cleverness does not have to be superficial; it can be a strategy of great seriousness. The style advocated by Molinier has much in common with the "wittiness" of English "Metaphysicals" like Donne and Andrewes.[64]

CONCLUSION

From this survey of schools of thought about preaching in France during the first half of the seventeenth century, it is clear that French Catholics shared with co-religionists in other countries and with Protestants the enthusiasm for preaching that was characteristic of the age. Preaching was as important in Catholic Reform as it was in the Protestant Reformation. The need for it had already been stressed in the emphasis of new religious orders on the improvement of parochial ministry. The Jesuits even went so far as to have special training programs in preaching. Leaders in all these orders, however, were among the more active advocates of reform in ministry at the Council of Trent. They also had a missionary vision and zeal that sent their brothers all over the world preaching the gospel at a time when other Christian bodies were content to minister to their members at home.

No one embodied the Tridentine ideal and program for the renewal of ministry, including its emphasis on preaching, so much as Charles Borromeo. He wrote on preaching himself and encouraged others to create both theoretical and practical literature about it. His example was copied in both Spain and France, with the result that in both countries clergy worked energetically to discover more effective ways of preaching, and laypeople flocked to hear the products of their labor. In this preaching of Catholic Reform, there was not the single hermeneutical principle that directed the whole preaching enterprise in the way that justification dominated all Lutheran preaching. Nor was there the emphasis on exegesis that characterized the preaching of Calvinists. Instead, the subject matter—and therefore the form—of early-seventeenth-century Catholic preaching was more diverse than that of the Protestants. It cannot be doubted, however, that a new outpouring of preaching characterized all European Christianity during the period of the Reformation.

FOR FURTHER READING

Bayley, Peter. *French Pulpit Oratory 1598–1650: A Study in Themes and Styles with a Descriptive Catalogue of Printed Texts.* Cambridge: Cambridge University Press, 1980.

———. *Selected Sermons of the French Baroque (1600–1650).* New York and London: Garland, 1983.

Catholicism in Early Modern History. Edited by John O'Malley. St. Louis: Center for Reformation Research, 1988.

Dickens, A.G. *The Counter Reformation*. New York: W. W. Norton & Co., 1968.

O'Malley, John. *The First Jesuits*. Cambridge: Harvard University Press, 1993.

Smith, Hilary Dansey. *Preaching in the Spanish Golden Age: A Study of Some Preachers in the Reign of Philip III*. Oxford: Oxford University Press, 1978.

Notes

1. The first draft of this chapter was revised in light of suggestions made by John O'Malley in a letter dated July 9, 1991.

2. Steven Ozment, *The Age of Reform 1250–1550: An Intellectual and Religious History of Late Medieval and Reformation Europe* (New Haven, Conn.: Yale University Press, 1986), 397.

3. Quoted ibid., citing Henry Outram Evennett, *Spirit of the Counter Reformation*, 1951, Birkbeck Lectures in Ecclesiastical History (Cambridge: Cambridge University Press, 1968), 9.

4. John O'Malley, "Catholic Reform" in *Reformation Europe: A Guide to Research*, ed. Steven Ozment (St. Louis: Center for Reformation Research, 1982), 304.

5. In John O'Malley, "Content and Rhetorical Forms in Sixteenth-Century Treatises on Preaching," in *Renaissance Eloquence: Studies in the Theory and Practice of Renaissance Rhetoric*, ed. James J. Murphy (Berkeley: University of California Press, 1983), 238 n. 2.

6. Originally posed in his 1946 work, *Katholische Reformation oder Gegenreformation?*, his thesis is concisely stated in Erwin Iserloh, Joseph Glazik, and Hubert Jedin, *Reformation and Counter Reformation*, vol. 5 of *History of the Church*, ed. Hubert Jedin and John Dolan, trans. Anselm Biggs and Peter W. Becker (New York: Seabury, 1980), 431-32. An example of an effort to observe this distinction can be seen in a work of the English Lutheran scholar A. G. Dickens, *The Counter Reformation* (New York: W. W. Norton & Co., 1968), 7: "I shall try to use each in its appropriate place: Catholic Reformation for the more spontaneous manifestations, Counter Reformation for the developed movement with resistance and reconquest high on its agenda." Recently, however, John O'Malley has proposed the more inclusive term "Early Modern Catholicism" on the grounds that not all the activity in the Catholic Church during that period was motivated by a desire to reform; the Jesuits, for example, seem to have thought of their work much more in terms of the care of souls. See his 1990 presidential address to the American Catholic Historical Association, "Was Ignatius Loyola a Church Reformer? How to Look at Early Modern Catholicism," *CHR* 77 (1991): 177-93.

7. Dickens, *The Counter Reformation*, 63-65.

8. The Italian name for the group is *Fraternita del divino amore sotte la protezione di San Girolamo*.

9. All three became cardinals, and Caraffa became Pope Paul IV.

10. B. J. Kidd, *The Counter-Reformation 1550–1600* (London: SPCK, 1933), 13-14. For the Latin text, see B. J. Kidd, *Documents Illustrative of the Continental Reformation* (Oxford: Clarendon, 1911), 314.

11. There were, however, a number of pirated editions published. One of these ended up in Germany and was republished by Luther with his sarcastic comments.

12. The Jesuits received this model from them.

13. About whom we shall hear more later.

14. A true religious order, not to be confused with the Oratory of Divine Love, which was only a confraternity or sodality.

15. One of the members of this group was Palestrina, the papal choirmaster. The musical genre of "oratorio" grew out of his compositions for these gatherings.

16. John Henry Newman brought it to England in the nineteenth century. Like Gaetano, Philip Neri was eventually canonized.

17. Owen Chadwick, *The Reformation*, Pelican History of the Church, vol. 3 (Grand Rapids, Mich.: Eerdmans, 1964), 255. Cf. John O'Malley's statement: "For Jedin, the heart of the Tridentine reform was an episcopacy animated by a renewed (or even a new) sense of ministry, as the bishop was transformed from feudatory to pastor" (O'Malley, "Catholic Reform," 297).

18. *Regimini militantis ecclesiae,* promulgated on September 27, 1540, and based upon the society's provisional rule, *Prima summa institute.* See André Ravier, *Ignatius of Loyola and the Founding of the Society of Jesus,* trans. Maura, Joan, and Carson Daly (San Francisco: Ignatius, 1987), 102.

19. Translation in Kidd, *The Counter-Reformation 1550–1600*, 28; Latin in Kidd, *Documents Illustrative of the Continental Reformation*, 337.

20. The quotation at the beginning of this section is taken from that summary.

21. John O'Malley, *The First Jesuits* (Cambridge: Harvard University Press, 1993), 104-10. I am grateful to Father O'Malley for a prepublication copy of his draft for the chapter containing this section.

22. *Trento*, in Italian.

23. For a much more nuanced understanding of the complexities of the council, see Giuseppe Alberigo, "The Council of Trent," in *Catholicism in Early Modern History: A Guide to Research,* ed. John O'Malley (St. Louis: Center for Reformation Research, 1988), 211-26. See also the chapter by Jared Wicks, "Doctrine and Theology," in ibid., 227-51.

24. J. Waterworth, trans., *The Canons and Decrees of the Sacred and Oecumenical Council of Trent, Celebrated Under the Sovereign Pontiffs, Paul III, Julius III, and Pius IV* (New York and London: E. Dunigan & Brother and C. Dolman, 1848), 2:27.

25. Ibid. John O'Malley points out that in this decree "is found a paraphrase of the 'Second Rule' of St. Francis of Assisi, viz., that preaching concerns 'virtues and vices, punishment and reward.'" "St. Charles Borromeo and the *Praecipuum Episcoporum Munus*: His Place in the History of Preaching," in *San Carlo Borromeo: Catholic Reform and Ecclesiastical Politics in the Second Half of the Sixteenth Century,* ed. John M. Headley and John B. Tomaro, Folger Books

(Washington: Folger Shakespeare Library, 1988; London and Toronto: Associated University Presses, 1988), 141, 152 n. 19.

26. Waterworth, *The Canons and Decrees of the Oecumenical Council of Trent,* 2:211-12.

27. Ibid., 2:187.

28. Ibid.

29. Peter Bayley, *French Pulpit Oratory 1598–1650: A Study of Themes and Styles, with a Descriptive Catalogue of Printed Texts* (Cambridge: Cambridge University Press, 1980), 38.

30. Evennett, *Spirit of the Counter Reformation,* 121.

31. "Missions," *ODCC.* For a report on research, see John W. Witek, "From India to Japan: European Missionary Expansion, 1500–1650," in O'Malley, *Catholicism in Early Modern History,* 193-210.

32. Peter Bayley, "Preaching After the Counter Reformation," in ibid., 308-9.

33. Ibid., 299.

34. The limitation of attention to two countries does not imply that there was not abundant homiletical activity in other countries as well, but only that I do not know of studies of that activity. In a letter dated March 25, 1991, John O'Malley listed the places where Catholic Reform preaching has been actively pursued as "Spain, Latin America, Portugal, Italy, Catholic France, Catholic Germany, Poland, etc." The list was intended to be suggestive rather than definitive.

35. O'Malley, "St. Charles Borromeo and the *Praecipuum Episcoporum Munus*" 139. On the importance of Borromeo's example, see Alberigo, "The Council of Trent," 219-21. Not everyone was enthusiastic about what Borromeo was doing, as Alberigo points out. Some of his enemies went so far as to try to have him assassinated, and even saintly Robert Bellarmine saw to it that Borromeo's canonization was for his private virtues rather than his pastoral concerns and activity.

36. Marc Fumaroli, *L'Age de l'éloquence: Rhétorique et res literaria de la Renaissance au seuil de l'époque classique,* Hautes Études Médiévales et Modernes, no. 43 (Geneva: Librairie Droz, 1980), 122-22, 135-36.

37. This is found in *Acta Ecclesiae Mediolanensis* 2:1205-48 and has been reprinted many times, but I have not been able to consult it.

38. O'Malley, "St. Charles Borromeo and the *Praecipuum Episcoporum Munus,*" 142.

39. Ibid.

40. Ibid., 143. He sometimes preached three or four times a day, preparing different sermons for each occasion.

41. In ibid., 144, 154 n. 41, with a reference to de Sales's letter to André Frémyot of October 5, 1604, and a quotation of the French text.

42. O'Malley, "St. Charles Borromeo and the *Praecipuum Episcoporum Munus,*" 147. For more detailed descriptions of these works, see Bayley, *French Pulpit Oratory 1598–1650,* 145-56.

43. O'Malley, "St. Charles Borromeo and the *Praecipuum Episcoporum Munus,*" 149.

44. Hilary Dansey Smith, *Preaching in the Spanish Golden Age: A Study of Some Preachers in the Reign of Philip III* (Oxford: Oxford University Press, 1978), 5. The

years of Philip's reign were 1598–1621. An example of the prose fiction is Padre Isla, *Historia del famoso predicador Fray Gerundio de Campazas,* which Bayley describes as "the satirical novel that did for post-Tridentine preaching what *Don Quixote* did for chivalric romances" (Bayley, "Preaching After the Counter Reformation," 307 n. 44). The only English translations I have been able to learn about were made in the eighteenth century.

45. Ibid., 17.

46. Ibid., 30.

47. Ibid., 44. The medieval practice of division by words or letter-by-letter in cabalistic fashion continued in common but not standard use.

48. Ibid., 54. "This is a term used ... to denote a sermon which weaves together, or contrasts one with the other, a Gospel text and an *Autoridad* (which may be from the Epistle for the day, or from the Breviary)."

49. Ibid., 75.

50. The rhetorical term for this is *ecphrasis.*

51. Ibid., 94-95.

52. Ibid., 109. A picture, usually printed in a collection of such things, accompanied by a statement about its significance, which is essentially enigmatic because true emblems are "composed of a set of secret relationships which at first puzzle the beholder."

53. Bayley, *French Pulpit Oratory,* and its companion volume, *Selected Sermons of the French Baroque (1600–1650)* (New York and London: Garland, 1983), which provides examples of the different kinds of sermons discussed in the first book.

54. Bayley, *French Pulpit Oratory,* 14.

55. Ibid., 19, 22. For more on Ramism, see below, chapters 15 and 18.

56. Ibid., 38.

57. Ibid., 56-60.

58. Ibid., 77.

59. Ibid., 78.

60. Ibid., 85.

61. Ibid. The internal reference is to Jean Descrains, "La Rhétorique dans les homélies de Jean-Pierre Camus aux Etats Généraux de 1616," *XVIIe Siècle,* 80-81 (1968): 61-78.

62. Ibid., 86.

63. Ibid., 94.

64. Bayley goes on, pp. 97-100, to discuss what he calls "orhestrated prose," but since that sort of preaching was found more among Protestants than Roman Catholics, it does not need to be discussed here.

UPHEAVAL IN BRITAIN

CUIUS REGIO

The beginning of this chapter marks a decisive shift in the orientation of my account of the history of preaching because from here on the preoccupation of the narrative will be with preaching in English; the homiletical tradition in other languages will be referred to only to the extent that it casts light on developments in preaching in English. While that shift could be thought to portend some simplification of the story, such optimism is destined for disappointment. From its beginning, the Reformation and post-Reformation history of English-speaking Christianity has been variegated and occasionally many-splendored.

A partial explanation for this complexity is given in a now-classic statement from F. M. Powicke: "The one definite thing which can be said about the Reformation in England is that it was an act of state."[1] In making the statement, however, Powicke was not explicitly contrasting what took place in England with what occurred on the Continent, but rather with medieval traditions of papal authority that had culminated in the pontificate of Boniface VIII (1294–1303). The role of the German princes in the Lutheran Reformation, that of the Swiss city councils in the Calvinist, and the establishment of the principle of *cuius regio eius religio*[2] as the means for settling which territories were to remain Catholic and which were to become Protestant show that all religious developments of the sixteenth century were very much acts of state, whatever superiority over princes previous theory may have given to popes.

At the time it was inconceivable to anyone that there could be a unified state that was religiously divided; indeed, the knowledge that religious pluralism did not entail civil anarchy is one of the eventual contributions of the English experience to Christendom. Furthermore, ever since Constantine had called the Council of Nicaea there had been theorists who were convinced that the state should have supremacy in spiritual as well as temporal matters; conciliarists such as Marsilius of Padua had so argued, and their thought had been persuasive to Catholic monarchs up until the Council of Trent.

Thus, in respect to its involvement with secular government, the essential difference between the Reformation in England and what happened on the Continent resulted from the fact that one English monarch's religious commitments differed so dramatically from another's; and so the pattern that religious reform took varied considerably from reign to reign. Indeed, there had not been such religious instability even in late antiquity when Roman emperors were either orthodox or Arian.

On the whole, Henry VIII had not wished for any religious change in England beyond the replacement of papal authority in the church with royal, even though he was willing to sound more Lutheran when diplomatic dickering with Germany called for his doing so. After Henry was succeeded by his ten-year-old son, Edward VI, in 1547, the two successive protectors, Somerset and Northumberland, moved the English church in a more Calvinist direction for a variety of political and theological reasons. When Edward died in 1553, his half sister Mary, daughter of Catherine of Aragon and wife of Philip II of Spain, acquired the sobriquet "Bloody" from the ardor with which she returned the Church of England to papal obedience.

Five years later when Queen Mary died, Elizabeth inherited a land deeply divided over issues of faith, with some subjects loyal to Rome, others who had lived during Mary's reign as exiles in Geneva where they acquired a vision of a "truly" Reformed church, and many others in between. For forty-five years Elizabeth refused to submit to pressure from either extreme, fostering instead a settlement in which the English church acquired the balance of Catholic and Reformed elements that has characterized it ever since, the balance that came in the nineteenth century to be called Anglicanism.

The Elizabethan Settlement, however, did not mean that matters were settled permanently. When James VI of Scotland became James I of Great Britain in 1603, his experience of the Presbyterianism that had been the religion of Scotland since John Knox had reformed the national church in 1560 led him to resist the pressure of Puritans to make the English church more Calvinistic. Then, under his son Charles I and Charles's archbishop, William Laud, considerable effort was made to emphasize the Catholic aspect of Anglican tradition.

The *religious* resistance to the efforts of this king and his primate by the group called "Puritans" since the reign of Elizabeth,[3] together with the *political* resistance of Parliament to the way Charles acted on his understanding of the divine right of kings, resulted in revolution, with Laud's execution in 1645 and that of the king in 1649. Under the Commonwealth, which lasted from the death of Charles I to the Restoration of Charles II in 1660, the English church (or, at least, the part of it under control of Parliament) was given at first a Presbyterian and then an Independent (Congregationalist) complexion.

At the Restoration it became obvious that the ideal of a realm united religiously as well as politically was no longer achievable. The established church could never again claim to embrace all citizens. Dissent was allowed, but those remaining within the establishment—freed from the necessity of accommodating disagreement—could now emphasize their differences from Presbyterians, Independents, and Baptists. The equilibrium thus established was threatened later when James II used his position to ease the situation of his fellow Roman Catholics, but the "Glorious Revolution" replaced him as monarch with his daughter Mary and her husband, William of Orange.

They, in turn, were followed by Queen Anne, Tory and High Church, but already weariness over religious controversies had made welcome a latitudinarianism to which any "enthusiasm" or fanaticism was foreign. This characterized the mood of the Church of England until it was finally vanquished by the Evangelical revival of the eighteenth century and the Catholic renewal (the "Oxford movement") of the nineteenth. Since then the major influence on the religious life of England has been the secularization of Western thought, which has left churches there as sparsely filled with worshipers as those of Roman Catholics and Protestants on the Continent.

It can be seen that English Christianity has been in a continual state of upheaval since the Reformation and that many of the disturbances upsetting it were induced by the Crown until the reign of William and Mary, when the monarchy became too constitutional to have any real power over the religious life of the realm.[4]

ON AGAIN, OFF AGAIN: THE TUDOR PERIOD

Periods and Characteristics

This ecclesiological flux and vacillation at the behest of sovereigns, especially clear during the reigns of Henry VIII and his three children, had homiletical implications. These have been traced by J. W. Blench in *Preaching in England in the Late Fifteenth and Sixteenth Centuries: A Study of English Sermons 1450–c.1600.*[5] So impressed was Blench with the influence of reign changes on preaching that each of his chapters is divided into four sections:

1. The Pre-Reformation Catholic Preachers, including the Conservative Henricians (1450–1547),
2. The Early Reformers (1547–1553),
3. The Preachers of Mary's Reign (1553–1558), and
4. The Elizabethan Preachers (1558–1603).

Indeed, he gives the impression at times that the preaching of a particular reign was monochrome when in fact, most of the ways of preaching were found in every period.

Tudor Hermeneutics

Blench begins his study by showing what forms of biblical interpretation were in use by preachers of different parties during the various reigns. Before the Reformation, the four medieval senses of Scripture dominated exegesis until Catholic-thinking clergy came under the influence of Erasmus and other humanists, and Reform-minded preachers came to accept Luther's demand for literal interpretation.[6]

As noted in the discussion of Luther (above, chap. 12) the literal sense recognized in the sixteenth century is very different from that of twentieth-century biblical scholars; it is a timeless theological interpretation rather than an effort to discover what the sacred authors intended their first readers to understand—and its hermeneutical key was the theological system of the preacher. Blench is able to say of a construal of scripture in a sermon by Bishop John Hooper that while "it does start with a theological position which it proceeds to find in the words of the sacred writer, it is very far removed from anything resembling the later 'higher criticism.'"[7] He goes on to say: "It is interesting also to notice that Latimer, while he will not admit pro-Catholic allegories, nevertheless introduces anti-

Catholic accommodations."[8] So a great deal of the preaching of the period was polemical, and the needs of controversy often dominated not only sermon strategy but also biblical interpretation as well.

Homiletical Genres

For his discussion of sermon form *(dispositio)*, Blench uses the medieval terms of "ancient" and "modern" to refer to the homily and thematic sermon forms,[9] although, by the time he wrote about, this vocabulary had already become anachronistic: the thematic sermon was no longer modern and the homily was in the process of revival. Thematic sermons were still the norm on the eve of the Reformation, but some preachers inspired by the humanists, such as Colet, had reverted to the patristic homily form. The preferred type for those influenced by continental Reformers was the exegetical homily that proceeded *secundum ordinem textus*.

While there was some resurgence of thematic preaching during the reign of Queen Mary I, the influence of humanism had tamed somewhat the ardor for "the subdividing mentality," with its infinite capacity for elaborate divisions. Preachers of the period, therefore,

> content[ed] themselves with an Exordium, Prayer, Division into (most frequently) three topics (which usually do not depend on the words of the text) and Confirmation of the Division with little if any subdivision. [10]

Blench notes correctly that this simplification of the thematic sermon, which had already begun to appear in the time of Edward, "approximates to the essentials of the classical oration."[11] This is to say that it represents the influence of the sort of ecclesiastical rhetoric that was a primary influence of the Renaissance on both Catholic and Protestant preaching. I will say more about this below.

Blench calls attention to the appearance during Elizabeth's reign of "the new Reformed method" found in the lectures of the extreme Puritans, but he devotes less than a page to this sermon form.[12] While the number of preachers who used it in the Tudor period may have been relatively small, the method later became so influential in both England and New England that I discuss it below.

Plain or Fancy

While Blench's analysis of the exegesis and form of Tudor preaching is generally accepted as accurate, what he has to say about style has recently been brought into question by implication. Classical rhetorical theory spoke of three styles: plain, moderate, and grand. For his period, however, Blench spoke of the "plain, but uncolloquial," the "colloquial," and the "ornate" styles.[13] The difficulty with this taxonomy is that it overlaps without duplicating the classical distinctions and thus misleads the reader into thinking that the traditional categories are being invoked. This danger of confusion is increased by the way Blench uses a good bit of classical vocabulary to talk about style.

What he does is coherent enough in itself. The plain but uncolloquial style is characterized by a spare use of *exempla* and schemata (figures of speech [or sound] as opposed to figures of thought) and these employed "not for display, but as an aid to cogent expression." The colloquial style "used a racy and pungent speech idiom, and avoids the schemata, but is enriched by frequent homely *exempla.*" The ornate style, as might be expected, "is highly embellished by the schemata, employs many *exempla* (often from literary sources) and aims distinctly at oratorical display."[14]

The difficulties with this categorization of styles are: (1) the danger of confusion with classical nomenclature, and (2) an importation of value judgments into descriptions in a way that obscures classifications. This latter difficulty is exaggerated by the resemblance of Blench's scheme to a modern critical misunderstanding of the way the three classical styles were distinguished in the ancient world, deriving from the 1905 analysis of G. L. Hendrickson.[15] He claimed there were originally only two ancient styles, one of which he called "oratorical" and the other "plain." The first was an emotional appeal while the second was a rational one.[16]

The whole discussion of style in Tudor sermons has been set on a more sure footing by Debora K. Shuger in *Sacred Rhetoric: The Christian Grand Style in the English Renaissance.*[17] She argues that this interpretation represents a distortion of both classical and Renaissance rhetorical theory. The ancient denotation of grand style was not the use of showy speech forms to convince an audience through psychological manipulation.[18]

> Beginning with the Greeks, the grand style was not described as primarily periodic, schematic, or playful but as passionate. The grand style moves the emotions . . . [It] expresses a passionate seriousness about the most important issues of human life; it is thus the style of Plato and the Bible as well as Cicero and Demosthenes.[19]

In the ancient world, a common way of contrasting the grand style to its alternative was to use the analogy of soldiers and athletes. The contests of athletes may be more aesthetic, but soldiers engage in life-and-death struggles. An audience of Isocrates might have responded by saying, "O how eloquent!" but an audience of Demosthenes would have responded by saying, "Let's go to war against the Macedonians!" Thus it was Demosthenes rather than Isocrates who would have been said to use the grand style.

The preachers of the English Renaissance, however, did not have a grand style that was identical with that of the classical rhetoricians, whose speech making was for courts of law, legislative assemblies, and ceremonial occasions. Nothing in their oratorical theory, therefore, had so exalted a subject as Christian preaching about the triune God. It remained for Augustine to point out that speaking of such a God required an elevated speech aimed at expressing and inculcating love of this God. His theories led medieval homileticians to develop what is called a "passionate plain style." Puritan preaching theory is a development of that medieval approach to proclamation.

Other English preachers, however, under the influence of continental Neo-Latin textbooks of both rhetoric and homiletics, developed a Christian grand style (even if they did not refer to it by that term). It drew on late Hellenistic rhetorical traditions connected with Longinus and Hermogenes, who wrote of "the sublime" and saw the need for a sense of grandeur in religion. They also began to address issues of affective psychology, a type of consideration absent from ancient rhetoric, because Greek and Roman culture had deep distrust of "the passions" as the antithesis of reason. This homiletical emphasis reflected the development of "faculty" psychology.

Shuger's reconstruction is convincing. The one caveat to be entered is that although she gives incidental expression to her familiarity with English Renaissance preaching that did not represent the grand style, on the whole she confines her book to its subject. A careless reader could be left with the impression that grand style was the only sort of homiletical theory or preaching there was. In an excellent chapter on textbooks, however, she indicates that preachers in the grand style were instructed using Latin textbooks from the Continent, whether liberal Protestant and Tridentine works on homiletics or general rhetorics. Hence they are squarely in the tradition of Erasmus and the humanists. Yet she recognizes that there were also textbooks in the vernacular, often very short—like that of William Perkins, to be studied below. These had an entirely different readership, one that was the heir of the medieval passionate plain style, even though it resisted almost every other aspect of medieval theology.

That is to say, the advocates of the plain style were Puritans. Proponents of the grand style were much more central Anglicans. The latter would reach their apogee, not only in eloquence but also in learning and sanctity, in the early seventeenth century with practitioners like Lancelot Andrewes and John Donne.

A DISPLAY OF PREACHERS

The Tudor preaching scene was so kaleidoscopic that it is difficult to hold any picture from it in view long enough to acquire distinct impressions of what it was like. A few thumbnail sketches at this point may be helpful in getting some sense of the phenomena. While these sketches cannot claim to be representative of all elements of the scene, at least they can give a sense of concretion to some of them.

The Book of Homilies

The first is not of a person but a book and the reality that necessitated it. When the power of the Crown was placed behind the Reformation by the regents of Edward VI, two truths were recognized: (1) that the new doctrines needed to be taught in a wholesale way, and (2) that many of the clergy were not well enough trained to teach them. To meet the need, a collection of sermons was published to inculcate the new doctrines. Known popularly as *The Book of Homilies*, it bore the full title of *Certain Sermons, or Homilies, appoynted by the Kynges Maiestie, to be declared and redde, by all Persones,*[20] *Uicars, or Curates euery Sonday in their Churches, where they haue Cure,* a designation stating the program as well as the contents of the work.[21]

The sermons are topical in their construction and constitute a catechetical enterprise, as may be seen from a listing of their titles. These, together with the authors to whom some have been attributed, are: (1) "A Fruitful Exhortation to the Reading of Holy Scripture," Archbishop Thomas Cranmer; (2) "Of the Misery of All Mankind," Archdeacon John Harpesfield; (3) "Of the Salvation of All Mankind," Cranmer; (4) "Of the True and Lively Faith," Cranmer; (5) "Of Good Works," Cranmer; (6) "Of Christian Love and Charity," Bishop Edmund Bonner; (7) "Against Swearing and Perjury"; (8) "Of the Declining from God"; (9) "An Exhortation to Obedience"; (11) "Against Whoredom and Adultery," possibly Cranmer's chaplain, Thomas Becon; and (12) "Against Strife and Contention," possibly by Becon.[22]

It has been cogently argued by John N. Wall Jr. that these homilies reflect a program of religious renewal for England that owes its inspiration not so much to any continental Reformer as it does to the northern tradition of Christian humanism represented by Erasmus.[23] His basic thesis is that these English humanists shared with Erasmus three convictions: that obedience to God is aimed not so much toward holy dying as toward obedience to God in the world as a way that improves social living, that such obedience is to the will of God as revealed in the Bible, and that this reform is communicated through human speech. In this view Wall is following the insight of Marjorie O'Rourke Boyle that "for Erasmus, the Christ is God's eternally thought speech; men imitate the Father when they imitate the divine discourse made flesh in Jesus."[24] On the basis of this theology,

> Cranmer and his followers set out to reform England with a collection of written documents intended to be read aloud, a collection of documents including among them the Bible itself, Erasmus' own commentary[25] on the New Testament heart of it for Christina speakers, and a collection of rhetorically constructed sermons expounding its meaning.[26]

All of these documents were begun during the reign of Henry VIII before the fall of his vicar general, Thomas Cromwell, but Henry's conservatism held back their distribution until the reign of Edward VI. Yet those who sponsored them included not only Cromwell, but Henry's archbishop of Canterbury, Thomas Cranmer, and even Catherine Parr, Henry's last wife, as well. So important was this ministry of the Word to Cranmer that all the books necessary for it were completed before the appearance in 1549 of the first Book of Common Prayer, which provided the English church with its liturgy in the language of the people. Central to this project was a vision of the Christian commonwealth that Erasmus had communicated through his *Enchiridion.* "The *Book of Homilies* is at once the fullest Tudor expression of the vision of a Christian commonwealth attainable through universal humanist education and the basic work in a program of universal education aimed at realizing this vision."[27]

One of the clearest indications of Cranmer and his associates' success in getting the Homilies used was the Puritan opposition to them. Millar Maclure summed it up when he said that "the drone of the Homilies replaced the mutter of the Mass."[28] The grounds for opposing them were that they were not tailor made for the sins of the priest's congregation and that they did not penetrate hearts as did sermons prepared with the particular congregation and occasion in mind. While insisting that the Puritans exaggerated the differences between the effects of reading a sermon from *The Book of Homilies* and preaching one freshly created, even Hooker had to agree that people may not pay too much attention to something they can read themselves at any time and that sermons "come always new."[29] Yet such complaints are a tribute to the extent to which the policy of the English humanists succeeded in providing for sound Anglican doctrine to be delivered orally to the people on a regular basis.

Hugh Latimer

The next representative of Tudor preaching to be considered, the Right Reverend Hugh Latimer (ca. 1485–1555), can be understood as a perfect exemplar of the English Erasmian tradition. He certainly was committed to an understanding of Christian living as devoted to the establishment of the Commonweal, preaching out against what he considered to be the social evils of his day.[30] His preaching shows consistently that he believed the Bible to be the only source of Christian doctrine and shows as well that few were as gifted as he in the oral communication of the biblical faith and its behavioral implications.

The son of a yeoman farmer who could afford to send him to school, Latimer was a fellow of Clare Hall at Cambridge when Erasmus was there. He was already recognized enough for his ability in the pulpit to be selected as one of the university's twelve scholars licensed to preach anywhere in England. Yet at first he did not support the New Learning. It was one of his fellow dons, Thomas Bilney—"Little Bilney," as Latimer called him—who won him to its cause.[31] Not long afterward, his preaching began to get him in trouble with the bishop of Ely, in whose diocese Cambridge is located, but at the time he had an unlikely rescuer in Cardinal Wolsey. Along with Cranmer, Latimer was active in obtaining Cambridge's approval for the annulment of Henry VIII's marriage to Catherine of Aragon, following which he received the first of many invitations to preach at court, and was appointed rector of a parish in Wiltshire.

Even though he continued in his outspoken preaching of the Reformation cause,[32] he was made bishop of Worcester in 1535. When, however, Henry's conservatism effected the enactment of the Six Articles that retained most elements of traditional practice, he resigned his see. Under house arrest for a while, he was then given a pension to live in retirement.

The death of Henry and accession of Edward VI came when he was in the Tower of London for having been supportive of another Reformer, Dr. Edward Crome. Even under the auspicious new reign, however, he did not resume his diocese, although he was continually invited to preach, delivering eight sermons at Paul's Cross and seven Lenten sermons before the king. When he preached another sermon at court the following Lent (1550), he spoke of himself as an old man and suggested that it would be his last at that place. He lived in semiretirement on the estate of his friend the duchess of Suffolk, preaching in the neighborhood twice every Sunday.

When, however, the sickly young king died and was succeeded by his older sister Mary, the fortunes of Latimer changed with those of the Reformation cause. Confined to the Tower with Cranmer and Ridley in September of 1553 and then transferred to prison in Oxford, he and Ridley anticipated Cranmer slightly in their trial for heresy and their deaths at the stake on October 16, 1555. Throughout his ordeal, Latimer maintained a sober gaiety. Foxe tells us that when the flame was set to the pyre he said, "Be of good comfort, master Ridley, and play the man. We shall this day light such a candle, by God's grace, in England, as I trust shall never be put out."[33]

As a preacher, Latimer is more reminiscent of Luther than anyone else because of his colloquial style, his sermons approaching what someone has called "matey chats."[34] Yet, unlike Luther, he had no theory of a single task that all sermons must accomplish. Indeed, some of the conventions of the thematic sermon still linger in his work,[35] such as an occasional protheme followed by a bidding prayer. Some of his longer efforts were delivered in two parts, with the prayer coming at the end of the first. He also used *exempla*. Yet there is nothing of the subdividing mentality in him. Rather, his sermons have been said to "suffer from looseness of structure and (to be) encumbered with digressions."[36] While most are constructed *secundum ordinem textus*,[37] and such expository homilies are not notorious for their coherence, Latimer is also like Luther in his tendency to ramble.

All this may be seen in an analysis of his "Sixth Sermon Preached Before King Edward the Sixth."[38] (For the text of this sermon, see **Vol. 2, pp. 296-312**.) The whole Lenten series shares the common text of Romans 15:4, but little is said about it here. Rather, Latimer begins with a summary of his previous sermon and then, through six long paragraphs, defends himself against a misunderstanding of something he said in it. He next announces that his text for the day will be the story of the miraculous draft of fishes in Luke 5, saying that he will refute a papal interpretation given the passage by Cardinal Reginald Pole, and bids prayer.

In response to the statement that the people pressed upon Jesus to hear him, Latimer wonders at the prevalence of "unpreaching prelates." In the process of doing so he tells an *exemplum* about a woman who went to hear the sermons at a certain church because she needed the sleep. But that reminds him of how Augustine was converted by Ambrose's preaching even though he had gone to church with unworthy motives. The importance of preaching is demonstrated by reference to the devil's efforts to stop it, including hardships in educating sons for the ministry and the impoverishment of clergy through the fee farming of benefices.

The people listened reverently to Jesus, unlike Latimer's restless audience at Westminster Palace. Jesus' getting into Peter's boat did not indicate that he was the future pope; Jesus just chose the most convenient boat in the manner that Latimer had picked his wherry over from Lambeth Palace that day. A good bit of antipapal interpretation is given, interlarded with a tale of a bishop who was angry when he was not rung into town for his visitation because the local bell lacked a clapper, and another story about his own visitation of a town where the people were too busy celebrating Robin Hood's day to gather for his sermon.

The way the fish came to be caught at Jesus' command, but still the disciples had to lower their nets to catch them, shows a synergism between the activity of God and human evangelistic endeavor. Jesus worked at being a carpenter until he began to preach, and then he worked at that. Everyone else should work as well, including the king, who has his own distinctive duties. As disjointed as the sermon may sound from this summary, it was tied together by the motif of the importance of preaching the Word of God.

Even from so sketchy an outline, it is possible to feel both the passion of Latimer's polemic and the pleasure of his style. Blench calls him "the greatest exponent of the colloquial style in the century"[39] and points out some of the stylistic devices by which he achieves this effect. These include the use of humorous compounds such as "claw-backs," "flibbergibs," "by-walkers," "merit-mongers," "bell-hallowers," and "card-gospellers." He frequently places words close together that sound alike but have different meanings (paronomasias), such as homily/homely, or supper/dupper. "Alliteration's artful aid" is employed, as in "boils, botches, blains, and scabs."[40] He loves to quote proverbs and folk wisdom and invents homely comparisons. He has an extremely sharp ear for the sound of conversation. He tells many *exempla* and, a much rarer thing, tells personal anecdotes, especially related to farm life—although he can tell about the perils of the episcopate as well.

From this depiction alone, it would be possible to confuse Latimer with mere entertainers who have taken the pulpit for their stage, a real temptation in times when preaching is popular. But as Horton Davies said:

> Latimer's preaching was too courageous, too direct, and too compassionate ever to be mistaken for demagoguery. It was, whether in denunciation, retelling a Biblical narrative, or in exposition, ... popular preaching at its best.[41]

His passion for the gospel was paramount, his concern for the suffering unending, and his willingness to speak the Word of God in season and out of season, at whatever cost to himself or others, makes the likes of him rare in any age.

Puritan Sermon Form

While Blench calls attention to the appearance of Puritan preaching in the reign of Elizabeth, he says little about it, because it was not yet very popular. Though the number of preachers who used it in the Tudor period may have been relatively small, the method became so influential later both in England and in New England that it deserves identification at its first appearance. From the time of Elizabeth through the beginning of the Commonwealth, most English clergy operated out of an essentially Calvinist theological framework. As a result, Calvin's highly exegetical understanding of the work of the preacher inevitably had its influence, especially among the more thoroughgoing Calvinists, those called Puritans.

The normative statement of Puritan homiletical method in England is generally recognized to have been made in William Perkins's *The Arte of Prophesying*.[42] In Perkins's formula the method was reduced to tabular form:

1. To read the Text distinctly out of the canonicall scripture.
2. To give the sense and understanding of it being read by the scripture itself.
3. To collect a few and profitable points of doctrine out of the naturall sense.
4. To applie (if he have the gift) the doctrine rightly collected to the manners of men in a simple and plain speech.[43]

This formula, commonly summarized as "Understanding, Doctrines, and Uses," has been explicated by Perry Miller:

The Puritan sermon quotes the text and "opens" it as briefly as possible, expounding circumstances and context, explaining its grammatical meanings, reducing its tropes and schemata to prose, and setting forth its logical implications; the sermon then proclaims in a flat, indicative sentence the "doctrine" contained in the text or logically deduced from it, and proceeds to the first reason or proof. Reason follows reason, with no other transition than a period and a number; after the last proof is stated there follow the uses or applications, also in numbered sequence, and the sermon ends when there is nothing more to be said.[44]

The only thing that needs to be added theologically is that while Perkins insisted the "onlie" sense of Scripture is the "literall," he also believed the Holy Spirit inspired the sacred writers in such a way that the meaning of all parts of the Bible is consistent. That means passages not necessarily showing that consistency were still to be interpreted "by the analogie of faith," in other words, in accordance with the Apostles' Creed—and even more with Paul's Epistle to the Romans as interpreted by Calvin. Perkins also divided texts into those of gospel and those of law in a manner reminiscent of Luther.[45]

Philosophically, an extremely important additional insight is that Perkins's homiletical theory reflects the perspective of the French logician Pierre Ramus and his rhetorical aide-de-camp, Omer Talon. Ramus represents a stage of development in logical thought between late scholasticism, on the one hand, and Bacon and Descartes, on the other, that was extremely influential on continental Reform thought and English and American Puritanism.[46] The essence of Ramus's system was to say that the material of any discipline could be classified by going through what today is called a "decision tree," opting between mutually exclusive alternatives.[47]

He also eliminated invention, disposition, and memory from the classical tasks of rhetoric, leaving only style *(elocutio)* and delivery *(actio)*, on the grounds that invention and disposition were parts of logic or dialectic rather than rhetoric. This does not mean that composers of sermons and other speeches no longer engaged in invention and arrangement in their work, but only that they were wearing their dialectical rather than their rhetorical hats when they engaged in such activities. Besides the implied diminution of rhetoric (always a popular pastime), the adoption of Ramist theory (as worked out in reference to rhetoric by Talon) gave sermons the form of logical demonstrations rather than oral persuasions.

Ramist principles were congenial to Puritans for a number of reasons, particularly that since sermons were the usual vehicle of conversion or election, they had to combine logical and emotional appeals. Because logic is a gift of God, the sermons had to be consistent with human reason, but the suggestion that preaching could persuade by force of intellect alone implied that conversion could be a human rather than a divine activity—a blasphemous idea.

This psychology of the Puritans called for election to be accompanied by a physical stimulus, in the belief that this reservation would allow for election to be an exclusively divine act, but one that was at the same time accepted in human freedom. Furthermore, they wanted to avoid any implication that the saving work of God was dependent upon human emotional manipulation or even that preaching was merely an aesthetic experience and thereby a sensual indulgence. Thus they felt that Ramus's humbling of rhetoric was consistent with the needs of the saints: it allowed for preaching that was both reasonable and passionate, but that nevertheless left results entirely in the hands of God.[48]

So much for Ramist theory, but what evidence is there that it is reflected in the "new Reformed method" of Puritan preaching inculcated by Perkins's *Arte of Prophesying*? The case has been well argued by Miller:

> The laws of invention applied to extracting arguments from a Biblical text would teach [a Ramist] how to "open" it and how to formulate the doctrine; Ramus' rules for memory would instruct him to "porte" his text into a few doctrines; the whole of the *Dialecticae* would teach him how to prove them and how to dispose doctrines and proofs in order. Ramus' constant insistence upon "use" would show him the necessity for applying each doctrine to the auditors "as euery heade shall geue the occasion." For the embellishment with figures and tropes and for the methods of oral delivery, Talon's rhetoric would teach him that these are secondary to the analysis of arguments and the genesis of a method, that they are to be added only after the theme and the demonstration are worked out.[49]

It can be seen that, along with the preaching patterns of the patristic homily and the medieval thematic sermon, pulpits of the English Reformation exhibited a third, Puritan pattern based on Ramist logic that received its classical statement in William Perkins's *The Arte of Prophesying*.[50]

"Silver-Tongued" Smith

Very little is known about the life of the third example of Tudor preaching. The "silver-tongued preacher,"[51] as Henry Smith was called, came from a wealthy and well-connected Leicestershire family; William Cecil (Lord Burghley), Elizabeth's treasurer, was the brother of his step-mother, and one of Smith's cousins married Francis Bacon. Although he was an eldest son, he did not inherit the family estate because he lived only a little over thirty years. He studied at Oxford, but his name was far too common for university records to furnish any certainty about whether he received a degree.[52]

An early-nineteenth-century life of John Aylmer, Bishop of London in Smith's time, furnishes what little additional information there is about his training for the ministry:

> Soon after his coming to Oxford, he lived and followed his studies with Richard Greenham, a pious minister in the country, but not thorough-ly affected to the orders of the church established; and his principles he seems to have infused into Smith.[53]

Saying that he was not "thoroughly affected" was a quaint Georgian way of saying that Henry Smith was a Puritan. The extent to which he was "Puritan," though, was very different from conventional associa-tions with the term. His only certain ministerial appointment was, to be sure, in that most Puritan of all arrangements, a readership.

> If an incumbent minister could not or would not preach the number and kind of sermons demanded, the laity could hire another minister, the lecturer, to preach at times when the church was not being used for regular services.[54]

Smith became reader at St. Clement Danes church near the Temple Inns of Court in 1587. The next year the bishop of London suspended him under the impression that he was not licensed, and that he had spo-ken disrespectfully of the Book of Common Prayer and not subscribed to the Articles of Religion. His reply, however, showed that he had no wish to do any of those things, and he was restored.[55] Indeed, in *God's Arrow Against Atheism and Irreligion*, he says that church people should not argue about such perennial Puritan concerns as set prayers, saints' days, fasting, and vestments:

> Inasmuch therefore as we have the preaching of God's holy word, and the right administration of the sacraments, which be the essential marks of the true church, none ought to forsake our church for any other defect, corruption, or imperfection.[56]

He opposed any sort of Separatism, although he believed in working within the Church of England to reform it in some ceremonial matters. Horton Davies has said that the difference between Smith's view of the importance of preaching and Hooker's view was that Smith believed it was "the one thing necessary," while Hooker taught that the gospel was equally conveyed in the reading of the lectionary in church and in the dramatic enactments of the gospel in baptism and the Eucharist.[57]

Certainly Smith's preaching is not preoccupied with controversial theological issues. Rather, his concern is greater for issues of morality, making him sound more like the popular image of a Puritan in the following catalog than many who had better claims to the title:

> What! Do you think that God doth not remember our sins, which we do not regard; for while we sin, the score runs on, and the judge setteth down all in the table of remembrance, and his scroll reacheth up to heaven.
>
> Item, for lending to usury; item, for racking of rents; item, for deceiving thy brethren; item, for starching thy ruffs; item, for curling thy hair; item, for painting thy face; item, for selling of benefices; item, for starving of souls; item, for playing at cards; item, for sleeping in church; item, for profaning the Sabbath day; with a number more hath God to call account, for every one must answer for himself: the fornicator for taking filthy pleasure; O son, remember thou hast taken thy pleasure, take thy punishments; the careless prelate for murdering so many thousand souls; the landlord, for getting money from his poor tenants by racking of his rents.[58]

This list, however, which seems to place on a par breaches of traditional Christian morality, social evils, ecclesiastical conditions that horrified Puritans, and petty vanities, can give an impression of small-mindedness that was by no means typical of Smith. He was concerned with the temptations of his flock. Their station in life can be inferred from the occupations of those who petitioned that Smith be made the incumbent of the parish where he was the reader: the wardens were a grocer and a locksmith, and their cosigners included "ordinary tradesmen, as smiths, tailors, saddlers, hosiers, haberdashers, glaziers, cutlers, and such like." For them, what he said was as practical as it was sweetly reasonable. But he could also keep them alert to the larger issues of society.[59] In its social witness, his sermon on poverty called "The Poor Man's Tears" compares favorably not only with the sermons of Latimer but with the best sermons of today's social prophets.

The style of Smith's preaching eludes easy categorization. Davies, drawing on the categories of Blench, says that Smith used the fully ornate style,[60] but Blench himself invents a category between the plain and the ornate for him:

> The truth surely lies between these extremes, for although his diction is simple, and often his use of the schemata[61] is, as Herr says, "stolid," nevertheless his sermons are given rich and varied colour by very frequent masterly similes, which are often combined in a series, each member of which throws some illumination on the subject.[62]

In speaking of the clarity of Smith's preaching, his nineteenth-century editor says:

> So free are (his sermons) from the affectations that disfigure most of the pulpit productions of the time, that there is scarcely an expression that would require alteration in order to adapt them to the tastes of the present day. They probably do not contain a dozen words that would not be understood by an ordinary modern audience.[63]

In much the same tone, John Lievsay speaks of Smith as a "bright rift in the fog of dullness" of Elizabethan sermons in general.[64] No wonder, then, that Fuller tells us:

> His church was so crowded with auditors, that persons of good quality brought their own pews with them, I mean their legs, to stand thereupon in the alleys.[65]

A look at the popularity Smith acquired, not only with his contemporaries but with succeeding generations as well, brings amazement that this is a response to the ministry of a man who died in his early thirties, a ministry that appears to have lasted only about four years and from which there remain less than sixty sermons.

The Judicious Hooker

The final example of Tudor preaching is very different from the others. Richard Hooker, who was born about the time Latimer died and who himself died three years before Elizabeth, comes nearer to being its definitive theologian than anyone else the Church of England has produced, with his *Treatise on the Laws of Ecclesiastical Polity* being the nearest approximation to an Anglican summa. Nor is he well known or attested as a preacher. Only ten of his sermons survive, and three of those were regarded as the work of Archbishop Ussher until the latest publication of his *Tractates and Sermons.*[66]

These homiletical works owe their survival to being relevant to the controversies of the period. The big issue of the time was the Church of Rome because in 1570 Pope Pius V had excommunicated Queen Elizabeth, declared that she was no longer queen, and forbade Roman Catholic English to obey her "orders, mandates, and laws" upon pain of excommunication themselves. The Spanish Armada and the various plots that centered around Mary Queen of Scots show that the dangers of revolt and regicide were not paranoid fancies. The "Two Sermons Upon S. Jude's Epistle" represent some of Hooker's polemic against Rome; it is, of course, far more measured and theological than most of what was going around at the time. Indeed, the long "Learned Discourse on Justification" (a tractate in the sense defined above) is largely an argument that not only pre-Reformation English forebears but even cardinals and popes were not necessarily excluded from salvation.

A reaction to this liberalism prompted the controversy that eventuated in the writing of the *Ecclesiastical Polity.* Hooker's most prestigious appointment was to be as master of the Temple, the minister in charge of the old Norman round church of the Knights Templar in London that became a parish church when the Templar property was taken over by the Inns of Court of the Inner and Middle Temple. That position, however, had its built-in difficulties, since there was another cleric at the Temple in the position of reader who was employed to preach in the afternoon. The reader in question was Walter Travers, a Presbyterian minister of strict Calvinist persuasion who had been disappointed in not being made master himself. To some extent Travers enjoyed the support of the lawyers who were the parishioners of the Temple, because many of their profession were Puritans.[67] At any rate, Travers began to use the time of his sermons in the afternoon to refute what Hooker had preached in the morning, especially his point that "the Church of Rome might be considered a part of Christ's church whose members might be saved in spite of erroneous official teaching."[68] Thus the situation became what was classically defined by Thomas Fuller as Canterbury speaking in the morning and pure Geneva in the afternoon.

Travers's behavior is not irrelevant to Hooker's "Learned Sermon on the Nature of Pride." "A Remedie Against Sorrow and Fear" is a sermon Hooker preached at the funeral of an otherwise unidentified "virtuous gentlewoman." The "Sermon Found in the Study of Bishop [Lancelot] Andrewes" is, appropriately enough, about prayer. The three sermon fragments previously attributed to Ussher do not specify the occasion of their delivery, but one may have been for Holy Week and another for Easter.

Thomas Fuller, who heard both Hooker and Travers, gives an unencouraging report of the former's delivery:

> His voice was low, stature little, gesture none at all, standing stone-still in the Pulpit.... Where his eye was left fixed at the beginning, it was found fixed at the end of his Sermon.[69]

Yet the sermons were masterfully crafted. Hooker had full knowledge of rhetorical theory, and his sermons followed the pattern of a classical oration. His sentences had the periodic structure of Latin prose, so his style has been called "Ciceronian," but his vocabulary was colloquial, candid, and intimate.[70] His range of biblical citation and allusion was enormous. He was concerned with the "on-going struggle within the individual believer's soul,"[71] and his theme was God's infinite love and mercy. As a final assessment, P. E. Forte's judgment has much to recommend it:

> If he rarely matches the eloquence of Donne or Andrewes or Taylor, he lacks their mannerisms as well, so that his sermons are among the least self-conscious and declamatory of the period.... Quiet, observant, concerned, he is the most reflective of the great English preachers.[72]

The Metaphysicals

Queen Elizabeth died and was succeeded by James I in 1603, thus ending the Tudor period and inaugurating the Stuart barely into the new century. "The seventeenth century in England was *par excellence* an age of sermons,"[73] but they were not all of a single type. Rather, preaching during this period suffered extraordinary shifts in taste. At the beginning of the century, the vogue was for pyrotechnic displays of amazing virtuosity; it was a time when some of England's best poets were also preachers. The middle of the century reflected the triumph of the Puritans in first the Presbyterian and then the Independent phases of the Commonwealth. Then the century ended with a reaction against theological partisanship in which lucid moral essays became more fashionable in pulpits that were themselves very fashionable. By that time, the period of Renaissance and Reformation had ended and the early modern era had begun.

The style of preaching popular at the beginning of the century when Elizabeth's long reign was ending and that of James I beginning is

referred to variously as being "witty" or "metaphysical." The understanding of "wit" in this context is characteristic of that period rather
than the current. Instead of designating either intelligence or humor *as
such,* it had the ninth meaning assigned to the word in *Webster's:* "felic-
itous perception or expression of associations between ideas or words
not usually connected, such as produce an amusing surprise."[74] Mitchell
expresses the idea of wit in preaching as "the facility in discovering
resemblances between the most disparate things, especially where one of
these happened to be of a religious character."[75] That is to say, wit is the
ability to coin *conceits* in the literary sense of the word.[76]

Such preaching could sound supercilious unless one remembers the
paradoxical nature of the Christian religion in which the most divine
things are communicated through the most mundane media and human
values are turned upside down. In the perspective of that memory, however, a peculiar appropriateness and even holiness can be imagined for
such preaching.

The description of this style of preaching as "metaphysical" is derived
from its association with the poetry that had been given this designation
by Samuel Johnson, partially out of recognition that one of the metaphysical poets, John Donne, became one of the most respected witty
preachers. The near equivalence of the two terms can be seen in
Johnson's complaint that by the metaphysical poets "the most heteroge-
neous ideas are yoked by violence together."[77]

There is more to the definition than that, though. There is an element
of the source of the ideas. Mitchell says:

> When . . . we speak of preaching as "metaphysical" we mean that it
> is quaint and fantastic, not because it employs unusual or whimsical
> expressions or images, but that when it does employ such it derives
> them from a background of remote learning, and adapts them to use by
> a curious transmutation effected by means of the peculiar temperament
> or deliberate endeavor of the preacher.[78]

The association of witty preaching with metaphysical poetry suggests
what is indeed true, that the homiletical phenomenon does not represent
a rarified taste confined to the pulpit, but is instead indicative of a characteristic of English and indeed European culture at the time, a fashion
in taste that came and went.

That, in turn, suggests another truth, that the metaphysical style was
not confined to one ecclesiastical party. It is the case, however, that it was
more characteristic of Anglo-Catholics than of any other group.[79] These

English theologians had reached a stage in their understanding of church reform and renewal in which they no longer regarded Luther and Calvin as new founding fathers. Rather, they believed the Church of England to be in continuity with the church through the ages, the Body of Christ, the Holy Catholic Church. They saw that continuity in the succession of their bishops from the apostles and in the continuation of the sacramental life of the church.

Their objection to Rome, beyond the (as they viewed them) unjust pretensions of the pope, was not that it was catholic, but rather that it was insufficiently catholic. It had made additions to the original and apostolic deposit of faith and practice. The English Reformation, therefore, had been a removal of such accretions without any jettisoning of essentials in the manner of continental Protestants. The English had been careful, as their descendants loved to say, not to throw the baby out with the bathwater. They considered their church to represent a reformed Catholicism "such as Chrysostom or Alfred would feel at home in, and David, Boniface, Chad or Anselm would not repudiate as alien."[80]

This conviction of their continuity with the church through the ages led the Anglo-Catholics to find their theological inspiration not in the continental Reformers but in the Fathers of the early church. Indeed, they did not eschew the medieval theologians either. But in returning to what they regarded as the fonts of their faith, they learned things from their reading in addition to dogmatics. They learned, for instance, a way of writing and speaking.

As noted in part 1, the patristic giants had all been trained as rhetors before they were ordained, and they did not forget the style they had learned when they became Christian authors. The Fathers who most influenced Anglo-Catholic style, such as Tertullian, represented not the balanced periods of Cicero, but the more aphoristic style of the Stoics, especially Seneca. "Senecan brevity, abruptness, and point characterize the sentences of Andrewes, and affect those of Donne."[81] And this at a time when Seneca's appeal was felt by English authors in fields other than theology.

The Anglo-Catholic metaphysical preachers acquired a number of stylistic traits from the Fathers. Basil's *isocola* and *antitheses* were effective vehicles for communicating the paradoxical gospel of the God who became a human being, the immortal God who died in behalf of mortals. Chrysostom, the "Golden-tongued," had "an oriental richness and profusion of epithets and images."[82] Ambrose's rich imagination found full play in allegorical interpretation of the Scriptures. He also introduced his seventeenth-century readers to the Cabalists and, with the aid of his contemporaries, to the natural history of Pliny and the *Physiologus,* from which so many morals could be derived. The Hermetic literature became known in a similar way. A sense of drama was acquired from the "last of the Fathers," Bernard of Clairvaux. The Anglo-Catholics shared the fashion for the use of "conceits" like those employed by the Fathers with Spanish, Italian, and French preachers. With them as well they shared a rhetorical education that taught them to keep commonplace books in which they could note for future use all such wonderful treasures from the Fathers. Thus imitation and quotation of the Fathers were common in the sermons of both Catholic Reform and Anglo-Catholic preachers.

Stella Praedicantium

The first and certainly one of the greatest of the Metaphysicals was Lancelot Andrewes (1555–1626),[83] who was known to his contemporaries as *stella praedicantium,* the "star of preaching," and an "Angell in the Pulpit." Born the year after his friend Hooker, he outlived him by twenty-six years. A London native and the son of a successful mariner who became a master of Trinity House, he was sent to Cooper's Free School and the Merchant Taylors' School. He achieved such a proficiency in Latin, Greek, and Hebrew by the age of sixteen that he became one of the first to receive a Greek scholarship to Pembroke College, Cambridge. There he continued to make rapid progress, receiving his B.A. in 1575. Elected a fellow of his college, he stayed on to receive his B.D. in 1585, and his D.D. around 1588.[84]

A naturally studious youth who allowed himself no recreation beyond walks on which he studied nature,[85] he became one of the most learned men in England. When he was appointed catechist of his college about the time he received his M.A., he quickly attracted a wide following both within and beyond the university. He then became Pembroke's treasurer and showed himself to be an effective administrator.

His fame had already begun to spread beyond Cambridge, and in 1586 he was appointed as one of the chaplains of both the queen and the archbishop of Canterbury, John Whitgift. Three years later he became vicar of St. Giles in the new Cripplegate section of London and also a prebendary (canon) of St. Paul's Cathedral. He was also made master of his Cambridge college at about this time.

Honors and duties were heaped upon him, and he was humble about the one and conscientious about the other. For instance, after his death a manual was published on ministering to the sick that he had drawn up for his pastoral work at St. Giles. Further, his stall at St. Paul's had been traditionally connected with hearing confessions, a responsibility he reinstituted. In 1601 he became dean of Westminster Abbey; in addition to his other activities in connection with the position, he became a beloved teacher of the boys at Westminster School.

King James I was, whatever his other shortcomings, well trained in theology. He took an immediate liking to Andrewes, appointing him to such duties as meeting with the Puritans at the Hampton Court Conference, heading the London group of translators of the Authorized Version of the Bible,[86] and engaging in controversy with Cardinal Bellarmine. Under this royal patronage, Andrewes became successively bishop of Chichester (1605), Ely (1609), and Winchester (1618). His presence at court was highly valued; he was made a privy councilor of England in 1616 and of Scotland the next year. He was appointed dean of the Chapel Royal, and, among other assignments in connection with the royal family, carried the paten in the coronation procession of Charles I in 1626. He died the same year.

He never sought the honors that came to him in such abundance; his first sense of duty was always to God. He was reputed to have spent five hours a day in prayer, a statement that is rendered credible by the manual of prayers he compiled for his own use, his *Preces Privatae*, first published in 1675 and in print to this day.[87]

It was, however, for his preaching that Andrewes was best known. Shortly after his death, King Charles I ordered that his sermon manuscripts be collected and published. Those given the task found ninety-six sermons in the form in which the bishop had delivered them. Most of them had been preached in court: seventeen for Christmas, eight on prayer and fasting for Ash Wednesday, six for other days in Lent, three for Good Friday, eighteen for Easter, fifteen for Whitsunday (Pentecost), and eighteen in thanksgiving for deliverance from conspiracies (eight for the Gowries and ten for the Gunpowder Plot).[88] There is one that was preached at St. Mary's hospital and two at St. Giles, six delivered at court on less solemn days in the Christian year, and three more on state occasions. In addition to his XCVI Sermons there remain his Cambridge catechetical sermons, in which there are nineteen on prayer (especially the Lord's Prayer) and seven on Christ's temptation in the wilderness. Of the court sermons it can be said that those before Elizabeth were for penitential seasons, while, for most of the years of his reign, James I heard Andrewes preach on Christmas, Easter, and Whitsunday, the great feasts of the year.

While some general characteristics of metaphysical preaching have been indicated above, a sample of the sort of thing Andrewes did could be a helpful preface to listing the attributes of his preaching. The passage chosen is from "Sermon IX of the Nativity," on the text: "Behold a virgin shall conceive and bear a Son and she shall call his name Immanuel":

And now, to look into the name. It is compounded, and to be taken in pieces. First, into *Immanu* and *El*; of which, *El* the latter is the more principal by far; for *El* is God. Now, for any thing yet said in *concipiet* and *pariet*, all is but man with us; not "God with us" till now. By the name we take our first notice that this Child is God. And this is a great addition, and here, lo, is the wonder. For, as for any child of a woman to "eat butter with honey," (Isa. vii.15), the words that next follow, where is the *Ecce*? but for *El*, for God to do it—that is worth an *Ecce* indeed.

El is God; and not God every way, but as the force of the word is, God in His full strength and virtue; God *cum plentudine potestatis* as we say, "with all that ever He can do"; and that is enough I am sure.

For the other, *Immanu*; though *El* be the more principal, yet I cannot tell whether it or *Immanu* do more concern us. For as in *El* is might, so in *Immanu* is our right to his might, and to all He hath or is worth. By that word we hold, therefore we to lay hold of it. The very standing of it thus before, thus in the first place, toucheth us somewhat. The first thing ever that we look for is *nos, nobis,* and *noster*, the possessives; for they do *mittere in possessionem*, "put us in possession." We look for it first, and lo, it stands here first; *nobiscum* first, and then *Deus* after.

I shall not need to tell you that in *nobiscum* there is *mecum*; in *nobiscum* for us all a *mecum* for every one of us. Out of this generality of "with us," in gross, may every one deduce his own particular—with me, and me, and me. For all put together make but *nobiscum*.

The Wise Men out of Immanuel, that is *nobiscum Deus*, doth deduce Ithiel (Prov. xxx.1), that is *mecum Deus*, "God with me"—his own private interest. And St. Paul when he had said to the Ephesians of Christ, "Who loved us, and gave Himself for us," (Eph. v. 2). might with good right say to the Galatians, "Who loved me and gave Himself for me." (Gal. ii. 20).

This *Immanu* is a compound again; we may take it in sunder into *nobis* and *cum*; and so then have we three pieces. 1. *El*, the mighty God; 2. and *anu*, we, poor we,—poor indeed if we have all the world beside if we do not have Him to be with us; 3. and *Im*, which is *cum*, and that *cum* in the midst between *nobis* and *Deus*, God and us—to couple God and us; thereby to convey the things of the one to the other. Ours to God; alas, they be not worth the speaking of. Chiefly, then, to convey to us the things of God. For that is worth the while; they are indeed worth the conveying.

This *cum* we shall never conceive to purpose, but *carendo*;[89] the value of "with" no way so well as by without, by stripping of *cum* from *nobis*. And so let *nobis*, "us," stand by ourselves without Him, to see what our case is but for this Immanuel; what, if this virgin's Child had not this day been born us: *nobiscum* after will be the better esteemed. For if this Child be "Immanuel, God with us," then without this Child, this Immanuel, we be without God. "Without Him in this world," (Eph. ii. 12), saith the Apostle; and if without Him in this, without Him in the next; and if without Him there—if it be not *Immanu-el*, it will be *Immanu-hell*; and that and no other place will fall, I fear me, to our share. Without Him, this we are. What with Him? Why, if we have Him, and God by Him, we need no more; *Immanu-el* and *Immanu-all*. All that we can desire is for us to be with Him, with God, and He to be with us; and we from Him, or He from us, never to be parted. We were with Him once before, and we were well; and when we left Him, and He no longer "with us," then began all our misery. Whensoever we go from Him, so shall we be in evil case, and never be well till we be back with Him again.

Then, if this be our case that we cannot be without Him, no remedy then but to get a *cum* by whose means *nobis* and *Deus* may come together again. And Christ is that *Cum* to bring it to pass. The parties are God and we; and now this day He is both. God before eternally, and now to-day Man; and so both, and takes hold of both, and brings both together again. For two natures here are in Him. If conceived and born of a woman, then a man; if God with us, then God. So Esay offered his "sign from the height above, or from the depth beneath," (Isa. vii. 11); here it is. "From above," *El*; "from beneath," *anu*; one of us now. And so, His sign from both. And both these natures in the unity of one Person, called by one name, even this name Immanuel.[90]

The first and most obvious comment to make is that the text from which Andrewes preaches is the Latin Vulgate, although he always translates the Latin (or other foreign language) after he quotes it. Anyone at the court of James I could have been expected to know the Latin, but he takes no chance of being misunderstood. The second point to be made, almost as obvious as the first, was stated by the one who did more than anyone else to call Andrewes to modern attention, T. S. Eliot:

> Andrewes takes a word and derives the world from it; squeezing and squeezing the word until it yields a full juice of meaning which we should never have supposed any word to possess.[91]

Other characteristics of Andrewes's preaching come out in the following passage from Mitchell, which characterizes this preaching so concisely that it deserves extended quotation:

It was not . . . so much the material as the use to which the material was put that distinguished the "metaphysical" preacher; the greater ingenuity with which he adapted his examples, the more unexpected parallels which he produced, and the more subtle, psychological, and learned images which he employed—these were the characteristic traits. Not mere quotation, but quotation leading up to an unexpected "point,"[92] and a "point," which, while it was verbal, conveyed something of much greater import; not punning and quibbling merely for their own sakes, but because amid the jingle of human phrases might be caught the accents of a divine message—these were the things that counted.[93]

In spite of his appreciation for Andrewes, Mitchell does fault him for what he calls the jerkiness or abruptness of his style, "the inability to achieve the *lexis eironmene* on which literary grace so largely depends."[94] This criticism, however, needs to be understood in the perspective of Mitchell's concern with sermons as literature, as representing a written rather than an oral medium. From this perspective, he finds the sermons of John Donne more satisfactory. Yet T. S. Eliot, a literary critic at least as perceptive as Mitchell, has found the advantage the other way in comparing the sermons of the two.[95]

In addition to Andrewes and Donne, many other early seventeenth-century preachers belonged to the metaphysical school. Among them Mitchell discusses the pulpit work of Ralph Brownrig, John Hacket, Richard Corbet, Henry King, Thomas Playfere, John Cosin, and Mark Frank.[96] Before leaving this school, however, it is necessary to pay attention to the rapid loss of respect that it suffered. It is represented in the attitudes of George Bull, who became bishop of St. David's in 1705. Although his theological position was very close to that of the earlier Anglo-Catholics, his former curate wrote of him:

He abhorred Affectations of Wit, Trains of fulsom Metaphors, and nice Words wrought up with tuneful, pointed Sentences, without any substantial Meaning at the Bottom of them. He looked upon Sermons consisting of these Ingredients . . . as inconsistent with the Dignity of serious and sacred Things, and as an Indication of a weak Judgment.[97]

A similar point of view was expressed by a Scottish lord who heard Andrewes preach at Holyrood during the royal visit of 1617: "He rather plays with his text than preaches on it."[98] The frequent imputation was that the metaphysical preachers were merely showing off.

To anyone who does not recognize the fundamental seriousness of the sermons of Andrewes, about the only thing that can be said is to call attention to the sermon that Archbishop William Laud preached from the scaffold on Tower Hill before he was beheaded by the Roundheads on January 10, 1645. It begins this way:

Good People,
You'l pardon my old Memory, and upon so sad occasions as I am come to this place, to make use of my Papers, I dare not trust my self otherwise. This is a very uncomfortable place to Preach in, and yet I shall begin with a Text of Scripture, in the twelfth of the Hebrews,
Let us run with patience that race that is set before us, looking unto Jesus the author and finisher of our faith, who for the joy that was set before him, endured the Crosse, despising the shame, and is set downe at the right hand of the Throne of God.
I have been long in my race, and how I have looked unto Jesus the Author and finisher of my Faith, is best known to him: I am now come to the end of my race, and here I finde the Crosse, a death of shame, but the shame must be despised, or there is no coming to the right hand of God; Jesus despis'd the shame for me, and God forbid but I should despise the shame for him; I am going apace, as you see, towards the Red-sea, and my feet are upon the very brinks of it, an Argument, I hope, that God is bringing me to the Land of Promise, for that was the way by which of old he led his people; But before they came to the Sea, he instituted a Passeover for them, a Lamb it was, but it was to bee eaten with very soure Herbs, as in the Twelfth of *Exodus.*
I shall obey, and labour to digest the sowre Herbs, as well as the Lamb, and I shall remember that it is the Lords Passeover; I shall not think of the Herbs, nor be angry with the hands which gathered them, but look up only to him who instituted the one, and governeth the other: For men can have no more powre over me, then that which is given them from above; I am not in love with this passage through the red Sea, for I have the weaknesse and infirmity of flesh and blood in me, and I have prayed as my Saviour taught me, and exampled me, *Vt transiret calix ista,*
That this Cup of red Wine might passe away from me, but since it is not that my will may, his will be done; and I shall most willingly drink of this Cup as deep as he pleases, and enter into this Sea, ay and passe through it, in the way that he shall be pleased to leade me.[99]

To imagine that such a witness of faith and demonstration of grace is less than serious requires an uncommon lack of imagination.[100] Although the metaphysical style of preaching, like all other homiletical styles, had its imitators who aped the conventions without aspiring to its substance, later generations' criticism of its true practitioners betrays an extraordinary capacity to miss the point.[101] But perhaps such a lack of imagination was epidemic at the time. T. S. Eliot suggests that "in the seventeenth century a dissociation of sensibility set in, from which we have never recovered."[102] This dissociation is a separation of thought from experience. Perhaps it was necessary for the development of scientific thought and modernism in general, but a price was paid: the loss of the ability of human beings to respond to their world as total persons whose thoughts are felt.

These examples of Tudor and Stuart preaching show that after a beginning in the reign of Edward VI, when the lack of trained preachers required sermons that could be read to congregations, the cause of preaching received considerable impetus. It was certainly supported by Latimer, the colloquial preacher of Reform. By the time of Elizabeth, Puritans were demanding extra preaching through the ministry of readers, and preaching of the clarity and grace of Henry Smith's could acquire an enormous following. Even a philosophical theologian like Hooker, with no skill in delivery, could attract an audience by the profundity of his thought. At the end of the Tudor period and the beginning of the Stuart, some of the greatest theologians, spiritual writers, and poets in the history of England were preaching witty sermons in the metaphysical style. No wonder that

> preaching played a more important role in the life of the times than ever before or since. Not only did the pulpit outdraw bearbaiting and morris dancing, but even in sophisticated London the popular preachers attracted larger audiences week after week than Shakespeare and Jonson in their prime.[103]

By any standard, it must be admitted that the goals of the English Erasmians were met beyond anything they could have imagined.

FOR FURTHER READING

Blench, J. W. *Preaching in England in the Late Fifteenth and Sixteenth Centuries: A Study of English Sermons 1450–c.1600.* Oxford: Basil Blackwell; New York: Barnes & Noble, 1964.

Certain Sermons, or Homilies, appoynted by the Kynges Maiestie, to be declared and redde, by all Persones, Uicars, or Curates euery Sonday in their Churches, where they haue Cure. London: R. Grafton, 1547.

Hooker, Richard. *Tractates and Sermons.* Edited by W. Speed Hill, general; Laetitia Yeandle, text; and Egil Grislis, commentary. Vol. 5 of *Folger Library Edition of the Works of Richard Hooker.* Cambridge: Belknap Press of Harvard University Press, 1990.

Lancelot Andrewes: Sermons. Selected and edited with introduction by G. M. Story. Oxford: Clarendon, 1967.

Selected Sermons of Hugh Latimer. Edited by Allan G. Chester. Folger Documents of Tudor and Stuart Civilization. Charlottesville, Va.: University of Virginia Press for the Folger Shakespeare Library, 1968.

Shuger, Debora K. *Sacred Rhetoric: The Christian Grand Style in the English Renaissance.* Princeton: Princeton University Press, 1988.

The Works of Henry Smith, Including Sermons, Treatises, Prayers, and Poems. Edited by Thomas Smith. Nichol's Series of Standard Divines: Puritan Period, vols. 39, 40. Edinburgh: James Nichol; London: James Nisbet and Co.; Dublin: G. Herbert, 1866.

The Works of William Perkins. Edited and introduction by Ian Breward. The Courtenay Library of Reformation Classics, vol. 3. Appleford, Abingdon, and Berkshire: Sutton Courtenay, 1970.

Notes

1. F. M. Powicke, *The Reformation in England* (London: Oxford University Press, 1941), 1.

2. The principle that the religion of the sovereign determines that of the realm.

3. The Puritans were not uniformly a group of Presbyterian separatists but included as well many who were loyal to the Church of England and who could live comfortably with episcopacy. See Patrick Collinson, *The Religion of Protestants: The Church in English Society 1559–1625* (Oxford: Clarendon, 1982), 1-38.

4. For a concise history of the Church of England, see William P. Haugaard, "From the Reformation to the Eighteenth Century," and Perry Butler, "From the Eighteenth Century to the Present Day" in *The Study of Anglicanism,* ed. John Booty and Stephen Sykes (London: SPCK; Philadelphia: Fortress, 1988), 3-47.

5. J. W. Blench, *Preaching in England in the Late Fifteenth and Sixteenth Centuries: A Study of English Sermons 1450–c.1600* (Oxford: Basil Blackwell; New York: Barnes & Noble, 1964).

6. Although it was not as clear when Blench was writing as it has become recently, both the Catholic and Protestant approaches were indebted to the humanists for their biblical literalism, as the grammatical basis of Luther's exegesis indicates. See above, chapter 12.

7. Blench, *Preaching in England in the Late Fifteenth and Sixteenth Centuries,* 47.

8. "Accommodations" were analogical extensions of biblical texts that theoretically were not claimed to be explicit biblical teaching but only inferences from such teaching or illustrations employing biblical metaphors or narratives. Blench (ibid.,

39) gives an excellent quotation from Tyndale explaining this procedure, although the word *accommodation* does not appear in the passage quoted.

9. Ibid., 71-72.

10. Ibid., 97.

11. Ibid., 88. The *partes* of the classical oration adapted to the sermon form were spelled out in an English translation of a homiletics textbook by Hyperius of Marburg as: (A) "Reding of the sacred scripture," (B) "Inuocation," (C) "Exordium," (D) "Proposition or division," (E) "Confirmation," (F) "Confutation," and (G) "Conclusion" (cited, ibid., 102). As Blench points out, "The last five are the stock parts of the classical oration."

12. Ibid., 101-2. Perhaps one reason for the short shrift given this method of sermon construction is that Blench found the form "unbearably tedious to the modern reader after a few pages."

13. Ibid., 113.

14. Ibid.

15. Ibid., 3. The G. L. Hendrickson article, "The Origin and Meaning of the Ancient Characters of Style," appeared in a journal identified by Shuger as *AJP* XXVI (1905), 249-90.

16. This misunderstanding of style is similar to the way the word *rhetoric* is often used pejoratively today to refer to only flowery or manipulative speech, as though legitimate persuasion were somehow unrhetorical.

17. Debora K. Shuger, *Sacred Rhetoric: The Christian Grand Style in the English Renaissance* (Princeton: Princeton University Press, 1988).

18. What the comic-strip character Pogo once described as "the twenty-four karat bamboozle."

19. Shuger, *Sacred Rhetoric*, 6.

20. That is, "parsons," from the Latin *persona*, the person who represents a parish church in its corporate and ecclesiastical capacities, which is to say, the priest who has been appointed to the benefice.

21. *Certain Sermons, or Homilies, appoynted by the Kynges Maiestie, to be declared and redde, by all Persones, Uicars, or Curates euery Sonday in their Churches, where they haue Cure* (London: R. Grafton, 1547).

22. Horton Davies, *From Cranmer to Hooker, 1534–1603*, vol. 1 of *Worship and Theology in England* (Princeton: Princeton University Press, 1970), 229, citing J. T. Tomlinson, *The Prayer Book, Articles, and Homilies*, an 1897 publication that I have not seen. Most of the same attributions are given in the articles on "Homilies, the Books of" in *ODCC*. Perhaps some of these attributions will have to be revised in the light of John N. Wall Jr.'s unpublished 1973 Harvard Ph.D. dissertation, "The Vision of a Christian Commonwealth in the Book of Homilies of 1547." A "Second Book" of twenty-one more homilies, most written by John Jewel, was issued under Elizabeth I around 1571.

23. "Godly and Fruitful Lessons: The English Bible, Erasmus' *Paraphrases*, and the *Book of Homilies*," in *The Godly Kingdom of Tudor England: Great Books of the English Reformation*, ed. John E. Booty (Wilton, Conn.: Morehouse-Barlow, 1981), 47-135.

24. Ibid., 56, referring to Marjorie O'Rourke Boyle, *Erasmus on Language and Method in Theology* (Toronto: University of Toronto Press, 1977), 53.

25. The *Paraphrases.*

26. Ibid., 57.

27. Ibid., 93.

28. Millar Maclure, *The Paul's Cross Sermons, 1534–1642,* University of Toronto Department of English Studies and Texts, no. 6 (Toronto: University of Toronto Press, 1958), 54. This study gives an account of a remarkable series of sermons preached outside St. Paul's Cathedral in London.

29. Davies, *From Cranmer to Hooker, 1534–1603,* 296-97. The Hooker reference is to *Ecclesiastical Polity* 5.22.

30. On the social conditions reflected in Latimer's sermons and his recommendations on what to do about them, see A. G. Dickens, *The English Reformation* (New York: Schocken Books, 1964), 151-54, and Charles Montgomery Gray, *Hugh Latimer and the Sixteenth Century: An Essay in Interpretation,* Harvard Phi Beta Kappa Prize Essays (Cambridge: Harvard University Press, 1950).

31. For Latimer's account of his conversion, see the first of his sermons on the Lord's Prayer, *The Works of Hugh Latimer, Sometime Bishop of Worcester, Martyr, 1555,* ed. for the Parker Society by George Elwes Corrie (Cambridge: The University Press, 1844), 2:334-35. For more about Bilney, see "The Seventh Sermon Before Edward VI," 2:222. Both of these sermons are included in *Selected Sermons of Hugh Latimer,* ed. Allan G. Chester, Folger Documents of Tudor and Stuart Civilization (Charlottesville: University of Virginia Press for Folger Shakespeare Library, 1968). Biographies of Latimer tend to be hagiographic, but one that is less so while still admiring is that of Allan G. Chester, *Hugh Latimer, Apostle to the English* (Philadelphia: University of Pennsylvania Press, 1954). Some critical distance is also maintained in Harold S. Darby, *Hugh Latimer* (London: Epworth, 1953). All must draw on John Foxe's *Acts and Monuments of Matters Happening in the Church* ("Foxe's Book of Martyrs"), whose account is reprinted in Latimer's *The Works of Hugh Latimer,* 1:ix-xxxi. I regret that Michael Pasquarello's University of North Carolina dissertation on the preaching of Latimer was not completed in time to influence this chapter.

32. Always, apparently, in the English humanist tradition. At any rate, he said: "I will not take upon me to defend (Luther) in all points. I will not stand to it that all that he wrote was true; I think he would not so himself: for there is no man but he may err. He came to further and further knowledge: but surely he was a goodly instrument." "Sixth Sermon Preached Before King Edward the Sixth" (Latimer, *The Works of Hugh Latimer,* 2:212).

33. John Foxe, *Acts and Monuments,* ed. R. R. Mandham and Josiah Pratt, 4th ed. rev. (London, 1875), 8:289.

34. Quoted without attribution in *The English Sermon, An Anthology,* vol. 1, ed. Martin Seymour-Smith (Cheadle and Cheshire: Carcanet, 1976), 54.

35. Charles Smyth says that Latimer was "a typically medieval preacher," in *The Art of Preaching: A Practical Survey of Preaching in the Church of England, 747–1939* (London: Society for Promoting Christian Knowledge, 1940), 107-8.

36. Blench, *Preaching in England in the Late Fifteenth and Sixteenth Centuries,* 92.

37. "Following the order of the text."

38. On at least one occasion he apologized for not preaching on either the Epistle or the Gospel appointed for the day. Latimer, "Last Sermon Preached Before King Edward the Sixth," in Chester, ed., *Selected Sermons of Hugh Latimer,* 90-113.

39. Blench, *Preaching in England in the Late Fifteenth and Sixteenth Centuries,* 142. He also gives a concise analysis of the construction of all seven sermons preached before Edward VI on pp. 92-94.

40. For the amount of his alliteration and also for the rhythm of his speech see Longinus, *On the Sublime,* trans. with commentary, James A. Arieti and John M. Crossett, Texts and Studies in Religion, vol. 21 (New York: Edwin Mellen, 1985), 207 n.

41. Horton Davies, *From Cranmer to Hooker, 1534–1603,* in *Worship and Theology,* 1:248.

42. Written originally in Latin by Perkins in 1592, *The Arte of Prophesying* was translated into English by Thomas Tuke in 1607. The edition followed here is the slightly condensed version contained in *The Works of William Perkins,* ed. and intr. Ian Breward, Courtenay Library of Reformation Classics (Appleford, Abingdon (Berkshire): Sutton Courtenay, 1970), 3:331-49, supplemented by references to the 1626–31 I. Legatt edition of *The VVorkes of . . . Mr. William Perkins.* The edition used by Breward, however, is that of John Legate and Cantrell Legge published between 1616 and 1618. Both of these seventeenth-century editions were published in London.

43. Breward, ed., *The Arte of Prophesying, Works of Perkins,* 3:349. The form of seventeenth-century spelling followed is that of Teresa Toulouse, *The Art of Prophesying: New England Sermons and the Shaping of Belief* (Athens: The University of Georgia Press, 1987), 20. A brief form of this method was imposed as a standard for clergy by *A Directory for the Public VVorship of God Throughout the Three Kingdoms of England, Scotland, and Ireland. Together with an Ordinance of Parliament for the taking away of the Book of Common-Prayer and For establishing and observing of this present Directory throughout the Kingdom of England, and Dominion of Wales* (London: Evan Tyler, Alexander Fifield, Ralph Smith, and John Field, 1644), 27-36.

44. Perry Miller, *The New England Mind: The Seventeenth Century* (Cambridge: Belknap Press of Harvard University Press, 1939), 332-33.

45. For a convenient summary of Perkins's theory of interpretation see Toulouse, *The Arte of Prophesying,* 14-23.

46. For an evaluation of the Ramist movement see Walter J. Ong, *Ramus: Method, and the Decay of Dialogue from the Art of Discourse to the Art of Reason* (Cambridge: Harvard University Press, 1958), ix. For a critique of Ong, see Brian Vickers, *In Defence of Rhetoric* (Oxford: Clarendon; New York: Oxford University Press, 1988), 475-77.

47. Bacon's objection to this procedure is that "men of this sort torture things with their laws of method, and whatever does not conveniently fall in these dichotomies, they either omit or pervert beyond nature, so that, so to speak, when the seeds and kernels of science are springing forth, they gather so many dry and empty husks." Quoted from the Spedding, Ellis, and Heath edition of Bacon's *Works,* 1:663, by Perry Miller, *The New England Mind,* 127.

48. For the psychology behind the Puritan understanding of conversion, see the chapter on "The Means of Conversion" in Perry Miller, *The New England Mind,*

280-99. For Ramist influence on Puritan homiletics, see the two following chapters on "Rhetoric" and "The Plain Style," 300-362.

49. Ibid., 338-39.

50. For the popularity of Talon among continental Reformed preachers, see Peter Bayley, *French Pulpit Oratory 1598–1650: A Study in Themes and Styles with a Descriptive Catalogue of Printed Texts* (Cambridge: Cambridge University Press, 1980), 29-31, 97.

51. From Thomas Fuller, "The Life of Mr. Henry Smith," which prefaced his 1675 edition of Smith's works and was reprinted in *The Works of Henry Smith, Including Sermons, Treatises, Prayers, and Poems,* ed. Thomas Smith, Nichol's Series of Standard Divines: Puritan Period, vols. 39, 40 (Edinburgh: James Nichol; London: James Nisbet and Co.; Dublin: G. Herbert, 1866), 1:ix. Unfortunately, the only modern book-length treatment of Smith is R. B. Jenkins, *Henry Smith: England's Silver-Tongued Preacher* (Macon, Ga.: Mercer University Press, 1983), which shows very little knowledge of Smith's period or understanding of the religious scene. For instance, the author thinks Thomas Fuller was a bishop and calls Lancelot Andrewes, Richard Hooker, and even Richard Bancroft "Puritans." He further considers Puritan "prophesyings" to have been only sermons rather than a homiletical training program (see Collinson, *The Religion of Protestants,* 129-30) and thinks the *Book of Homilies* was a set of lay-readers' sermons that were "devoid of theological controversy, political overtones, and sectarianism" (p. 26). Much shorter but far more reliable is John L. Lievsay, "'Silver-Tongued Smith,' Paragon of Elizabethan Preachers," *Huntington Library Quarterly* 11 (1947–48): 13-36. The implication of the epithet "silver-tongued" is that Smith was second in preaching ability only to John of Antioch and Constantinople, who was called *Chrysostomos,* the "Golden-tongued."

52. Thomas Smith argued that the title of "Mr. Henry Smith" under which he published his sermons would have been the equivalent at the time of "Henry Smith, M.A." *The Works of Henry Smith,* 1:xii. Jenkins, *Henry Smith,* 11, credits this opinion to Fuller rather than Thomas Smith, not having noticed, apparently, that the Fuller account ended two pages earlier.

53. Quoted in Thomas Smith, *The Works of Henry Smith,* 1:xiii.

54. Paul Seaver, *The Puritan Lectureships: The Politics of Religious Dissent, 1560–1662* (Stanford: Stanford University Press, 1970), 6. For a slightly different perspective see Collinson, *The Religion of Protestants,* 170-77.

55. No doubt the intercession of his powerful stepuncle also assisted in this restoration.

56. Thomas Smith, *The Works of Henry Smith,* 2:447.

57. *Worship and Theology,* I, 294. *Sed contra,* Smith's statement quoted above that the administration of the sacraments is one of the "essential marks of the true church."

58. Thomas Smith, *The Works of Henry Smith,* 2:328.

59. Ibid., 1:xvi.

60. Davies, *From Cranmer to Hooker, 1534–1603,* in *Worship and Theology,* 1:309. In *Like Angels from a Cloud: The English Metaphysical Preachers, 1588–1645* (San Marino, Calif.: Huntington Library, 1986), 12 *et passim,* Davies treats Smith as one of the Metaphysical preachers.

61. Blench defines schemata as "artificial word patterns" (*Preaching in England in the Late Fifteenth and Sixteenth Centuries,* 113), but the more ordinary term is "figures of speech."

62. Ibid., 184.

63. Thomas Smith, *The Works of Henry Smith*, 1:xx.

64. Lievsay, "Silver-tongued Smith," 13.

65. Thomas Smith, *The Works of Henry Smith*, 1:ix.

66. Hooker, *Tractates and Sermons*, vol. 5 in *Folger Library Edition of the Works of Richard Hooker*, gen. ed. W. Speed Hill, text, Laetitia Yeandle, comm., Egil Grislis (Cambridge: Belknap Press of Harvard University Press, 1990). See my review article in *ATR* 74 (1992), 112-16. In the usage of the time, "sermons" were delivered from notes rather than a full manuscript, "lectures" were read verbatim from the pulpit, and "tractates" were preached in church but published to be read as treatises. Yet the terms were not used with such consistency that one can infer from the title the extent to which a particular Hooker text represents what was actually said from the pulpit.

67. This affiliation reflects in part the objection of the common lawyers of the Inns of Court to their not being allowed to practice in church courts of canon law. Possibly relevant to this partisanship is the fact that Hooker argued from the principles of natural law, which is related to the Roman tradition of civil law (taught in the universities but not at the Inns of Court, where most British barristers received their legal education) while the lawyers were trained in the English tradition of common law.

68. William P. Haugaard, "The Controversy and its Dissemination," in Hooker, *Tractates and Sermons*, 268.

69. Thomas Fuller, *Church History of Britain* (London: 1655; reprint, London: Thomas Tegg, 1842), 9.7.53 (2:216).

70. Fuller says of his style: "The doctrine he delivered had nothing but itself to garnish it. His style was long and pithy, driving-on a whole flock of several clauses before he came to the close of a sentence. So that when the copiousness of his style met not with proportionable capacity in his auditors, it was unjustly censured for perplexed, tedious, and obscure" (ibid.). This Ciceronian complexity of sentence structure has caused, for example, Blench to speak of Hooker as a representative of the "fully ornate style" (Blench, *Preaching in England in the Late Fifteenth and Sixteenth Centuries*, 188), but Shuger is right in seeing that it is rather the passion of his preaching, a passion that results from the union of *magnitudo* and *praesentia* that makes his style "grand" in the sense in which the term was used in the Renaissance (Shuger, *Sacred Rhetoric*, 223). This union is further defined as that of "the greatest object (of love) with the most vivid representation" (199)—which, of course, is what the rhetorical terms *magnitudo* and *praesentia* mean.

71. P. E. Forte, "Hooker as Preacher," in Hooker, *Tractates and Sermons*, 650.

72. Ibid., 682. Cf. W. Fraser Mitchell, *English Pulpit Oratory from Andrewes to Tillotson: A Study of Its Literary Aspects* (1932; New York: Russell & Russell, 1962), 65.

73. Mitchell, *English Pulpit Oratory from Andrewes to Tillotson*, 3. This is the standard work on the period although (a) much new light has been shed in the two generations since it originally appeared, and (b) its primary concern with the literary aspects of seventeenth-century preaching means that the criteria of judgment often reflect written more than oral standards, and aesthetic more than theological.

74. *Webster's New International Dictionary (Unabridged)*, 2nd ed., s.v. "wit."

75. Mitchell, *English Pulpit Oratory*, 6.

76. "An elaborate metaphor comparing two apparently dissimilar objects or emotions, often with an effect of shock or surprise." *The Oxford Companion to English Literature*, ed. Margaret Drabble, 5th ed. (Oxford: Oxford University Press, 1985), 222.

77. Quoted without documentation in T. S. Eliot, "The Metaphysical Poets" in *Selected Prose of T. S. Eliot*, ed. with intro. Frank Kermode (New York: Harcourt Brace Jovanovich, 1975), 60. Eliot's essay was originally published in 1921.

78. Mitchell, *English Pulpit Oratory*, 7.

79. While the term "Anglo-Catholic" was coined in 1838, the essential elements of the point of view so labeled go back to the seventeenth century.

80. Douglas Macleane, *Lancelot Andrewes and the Reaction* (London: Allen, 1910), 2. Quoted in Mitchell, *English Pulpit Oratory*, 139.

81. George Williamson, *The Senecan Amble: A Study in Prose Form from Bacon to Collier* (Chicago: University of Chicago Press, 1951), 231-74. The quotation is from p. 239.

82. Mitchell, *English Pulpit Oratory*, 142. The influence of the Fathers on the Anglo-Catholics is discussed on pp. 141-48. Davies, *Like Angels from a Cloud*, 2-3, 45-98, lists eleven characteristics of metaphysical sermons: patristic learning; classical lore; citations from Greek, Latin, and occasionally Hebrew originals; illustrations from "unnatural" natural history; allegorical exegesis; plans with complex divisions and subdivisions; a Senecan and staccato style; the use of paradoxes, riddles, and emblems; fondness for speculation; and the relation of doctrinal and devotional preaching to the Christian calendar. While the way of stating them is different, this list parallels closely the traits listed in the text.

83. The main contemporary biographical sources are the sermon preached at his funeral by the bishop of London, John Buckeridge, and a life written by his secretary and friend Henry Isaacson, both of which are reprinted in the edition of his *Works*, ed. J. P. Wilson and James Bliss, 11 vols., in The Library of Anglo-Catholic Theology (Oxford: John Henry Parker, 1841–54). The locations of these are, respectively, *Works* 5:257-98, and 11:i-xxxiv. The standard modern biography is Paul A. Welsby, *Lancelot Andrewes, 1555–1626* (London: SPCK, 1958), even though his negative view of some of Andrewes's actions is not shared by all scholars. A handy introduction to the man and his preaching is Trevor A. Owen, *Lancelot Andrewes,* Twayne's English Authors Series, no. 325 (Boston: Twayne, 1981). In addition to the complete edition of the sermons in the *Works*, sermons are found in *Seventeen Sermons on the Nativity by the Right Honourable and Reverend Father in God Lancelot Andrewes,* Ancient and Modern Library of Theological Literature (London: Griffith, Farran, Okeden, and Welsh; New York: E. P. Dutton, n.d.), and *Lancelot Andrewes: Sermons,* selected and ed. with intro. by G. M. Story (Oxford: Clarendon, 1967). The latter contains twelve sermons. Marianne Dorman has edited the sermons for devotional reading in *The Liturgical Sermons of Lancelot Andrewes,* 2 vols. (Edinburgh, Cambridge, and Durham: Pentland, 1992–93), but in making the sermons more accessible to modern readers, she has rendered them useless for scholarly study.

84. In the Oxford and Cambridge of Andrewes's time, these English degrees did not have the same meaning as do current American degrees with the same names.

The M.A. represented continuing residence and study, but not a thesis, and principally signified a change of status in the university whereby one became a "senior member" and thus a member of the university's governing body. The B.D. was (and is) not pre-ordination training but represents the completion of a definitive thesis in one of the theological disciplines, being therefore closely akin to our modern Ph.D. The D.D., far from being honorary, represents further publications or a further thesis regarded as embodying original research. The number of years of residence after which one became eligible for such degrees was closely regulated. I am indebted to Prof. Peter Bayley of Cambridge for this information.

85. He is said to have spent his school holidays learning new languages with the help of a tutor.

86. Andrewes and his committee were responsible for Genesis through 2 Kings in the King James version.

87. Although Andrewes compiled his manual from a variety of biblical and liturgical sources in their original languages, the edition most often referred to is the translation with notes and introduction by F. E. Brightman (London: Methuen, 1909; reprint, Gloucester, Mass.: Peter Smith, 1983).

88. Parliament had decreed liturgically observed days of annual national thanksgiving to commemorate the escape of James from the conspiracy of the Gowrie brothers in Perth on August 5, 1600, and the frustration of the plan of Guy Fawkes to blow up the Houses of Parliament on November 5, 1605, when the king and all the lords and commons were there.

89. "By being deprived" of it.

90. *Seventeen Sermons on the Nativity by the Right Honourable and Reverend Father in God Lancelot Andrewes, Sometime Lord Bishop of Winchester. A New Edition.* The Ancient and Modern Library of Theological Literature (London: Griffith, Farrar, Okeden, and Welsh, n.d.), 140-42.

91. Eliot, "Lancelot Andrewes," in *Selected Prose of T. S. Eliot*, 184. This essay was originally published in 1926. The theology, as opposed to the rhetorical form, of Andrewes's sermons is well treated in Nicholas Lossky, *Lancelot Andrewes the Preacher (1555–1626): The Origins of the Mystical Theology of the Church of England*, trans. Andrew Louth (Oxford: Clarendon, 1991). Not as sympathetic to the man or his thought is Maurice F. Reidy, *Bishop Lancelot Andrewes, Jacobean Court Preacher: A Study of Early Seventeenth-Century Religious Thought* (Chicago: Loyola University Press, 1955).

92. "Point" is a key term in the vocabulary about witty preaching, so much so that the style is also called "pointed." It means that the "wit" is used to enhance meaning rather than as a mere ornament.

93. Mitchell, *English Pulpit Oratory*, 149. A more nuanced analysis of the way Andrewes achieved his effects that employs the techniques of modern linguistics appears in Joseph C. Beaver, "A Study of the Sermon Styles of Lancelot Andrewes and John Donne" (unpublished M.T.S. thesis, Seabury-Western Theological Seminary, 1986), 8-15.

94. Mitchell, *English Pulpit Oratory*, 163. Mitchell seems to have misunderstood rhetorical terminology here. This "run-on" or "strung-out" continuous style, far from being the basis of good writing, is contrasted unfavorably with the periodic

style by Aristotle in *Rhetoric* 3.9.1 (1409a). And what Mitchell calls jerkiness or abruptness is simply the Senecan style taken into English.

95. Eliot, "Lancelot Andrewes," 181-88.

96. Mitchell, *English Pulpit Oratory,* 163-94. In *Like Angels from a Cloud,* Davies discusses many more—more than forty.

97. Quoted, Mitchell, *English Pulpit Oratory,* 120-21, from William Lupton as cited in Robert Nelson, *The Life of Dr. George Bull* (London: 1713).

98. Ibid., 161.

99. Reprinted, *In God's Name: Examples of Preaching in England from the Act of Supremacy to the Act of Uniformity, 1534–1662,* chosen and ed. with intro. and annotations by John Chandos (Indianapolis and New York: Bobbs-Merrill, 1971), 415-16.

100. The judgment required in the case of Laud's sermons is not unlike that expected in a cartoon that appeared in the *New Yorker* a number of years ago. Two men were depicted walking on a beach. From the sea they could hear someone shouting, *"Au secours! Sauvez moi!"* In the caption one man observed to the other: "Either he's French or the worst snob I ever saw."

101. See also Davies, *Worship and Theology in England,* 2:142-54.

102. Eliot, "The Metaphysical Poets" in *Selected Prose of T. S. Eliot,* 64.

103. Seaver, *The Puritan Lectureships,* 5. See also the chapter on "The Vogue of the Sermon" in Alan Fager Herr's dissertation, *The Elizabethan Sermon: A Survey and Bibliography* (Philadelphia: University of Pennsylvania, 1940), 11-29.

PART IV

THE MODERN ERA: FROM THE RESTORATION TO WORLD WAR I

CHAPTER 16

THE DAWN OF MODERNITY (A)

THE RESTORATION AND THE AGE OF REASON

There are a few moments in history in which it is possible to discern a shift in consciousness, a point in time when it seems that the whole world has suddenly awakened seeing things in a different way. One such moment occurred in Europe in the late-seventeenth century. That moment can be characterized in a number of ways. One is in terms of the aftermath of the religious wars that followed the Reformation, wars to determine not only whether a particular area would remain under the spiritual jurisdiction of the pope or be given over to the teachings of one of the Reformers, but also to see which of competing versions of Protestantism would prevail. At the end of these wars, the world was sick of bloodshed and devastation and would have been willing to live under any religious system or none, rather than continue what appeared in retrospect to have been a war over iotas.

Then, too, this was the age of Francis Bacon and Isaac Newton, a time when the scientific method was being used for the first time to investigate nature and was producing extraordinary results. It was also the time when philosophy ceased to presuppose revelation and began to depend on human reason alone, the time of Spinoza, Descartes, and Locke. And, finally, this was a time when the interests of the mercantile classes began to take priority over those of the nobility and royalty. The christocentric culture that had begun with the conversion of Constantine had begun visibly to disintegrate.

In Great Britain, when Richard Cromwell proved in 1660 to be lacking in his father's great ability, Presbyterians joined with Royalists to recall Charles II to the throne. Although Charles himself had little interest in religion, under him the Royalists succeeded in excluding Puritans and Independents from the established church. Thus, for the first time, one can speak of the Church of England as Anglican (although the term is of later coinage) and note that there were dissenting churches in the realm, the Presbyterians and Congregationalists. Charles's brother, James II, who succeeded him, was unlike him in that he had a great deal of religious commitment—and it was all Roman Catholic. When the "Glorious Revolution" against him in 1688 brought his daughter Mary to the throne with her husband, William of Orange, a leader of the Dutch Protestants, it became inevitable that dissent should be tolerated. For the first time it was recognized in England that the country could be politically united and yet religiously divided.

HOMILETICAL THEORY

A New Taste in Preaching

Inevitably, this shift in consciousness that was the dawn of modernity came to be reflected in preaching. It expressed itself as a growing distaste for the styles of either Anglo-Catholics like Andrewes or Puritans following the rules of Perkins. Originally, the basis for this change of taste was expressed exclusively in terms of homiletical and rhetorical values without reference to the cultural changes that occasioned the shift.

One of the first to articulate this dissatisfaction with former styles was Robert South (1634–1716), a staunch Anglican who nevertheless seemed to say to both parties from earlier in the century, "A plague on both your houses." The Anglo-Catholics he designated as "such as disparage, and detract from the Grandeur of the Gospel, by a puerile and indecent Levity" and the Puritans as "such as depreciate and (as much as in them lies) debase the same, by a coarse, careless, rude and insipid Way of handling the great and invaluable Truths in it."[1]

Since the canons of taste enunciated by South are, on the one hand,

392

such a reversal of the standards that prevailed earlier in the century, and yet are, on the other hand, so typical of the period that was beginning, there is no better way to state the objections to former tastes more economically than to quote South at length. Of the Anglo-Catholics with whom he shared so many theological positions, he says:

> All vain, luxuriant Allegories, rhiming *Cadences* of similary Words, are such pitiful Embellishments of Speech, as serve for nothing, but to embase Divinity; and the Use of them, but like the Plaistering of Marble, or the Painting of Gold, the Glory of which is to be seen, and to shine by no other Lustre but their own. What *Qunitilian* most discreetly says of *Seneca's* handling Philosophy, that he did *rerum pondera minutissimis sententiis frangere,* break, and (as it were) emasculate the Weight of his Subject by little affected Sentences, the same may with much more Reason be applyed to the Practice of those, who detract from the Excellency of Things Sacred by a comical Lightness of Expression: As when their Prayers shall be set out in such a Dress, as if they did not supplicate, but compliment Almighty God, and their Sermons so garnished with Quibbles and Trifles, as if they played with Truth and Immortality; and neither believed these Things themselves, nor were willing that others should. . . . And as this can by no means be accounted Divinity, so neither indeed can it pass for Wit; which yet such chiefly seem to affect in such Performances. . . . Such are wholly mistaken in the Nature of *Wit:* For *true Wit* is a severe and manly Thing. Wit in Divinity is nothing else, but Sacred Truths suitably expressed. 'Tis not Shreds of *Latin* or *Greek,* nor a *Deus dixit,* and a *Deus benedixit,* nor those little Quirks, or Divisions into the [ ], the [ ], and the [ ], or the *Egress, Regress,* and *Progress,* and other such Stuff (much like the Style of a Lease) that can properly be called *Wit.* For that is not *Wit,* which consists not with *Wisdom.*[2]

As sharp as South was with his fellow High Churchmen, he was much more acerbic in treating the Puritans and Independents, whom he despised, devoting almost five times as much space to his list of their shortcomings as he had to that of their opponents.

> First of all they seize upon some Text, from whence they draw something (which they call a *Doctrine*) and well may it be said to be *drawn* from the Words; forasmuch as it seldom naturally flows, or *results* from them. In the next place, being thus provided, they branch it into several Heads; perhaps twenty, or thirty, or upwards. Whereupon, for the Prosecution of these, they repair to some *trusty Concordance,* which never fails them, and by the Help of that, they range six or seven

393

Scriptures under each Head; which Scriptures they prosecute one by
one; first amplifying and enlarging upon one, for some considerable
Time, till they have spoiled it; and then that being done, they pass to
another, which, in its Turn, suffers accordingly. And these impertinent,
and unpremeditated Enlargements they look upon as *the Motions and
Breathings of the Spirit,* and therefore much beyond those *carnal
Ordinances of Sense and Reason,* supported by Industry and Study; and
this they call a *saving* Way of Preaching, as it must be confessed to be
a Way to save much Labour, and nothing else that I know of. . . . But
to pass from these indecencies to others, as little to be allowed in this
Sort of Men, can any tolerable Reason be given for those strange new
Postures used by some in the Delivery of the Word? Such as *shutting the
Eyes, distorting the Face, and speaking through the Nose,* which I think
cannot so properly be called *Preaching,* as *Toning of a Sermon.* Nor do
I see, why *the* Word may not be altogether as effectual for *the
Conversion of Souls,* delivered by one, who has the Manners to look his
Auditory in the Face, using his own Countenance, and his own native
Voice without straining it to a lamentable and doleful *Whine,* (never
serving to any Purpose, but where some religious Cheat is to be carried
on). . . . And here, I humbly conceive, that it may not be amiss to
take Occasion to utter a great Truth, as both worthy to be considered,
and never to be forgot: Namely, That if we reflect upon the late Times
of Confusion, which passed upon the Ministry, we shall find, that the
grand Design of the Fanatick Crew was to persuade the World, That a
standing, settled Ministry was wholly useless. This, I say, was the main
Point which they then drove at. And the great Engine to effect this, was
by engaging Men of several Callings (and those the meaner still the better) to hold forth, and harangue the Multitude, sometimes in Streets,
sometimes in Churches, sometimes in Barns, and sometimes from
Pulpits, and sometimes from Tubs. . . . But on the contrary, had
Preaching been made, and reckoned a Matter of solid and true
Learning, of Theological Knowledge, and long, and severe Study, (as
the Nature of it required it to be) assuredly, no *preaching Cobbler*
amongst them all, would ever have ventured *so far beyond his Last,* as
to undertake it.[3]

Eight years later, in a sermon delivered at the cathedral rather than the
university church at Oxford, South stated his ideal of preaching in positive terms. The sermon, on "Christ's Promises to the Apostles," treated
the preaching of the apostles as the norm for that of latter-day clergy. He
considered them to have miraculously been given an ability to speak that
those to come later would have to acquire by study. The speaking
enabled by that gift had three properties:

   i. Great clearness and Perspicuity.
   ii. An unaffected Plainness and Simplicity. And
   iii. A suitable and becoming Zeal or Fervour.[4]

In a word, the Apostles Preaching was therefore mighty, and successful, because plain, natural, and familiar, and by no means above the Capacity of their Hearers: nothing being more preposterous than for those, who where professedly aiming at Men's *Hearts,* to miss the Mark, by shooting *over their Heads.*[5]

Foreshadowing

These criteria characterize a homiletical norm and style that was to remain in effect until well into the nineteenth century. It is, therefore, worthwhile to trace its origins.

One of the first groups to call for greater simplicity in preaching was the Cambridge Platonists. During the interregnum, this group of scholars had begun to feel disquiet over the Calvinism that pervaded the university. This theological position, together with the Laudianism of the opposition, was objected to, not so much because of its beliefs, as because of the spirit that promotion of the position seemed to engender, a pride and querulousness foreign to the spirit of Christ. Members of the group combined an irenicism of spirit with a trust in the God-given powers of human reason, a reason that had discovered truth even when employed by practitioners of other religions or by pagan philosophers.

Their philosophical stance, however, was not the Aristotelianism that had been regnant since its reintroduction into Europe in the Middle Ages. Nor was it the contemporary thought of Descartes and Hobbes, both of whom seemed to describe a materialistic and mechanistic universe in which there was little opening to the immanence of God. Instead, they liked Plato and Plotinus and shared with them a mystical orientation.

While the Platonists were not a homiletical movement as such, their contribution to English preaching has been summarized by Mitchell: "From the elevation of their thoughts they supplied it with a new sublimity, and from the necessity of conveying their ideas to the many they materially aided in the fight for simplicity."[6] Their greatest contribution, however, was through the later preachers whom they influenced. Of whom, I will say more later.

It has been claimed in the past that one of the major forces leading to the plain style of preaching was the standard of prose composition the newly founded Royal Society expected of its members in the communication of the results of their scientific investigations:

They have exacted from all their members a close, naked, natural way of speaking, positive expressions, clear sense, a native easiness, bringing all things as near the Mathematical plainness as they can, and preferring the language of Artizans, Countrymen, and Merchants, before that, of Wits or Scholars.[7]

Their goal, in short, was to deliver "so many *things* almost in an equal number of *words.*" Yet while some of the people calling for the change in preaching style were involved in the formation of the Royal Society, it seems that both movements were responses to the same social forces rather than that one was an outgrowth of the other.

A third influence that might be thought to account for the new demand for plain preaching is that of the contemporary French pulpit. This was, after all, the golden age of French preaching, with such giants as Bossuet, Bourdaloue, Claude, Fénelon, Massillon, and Rapin. And many of the Royalist clergy had been in exile with Charles II in France during the Commonwealth. Yet Charles Smyth is convinced that the first real impact of French homiletics on English preaching did not occur before 1778–79, when Charles Simeon annotated Robert Robinson's translation of Jean Claude's *Traité du la composition d'un sermon.*[8] The main explanation usually given for this lack of influence is what Mitchell has called the French sermon's "declamatory style foreign to the majority of English preachers."[9] This difference in national temperament and taste is well summarized by Hugh Blair's biographer, John Hill:

The French preacher generally addresses the imagination and passions; rouses his audience by an animated harangue; and is at more pains to embellish a few thoughts thinly spread out, than to exhibit any rich variety of sentiment. The English preacher, on the other hand, who is often of a temper more cold and phlegmatic, tries to accomplish his purpose by very different means. He regards his hearer as an intellectual, rather than as a sensitive, being.[10]

In addition to these matters of temperament, there is a deeper difference in the purpose of preachers, noted by Irène Simon in comparing funeral sermons of Bossuet and Gilbert Burnet:

Though both preachers agree on what corrupts sacred eloquence, their standards are altogether different: plain, solid, edifying sermons for the one; for the other "la parole de l'Evangile . . . vive, pénétrante, animée, toute pleine d'esprit et de feu."[11]

396

Thus the influence of French neoclassicism also fails to account for the emergence of the plain style. The most it seems possible to say is that the world woke up one morning with differences of taste that affected different countries as well as different aspects of intellectual life. Perhaps a sociologist of knowledge could account for this broad shift, but so far no historian appears to have done so.

Genesis in Ecclesiastes

The person in whom the demand for a plain style in preaching first makes its definitive appearance is **John Wilkins** (1614–72). The grandson of the great moderate Puritan John Dod and son of an Oxford goldsmith, Wilkins, upon the completion of his education and ordination, became in turn the chaplain of several distinguished political and scientific figures, including the Elector Palatine. In London and later, after he returned to Oxford as warden of Wadham College, he became a leading popularizer of the new science and the key figure in the organization of the Royal Society. After the Restoration he was made bishop of Chester. For his vigorous participation in the intellectual life of the period, ranging from the liberalization of English religious life through the acceptance of the scientific revolution to the advocacy of simpler modes of intellectual communication, he appears to have deserved being called "the most dynamic force in seventeenth-century England."[12]

Wilkins's contribution to preaching theory occurred early in his career with the 1646 publication of *Ecclesiastes: or, A Discourse Concerning the Gift of Preaching, As it falls under the Rules of Art.*[13] The book is divided into five sections, the first of which (after the short introduction) is on homiletical method and the last of which concerns "Expression"— style and delivery, in the vocabulary of classical rhetoric. By far the largest portion of the volume (pp. 32-251 in the edition consulted) is devoted to providing bibliographical assistance to the preacher in finding appropriate content for the sermon: section 3 on "Matter and Authors," and section 4, which provides "*A regular* Scheme *of the chief Heads in* Divinity."

The section on method deals with the parts of a sermon and what may be said in each part to render it most effective. This latter is, of course, what classical rhetoricians called "invention"—discovering in every case the available means of persuasion. It lists the topics that could be discussed in each part of the sermon, stating the alternatives first in an outline form that is typographically reminiscent of Ramist charts. That is not surprising, since Wilkins was influenced by Ramist logic as part of the entire system of Puritan homiletics taught by Perkins.[14] In modern typography and eliminating the distracting brackets Wilkins's printer used, such an outline looks like this:

3. **Application** is either,
    Doctrinal, for our information; whether more
        General, in some truths to be acknowledged;
            Dialectical, for Instruction, by inferring such corollaries as do naturally flow from the truth we have proved.
            Elenctical, by confuting such errors as are inconsistent with what we have asserted.
        Particular, as to the discovery of our own estates and conditions, whether we do really believe such a truth or practice such a duty, to be examined by signs or marks, which are derived either from the
            Cause or Original from which a thing must proceed.
            Effects or Consequences of it.
            Properties belonging to it
    Practical, either for
        Reproof, which may consist of two parts
            Dissuasive, from the aggravation of any sin, as to the
                Nature of it, its unreasonableness, deformity, etc.
                Threats denounced.
                Judgments executed upon it.
            Directive, to be amplified by
                Cautioning against impediments that hinder.
                Setting down the most proper means to promote such an end, whether more remote, immediate.
                Consolation, either in a state of
                    Suffering, by losses, etc.
                    Doubt or desertion. Against which men are to be supported by
                        The **consideration** of the nature of God, ourselves, afflictions.
                        Promises.

> **Experience.**
> **Removal** of scruples.
> **Exhortation,** to be further enlarged by
> **Motives,** to excite the affections
> from those general heads of
> **Benefit** or profit,
> **Hurt** or danger.
> **Means,** to direct the actions, whether
> **General.**
> **Special**[15]

Although Wilkins develops all of this in essay form later, most of the possible ways of relating the message of a text to a congregation are already apparent in this outline.

In the Wilkins method, the parts of a sermon are similar to the old Puritan "doctrines and uses." The principal parts are *explication* of the biblical text and its teaching, the *confirmation* of that doctrine by appeal to authority or reason, and the *application* of that teaching to a congregation. These parts may be preceded by a *preface,* although Wilkins did not consider one to be necessary on most occasions. A *transition* should be made from the explication to the confirmation, to render the method more "perspicuous." "The *Conclusion* should consist of some such matter as may engage the hearers to a serious *remembrance* and *consideration* of the truths delivered."[16]

The topics for an explication or confirmation are developed as fully as those of the application in the outline above, and the expository treatment of each part contains further subpoints. Indeed, the section on explication offers an excellent concise handbook on the best exegetical method of the time and on the means for drawing correct theological inferences from the text. Stated in such detail, the method sounds very complex, but what remains after all the options are explored is a simple, straightforward sermon pattern. The minute subdivisions of Puritan homiletics have been eliminated from sermons using the Wilkins method.

Wilkins's insistence upon simplicity of style is as important for the development of the plain sermon as this simplification of sermon outline. Dividing expression into *phrase* and *elocution,* he says the phrase must be:

> plain and natural, not being darkened with the affectation of *Scholastical* harshness, or *Rhetorical* flourishes. Obscurity in the discourse, is an Argument of Ignorance in the mind. The greatest learning

is to be seen in the greatest plainness. The more clearly we understand anything ourselves, the more easily we may expound it to others. When the notion it self is good, the best way to set it off, is in the most obvious plain expression.[17]

Wilkins seems to have anticipated the way that homiletical taste was ready to turn and set forth a clear method for constructing sermons that would satisfy that taste. The number of editions in which his textbook appeared in such a short time shows that the homiletical world was ready for such an approach. With his emphasis on simplicity of construction and plainness of diction, he was able to articulate norms for sermons that remained unconscious until he stated them. As soon as he put them into print, the world seemed to recognize that this was what they had been waiting for.

The Theory and Message of Eighteenth-Century Preaching

The closest study of neoclassical or latitudinarian British preaching as a whole is that of Rolf Lessenich in his handbook of eighteenth-century homiletics and theology.[18] No simpler way of surveying the subject exists than merely summarizing his treatment. He also writes as something of an advocate, trying to prove that the pulpit literature of the period is not as dull and dry as reputation would have it.

He begins by showing that the objective prose style of the Royal Society was not the ideal of the preachers. Accepting the recent faculty psychology, they knew that it was as necessary to move hearts as it was to convince minds.[19] The call for a plain style was in part motivated by this desire to make an emotional impact, since it was assumed that the two extremes to be avoided—ostentation and rusticity—made a negative impression on a congregation.

Another way of asserting the emotional appeal of eighteenth-century preaching is to note not only its status as literature at the time but also its influence on the prose style of other literature as well. Samuel Johnson was able to say: "Why, Sir, you are to consider, that sermons make a considerable branch of English literature; so that a library must be very imperfect if it has not a numerous collection of sermons."[20] Further, preachers were urged to deepen the appeal of their preaching by studying the best ancient and modern rhetorical handbooks and examples of oratory.

Yet the solemn purpose of preaching was never forgotten, so that the pleasure of listening or reading was always regarded as subordinate to instruction. To have this combined appeal to the mind and to the emotions, sermons had to be comprehensible to persons of a wide range of social status and education.[21]

The strategy by which the mind was persuaded and the passions moved was tandem, with appeal first to the mind and then to the emotions. This task, however, was set within the framework of a forensic speech of classical rhetoric. Thus the pattern was: exordium, explication, proposition, partition, argumentative part, application, and conclusion. Although the pattern was concealed in the outline recommended by Wilkins, the structure was there. His preface was an exordium or introduction, his explication included the statement of a proposition, his transition was a partition, his confirmation the argumentative part, and he used the same terms for application and conclusion.

Eighteenth-century exordia, prefaces, proems, or introductions served the classical purposes of rendering the audience benevolent, attentive, and teachable and of preparing them for what was to come, thus leading smoothly into the explication.

The way the neoclassical preachers solved the historic problem of fitting the explication of a text into the pattern of a forensic oration was by having it serve the function of the narration, the summary of a case made by a lawyer that led up to an identification of the issues to be contested in the trial. This exegetical section, however, was much simpler than it had been in previous Puritan practice. It aimed neither at some abstruse point of doctrine nor at controversy, but at practical moral instruction. This choice of purpose had already determined the choice of the text to be explicated, since lectionary preaching was not an ideal of the day. Indeed, some neoclassical sermons were topical rather than textual.

If, as was most common, there was a text, its explication was not to be technical and complex, but as "artistic" as the rest of the sermon. The explication enabled the preacher to show that the proposition to be proved by the sermon did derive from the scriptural passage on which it was based. Being thus prepared for, the proposition was stated concisely. Then the partition outlined what was to come by giving "a short and precise enumeration of the separate points of view under which the subject was consecutively treated."[22] The purpose of the partition was to help the congregation remember what was said.[23]

In the argumentative part, which was considered the most important, a preacher would either try to teach the congregation the message of the text or would use the text almost as a pretext, as a jumping-off place for the consideration of a wider topic. The first of these two sermon types was called "analytic" and the other was called "synthetic," but by the vocabulary of later generations, they are not very different from textual and topical developments.

Each of these two types could be divided into two more, giving four genera to neoclassical preaching. The subcategories of analytic sermons were "explicatory" and "observatory," while those of the synthetic sermon were "applicative" and "propositional." The *explicatory* seeks to illustrate the doctrine of the text by exploring the meaning of its most important theological terms, solving difficulties raised, and removing obscurities. Such sermons, of course, are on texts of which the meaning is not clear. For those that have an obvious meaning, the argument needed to consist only of observations about that meaning—hence the designation *observatory*. This method was often used for historical texts.

The *applicative* sermon did not develop the explication of the text so much as it did its practical application to the hearers' lives. Such sermons were essentially hortatory, calling upon the members of the congregation to repent or to lead holier lives. Such sermons, however, were not without the support of rational argument, although they did call for more warmth than the other genera. The *propositional* sermon, on the other hand, was in some ways like the explicatory, but differed in deriving a number of propositions from the text rather than just one. But the development of these propositions was not limited to the implications of the one text; it could be expanded to draw in other material. This genus was a favorite medium for systematic theological instruction from the pulpit.

The preaching theorists of the period disagreed about the way arguments should be introduced in a sermon, some holding that there should be a formal statement of each "head" or topic that would be discussed, while others insisted that transitions from point to point should be unobtrusive. The arguments for the first method are pedagogical and mnemonic, while those for the second are essentially aesthetic, an assumption that the best art is that which covers up art *(ars est celare artem)*. In either case, however, it was assumed that the arguments should be presented in a logical order, and that arguments of the same kind should be grouped together. By the same token, it was expected that the arguments should be presented in an order that built to a climax. And it was recognized that the multiplication of arguments generated more confusion than persuasion.[24]

The epilogue (peroration, conclusion) of the sermon could either recapitulate what had already been said or it could be an emotional appeal to the congregation to act on what had been said. Many theorists thought the latter method far more effective than the former. A variety of emotional appeals was recognized, as for instance in this catalog of Jean Claude:

There are three sorts of dispositions, or emotions, the violent—the tender, and the elevated. The *violent* are, for example, indignation, fear, zeal, courage, firmness against temptations, repentance, self-loathing, &c. The *tender* emotions are joy, consolation, gratitude; tender subjects are pardon, pity, prayer, &c. The *elevated* are admiration of the majesty of God, the ways of providence, the glory of Paradise, the expectation of benefits, &c.[25]

A number of these emotional appeals in the conclusion involved references to judgment and eternal life or damnation.[26]

Like all good manuals of rhetoric, the homiletical writings of the eighteenth century were not only concerned with composition but with delivery as well. Their writers accepted the wisdom of Demosthenes, who told an inquirer that the most important aspect of oratory is "delivery." When asked what the second and third most important parts are, he repeated, "delivery," and "delivery." Yet Thomas Sheridan, founder of the elocution movement and father of the playwright Richard, was convinced that this was the most neglected aspect of preaching in England.[27] Delivery (also called "pronunciation" or "elocution") was recognized to consist of two parts, voice and gesture.

In delivery, as in everything else, however, the eighteenth century sought the golden mean between extremes. Dryness was to be avoided on the one hand, ecstasy on the other.[28] The soporific qualities of sermons were proverbial. Yet the enthusiasm of such as the Methodists was equally to be avoided. A liveliness of voice and gesture that did not spill over into hysteria was the ideal. Another Scylla and Charibdes to be steered between were meanness and affectation. One was neither coarse nor pretentious in the pulpit. In delivery as in style, the latitudinarian ideal was naturalness.[29]

To summarize all of this preaching theory, the ideal preacher was seen to be one who combined learning with forceful delivery. "Next to convincing his hearers with solid learning the preacher had to persuade them, to raise their emotions and stir their passions in favor of his cause."[30] Finally, for a preacher to be truly effective, it was necessary that he support these gifts with the moral qualities of sincerity and behavior consistent with what was enjoined. This combination was the ideal of the neoclassical homileticians.[31]

In addition to their thoughts about preaching, it helps to understand the theology of the latitudinarians, since in some ways their homiletic was a function of their beliefs about God—which is probably true of all preaching. The theology of the latitudinarians was probably neither so bad as it is regarded by some (hardly better than deism), nor so good as it is regarded by others (straightforward Christian orthodoxy expressed in the vocabulary of the time). To begin with, those who held it were not Calvinists; they did not believe in predestination or a God of wrath. The order and regularity of the universe as discovered by the new science had convinced these thinkers of God's benevolence toward humanity.

Everything that existed was a provision of an all-wise and all-loving Creator, the God of "the spacious firmament on high." It was assumed that nature revealed the glory of God and that there was, therefore, universal human consent to the existence of such a Being. The Calvinist doctrine of election was seen to be inconsistent with divine benevolence: How could an all-loving God consent even passively to the damnation of most of the human race? Human beings, therefore, must be free to choose good or evil. Inevitably, some would choose evil, and God would reluctantly allow them the fate upon which they had insisted.

Indeed, human reason and will had been incapacitated by the fall, but God's will for the salvation of all expressed in the redemption of the world by God's Son, Jesus Christ, meant that anyone who wished grace to overcome original sin would find it available in abundance. Since human reason had not been so distorted by the fall as to be unable to recognize the advantages of good over evil both here and hereafter, and since in any case the Scriptures revealed these advantages for those who had any difficulty in seeing them, there was nothing really to inhibit the salvation of anyone who wished it.

Accepting this salvation was largely a matter of living in the way of God's will, the practical goodness apparent to natural reason but made abundantly clear in biblical revelation. Holiness could hardly be distinguished from what Jeremy Bentham was later to call "enlightened self-interest." The advantages of righteousness were so patent that it was hard to understand how even a reason and will corrupted by the fall could fail to choose the way of life. But to ensure that this benighted option was even less likely to be elected, sermons were preached urging all people to reform their ways and live the moral life that was the commandment and gift of God. The faith that appropriated this way of life was simply a fervent conviction that this view of the universe was correct.[32]

Popular as such preaching was for a long time, consciousness has shifted again so completely that many modern readers find neoclassical preaching as hard to appreciate as the Restoration congregations found the sermons of the Metaphysicals and Puritans. To contemporary ears it has a sound of smugness, of self-satisfaction, of comfort in the universe and ease in Zion that is almost impossible to empathize with. Its serene good taste and its abhorrence of enthusiasm as nature abhors a vacuum make it guilty of breaking the eleventh commandment for all public speakers: "Thou shalt not bore!" To say that, however, is only to admit that contemporary consciousness is as provincial as any that preceded it, because there can be no doubt that neoclassical latitudinarian preaching fitted the consciousness of its time like a custom-tailored garment. Further, it was the style of preaching that was developed during the Enlightenment, a time when Christianity was very much on the defensive. In an atmosphere in which deists and atheists were attacking the roots of faith, neoclassical preaching may have been as much of the gospel as could be heard.

PRACTICE IN PREACHING

In order to understand the careers and homiletical practice of the Restoration and the eighteenth-century preachers who set the style that was to last so long and be so pervasive,[33] it is necessary to know something about the close involvement of church and state during this period. Since the Reformation, it had been assumed in England that many of the administrative responsibilities of the pope during the Middle Ages had been transferred (or, according to the theory, restored) to the monarch, God's vicegerent in the realm. As constitutional theory came to be debated in the early-seventeenth century, when Puritans began to say that divine authority rested in the law (enacted by Parliament), the issue was not over the legitimate role of the state in the government of the church, but over who should exercise that role.

Thus the two sides in the English Civil War each had characteristic positions on civil and church government. Royalists tended to be Episcopalians, and Puritans were Parliamentarians. (The Independents who were so much at the center of things during the Protectorate were opposed to both doctrines of ministry and to the establishment of any church.) After the Restoration, these coalitions became High Church Tories and latitudinarian Whigs. The High Churchmen were devoted equally to bishops and the monarchy, while the latitudinarians were tolerant toward Dissenters and considered the king to be subordinate to the law.

Throughout the seventeenth century and during the early part of the eighteenth, there were constant changes in which coalition was in power. James I and Charles II had combined a belief that they ruled by divine right with an Anglo-Catholic theology. The Civil War was an effort of a Puritan Parliament to overthrow both the monarchy and the episcopal establishment. As the Commonwealth moved into the Protectorate of Oliver Cromwell, Independency came to the fore. At the Restoration, High Church heirs of Laudian Anglo-Catholicism took control of the church as the reward of their loyalty to the monarchy. The refusal of James II to support the established church and his efforts to restore Roman Catholicism created an intolerable bind for High Church Tories, because it forced them to choose between their doctrine of the church and their theology of government.[34] Under William and Mary, the Whigs were in power. Queen Anne was High Church and Tory and tried to reward those who agreed with her, but the Whig hegemony was restored with the Hanoverian succession and lasted longer than the Georges.

What makes all of this so important for the history of preaching during that period is that most church offices beyond the parochial level were royal (that is to say, governmental) appointments. University positions, cathedral canonries and deanships, and bishoprics were bestowed by the political party in power. Not surprisingly, plums went to their supporters among the clergy. This was especially true with regard to the episcopate because bishops were members of the House of Lords, and a loyal episcopal bench could often swing a close vote to the side that had appointed them. In spite of laws to the contrary, this was still a time when clergy could enjoy appointment to a number of positions simultaneously, even when these were geographically distant from one another. This pluralism rendered absenteeism inevitable. And bishops were absent from their dioceses most of the year because of their need to be in London when Parliament was sitting. Although the ethical standards of a later generation make it hard to credit, many of even the most exemplary clergy of this period (among them most of those to be considered below) were caught up in an endless quest for preferment to influential and lucrative positions in the church.[35]

The Pioneers

It is generally recognized that the style of plain preaching was set in the last third of the seventeenth century by three masters: Robert South, Isaac Barrow, and John Tillotson. A brief look at the contribution of each of them is necessary for an understanding of how the taste was formed.

Robert South (1634–1716)

Although South was slightly the youngest of the three, Mitchell credits him with being the first to achieve the plain style:

> All the competing and, from different points of view, extravagant styles which had fascinated men and absorbed their attention during the first sixty years of the century were successfully fused together [by South], and the result was a plain, perspicuous and harmonious whole.[36]

Certainly he was the most explicit theorist of the style, as may be seen above in his critique of sermons constructed according the methods of the Metaphysicals or Perkins. Yet he was an odd person for this achievement, being far from a latitudinarian. He came from a background of affluence and loyalty to the Royalist cause.[37] Indeed, the most traumatic and significant moment of his life, the execution of Charles I, occurred when he was a youth at nearby Westminster School, where Latin prayers were being said for the king on the morning of his death. Growing up with such passionate convictions when the detested enemy was in power must have been galling for South, but at Westminster he was taught how to survive in such a period. The sincerity of his conviction was shown when he moved on to Christ Church, Oxford, where he was a member of a small group that met for clandestine worship according to the outlawed Prayer Book.

With the Restoration, things began to look up for South. It was during the year in which it occurred that he preached "The Scribe Instructed," the first of his two sermons in favor of the plain style. His brilliance was noted and he became the Orator of the University, the person who made the official Latin addresses upon auspicious public occasions. Preferment came his way: he was made a canon of Westminster in 1663 when he was only twenty-nine, vicar of a Welsh parish in 1667, canon of Christ Church[38] in 1670, and rector of Islip in 1678.

Seven years later, James II came to the throne. Even though he had earlier been one of James's chaplains while he was still Duke of York, South shared with all his fellow English a hysteria about Roman Catholicism; the so-called Popish Plot was quite a recent memory. Yet the accession of William and Mary was no relief to South, since their openness to Dissenters was at least as abhorrent to him as James's attitude toward Roman Catholics. Thus, in his final decades, South's lifelong and passionate devotion to the Royalist cause had to contend with the reality that the kings whom his theology idealized were quite capable of encouraging religious systems deeply at odds with his own. South's brilliant climb had stalled.

In addition to his advocacy of the plain style and his proclamation of his High Church Tory convictions, South's preaching is known for two main characteristics: his use of humor and his elaboration of metaphor. South was "witty" in the modern sense of brilliant joking rather than in the early-seventeenth-century sense of employing conceits.[39] This trait, which can be seen clearly in his criticism of other preaching styles, has drawn disapproval both in his own time and since. Some believed that levity could never be used to press home serious messages and that it was, in any case, inconsistent with the dignity of preaching's divine subject matter. Others have found his biting sarcasm at times to accord ill with Christian charity. Yet others delight simply in his being funny and charming, and recognize the rhetorical effectiveness of the way he used wit to surprise his audience into considering seriously points they might have passed over in a more sober presentation.

South also used metaphors at a time when their legitimate employment in sermons was debated, and he used them more extensively than any of his contemporaries.[40] Some of the metaphors are quite extended; they are often incorporated into broader patterns of imagery. He used metaphor to develop the argument of his sermons, at times employing a complex metaphor in which there was more than one point of comparison. Sometimes a complex pattern of imagery was mixed in with other elements, such as biblical and historical allusions and quotations. His preaching relied as heavily upon metaphor as Jesus' preaching relied upon parable.

As disturbing as elements of his style have been to various people then and now, many others undoubtedly agree with Simon that he was "probably the best preacher of his age, and he had a mind of the highest order"[41] and regret with her that his influence was not more widespread in the century to follow. While one cannot convey the religious depth of much of his preaching by quoting a short passage, something of his charm may be seen in a letter he wrote to respond to an offer of the deanship of Westminster Abbey shortly before his eightieth birthday:

> My Most Honoured Lord,
>   Could my present circumstances and condition, in any Degree come up to the Gracious, and surpriseing offer lately brought me from her Majesty, I should with the utmost Gratitude, and Deepest Humility Cast my self at Her Royall Feet, and with Both Armes Embrace it.
>   But alas, my Lord, That Answer which Alexander the Great once gave a Souldier petitioning Him for an Office in his Army may no lesse properly become her majesty to my Poor Self, (though not *Petitioning for,* but *prevented by*[42] her Princely Favour,) *Freind* [sic], said He, *I own that I can give thee this Place, but I cannot make thee Fitt for it.* And this, my Lord, is my unhappy case.

For haveing, for now above these *Fourty years*, the Best, the Ablest, and most usefull part of my Age, not bin thought fitt by my Superiors, to serve the Crown or Church in any other way, or Station, than what I have held hitherto, I cannot, but in modesty (and, even, in *Respect to them*) judge myself unworthy and unfitt to serve them in any higher, or greater Post now; being grown Equally superannuated to the *Active*, as well as the *Enjoying* Part of Life.

For Age, my Lord, is not to be *Defyed*, nor forced by All, that Art, or Nature can doe, to retreat one step backward: And even the Richest Spread Table, with the Kindest Invitations to it, Come but too late to one, who has lost both his Stomack, and his Appetite too.

In fine, my good Lord, after the Utmost Acknowledgement, Duty and Devotion paid to the Sacred *Fountain-Head* from which all this Goodnesse flowes, the same Gratitude, in the *very next place,* commands me, with the Profoundest Deference to Own, and Blesse that Noble Channell, by which it has so liberally passed upon,

(Great Sir)

Your Honours most obliged, Humble, and obedient Servant

Robert South.

Westminster Abbey,

8 June, 1713,

Nothing, my Lord, afflicts me more than that I am disabled from bringing your Honour, these my Acknowledgements (and many more with them) in Person my Self.[43]

Isaac Barrow (1630–77)

A Royalist like South, Barrow seems to have been less troubled by his allegiance. Somehow he managed to go through Cambridge during the Puritan reign without having to sign either the Covenant or the Engagement, and he died before either James II or William and Mary could test his conscience. On the whole, he seems to have led a carefree existence in an academic setting most of his life. It is only when one looks at the diversity of his accomplishments that it becomes clear what an extraordinarily gifted person he was.

Apparently his original intention had been to become a physician; he studied science in preparation for such a career. His election as a fellow of Trinity College, however, obligated him to study theology. An interest in biblical chronology led him into astronomy and geometry. Taking up mathematics, he was eventually made a professor of Gresham College, the London center of scientific study so closely related to the founding of the Royal Society (of which Barrow became a member). Elected from there to the first chair of mathematics at Cambridge, he became one of the predecessors of Isaac Newton and Gottfried Leibniz in the discovery of differential calculus. Yet he recognized the superior genius of his pupil and in time resigned the chair in favor of Newton.

At points along the way, his great classical learning caused him to be considered for various chairs before he became regius professor of Greek at the Restoration. He had, after all, gone to Constantinople to study the works of Chrysostom. On the voyage home, pirates attacked his ship and he, who had been notorious for fighting as a schoolboy, joined the struggle against them.

He was ordained shortly before the Restoration, but his other duties kept him from writing the theological treatises that were prerequisite to appointment as a preacher at Trinity College. After resigning in favor of Newton, however, he quickly satisfied that requirement and immediately became much in demand as a preacher at court as well as the university. When he was appointed Master of Trinity in 1672, he devoted himself to refuting Roman Catholic claims and to building up a library for his college, the university not having one at the time. So charmed was his life that it seems inevitable that it should have been he who commissioned Christopher Wren to build Trinity's magnificent library. It would be hard to quarrel with the judgment of Charles II when he appointed Barrow as Master of Trinity: the king called him the best scholar in England.[44]

Since Barrow was appointed a preacher to his college only six years before his death, it is extraordinary that his sermons should have the respect they do. Mitchell calls him "the most continuously and uniformly eloquent of English preachers."[45] What accounts for this reputation? Two things, apparently: the profundity of his mind, which permitted him to treat his subjects comprehensively, not to say exhaustively, and his having learned style from transcribing the works of Demosthenes and Chrysostom until he fell into the English equivalent of the patterns of their speech. Both of these qualities can be seen in a short passage from his sermon on "The Profitableness of Godliness":

> The gain of money, or of somewhat equivalent thereto, is therefore specially termed Profit, because it readily supplieth necessity, furnisheth convenience, feedeth pleasure, satisfieth fancy and curiosity, promoteth ease and liberty, supporteth honour and dignity, procureth power, dependencies, and friendships, rendreth a man somebody, considerable in the world; in fine, enableth to doe good, or to perform works of beneficence and charity.[46]

One is left with the contradictory feelings that, on the one hand, everything has been said that could be, and, on the other, that Barrow could have gone on indefinitely. Apparently he sometimes did; it is reported that one of his sermons lasted three hours and forty-five minutes. His use of appositives, parallel construction, and anaphora allow him to roll along forever, never repeating himself, always saying something worthwhile. To acquire such a reputation for preaching, however, it is usually necessary that spiritual depth be accompanied by literary grace. Although Barrow appears in some ways to have given as little thought to the way his sermons sounded as he did to his own personal appearance, there can be no doubt that the charm was there. Anyone who questions that has but to read his defense of legitimate humor in his sermon "Against Foolish Talking and Jesting."[47]

John Tillotson (1630–94)

The preacher who is universally admitted to have set the style for plain, latitudinarian, neoclassical preaching is one who was in touch with all of the trends and influences that anticipated the taste. Born into the strict Puritan family of a Yorkshire clothier, John Tillotson went to Cambridge where, in addition to some of the leading Puritans of the day, he came under the influence of the Cambridge Platonists and others.

Being of a naturally irenic disposition and willing to consider a number of points of view, he remained for a while within the Puritan camp without presupposing, as so many did, that his was the only position worthy of respect. Although he was in London at the time of Cromwell's death, eventually married Cromwell's niece, and sat with the Presbyterians at the Savoy Conference in its abortive effort to work out a Restoration settlement that would include them, Tillotson was ordained by a bishop and served various appointments in Church of England parishes. His fame began to build in his early thirties, when he was appointed to preach on Sundays to the lawyers at Lincoln's Inn and on Tuesdays at the parish of many who were influential in the city government of London, St. Lawrence Jewry.

During this London ministry he became close to John Wilkins, the author of *Ecclesiastes,* who was his vicar at St. Lawrence. Indeed, the Cromwell niece whom Tillotson married in 1664, a year after arriving at St. Lawrence, was Wilkins's stepdaughter. Tillotson must have been an eager disciple of his father-in-law's homiletical principles; he certainly became deeply involved in another of his causes in communication, that which resulted in the 1668 publication of Wilkins's *Essay Towards a*

Real Character and Philosophical Language. This project was devoted to an effort to help the scientists of the Royal Society achieve their goal of "so many *things* almost in an equal number of *words.*"[48] Indeed, Tillotson himself became a member of the society. And when Wilkins was consecrated to be bishop of Chester, his son-in-law preached. He also edited Wilkins's sermons after his death.

Tillotson's broad-mindedness and irenic spirit continued to manifest themselves, especially in his efforts to ease the legal situation of Dissenters and even include them in the establishment. The only area of his thought in which his charity was not apparent was his attitude toward Roman Catholics; like both South and Barrow, he wrote polemical works against them. Barrow was a great friend, and Tillotson also became his posthumous editor.[49] In fact, it is difficult to discover anyone who was not his friend, so universal was his capacity to appreciate fellow human beings!

Inevitably, preferment came his way. In 1668 he became one of the chaplains of Charles II, in 1670 a prebendary, and in 1672 the dean of Canterbury, becoming as well a canon of St. Paul's. When James II came to the throne, he continued to preach passive obedience to the civil magistrate, but he also urged Dissenters not to go along with the king's efforts to grant indulgence to Dissenters as a means of acquiring it for his co-religionists as well. Tillotson was among those called together by Archbishop Sancroft when James ordered the proclamation of the Declaration of Indulgence in churches, but, not being a bishop, he was not one of the seven sent to the tower for refusing to have it read.

Neither was he directly involved in the invitation to William and Mary to take over the throne, but, an old friend of William's, he was invited to preach at court three days after their coronation. He then was made dean of St. Paul's, having refused a bishopric, pleading little taste for "either the ceremony or the trouble of a great place."[50] It was only with great reluctance that he acceded to William's request that he succeed the nonjuring Sancroft as archbishop of Canterbury, becoming, in the words of Charles Smyth, "the only Primate of All England to enjoy the reputation of being the greatest preacher of his day."[51] He found, as he expected, the role to be very onerous, especially as there were many who questioned his orthodoxy, and he survived in the position only three years.

In some ways, his preaching style could be described as meeting an ideal of today: it was conversational. (For a sermon by Tillotson, **see Vol. 2, pp. 329-48**.) That trait, however, is not recognizable to many modern readers because ordinary speech has changed so much since his time. Even then, it was the ordinary speech of a particular social group, that of "gentlemen." It was not the sophisticated parlance that had been popular at the court of James I, where the diction of Lancelot Andrewes could have been considered conversational, nor yet was it the language of "lower classes" in either the city or the country.

Tillotson carried plainness to the extreme of actively seeking to avoid any expression that was either dramatic or poetic. He wished to avoid persuading anyone by any tricks of language, depending instead entirely upon the reasonableness of the thought he presented so calmly. Nor was his thought particularly demanding or profound; he wished to be sure that his audience could understand and accept what was said. Pellucidity, even obviousness, was his great aim.

As for structure:

> He usually begins a discourse with a short proem which seeks to introduce his subject, impress its high seriousness upon his hearers, and prejudice them in his favour. As though outlining a problem in logic, he makes every sentence count; there are no embellishments and no redundant phrases. In turn he considers the several divisions into which his subject logically falls. There is no peroration; no impassioned pleading with sinners; no final "call." When the argument is concluded, the counsel for the Prosecution rests his case.[52]

When his preaching is thus described, it is hard for ordinary people of today to understand how it could have been so popular at the time. It is even hard for specialists who have studied it to understand its appeal. Simon, for instance, says:

> It is doubtful . . . whether such a style could have riveted the attention of less eager listeners. While Barrow's verbal imagination or South's manly wit arouse our interest in the themes they treat, the reader who does not come to Tillotson's sermons for edification is likely to appreciate the clear and easy style only when the matter treated is of particular interest, that is, defines the preacher's position and belief as a Church-of-England man of the time, for the prosaic quality of his thought and mind is made all the more obvious by the plainness and simplicity of his style.[53]

Smyth speaks of "the dull sobriety, the unadventurous reasonableness of Tillotsonian homiletics."[54] He also indicates the theological shortcoming of the content of these sermons: "Beyond a general impression that it was more prudent on the whole to believe the Gospel, in a modified sort of way, than not, what impression does Tillotson convey?"[55] Yet Smyth also recognizes what made such a style so welcome in its generation, "the real horror of fanaticism that lay at the heart of the Anglican piety for more than a hundred years" after the Civil War, Commonwealth, and Protectorate.[56]

The popularity of Tillotson's preaching, however, does not entirely account for the influence of his style on preachers for a century afterward. James Downey says:

> Above all, and herein lies the reason for his influence, Tillotson was imitable. In both structure and language his sermons are easy to emulate. Barrow, South, Burnet, and Stillingfleet were all perhaps better preachers; but none of them was really imitable. Lesser men attempting to emulate their styles were in danger of falling victims to bombast, or bathos, or both.[57]

There must have been more to it than that. Tillotson set a style that was to remain popular for some time, not only for preachers, but for all writers of English prose. There must have been something in the spirit of the age to which such prose spoke.

PREACHING AND THE LIFE OF THE MIND IN THE EIGHTEENTH CENTURY

Several connections have already been suggested between homiletics and the rest of the intellectual life of England at the Restoration and afterward: the number of outstanding preachers closely connected with the new science and the founding of the Royal Society, the influence of the homiletical plain style on essayists such as Addison, Steele, Dryden, and others. There is probably no other time in British history when ties were so numerous between preachers and secular high culture. Thus this chapter would be incomplete without at least a simple listing of preachers who are also well known today for their contributions to literature and philosophy: Swift, Sterne, Johnson, Butler, and Berkeley.

The list begins a little before this exact period with someone who anticipated the plain style. While **George Herbert** is classified as one of the metaphysical poets, his homiletical taste was much simpler than that of the preachers who share that adjective. Born into a noble family active in both government and letters, Herbert was educated at Westminster and Cambridge, was made a Major Fellow of Trinity, gave university lectures in rhetoric, and became Orator of the university. Although devout all his life, he seemed attracted at first to serving God in government; he spent a year as a member of Parliament. That seemed to disillusion him thoroughly with the idea of a unified realm of church and state. At the end of it, late in 1624 when he was thirty-one years old, he was ordained deacon. While he was appointed to livings then,[58] his health seems to have delayed his ordination to the priesthood for six years. By that time he had already been installed for a few months at Bemerton, his only parish. He did not live to serve there a full three years.

His ministry is best known for its ideals, stated in a work that was near completion when he moved to Bemerton, his *A Priest to the Temple, or, The Country Parson, His Character and Rule of Life.* In this spiritual classic, he set forth his standards for preaching and for all other aspects of his ministry. He seemed to consider no work more important than preaching, saying: "The Country Parson preacheth constantly, the pulpit is his joy and his throne."[59] The way in which he anticipated the plain style can be seen in what he had to say about explication.

> The Parson's Method in handling of a text consists of two parts; first, a plain and evident declaration of the meaning of the text; and, secondly, some choice Observations drawn out of the whole text, as it lies entire, and unbroken in the Scripture itself. This he thinks natural, and sweet, and grave. Whereas the other way of crumbling a text into small parts, as, the Person speaking, or spoken to, the subject, and object, and the like, hath neither in it sweetness, nor gravity, nor variety, since the words apart are not Scripture, but a dictionary, and may be considered alike in all the Scripture.[60]

But for the kindness and humility, this could sound like South, although it anticipates "The Scribe Instructed" by twenty-eight years.

A less obviously saintly soul was the satirist and political pamphleteer **Jonathan Swift** (1667–1745). Most literary critics who have studied his work have been able to neglect or dismiss his priesthood.[61] Yet there is plenty of evidence to suggest that the dean of St. Patrick's, Dublin, was not only conscientious in the performance of his official duties by the standards of his time and a High Churchman in his beliefs, but that he was also a man of prayer, a good pastor, and a generous almsgiver.[62] His satire shows him to have been a person of such lofty ideals and such outrage over their contradiction in the way people lived that he could not contain his indignation, having it build up inside him like steam in a pressure cooker until it came hissing out of the safety valve. The epitaph that he wrote for himself says what needed to be said:

> Here lies the body of Jonathan Swift, Doctor of Divinity and Dean of this Cathedral Church, where savage indignation can no more lacerate

his heart. Go, traveller, and imitate if you can one who strove with all his might to champion liberty.[63]

The homiletical theory and practice of such a person can hardly be expected to be ordinary, nor was it. His "Letter to a Young Clergyman Lately Entered into Holy Orders" states his theory of preaching, but does so with such irony that it would be easy to forget the sound advice in appreciation of the sardonic manner in which it is given.[64] He begins by observing that most clergy do not stay at the university long enough to acquire the learning preaching requires—a minimum of ten years. Then he says that clergy should learn how to deliver sermons in rural congregations before they preach to those in the city.

The study of English is a necessity, including as a minimum the ability to use words that people understand rather than technical jargon (although it is possible to use language that is too common or coarse). Clichés are to be avoided like the plague. Sermons that persuade by reason are more effective in the long run (at least in northern climates) than those that move the emotions:

> A plain convincing reason may possibly operate upon the mind, both of the learned and the ignorant hearer, as long as they live, and will edify a thousand times more than the art of wetting the handkerchiefs of a whole congregation, if you were sure to attain it.[65]

"The two principal branches of preaching," according to Swift, "are, first to tell the people what is their duty, and then to convince them that it is so." The heads of divisions should be expressed in a few clear words so that the outline can be remembered. Clergy should prepare their manuscripts in such a way and practice their delivery so that they may appear to preach without looking at their notes. Few preachers are capable of wit in the pulpit, and the rest should avoid trying.

While Swift is clear that saving truth is a matter of revelation, he nevertheless wishes that clergy would be grateful for the help they can receive from pagan philosophers in teaching practical morality and not bite the hand that feeds them. Yet quotations, except from the Bible, should be kept to a minimum; clergy should never have been encouraged to collect them in commonplace books. The reasoning of the preacher is more convincing than "a manifest incoherent piece of patchwork." The mysteries of the Christian religion should be accepted rather than explained, and controversial preaching against the heresies of the day is pointless since those who hold them are not in church. But at least clergy had given up preaching on the doctrinal issues of the Puritans.

One cannot be entirely sure of the extent to which Swift practiced what he preached, because only about a dozen of his sermons have survived. He was as ironic about his preaching as everything else, telling Thomas Sheridan when he gave him a bundle of them: "They may be of use to you, they never were of any to me."[66] His sermon on the Trinity certainly followed his advice on recognizing that mysteries are mysteries:

> There is some kind of unity and distinction in the divine nature, which mankind can not possibly comprehend; thus the whole doctrine is short and plain, and in itself incapable of any controversy, since God himself both pronounced the fact, but wholly concealed the manner.[67]

The majority of his surviving sermons do deal with Christian behavior. Occasionally his political convictions entered his preaching, but did so because of his deep moral commitments. His sermon on "Brotherly Love," for instance, would seem to the ecumenically minded modern Christian to be commending its opposite in his opposition to political rights for Roman Catholics and Dissenters, but he saw the Whig policy of comprehension to be a cynical indifference to religion for political advantage.[68] His sermon on "Doing Good" (public service) was occasioned by the issue that prompted his *Drapier's Letters,* William Wood's patent to circulate his halfpence in a way that would exploit the Irish for the profit of the English.

The true value of Swift's preaching, however, can best be seen in his sermon on "Mutual Subjection." In a world rife with class consciousness, smugness, and condescension, he undercuts it all:

> It plainly appears from what hath been said, that no human creature is more worthy than another in the sight of God, farther than according to the goodness or holiness of their lives; and that power, wealth, and the like outward advantages, are so far from being the marks of God's approving or preferring those on whom they are bestowed, that, on the contrary, he is pleased to suffer them to be almost engrossed by those who have least title to his favour. Now, according to this equality wherein God hath placed all mankind with relation to himself, you will observe, that in all the relations between man and man, there is a mutual dependence, whereby the one cannot subsist without the other.[69]

A writing cleric whose religious seriousness has been at least as suspect among the critics as Swift's is **Laurence Sterne** (1713–68), the author of *Tristram Shandy* and *A Sentimental Journey.*[70] The morality of both his life and his works was severely attacked by Thackery and other

Victorians. And some question of seriousness could be raised by the way the sermons were published, not as Sterne's own, but as those of the fictitious Mr. Yorick in *Tristram Shandy*. It was only posthumously that any sermons were published under his own name, and those were inferior to Yorick's, consisting largely of borrowings from imminent divines of the day. Apparently the Yorick sermons were his own, preached during the thirty years he had been a parish priest in Yorkshire, the last twenty of which he was a prebendary of York Minster.[71] The sermons published as Yorick's were his best, but after his death, his heirs issued his earlier and less skillful sermons under his own name. He seems to have developed the literary talent manifest in the novels by writing sermons in which he dramatized biblical stories through his ability to imaginatively construct scenes, characters, and dialogue. He appears to have achieved in his preaching the ideal that he set forth in a letter: "Preaching (you must know) is a theological flap upon the heart, as the dunning for a promise is a political flap upon the memory."[72]

Sermons were written by at least one eighteenth-century author who was not ordained, **Samuel Johnson** (1709–84). While the famous doctor was a very devout High Church Tory with an almost encyclopedic knowledge of English homiletical literature, the sermons appear to have been part of the literary work he did to support himself. He claimed to have written around forty, although only twenty-eight have survived. Of these, one was for his friend the Reverend Henry Hervey Aston to deliver to the Sons of the Clergy, another was for a priest convicted of forgery to deliver to fellow prisoners at Newgate.

The rest were for his oldest and closest friend, the Reverend John Taylor, including one for the funeral of Johnson's wife. Taylor, under whose name most of the sermons were originally published, was a sort of Dr. Syntax, though more of a stockbreeding than a hunting parson. Yet it was to him that Johnson himself turned when he was in need of pastoral care. Sometimes the sermons seem to have emerged from a dialectical process in which Johnson would draft something according to the specifications of his client, and the client would then tailor that to make the work his own. In any case, the sermons were consistent with Johnson's own theological principles while being fair to those of the preacher when there was a difference—as there was between Johnson and Taylor.[73]

Finally, to show the extent of homiletical involvement in the intellectual and artistic life of England in the eighteenth century, two bishops need to be mentioned, one of whom was a theologian and the other of whom was a philosopher. **Joseph Butler** (1692–1752), who became bishop first of Bristol and then of Durham, is chiefly remembered for his great refutation of deism: *The Analogy of Religion Natural and Revealed to the Constitution and Course of Nature* (1736). Since, however, all good apologetic builds on principles mutually acknowledged by the opponent and the defender, the *Analogy* lost some of its force as a defense of Christianity when those who attacked it became atheists instead of deists.

Thus Butler's other great work, his *Fifteen Sermons Preached at the Rolls Chapel,* written to oppose Hobbes's position that human behavior is motivated exclusively by self-interest, has continued to have relevance. The abiding interest of these sermons, which argue from the human experience of having a conscience, is even more impressive when one notes that they were preached in Butler's first assignment after ordination during the years between his twenty-sixth and thirty-fifth birthdays.[74]

The philosopher bishop was **George Berkeley** (1685–1753) of the Irish diocese of Cloyne. Known as a philosophical idealist, Berkeley pointed out that there is no necessary connection between our stream of sensation in consciousness and any external universe, thus becoming an important epistemological link between Locke and Hume. He also looked on the Americas as a place where Christianity could begin afresh, served for a while in Newport, Rhode Island, and had a scheme for building a college in Bermuda to train colonists and natives for the ministry and other useful service.[75] Yet in the rationalistic age in which he lived, the sermons of Berkeley the philosopher represent for Downey not so much the latitudinarian beginning of his century as something proleptic of the evangelical preaching of the century's end.[76] This is in part because, for Berkeley, the church was not so much "the temporal custodian of virtue and a bulwark for morality" as it was the mystical Body of Christ, in which souls could be saved from sin and damnation by an appeal to the heart. Unfortunately, only ten of Berkeley's sermons and fourteen sets of pulpit notes have been preserved. Still, they represent yet another way in which preaching has been connected to the very center of eighteenth-century intellectual and artistic life.

FOR FURTHER READING

Downey, James. *The Eighteenth Century Pulpit: A Study of the Sermons of Butler, Berkeley, Secker, Sterne, Whitefield, and Wesley.* Oxford: Clarendon, 1969.

In God's Name: Examples of Preaching in England from the Act of Supremacy to the Act of Uniformity, 1534–1662. Edited with introduction and notes by John Chandos. Indianapolis: Bobbs-Merrill, 1971.

Lessenich, Rolf P. *Elements of Pulpit Oratory in Eighteenth-Century England (1660–1800)*. Cologne and Vienna: Böhlau Verlag, 1972.

Simon, Irène. *Three Restoration Divines: Barrow, South, Tillotson: Selected Sermons*. Bibliotèque de la Faculté de Philosophie et Lettres de l'Université de Liège, Fascicules 171 and 213. Paris: Société d'Editions Les Belles Lettres, 1967–76.

Swift, Jonathan. "Letter to a Young Clergyman Lately Entered into Holy Orders." In *Works*, vol. 5. London: John Nichols, 1801.

The Works of Dr. John Tillotson, Late Archbishop Of Canterbury. With the Life of the Author, By Thomas Birch, M. A. Also, A Copious Index, And The Texts Of Scripture Carefully Compared. In Ten Volumes. London: J. F. Dove for Richard Priestley, 1820.

Notes

1. "The Scribe Instructed, Preached at St. Mary's, Oxford, on 29 July, 1660, Being the Time of the KING'S Commissioners meeting there, soon after the *Restoration*, for the Visitation of that *University*," in Irène Simon, *Three Restoration Divines: Barrow, South, Tillotson: Selected Sermons*, Bibliotèque de la Faculté de Philosophie et Lettres de l'Université de Liège, Fascicules 171 and 213 (Paris: Société d'Editions Les Belles Lettres, 1967–76), 2.1.245.

2. Ibid. The complaints of South against metaphysical preaching may be compared with the list Mitchell has culled from a considerable body of contemporary criticism: "its partiality for strange and unexpected figures, its 'wit,' its passion for quotations, particularly in Latin and Greek, the exaggerated importance it attached to particular words or expressions, and its illogical and unnecessary divisions and subdivisions" (W. Fraser Mitchell, *English Pulpit Oratory from Andrewes to Tillotson: A Study of Its Literary Aspects* (1932; New York: Russell & Russell, 1962), 352-53). A characteristic interpretation of the time was that the quotations from the Fathers and classical writers were an effort to show off one's scholarship.

3. Ibid., Simon, 2:246-50. South's prejudice can be seen here in the way that he lumps together the preaching of often very learned Puritans with that of many uneducated Independents. For a parody of the preaching of Independents, see *In God's Name: Examples of Preaching in England from the Act of Supremacy to the Act of Uniformity, 1534-1662*, ed., with intro. and notes, John Chandos (Indianapolis: Bobbs-Merrill, 1971), 388-93.

4. "[Christ's Promises to the Apostles] Preached at Christ Church, Oxford, on 30 April, 1668, Being Ascension-Day," ibid., Simon, 2.2.323.

5. Ibid., 2.2.326.

6. Mitchell, *English Pulpit Oratory from Andrewes to Tillotson*, 307.

7. Thomas Sprat, *The History of the Royal Society of London, For the Improving of Natural Knowledge* (London: 1667), 2:20.

8. Charles Smyth, *The Art of Preaching: A Practical Survey of Preaching in the*

Church of England 747–1939 (London: SPCK; New York: Macmillan 1940), 183. Robert Robinson's translation of Claude's work was published in 1688 under the title of *An Essay on the Composition of a Sermon.*

9. Mitchell, *English Pulpit Oratory from Andrewes to Tillotson,* 124.

10. *An Account of the Life and Writings of Hugh Blair* (Edinburgh, 1807), 131-33, as cited in Rolf P. Lessenich, *Elements of Pulpit Oratory in Eighteenth-Century England (1660–1800)* (Cologne and Vienna: Böhlau Verlag, 1972), 62.

11. Simon, *Three Restoration Divines,* 1:11.

12. Barbara J. Shapiro, *John Wilkins 1614–1672: An Intellectual Biography* (Berkeley and Los Angeles: University of California Press, 1969), 2. The quotation is from Grant McColley, "The Ross-Wilkins Controversy," *Annals of Science* 3 (1938): 155.

13. Immediately influential, the book was reprinted in 1646, 1647, 1651, 1653, 1659, 1669, 1675, 1679, 1693, 1704, and 1718, with many revisions and expansions. Shapiro, *John Wilkins 1614–1672,* 272. The edition I have consulted is the eighth of 1704, which incorporates the 1693 additions of John Williams.

14. "Wilkins's *Ecclesiastes* was a part of the Puritan preaching tradition. In time, however, the Puritan's emphasis on plain language was obscured by the tremendous complexity of their 'method,' with its countless subdivisions and their minute discussions of the text. Wilkins and later Restoration writers retained the natural, direct language, but reduced the method to a simple outline form and eliminated textual division." Shapiro, *John Wilkins 1614–1672,* 75.

15. John Wilkins, *Ecclesiastes: or, A Discourse Concerning the Gift of Preaching, As it falls under the Rules of Art* (London: J. Lawrence; A. and J. Churchill, 1704), 10, 11.

16. Wilkins, *Ecclesiastes: or, A Discourse Concerning the Gift of Preaching,* 32.

17. Ibid., 251.

18. Lessenich, *Elements of Pulpit Oratory in Eighteenth-Century England (1660–1800).*

19. One of the ways that Lessenich was able to argue this was to insist that "the theory of preaching and latitudinarian theology remained virtually unchanged from the beginning to the end of the neoclassic era" (p. xi), a point that will be challenged below in the consideration of Hugh Blair and the Belles Lettres movement.

20. Quoted by Lessenich, *Elements of Pulpit Oratory in Eighteenth-Century England (1660–1800),* 13, from James Boswell, *The Life of Samuel Johnson* (1791). He cites the edition of Birbeck Hill (Oxford: Oxford University Press, 1887), 4:105-6.

21. Ibid., 1-36.

22. Ibid., 76.

23. Ibid., 37-81.

24. Ibid., 82-119.

25. Robinson, *An Essay on the Composition of a Sermon,* 2:489-94, quoted in Lessenich, *Elements of Pulpit Oratory in Eighteenth-Century England (1600–1800),* 123.

26. Lessenich, *Elements of Pulpit Oratory in Eighteenth-Century England (1660–1800),* 120-27.

27. Lessenich does not pay enough attention to the elocutionary movement. While its standard for gestures was naturalness, its writers came to think that these could

be reduced to a science. Thus in 1768 James Burgh described seventy-two different emotions and the facial and bodily movements to be used to suggest them. This tendency reached its *reductio ad absurdum* in the 1806 publication of Gilbert Austin's *Chironomia*, which came complete with charts including foot positions for the expression of the entire range of emotions. See *The Rhetoric of Western Thought*, eds. James L. Golden, Goodwin F. Berquist, and William E. Coleman, 3rd ed. (Dubuque: Kendall/Hunt, 1976–83), 174-87.

28. William Hogarth did two satirical engravings of preachers, one showing an Anglican parson putting his flock to sleep with his sermon and the other showing a Methodist preacher whose effects on his congregation were measured by an emotional thermometer registering everything between the high of madness and the low of suicide.

29. Lessenich, *Elements of Pulpit Oratory in Eighteenth-Century England* (1600–1800), 128-50.

30. Ibid., 154.

31. Ibid., 151-61.

32. Ibid., 162-232.

33. While the few individual trendsetters to be discussed below were all clergy of the established church, their style of preaching was adopted by clergy of all denominations. See, for example, Lessenich, *Elements of Pulpit Oratory in Eighteenth-Century England (1600–1800)*, x: "The large majority of post-Restoration Protestant preachers quickly forgot their petty differences of belief, as between Anglicans and Dissenters, Congregationalists, Baptists, Presbyterians, and Unitarians, and united their strength in a joint oratorical crusade against vice." As he makes clear in the passage that follows this, Lessenich believed that this agreement included homiletical form as well as content.

34. Many of their best and most capable leaders, including Archbishop Sancroft, went into schism from the Church of England rather than swear allegiance to William and Mary, feeling that their ordination oaths of loyalty to James II were still in effect even though he was deposed. For this refusal to swear, they were called nonjurors.

35. This combination of circumstances made it possible for Professor Norman Sykes to deliver a course of lectures at Cambridge in 1951–52 on church, state, and society in England from the Restoration through the reign of Queen Anne that was structured around a satirical song, "The Vicar of Bray" (*The British Musical Miscellany*, 1734, reproduced in *The Oxford Book of Light Verse*, ed. W. H. Auden [Oxford: Clarendon, 1939]), 260-62:

In good King Charles's golden days,
   When loyalty no harm meant;
A furious high-church man I was,
   And so I gain'd preferment.
Unto my flock I daily preach'd,
   Kings are by God appointed,
And damn'd are those who dare resist,
   Or touch the Lord's anointed.
     And this is law, I will maintain
     Unto my dying day, Sir,

When glorious Ann became our Queen,
   The Church of England's glory,
Another face of things was seen,
   And I became a Tory:
Occasional conformists base,
   I damn'd, and moderation,
And thought the church in danger was,
   From such prevarication.
     And this is law, &c.

That whatsoever King shall reign,
   I will be Vicar of Bray, Sir!

When Royal James possessed the crown,
   And popery grew in fashion;
The penal law I houted down,
   And read the declaration:
The Church of Rome, I found would fit,
   Full well my constitution,
And I had been a Jesuit,
   But for the Revolution.
     And this is law, &c.

When William our deliverer came,
   To heal the nation's grievance,
I turned the cat in pan again,
   And swore to him allegiance:
Old principles I did revoke,
   Set conscience at a distance,
Passive obedience is a joke,
   A jest is non-resistance.
   And this is law, &c.

When George in pudding time came o'er,
   And moderate men looked big, Sir,
My principles I chang'd once more,
   And so became a Whig, Sir:
And thus preferment I procur'd,
   From our Faith's Great Defender,
And almost every day abjur'd
   The Pope, and the Pretender.
    And this is law, &c.

The illustrious House of Hanover,
   And Protestant succession,
To these I lustily will swear,
   Whilst they can keep possession:
For in my faith, and loyalty,
   I never once will falter,
But George, my lawful King shall be,
   Except the times should alter.
    And this is law, &c.

---

36. Mitchell, *English Pulpit Oratory from Andrewes to Tillotson*, 320-21.

37. The best studies of South and his work are Simon, *Three Restoration Divines*, 1:228-7 (a selection of his sermons makes up 2.1.1-331), and Gerard Ready, *Robert South (1634–1716): An Introduction to His Life and Sermons*, Cambridge Studies in Eighteenth-Century English Literature and Thought, no. 12 (Cambridge: Cambridge University Press, 1992).

38. The chapel of Christ Church, South's college, serves also as the cathedral of the diocese of Oxford.

39. For the best discussion of South's wit, see Simon, *Three Restoration Divines*, 1:253-74.

40. See Ready, *Robert South (1634–1716)*, 48-52, 109-10 passim.

41. Simon, *Three Restoration Divines*, 1:231.

42. In the usage of the time, "prevented" meant "preceded."

43. Quoted, Simon, *Three Restoration Divines*, 1:232, from British Museum MS Loan (Portland Papers) 29/200.

44. This section is drawn from Simon, *Three Restoration Divines*, 1:213-28. Barrow's sermons appear ibid., 1:301-510. The other easily accessible source for Barrow is Mitchell, *English Pulpit Oratory from Andrewes to Tillotson*, 321-33 and passim.

45. Mitchell, *English Pulpit Oratory from Andrewes to Tillotson*, 324.

46. Quoted in Simon, *Three Restoration Divines*, 1:219-20, from the 1683 edition of his *Works*, 1:14.

47. Simon, *Three Restoration Divines*, 1:315-26.

48. This ideal seems not unlike the Chinese use of pictograms for writing instead of an alphabet that transcribed the sounds of words.

49. The bad press Tillotson has received for this editing, in which he has been accused in effect of transmitting his own blandness to Barrow's prose, is undeserved. See Simon, *Three Restoration Divines,* 1:303-14.

50. Smyth, *The Art of Preaching,* 104.

51. Ibid., 103.

52. James Downey, *The Eighteenth Century Pulpit: A Study of the Sermons of Butler, Berkeley, Secker, Sterne, Whitefield, and Wesley* (Oxford: Clarendon, 1969), 25.

53. Simon, *Three Restoration Divines,* 1:291.

54. Smyth, *The Art of Preaching,* 146.

55. Ibid., 162. Cf. Horton Davies, *Worship and Theology in England: From Andrewes to Baxter and Fox, 1603–1690* (Princeton: Princeton University Press, 1975), 2:183-84: "Here is an unequalled combination of eudaemonism, utilitarianism, and pelagianism, masquerading as Christianity. It was left to the men of latitude to conceive of a contradiction, Christian discipleship without the taking up of a cross."

56. Smyth, *The Art of Preaching,* 146.

57. Downey, *The Eighteenth Century Pulpit,* 27.

58. That is, given preferment; appointed to receive the income of church positions while hiring someone else to do the actual ministerial work.

59. The edition consulted is that of Western Spiritual Classics, with a preface by A. M. Allchin, ed. and intro. John N. Wall Jr. (New York, Ramsey, and Toronto: Paulist, 1981). The quotation is from p. 62.

60. Ibid., 64.

61. This is true even of so perceptive a critic as David Nokes, who entitled his critical biography *Jonathan Swift, A Hypocrite Reversed* (Oxford: Oxford University Press, 1985). On the title page he quotes the relevant passage from Thomas Sheridan's 1784 *Life of Jonathan Swift:*

> He had, early in life, imbibed such a strong hatred to hypocrisy, that he fell into the opposite extreme; and no mortal ever took more pains to display his good qualities, and appear in the best light to the world, than he did to conceal his, or even to put on the semblance of their contraries. . . . Lord Bolingbroke, who knew him well, in two words summed up his character in that respect, by saying that Swift was a hypocrite reversed.

Yet even Nokes seems incapable of understanding any of the religious activities of Swift in anything but the worst light. In doing so he reminds me of Roland Barthes's description of all biography as inevitably a "counterfeit integration of the subject." (Quoted by Carolyn G. Heilbrun in "Dorothy L. Sayers: Biography Between the Lines" in *Dorothy L. Sayers: The Centenary Celebration,* ed. Alzina Stone Dale (New York: Walker & Co., 1993), 2. The data of a person's life is filtered through the biographer's capacity to perceive.

62. While there may be a rose-colored tint to the lens through which Robert W. Jackson views Swift, there can be no doubt that he has amassed some real and objective

data in *Jonathan Swift, Dean and Pastor* (London: SPCK, 1939) that shows the sincerity of Swift in his exercise of his ministry.

63. *Hic depositum est corpus Jonathan Swift, S.T.D. huius cathedralis decani, ubi saeva indignationio ulterius cor lacerare nequit, abi viator, et imitare, si poteris, strenuum pro virili libertatis vindicatorem.* The translation is that of Nokes, *A Hypocrite Reversed,* 412.

64. The edition consulted is that of 1801 by John Nichols in London, 5:85-110. The date of the original is January 9, 1719–20 (the two years reflect the shift from treating March 25, the Feast of the Annunciation, as the beginning of the New Year to starting it on January 1).

65. Ibid., 5:95.

66. Quoted in Jackson, *Jonathan Swift, Dean and Pastor,* 123.

67. Quoted ibid., 121.

68. This and the other two sermons to be discussed are contained in *The English Sermon: Volume II: 1650–1750,* ed. C. H. Sisson (Cheadle, Cheshire: Carcanet, 1976), 286-313.

69. Ibid., 309.

70. What follows is based on Downey, *The Eighteenth Century Pulpit,* 115-54.

71. In this case, being a prebendary meant being a non-residentiary canon who, among other duties, preached twice a year at the cathedral.

72. Quoted from a letter to George Whateley in Downey, *The Eighteenth Century Pulpit,* 137.

73. James Gray, *Johnson's Sermons: A Study* (Oxford: Clarendon, 1972). With Jean Hagstrom, Gray edited the sermons for *The Yale Edition of the Works of Samuel Johnson* (New Haven: Yale University Press, 1958–85).

74. See Downey, *The Eighteenth Century Pulpit,* 30-57, and *The Works of Bishop Butler: Vol. I: Sermons, Charges, Fragments, and Correspondence,* ed. with intro. and notes J. H. Bernard (London: Macmillan, 1900).

75. For his reaction to his American experience, see his "Sermon Preached before the Incorporated Society for the Propagation of the Gospel in Foreign Parts" in Sisson, *The English Sermon,* 315-30.

76. Downey, *The Eighteenth Century Pulpit,* 58-88. The quoted words appear on p. 62.

CHAPTER 17

THE DAWN OF MODERNITY (B)

THE RECOVERY OF FEELING

"RELIGIONS OF THE HEART"

The beginning of the demand for plainness in preaching was seen in the previous chapter as a response to a number of simultaneous historical conditions: the weariness with theological disputes at the end of the wars of religion, the beginnings of modern science, the emergence of philosophical systems that did not presuppose revelation, and the growing ascendancy of the mercantile class over the aristocracy. The rationalism of the group that became the latitudinarians was only one of the possible responses to the same set of circumstances.[1] Another would strike many people as being as near to diametrically opposed as one could get: an emphasis on emotion instead of reason.

The one response was as widespread as the other.[2] Throughout Europe in the sixteenth and seventeenth centuries, there suddenly emerged in all religious traditions an insistence that in order to be real, religion had to be experienced affectively. It is impossible to account for this diversity of movements in terms of the historical influence of some on others. Rather, there appears to have been a spontaneous emergence of the same demand

426

for an engagement of feelings in a wide variety of religious systems, systems that had little in common with one another beyond this new emphasis that they shared.

All the major religious groups of Europe were involved. Roman Catholic manifestations included Jansenism, quietism, and devotion to the Sacred Heart. In seventeenth-century British Christianity, the hunger for religious involvement that stirred the emotions was observable in strands of Puritanism, the Scots-Irish revivals, and the birth of the Quakers. The form of religion of the heart most related to this history of preaching in the English-speaking world, the Evangelical Awakening, appeared in Great Britain and America in the eighteenth century.

Among continental Protestants the expression was Pietism, first in its Dutch Reformed emergence and then in the German Lutheran. In Russia, some stirrings could be seen that remained within the Orthodox Church, while others separated into sects of varying degrees of radicality. Of all these aspects, some could be attributed to the influence of European Protestantism and Pietism, while others appeared to be entirely indigenous. The emergence of Hasidic Judaism in the eighteenth century has to be reckoned as another example of the tendency to value the affective dimensions of religion.

The preaching of those in groups that found their discriminating characteristic in experience would be very different from the preaching of those who based everything on an appeal to reason. Thus religions of the heart have an important place in the history of preaching. While only the movements from this group that had a direct influence on the development of preaching in the English-speaking world will be considered in what follows, those that do concern this story cannot be understood adequately unless they are seen in the context of this wider spirit of the times.[3]

EARLY STIRRINGS OF BRITISH HEARTS

The first manifestations in Great Britain of the tendency to estimate the value of religion on the basis of its affective dimensions occurred among the Puritans. The treatment of the Puritans in part 3 concentrated on their agenda to bring the Church of England to what they considered the scriptural perfection of the model of Geneva and the way their understanding of how sermons should be shaped had been influenced by Ramist logic. As early as the reign of Charles I, however, a change can be detected in the Puritan program. Preoccupation with purification of the polity and liturgy of the national church gave way to consideration of the life of the individual Christian. As good Calvinists, Puritans agreed that one's salvation is entirely in the hands of God, a matter of the eternal decree of God by which one was elected to salvation or reprobation. But the question arose as to whether those who were elected to grace knew they were.

It came to be Puritan orthodoxy that those who were elected to grace had assurance of their salvation. The pioneers in this line of thought were William Perkins[4] and his disciple, William Ames. Their work in this area grew out of a recognition that the way election occurred was not simply in God's having decided the issue at the dawn of creation or even in the Holy Spirit's causing a person to respond to the proclamation of the gospel in a sermon (which, according to Calvin, was the medium through which justification occurred). Rather, salvation was communicated in an inevitable sequence of stages (*ordo salutis,* the "order of salvation").

Calvinist biblical interpreters had found that pattern in Romans 8:30: "And those whom he predestined he also called; and those whom he called he also justified; and those whom he justified he also glorified." Perkins saw the "degrees" of salvation to be:

1. Effectual calling—or conversion, the event by which someone is brought to repentance and faith by the proclamation of the law and the gospel.

2. Justification—the imputation of Christ's righteousness to the sinner so that the sinner is accounted righteous by God on the basis of faith.

3. Sanctification—the Christian's continuing death to sin (mortification) and coming to life in Christ (vivification).

4. Glorification—the completion of the Christian's conformity to the likeness of Christ that occurs between death and judgment.

While Perkins had already insisted that the highest degree of faith is assurance of one's own salvation, Ames identified the appearance of this assurance as "adoption" and added it to the order of salvation as a stage between justification and sanctification.[5] The lack of assurance that one was saved came to be treated as evidence that one was not, a position that in time would offer a powerful appeal for conversion in evangelistic preaching not only by Calvinists but also by "Arminians" (those like Wesley who believe that human freedom of the will is consistent with the sovereignty of God).

While the doctrine of assurance would give important theological content to the later preaching of revivals, some of the external forms of such preaching also can be traced back to British Calvinists in the early-seventeenth century—although in this case they were not English Puritans, but Scottish and Irish Presbyterians. Among them a tradition had developed of preparing for their infrequent celebrations of the Eucharist by having sacramental meetings at which people were encouraged to ready themselves to receive Holy Communion by repenting of their sins in the assurance that justification should produce a sanctified life. The preaching was often quite emotional, and people came under conviction of their sins and experienced conversion.

Such meetings began as activities of the local congregation, but they came to be such moving experiences that visitors from some distance were attracted. At times the crowds were so large that the meeting had to be moved out-of-doors. These meetings were suppressed by Charles I, but, by the time of the Restoration when they were outlawed again, they had become the principal institutional form of the religious life of the Scottish and Irish Calvinists, who continued to hold such meetings under clandestine conditions. Access to the churches being forbidden them, open-air meetings became the norm. Since their clergy had been ejected from their "livings," they wandered around preaching revivals at these sacramental meetings. These conditions continued until the Glorious Revolution of 1688, when William and Mary came to the throne.

> By 1688 there was a long-established tradition of periodic sacramental meetings, involving enthusiastic preaching and the expectation of experiences of conviction and conversion, hosted by a semi-independent fellowship of traveling (or itinerant) preachers. The precedents for the Evangelical Revival (and American Awakenings) were well in place.[6]

THE EVANGELICAL REVIVAL

Wales

Although the Evangelical revival is explained by some historians against the background of the industrial revolution, deism, Lockean psychology and epistemology, and the emergence of moralism and voluntary societies in the sphere of religion, its first manifestation was in one area of the British Isles least affected by all of these forces, Wales. Unlike the movement a century before among Scottish and Irish Calvinists, this one began (although it did not remain) within the established church. Nor was the Welsh revival unhoped for. **The Reverend Griffith Jones** of the parish of Llandowrer, who served as a sort of godfather for the movement, had been praying for it as far back as 1714. His own way of preparing the way of the Lord was to establish schools in which children could become literate enough to read the Bible in Welsh. He was able to found 3,225 such schools, in which 150,000 had learned to read before he died in 1761; he also distributed 30,000 Welsh Bibles.

Two young men in particular are credited with the first preaching of the revival. One of them, **Howell Harris,** was not ordained. After a dramatic conversion experience in 1735 when he was twenty-one, he went to Oxford with the ministry in mind, but he was so distressed by the low moral level of the university that he stayed only a few weeks. Returning home, he began a ministry of teaching and preaching. He became an overseer of some of Griffith Jones's schools and began evangelizing from house to house, establishing societies of his converts.

Soon his witnessing attracted crowds, and he began preaching out-of-doors and itinerating between his congregations. Harris's preaching drew power from his strongly emotional nature, a nature that also made him hard to get along with. In fact, at one time he dropped out of the Methodist conference for twelve years, establishing instead a community not unlike Zinzendorf's Herrnhut at his home at Trevecka. Later, though, he became reconciled. Through him the Welsh revival was to influence the British revival, especially through his contacts with George Whitefield, John Wesley, and Lady Huntingdon.

The other young man, **Daniel Rowland,** was ordained in the established church and presented to the parish of Llangeitho, which served both as a base for his itinerate preaching and as a center for the revival. Although no direct influence has been traced, Rowland's work bore many resemblances to the Scottish and Irish revivals of the previous century. Harris has left an account of the preaching in preparation for a celebration of the Eucharist in Rowland's parish:

> I was last Sunday at the Ordinance with Brother Rowlands where I saw, felt, and heard such things as I cant send on Paper any Idea of. . . . Such Crying out and Heart Breaking Groans, Silent Weeping and Holy Joy, and shouts of Rejoicing I never saw. Their Amens and Cryings Glory in the Highest &c would inflame your soul was you there. Tis very common when he preaches for Scores to fall down by the Power of the Word, pierced and wounded or overcom'd by the love of God and Sights of the Beauty and Excellency of Jesus, and lie on the ground.[7]

It was upon the foundation of these two men that the Methodist movement, which became the most notable aspect of Welsh culture for generations to come, was built.

A study of the preaching of the Welsh pioneers was made by one of their successors, Gwyn Walters, who taught preaching for many years at Gordon-Conwell Theological Seminary.[8] He described the preaching style of the Welsh folk preachers covering a period of 250 years, demonstrating what remarkable eloquence in the gospel some of them attained. Several characteristics of their style remind one of classical African American preaching, especially a form of dialogue with the elders in the "amen corner" that resembles the black tradition of "call and response," and the way preachers would break out in an extemporaneous singing of their words, what the Welsh call the *hwyl*, which resembles the chanted portions of American folk preaching.

The Homeless Pilgrim with Dubious Name[9]

The link between the Welsh and British expressions of the Evangelical Awakening was in the person of Howell Harris, who came to have close association with both Whitefield, for whom he furnished the model of field preaching and later served as a marriage broker, and Wesley, in an association to be discussed below.[10]

Born to innkeeping parents[11] in Gloucester in 1714, **George Whitefield** showed great interest in both religion and drama as a child. Changing financial circumstances of the family meant that the only way he could go to the university to prepare for ordination was as a "servitor," who had to perform chores for his college and for "gentleman" scholars. There he met the Wesley brothers (who occupied the middle status of "commoners") and became involved in their pious circle, known in the university by such opprobrious terms as the "Holy Club" or "Methodists."

Although the name Methodists was later to be picked up and proudly worn as a badge, what it came to stand for was very different from that to which it was originally applied. The circle at Oxford was typical of a sort of voluntary association being formed at the time, one that owed something to the influence of both the Puritan "conventicles" of the previous century and the *collegia* of Spener and the German Pietists. These "societies," founded on models established by Anthony Horneck and Josiah Woodword, were "a means by which Christians could hold each other accountable for their personal moral behavior and for their pursuit of benevolent enterprises."[12]

Although all forms of the Methodist revival would use societies as one of their basic methods of organization, they would envision them as associations of the converted. The Holy Club at Oxford, however, had its heyday before any of its members had undergone a conversion experience. Its members, therefore, would look back on its activities as fruitless works before grace. Whitefield was the only member of the group who underwent that experience while he was still at the university, which he did under the influence of a book to which Charles Wesley introduced him.

Ordained a deacon on June 20, 1736, about a month before he received his B.A., Whitefield began preaching around London, not having been appointed to a cure. In what Stout calls the "filiopietistic" accounts of the beginning of the Methodist revival, a good bit of shock is expressed over the way that the founders were denied pulpits in the Church of England. Such a reaction is hardly justified. The account of the latitudinarian church in the previous chapter does not reveal it to be seething with zeal, but the synagogue at Nazareth when our Lord preached there may have been the last pulpit open to anyone who wanted to occupy it. The clergy appointed to the parishes were the only persons with an automatic right to preach in them. Those who complain today about the exclusion of Whitefield and the Wesleys probably keep close watch over who preaches in their own churches, and it is only the conviction that the Methodist leaders were voices crying in the wilderness that makes the closed pulpits seem at all exceptional.

The truly extraordinary fact is that they received so many invitations to preach so early in their ministries. That does not happen today to many twenty-two-year-old, newly ordained deacons. Yet young Whitefield seems to have been the sensation of the season. The Wesleys had already gone to Georgia as missionaries of the Society for the Propagation of the Gospel, and Whitefield soon came to see it as his vocation to follow them there. Meanwhile, he took advantage of every opportunity to preach the necessity of the rebirth he had just experienced.

The effects were astonishing: someone complained to the bishop of London that in his first sermon, Whitefield had driven fifteen people mad. The bishop's response was to wish that "the madness might not be forgotten before the next Sunday." Other clergy must have felt the same way because invitations poured in and, wherever he went, the churches were overflowing. In the year and a half before he could sail to America, Whitefield created such a taste for his sermons that it had to be met by printed transcripts for those unable to hear them. Indeed, most of the